HISTORICAL DICTIONARY

The historical dictionaries present essential information on a broad range of subjects, including American and world history, art, business, cities, countries, cultures, customs, film, global conflicts, international relations, literature, music, philosophy, religion, sports, and theater. Written by experts, all contain highly informative introductory essays of the topic and detailed chronologies that, in some cases, cover vast historical time periods but still manage to heavily feature more recent events.

Brief A–Z entries describe the main people, events, politics, social issues, institutions, and policies that make the topic unique, and entries are cross-referenced for ease of browsing. Extensive bibliographies are divided into several general subject areas, providing excellent access points for students, researchers, and anyone wanting to know more. Additionally, maps, photographs, and appendixes of supplemental information aid high school and college students doing term papers or introductory research projects. In short, the historical dictionaries are the perfect starting point for anyone looking to research in these fields.

HISTORICAL DICTIONARIES OF LITERATURE AND THE ARTS

Jon Woronoff, Series Editor

Science Fiction Literature, by Brian Stableford, 2004.

Hong Kong Cinema, by Lisa Odham Stokes, 2007.

American Radio Soap Operas, by Jim Cox, 2005.

Japanese Traditional Theatre, by Samuel L. Leiter, 2006.

Fantasy Literature, by Brian Stableford, 2005.

Australian and New Zealand Cinema, by Albert Moran and Errol Vieth, 2006.

African-American Television, by Kathleen Fearn-Banks, 2006.

Lesbian Literature, by Meredith Miller, 2006.

Scandinavian Literature and Theater, by Jan Sjåvik, 2006.

British Radio, by Seán Street, 2006.

German Theater, by William Grange, 2006.

African American Cinema, by S. Torriano Berry and Venise Berry, 2006.

Sacred Music, by Joseph P. Swain, 2006.

Russian Theater, by Laurence Senelick, 2007.

French Cinema, by Dayna Oscherwitz and MaryEllen Higgins, 2007.

Postmodernist Literature and Theater, by Fran Mason, 2007.

Irish Cinema, by Roderick Flynn and Pat Brereton, 2007.

Australian Radio and Television, by Albert Moran and Chris Keating, 2007.

Polish Cinema, by Marek Haltof, 2007.

Old Time Radio, by Robert C. Reinehr and Jon D. Swartz, 2008.

Renaissance Art, by Lilian H. Zirpolo, 2008.

Broadway Musical, by William A. Everett and Paul R. Laird, 2008.

American Theater: Modernism, by James Fisher and Felicia Hardison Londré, 2008.

German Cinema, by Robert C. Reimer and Carol J. Reimer, 2008.

Horror Cinema, by Peter Hutchings, 2008.

Westerns in Cinema, by Paul Varner, 2008.

Chinese Theater, by Tan Ye, 2008.

Italian Cinema, by Gino Moliterno, 2008.

Architecture, by Allison Lee Palmer, 2008.

Russian and Soviet Cinema, by Peter Rollberg, 2008.

African American Theater, by Anthony D. Hill, 2009.

Postwar German Literature, by William Grange, 2009.

Modern Japanese Literature and Theater, by J. Scott Miller, 2009.

Animation and Cartoons, by Nichola Dobson, 2009.

Modern Chinese Literature, by Li-hua Ying, 2010.

Historical Dictionary
of Modern
and Contemporary
Classical Music

Nicole V. Gagné

The Scarecrow Press, Inc.
Lanham • Toronto • Plymouth, UK
2012

Published by Scarecrow Press, Inc.
A wholly owned subsidiary of The Rowman & Littlefield Publishing Group, Inc.
4501 Forbes Boulevard, Suite 200, Lanham, Maryland 20706
http://www.scarecrowpress.com

Estover Road, Plymouth PL6 7PY, United Kingdom

British Library Cataloguing in Publication Information Available

Library of Congress Cataloging-in-Publication Data

Gagné, Nicole V.
    Historical dictionary of modern and contemporary classical music / Nicole V. Gagné.
        p. cm. — (Historical dictionaries of literature and the arts)
    Includes bibliographical references.
    ISBN 978-0-8108-6765-9 (cloth : alk. paper) — ISBN 978-0-8108-7962-1 (ebook)
    1. Music—Dictionaries. I. Title.
    ML100.G13 2012
    780.9'0403—dc23   2011023969

Contents

Editor's Foreword

Although this is a book about modern and contemporary music, referring to a period of time in which many potential readers have been living, it takes a bit more explanation. This is not the music many of us hear most of the time, such as pop, rock, jazz, or world music. It addresses modern and contemporary music of the type commonly called "classical"—the sort one hears in concert halls, occasionally on the radio, and sometimes as background for films. Some of its composers are known and admired, like Béla Bartók, Alban Berg, Benjamin Britten, and others further down the alphabet, even if they are still not as widely recognized as Bach, Beethoven, and Brahms, but this variety of music is still a mystery to many people today. While it has its roots in older music, for more than a century it has taken many twists and turns, introduced innovations and variations, and experimented with things that do not readily appeal to the public, such as atonality, dissonance, minimalism, serialism, and unfamiliar sounds and instruments. This is why a *Historical Dictionary of Modern and Contemporary Classical Music* is a particularly important addition to Scarecrow Press's series on literature and the arts.

The best place to start is the introduction, which provides a broad overview of the subject, describing why modern and contemporary classical music has moved in the general directions it has and why some composers have modified traditions and inserted new, sometimes totally unexpected, elements. This has taken place over more than a century, and the chronology lists when famous compositions were written and how techniques and technology interacted with the art. But the most important section, as always, is the dictionary, with almost four hundred entries on composers and musicians, from all over the world and often with quite varied musical backgrounds. Some are quite familiar, while others—actually, most—are known only in more limited circles, yet all have contributed in their own way. Important as these people are, it is actually the techniques and practices they have used, and sometimes devised, that deserve the most attention, since they provide an understanding of what has been going on in the world of classical music all this time. This will be quite adequate for many readers, but others will hopefully want to learn more, and a good starting place for further research is the bibliography.

Nicole V. Gagné, the author of this volume, has an amazingly broad and deep understanding of modern and contemporary classical music, and she has been writing on the topic for about three decades. During this period, she has written or cowritten *Soundpieces: Interviews with American Composers*, *Sonic Transports: New Frontiers in Our Music*, and *Soundpieces 2*, as well as numerous articles about music of specialized periodicals. She has also contributed to *The New Grove II*. In 2004, her essay "The Beaten Path," a history of percussion in American music, won the Deems Taylor Award for best magazine article about music. In addition to her admirable qualifications for writing this volume, Ms. Gagné was also the librettist and co-composer of the opera *Agamemnon*. And music is only one of her interests; she has also been a magazine editor for home journals and contributor to film periodicals, as well as a lecturer. With this book as a guide, readers will certainly find their way through a lively and intriguing field more readily, and with greater understanding will hopefully come greater appreciation and enjoyment.

Jon Woronoff
Series Editor

Preface

The bulk of this volume deals with composers, but it also contains a representative sampling of entries on musicians who have specialized in modern and contemporary music, along with more than 60 topic entries, covering an array of musical subjects developed over the late 19th and 20th centuries. Omitted are several important composers born in the 19th century, whose music falls within its chronology but who were essentially postromantics, among them Edward Elgar, Giacomo Puccini, Sergey Rachmaninoff, and Jean Sibelius. Also excluded from this survey are composers of pop, jazz, and rock music, genres so large and ramified that they require their own studies. Instead, this dictionary contains entries on those postromantics who also had a foot in modernism, such as Leos Janácek, Gustav Mahler, Carl Nielsen, and Richard Strauss. It also has entries for certain pop, jazz, and rock composers whose work either overlaps the realm of concert music—including Ornette Coleman, Duke Ellington, Fred Frith, George Gershwin, Scott Joplin, and Frank Zappa—or else is so radical within its own field that it merits discussion in this context, such as the Beatles, Robert F. Graettinger, the Residents, Sun Ra, and Cecil Taylor.

My work on this book is especially indebted to two eminent music historians and authors, Sabine Feisst and Don C. Gillespie. I am profoundly grateful to them for their support, guidance, corrections, and kindness. What I have done is as good as it is because of their input. Sarah Cahill, Frank de Falco, Anne LeBaron, Michael Musgrave, Bruce Posner, "Blue" Gene Tyranny, La Monte Young, and Marian Zazeela were also generous in helping me with my research, and they have my deepest appreciation. Further thanks go to Jonathan Hiam of the New York Public Library for the Performing Arts for his kind efforts on my behalf, and a special thank-you to Scarecrow Press's series editor for the Historical Dictionaries of Literature and the Arts, Jon Woronoff. Any errors or misrepresentations in this dictionary are my own responsibility, and I welcome corrections and comments from readers.

This book is respectfully dedicated to Kevin Lally and to the cherished memory of David Avidor, Gene Bagnato, and Tracy Caras.

Acronyms and Abbreviations

AACM	Association for the Advancement of Creative Musicians
a.k.a.	Also Known As
BA	Bachelor of Arts
BBC	British Broadcasting Corporation
BMus	Bachelor of Music
c.	Circa
CD	Compact Disc
CD-ROM	Compact Disc–Read-Only Memory
CEMAMu	Centre d'Études de Mathématiques et Automatiques Musicales
DMus	Doctor of Music
EVI	Electronic Valve Instrument
GRM	Groupe de Recherches Musicales
IRCAM	Institut de Recherche et de Coordination Acoustique/Musique
LP	Long-Playing [record]
MEV	Musica Elettronica Viva
MIDI	Musical Instrument Digital Interface
MMus	Master of Music
NHK	Nippon Hoso Kyokai [Japan Broadcasting Corporation]
No.	Number
NRC	National Research Council of Canada
Op.	Opus (plural: Opp., Opera)
orch.	Orchestrated
POW	Prisoner of War
RCA	Radio Corporation of America
rev.	Revised
RTF	Radiodiffusion-Télévision Française
UCLA	University of California, Los Angeles
UNESCO	United Nations Educational, Scientific, and Cultural Organization
UPIC	Unité Polyagogique Informatique du CEMAMu
WDR	West-Deutscher Rundfunk

Chronology

1890   Satie: *Trois Gnossiennes*.

1894   Debussy: *Prélude à l'apres-midi d'un faune*; Ives: *Song for Harvest Season*; Mahler: Symphony No. 2.

1897   Thaddeus Cahill patents his electrical instrument the telharmonium.

1898   Scriabin: Piano Sonata No. 3, *Réverie*; Strauss: *Ein Heldenleben*.

1899   William Duddell builds his electrical instrument the singing arc. Debussy: *Nocturnes*; Joplin: *The Ragtime Dance*; Schoenberg: *Verklärte Nacht*.

1901   Debussy: *Pélléas et Mélisande*; Delius: *A Village Romeo and Juliet*; Farwell: *American Indian Melodies*; Mahler: Symphony No. 4; Ravel: *Jeux d'eau*.

1903   Janácek: *Jenufa*; Ravel: String Quartet; Satie: *Trois morceaux en forme de poire*.

1904   **October:** Alban Berg and Anton Webern become pupils of Arnold Schoenberg. Busoni: Piano Concerto; Ives: Symphony No. 3; Mahler: Symphony No. 6; Scriabin: Symphony No. 3; Vaughan Williams: *In the Fen Country*.

1905   Debussy: *La mer, Images*; Delius: *A Mass of Life*; Falla: *La vida breve*; Mahler: Symphony No. 7; Ravel: *Introduction and Allegro*; Strauss: *Salome*.

1906   **November:** Ferruccio Busoni completes *Sketch of a New Esthetic of Music*. Bartók and Kodály: *Twenty Hungarian Folksongs*; Falla: *Cuatro piezas españolas*.

1907   Delius: *Brigg Fair*; Scriabin: Piano Sonata No. 5, *Le poème de l'extase*.

1908   Bartók: *14 Bagatelles*; Farwell: *Three Indian Songs*; Ives: *The Unanswered Question*; Ravel: *Gaspard de la nuit*; Schoenberg: String Quartet No. 2; Strauss: *Elektra*.

1909 Bartók: String Quartet No. 1; Ives: Piano Sonata No. 1; Mahler: *Das Lied von der Erde*; Schoenberg: *Erwartung*, *Five Orchestral Pieces*; Webern: *Six Pieces* for Orchestra.

1910 Busoni: *Fantasia contrappuntistica*; Mahler: Symphonies Nos. 9 and 10; Scriabin: *Prométhée*; Strauss: *Der Rosenkavalier*; Stravinsky: *L'oiseau de feu*; Vaughan Williams: *Fantasia on a Theme of Thomas Tallis*, Symphony No. 1.

1911 Bartók: *Duke Bluebeard's Castle*; Joplin: *Treemonisha*; Prokofiev: Piano Concerto No. 1; Scriabin: Piano Sonatas Nos. 6 and 7; Stravinsky: *Petrushka*.

1912   16 October: Arnold Schoenberg premieres his *Pierrot lunaire* in Berlin. Berg: *Altenberg Leider*; Butterworth: *Bredon Hill*; Debussy: *Jeux*; Delius: *On Hearing the First Cuckoo in Spring*; Ravel: *Daphnis et Chloé*; Roslavets: String Quartet No. 1.

1913   29 May: Igor Stravinsky's *Le sacre du printemps* has its premiere in Paris. **1 July:** Luigi Russolo publishes his futurist manifesto *The Art of Noises*. Ives: String Quartet No. 2; Ravel: *Trois poèmes de Stéphane Mallarmé*; Schoenberg: *Die glückliche Hand*; Scriabin: Piano Sonatas Nos. 8, 9, and 10; Vaughan Williams: Symphony No. 2.

1914 Ives: *Three Places in New England*; Joplin: *Magnetic Rag*; Lourié: *Synthèses*; Ornstein: *Three Moods*; Prokofiev: *Sarcasms*; Vaughan Williams: *The Lark Ascending*.

1915   18 December: Edgard Varèse leaves France and immigrates to the United States. Falla: *El amor brujo*, *Noches en los jardines de España*; Ives: Piano Sonata No. 2; Milhaud: *Les choéphores*; Prokofiev: *Scythian Suite*; Szymanowski: *Mythes*.

1916 Bloch: *Schelomo*; Cowell: *Dynamic Motion*; Grainger: *The Warriors*; Holst: *The Planets*; Ives: Symphony No. 4; Nielsen: Symphony No. 4; Satie: *Parade*.

1917 Bartók: String Quartet No. 2; Bax: *Tintagel*; Boulanger: *Psalm 130*, *Vieille prière bouddhique*; Griffes: *The Pleasure-Dome of Kubla Khan*; Prokofiev: Symphony No. 1.

1918 Milhaud: *L'homme et son désir*; Satie: *Socrate*; Stravinsky: *L'histoire du soldat*.

1919 Bartók: *The Miraculous Mandarin*; Cowell: *Two Rhythm-Harmony Quartets*; Griffes: Piano Sonata; Hauer: *Nomos*; Milhaud: *Le bouef sur le toit*; Ruggles: *Toys*.

1920 **January:** Henri Collet publishes "Les cinq Russes, les six Français, et M. Satie," conferring the name "Groupe des Six" upon Georges Auric, Louis Durey, Arthur Honegger, Darius Milhaud, Francis Poulenc, and Germaine Taillefaire. **March:** Erik Satie's *Musique d'ameublement* is performed to enhance and complement ambient sound at an art gallery exhibition in Paris. Hába: String Quartet No. 2; Hindemith: *Das Nusch-Nuschi*; Ravel: *La valse*; Stravinsky: *Symphonies of Wind Instruments*.

1921 **23 June:** Leon Theremin patents his electrical instrument the theremin. Honegger: *Le Roi David*; Milhaud: *Saudades do Brasil*; Ruggles: *Angels*; Varèse: *Amériques*; Vaughan Williams: Symphony No. 3; Walton: *Façade*.

1922 Berg: *Wozzeck*; Nielsen: Symphony No. 5; Warlock: *The Curlew*.

1923 **March:** Arnold Schoenberg completes the Piano Suite, his first fully twelve-tone composition. Hindemith: *Das Marienleben*; Honegger: *Pacific 2.3.1*; Milhaud: *La création du monde*; Ruggles: *Vox clamans in deserto*; Stravinsky: *Les noces*.

1924 Gershwin: *Rhapsody in Blue*; Ruggles: *Men and Mountains*; Varèse: *Octandre*.

1925 Antheil: *Ballet mécanique*; Berg: Chamber Concerto; Cowell: *The Banshee*; Mosolov: Piano Sonata No. 5; Shostakovich: Symphony No. 1; Varèse: *Intégrales*.

1926 Berg: *Lyrische Suite*; Copland: Piano Concerto; Falla: Harpsichord Concerto; Janácek: *Glagolitic Mass*; Krenek: *Jonny spielt auf*; Ruggles: *Portals*; Salzedo: Concerto.

1927 Bartók: String Quartet No. 3; Riegger: *A Study in Sonority*; Rudhyar: *Three Paeans*; Schoenberg: String Quartet No. 3; Stravinsky: *Oedipus Rex*; Varèse: *Arcana*.

1928 **October:** Eric Fenby arrives at Grez-sur-Loing, France, and begins working as amanuensis for the blind and paralyzed Frederick Delius. Bartók: String Quartet No. 4; Mosolov: *Zavod*; Ravel: *Boléro*; Schoenberg: Variations for Orchestra; Thomson: *Four Saints in Three Acts*; Webern: Symphony; Weill: *Die Dreigroschenoper*.

1929 Copland: *Vitebsk*; Cowell: Piano Concerto; Delius: *A Song of Summer*; Foulds: *Dynamic Triptych*; Rudhyar: *Granites*; Weill: *Happy End*; Wellesz: *Die Bakchantinnen*.

1930 **January:** Publication of Cowell's *New Musical Resources*. Carrillo: *Fantasia Sonido 13*; Copland: Piano Variations; Crawford: *Piano Study in*

Mixed Accents; Delius: *Songs of Farewell*; Foulds: *Three Mantras*; Roldán: *Ritmicas*; Roussel: Symphony No. 3; Sorabji: *Opus clavicembalisticum*; Stravinsky: *Symphony of Psalms*; Weill: *Der Jasager*.

1931 Cowell: *Rhythmicana*; Crawford: *String Quartet 1931*; Varèse: *Ionisation*.

1932 Schoenberg: *Moses und Aron*; Shostakovich: *Lady Macbeth of Mtsensk*.

1933 October: Arnold Schoenberg settles in the United States. Partch: *17 Lyrics of Li Po*; Pound: *Le testament*; Ruggles: *Sun-Treader*; Still: Symphony No. 1.

1934 Berg: *Lulu Suite*; Varèse: *Ecuatorial*; Vaughan Williams: Symphony No. 4; Webern: Concerto for Nine Instruments; Weill: Symphony No. 2.

1935 Bartók: String Quartet No. 5; Becker: *A Marriage with Space*; Berg: Violin Concerto; Chávez: *Sinfonía India*; Cowell: *Mosaic Quartet*; Gershwin: *Porgy and Bess*.

1936 Barber: *Adagio for Strings*; Bartók: *Music for Strings, Percussion, and Celesta*; Blitzstein: *The Cradle Will Rock*; Copland: *El salón México*; Grainger: *Free Music Nos. 1 and 2*; McPhee: *Tabu-Tabuhan*; Orff: *Carmina Burana*; Schoenberg: Violin Concerto, String Quartet No. 4; Shostakovich: Symphony No. 4; Varèse: *Density 21.5*.

1937 Bartók: Sonata for Two Pianos and Percussion; Shostakovich: Symphony No. 5.

1938 December: Stefan Wolpe settles in the United States. Beyer: *Music of the Spheres*; Caturla: Suite; Copland: *Billy the Kid*; Harris: Symphony No. 3; Revueltas: *Sensemayá*; Stravinsky: *Dumbarton Oaks Concerto*; Webern: String Quartet.

1939 30 September: Igor Stravinsky arrives in New York and settles in the United States. **2 October:** Manuel de Falla leaves Spain to settle in Argentina. Bartók: String Quartet No. 6; Cage: *Imaginary Landscape No. 1*; Prokofiev: *Alexander Nevsky*; Webern: *First Cantata*.

1940 February: Paul Hindemith immigrates to the United States. **8 October:** Béla Bartók gives his farewell concert in Budapest; he immigrates to the United States later that month.

1941 15 January: Olivier Messiaen premieres his *Quatuor pour la fin du Temps* in the German POW camp where he and his fellow musicians are prisoners. Eisler: *Fourteen Ways to Describe Rain*; Nancarrow: *Sonatina*; Shostakovich: Symphony No. 7.

1942 Cage: *The Wonderful Widow of Eighteen Springs*; Copland: *Lincoln Portrait, Rodeo, Fanfare for the Common Man*; Hindemith: *Ludus Tonalis*; Krenek: *Lamentatio Jeremiae prophetae*; Schoenberg: *Ode to Napoleon Buonaparte*, Piano Concerto.

1943 Bartók: Concerto for Orchestra; Britten: *Serenade*; Prokofiev: *War and Peace*; Ruggles: *Evocations*; Vaughan Williams: Symphony No. 5; Webern: *Second Cantata*.

1944 Copland: *Appalachian Spring*; Hovhaness: *Lousadzak*; Martinu: *Fantasia*; Messiaen: *Vingt regards sur l'Enfant-Jésus, Trois petites liturgies de la Présence Divine*; Poulenc: *Les mamelles de Tirésias*; Prokofiev: *Cinderella*, Symphony No. 5.

1945 **14 September:** Anton Webern is killed by an American soldier in Austria. Bartók: Piano Concerto No. 3; Britten: *Peter Grimes*; Shostakovich: Symphony No. 9.

1946 Boulez: *Première sonate*; Copland: Symphony No. 3; Schoenberg: String Trio.

1947 Babbitt: *Three Compositions for Piano*; Ellington: *The Clothed Woman*; Graettinger: *Thermopylae*; Schoenberg: *A Survivor from Warsaw*; Stravinsky: *Orpheus*; Thomson: *The Mother of Us All*; Vaughan Williams: Symphony No. 6.

1948 **10 February:** The Central Committee of the Communist Party denounces formalist Soviet composers, including Sergey Prokofiev and Dmitry Shostakovich. **5 October:** Radiodiffusion-Television Française broadcasts *Concert de bruit*, Pierre Schaeffer's first *musique concrète* compositions. Babbitt: *Composition for Four Instruments*; Boulez: *Deuxième sonate*; Cage: *Sonatas and Interludes*; Copland: Concerto for Clarinet and String Orchestra; Dallapiccola: *Il prigioniero*; Messiaen: *Turangalîla-symphonie*; Strauss: *Vier letzte Lieder*; Thomson: *"Louisiana Story" Suite*.

1949 **17 March:** Publication of Harry Partch's *Genesis of a Music*. Blitzstein: *Regina*; Bowles: *Night Waltz*; Dlugoszewski: *Moving Space Theater Piece for Everyday Sounds*; Nancarrow: Study No. 1; Russell: *A Bird in Igor's Yard*; Schoenberg: *Phantasy*.

1950 Cage: *String Quartet in Four Parts, Six Melodies*; Carter: String Quartet No. 1; Copland: Piano Quartet; Feldman: *Projection No. 1*; Henry and Schaeffer: *Symphonie pour un homme seul*; Messiaen: *Quatre études de rythme*; Wolpe: Quartet.

1951　Boulez: *Structures, Premier Livre*; Britten: *Billy Budd*; Cage: *Music of Changes, Imaginary Landscape No. 4*; Partch: *Oedipus*; Stravinsky: *The Rake's Progress*.

1952　**29 August:** David Tudor premieres John Cage's silent piece *4'33"* at the Maverick Concert Hall near Woodstock, New York. Barraqué: Piano Sonata; Brown: *December 1952*; Ginastera: Piano Sonata No. 1; Vaughan Williams: Symphony No. 7.

1953　Babbitt: *Du*; Brant: *Antiphony One*; Brown: *Twenty-Five Pages*; Henry and Schaeffer: *Orphée 53*; Shostakovich: Symphony No. 10; Stockhausen: *Kontra-Punkte*.

1954　Cowell: Symphony No. 11; Glanville-Hicks: *Etruscan Concerto*; Luening and Ussachevsky: *Rhapsodic Variations*; Varèse: *Déserts*; Yardumian: *Armenian Suite*.

1955　Boulez: *Le marteau sans maître*; Harrison: *Strict Songs*; Hovhaness: Symphony No. 2; Le Caine: *Dripsody*; Partch: *The Bewitched*; Poulenc: *Les dialogues des Carmélites*; Vaughan Williams: Symphony No. 8; Xenakis: *Metastasis*.

1956　**9 August:** Lejaren Hiller and Leonard Isaacson premiere selections from their string quartet *Illiac Suite*, created with computer composition programs. Cowell: *Variations for Orchestra*; Henze: *Undine*; Nono: *Il canto sospeso*; Stockhausen: *Klavierstück XI, Gesang der Jünglinge*; Wolpe: Symphony; Xenakis: *Pithoprakhta*.

1957　Babbitt: *All Set*; Boulez: *Troisième sonate*; Copland: *Piano Fantasy*; Feldman: *Piece for Four Pianos*; Pousseur: *Scambi*; Stockhausen: *Gruppen*; Stravinsky: *Agon*; Takemitsu: *Requiem for Strings*; Vaughan Williams: Symphony No. 9; Young: *for Brass*.

1958　Boulez: *Pli selon pli*; Carrillo: *Balbuecos*; Lutoslawski: *Musique funèbre*; Mayuzumi: *Nirvana Symphony*; Varèse: *Poème électronique*; Young: *Trio for Strings*.

1959　Barraqué: . . . *au-délà du hasard*; Bussotti: *Five Piano Pieces for David Tudor*; Carter: String Quartet No. 2; El-Dabh: *Fantasia-Tahmeel*; Johnson: *November*; Maxfield: *Sine Music*; Scelsi: *Quattro pezzi su una nota sola*; Schuller: *Seven Studies on Themes of Paul Klee*; Stravinsky: *Movements*.

1960   Cage: *Cartridge Music*; Coleman: *Free Jazz*; Dlugoszewski: *Suchness Concert*; Foss: *Time Cycle*; Jennings: String Quartet; Partch: *Revelation in the Courthouse Park*; Penderecki: *Threnody for the Victims of Hiroshima*; Young: *Compositions 1960*.

1961   Babbitt: *Composition for Synthesizer*; Brown: *Available Forms I*; Cage: *Atlas Eclipticalis*; Carter: Double Concerto; Ligeti: *Atmosphères*; Lutoslawski: *Jeux Venitiens*.

1962   Britten: *War Requiem*; Copland: *Connotations*; Feldman: *Structures*; Reynolds: *The Emperor of Ice Cream*; Sessions: *Montezuma*; Shostakovich: Symphony No. 13.

1963   **9–11 September:** Erik Satie's *Vexations* is performed 840 times in succession by John Cage and a team of pianists at New York's Pocket Theater. Berio: *Epiphanie*; Cowell: *26 Simultaneous Mosaics*; Foss: *Echoi*; Harrison: *Pacifika Rondo*; Maxfield: *Bacchanale*; Stockhausen: *Plus-Minus*; Xenakis: *Eonta*; Zimmermann: *Die Soldaten*.

1964   Ashley: *The Wolfman*; Britten: *Curlew River*; Nono: *La fabbrica illuminata*; Riley: *In C*; Scelsi: String Quartet No. 4; Wolff: *For One, Two, or Three People*; Xenakis: *Akrata*; Young: *The Tortoise, His Dreams and Journey, The Well-Tuned Piano*.

1965   Boulez: *Éclat*; Carter: Piano Concerto; Jennings: *Winter Trees*; Johnston: *Sonata for Microtonal Piano*; Lucier: *Music for Solo Performer*; Oliveros: *Bye Bye Butterfly*; Rochberg: *Music for the Magic Theater*; Rorem: *Miss Julie*; Sun Ra: *The Magic City*.

1966   The Beatles: *Revolver*; Hovhaness: Symphony No. 19; Ligeti: *Lux aeterna*; Partch: *Delusion of the Fury*; Stravinsky: *Requiem Canticles*; Taylor: *Unit Structures*.

1967   The Beatles: *Sgt. Pepper's Lonely Hearts Club Band, Magical Mystery Tour*; Birtwistle: *Punch and Judy*; Cardew: *Treatise*; Copland: *Inscape*; Reich: *Piano Phase*; Subotnick: *Silver Apples of the Moon*; Takemitsu: *November Steps*; Zappa: *Lumpy Gravy*.

1968   The Beatles: *The White Album*; Berio: *Sinfonia*; Braxton: *For Alto*; Cage and Hiller: *HPSCHD*; Kagel: *Der Schall*; Martirano: *L's G.A.*; Thomson: *Lord Byron*.

1969   The Beatles: *Abbey Road*; Carter: Concerto for Orchestra; Davies: *Eight Songs for a Mad King*; Maderna: *Quadrivium*; Moondog: *Moondog*;

Musgrave: Clarinet Concerto; Shostakovich: Symphony No. 14; Stockhausen: *Fresco*; Wolpe: String Quartet.

1970 Crumb: *Black Angels, Ancient Voices of Children*; Davidovsky: *Synchronisms No. 6*; Johnston: *Carmilla*; Lucier: *I Am Sitting in a Room*; Reich: *Four Organs*.

1971 Bernstein: *Mass*; Bryars: *Jesus' Blood Never Failed Me Yet*; Cardew: *The Great Learning*; Carter: String Quartet No. 3; Dlugoszewski: *Tender Theatre Flight Nageire*; Feldman: *Rothko Chapel*; Finney: *Landscapes Remembered*; Harrison: *Young Caesar*; Oliveros: *Sonic Meditations I–XII*; Shapey: *Praise*; Tenney: *Quiet Fan*; Wolff: *Burdocks*.

1972 Andriessen: *De volharding*; Carlos: *Sonic Seasonings*; Coleman: *Skies of America*; Dodge: *Speech Songs*; Rochberg: String Quartet No. 3; Tal: *Massada 967*.

1973 Britten: *Death in Venice*; Davies: *Stone Litany*; Eastman: *Stay on It*.

1974 Frith: *Guitar Solos*; Glass: *Music in Twelve Parts*; Grisey: *Dérives*; Henze: *Tristan*; Messiaen: *Des canyons aux étoiles . . .*; Shostakovich: String Quartet No. 15.

1975 Boulez: *Rituel in memoriam Bruno Maderna*; Cage: *Etudes Australes*; Dlugoszewski: *Abyss and Caress*; LeBaron: *Concerto for Active Frogs*; Rzewski: *The People United Will Never Be Defeated*; Wuorinen: *A Reliquary for Igor Stravinsky*.

1976 **21 November:** Philip Glass's minimalist opera *Einstein on the Beach* has its American premiere at New York's Metropolitan Opera House. Górecki: Symphony No. 3; Reich: *Music for 18 Musicians*; the Residents: *The Third Reich 'n' Roll*.

1977 Andriessen: *Hoketus*; Berio: *Opera*; Feldman: *Neither*; Pärt: *Tabula Rasa*.

1978 Adams: *Shaker Loops*; Braxton: *Composition No. 82*; Eno: *Music for Airports*; Shapey: *21 Variations*; Tyranny: *Harvey Milk (Portrait)*; Wolff: *Wobbly Music*.

1979 Ashley: *Automatic Writing*; Branca: *The Spectacular Commodity*; Brant: *Orbits*; Glass: *Satyagraha*; Lutoslawski: *Novelette*; the Residents: *Eskimo*; Taylor: *3 Phasis*.

1980 Ashley: *Perfect Lives*; Branca: *The Ascension*; Denisov: *Requiem*; Frith: *Gravity*.

1981 Boulez: *Répons*; Branca: *Indeterminate Activity of Resultant Masses*; Eastman: *The Holy Presence of Joan d'Arc*; Frith: *Speechless*; Harrison: Double Concerto; Sun Ra: *Nuits de la Fondation Maeght*; Tavener: *Prayer for the World*; Tower: *Sequoia*.

1982 Brant: *Meteor Farm*; Eno: *On Land*; Oliveros: *The Wanderer*; the Residents: *The Tunes of Two Cities*; Riley: *The Ethereal Time Shadow*; Tyranny: *The Intermediary*.

1983 Anderson: *United States*; Branca: Symphony No. 3; Hykes: *Hearing Solar Winds*; Monk: *The Games*; Radigue: *Songs of Milarepa*; Zwilich: Symphony No. 1.

1984 Frith: *Live in Japan*; Sharp: *Tessalation Row*; Tenney: *Bridge*; Zorn: *Cobra*.

1985 Feldman: *Coptic Light*; Grisey: *Les espaces acoustiques*; Taylor: *Segments II*.

1986 **January:** The MacWorld Expo in Boston introduces Laurie Spiegel's *Music Mouse* program for playing real-time computer music. Bolcom: *12 New Etudes*; Braxton: *Composition No. 125*; Carter: String Quartet No. 4; Eastman: *Piano 2*; LeBaron: *Noh Reflections*; Moran: *Open Veins*; Vierk: *Simoom*; Zappa: *Jazz from Hell*; Zorn: *Spillane*.

1987 Adams: *Nixon in China*; Ashley: *Atalanta (Acts of God)*; Cage: *Europeras I/II*.

1988 Galás: *Masque of the Red Death*; Kurtág: *. . . quasi una fantasia . . .* ; Lewis: *Voyager*; Oswald: *Plunderphonics EP*; Lucier: *Silver Streetcar for the Orchestra*; Reich: *Different Trains*; the Residents: *God in Three Persons*; Taylor: *Legba Crossing*.

1990 Berio: *Rendering*; Globokar: *L'armonia drammatica*; Spiegel: *Sound Zones*; Young: *The Lower Map of the Eleven's Division in the Romantic Symmetry (over a 60-Cycle Base) in Prime Time from 144 to 112 with 119, Chronos kristalla*.

1991 LeBaron: *The E&O Line*; Monk: *Atlas*; Xenakis: *Gendy3*; Zorn: *Elegy*.

1992 Cage: *Sixty-Eight*; Nancarrow: Study No. 51; Messiaen: *Éclairs sur l'au-délà*; Ostertag: *All the Rage*; Rzewski: *De profundis*; Westerkamp: *Beneath the Forest Floor*.

1993 Boulez: *. . . explosante-fixe . . .* ; Branca: Symphony No. 9; Lam: *The Child God*.

1994   Risset: *Variants*; Takemitsu: *Archipelago S.*; Tyranny: *Country Boy Country Dog.*

1995   Babbitt: Piano Quartet; Carter: String Quartet No. 5; Zorn: *Kristallnacht.*

1998   Ashley: *Dust*; Carter: *What Next?*; Gubaidulina: *In the Shadow of the Tree.*

2000   Deyhim: *Madman of God: Divine Love Songs of the Persian Sufi Masters.*

2001   Branca: Symphony No. 13; Brant: *Ice Field*; Frith: *Clearing*; Monk: *Mercy.*

2002   Ferrari: *Les anecdotiques*; Kancheli: *Warzone*; LeBaron: *Hsing*; León: *A Row of Buttons*; Shea: Chamber Symphony No. 2; Tavener: *The Veil of the Temple.*

2003   Ashley: *Celestial Excursions*; Oswald: *Aparenthesi*; Schuller: *Encounters.*

2005   Adams: *Doctor Atomic*; Chin: *Cantatrix sopranica*; Teitelbaum: *Z'vi.*

2006   Carter: Horn Concerto; El-Dabh: *Symphony for 1,000 Drums*; Goehr: *Broken Lute*; Gosfield: *A Sideways Glance from an Electric Eye*; Takahashi: *Yoru, ame, samusa.*

2007   Adams: *The Light Within*; Henze: *Phaedra*; Zorn: *Six Litanies for Heliogabalus.*

2010   Branca: Symphony No. 15; Tyranny: *Scriabin's Chord, George Fox Searches.*

Introduction

This dictionary of modern and contemporary classical music surveys the years 1890 to the present. The last decade of the 19th century was selected as a convenient starting point because it was a time when modernist sensibilities were reaching a critical mass and emerging more frequently in music. Along with that focus, this dictionary also includes 20th-century composers who basically eschewed modernist devices and wrote accessible works in a tonal idiom, drawing chiefly on classical, romantic, and folk models.

Twentieth-century tonality is represented herein as another form of modern music, along with more specifically modernist composition, employing dissonance and polyrhythm, and what was known in the 1910s and 1920s as ultramodernism, involving the use of atonality and densities. From there, atonal composition evolved by midcentury into two basic subgroups, serial and nonserial. But by the 1950s, atonal composition had also been stripped of its modernist methods and rhetoric by chance and indeterminate music, as part of a cultural shift that has grown since the second half of the 20th century. The postmodern sensibility, with its enthusiasm for the unprecedented availability of virtually every type of music, has engendered numerous subgroups, and this dictionary includes entries on multiculturalism, minimalism, multimedia, free improvisation, and other postmodern genres and artists.

The contemporary music scene thus embodies a uniquely broad spectrum of activity, which has grown and changed down to the present hour. With new talents emerging and different technologies developing in the coming years of the 21st century, no one can predict what paths music will take next. All we can be certain of is that the inspiration and originality that make music live will continue to bring awe, delight, fascination, and beauty to the people who listen to it.

FROM MODERN TO MODERNIST

Throughout the history of music, generations of composers have perceived themselves as modern in comparison to their predecessors. Johannes de Muris's 1321 treatise *Notitia artis musicae* (a.k.a. *Ars novae musicae*, The art of new music) praises the "moderni musici."[1] Almost 300 years later, another theorist, Giovanni Maria Artusi, attacked the innovative madrigals of Claudio Monteverdi (without citing the composer's name) in his 1600 publication *Della imperfettione della moderna musica* (*Of the Imperfection of Modern Music*). Hector Berlioz called his 1844 book *Traité d'instrumentation et d'orchestration modernes* (*Treatise on Modern Instrumentation and Orchestration*). But by the first decade of the 20th century, music was no longer only modern, it had also become modernist in a radical break from long-standing traditions of tonal organization, melody, harmony, rhythm, and instrumentation.

The development of modernist music can be traced in two paths that share a common starting point: Richard Wagner. Late romantic and postromantic devices that derived from German music in general, and the operas of Wagner in particular, were rejected by French composers Claude Debussy, Erik Satie, and Maurice Ravel. They developed a new sound employing staticism, repetition, and subtlety and refrained from heavy philosophical or emotional content. Satie's piano music drew on medieval influences (*Ogives*, 1886), employed irregular phrasing (*Trois Gymnopédies*, 1888; *Trois Gnossiennes*, 1890), and featured cabaret tunes (*Trois morceaux en forme de poire*, 1903). In 1887, Debussy was told by the Académie des Beaux-Arts, "Beware of this vague impressionism."[2] To his credit, he ignored their warnings, and with such classics as *Prélude à l'après-midi d'un faune* (1894) for orchestra, the opera *Pelléas et Mélisande* (1901), and *Images* (1905) for piano, Debussy launched a new era in music, displacing drama and development with sensuous harmonies and tone colors and evoking subtle and nuanced moods and feelings. Ravel brought a melodic sensibility and a classicist's concern for clarity and precision to such great works as *Jeux d'eau* (1901) for piano, String Quartet in F Major (1903), and *Introduction and Allegro* (1905) for harp and sextet. Impressionist qualities also characterized the music of Frederick Delius and Charles T. Griffes and shaped the early works of Igor Stravinsky, Béla Bartók, Manuel de Falla, and many other modernists.

Another pathway to modernism pursued the practices that the French had rejected. The dissonance, ambiguous tonalities, and massive orchestral sonorities that characterized Wagnerian opera were taken further in the symphonies of Anton Bruckner and Gustav Mahler and the tone poems and operas of Richard Strauss. These composers outlined a tradition that culminated with Arnold Schoenberg's epochal 1909 scores *Erwartung* and *Five Orchestral Pieces*. Schoenberg intensified the dramatic and emotional content of his predecessors' music into the startling distortions of expressionism. Relinquishing the tonal center and its hierarchical organization of harmonic movement, he used dissonance freely and featured angular and fragmentary melodic lines with wide leaps and asymmetrical forms.

Russian-born Igor Stravinsky became the leading modernist composer within the French sphere of influence with the polytonal and polyrhythmic music of his classic ballets *L'oiseau de feu* (1910), *Petrushka* (1911), and *Le sacre du printemps* (1913). Despite the uproar that attended its premiere, *Le sacre* became one of the most influential of all 20th-century scores. The dance attracted several innovative French composers. Ravel developed into a brilliant orchestrator with *Ma Mère l'Oye* (1911) and *Daphnis et Chloé* (1912). Satie's *Parade* (1916), with its noises and ragtime dance, was structured in symmetrical time units rather than a foundation of harmonic movement. Darius Milhaud brought a novel approach to percussion and explored spatial and multicultural techniques in *L'homme et son désir* (1918) and *Le boeuf sur la toit* (1919).

Schoenberg delved further into atonal composition in the 1910s, producing a masterpiece with *Pierrot lunaire* (1912) for soprano and quintet. His pupils Alban Berg and Anton Webern followed Schoenberg into atonality, and collectively they came to be known as the Second Viennese School. Berg caused a scandal when his *Altenberg Lieder* (1912) for voice and orchestra was premiered in 1913. Webern explored extreme compression in his *Five Pieces* (1913) for orchestra.

A short-lived ultramodernist movement—futurism—took atonality into a different direction. Italian artist and composer Luigi Russolo, author of the 1913 manifesto *L'arte dei rumori* (*The Art of Noises*), designed and built different noisemaking machines and invented a graphic notation to score his octet *Risveglio di una città* (1914).

Hungary's Béla Bartók, essentially a tonal composer, struck a balance between tonality and atonality with his concept of "pantonality," evoking the sensation of a key signature through repeated or sustained tones rather than tonal harmonic structures, thus opening the music to any available pitch or sound.[3] Bartók had a foot in both impressionism and expressionism and made those sound worlds his own through his original use of folk-derived rhythms and melodies, creating such great works as String Quartets Nos. 1–6 (1909–1939), the opera *Duke Bluebeard's Castle* (1911), the pantomime score *The Miraculous Mandarin* (1919), Piano Concertos Nos. 1–3 (1926–1945), *Music for Strings, Percussion, and Celesta* (1936), Sonata for Two Pianos and Percussion (1937), and Concerto for Orchestra (1943).

The link to folk music brought vitality and urgency to the tonal composition of English composer Ralph Vaughan Williams as well. It also kept him from imitating his teachers: He recalled Maurice Ravel "telling me that I was the only pupil who 'n'ecrit pas de ma musique.'"[4] Folk music freed Vaughan Williams from postromantic rhetoric, and he became arguably the finest symphonist of the 20th century with nine individual and compelling symphonies spanning the years 1910 to 1957, which owe precious little to the influence of Johannes Brahms, Mahler, or Strauss.

A few maverick composers during the 1900s and 1910s mostly bypassed both the French and the Viennese and came to dissonance, polyrhythm, and atonality on their own. The Russian Alexander Scriabin and the Americans Charles Ives and Henry Cowell were also groundbreakers in their use of overtones and densities and in the development of pleroma music, where specialized musical aggregates produce a singular resonance or meaning. Along with generating and reinforcing overtones through loudness, attack, and trills, Scriabin derived the six pitches of his "Chord of the Pleroma" (C, F-sharp, B-flat, E, A, D) from partials in the overtone series; more commonly known as the Mystic Chord, it informs all his late music, most notably his Piano Sonatas Nos. 6–10 (1911–1913).[5] Ives, a polytonal composer by the 1890s, increased his music's activity into epic densities, quoting popular, sacred, and classical tunes in startling new aggregates with such works as Piano Sonatas Nos. 1 and 2 (1909, 1915), String Quartet No. 2 (1913), *Three Places in New England* (1914), and Symphony No. 4 (1916). Cowell created densities and resonances with his tone-cluster music for piano, such as *Dynamic Motion* (1916) and *The Tides of Manaunaun* (1917), and used ratios from the overtone series to derive the harmonies and near-unplayable rhythms of *Two Rhythm-Harmony Quartets* (1919).

Interest in atonal and pleroma music continued to grow in the 1920s, especially in the United States. Edgard Varèse, who had emigrated from France in 1915, produced a series of dissonant crystalline scores in the 1920s, including *Offrandes* (1922), *Intégrales* (1925), and *Arcana* (1927), which featured winds and percussion in propulsive rhythms, densities, and sonorities. In 1931, Varèse composed an all-percussion score, *Ionisation*, and defined a new form of 20th-century ensemble music. Carl Ruggles imbued his dissonant and atonal music with a lyrical and visionary sensibility in such great scores as *Angels* (1921), *Vox clamans in deserto* (1923), *Portals* (1926), and *Sun-Treader* (1933). Dane Rudhyar, another French immigrant, explored resonant piano sounds and rhythmic patterns derived from speech in his atonal piano works, which include *Pentagrams Nos. 1–4* (1924–1926), *Three Paeans* (1925–1927), and *Granites* (1929). Ruth Crawford's nine Preludes for piano (1925–1928) and *Piano Study in Mixed Accents* (1930) brought a new voice to the use of tone-clusters and dissonant counterpoint.

Modernist music underwent a split over the 1920s with the emergence of neoclassicism, in which modernist harmonies and rhythms were adapted to classical and Baroque forms. Anticipated in the 1900s and 1910s by Ferruccio Busoni and Sergey Prokofiev, neoclassicism had its great champion in Stravinsky, with such major works as *Oedipus Rex* (1927) and *Symphony of*

Psalms (1930). Popular with audiences, neoclassicism proved widely influential. Paul Hindemith celebrated the German Baroque with his *Kammermusik Nos. 1–7* (1922–1927), and Manuel de Falla's Harpsichord Concerto (1926) was steeped in the sound of Domenico Scarlatti. Neoclassicism offered a path for French and American composers, among them Francis Poulenc, Albert Roussel, Elliott Carter, Louise Talma, Roger Sessions, and Ross Lee Finney, who had come to regard impressionism as passé yet resisted atonality.

In 1923, the year Stravinsky set his hand anew to sonata form in completing his Octet, Schoenberg finished the Piano Suite, in which he made the first full use of his twelve-tone, or dodecaphonic, method for atonal composition. As its name implies, twelve-tone music enables all 12 tones of the chromatic scale to have equal importance, with no individual tone exerting a tonal pull or dominance. Schoenberg's method involved patterning the 12 tones into a specific sequence, called the twelve-tone set, or row, which is heard forward, backward, and upside down (both forward and backward) in melodic, harmonic, and polyphonic expressions based on traditional development techniques such as transposition, augmentation, and diminution.

This methodology had been anticipated in the 1910s and early 1920s by Scriabin, Berg, Josef Matthius Hauer, Arthur Lourié, Nikolai Roslavets, Bartók, and Ruggles, but Schoenberg became its primary exponent. Dodecaphony also greatly enhanced the works of certain of his pupils. For Webern, it brought a new precision and rigor in composing purely instrumental atonal music, which led to such masterpieces as his Symphony (1928), Concerto for Nine Instruments (1934), and Variations for Orchestra (1940). Berg, who had achieved a major success with his classic expressionist opera *Wozzeck* (1922), brought tonal qualities to several outstanding twelve-tone works, among them *Lyrische Suite* (1926) for string quartet and his Violin Concerto (1935).

Having studied the scores of the impressionists and Stravinsky, Aaron Copland brought a distinctly American approach to polytonality and polyrhythm in the Symphony for Organ and Orchestra (1924), Piano Concerto (1926), and *Dance Symphony* (1929). Denounced right from the start as "ultramodern," Copland's music in fact resisted familiar schools—although he did employ twelve-tone techniques in his Piano Variations (1930) and neoclassical elements in *Short Symphony* (1933), two of his finest works.[6] Like Bartók and Vaughan Williams, Copland reached a new level of expression and artistry in his tonal composition through his use of folk music, with such classics as the ballet scores *Billy the Kid* (1938) and *Appalachian Spring* (1944).

Also impacted by folk music were two other outstanding tonal composers of the era: Dmitry Shostakovich, whose major works include 15 symphonies (1925–1971) and 15 string quartets (1937–1974), and Benjamin Britten, creator of such great vocal scores as *Les illuminations* (1939), *Serenade* (1943), *War*

Requiem (1962), and the operas *Peter Grimes* (1945), *Billy Budd* (1951), and *Death in Venice* (1973). They further shared with Copland an affinity for the blazing postromantic voice of Mahler, although neither Shostakovich nor Britten wrote music that was as free of postromantic rhetoric as Copland's was.

Copland, Ruth Crawford, John Cage, Ernst Krenek, Frank Martin, and Stefan Wolpe were among the composers who investigated the twelve-tone method during the 1930s. Schoenberg's relocation to the United States in 1933 brought a greater understanding and appreciation of his music, and he produced such great scores as the Violin Concerto (1936), String Quartet No. 4 (1936), Piano Concerto (1942), and String Trio (1946). After World War II, composer/conductor René Leibowitz helped revitalize European interest in twelve-tone music by teaching and performing works of the Second Viennese School. Leibowitz also coined the term *serial* for this music, after the series of pitches that constitute a specific set.

Before the end of the 1940s, Milton Babbitt in the United States and Olivier Messiaen in France had extended the twelve-tone method of pitch organization to the organization of duration, dynamics, and timbre, in what came to be known as total serialism. Babbitt's approach, based on Schoenberg's music, resulted in such notable works as *Composition for Four Instruments* (1948) and *All Set* (1957) for jazz ensemble; he was influential not just for Americans such as Lejaren Hiller and Charles Wuorinen, but also for England's Manchester School composers, including Peter Maxwell Davies and Harrison Birtwistle. Messiaen, although he had outlined total serialism in his *Quatre études de rythme* (1950) for piano, kept to his own impressionist-inspired nondevelopmental music: a personal blend of ancient Greek and Hindu rhythms, Gregorian plainchant and church modes, birdsong, and the evocation of color, invariably expressive of religious awe and contemplation, as in his classic scores *Quatuor pour la fin du Temps* (1941), *Vingt regards sur l'Enfant-Jésus* (1944) for piano, the choral work *Trois petites liturgies de la Présence Divine* (1944), and *Turangalîla-symphonie* (1948).

Two of Messiaen's pupils, Karlheinz Stockhausen and Pierre Boulez, saw themselves in the serial tradition of Webern and championed total serialism. Stockhausen developed an extreme pointillism in his 1952 orchestral scores *Spiel* and *Punkte*. Boulez brought rigor, energy, and fresh sonorities to his landmark *Le marteau sans maître* (1955) for alto and six instruments. Other composers of totally serialized music in the 1950s include Bruno Maderna, Luciano Berio, and Luigi Nono. By then, it was neoclassicism's turn to be regarded as passé, and many former exponents, including Stravinsky, Talma, Sessions, and Arthur Berger, began composing serial music. New ways of melding twelve-tone techniques with tonal methodologies were devised by Copland, Martin, Finney, Irving Fine, George Perle, Egon Wellesz, Luigi Dallapiccola, and Hans Werner Henze.

Other major late modernists found their own paths into atonality. Wolpe coordinated his music's chromatic circulation with its structural transformation in *Enactments* (1953) for three pianos, his Symphony (1956) and String Quartet (1969), and other outstanding scores. Elliott Carter assigned specific intervallic and tempo relationships to instruments and created dense works that featured multiple shifting tempi, notably the String Quartet No. 2 (1959), Double Concerto (1961), and Concerto for Orchestra (1969). Conlon Nancarrow, restricting himself to the medium of the player piano, created a piano music of surrealistic speeds, articulations, and densities in his 51 Studies for Player Piano, composed from the late 1940s to 1992. Also interested in densities, Iannis Xenakis employed stochastic processes and related structures that he derived from higher mathematics in *Metastasis* (1955), *Herma* (1961), and *Akrata* (1964).

Xenakis was one of many in the mid-1950s who used randomness to bring character into a totally chromatic music that had become increasingly formularized and constricting. In his 1957 article "Alea," Boulez decried the "purely mechanistic, automatic, fetishistic" conception that had dominated and suggested the composer leave certain parameters up to the performer—which Stockhausen had done in 1956 with *Klavierstuck XI*.[7] Other composers who started using aleatoric methods in the 1950s and 1960s include Berio, Lukas Foss, Witold Lutoslawski, and Jacob Druckman.

That aleatoric music had to be invented is something of a vindication of the work of John Cage. Rejecting the serial fixation on control, Cage used chance procedures to compose atonal music, employing random processes to select the musical materials for his breakthrough 1951 compositions *Music of Changes* for piano and *Imaginary Landscape No. 4* for 12 radios. The latter piece perforce sounds different in every realization, which introduces the concept of indeterminate composition, where the composer cannot control how the music sounds. Cage had taken a Buddhist-inspired path into making music without relying on his own tastes and memories. In *4'33"* (1952), no sound is played for four minutes and 33 seconds; its music is any and all sounds going on during that time. With Cage, music was no longer a method for the manipulation of particularized sounds, but rather a way of listening: When you listen attentively to a sound's own special character, without introducing intellectual and emotional responses, you're hearing music.

FROM MODERNIST TO POSTMODERN—AND BEYOND

Cage provided a necessary break from modernist definitions of composition, which were fundamentally extensions of classical and romantic mindsets, for all the shocking new liberties in modernist forms and content. His chance and indeterminate music represents an important turning point from modernism to postmodernism, in which modernist freedoms are extended to nonmodernist materials and conceptualizations, and other composers around him quickened to his ideas. Morton Feldman utilized new methods of graphic notation in his five *Projection* scores (1950–1951) and developed indeterminate rhythms with free-duration works such as *Piece for Four Pianos* (1957). Earle Brown's open-form music included graphic notation in his *Folio* series (1952–1954), proportional notation in *Music for Cello and Piano* (1955), and improvisation in *Centering* (1973) for violin and 10 instruments. Christian Wolff used cueing techniques in *For Five or Ten Players* (1962) and *For One, Two or Three People* (1964), and wrote purely verbal instructions in his *Prose Collection* (1968–1971).

Another essential innovator for the postmodern sensibility was Harry Partch, who abandoned most of the instruments of Western music along with their equal-tempered tuning system and built new instruments tuned to his own just-intonation-based system. Partch's major compositions, which include *Oedipus* (1951), *Revelation in the Courthouse Park* (1960), and *Delusion of the Fury* (1966), were music-theater works with his instruments displayed onstage as sculptural objects, played by costumed musicians who sang and acted with the rest of the cast.

The medium of electronic music was a game changer for postmodern music, offering not only new sounds but also a new sensibility of composition. "With electronics, the keyboard is no longer the standard of musical thought. We aren't thinking just in terms of a gamut of pitches laid out linearly; we're thinking of the world of sound," noted Ben Johnston, who studied with both Partch and Cage.[8] With his *Cinq études de bruit* in 1948, Pierre Schaeffer introduced a new idea of what constitutes music with *musique concrète*: tape music derived from prerecorded sounds. Magnetic tape recorders became generally available in the early 1950s, and an array of major works arose internationally, among them Hugh Le Caine's *Dripsody* (1955), Xenakis's *Concret PH* (1956) and *Bohor* (1962), Stockhausen's *Gesang der Jünglinge* (1956) and *Hymnen* (1967), Toru Takemitsu's *Vocalism A-I* (1956) and *Water Music* (1960), Varèse's *Poème électronique* (1958), Luciano Berio's *Thema (Omaggio a Joyce)* (1958) and *Visage* (1961), and Richard Maxfield's *Cough Music* (1961) and *Radio Music* (1961).

Building on the tape-music facilities of the early 1950s, a number of music studios pursuing electrical synthesis emerged internationally, and an important body of electrically synthesized music emerged in the 1960s. Along with purely electronic works, composers such as Babbitt, Wuorinen, Mario Davidovsky, and Morton Subotnick also created electroacoustic pieces that combined live musicians with electronic sounds on tape. Systems for the real-time performance of electronic music were devised by Stockhausen, Robert Ashley, Pauline Oliveros, Charlemagne Palestine, David Tudor, Salvatore

Martirano, and Jerry Hunt. Synthesizers entered the marketplace at the end of the 1960s, bringing the studio's electronic palette with them, and electronic sound eventually became part of almost every young composer's education and vocabulary.

Economical, ubiquitous, and responsive, computers eventually became an essential medium for synthesizing sound; they enabled Charles Dodge to synthesize speech in the 1970s and became playable instruments in real time with Laurie Spiegel's *Music Mouse* program in the 1980s. They brought new possibilities to the creation of electroacoustic instruments, with such composer/improvisers as Oliveros and her expanded accordion and trombonist George Lewis in his *Voyager* performances. The postmodern need for better ways to appropriate, deconstruct, and recontextualize sounds had its perfect instrument with sampling technology, a wedding of synthesizers and computers, which became generally available in the early 1980s. Samplers displaced tape as the medium for recording and transforming fragments of sound, and produced notable works by the Residents, Frank Zappa, John Oswald, Bob Ostertag, and many others.

Electronics have also been a frequent factor in multimedia music, with film, video, lighting, projections, and computer-generated effects visual and aural transforming the musical experience—especially when theatrical elements are also involved, as in the operas of Ashley, the sound and light environments of La Monte Young and Marian Zazeela, or works by Oliveros, Mauricio Kagel, Meredith Monk, and Laurie Anderson.

A different deconstruction of the listening experience is offered by spatial music. In assigning the physical placement of musicians, such composers as Henry Brant, Stockhausen, Oliveros, Gyorgy Kurtág, Thea Musgrave, George Crumb, and Lucia Dlugoszewski redefined the relationship between performer and listener, creating new forms of drama and ritual and enjoying a heightened clarity of sound.

As developments in recording technology over the second half of the 20th century made available a seemingly endless spectrum of musical expression, postmodern music responded with techniques for appropriating, deconstructing, and recontextualizing any and all of it. World music came to shape the sound of later 20th-century music, from such multicultural composers as Henry Cowell and Lou Harrison to notable innovators outside the field of concert composition, such as jazz leader Sun Ra and the legendary rock band the Beatles—both of whom also worked with dissonance, atonality, densities, and noise instrumental and electronic, further blurring the boundaries between genres.

The most popular and successful postmodern development has been minimalist music—or more precisely, one specific type of musical minimalism: pulse-driven repeated-pattern music, which had roots in the energy and drive of jazz and rock. The trend was launched by *In C* (1964) for large ensemble by Terry Riley, who became an important improviser on electronic keyboards tuned in just intonation with the LPs *Shri Camel* (1978) and *The Descending Moonshine Dervishes* (1982). Philip Glass defined his own sound with an amplified ensemble of two electric organs, woodwinds, and voice in such landmark works as *Music with Changing Parts* (1970), *Music in Twelve Parts* (1974), and the non-narrative opera *Einstein on the Beach* (1975). Also performing with his own ensemble, Steve Reich hit his stride with such acclaimed scores as *Drumming* (1971), *Music for Eighteen Musicians* (1976), and *Tehillim* (1981) for four female voices and orchestra. Other notable works in this style came from Julius Eastman, Louis Andriessen, John Adams, and Meredith Monk.

Minimalist composers who used repeated patterns without a constant beat, however, had a tougher time finding an audience. Improvising vocalist and pianist La Monte Young used repeated patterns in his pleroma and drone music, launching two ongoing minimalist classics in 1964 with *The Tortoise, His Dreams and Journeys* for voices, various instruments, and sine waves, and *The Well-Tuned Piano* for piano retuned in just intonation. By the 1970s, Morton Feldman was traditionally notating his sound world of quiet and unpulsed pitch patterns that repeat and subtly change with such great works as the vocal scores *Rothko Chapel* (1971) and *Neither* (1977) and the orchestral pieces *Coptic Light* (1985) and *For Samuel Beckett* (1987).

Young and Feldman proved every bit as daunting for audiences as the earlier generation of modernists had been in their day—especially when they turned to expanded time scales and created works lasting several hours. So did most other forms of minimalist music, regardless of scale, such as gradual-process music—slowing down and amplifying the transformation of a sound, as in works by Charlemagne Palestine, Frederick Rzewski, and Alvin Lucier—or singular-event music, focusing on an individual action, long or short, favored by such Fluxus composers as Young, George Maciunas, George Brecht, and Alison Knowles. Pauline Oliveros explored consciousness in her *Sonic Meditations I–XII* (1971) and *XIII–XXV* (1973). Another minimalist form that achieved popularity was ambient music—also anticipated by Satie in the 1920s—which seeks to complement ambient sound, not displace it. Brian Eno coined the term with his landmark LP *Music for Airports* (1978) and started an entire art-rock subgenre that includes music by John Zorn and Fred Frith.

All these subgroups of minimalist music can be considered nondramatic, insofar as they create coherence without contrast or development. From this perspective, minimalism arises with the chance and indeterminate works of Cage. In modernist serial music, each tone is as important as all the others by virtue of the unique place that it occupies in the composition's overall structure. In Cage's postmodern music, each sound, whether a tone or a noise, is as important as all the others in and of itself, because listening to it is worth doing, not because of any relationship that could be drawn between its frequency or duration or dynamic level or timbre or moment of appearance and those of any other sounds in the piece.

Similarly, the long shadow of Harry Partch can be seen in two other important fields of musicmaking in the late 20th century: alternate tuning systems and instrument building. The two have frequently overlapped, as Partch was not the only composer who had to design and/or build the instruments that could play his tunings: Hans Barth, Alois Hába, Julián Carrillo, and Percy Grainger all pursued microtonal systems on new instruments. But Partch also blazed a trail for composers who tune in just intonation, following the intervals of the overtone series; Young, Riley, Oliveros, Harrison, James Tenney, and Ben Johnston are among the many who have retuned their instruments in just systems. A different approach to the octave is to subdivide the half-tone into such gradations as third-, quarter-, sixth-, and eighth-tones, heard in the microtonal scores of John Foulds, Ivan Wyschnegradsky, Giacinto Scelsi, György Ligeti, Gérard Grisey, Horatiu Radulescu, and others.

Mauricio Kagel called for homemade instruments in *Acustica* (1970), and Tan Dun has written for ceramic and paper instruments. More common is the designing or building of new instruments by the composer/musicians who play them, such as Dlugoszewski, Moondog, Glenn Branca, Ellen Fullman, Frith, and Elliott Sharp. The postmodern attitude to new instruments also includes the appropriation of noninstruments, with such groups as Music for Homemade Instruments, making instruments from trash and found objects, or the Vienna Vegetable Orchestra. The deconstruction of traditional instruments can take the form of retuning, as with the just-intonation composers mentioned above, or extended performance techniques, as in works by Dlugoszewski, Krzysztof Penderecki, George Crumb, and Helmut Lachenmann.

Instrument building, noninstruments, new tunings, and extended performance techniques all became important factors in free improvisation, which featured polyrhythm, dissonance, atonality, noise, and densities. The genre arose in the United States and Europe during the late 1960s, drawing on the free-jazz composer/musicians Ornette Coleman, Cecil Taylor, and Sun Ra, the amplification and intensity of rock, and the simultaneities and noise of such composers as Varèse and Cage. This postmodern approach to improvisation, which embraces multimedia, multiculturalism, electronic music, and electroacoustic instruments, has engaged such important composer/musicians as reed player Zorn, guitarists Frith and Sharp, harpist Anne LeBaron, and percussionist Susie Ibarra.

CONTEMPORARY MUSIC AND PERSONAL MUSIC

In looking beyond modernist and traditional music, postmodernism has embraced popular music—a development anticipated by Erik Satie, who used pop materials for non-pop purposes during the 1910s and 1920s, and taken further in the jazz-influenced concert works of Milhaud, Poulenc, Copland, Kurt Weill, George Gershwin, William Russell, and others. What made vocalist and composer Robert Ashley postmodern was that he used the sounds of pop, jazz, and rock without relying on the modernist compositional mindset that he summed up as "You write a piece of music and then you give it to somebody and they give it to somebody else and finally it gets played."⁹ Ashley sidestepped the music publishers, opera houses, and other performing institutions and created intimate, nondramatic multimedia operas, rich in improvisation and simultaneities, always new in every realization. They include *Perfect Lives* (1977–1980), *Atalanta (Acts of God)* (1982–1987), *Now Eleanor's Idea* (1985–1994), *Dust* (1998), and *Celestial Excursions* (2003).

Ashley followed the path of composers who performed their own music, crediting John Cage and David Tudor as "just amazing pioneers in inventing the idea of a personal music. That change is a huge one, it's an amazing change in point of view. . . . It has caused a crossover of popular music and so-called concert music, which is going to change the audience for new music entirely."¹⁰ Postmodern musicmaking as Ashley has described it could indeed be the key in expanding the audience for new music. If so, it would represent a valuable healing to a century-old rift between audiences and composers. Stravinsky's *Le sacre du printemps*, although its Paris premiere provoked a near riot in 1913, became a staple of the repertory. Other types of modern music, however, have retained their disagreeability. Varèse's *Déserts* (1954) for 14 winds, piano, five percussionists, and two channels of magnetic tape had its premiere at Le Théatre de Champs-Elysées in Paris, where Stravinsky was met with such hostility four decades earlier, and it too provoked a scandal: "Murmurs at first, then, crescendo, waves of vociferous protest mingled with wavering applause, baritones and tenors hurling shouts of 'That's enough,' 'Shame, shame,' etc., ladylike cluckings."¹¹ But Varèse's masterpiece—dissonant and atonal, with interludes of electronic music—has remained at the fringe of the repertory, along with the rest of his works.

Much of the music surveyed in this dictionary has made itself less accessible to listeners insofar as its materials can be disagreeable or contradictory; indeed, some of it has been *so* novel and original as to render itself virtually unrecognizable. And almost none of it has had any real impact on the consciousness of the general public, which largely prefers entertainment to art and has turned to music by pop and rock composer/musicians. Yet the majority of people who listen to music, no matter how disinterested any of them might be in concert music, still recognize the names of Johann Sebastian Bach, George Frideric Handel, Wolfgang Amadeus Mozart, Ludwig van Beethoven, Frédéric Chopin, Franz Liszt, Richard Wagner, and Pytor Tchaikovsky as composers. The only names in this book certain to be likewise identified are Igor Stravinsky and Aaron Copland. The few others who would evoke such recognition—Scott Joplin, George Gershwin, Duke Ellington, Leonard Bernstein, the Beatles—all gained renown in popular music.

The growth of personal music has already transformed the audience for new music as Ashley envisioned, being responsible for some of the most vital and important musicmaking of the last 50 years, starting with the works of Ashley, Oliveros, and Young. Subsequent generations of composer/musicians include several major figures who brought a range of expression to their changing involvements with pop, jazz, blues, rock, and world music. Composer and improvising saxophonist Anthony Braxton has produced more than 350 compositions, all fundamentally interrelated with recombinable parts; they include the solos of his 1968 double LP *For Alto*, *Composition No. 82* (1978) for four orchestras and his *Trillium* series of operas (1984–present). In his instrumental compositions, electronic music, and piano improvisations, "Blue" Gene Tyranny has evoked emotion while remaining nondramatic and nonrepresentational; among his major works are *Harvey Milk (Portrait)* (1978), *The Intermediary* (1982), *Country Boy Country Dog* (1994), and *The Somewhere Songs* (1988–2001) and *George Fox Searches* (2010) for piano.

Fred Frith, as the improvising guitarist of *Guitar Solos* (1974), *Live in Japan* (1984), and *To Sail, To Sail* (2008), has redefined the instrument's sound; his notable compositions include the multicultural albums *Gravity* (1980) and *Speechless* (1981), *Lelekovice* (1990) for string quartet, and the Pablo Neruda settings *Pacifica* (1998). Anne LeBaron also uses extended performance techniques as an improvising harpist and has composed such important scores as *Lamentation/Invocation* (1984) for baritone and three instruments; the theatrical works *Concerto for Active Frogs* (1975) for voices, instruments, and tape; and *Hsing* (2002) for harp; and the operas *The E&O Line* (1991), *Croak (The Last Frog)* (1996), *Wet* (2005), and *Crescent City* (2010). Saxophonist John Zorn, one of the leading free improvisers, has composed works for improvising musicians (*Archery*, 1979; *Cobra*, 1984) and outstanding studio pieces (*Elegy*, 1991; *Kristallnacht*, 1995; *Interzone*, 2010); among his major concert scores are *The Dead Man* (1990) for string quartet and the opera *Rituals* (1998) for mezzo-soprano and 10 instruments.

Glenn Branca adapted minimalist techniques to ensembles of electric guitars, creating a visceral, high-volume pleroma music with 10 guitar symphonies: Nos. 1–6 (1981–1988), 8 (1992), 10 (1994), 12 (1998), and 13 (2001).

Equally dense and hallucinatory have been his instrumental symphonies, Nos. 7 (1989), 9 (1993), 11 (1998), and 14 (2008). Symphony No. 15 (2010) used guitars along with other instruments.

The Residents have created a unique sound world of dissonance, noise, synthesizers, samplers, and vocal and instrumental distortions. They also built instruments with new tunings for *Six Things to a Cycle* (1975) and *Eskimo* (1979). The Residents dissected pop consumerism in *The Third Reich 'n' Roll* (1976) and *The King & Eye* (1989), class warfare in *Mark of the Mole* (1981) and *The Tunes of Two Cities* (1982), and the huckstering of religion in *God in Three Persons* (1988). They have even brought their vision onstage with such live shows as *Wormwood* (1998) and *The Bunny Boy* (2008).

These and other composer/musicians have found their own vital ways through the contemporary expansion of possibilities, which has changed composition and improvisation and reshaped both new music and pop music. They have gained enough of an audience to permit their music to continue and grow without influence or compromise, and that is all the public any creative person really wants or needs.

NOTES

1. Don Michael Randel, *The Harvard Dictionary of Music* (Cambridge, Mass.: Harvard University Press, 2003), 59.

2. Léon Vallas, *Claude Debussy: His Life and Works* (New York: Dover, 1973), 42.

3. Dane Rudhyar, *The Magic of Tone and the Art of Music* (Boulder, Colo.: Shambhala, 1982), 103n.

4. Ralph Vaughan Williams, *National Music, and Other Essays* (New York: Oxford University Press, 1987), 191.

5. Anatole Leikin, "From Paganism to Orthodoxy to Theosophy: Reflections of Other Worlds in the Piano Music of Rachmaninov and Scriabin," in *Voicing the Ineffable: Musical Representations of Religious Experience*, edited by Siglind Bruhn (Hillsdale, N.Y.: Pendragon, 2002), 41.

6. Aaron Copland and Vivian Perlis, *Copland: 1900 through 1942* (New York: St. Martin's/Marek, 1984), 110.

7. Pierre Boulez, "Alea," in *Perspectives on Contemporary Music Theory*, edited by Benjamin Boretz and Edward T. Cone (New York: Norton, 1972), 47.

8. Cole Gagne and Tracy Caras, *Soundpieces: Interviews with American Composers* (Metuchen, N.J.: Scarecrow Press, 1982), 262.

9. Gagne and Caras, *Soundpieces*, 18.

10. Gagne and Caras, *Soundpieces*, 19.

11. Fernand Ouellette, *Edgard Varèse* (New York: Orion, 1968), 185–86.

ABRAMS, MUHAL RICHARD (1930–). American composer and musician. A multi-instrumentalist who is best known as a pianist, Muhal Richard Abrams is largely self-taught. He cofounded the Association for the Advancement of Creative Musicians, and his skill at playing both traditional and **free jazz** made Abrams a leader in creative African-American music. His recordings include solo performances (*Afrisong*, 1975; *Vision towards Essence*, 2007) and large-ensemble works (*Mama and Daddy*, 1980; *The Hearinga Suite*, 1990). *Visibility of Thought* (2001) featured Abrams on **computer** and **synthesizer**. Abrams has also worked with such composer/musicians as **Leroy Jenkins, Anthony Braxton, Anne LeBaron, Roscoe Mitchell**, and **George Lewis**. Among his compositions are *Quintet* (1982) for soprano, piano, harp, violin, and cello; *Piano Duet #1* (1986); *Saturation Blue* (1986) for chamber orchestra; and the orchestral scores *Transversion 1, Op. 6* (1991) and *Tomorrow's Song, as Yesterday Sings Today* (1999).

ADAMS, JOHN (1947–). American composer, musician, and educator. John Adams's teachers at Harvard University included **Roger Sessions** and **Leon Kirchner**, and he has taught at the San Francisco Conservatory of Music. Using a **minimalist**-influenced style, Adams composed such notable works as *Phrygian Gates* (1977) for piano, *Shaker Loops* (1978) for string septet or string orchestra, *Harmonium* (1981) for chorus and orchestra, and the orchestral scores *Grand Pianola Music* (1982) and *Harmonielehre* (1985). He is especially admired for his **operas**, which include *Nixon in China* (1987), *The Death of Klinghoffer* (1991), and *Doctor Atomic* (2005). A frequent conductor of 20th-century music, Adams is also the author of *The John Adams Reader* (2006) and *Hallelujah Junction* (2008). *See also* METRIC MODULATION; POSTMODERNISM.

ADAMS, JOHN LUTHER (1953–). American composer. John Luther Adams studied with **James Tenney** and Leonard Stein at the California Institute of the Arts. In 1978, he relocated to Alaska, and he has frequently evoked its landscape in **minimalist** works that rely on imaginative sonorities, atmosphere, and stillness. Adams's music includes *Night Peace* (1976) for antiphonal mixed chorus, soprano, harp, and percussion; the orchestral scores *The Far Country of Sleep* (1988), *In the White Silence* (1998), and *The Light That Fills the World* (2000); the percussion-ensemble works *Strange and Sacred Noise* (1997) and *Inuksuit* (2009); and pieces for mixed chamber ensembles such as *The Farthest Place* (2001) and *The Light Within* (2007). The creator of a permanent **sound installation** in Fairbanks's Museum of the North, Adams is also the author of *Winter Music* (2004) and *The Place Where You Go to Listen* (2009). *See also* POSTMODERNISM.

ALEATORY. The term *aleatory* has its origin in a 1957 article by **Pierre Boulez** entitled "Alea," the Latin word for dice. His polemical essay dismissed the **chance music** of **John Cage** (without mentioning his name), accusing it of poverty of compositional invention. Yet Boulez also sought to bring spontaneity into the rigidly formulated **total serialism** that he had embraced. He proposed an approach in which an otherwise strictly composed piece could leave certain parameters to the discretion of the performer, such as the sequencing of events or the selection of specific pitches or tempi, and thus introduce newness without obliging composer, musician, and listener to abandon their memories and tastes, which Cage saw as the true value of chance and **indeterminacy**.

Notable **open-form** precedents for aleatoric music include **Percy Grainger**'s *Random Round* (1915), **Henry Cowell**'s **elastic-form** scores of the 1930s, and the **free-rhythm** music of **Alan Hovhaness** in the 1940s. Unlike those innovations, however, aleatory was taken up internationally — Boulez was one of many composers in the mid-1950s who felt stifled by the inflexibility of their **serial** methods. By the time he began using aleatoric techniques in his *Troisième sonate* (1957) and *Pli selon pli* (1958), Boulez had been beaten to the punch by two 1956 works: **Karlheinz Stockhausen**'s *Klavierstuck XI* utilized randomness, and **Iannis Xenakis**'s *Pithoprakhta* introduced **stochastic music**. The idea of aleatory spread quickly and was used by many, including **Lukas Foss, Luciano Berio, Ernst Krenek, Witold Lutoslawski, Bruno Maderna, Alberto Ginastera, Jacob Druckman, Barbara Kolb, Mel Powell**, and **George Russell**.

ALTERNATE TUNING SYSTEMS. Although any conceivable division of the octave is available, by the mid-19th century, the standard tuning system in Western music was equal temperament, which divides the octave into 12 more or less equivalent intervals known as *semitones*. These intervals define the 12 tones of the chromatic scale and permit a work to be transposed into any key without losing the intervallic relationships that make the music identifiable to the ear. In the 20th century, two traditions of alternate tuning systems emerged. **Microtonal** music splits the semitone into smaller divisions, such as **quarter-tones**. **Just intonation** discards equal-tempered tunings and uses instead the intervals that are produced naturally as overtones in the harmonic series.

AMACHER, MARYANNE (1938–2009). American composer, musician, and educator. Maryanne Amacher studied in the United States and Europe; among her teachers were **George Rochberg** and **Karlheinz Stockhausen**. She taught **electronic music** at Bard College (2000–2009) and composed such electronic works as *Torse* (1976) and *TEO! A Four-Part Sonic Sculpture* (2008). Amacher is best known for her series of site-specific **sound installations**, which include "City Links" Nos. 1–21 (1967–1979), uniting distant locations over telephone lines, and "Music for Sound-Joined Rooms" (1980–2002).

AMBIENT MUSIC. The notion of music that tints and complements ambient sound rather than obliterating it emerges with **Erik Satie**, whose *Musique d'ameublement* of the early 1920s gave musicians fragmentary phrases to perform in public areas. Satie's innovation, however, failed to attract immediate successors. Only **John Cage** was more willing to efface himself than Satie had been: Cage's landmark tacet score *4'33"* (1952) had audiences listening to the ambient sounds of the performance space. But as **minimalism** entered the musical mainstream, other composers began building upon Satie's approach. **Karlheinz Stockhausen** was ahead of the curve with the lengthy and meditative *Fresco* (1969) for four orchestra groups; so was **Wendy Carlos** with her **electronic-music** double LP *Sonic Seasonings* (1972).

The breakthrough came with **Brian Eno**, who coined the term *ambient music* for his classic LP *Music for Airports* (1978), which used subtly changing phrases as a calming and contemplative background sound that could be listened to or ignored. Harold Budd joined Eno for *The Plateaux of Mirror* (1979), and this genre soon took on a life of its own, attracting such art-rock composer/musicians as **John Zorn, Fred Frith**, Klaus Schulze, Robert Fripp, and Jean-Michel Jarre. *See also* POSTMODERNISM.

AMIRKHANIAN, CHARLES (1945–). American composer and musician. Charles Amirkhanian was music director of KPFA/Berkeley (1969–1992) and since 1993 has directed the Other Minds music festivals. Amirkhanian's works are mostly **electroacoustic music** (*His Anxious Hours* for chamber ensemble and **tape**, 1987; *Ripping the Lamp* for violin and tape, 2007) and text-sound compositions (*Just*, 1972; *Loudspeakers*, 1990). His **electronic music** with **sampled** sounds includes *Walking Tune* (1987).

AMM. The **free-improvisation** ensemble AMM was formed in London in 1965 by jazz musicians Lou Gare (tenor saxophone), Eddie Prévost (percussion), and Keith Rowe (electric guitar), who were soon joined by **Cornelius Cardew** (piano, cello). AMM turned to live electronics, using Rowe's guitar, transistor radios, contact microphones, and other devices. Their **electroacoustic** performances defined the group, which has performed internationally. Others who have played with AMM include Lawrence Sheaff, Christopher Hobbs, John Tilbury, and **Christian Wolff**. Notable recordings include *The Crypt 12th June 1968* (1969), *To Hear and Back Again* (1973), *Generative Themes* (1983), *The Nameless Uncarved Block* (1990), *Laminal* (1994), *Fine* (2001), and *Sounding Music* (2010). *See also* ELECTRONIC MUSIC; POSTMODERNISM.

ANALOG NOTATION. *See* PROPORTIONAL NOTATION.

ANDERSON, LAURIE (1947–). American composer and musician. Laurie Anderson featured music with the characterizations and commentaries of her performance art, as in the 1977 pieces *New York Social Life* and *Time to Go (for Diego)*. Her work reached epic length with the popular *United States* (1979–1983), a **multimedia** piece featuring **tape**, projections, and electronics that altered her voice and her violin playing. Also a filmmaker (*Home of the Brave*, 1986), Anderson has composed **electroacoustic music** for orchestra (*Born, Never Asked*, 1980; *It's Cold Outside*, 1981) and has worked with such composer/musicians as **Brian Eno**, **George Lewis**, **"Blue" Gene Tyranny**, and **Peter Gordon**. Among her art-rock albums are *Strange Angels* (1989) and *Bright Red* (1994). Her recent stage works include *Songs and Stories from Moby Dick* (1999) and *Delusion* (2010). *See also* COMPUTER MUSIC; FILM MUSIC; POSTMODERNISM.

ANDRIESSEN, LOUIS (1939–). Dutch composer, musician, and educator. Louis Andriessen studied with his father, composer Hendrik Andriessen; with Kees van Baarren at the Royal Conservatory in The Hague (1957–1962); and with **Luciano Berio** (1962–1964). He has taught at the Royal Conservatory since 1974 and was a founder and pianist of Orkest de Volharding (1972–present) and Hoketus (1976–1986), ensembles named after his compositions. Andriessen's approach to **minimalism** employs driving rhythms and colorful orchestrations, sometimes massing or opposing like voices; repeated patterns are utilized within a larger formal structure that can reflect social or spiritual concerns. Major works include *De volharding* (1972) for three saxophones, three trumpets, three trombones, and piano; *Hoketus* (1977) for two amplified ensembles; and *De snelheid* (1983, rev. 1984) for three amplified ensembles.

Female voices are featured in *De staadt* (1976), *De tijd* (1981), and *TAO* (1996). Andriessen has composed music-theater works such as *George Sand* (1980) and *Inanna* (2003) and the **operas** *Writing to Vermeer* (1998) and *La Commedia* (2008). Among his notable smaller-scale works are *Symfonie voor losse snaren* (1978), for 12 string instruments retuned to provide a full spectrum of pitches on open strings; *Hout* (1991) for tenor saxophone, marimba, guitar, and piano; and *Fanfare, om te beginnen* (2001) for six groups of French horns. *See also* ALTERNATE TUNING SYSTEMS; PLEROMA; POSTMODERNISM.

ANTHEIL, GEORGE (1900–1959). American composer and musician. George Antheil studied with Constantine von Sternberg and **Ernest Bloch**. He left the United States in 1922 and performed in Europe, creating *scandales* with his percussive and **dissonant** piano music such as Sonata No. 2, "Airplane" (1922), *Sonata Sauvage* (1923), and *Sonatina: Death of the Machines* (1923). The pianist doubles on drums in Sonata No. 2 for Violin and Piano with Drums (1923), which **quotes** pop and salon music of the day. Antheil's Piano Concerto No. 1 (1922) and String Quartet No. 1 (1924) were also **modernist** works, and jazz informed his Symphony No. 1 (1920), *Jazz Sonata* (1922) for piano, and *Jazz Symphony* (1925, rev. 1955) which was premiered in 1927 by the W. C. Handy Orchestra.

Antheil settled in Paris in 1923, and his music was promoted by **Ezra Pound**. *Ballet pour instruments mécaniques et percussion* (1925, rev. 1952) was Antheil's greatest provocation. The ensemble for the 1926 Paris premiere included eight pianos, a player piano, four xylophones, glockenspiel, gong, cymbal, triangle, wood block, various drums, two electric bells, and electric fans doctored with strips of leather that slapped a thin board to create the sounds of small and large airplane propellers. The resulting din, punctuated with extended oases of silence, elicited praise and shock. When *Ballet mécanique* premiered in America in 1927—with extra pianists and a real propeller—it was met with disdain. The Frankfurt production of Antheil's **opera** *Transatlantic* (1928) was also a failure, and he returned to the United States in 1933. Antheil's subsequent music—Symphonies Nos. 2–6 (1938–1947), Violin Concerto (1946), Piano Sonatas Nos. 3–5 (1947–1950)—was tonal and traditional. He also composed numerous **film** scores and wrote an autobiography, *Bad Boy of Music* (1945). *See also* MINIMALISM.

ASHLEY, ROBERT (1930–). American composer, musician, and educator. Robert Ashley's innovations in music theater, **opera**, and **electroacoustic music** make him one of the most important **postmodern** composers in American music. Born in Ann Arbor, Michigan, Ashley trained as a pianist.

He graduated with a BMus from the University of Michigan in 1952 and attended the Manhattan School of Music, receiving his MMus in 1954; he also studied privately with **Wallingford Riegger**. During these years, Ashley lost interest in playing jazz and concert music, feeling that they had no relation to his everyday experience of life. He returned to the University of Michigan and studied composition with **Ross Lee Finney**, **Roberto Gerhard**, and Leslie Bassett (1957–1960). He also utilized the Speech Research Laboratories there to study psychoacoustics and cultural speech patterns—areas that would inform most of his later music.

Ashley formed the Cooperative Studio for Electronic Music (1958–1966) with composer **Gordon Mumma**, gathering equipment for **tape** and **electronic music** in real-time performance. He had been performing his Piano Sonata since the mid-1950s, but in 1959 he stopped trying to notate his jazz-derived piano playing. He organized the legendary **ONCE Group** in 1960, bringing together his first wife Mary Ashley, a visual and performance artist, light sculptor Milton Cohen, Mumma, **Roger Reynolds**, and other like-minded creative people. Their series of ONCE Festival performances (1961–1969) became a national showcase for new and experimental music.

Seeking to write down different techniques for achieving the spontaneity of jazz performance, Ashley used **graphic notation** for several scores in the early 1960s, including *Maneuvers for Small Hands* (1961) for piano and *Trios (White on White)* (1963) for various instruments. The four *In memoriam . . .* pieces (1963) employed a range of performers and were each subtitled with a traditional genre; the fourth, *Kit Carson*, was scored for eight-part ensemble and was Ashley's first designated opera. Perhaps most admired and notorious was *The Wolfman* (1964) for amplified voice and tape.

Ashley created **multimedia** music theater with the ONCE Group such as *Combination Wedding and Funeral* (1964) and *Orange Dessert* (1965). With Mary Ashley, he co-composed *The Lecture Series* (1964) and *Night Train* (1966). His second opera was *That Morning Thing* (1967) for solo voices, women's chorus, dancers, and tapes, from which Ashley derived *She Was a Visitor* (1967) for speaker and chorus. The **Sonic Arts Union**, a composers collective he cofounded in 1966 with Mumma, **Alvin Lucier**, and **David Behrman**, performed in the United States and Europe for a decade, presenting such works as his electronic music theater piece *Purposeful Lady Slow Afternoon* (1968) and *Fancy Free, or It's There* (1970) for male speaker and four cassette-recorder operators.

Serving as director of the Center for Contemporary Music at Mills College from 1969 to 1981, Ashley discouraged students from writing scores for other musicians, and instead had them playing their own music. The results confirmed his belief in a personal music, realized without mediation, which would further the intermingling of popular and concert music. Ashley proved his point with a masterpiece: the epochal *Perfect Lives*, completed in 1980, a video opera for television consisting of seven 30-minute episodes. He had performed versions of the different episodes since 1977 and would continue to do so into 1983, changing the pieces with every realization and evoking new spontaneities.

In 1976, Ashley produced and directed *Music with Roots in the Aether*, seven video portraits of composers and their music: himself, Mumma, Lucier, Behrman, **Philip Glass**, **Pauline Oliveros**, and **Terry Riley**. Ashley's 1979 release *Automatic Writing* for voices and electronic sounds was a dreamlike excursion into involuntary speech. *Perfect Lives* was followed by the opera *Atalanta (Acts of God)*, realized in 1982–1987, which yielded the television opera *Atalanta Strategy* (1984). *Now Eleanor's Idea*, the third part of a trilogy with *Perfect Lives* and *Atalanta*, is itself a tetralogy consisting of *Improvement (Don Leaves Linda)* (1985), *el/Aficionado* (1987), *Now Eleanor's Idea* (1993), and *Foreign Experiences* (1994). Musicians who have performed in Ashley's operas include **Peter Gordon**, **Thomas Buckner**, **Joan La Barbara**, and **"Blue" Gene Tyranny**.

With a **minimalist** disdain for drama, Ashley writes texts of monologues with a stream-of-consciousness quality, although he did set a libretto by Maria Irene Fornes for the opera *Balseros* (1997), commissioned by the Florida Grand Opera. Among his later instrumental works are *Basic 10* (1988) for snare drum or other percussion instruments, *Outcome Inevitable* (1991) for chamber orchestra, and *Van Caos' Meditation* (1992) for piano. He has also composed two operas that reflect on mortality: *Dust* (1998) and *Celestial Excursions* (2003). Ashley's recent vocal works include *Hidden Similarities* (2005) for voices and eight instruments and the operas *Concrete* (2006) and *Quicksand* (2008). *See also* INDETERMINACY; MULTICULTURALISM; SYNTHESIZER.

ATONALITY. The second half of the 19th century saw a relaxation of the traditionally strict reliance on a tonal center to anchor and define a score and its harmonic movement, due in large part to the pronounced chromaticism of Richard Wagner's operas, most notably *Tristan und Isolde* (1859) and *Parsifal* (1882). Franz Liszt's *Bagatelle sans tonalité* (1885) for piano is perhaps the most extreme and prophetic work of that time. **Claude Debussy**, **Gustav Mahler**, **Charles Ives**, and **Alexander Scriabin** all pushed against the limits of tonal composition in the first decade of the 20th century, and by 1909 **Arnold Schoenberg** was composing without tonality in such works as *Erwartung*. When his **modernist** music was called "atonal," however, Schoenberg resisted the label as a misnomer, describing a music without tones. He preferred the term *pantonal*, an equal importance of all the pitches, as opposed to the pecking orders of tonal organization. But the term *atonal* stuck as a designation for music that is not tonal.

Schoenberg developed his **twelve-tone** method in the early 1920s, and this technique was embraced by many composers over the decades; it also impacted the music of independent atonal chromatic composers such as **Elliott Carter, Stefan Wolpe, Miriam Gideon,** and **Ralph Shapey.** Other methods for avoiding tonality include **chance** and **indeterminate** procedures, as employed by **John Cage** and his followers; developing new sounds with **tape music, electronic music,** and **electroacoustic music;** and the use of density and noise, as in the music of **Conlon Nancarrow, Iannis Xenakis, Karlheinz Stockhausen, Sun Ra,** or the **free improvisers.** *See also* BABBITT, MILTON; BARRAQUÉ, JEAN; BARTÓK, BÉLA; BECKER, JOHN J.; BERG, ALBAN; BERIO, LUCIANO; BEYER, JOHANNA M.; BIRTWISTLE, HARRISON; BOULEZ, PIERRE; BRAXTON, ANTHONY; BROWN, EARLE; CARDEW, CORNELIUS; COLEMAN, ORNETTE; COWELL, HENRY; DALLAPICCOLA, LUIGI; DAVIDOVSKY, MARIO; DAVIES, PETER MAXWELL; DLUGOSZEWSKI, LUCIA; DRUCKMAN, JACOB; EISLER, HANNS; FELDMAN, MORTON; FERNEYHOUGH, BRIAN; FERRARI, LUC; FINE, VIVIAN; FINNEY, ROSS LEE; FOSS, LUKAS; FREE JAZZ; GERHARD, ROBERTO; GOEHR, ALEXANDER; HAUER, JOSEF MATTHIAS; HENRY, PIERRE; HILLER, LEJAREN; HUNT, JERRY; KIRCHNER, LEON; KOSUGI, TAKEHISA; KRENEK, ERNST; LEÓN, TANIA; LIGETI, GYÖRGY; LUENING, OTTO; LUTOSLAWSKI, WITOLD; MADERNA, BRUNO; MAMLOK, URSULA; MARTIN, FRANK; NONO, LUIGI; POSTMODERNISM; POUSSEUR, HENRI; POWELL, MEL; REYNOLDS, ROGER; RIEGGER, WALLINGFORD; ROCHBERG, GEORGE; RUDHYAR, DANE; RUGGLES, CARL; SCHAEFFER, PIERRE; SCHULLER, GUNTHER; SEEGER, RUTH CRAWFORD; SESSIONS, ROGER; STRAVINSKY, IGOR; SUBOTNICK, MORTON; TAKAHASHI, YUJI; TAKEMITSU, TORU; TAL, JOSEF; TALMA, LOUISE; TAYLOR, CECIL; TENNEY, JAMES; TUDOR, DAVID; USSACHEVSKY, VLADIMIR; VARÈSE, EDGARD; WEBER, BEN; WEBERN, ANTON; WOLFF, CHRISTIAN; WUORINEN, CHARLES; ZIMMERMANN, BERND ALOIS; ZORN, JOHN.

AURIC, GEORGES. *See* GROUPE DES SIX.

AUSTIN, LARRY (1930–). American composer, musician, and educator. Larry Austin studied with **Darius Milhaud,** Violet Archer, and Andrew Imbrie. He taught at the University of North Texas (1978–1996) and other institutions and is the coauthor of *Learning to Compose* (1989). The founder and conductor of the New Music Ensemble (1963–1968), Austin also founded and edited the new-music journal *Source* (1967–1973). Frequently utilizing randomness and **indeterminacy**, Austin first gained renown with such compositions as *Improvisations for Orchestra and Jazz Soloists* (1961) and *Changes* (1965) for trombone and tape. Among his **multimedia** works are *Bass* (1966), *Tableaux vivants* (1973, rev. 1981), and *Catalogo voce* (1979). His **electronic music** includes *Phoenix* (1974), **Stars* (1982), *Djuro's Tree* (1997), and *John Explains* (2007). Austin's recent **electroacoustic** scores have combined **computer** with violin in *Redux* (2007) and piano in *Redux-Two* (2008). *See also* IVES, CHARLES; POSTMODERNISM.

B

BABBITT, MILTON (1916–2011). American composer and educator. Milton Babbitt studied with **Marion Bauer** at New York University in 1934 and began private studies with **Roger Sessions** the following year. He later joined Sessions on the faculty at Princeton University (1938–1984), where his students included **Lejaren Hiller, Jonathan Harvey, Richard Maxfield,** and **Harrison Birtwistle.** Babbitt originated the techniques of **total serialism,** extending **Arnold Schoenberg**'s **twelve-tone** method of pitch organization to rhythm, dynamics, and timbre in *Three Compositions for Piano* (1947), *Composition for Four Instruments* (1948), *Composition for 12 Instruments* (1948), and such 1950s works as the vocal scores *The Widow's Lament in Springtime* (1950), *Du* (1953), and *Two Sonnets* (1955); *Composition for Viola and Piano* (1950); and *All Set* (1957) for jazz ensemble.

Babbitt was codirector of the Columbia-Princeton Electronic Music Center, founded in 1958, and consulted in the creation of its RCA Mark II **Synthesizer.** Prizing **electronic music** for its precise articulation of highly complex rhythms, he created *Composition for Synthesizer* (1961) and *Ensembles* (1964) for synthesizer. He also combined electronic sounds with other instruments: soprano voice in *Vision and Prayer* (1961), *Philomel* (1964), and *Phonemena* (1974); string orchestra in *Correspondences* (1967); piano in *Reflections* (1975); violin and small orchestra in *Concerti* (1976); and saxophone in *Images* (1979).

Although the rigors of Babbitt's music made large-ensemble performances infrequent, he composed the orchestral pieces *Relata I* (1965), *Relata II* (1968), Piano Concertos Nos. 1 (1985) and 2 (1998), *Transfigured Notes* (1986) for string orchestra, and *Concerti for Orchestra* (2004). More frequently he wrote for chamber groups: *Four Play* (1984) for clarinet, violin, cello, and piano; *Counterparts* (1992) for brass quintet; *Quartet* (1995) for piano and strings; *Quintet* (1996) for clarinet and strings; *Swan Song No. 1* (2003) for six instruments, and six string quartets (1948–1993). His other major works for voice include *An Elizabethan Sextette* (1979) for six-part women's chorus, *Three Cultivated Choruses* (1982) for four-part chorus, *Four Cavalier Settings* (1991) for tenor and guitar, and *Autobiography of the Eye* (2004) for soprano and cello. *See also* ATONALITY; ELECTRO-ACOUSTIC MUSIC; MODERNISM; SERIALISM.

BARBER, SAMUEL (1910–1981). American composer and musician. Samuel Barber studied with Rosario Scalero at the Curtis Institute of Music. A baritone and pianist, he composed **neoromantic** music with his own lyrical sound, beginning with such major works of the 1930s as *Dover Beach* (1931) for voice and string quartet, the overture to *The School for Scandal* (1932) for orchestra, and his classic *Adagio for Strings* (1936). Barber's later music could be more **dissonant**, as in the ballet score *Medea* (1947) and Symphony No. 2 (1950). His Piano Sonata (1948) and Nocturne (1959) for piano explored **twelve-tone** techniques. Barber was also expert at writing for voice—with orchestra in *Knoxville: Summer of 1915* (1947) and with piano in *Hermit Songs* (1953). His notable later works include *Prayers of Kierkegaard* (1954) for soprano, mixed chorus, and orchestra; the **operas** *Vanessa* (1958) and *Antony and Cleopatra* (1966); Piano Concerto (1962); and *Third Essay for Orchestra* (1978).

BARRAQUÉ, JEAN (1928–1973). French composer and critic. Jean Barraqué studied with **Olivier Messiaen**. A dynamic personal approach to **serialism** characterizes his small output: Piano Sonata (1952); *Étude* (1953) for **tape**; *Séquence* (1955) for soprano and instruments; *Le temps restitué* (1957, orch. 1968) for soprano, mixed chorus, and orchestra; . . . *au-délà du hasard* (1959) for three female voices and four instrumental groups; *Chant après chant* (1966) for soprano, piano, and percussion sextet; and Concerto (1968) for clarinet, vibraphone, and six instrumental trios. Barraqué's critical writings include the book *Debussy* (1962). *See also* ATONALITY; MODERNISM.

BARTH, HANS (1897–1956). German-born American composer, musician, and educator. Hans Barth studied at the Leipzig Conservatory as a child and settled in the United States with his family in 1907, becoming a citizen in 1912. A concert pianist, he also taught at several American institutions. Barth designed a **quarter-tone** piano that he used in his Piano Concerto (1928), *Concerto for Quarter-Tone Piano and Quarter-Tone Strings* (1930), Quintet (1930) with strings, and *Ten Etudes for Quarter-Tone Piano and Orchestra* (1944). His other **microtonal** works include the chamber **opera** *Miragia* (1928) and Suite (1930) for quarter-tone strings, brass, and kettledrums. *See also* ALTERNATE TUNING SYSTEMS; INSTRUMENT BUILDING; MODERNISM.

BARTÓK, BÉLA (1881–1945). Hungarian-born American composer, musician, and educator. One of the crucial **modernists** of the first half of the

20th century, Béla Bartók transmuted folk music into radical new harmonies, rhythms, and timbres. Born in the village of Nagyszentmiklós in Hungary (today Sînnicolau Mare, Romania), Béla Viktor János Bartók received piano lessons from his mother at age five and was composing by nine. In 1899, he began studying at the Budapest Academy of Music with István Tomán (piano) and János Koessler (composition). Bartók's first scores showed the impress of Ludwig van Beethoven and Johannes Brahms; in the early 1900s, he was also drawn to the works of Franz Liszt, Richard Wagner, and **Richard Strauss**. The seismic shift in his composition occurred when he heard the folk music of Slovakia in 1904. For the rest of his life, Bartók studied, transcribed, and arranged what he referred to respectfully as "peasant music," becoming one of the great ethnomusicologists of his day in researching the folk music of Hungary, Romania, and Slovakia, as well as Turkish and Arabic music. He co-composed *Twenty Hungarian Folksongs* (1906) with his friend **Zoltán Kodály**, another folk-music enthusiast.

In 1907, Bartók was appointed to the piano staff of the Budapest Academy, where he taught until 1934. He encountered the music of **Claude Debussy** then, and the qualities of Hungarian folk music that he heard in Debussy's harmonies and melodies prompted Bartók to turn away from Germanic models in his music. **Impressionism** and folk music are reflected in the unusual motivic structures, lively rhythms, and **polytonal** passages of Bartók's first major works: Violin Concerto No. 1 (1908), *14 Bagatelles* (1908) for piano, String Quartet No. 1 (1909), and *Two Pictures* (1910) for orchestra. His music elaborated into fierce **dissonances** and dark **expressionist** shadings with three great theater works: the one-act **opera** *Duke Bluebeard's Castle* (1911), the ballet *The Wooden Prince* (1916), and the pantomime *The Miraculous Mandarin* (1919). He also relied less upon the use of a home key in his String Quartet No. 2 (1917) and such piano scores as *Allegro barbaro* (1911) and Suite (1916).

Utilizing drones and reiterated tones, Bartók would establish tonal emphases or levels, creating the sensation of a key while avoiding its harmonic limitations. This use of a centralizing tone to maintain musical character, which Bartók called **pantonality**, opened his musical sensibility to any available pitch or sound. His Sonatas Nos. 1 (1921) and 2 (1922) for violin and piano were unusually chromatic and dense, with affinities to the **atonal** and **twelve-tone** music of **Arnold Schoenberg**. After a 1923 encounter with the **tone-cluster** piano music of **Henry Cowell**, Bartók's use of densities and rhythmic complexity became even more extreme in his Piano Sonata (1926), Piano Concerto No. 1 (1926), and String Quartets Nos. 3 (1927) and 4 (1928). "*Musique nocturnes*," the fifth movement of *Out of Doors* (1926) for piano, gave a name to the atmospheric "night music" passages he developed during the 1920s. Impressionism and expressionism overlap in these mysterious sound worlds, rich with the unusual timbres of **extended performance techniques** and tiny enigmatic gestures suggestive of nocturnal nature.

Bartók's international reputation spread during the 1930s, thanks to his concertizing and the performances of such major scores as *Cantata profana* (1930) for soloists, chorus, and orchestra; Piano Concerto No. 2 (1933); *Music for Strings, Percussion, and Celesta* (1936); Sonata for Two Pianos and Percussion (1937); *Contrasts* (1938) for clarinet, violin, and piano; Violin Concerto No. 2 (1938); and String Quartets Nos. 5 (1935) and 6 (1939). But by the end of the 1930s, the Hungarian government was preparing to join the Axis nations, and so Bartók, an unwavering opponent of fascism, decided to leave his homeland. He emigrated to the United States, arriving in 1940.

Residing chiefly in New York, Bartók maintained a precarious existence, performing occasionally (often with his second wife, pianist Ditta Pásztory) and cataloging folk-music collections for Columbia University, where he received an honorary doctorate in 1940. He was plagued by ill health throughout his life, and his physical condition deteriorated drastically during his last years in America. Yet Bartók rallied from depression and illness to produce two of his finest and most popular scores: Concerto for Orchestra (1943) and Piano Concerto No. 3 (1945). He became a U.S. citizen in 1945, but by then had developed leukemia, and he soon died in a New York hospital at age 64. *See also* GEBRAUCHSMUSIK; MULTICULTURALISM; QUARTER-TONE MUSIC.

BAUER, MARION (1882–1955). American composer, musician, educator, and critic. Pianist Marion Bauer studied with **Nadia Boulanger** and taught at New York University (1926–1951) and other institutions; her students include **Milton Babbitt** and **Miriam Gideon**. Bauer developed an **impressionist** sensibility in *From the New Hampshire Woods* (1921) for piano and *A Lament on an African Theme* (1927) for orchestra; her more aggressively **modernist** scores include *Turbulence* (1924) for piano, String Quartet (1925), and Four Piano Pieces (1930). *Sun Splendor* (1926) for two pianos found success in her 1947 orchestration; so did more conservative works such as *Symphonic Suite for Strings* (1940), *American Youth Concerto* (1943) for piano and orchestra, and Symphony No. 1 (1950). Her piano pieces *Patterns* (1946) and *Moods* (1954) employed **twelve-tone** techniques. The author of *Twentieth-Century Music* (1933, rev. 1947) and other books, Bauer also wrote criticism for the magazines *Modern Music* and *The Musical Leader*.

BAX, (SIR) ARNOLD (1883–1953). English composer and musician. Arnold Bax studied composition and piano at London's Royal Academy of Music. He first gained attention with such works for voice and piano as *A Celtic*

Song Cycle (1904) and *The White Peace* (1906). Blending postromantic and **impressionist** qualities with Irish, Russian, and German folk song, Bax found his greatest success with orchestral music: *The Garden of Fand* (1913, orch. 1916), *November Woods* (1917), *Tintagel* (1917, orch. 1919), *Summer Music* (1917, orch. 1921, rev. 1932), and seven symphonies (1922–1939). He was knighted in 1937 and served as Master of the King's Musick (1942–1952). Bax's late works include his Violin Concerto (1938), *A Legend* (1944) for orchestra, Piano Trio (1945), and the score of David Lean's 1948 **film** *Oliver Twist*.

BEATLES, THE. English composers and musicians. Arguably the greatest band in the history of rock music, the Beatles also became the most commercially successful composers of 20th-century avant-garde music, creating innovative records that were internationally celebrated. They were a unique convergence of talent, with three major artists in singer/multi-instrumentalist/composers John Lennon (1940–1980), Paul McCartney (1942–), and George Harrison (1943–2001). Playing with drummer Ringo Starr (1940–), they released albums produced by George Martin, which exploited some of the new possibilities in processing and transforming vocal and instrumental tracks. *Revolver* (1966) featured remarkable **tape-music** effects for Lennon's "Tomorrow Never Knows"; Harrison's guitar is also heard backwards there and on Lennon's "I'm Only Sleeping." McCartney's "Eleanor Rigby" had a string quartet accompanying the voices. Harrison introduced a **multicultural** dimension, playing sitar on "Love You To" and employing Indian techniques in "Taxman" and "I Want to Tell You."

Indian elements also define Harrison's "Within You Without You" on *Sgt. Pepper's Lonely Hearts Club Band* (1967)—which included the face of **Karlheinz Stockhausen** on its cover. Lennon utilized startling instrumental densities in "A Day in the Life" and tape collages in "Being for the Benefit of Mr. Kite," qualities he also explored in "All You Need Is Love" and "I Am the Walrus" on *Magical Mystery Tour* (1967). His "Revolution 9" on the double LP *The Beatles* (1968, a.k.a. *The White Album*) was a work of pure *musique concrète*. *Abbey Road* (1969), the Beatles' final album, used segues, edits, and reprises to weave Lennon and McCartney's songs into a suite. It also featured one of the first **synthesizers** available, used on McCartney's "Maxwell's Silver Hammer," Harrison's "Here Comes the Sun," and Lennon's "I Want You (She's So Heavy)." Lennon pursued the tape experiments of "Revolution 9" with **Yoko Ono** on their LP *Two Virgins* (1968), Harrison released the synthesizer album *Electronic Sound* (1969), and McCartney collaborated with composer/arranger Carl Davis on *Liverpool Oratorio* (1991) for soloists, mixed chorus, and orchestra. *See also* POSTMODERNISM.

BECKER, JOHN J. (1886–1961). American composer, musician, and educator. John Joseph Becker graduated from Cincinnati Krueger Conservatory in 1905 and received his doctorate from the Wisconsin Conservatory in 1923. He also taught at the Kidd-Key Conservatory of North Texas (1906–1914) and the University of Notre Dame (1918–1928). His early music featured **impressionist** techniques, but a 1928 encounter with **Henry Cowell** encouraged Becker to pursue a more **modernist** path. His *Symphonia brevis* (1929) for orchestra and *Concerto arabesque* (1930) for piano and chamber orchestra featured **dissonant atonal** counterpoint, inspired by 16th-century polyphony. Becker was then chairing the Department of Fine Arts at St. Thomas College in St. Paul, Minnesota (1929–1933), where he founded a chamber orchestra that he led in music by Cowell, **Charles Ives, Carl Ruggles, Wallingford Riegger**, and himself.

Becker called for dancers in the 1932 scores *Abongo* for large percussion ensemble and *Dance Figure* for voice and orchestra. His search for a new music drama resulted in the **multimedia** work *A Marriage with Space* (1935) for orchestra, dancers, actors, colors, and lights, from which he derived his Symphony No. 4, "Dramatic Scenes" (1938). He also extracted an orchestral suite from his one-act dance play *When the Willow Nods* (1939). *Privilege and Privation* (1940) was a one-act **opera** with chamber orchestra.

Becker's other important compositions of the 1930s include *Missa symphonica* (1933) for male voices, Concerto for Horn and Orchestra (1933), *Psalms of Love* (1935) for soprano or tenor and piano, and his *Soundpieces* series of chamber works, launched with *Soundpiece for Piano and String Quartet* (1933). *Soundpiece No. 2* for string quartet and *No. 3* for violin and piano followed in 1936; *No. 4* for string quartet and *No. 5* for piano, in 1937.

Becker was director of the Federal Music Project in Minnesota (1935–1941) and taught at Barat College (1943–1957) and Chicago Musical College (1949–1953). His composition became less frequent in his last years, but includes such notable works as *At Dieppe* (1959) for voice and piano and his final soundpieces: *No. 6* (1942) for flute and clarinet, *No. 7* (1949) for two pianos, and *No. 8* (1959) for string quartet.

BEHRMAN, DAVID (1937–). Austrian-born American composer, musician, and educator. David Behrman learned the basics of **electronic music** from **Gordon Mumma** and was a student of **Henri Pousseur** in Brussels. He was a composer/musician for the Merce Cunningham Dance Company and has taught at Mills College, Rutgers University, and Bard College, among other institutions. A cofounder of the **Sonic Arts Union** (1966–1976), Behrman performed internationally with Mumma, **Robert Ashley**, and **Alvin Lucier**, playing such electronic works as *Wave Trains* (1967) and *Run-*

through (1970). He began using interactive **computers** in his **electroacoustic music** with *Figure in a Clearing* (1977), combining it with a cello. A computer was also used in *Interspecies Smalltalk* (1984) with violin, in *Leapday Night* (1986) with trumpets, and in *Navigation and Astronomy* (1990) with koto. *My Dear Siegfried* (2003) combined a **sampler** and computer with its vocalists and instrumentalists. Among Behrman's **sound installations** are *In Thin Air* (1997) and *Pen Light & View Finder* (2002). *See also* MULTICULTURALISM; POSTMODERNISM.

BERBERIAN, CATHY (1925–1983). American composer, musician, and educator. Mezzo-soprano Cathy Berberian studied at the Milan Conservatory and became an important performer of contemporary music. She was married (1950–1965) to **Luciano Berio**, who created for her *Circles* (1960), *Folk Songs* (1964), *Sequenza III* (1966), and *Recital I (for Cathy)* (1972). Other composers who wrote music for Berberian include **Igor Stravinsky, Hans Werner Henze, Sylvano Bussotti, Henri Pousseur**, and **John Cage**. She also composed the **graphic** score *Stripsody* (1966) for solo voice and taught at Vancouver University and Cologne's Rheinische Musikschule.

BERG, ALBAN (1885–1935). Austrian composer. An essential early **modernist** and one of the first great exponents of **twelve-tone** composition, Alban Berg developed new ways of joining tonal and **atonal** techniques and created a body of work that ranged from searing **expressionism** to the lyrical and romantic. Alban Maria Johannes Berg was born into a well-off family in Vienna and began teaching himself music in 1900. That same year, his father died, which left the family in hard financial straits—accepting Berg as a private student in 1904, **Arnold Schoenberg** waived his fee. Studying with Schoenberg proved invaluable to Berg, as it did for his friend and fellow pupil **Anton Webern**, and the trio's related activities eventually led to their being known as the Second Viennese School.

Berg's first works with opus numbers were composed in 1909, an accomplished Piano Sonata in a postromantic idiom and the more expressionistic *Vier Lieder* for voice and piano. After creating an ambiguously tonal String Quartet (1910), Berg stepped away from tonality in his *Fünf Orchesterlieder nach Ansichtskartentexten von Peter Altenberg* (1912) for voice and orchestra. When Schoenberg conducted the Vienna premiere of two of the *Altenberg Lieder* in 1913, there was bedlam in the audience and the performance had to be stopped. That year, Berg composed a miniaturist chamber piece, *Vier Stücke* for clarinet and piano. In this atonal score, which utilized **tone-clusters**, Berg left behind the themes and motives of the *Altenberg Lieder* and worked instead with small motivic cells. His *Drei Orchesterstücke* in 1914 anticipated aspects of the twelve-tone method that Schoenberg would introduce a decade later. That same year, Berg began writing an **opera** based on Georg Büchner's play *Woyzeck*, but halted his work on the libretto and music to serve in the Austrian army (1915–1918) during World War I.

Berg's opera, entitled *Wozzeck*, was completed in 1922 and premiered in Berlin in 1925, where it generated scandal and controversy, but the power of the music and the intensity of the drama brought *Wozzeck* international attention and other European opera houses soon were staging it. Combining an array of vocal styles—operatic singing, Schoenbergian *Sprechstimme*, lines spoken in rhythmic synchronization with the music—*Wozzeck* became the classic expressionist opera and a fixture in the repertory. Berg's **dissonant** and atonal score made real Büchner's hallucinatory account of a lowly soldier who murders his unfaithful lover. Berg also completed the Chamber Concerto for piano, violin, and 13 wind instruments in 1925. His natural warmth and expressivity adapted readily to procedures from Schoenberg's new method of twelve-tone organization, and his score included **quarter-tones** for the violin. Berg's first full twelve-tone piece was the 1925 song *Schliesse mir die Augen beide* for voice and piano, with a text that he had previously set in the late 1900s.

In the 1920s and 1930s, Berg taught private composition students, among them **Ross Lee Finney** and Theodor Adorno. During these years, his music melded tonal techniques with Schoenberg's method and achieved a haunting and personal voice, exemplified by one of his greatest works, the *Lyrische Suite* (1926) for string quartet. The piece has autobiographical content as well: Berg encoded a confessional program of an illicit love affair within his composition, which he detailed in an annotated score (discovered in 1976 by composer and Berg scholar **George Perle**). Berg began his second opera, *Lulu*, in 1928, writing the libretto from two plays by Frank Wedekind, *Erdgeist* and *Büsche der Pandora*, in which a woman brings destruction to everyone who loves and desires her. Berg stopped work on *Lulu* to compose *Der Wein* (1929), a concert aria for soprano and orchestra, which set poetry by Charles Baudelaire. He incorporated jazz and the tango into this twelve-tone work and inflected *Lulu* with traditional strains as well.

Berg extracted the *Lulu Suite* for soprano and orchestra from his work in progress in 1934, but the following year he set *Lulu* aside once again, the instrumentation of its last act not yet finished, to compose a masterpiece: the elegiac Violin Concerto (1935), dedicated by Berg to the memory of 18-year-old Manon Gropius, whose mother had previously been married to **Gustav Mahler**, a composer whom Berg adored and whose music informed his own. The Violin Concerto, which includes a **quotation** from the chorale of Johann Sebastian Bach's Cantata No. 60, became Berg's most popular orchestral score. It was also his last: A few months later, Berg died in Vienna at age 50, having developed blood poisoning from an abscess. The full *Lulu* was premiered in Paris in 1979 with a performing version of the third act prepared by **Friedrich Cerha**.

BERG, CHRISTOPHER (1949–). American composer and musician. Christopher Berg studied piano with Robert Helps at the Manhattan School of Music and has championed the music of **Kaikhosru Shapurji Sorabji**. Among Berg's compositions are *Mass* (1979) for soprano, mixed chorus, and orchestra; *Tango Meditation* (1986) for piano; *Many Rooms* (1992) for piano; *We Have Heard the Chimes at Midnight* (2004) for orchestra; and the **opera** *Cymbeline* (2007). His tuneful songs include *Songs on Poems of Frank O'Hara* (1985–1988) for medium voice and piano, *Five "Russian" Lyrics* (1994) for baritone and piano trio, and *Two Oscar Wilde Sonnets* (1999) for voice and piano.

BERGER, ARTHUR (1912–2003). American composer, musician, educator, and critic. Arthur Berger studied with **Walter Piston, Nadia Boulanger**, and **Darius Milhaud**. A **neoclassicist** with his Wind Quartet (1941) and *Serenade concertante* (1944, rev. 1951) for orchestra, Berger adopted **twelve-tone** methods to that idiom in *Chamber Music for 13 Players* (1956) and String Quartet (1958). His other notable works include Septet (1966); Trio (1972) for guitar, violin, and prepared piano; *Perspectives II* (1985) for orchestra; and the quintet *Diptych: Collages 1 & 2* (1990, rev. 1995). He wrote music criticism for newspapers and journals and the books *Aaron Copland* (1963) and *Reflections of an American Composer* (2002). Berger also taught at Brandeis University (1953–1980) and other institutions; his students include **Charles Dodge, William Flanagan**, and **Alvin Lucier**. *See also* MODERNISM.

BERIO, LUCIANO (1925–2003). Italian composer, musician, and educator. With a sure lyrical gift and a memorable feeling for texture and color, Luciano Berio synthesized different ideas and methodologies and became one of Europe's most important late 20th-century composers. Born into a family of musicians in Oneglia (now Imperia), Italy, Berio attended the Milan Conservatory (1946–1950) and studied with composers G. F. Ghedini and G. C. Paribeni and conductor Carlo Maria Giulini. He married singer **Cathy Berberian** in 1950, and her unique talents informed many of his best vocal works, even after their marriage ended in 1965. Berio's early music, such as *Magnificat* (1948) for two sopranos, mixed chorus, and orchestra and *Due pezzi* (1951) for violin and piano or orchestra, showed the impact of **Béla Bartók**,

Igor Stravinsky, and **Paul Hindemith**. More original was the expressive instrumental color of *El mar la mar* (1952) for soprano, mezzo-soprano, piccolo, two clarinets, accordion, harp, cello, and double bass, which used folk elements and **serial** procedures. Further investigating serialism, Berio studied with **Luigi Dallapiccola** at Tanglewood in 1952 and attended the Darmstadt Summer School for New Music the following year. Berio's *Cinque variazioni* (1953, rev. 1966) for piano was a serial work, and *Nones* (1954) for orchestra was **totally serialized**.

Berio began creating **tape music** with *Ritratto di città* (1954), a collaboration with **Bruno Maderna**. The two founded the Studio di Fonologia Musicale of the Italian Radio in 1955, with Berio as director until 1959, and he created the tape pieces *Mutazioni* (1955), *Perspectives* (1957), *Thema (Omaggio a Joyce)* (1958), *Momenti* (1960), and *Visage* (1961). *Thema* and *Visage* used Berberian's voice as the initial sound source.

Serenata 1 (1957) for flute and 14 instruments introduced **spatial** ideas into Berio's music, and *Allelujah* (1956) for orchestra, which featured **toneclusters**, was reworked into *Allelujah II* (1958) for five orchestral groups and two conductors. *Différences* (1959) combined five musicians with a tape of their prerecorded playing. *Sequenza* (1958) for flute, which used **proportional notation**, led Berio to a lifelong series of solos, from *Sequenza II* (1963) for harp to *Sequenza XIV* (2002) for cello; these also begat the *Chemins* pieces, starting with *Chemins I* (1965) for harp and orchestra, after *Sequenza II*, and ending with *Récit* (1996, a.k.a. *Chemins VII*) for alto saxophone, an ensemble of 12 saxophones, and percussion, developed from *Sequenza IXb* (1981) for alto saxophone.

With *Tempi concertati* (1959) for flute, violin, and small orchestra, Berio combined improvisation with strictly organized material. The seven orchestral sections and five pieces for solo voice of *Epiphanie* (1963, rev. 1965) can be performed in one of 10 different sequences. *Sincronie* (1964) for string quartet permits the players to select certain pitches. Berio also asserted his love of folk music in 1964, completing his set of arrangements *Folk Songs* for mezzo-soprano and seven instruments (or orchestra, 1972).

His other vocal music explored the relationship between phonetics and musical structures: *Circles* (1960) for female voice, harp, and two percussionists; *Sequenza III* (1966) for female voice; *O King* (1967) for mezzo-soprano and five instruments; and the theatrical *Recital I (for Cathy)* (1972) for mezzo-soprano and 17 instruments. *Passagio* (1962) for soprano, two mixed choruses, and orchestra distributed one chorus among the audience. *Laborintus II* (1965), a theatrical piece for three female voices, speaker, 17 instruments, mixed chorus, and tape, referred to (but did not quote) such composers as Claudio Monteverdi and Stravinsky. **Quotation** defined one of Berio's greatest works: *Sinfonia* (1968) for eight amplified voices and orchestra; section 2 is an expanded version of *O King*, and section 3 intercuts the third movement of **Gustav Mahler**'s Symphony No. 2 with an array of other quotations, from Johann Sebastian Bach and Ludwig van Beethoven to **Maurice Ravel**, **Charles Ives**, and **Karlheinz Stockhausen**.

During these years, Berio taught at Tanglewood (1960), Mills College (1962, 1963–1964), and Juilliard (1965–1971). His students include **Steve Reich** and **Robert Moran**. He founded the Juilliard Ensemble in 1967 and directed IRCAM's **electroacoustic** section (1974–1980). A conductor since the 1950s, Berio was artistic director of the Israel Chamber Orchestra (1975), Accademia Filarmonica Romana (1975–1976), Orchestra Regionale Toscana (1982–2003), and Maggio Musicale Fiorentino (1984–2003).

Berio's music-theater work *Opera*, completed in 1977, was essentially his first **opera**, and from it he derived such works as the theatrical *Melodrama* (1970) for voice and septet and *E vó* (1972), a Sicilian lullaby for soprano and chamber orchestra, which used **quarter-tones**. His operas *La vera storia* (1981) and *Un re in ascolto* (1983) were collaborations with writer Italo Calvino; *Outis* (1996) and *Cronaca del luogo* (1998) featured live electronics. Other notable late works include *Voci (Folk Songs II)* (1984) for viola and two instrumental groups and *Naturale* (1985) for viola, percussion, and recorded voice, both of which used Sicilian folk music; *Rendering* (1990) for orchestra, which used Franz Schubert's sketches for his unfinished Symphony No. 10; *Sequenza XIII* (1995, a.k.a. *Chanson*) for accordion; *Korót* (1998) for eight cellos; and *Stanze* (2003) for baritone, three male choruses, and orchestra, his last work. Berio died of cancer of the spine in Rome at age 77. *See also* ATONALITY; MODERNISM.

BERNSTEIN, LEONARD (1918–1990). American composer, musician, and educator. Leonard Bernstein took piano lessons in his youth and studied with **Walter Piston** and Edward Burlingame Hill at Harvard University; he also studied at the Curtis Institute with Isabella Vengerova (piano), Fritz Reiner (conducting), and Randall Thompson (orchestration) and at Tanglewood with conductor Serge Koussevitzky. Bernstein became assistant conductor of the New York Philharmonic in 1943 and later its music director (1958–1969), establishing himself as one of the great conductors of the era.

Bernstein's notable compositions begin with his Symphony No. 1, "Jeremiah" (1942), for orchestra and mezzo-soprano, and the ballet scores *Fancy Free* (1944) and *Facsimile* (1946), which featured jazz elements. Jazz also informed Bernstein's Symphony No. 2, "The Age of Anxiety" (1949, rev. 1965), for piano and orchestra; *Prelude, Fugue, and Riffs* (1949) for clarinet and jazz ensemble; the one-act **opera** *Trouble in Tahiti* (1951); and his score for the 1954 **film** *On the Waterfront*. Bernstein was equally active in popular music during these years, scoring the hit musicals *On the Town* (1944), *Wonderful Town* (1953), *Candide* (1956), and *West Side Story* (1957).

Although his music was tonal and tuneful, Bernstein also made use of **twelve-tone** techniques in such works as *Fancy Free*, *Candide*, the ballet score *The Dybbuk* (1974), and *Arias and Barcarolles* (1988), a song cycle for mezzo-soprano, baritone, and piano four-hands or strings and percussion. Among his later compositions are Symphony No. 3, "Kaddish" (1963, rev. 1977), for speaker, soprano, mixed chorus, boys' choir, and orchestra; *Chichester Psalms* (1965) for mixed or male chorus, boy soprano, and orchestra; the rock- and pop-inspired **multimedia** *Mass: A Theater Piece for Singers, Players, and Dancers* (1971); *Songfest* (1977) for six vocalists and orchestra; the three-act opera *A Quiet Place* (1984), which includes *Trouble in Tahiti*; and *Jubilee Games* (1986), revised in 1989 as Concerto for Orchestra with a baritone solo (live or on prerecorded **tape**). The author of *The Joy of Music* (1959), *The Infinite Variety of Music* (1966), and *Findings* (1982), Bernstein taught at Tanglewood (1942–1990) and presented the celebrated series of Young People's Concerts (1958–1972).

BEYER, JOHANNA M. (1888–1944). German-born American composer, musician, and educator. After completing conservatory studies in Germany, Johanna Magdalena Beyer relocated to New York in 1924. She received her degree from the Mannes College of Music in 1928 and studied composition with **modernists Henry Cowell**, **Dane Rudhyar**, **Ruth Crawford Seeger**, and **Charles Seeger**. Supporting herself as a piano teacher, Beyer began producing **dissonant** and **atonal** scores in the 1930s, which were distinguished by her **polyrhythmic** imagination; an original use of sliding tones, sustained tones, and **tone-clusters**; and her sly sense of humor.

Beyer composed for winds with her Suites for Clarinet 1 and 1b (1932), Quintet for Woodwinds (1933), and Suite for Clarinet and Bassoon (1933), and for voice in *Three Songs* (1933) for soprano, piano, and percussion and *The Robin in the Rain* (1935) for soprano, women's chorus, and piano. In 1934, she combined the two with *Ballad of the Star-Eater* and *Three Songs*, both for soprano and clarinet. Beyer also created the impressive piano works *Gebrauchs-Musik* (1934) and *Clusters* (1936, a.k.a. *New York Waltzes*), the percussion-ensemble scores *Percussion Suite* (1933) and *IV* (1935), and her remarkable String Quartets Nos. 1 (1934) and 2 (1936).

During Cowell's imprisonment (1936–1940), Beyer looked after his New Music Quarterly publications and served as his secretary, agent, and advocate. She also composed more music for chorus (*The Federal Music Project*, 1936; *The Composers' Forum-Laboratory*, 1937; *The People, Yes*, 1937;

The Main-Deep, 1937) and for orchestra (*Symphonic Suite*, 1937; *Symphonic Opus 3*, 1939; *Symphonic Movement 1*, 1939; *Symphonic Opus 5*, 1940). Although her chamber music continued to rely on winds, with Sonata for Clarinet and Piano (1936), Suite for Oboe and Bassoon (1937), Movement for Woodwinds (1938), and Six Movements for Oboe and Piano (1939), she also produced Movement for Double Bass and Piano (1936), Movement for Two Pianos (1936), *Cyrnab* (1937) for chamber orchestra, and Suite for Violin and Piano (1937).

Beyer's political-themed **opera** *Status Quo* may never have been completed, but she did derive from it three 1938 scores: *Dance* for orchestra, *Movement* (a.k.a. *Dance*) for string quartet, and the forward-looking *Music of the Spheres* for three electrical instruments or strings with lion's roar and triangle. She produced her last works for percussion ensemble the following year with *March*, *Waltz*, *Three Movements*, and *Percussion, Opus 14*. By then she was already in the grip of amyotrophic lateral sclerosis, the debilitating disease that would take her life at age 55. Her last known composition is the tonal Sonatina in C (1943) for piano. *See also* ELECTROACOUSTIC MUSIC.

BIRTWISTLE, (SIR) HARRISON (1934–). English composer and educator. Harrison Birtwistle studied with Richard Hall at the Royal Manchester College of Music (1952–1955), where he was first exposed to **serial** techniques. He also investigated the music of **Igor Stravinsky** and **Olivier Messiaen** during these years and studied with **Milton Babbitt** in 1966. Birtwistle and his fellow students **Peter Maxwell Davies** and **Alexander Goehr** came to represent what was called the Manchester School of **atonal modernism**. Birtwistle was admired for his *Refrains and Choruses* (1957) for wind quintet; *Monody for Corpus Christi* (1959) for soprano, flute, horn, and violin; and *Entractes* (1962) for flute, viola, and harp. A devotion to the cultural history of England characterizes *Narration* (1963) for chorus and his **operas** *Punch and Judy* (1967), *Down by the Greenwood Side* (1969), and *Gawain* (1991; rev. 1994, 1999).

A fascination with ancient Greece was also formative for Birtwistle's vocal music, with *Entractes and Sappho Fragments* (1962) for soprano and instruments, . . . *agm* . . . (1979) for mixed chorus and three instrumental ensembles, and the operas *The Mask of Orpheus* (1983) and *The Minotaur* (2007). Opera became a specialty for Birtwistle, with such other successful works as *Yan Tan Tethera* (1984), *The Second Mrs. Kong* (1994), and *The Io Passion* (2003). His important scores for orchestra include *The Triumph of Time* (1972), *Earth Dances* (1986), *Exody* (1997), and *The Shadow of Night* (2001); among his chamber-ensemble pieces are *Tragoedia* (1965), *Silbury*

Air (1977), *Secret Theatre* (1984), *Ritual Fragment* (1990), and *Cantus Iambeus* (2005). Birtwistle has taught at King's College London and the Royal Academy of Music in London. He was knighted in 1988. *See also* FILM MUSIC; TWELVE-TONE MUSIC.

BISCARDI, CHESTER (1948–). American composer, musician, and educator. Chester Biscardi studied at the University of Wisconsin, Madison, and at Yale University; his teachers included **Krzysztof Penderecki** and **Toru Takemitsu**. He has taught at Sarah Lawrence College since 1977. Biscardi composed in an **atonal** idiom in *At the Still Point* (1977) for orchestra, and **twelve-tone** techniques are featured in *Trasumanar* (1980) for 12 percussionists and piano. Tonal and melodic materials informed his Piano Concerto (1983), the chamber **opera** *Tight-Rope* (1985), and such lyrical recent works as *Resisting Stillness* (1996) for two guitars and *Modern Love Songs* (2002) for voice and piano. A skilled pianist, Biscardi has written compellingly for the instrument with *Mestiere* (1979), Piano Sonata (1986, rev. 1987), *Companion Piece (for Morton Feldman)* (1991), and *In Time's Unfolding* (2000). *See also* NEOROMANTICISM.

BITONALITY. Bitonal music involves the simultaneous use of two different key signatures. This form of **polytonality** can be heard in such early **modernist** works as **Charles Ives**'s *Variations on "America"* (1892) and *Psalm 67* (1898) and **Béla Bartók**'s *14 Bagatelles* (1908). **Igor Stravinsky** brought international attention to this **dissonant** technique with his ballet scores *Petrushka* (1911) and *Le sacre du printemps* (1913). Other examples of bitonal composition include **Erik Satie**'s *Sports et divertissements* (1914), **Aaron Copland**'s *Music for the Theatre* (1925), **Nicolas Slonimsky**'s *Studies in Black and White* (1928), **Gustav Holst**'s Double Concerto (1929), **Silvestre Revueltas**'s *Cuauhnáhuac* (1930) and *Colorines* (1933), and **Duke Ellington**'s "Main Stem" (1942).

BLITZSTEIN, MARC (1905–1964). American composer and musician. A talented concert pianist by his teens, Marc Blitzstein turned to composition and studied with Rosario Scalero at the Curtis Institute. He relocated to Paris in 1926 to study with **Nadia Boulanger**, but a few months later in 1927 left her and went to Berlin to study with **Arnold Schoenberg**—whom he also left some months later. Back in the United States, Blitzstein began composing tonal **modernist** scores: Piano Sonata (1927), *Percussion Music for the Piano* (1929), and Piano Concerto (1931). Involved with left-wing politics by the mid-1930s, he stepped away from modernism and began composing more accessible songs with progressive social content. Blitzstein had a keen ear for the rhythms of American speech, and his efforts rapidly coalesced into the musical play *The Cradle Will Rock* (1936), a classic cry of defiance from Depression-era America. He also wrote the book and lyrics for this biting satire, in which he delivered a passionate pro-labor message.

Blitzstein wrote the texts for almost all his theater music. He followed *The Cradle Will Rock* with an **opera**, the political-themed *No for an Answer* (1940), and the *Airborne Symphony* (1946), a rousing flag-waver for narrator, soloists, chorus, and orchestra. Blitzstein adapted Lillian Hellman's play *The Little Foxes* for his most admired opera, *Regina*, which he completed in 1949, and found success in the early 1950s writing a popular English translation of Bertolt Brecht's lyrics for **Kurt Weill**'s *The Threepenny Opera*. But his Faustian opera *Reuben, Reuben* (1955) fared badly; also unsuccessful were the music and lyrics for *Juno* (1959), a musical based on Sean O'Casey's *Juno and the Paycock*. While he was on a working vacation in Martinique early in 1964, three men robbed the 58-year-old Blitzstein and beat him to death. Leonard J. Lehrman utilized the composer's sketches and notes to complete two operas that Blitzstein left unfinished: *Idiots First* (1973), a one-act adaptation of the Bernard Malamud story, and a full-length original, *Sacco and Vanzetti* (2003).

BLOCH, ERNEST (1880–1959). Swiss-born American composer, musician, and educator. Ernest Bloch studied in Geneva and Brussels and came to the United States in 1916; he became a citizen in 1924. A violinist and conductor, Bloch taught at several American institutions and founded the Cleveland Institute of Music in 1920; among his students were **Roger Sessions** and **George Antheil**. Best known for such Jewish-themed works as *Trois poèmes juifs* (1913) for chamber orchestra, *Israel* (1916) for five voices and orchestra, *Schelomo* (1916) for cello and orchestra, and *Sacred Service* (1933) for baritone, mixed chorus, and orchestra, he also composed **neoclassical** scores, including Concerto Grosso No. 1 (1925) for strings with piano obbligato, Violin Concerto (1938), and String Quartet No. 2 (1945). Bloch's other notable works include Piano Quintet No. 1 (1923), which included **quarter-tones**, and *America* (1926) for mixed chorus and orchestra.

BOLCOM, WILLIAM (1938–). American composer, musician, and educator. William Bolcom studied with **Darius Milhaud** and **Olivier Messiaen** in Paris and taught at the University of Michigan (1973–2008). Bolcom's music is frequently eclectic: His massive oratorio *Songs of Innocence and Experience* (1956–1981) used romantic, **modern**, rock, and pop musical styles. His other notable works include *12 New Etudes* (1977–1986) for piano; *Gospel Preludes* (1979–1984) for organ; the **operas** *McTeague* (1992), *A View from* *the Bridge* (1999), and *A Wedding* (2004); 11 string quartets (1950–2002); four violin sonatas (1956–1994); eight symphonies (1957–2005); and numerous cabaret songs and piano rags. An accomplished pianist, Bolcom has also recorded works by Milhaud, **George Gershwin**, **Scott Joplin**, and others. *See also* POSTMODERNISM.

BOULANGER, LILI (1893–1918). French composer and musician. Sister of **Nadia Boulanger**, Lili Boulanger was a singer and organist; she studied composition with Paul Vidal and Georges Caussade. Among her early noteworthy scores are *Nocturne* (1911) for violin and piano and the cantata *Faust et Hélène* (1913). **Impressionism** informs such works as *Cortège* (1914) for violin and piano, *Clairières dans le ciel* (1914) for high voice and piano, and her orchestral scores *D'un matin de printemps* (1917) and *D'un soir triste* (1918). Especially admired are Boulanger's religious works *Psalm 24* (1916) for chorus, orchestra, and organ; *Psalm 130* (1917) for contralto, tenor, chorus, orchestra, and organ; *Vieille prière bouddhique* (1917) for tenor, chorus, and orchestra; and *Pie Jesu* (1918) for mezzo-soprano, string quartet, harp, and organ, her final composition. Afflicted by ill health all her life, she succumbed to intestinal tuberculosis at age 24.

BOULANGER, NADIA (1887–1979). French composer, musician, and educator. Sister of **Lili Boulanger**, Nadia Boulanger studied organ with Louis Vierne and composition with Gabriel Fauré and Charles-Marie Widor at the Paris Conservatoire. Although Boulanger performed regularly as an organist and conductor and composed skillful works such as the 1918 scores *Vers la vie nouvelle* for piano and *Lux aeterna* for mezzo-soprano, string quartet, harp, and organ, she devoted herself mostly to teaching. An influential champion of **Igor Stravinsky** and **neoclassicism**, Boulanger taught in France and the United States and instructed several generations of composers, among them **Marion Bauer**, **Aaron Copland**, **Virgil Thomson**, **Elliott Carter**, **Ross Lee Finney**, **Walter Piston**, **David Diamond**, **Thea Musgrave**, **Pierre Henry**, **Peggy Glanville-Hicks**, **Alejandro Caturla**, **Roy Harris**, **Mildred Couper**, **Arthur Berger**, **Louise Talma**, **Paul Bowles**, **Nicholas Maw**, **Yvar Mikhashoff**, **Irving Fine**, and **Philip Glass**. *See also* MODERNISM.

BOULEZ, PIERRE (1925–). French composer and musician. Among the most influential and respected European composers since the 1950s, Pierre Boulez extended **serial** methods, introduced the concept of **aleatory**, and composed vocal, instrumental, and **electroacoustic music** that is as attractive and original in sonority as it is rigorous in design. Born in the town of Montbrison, Boulez entered the Paris Conservatoire in 1943. His teachers included

Olivier Messiaen, who revealed to him the music of **Claude Debussy** and **Igor Stravinsky**. After quitting the academic atmosphere of the Conservatoire in 1945, Boulez began independent studies with **René Leibowitz**, who exposed him to the **twelve-tone music** of **Arnold Schoenberg** and **Anton Webern**.

The serial method liberated Boulez as a composer, providing him with a structure for his own unusual sonorities and demanding **polyrhythms**, and he would become one of its most ardent and persuasive exponents. In 1946, he created a pair of notable chamber scores, *Sonatine* for flute and piano and *Première sonate* for piano—quick and aggressive works, filled with wide leaps and biting attacks. That same year, he also produced his first version of *Le visage nuptial*, a setting of poet René Char for soprano, piano, percussion, and two **ondes martenots**. Boulez played this **electronic** instrument with Jean-Louis Barrault's theater company, where he was music director (1946–1957); it enabled him to use **quarter-tones** in the score, although these passages were eliminated in 1951 when he revised *Le visage* as a cantata for soprano, alto, women's chorus, and orchestra.

The savagery of Boulez's *Première sonate* was taken further in *Deuxième sonate*, completed in 1948. This percussive piece was even more severe in its serial organization, and Boulez transferred that rigor, although with a more restrained sound, to string quartet with *Livre pour quatour*, completed in 1949. He also set another Char text for *Le soleil des eaux*, which he composed in 1950 for three solo voices and chamber ensemble; like *Le visage nuptial*, it was revised and expanded, in a 1958 version for three soloists, mixed chorus, and orchestra (which was revised again in 1965).

Messiaen's *Quatre études de rythme* (1950) had extended serial organization from pitch to rhythm, dynamics, and timbre, and Boulez expanded upon this technique of **total serialism** in *Polyphonie X* (1951) for 18 instruments and in his first efforts at **tape music**, *Deux études* (1952). He conceived *Structures* for two pianos as a massive series that would investigate all aspects of serial composition. *Structures, premier livre* was completed in 1951 and performed by Boulez and Messiaen the following year.

Boulez set Char once again with *Le marteau sans maître* (1955), scored for alto and six instruments. This landmark piece was performed internationally and made Boulez one of Europe's most admired composers. Afterward, however, he came to regard total serialism as restrictive, and *Polyphonie X* and *Deux études* were both withdrawn. In the 1957 article "Alea," Boulez decried the loss of spontaneity in serial music and proposed different performance freedoms, with the musicians selecting specific aspects of pitch, tempo, and the continuity of material. This aleatoric approach characterized two major works of his: *Troisième sonate* (1957) for piano and *Pli selon pli* (1958; rev.

1962, 1989) for soprano and orchestra, both of which can be performed in whole or in part. The latter, a setting of poet Stephane Mallarmé, includes three *Improvisation* sections. Neither work was ever formally completed; Boulez has regarded them as works in progress, an open-ended attitude reflected in his penchant for revising his earlier music.

In 1953, Boulez founded the Domaine Musical concert series of 20th-century music, and its performances provided his training as a conductor. He was invited to conduct other orchestras in the late 1950s and, by the 1970s, became music director of the BBC Symphony Orchestra (1971–1975) and New York Philharmonic (1971–1977), entering the front rank of international conductors—a preeminence he has maintained to the present. Although his composition became more sporadic as conducting gained ascendancy, his 1960s and 1970s works include *Structures, deuxième livre* (1961) for two pianos, *Éclat* (1965) for 15 instruments, and *Rituel in memoriam* **Bruno Maderna** (1975) for orchestra.

With a special interest in **microtonal** and electroacoustic music, Boulez founded the Institut de Recherche et de Coordination Acoustique/Musique (IRCAM) in Paris in 1976, along with its contemporary-music group Ensemble InterContemporain. Boulez's works combining instruments and electronics include *Répons* (1981), for six soloists and chamber orchestra with **computer** sounds and live electronics, and . . . *explosante-fixe* . . . (1993) for flute with live electronics, two flutes, and chamber orchestra. His other notable recent compositions include *Incises* (1994, rev. 2001) for piano; *Sur incises* (1998) for three pianos, three harps, and three percussionists; and *Une page d'éphéméride* (2005) for piano. *See also* ATONALITY; MODERNISM.

BOWLES, PAUL (1910–1999). American composer, musician, and critic. Paul Bowles took piano lessons as a boy and studied composition with **Aaron Copland** in 1929; in the early 1930s, he also took intermittent lessons with **Nadia Boulanger**, **Virgil Thomson**, **Roger Sessions**, and Israel Citkowitz. Bowles's early music includes the piano scores *Aria, Chorale, and Rondo* (1930) and *Tamanar* (1931); Sonata for Oboe and Clarinet (1931); *Scenes d'Anabase* (1932) for tenor, oboe, and piano; and *Cantata "par le Detroit"* (1933) for soprano, four male voices, and harmonium. Averse to development, climaxes, and other familiar devices of European music, Bowles was drawn to shorter forms that explored psychological nuance. He turned to composing music for the theater, beginning with Orson Welles's productions of *Horse Eats Hat* and *Dr. Faustus* in 1936 and *Too Much Johnson* in 1938; Bowles found his greatest success scoring Tennessee Williams's plays *The Glass Menagerie* (1944) and *Summer and Smoke* (1948).

Using **neoclassical** techniques, Bowles also produced a suite of Mexican dances, *Mediodía* (1937), for 11 instruments; the 1938 works *Music for a Farce* for clarinet, trumpet, piano, and percussion and *Romantic Suite* for six winds and strings, piano, and percussion; *The Wind Remains* (1943), a zarzuela with his own libretto, based on a play by Federico García Lorca; Sonata for Two Pianos (1947); and Concerto for Two Pianos, Winds, and Percussion (1947, arranged in 1949 for two pianos and orchestra).

Bowles wrote music criticism for the *New York Herald Tribune* from 1942 to 1946, and in 1947 he permanently relocated to Morocco. After the 1949 publication of his first novel, *The Sheltering Sky*, writing prose largely displaced his interest in composition. Bowles's later music includes *Night Waltz* (1949) for two pianos; *A Picnic Cantata* (1953) for four female voices, two pianos, and percussion; *Yerma* (1958), an **opera** from the play by Lorca; and music for Williams's plays *Sweet Bird of Youth* (1959) and *The Milk Train Doesn't Stop Here Anymore* (1962). Late innovations came with his music for the theater in Morocco: *The Bacchae* (1969) employed Moroccan instruments, and *Hippolytus* (1992) and *Salome* (1993) utilized a **synthesizer**. *See also* MULTICULTURALISM.

BRANCA, GLENN (1948–). American composer and musician. An autodidact, Glenn Branca had his formative musical experience playing in Theoretical Girls, the band he formed with Jeffrey Lohn in 1977. He started his own band, the Static, the following year, pursuing the rich sounds he was hearing in the densities and loudness of electric guitars. When his ideas became too austere and complex for the rock band format, he developed an ensemble of electric guitars, playing with drummer Stefan Wischerth, to perform his compositions. A series of landmark works began in 1979 with *(Instrumental) for Six Guitars*, *The Spectacular Commodity*, *Dissonance*, and *Lesson No. 1*. Melding hard rock with the techniques of **minimalist** composers **Steve Reich** and **Philip Glass**, Branca created a visceral, high-volume sound unique to rock and new music, where the interaction of amplified partials generated a hallucinatory range of acoustic phenomena.

This music had its own emotional life, too, from hammer-blow attacks to states of ecstasy, and Branca pushed the limits still further with three major pieces: *The Ascension* (1980); Symphony No. 1, "Tonal Plexus" (1981); and *Indeterminate Activity of Resultant Masses* (1981). The last title acknowledges that he could not always predict or control the new sounds his music was making, which gave the work an **indeterminate** quality. Seeking greater precision, he used **alternate tuning systems** in Symphony No. 2, "The Peak of the Sacred" (1982), and built tiers of mallet guitars to work with a greater number of open strings. His understanding of this music was illuminated by

Dane Rudhyar's *The Magic of Tone and the Art of Music* (1982), which introduced him to the harmonic series and clarified the concept of **pleroma** music. For Symphony No. 3, "Gloria" (1983), dedicated to Rudhyar, Branca designed keyboard instruments that plucked their strings like harpsichords (and one that employed rotating leather wheels). Pickups amplified the partials from these vibrating strings, which were tuned to the first 127 intervals of the harmonic series. These instruments were also used in Symphony No. 4, "Physics" (1983).

Electric guitars were featured in Symphony No. 5, "Describing Planes of an Expanding Hypersphere" (1984), along with the six-foot-long harmonics guitar. In 1986, Branca used refretted guitars in *Chords* and untempered steel-wire guitars in *Hollywood Pentagon*. That same year, he composed string-orchestra music for the **film** *The Belly of an Architect* (1987). With the guitars, keyboards, and drums of Symphony No. 6, "Angel Choirs at the Gates of Hell" (1987, rev. 1988 as *Devil Choirs at the Gates of Heaven*), Branca reached a new level of expression, but he turned to the orchestra for his Symphony No. 7 (1989), a five-movement work from which he derived the independent pieces *Shivering Air*, *Freeform*, and *Harmonic Series Chords*.

Employing tunings developed from the harmonic series, Branca made an orchestra sound as hallucinatory as his guitar music, and his composition continued along both tracks. His other orchestral works include the dance score *The World Upside Down* (1990), Symphonies Nos. 9 (*"L'eve future,"* 1993) and 11 ("The Netherlands," 1998), and the first movement of Symphony No. 14, "The Harmonic Series," premiered in 2008. His later guitar symphonies are the paired Nos. 8 (1992) and 10 (1994), "The Mysteries"; No. 12, "Tonal Sexus" (1998); and No. 13, "Hallucination City" (2001), for 100 guitars. With the 12 musicians of Symphony No. 15, "Running through the World Like an Open Razor" (2010, a.k.a. *Music for Strange Orchestra*), Branca combined guitars and other instruments. *See also* POSTMODERNISM; TONE-CLUSTER.

BRANT, HENRY (1913–2008). Canadian-born American composer, musician, and educator. Born in Montreal of American parents, Henry Brant studied privately with **George Antheil**, **Aaron Copland**, and **Wallingford Riegger**, and at Juilliard with Rubin Goldmark. A maverick from his youth, Brant devised a conceptual harmonic approach that he called "oblique harmony" with *Variations* (1930) for four instruments and *Two Sarabandes* (1931) for piano. He massed like voices in *Angels and Devils* (1931; rev. 1956, 1979) for solo flute and flute orchestra, and used noninstruments in *Music for a Five and Dime* (1932) for clarinet, piano, and kitchen hardware. Humor became a Brant trademark, as in his 1938 scores *The Marx Brothers* for tin whistle and chamber ensemble and *Whoopee in D Major* for orchestra, and jazz was featured in *Statements in Jazz* (1945) and *Jazz Clarinet Concerto* (1946), both for clarinet and dance band.

Brant's **polytonal** and **polyrhythmic** music grew denser with *Millennium I* (1950) for eight trumpets, chimes, and glockenspiel and *Origins* (1952) for 18 percussionists. Seeking a clearer separation of polyphony, he built upon the innovations of **Charles Ives**'s *The Unanswered Question* (1908): keeping the musicians physically separated and abandoning strict rhythmic coordination. Beginning with *Antiphony One* (1953, rev. 1968) for five orchestral groups and *Millennium II* (1954) for soprano, brass, and percussion, **spatial music** became Brant's passion, from such chamber works as *Joquin* (1958) for piccolo and six instruments, *Prevailing Winds* (1974) for wind quintet, and *Lombard Street* (1983) for organ and four percussionists, to the large-ensemble scores *Sixty* (1973) for three bands, *Plowshares & Swords* (1995) for 74 solo musicians, and *Ice Field* (2001) for more than 100 players. Spatial music led Brant to **pleroma** composition, with densities of like voices in *Orbits* (1979) for 80 trombones, organ, and soprano, which included **quarter-tone** passages; *Rosewood* (1989) for 50 or more guitars; and *Jericho* (1996) for jazz drummer and four quartets of trumpeters. His **multimedia** spatial music includes *Grand Universal Circus* (1956) and *Violin Concerto with Lights* (1961).

Brant's three-hour *Bran(d)t aan de Amstel* (1984) filled the canals of Amsterdam with boatloads of musicians—100 flutes, four jazz drummers—and also used three brass bands, three mixed choruses, four church carillons, and four street organs. His *500: Hidden Hemisphere* (1992) combined a Caribbean steel-drum band with three concert bands. Other **multicultural** spatial scores by Brant include *Meteor Farm* (1982), with Javanese gamelan, West African drumming ensemble, Western and South Indian vocalists, big-band ensemble, symphony orchestra, and mixed chorus, and *Dormant Craters* (1995) for gamelan and steel-drum band. A regular conductor of his own music, Brant also taught at Columbia University, Juilliard, and Bennington College; his students have included **Joan Tower**, **Robert Macht**, and **James Tenney**. *See also* POSTMODERNISM.

BRAXTON, ANTHONY (1945–). American composer, musician, and educator. Anthony Braxton played clarinet and saxophone in bands in his late teens and joined the Association for the Advancement of Creative Musicians in 1966. He recorded two breakthrough LPs in 1968: *Three Compositions of New Jazz*, ensemble works that highlighted his commitment to multi-instrumentalism, and *For Alto*, which expanded the vocabulary of solo alto saxophone. These records also formed a basis for his use of **open-form** composition, systematic improvisation, and **extended performance techniques**.

Braxton has given each of his pieces three types of titles: a composition number representing the work's chronological sequence; a graphic image that offers a structural overview; and an alternative hieroglyphic-type code indicative of deeper philosophical and spiritual content. Braxton's **dissonant** and sometimes **atonal** music embraces the Western classical tradition, **modernist** and contemporary innovations, and the heritage of 20th-century creative African-American music, bringing together **free jazz** and avant-garde composition, including the use of **graphic notation**. Braxton investigated **pleroma** music in *Composition No. 19* (1971) for 100 tubas, *Composition No. 82* (1978) for four orchestras, and *Composition No. 103* (1983) for seven trumpets. His **multimedia** works include *Composition No. 96* (1980) for orchestra and four slide projectors and *Composition No. 125* (1986) for tuba, light show, and constructed environment.

Performing internationally since the early 1970s, Braxton has played with such notable composer/musicians as **Leroy Jenkins**, **Roscoe Mitchell**, **Muhal Richard Abrams**, **Alvin Lucier**, **Frederic Rzewski**, **Richard Teitelbaum**, **George Lewis**, **Anne LeBaron**, and **Fred Frith**. He has also given **multicultural** performances with creative musicians from Japan and India. Braxton's compositions, which now number over 350, are fundamentally interrelated, and musicians are free to combine parts from various compositions to create new versions of his music. His *Trillium* series, begun in 1984, encompasses 36 autonomous one-act **operas** and permits the interconnection of acts in any combination. The author of two multivolume books on music, *Tri-axium Writings* (1985) and *Composition Notes* (1988), Braxton has also taught at Mills College (1985–1990) and Wesleyan University (1990–present). *See also* FREE IMPROVISATION.

BRECHT, GEORGE. *See* FLUXUS.

BRIDGE, FRANK (1879–1941). English composer and musician. Frank Bridge studied at the Royal College of Music (1899–1903) with Sir Charles Villiers Stanford. His early works, such as String Quartet No. 1 (1906) and *Dance Rhapsody* (1908) for orchestra, were in a late-romantic idiom. Bridge was a conductor in the 1910s, and his interest in the music of the French **impressionists** informed his orchestral compositions *The Sea* (1912) and *Summer* (1914). In the 1920s and 1930s, he was also drawn to the music of the Viennese **expressionists**, and several of his works show these varied influences, including Piano Sonata (1925), *Enter Spring* (1927) for orchestra, *Oration* (1930) for cello and orchestra, *Phantasm* (1931) for piano and orchestra, and String Quartets Nos. 3 (1926) and 4 (1937). *See also* BRITTEN, BENJAMIN; MODERNISM.

BRITTEN, BENJAMIN (1913–1976). English composer and musician. A tonal composer especially admired for his lyricism, sense of atmosphere, and dramatic sensibility, Benjamin Britten became England's most important composer in the years after the death of **Ralph Vaughan Williams**. Born in Lowestoft, Suffolk, Edward Benjamin Britten began formal piano lessons at age seven. He had composed songs, string quartets, and piano sonatas when he began studying privately with **Frank Bridge** at age 14. He then attended the Royal College of Music (1930–1933) and studied with **John Ireland**. Britten attracted favor early with *A Boy Was Born* (1933) for mixed chorus and boys' choir and *Simple Symphony* (1934), derived from his juvenilia of the 1920s; *Variations on a Theme of Frank Bridge* (1937) for orchestra enjoyed even greater success.

In 1937, Britten was introduced to singer **Peter Pears** who became his lifelong companion. Britten wrote several outstanding song cycles for Pears's nuanced tenor, starting with *Les illuminations* (1939), a setting of Arthur Rimbaud with string orchestra, and *Seven Sonnets of Michelangelo* (1940) for voice and piano. His other important scores from this time include the Piano Concerto (1938, rev. 1945), Violin Concerto (1939), and *Sinfonia da Requiem* (1940) for orchestra. In 1941, Britten and **Colin McPhee** recorded McPhee's two-piano transcription *Balinese Ceremonial Music*; Britten also composed his String Quartet No. 1 and the comic operetta *Paul Bunyan* to a text by poet W. H. Auden.

During the war years, Britten produced *A Ceremony of Carols* (1942) for treble voices and harp and his classic *Serenade* (1943) for tenor, French horn, and string orchestra, which set an array of English poetry. The year 1945 saw his String Quartet No. 2, the ever popular *The Young Person's Guide to the Orchestra*, and most importantly, the completion of his first **opera**, the tragic *Peter Grimes*. The latter was performed internationally, as were the *Four Sea Interludes* (1945) for orchestra derived from it, and made Britten's reputation. Two more operas quickly followed: the stylized drama *The Rape of Lucretia* (1946) and the comic *Albert Herring* (1947). Britten settled in Aldeburgh in 1947, and the following year he and Pears launched an annual festival of concerts and operas there, which has continued to the present. Britten ended the decade with two notable works for soloists, chorus, and orchestra: *Saint Nicholas* (1948) and *Spring Symphony* (1949).

Both *Paul Bunyan* and *Peter Grimes* had used elements of gamelan music, and after a trip to Bali in 1955, Britten evoked its sound with his **multicultural** ballet score *The Prince of the Pagodas* (1956). His other large-scale works of the 1950s include two major operas from American texts: Herman Melville's *Billy Budd* (1951) and Henry James's *The Turn of the Screw* (1954). Britten also crafted intimate works in these years, such as *Lachrymae*

(1950) for viola and piano, *Six Metamorphoses after Ovid* (1951) for solo oboe, and *Songs from the Chinese* (1957) for tenor and guitar. The popular miracle play *Noye's Fludde* (1958), scored for adults' and children's voices, children's chorus, chamber ensemble, and children's orchestra, was one of the finest of Britten's many scores featuring boys' voices. He composed two important choral works in 1959—*Cantata academica* for soloists, mixed chorus, and orchestra and *Missa brevis* for treble voices and organ—and a masterpiece in 1962: *War Requiem* for soprano, tenor, baritone, mixed chorus, boys' choir, orchestra, chamber orchestra, and organ.

Britten's more traditional opera of Shakespeare's *A Midsummer Night's Dream* (1960) was followed by three unusual chamber operas intended as church parables, for all-male casts with no conductor: *Curlew River* (1964), based on the Japanese Noh play *Sumidagawa*, and two settings from the Bible, *The Burning Fiery Furnace* (1966) and *The Prodigal Son* (1968). Britten's friendship with cellist Mstislav Rostropovich in these years resulted in several major scores: Sonata (1961) for cello and piano, Symphony for Cello and Orchestra (1963), and three suites for solo cello (1964–1971). Made a member of the Order of Merit in 1965, he accepted a peerage in 1976, becoming Baron Britten of Aldeburgh. His music reached a new level of expressivity in the 1970s with the operas *Owen Wingrave* (1970) and *Death in Venice* (1973), both of which evoked the gamelan. Britten's final works were *Phaedra* (1975) for mezzo-soprano and small orchestra and String Quartet No. 3 (1975). Plagued by a congenitally weak heart, he finally succumbed in his Aldeburgh home at age 63. *See also* GEBRAUCHSMUSIK.

BROWN, EARLE (1926–2002). American composer, musician, and educator. Earle Brown studied **Joseph Schillinger**'s techniques of composition and orchestration with Kenneth McKillop and composition with Roslyn Brogue Henning. He wrote **twelve-tone music** with *Three Pieces for Piano* (1951) and *Music for Violin, Cello, and Piano* (1952), but was drawn to **John Cage**'s ideas and joined Cage's circle along with **Morton Feldman**, **Christian Wolff**, and **David Tudor**. Brown wrote music of **indeterminate** length and instrumentation with the **graphic** scores of his *Folio* series (1952–1954), which included the landmark works *December 1952* and *Four Systems*. *Twenty-Five Pages* (1953) for one to 25 pianos also used an **open form**, its unbound pages playable in any order or inversion. To notate duration more precisely in *Music for Cello and Piano* (1955), he used horizontal lines proportional in length to durations of time. **Proportional notation** also characterized *Four More* (1956) for one or more pianos.

With *Available Forms I* (1961), Brown began composing open-form orchestral scores; *Available Forms II* (1962) was for 98 instruments and two conductors. He exercised greater control over pitch assignment in *Corroboree* (1964) for two or three pianos and String Quartet (1965), using proportional notation in both. *Modules I and II* (1966) for two conductors and orchestra used simpler chordal structures; *Time Spans* (1972) for orchestra restricted itself to a single chord. In these works, the conductor decides what is played. In *Centering* (1973) for violin and 10 instruments, the soloist also improvises. *Sounder Rounds* (1983) for orchestra and *Tracking Pierrot* (1992) for chamber ensemble blended closed and open forms. Brown's other open-form scores were *Sign Sounds* (1972) for chamber ensemble, in proportional notation; the graphic scores *Folio II* (1970–1982); and the chamber ensemble pieces *Tracer* (1985) and *Oh, K* (1992). Brown also conducted his music and taught in the United States and Europe. *See also* ATONALITY; MADERNA, BRUNO; MINIMALISM; POSTMODERNISM; SOUND INSTALLATION.

BRYARS, GAVIN (1943–). English composer, musician, and educator. Gavin Bryars played jazz bass in the early 1960s and in 1968 worked with **John Cage** in the United States. Back in England, he worked with **Cornelius Cardew** and also taught at Portsmouth Polytechnic, where he cofounded the **Portsmouth Sinfonia** in 1970, and at Leicester Polytechnic. Bryars composed notable **indeterminate** works, such as *The Sinking of the Titanic* (1969), and the **minimalist** classic *Jesus' Blood Never Failed Me Yet* (1971, rev. 1993) for **tape** and ensemble. He also leads the Gavin Bryars Ensemble (1981– present) and has created **sound installations**. His later works include the **operas** *Medea* (1982, rev. 1984), *Doctor Ox's Experiment* (1997), and *G* (2001); three string quartets (1985–1998); Violin Concerto (2000); and sets of madrigals for vocal ensembles (1998–2007). *See also* POSTMODERNISM.

BUCKNER, THOMAS (1941–). American musician. A specialist in contemporary and improvised music, baritone Thomas Buckner has sung in numerous **operas** of **Robert Ashley** and collaborated with such composer/ musicians as **Roscoe Mitchell**, **Christian Wolff**, **Leroy Jenkins**, **Annea Lockwood**, **"Blue" Gene Tyranny**, and **Phill Niblock**. Buckner founded the new-music recording labels 1750 Arch Records and Mutable Music and has curated the World Music Institute's "Interpretations" concerts since 1989.

BUSONI, FERRUCCIO (1866–1924). Italian composer, musician, and educator. A piano prodigy, Ferruccio Busoni began concertizing at age seven. He studied composition with W. A. Mayer-Rémy and performed internationally while still a teenager, becoming one of the great virtuosi of all time. Busoni's development as a composer was slow, although he played his first compositions at age nine and published his Op. 1, *Ave Maria* for voice and piano, in 1878. He did not shake off the influence of Johannes Brahms until his Violin Sonata No. 2 (1898), which **quoted** Johann Sebastian Bach. Anticipating the **neoclassical** movement of the 1920s, Busoni composed the classically inspired Concerto (1904) for piano and orchestra with male chorus; *Turandot* (1905), an orchestral suite he developed into an **opera** in 1917; *Berceuse élégiaque* (1909) for orchestra; and *Fantasia contrappuntistica* (1910) for piano, an expansion on Bach's *Die Kunst der Fuge*.

Busoni's forward-looking treatise *Entwurf einer neuen Ästhetik der Tonkunst* (1907, rev. 1916) discussed **microtonal** tunings and **electronic music**. His music never strayed into these realms, but it did become more **modernist** in its chromaticism and tonal ambiguity, reaching an extreme with *Sonatina seconda* (1912) for piano and *Nocturne symphonique* (1913) for orchestra. Busoni's interest in Native American music is reflected in his *Indianische Fantasie* (1914) for piano and orchestra, *Indianisches Tagebuch* (1915) for piano, and *Gesang vom Reigen der Geister* (1915) for orchestra.

Busoni had lived in Berlin since 1894, but World War I compelled him to relocate to Switzerland in 1915. There he completed the one-act comic opera *Arlecchino* in 1916 and began scoring his full-length dramatic opera *Doktor Faust*, which featured **polytonal** counterpoint and harmonies based on fourths. He derived *Sarabande and Cortege* (1919) for orchestra from *Doktor Faust* and was still working on the score when he returned to Berlin in 1920. It was unfinished when Busoni died from a kidney infection four years later, at age 58, and Philipp Jarnach completed the score in 1926. Busoni taught mostly piano, but he also instructed such composition students as Jarnach, **Stefan Wolpe**, **Kurt Weill**, and **Otto Luening**. *See also* MULTICULTURALISM; TELHARMONIUM.

BUSSOTTI, SYLVANO (1931–). Italian composer, musician, and educator. Sylvano Bussotti studied with **Luigi Dallapiccola** at the Florence Conservatory and later taught at the Milan Conservatory. He used **graphic notation** and **extended performance techniques** in numerous scores, such as *Five Piano Pieces for David Tudor* (1959), *Coeur pour batteur* (1959) for solo percussionist, *Siciliano* (1962) for 12 male voices, and the absurdist chamber **opera** *La passion selon Sade* (1966), in which he performed with **Cathy Berberian**. Bussotti's other notable works include the ballet scores *Raramente* (1970), *Phaidra/Heliogabalus* (1980), and *Ermafrodito* (1999); the operas *Loranzaccio* (1972), *Nottetempo* (1976), *Phedre* (1988), *Tieste la tragedia* (1993), and *Izumi Shikibu* (2006); the orchestral series *Il catalogo è questo* (1976–1981), *I semi di Gramsci* (1971) for string quartet and orchestra, *Fogli d'album* (1984) for piano, *Lingue ignote* (1994) for bass voice and septet, and *Variazione Russolo* (2007) for piano and *intonarumori*. *See also* FILM MUSIC; FUTURISM; TUDOR, DAVID.

BUTTERWORTH, GEORGE (1885–1916). English composer, educator, and critic. George Butterworth studied with Thomas Dunhill and Sir Charles Hubert Parry, but found his true music education collecting folk songs with **Ralph Vaughan Williams** and **Gustav Holst**. Folk music invigorated Butterworth's feeling for nature in *A Shropshire Lad* (1912) for string orchestra and his orchestral scores *Two English Idylls* (1911) and *The Banks of Green Willow* (1913). Equally admired are his settings of A. E. Housman for voice and piano, *Six Songs from "A Shropshire Lad"* (1911) and *Bredon Hill and Other Songs* (1912). Butterworth wrote criticism for the London *Times* and taught at Radley College, but with the outbreak of World War I in 1914, he enlisted in the English army. Butterworth, age 31, was killed by a sniper at Pozières; his body was never recovered.

C

CAGE, JOHN (1912–1992). American composer, musician, and educator. The most influential composer in the second half of the 20th century, John Cage helped launch the **postmodern** era through his use of **chance, indeterminacy, minimalism**, improvisation, theater, and experimentation. John Milton Cage Jr. was born in Los Angeles and took piano lessons as a boy. After a brief stay at Pomona College (1929–1930), he studied independently with Richard Buhlig, **Henry Cowell**, Adolph Weiss, and **Arnold Schoenberg**. His Sonata for Clarinet (1933) and *Metamorphosis* (1938) for piano were **twelve-tone** scores, but rhythm became a greater concern and Cage turned to percussion music: Quartet (1935), Trio (1936), and *First Construction (in Metal)* (1939), a sextet.

In 1938, Cage met the dancer and future choreographer Merce Cunningham who would become his lifetime companion (Cage also served as administrative and musical director of the Merce Cunningham Dance Company, 1953–1992). With *Imaginary Landscape No. 1* (1939) for records of constant and variable frequency, large Chinese cymbal, and muted piano, Cage began employing a structure of rhythmic relationships. *Living Room Music* (1940) for percussion and speech quartet had the musicians playing household objects, furniture, or sections of the room's architecture. Cage and **Lou Harrison** gave a series of percussion-ensemble concerts (1939–1941) and collaborated on a quartet, *Double Music* (1941). Among Cage's other percussion works are the quartets *Third Construction* (1941) and *Credo in Us* (1942), the latter including a piano and radio or phonograph. The exterior of the piano became a percussion instrument in *The Wonderful Widow of Eighteen Springs* (1942) for voice and closed piano.

With *Bacchanale* (1940), Cage developed the "prepared piano"—inserting between the strings objects such as screws or weather stripping to alter the instrument's pitch and timbre and create a percussion-orchestra sound. Other prepared-piano works followed—*Tossed as It Is Untroubled (Meditation)* (1943), *The Perilous Night* (1944), *Music for Marcel Duchamp* (1947)—culminating in Cage's classic *Sonatas and Interludes* (1948). This music utilized a rhythmic system based on groups of measures having a square root, so that the small parts had the same relation to each unit as the units had to the whole. Other works with this system include *Suite for Toy Piano* (1948), *String Quartet in Four Parts* (1950), and *Six Melodies* (1950) for violin and piano.

A student of Zen Buddhism since the late 1940s, Cage developed a compositional methodology to bypass his tastes and memories and let sounds be themselves. In 1951, he used chance operations to make choices within the rhythmic structures of four groundbreaking scores, starting with the octet *Sixteen Dances*. His *Concerto for Prepared Piano and Orchestra* introduced the coin-tossing method used in consulting the ancient Chinese oracle *I Ching*, which Cage would employ for the rest of his life. He tossed coins to assign pitch, tempo, dynamics, duration, silences, and overlappings in the landmark *Music of Changes* for piano, which also used **tone-clusters**, **string-piano** techniques, and noises such as slamming the keyboard lid. Cage further removed himself from his music with *Imaginary Landscape No. 4 (March No. 2)*, scored for 12 radios.

Imaginary Landscape No. 4 had a fixed form, as did Cage's other chance-based pieces, but its music sounds different in every performance, and so it was also his entry into indeterminate composition. Indeterminacy led Cage to his most radical work, the epochal *4'33"* (1952), a score entirely tacet—no sound is performed in its four-minute-and-33-second duration, and the music of *4'33"* consists of whatever sounds are audible during the performance. Cage had defined *music* not as a method for manipulating specialized sounds but as a mode of listening: Listen to a sound for its own unique character, without reacting intellectually and emotionally, and you will hear music.

Cage's ideas drew other creative people to him, including **Morton Feldman, Earle Brown, Christian Wolff,** and pianist **David Tudor,** with whom he gave numerous concerts. He employed **graphic notation** in a series of solo pieces that included *59-1/2"* (1953) for a string player and *34'46.776"* (1954) for a pianist, and he explored indeterminacy with *Speech* (1955) for five radios and news reader and *Radio Music* (1956) for one to eight radios. *Winter Music* (1957) was scored as 20 unnumbered pages of keyboard aggregates, to be played in whole or part by up to 20 pianists. A similar approach characterized *Concert for Piano and Orchestra* (1958) and *Atlas Eclipticalis* (1961) for one to 86 players. Musicians translate graphic symbols to define the sound's parameters in *Cartridge Music* (1960), performed with phonograph cartridges, and in *Variations I* (1958) and *II* (1961) for any number of players and any sound-producing means.

By then, Cage was teaching, privately and at such institutions as the New School for Social Research (1956–1960); his students include Wolff, **Richard Maxfield, Toshi Ichiyanagi, Dick Higgins, Ben Johnston,** and **Horatiu**

Radulescu. His writings were collected in *Silence* (1961) and *A Year from Monday* (1967). Cage's indeterminate music became theatrical with *Theatre Piece* (1960) for eight players and **multimedia** with *HPSCHD* (1968) for one to seven harpsichords and one to 51 **tapes**, a collaboration with **Lejaren Hiller**, which was created with **computers**.

Cage combined indeterminacy with improvisation in *Child of Tree (Improvisation IA)* (1975) and *Branches (Improvisation IB)* (1976), scored for amplified plant materials: a perishable instrumentation that always requires new techniques. With *Etudes Australes* (1975) for piano and *Freeman Etudes* (1980–1989) for violin, he traced star maps for the sequencing of aggregates. Other notable late works include the **multicultural** *Apartment House 1776* (1976) for any number of musicians, which can be played with or without *Renga* (1976) for orchestra; *Postcard from Heaven* (1983) for one to 20 harps; *Europeras I/II* (1987), **operas** made entirely of **quotations**, which superimposed the vocal and orchestral music—and costuming, staging, and lighting—of European opera; and *Sixty-Eight* (1992) for orchestra, which uses only 15 pitches. Cage died of a stroke in a New York hospital at age 79. *See also* ALEATORY; AMBIENT MUSIC; ATONALITY; BRYARS, GAVIN; CARDEW, CORNELIUS; ELECTROACOUSTIC MUSIC; FLUXUS; FREE DURATION; FREE IMPROVISATION; INSTRUMENT BUILDING; POLYRHYTHM; STOCHASTIC MUSIC; TAKAHASHI, YUJI; TENNEY, JAMES.

CAHILL, SARAH (1960–). American musician. Pianist Sarah Cahill is a specialist in new American music and the American experimental tradition. She has commissioned works from numerous composers, including **Pauline Oliveros, Lou Harrison, Terry Riley, Annea Lockwood, Meredith Monk, Frederic Rzewski**, and the **Residents**.

CARDEW, CORNELIUS (1936–1981). English composer, musician, and educator. Cornelius Cardew studied piano, cello, and composition at the Royal Academy of Music in London (1953–1957) and later studied with Goffredo Petrassi and taught at Maidstone College of Art and Morley College of Art. Cardew worked as an assistant to **Karlheinz Stockhausen** (1958–1960) and collaborated in the composition of Stockhausen's *Carré* (1960); he also participated in the premieres of *Refrain* (1959) and *Plus-Minus* (1963). Another important figure for Cardew was **John Cage**, whose ideas of **chance music** and **indeterminacy** impacted Cardew's *Two Books of Study for Pianists* (1958).

In the 1960s, Cardew was performing his own music, as well as works by Cage, **Pierre Boulez, Morton Feldman, Christian Wolff, La Monte**

Young, Terry Riley, and others. His composition employed performance freedoms in *February Pieces* (1959–1961) for piano, *Autumn '60* for orchestra, *Octet '61 for Jasper Johns*, and *First Movement for String Quartet* (1961). **Graphic notation** was used in *Solo with Accompaniment* (1964) for variable performers and the piano scores *Memories of You* (1964) and *Three Winter Potatoes* (1965). Especially notable was the 193-page score *Treatise* (1967) for unspecified performer(s), often realized in **multimedia** performances.

Cardew wrote purely verbal scores as well: *The Tiger's Mind* (1967) used guided improvisation, and *Schooltime Special* (1968) was a series of questions and options for the performer. *The Great Learning* (1968–1971) for voices and sound-producing objects was a **free-duration** setting of texts by Confucius, which also permitted choices in pitch materials. Cardew cofounded the **Scratch Orchestra** in 1969 to explore both improvisation and composition, working with musicians and nonmusicians who had performed in *The Great Learning*. He also played with the **electroacoustic free-improvisation** group **AMM** from 1965 until 1972.

By then, Cardew had embraced revolutionary Maoist thought. He renounced his former compositions and activities and published such tracts as "Stockhausen Serves Imperialism" (1974). Devoting himself to the production and distribution of music that served the needs of the revolutionary political movement, Cardew turned to folk music and workers' tunes. His late piano works include *Piano Album* (1973), *Thälmann Variations* (1974), *Vietnam Sonata* (1976), and *Boolavogue* (1981) for two pianos. Among his songs are "Bethanien Song" (1974) and "Resistance Blues" (1976). At age 45, Cardew was killed by a hit-and-run driver in London. *See also* ALEATORY; ATONALITY; GEBRAUCHSMUSIK; POSTMODERNISM.

CARLOS, WENDY (1939–). American composer and musician. Born Walter Carlos, she studied with **Vladimir Ussachevsky** and **Otto Luening** at Columbia University. Carlos had a popular hit with the album *Switched-On Bach* (1968), featuring her **synthesizer** arrangements of the music of Johann Sebastian Bach. As a composer of **electronic music**, her first major work was the double LP *Sonic Seasonings* (1972), which anticipated **ambient music**. Carlos transitioned to female in 1972 and began releasing albums as Wendy Carlos with *Switched-On Brandenburgs* (1979). Her later works include *Beauty in the Beast* (1986), which featured **alternate tuning systems**, and the musical drama *Tales of Heaven and Hell* (1998), combining orchestra and voices with synthesizers. She composed electronic **film music** for Stanley Kubrick's *A Clockwork Orange* (1971) and *The Shining* (1980). *See also* ELECTROACOUSTIC MUSIC.

CARRILLO, JULIÁN (1875–1965). Mexican composer, musician, educator, and theorist. Julián Carrillo studied violin and composition at the National Conservatory in Mexico City and the Royal Conservatory in Leipzig, Austria. He later taught at the National Conservatory and formed and conducted its symphony orchestra.

Although Carrillo was investigating **microtonality** by 1895, such early compositions as String Sextet (1900) and Symphony No. 1 (1901) were traditional. He relocated to New York in 1914 and there outlined his "thirteenth sound" ideas for composing with intervals smaller than the semitone. Returning to Mexico in 1918, Carrillo resumed teaching and began conducting the Orquesta Sinfónica de México. His first microtonal works called for instruments tuned in quarter-, eighth-, and 16th-tones: *Preludio a Colón* (1925) for soprano and five instruments, the sextet *Sonata casi fantasía* (1926), and Concertino (1927) for microtonal sextet and orchestra. His music was championed by conductor Leopold Stokowski and eventually gained international attention. In 1930, Carrillo formed the all-microtonal ensemble Sonido 13 Orquesta Sinfónica and composed his *Fantasia Sonido 13* for it.

Along with such scores as Sonata (1931) for guitar in quarter-tones; *Horizontes* (1947) for violin, cello, harp, and orchestra in quarter-, eighth-, and 16th-tones; and Concertino (1948) for third-tone piano and orchestra, Carrillo also wrote non-microtonal **modernist** works such as the **polytonal** *8 de septiembre* (1930) for piano and orchestra and the **atonal** Symphony No. 3 (1940). He patented 15 *pianos metamorfoseadores* in 1940, each piano tuned in a different microtonal interval in a range up to 16th-tones. The first, tuned in third-tones, was built in 1949; all 15 were constructed by 1958.

Carrillo's notable late works include *Balbuecos* (1958) for 16th-tone piano and orchestra, Six Sonatas (1959) for cello in quarter-tones, and *Mass* (1962) for male voices in quarter-tones. He was also the author of several books, including *Pláticas musicales* (1923), *Génesis de la revolución musical del sonido 13* (1940), *Leyes de metamorfosis musicales* (1949), and *Sonido 13: Recorrido histórico* (1962). *See also* INSTRUMENT BUILDING.

CARTER, ELLIOTT (1908–). American composer, educator, and critic. Elliott Carter developed new rhythmic approaches to **atonal** composition and has become one of America's most respected composers. Born in New York City, Elliott Cook Carter Jr. studied piano as a teenager and attended Horace Mann School; there he discovered the music of **Charles Ives**, from whom he received encouragement. At Harvard University (1926–1932), Carter's teachers included **Walter Piston** and **Gustav Holst**. He then went to France, attending L'École Normale de Musique (1932–1935) and studying privately with **Nadia Boulanger**. Returning to New York in 1936, he wrote reviews for *Modern Music* magazine (1937–1946). Carter kept to a tonal and **neoclassical** idiom in his early works *To Music* (1937) for mixed chorus, the ballet score *Pocahontas* (1939), Symphony No. 1 (1942, rev. 1954), and *Holiday Overture* (1944, rev. 1961) for orchestra.

Polyrhythms and multiple tempi inform Carter's Piano Sonata (1946) and Sonata for Cello and Piano (1948). In the latter, he developed his method of **metric modulation**, changing tempi after the manner of harmonic modulation. Carter's music became more aggressively **modernist** and attained a new stature and individuality with the atonal String Quartet No. 1 (1950). A series of classics followed: Variations for Orchestra (1955); String Quartet No. 2 (1959); Double Concerto (1961) for harpsichord, piano, and two chamber orchestras; Piano Concerto (1965); and Concerto for Orchestra (1969). In these pieces, Carter avoided **serial** techniques and instead defined individual instruments or subgroups of instruments with specific intervallic and tempo materials, creating dense and exciting works in which instrumental speeds are sometimes changing continuously.

In the 1970s, Carter produced such noteworthy pieces as String Quartet No. 3 (1971), Brass Quintet (1974), Duo for Violin and Piano (1975), *A Symphony of Three Orchestras* (1977), and his first vocal works since the 1940s, *A Mirror on Which to Dwell* (1976) for soprano and chamber orchestra and *Syringa* (1979) for mezzo-soprano, bass, and chamber orchestra. His approach to density and simultaneities gradually became thinner and more relaxed with such important scores as *Night Fantasies* (1980) for piano, the sextet *Triple Duo* (1982), *Penthode* (1985) for five groups of four instruments, String Quartets Nos. 4 (1986) and 5 (1995), the orchestral trilogy *Symphonia: Sum fluxae pretium spei* (1993–1996), and Clarinet Concerto (1996).

Blessed with a remarkable longevity that has left his composition unimpaired, Carter completed his first **opera** at the age of 90: the 45-minute *What Next?* (1998), a comic account of the aftermath of an automobile accident, with a surreal libretto by Paul Griffiths. Carter's notable recent scores include the Cello Concerto (2000), Horn Concerto (2006), and Flute Concerto (2008) and the orchestral scores *Boston Concerto* (2002) and *Soundings* (2005). He has taught at such universities as Columbia, Yale, and Cornell and at the Peabody Conservatory, Tanglewood, and Juilliard; his students include **Ellen Taaffe Zwilich**.

CATURLA, ALEJANDRO (1906–1940). Cuban composer and musician. A student of Pedro Sanjuán and **Nadia Boulanger**, Alejandro Caturla founded and conducted the Orquesta de Conciertos de Caibarién. Drawing together Spanish, African, and Cuban musical genres with his own **polytonal** sensibility, Caturla's notable works include the orchestral scores *Tres danzas* *cubanas* (1927) and Suite (1938); *Bembé*, for piano, brass, woodwinds, and percussion (1929) or for percussion alone (1930); *Primera suite cubana* (1931) for winds and piano; and *Berceuse campesina* (1939) for piano. Also a lawyer, the 34-year-old Caturla was serving as a judge when he was shot to death by a criminal whom he had tried. *See also* MODERNISM; MULTICULTURALISM.

CERHA, FRIEDRICH (1926–). Austrian composer, musician, and educator. Violinist Friedrich Cerha studied at the Academy of Music and Dramatic Arts in Vienna, where he later taught, and at Darmstadt. In 1958, Cerha cofounded the new-music Ensemble die Reihe, which he directed and conducted until 1983. Taking an individual approach to **serial** composition, tonality, and **chance music**, he has produced such notable works as *Spiegel* (1960–1961), a cycle of seven scores for orchestra and **tape**, which also exists in a **multimedia** version; the music-theater piece *Netzwerk* (1967, rev. 1980); and the **operas** *Baal* (1980), *Der Rattenfänger* (1986), and *Der Riese vom Steinfeld* (1999). Cerha's recent music includes four string quartets (1989–2001), *Langegger Nachtmusik III* (1991) for orchestra, *Impulse* (1993) for orchestra, Violin Concerto (2004), and Percussion Concerto (2008). *See also* BERG, ALBAN; MODERNISM.

CHAMBERS, WENDY MAE (1953–). American composer and musician. Wendy Mae Chambers studied with **Charles Wuorinen**, **Roger Reynolds**, and **Pauline Oliveros**. She created **multimedia** pieces (*Music for Choreographed Rowboats* for 24 musicians in rowboats, 1979; *Ten Grand* for 10 pianos and laser lights, 1983), **multicultural** music (*One World Procession* for Tibetan horn and 50 percussionists, 1981), **spatial music** (*Symphony of the Universe* for chorus, horn, organ, jazz band, **tape**, and 100 timpani, 1989), and **pleroma** works (*Pluck* for 30 harps, 1984; *Marimba!* for 26 marimbas, 1985; *A Mass for Massed Trombones* for 77 trombones, 1993). Her music for solo instruments includes *Suite for Toy Piano* (1983), *Blues* (1995) for cello, *Mandala* (1997) for clarinet, and *Antarctica Suite* (1999) for piano. Chambers also performs on toy piano and car horn organ, a keyboard instrument she built that plays 25 car horns and is powered by a car-battery charger. *See also* INSTRUMENT BUILDING; POSTMODERNISM.

CHANCE MUSIC. Any music that employs chance or randomness, whether in compositional decisions or performance freedoms, can be referred to as "chance music." Early examples of this approach include **Henry Cowell's** **elastic-form** works and the **free-rhythm** scores of **Alan Hovhaness**. **John Cage** became the leading voice for composing with chance techniques, starting with such 1951 scores as *Music of Changes* for piano and *Imaginary Landscape No. 4 (March No. 2)* for 12 radios. As Cage's music moved further into **indeterminacy**, other composers developed different techniques for combining chance operations with strictly organized material, such as the **stochastic music** of **Iannis Xenakis** and **Pierre Boulez**'s approach of **aleatory**. Another form of chance music utilizes improvisation, as in the game pieces of **John Zorn**. *See also* ATONALITY; FREE IMPROVISATION; GRAPHIC NOTATION; OPEN FORM.

CHATHAM, RHYS (1952–). American composer and musician. Guitarist and trumpet player Rhys Chatham studied with **Morton Subotnick** and **La Monte Young**. A **minimalist** with such works as *Two Gongs* (1971), he first adopted the energy of rock to create **pleroma** music with *Guitar Trio* (1977), for multiple electric guitars tuned in **just intonation**, and followed with *Drastic Classicism* (1981), *Guitar Ring* (1982), and *Die Dönnergötter* (1986). *An Angel Moves Too Fast to See* (1989) was for 100 guitars; *A Crimson Grail Moves Too Fast to See* (2005), for 400. Chatham's notable works for other instruments include *For Brass* (1982) for brass octet and drums, *The Last World* (1985) for soprano and **tape**, and Symphony No. 4 (1995). *See also* POSTMODERNISM.

CHÁVEZ, CARLOS (1899–1978). Mexican composer, musician, and educator. Carlos Chávez studied piano with Manuel Ponce and Pedro Luis Ogazón, but was mostly self-taught. His Piano Sonata No. 2 (1919), like much of his early music, used romantic and **impressionist** techniques. But Chávez was drawn to indigenous Indian music and Aztec lore, creating the ballet scores *El fuego nuevo* (1921) and *Los cuatro soles* (1925). Traveling in Europe in 1922 and 1923, he was impressed by **modernist** approaches to **dissonance** and **polyrhythm**, which inform his piano scores *Seven Pieces* (1923–1930), Sonatina (1924), and Piano Sonata No. 3 (1928). An extended stay in New York (1926–1928) resulted in firm friendships with several major composers, including **Aaron Copland**, **Edgard Varèse**, and **Henry Cowell**; with the latter two, Chávez founded the Pan-American Association of Composers (1928–1934). His other important 1920s works include *Tres exágonos* (1924) for voice and piano or chamber ensemble, *Energía* (1925) for nine instruments, and the ballet score *HP* (1927, a.k.a. *Horsepower*).

Regarded as Mexico's most important composer, Chávez was appointed by the government to direct both the Conservatorio Nacional in Mexico City (1928–1934) and the Orquesta Sinfónica de México (1928–1949). His use of Indian and mestizo (Spanish-Indian) techniques became more accessible with Sonata for Four Horns (1929) and *Sinfonía de Antígona* (1934). *Llamadas (sinfonía proletaria)* (1934) for orchestra and mixed chorus was his music for the masses, but Chávez found his most enduring success with *Sinfonía India* (1935), a celebration of Indian music. *Xochipilli Macuilxochitl* (1940) was scored for traditional Indian instruments. An international sound characterized *Toccata for Percussion Instruments* (1942) and the dance score *Hija de Colquide* (1944); his Violin Concerto (1950) and Symphony No. 5 (1953) showed affinities with **neoclassicism**. Director of the Instituto Nacional de Bellas Artes (1947–1952), Chávez also taught at Tanglewood and the University of Buffalo. His later works include the **opera** *Panfilo and Lauretta* (1956, a.k.a. *Love Propitiated* or *The Visitors*), Symphonies Nos. 3–6 (1951–1961), and Trombone Concerto (1976). *See also* MULTICULTURALISM.

CHIN, UNSUK (1961–). Korean composer, musician, and educator. Pianist Unsuk Chin studied composition with Sukhi Kang at Seoul National University and **György Ligeti** in Hamburg; she settled in Berlin in 1988. Drawing from **spectral music**, Balinese gamelan, and medieval music, Chin has explored color and sonority in such works as *Spektra* (1985) for three cellos; *Die Troerinnen* (1986, rev. 1990) for three female voices, female chorus, and orchestra; *Gradus ad infinitum* (1989) for **tape**; Piano Etudes Nos. 1–6 (1995–2003); *ParaMetaString* (1996) for string quartet and tape; *Xi* (1998) for ensemble and electronics; *Miroirs des temps* (1999, rev. 2001) for four voices and orchestra; Double Concerto (2002); *Cantatrix sopranica* (2005) for two sopranos, countertenor, and ensemble; the **opera** *Alice in Wonderland* (2007); and *Su* (2009) for sheng and orchestra. *See also* ELECTROACOUSTIC MUSIC; MULTICULTURALISM.

CHOU WEN-CHUNG (1923–). Chinese-born American composer and educator. Chou Wen-chung came to the United States in 1946 and became a citizen in 1958. He studied at the New England Conservatory of Music and Columbia University, where he later taught (1964–1991) and established the Center for U.S.-China Arts Exchange (1978–present). His teachers included **Edgard Varèse, Otto Luening, Nicolas Slonimsky**, and **Bohuslav Martinu**. Chou's "variable modes" concept of composition blends Chinese traditions of Taoist thought and *qin* music with Western techniques and **microtonal** tunings. Among his notable works are *And the Fallen Petals* (1956) for orchestra, *Riding the Wind* (1964) for wind orchestra, *Pien* (1966) for chamber ensemble, *Echoes from the Gorge* (1989) for percussion quartet, Cello Concerto (1992), String Quartets Nos. 1 ("Clouds," 1997) and 2 ("Streams," 2003), and *Eternal Pine* (2008) for Korean instruments. His students include **Joan Tower, Charles Dodge, Anne LeBaron, James Tenney**, and **Johnny Reinhard**. *See also* MODERNISM; MULTICULTURALISM.

COLEMAN, ORNETTE (1930–). American composer and musician. One of the most innovative and influential figures in creative African-American music, Ornette Coleman taught himself to play saxophone and read music by his early teens and soon was performing professionally. He played alto and led small ensembles in his own works on the albums *Something Else!!!!* (1958), *Tomorrow Is the Question* (1958), and *The Shape of Jazz to Come* (1959). Coleman broke new ground with his free treatment of melody, his disregard for familiar harmonic progressions and a fixed tonal center, and his use of **dissonance** and **polyrhythm**. His music met with controversy at first, but Coleman's expressive blues roots and the power and beauty of such pieces as "Rejoicing" (1958) and "Lonely Woman" (1959) could not be denied. His sound refined into a celebrated quartet with Don Cherry (trumpet), Charlie Haden (bass), and Billy Higgins or Ed Blackwell (drums) in the albums *Change of the Century* (1959), *This Is Our Music* (1960), and *To Whom Who Keeps a Record* (1960). The culmination was the epochal *Free Jazz* (1960), an octet with Eric Dolphy (bass clarinet), Freddie Hubbard (trumpet), and Scott LaFaro (bass) performing an extended group **free improvisation**, a jazz first.

Over the 1960s, along with touring internationally and performing on trumpet and violin as well as saxophone, Coleman developed a **free-jazz** approach that he termed "harmolodics": an equality in melody, harmony, and rhythm that enabled multiple players to solo simultaneously on similar melodic material by modulating into different keys. He also brought harmolodic composition to other genres, such as the woodwind quintet *Sounds and Forms* (1965), the 1967 string quartets *Saints and Soldiers* and *Space Flight*, and *Skies of America* (1972) for his quartet and symphony orchestra. **Electronic music** by Emmanuel Ghent was featured in Coleman's *Man on the Moon* (1969).

Traveling through Morocco and Nigeria in the early 1970s, Coleman performed with local musicians, and he recorded the **multicultural** LP *Dancing in Your Head* (1976) with the Master Musicians of Jajouka. Other notable musicians who have performed with Coleman include **Gunther Schuller, Yoko Ono, Leroy Jenkins, Sussan Deyhim**, Bill Evans, Pharoah Sanders, and Coleman's son Denardo. Adapting rock and funk to his music, Coleman formed the harmolodic ensemble Prime Time in 1975, usually featuring pairs of electric guitarists, electric bassists, and drummers, as in the recordings *Opening the Caravan of Dreams* (1983) and *In All Languages* (1987). His notable recent CDs include the 1994 "Sound Museum" albums *Hidden Man* and *Three Women*, *Tone Dialing* (1995), along with *Sound Grammar* (2006). *See also* ATONALITY.

COMPUTER MUSIC. *This entry focuses on the use of computers to generate compositional material and to synthesize sound; separate entries deal with the use of computers in* **electroacoustic music** *and the* **sampling** *of preexisting sound.*

The mid-1950s saw the rise of the computer as a tool for composition. **Iannis Xenakis** used a computer to devise the complex glissandi of *Metastasis* (1955) and also relied upon computer calculations to employ **stochastic** procedures compositionally in *Pithoprakhta* (1956). **Lejaren Hiller,** collaborating with Leonard Isaacson, completed his String Quartet No. 4, "Illiac Suite," in 1957, with the ILLIAC I computer at the University of Illinois as a third co-composer; the piece describes a growing sophistication in composition programming across its four movements, from monody to simple four-part counterpoint in the first to stochastic music in the fourth. *HPSCHD* (1968), Hiller's collaboration with **John Cage,** required a program that re-created the *I Ching*–based process of random selection ordinarily employed by Cage in his **chance music.**

In 1957, Max Mathews, a researcher at Bell Labs, first demonstrated the use of a computer in synthesizing sound through a digital-to-analog converter that changed the binary digital information of the computer into analogous electrical output heard through loudspeakers. **James Tenney** utilized Mathews's digital-synthesis program to produce several groundbreaking works, among them *Analog #1: Noise Study* (1961) and *Ergodos II* (1964). Using the Bell Labs computers, **Jean-Claude Risset** synthesized the sound of a trumpet and **Charles Dodge** synthesized speech. **Laurie Spiegel** created *The Expanding Universe* (1975) there; in the 1980s, she devised her *Music Mouse* program for the performance of real-time computer music. The electronic protocol MIDI (Musical Instrument Digital Interface), developed in the early 1980s, enabled **synthesizers,** computers, and samplers to communicate and synchronize with each other, and musicians could play an array of different instruments from one keyboard. Over the 1980s, most composers of **electronic music** stepped away from synthesizer technology and were using computers. *See also* ABRAMS, MUHAL RICHARD; ANDERSON, LAURIE; AUSTIN, LARRY; BEHRMAN, DAVID; BOULEZ, PIERRE; DUCKWORTH, WILLIAM; ENO, BRIAN; FERRARI, LUC; GANN, KYLE; HARVEY, JONATHAN; HENRY, PIERRE; HUNT, JERRY; LA BARBARA, JOAN; LEÓN, TANIA; LEWIS, GEORGE; MARTIRANO, SALVATORE; MEV; MIMAROGLU, ILHAN; MUMMA, GORDON; MURAIL, TRISTAN; NIBLOCK, PHILL; OSTERTAG, BOB; OSWALD, JOHN; REYNOLDS, ROGER; SHEA, DAVID; TAKAHASHI, YUJI; TAPE MUSIC; TEITELBAUM, RICHARD; SUBOTNICK, MORTON; TYRANNY, "BLUE" GENE; USSACHEVSKY, VLADIMIR; ZORN, JOHN.

CONRAD, TONY (1940–). American composer and musician. As a teenager, Tony Conrad was retuning his violin in **just intonation**. He played **La Monte Young**'s **minimalist** music, including *The Tortoise, His Dreams and Journeys* (1964) with Young, **Terry Jennings**, **Angus MacLise**, **Marian Zazeela**, and John Cale. Conrad withdrew from music for many years and created experimental cinema such as *The Flicker* (1966). More recently, he has released recordings of his drone music (*Early Minimalism, Vol. 1*, 1997; *Joan of Arc*, 2006) and resumed performing on amplified violin with prerecorded drones; he has also played with **Pauline Oliveros**, **Charlemagne Palestine**, and others. *See also* ELECTROACOUSTIC MUSIC; PLEROMA; POSTMODERNISM.

COPLAND, AARON (1900–1990). American composer, musician, and educator. One of the 20th century's greatest composers, Aaron Copland created a distinctly American sound, combining rhythmic vitality and a lyrical voice in a body of work that ranged from astringent **modernism** to expressive tonality with elements of folk and popular music. Born in Brooklyn, Copland was taught piano by his mother and sister and studied with Leonard Wolfson (1913–1917). Already writing music, he studied theory and composition with Rubin Goldmark (1917–1921) and, on his own, investigated the works of **Claude Debussy**, **Maurice Ravel**, and **Alexander Scriabin**. **Dissonant** harmonies and complex rhythms, along with jazz qualities, informed Copland's early piano works *Humoristic Scherzo* (1920, a.k.a. *The Cat and the Mouse*) and *Three Moods* (1921).

In 1921, Copland began studying in France, at first briefly with Paul Vidal in Fontainebleau, then in private lessons with **Nadia Boulanger** in Paris (1921–1924). She became the formative musical experience of his life, providing him with an expert technique and exposing him to the music of **Gustav Mahler** and **Igor Stravinsky**, which opened doors for Copland's own expressivity and **polyrhythmic** invention. For Boulanger's classes, he produced the Four Motets (1921) for mixed chorus, Passacaglia (1922) for piano, and *As It Fell upon a Day* (1923) for soprano, flute, and clarinet. At her urging, he composed the ghoulish ballet score *Grohg* (1925), delving deeper into **polytonality** and polyrhythms and utilizing jazz qualities and **quartertone** passages. *Grohg* went unperformed, but Copland derived from it the *Cortège macabre* (1925) and *Dance Symphony* (1929).

Boulanger brought Copland to conductor Serge Koussevitsky, who commissioned a work for organ and orchestra. After returning to the United States in 1924, he composed the Symphony for Organ and Orchestra (arranged for orchestra alone as First Symphony, 1928). Other major scores followed: *Music for the Theatre* (1925) for small orchestra and Piano Concerto (1926), both jazz inspired; the dramatic *Symphonic Ode* (1929, rev. 1955); *Vitebsk* (1929) for piano, violin, and cello, which used a Russian-Jewish folk theme and quarter-tones; and the epigrammatic *Statements* (1934) for orchestra. Copland produced a masterpiece with the Piano Variations (1930, orch. 1957), a stripped-down work that utilized techniques from **Arnold Schoenberg**'s **twelve-tone** method. He also explored **neoclassical** elements in *Short Symphony* (1933, a.k.a. Symphony No. 2; arranged as the Sextet for clarinet, piano, and string quartet, 1937).

Copland had a popular success with *El salón México* (1936), a vibrant collage of Mexican folk music, and produced more works of greater accessibility. The high school **opera** *The Second Hurricane* (1937) marked his first use of American folk music, a sound that permeated his brilliant ballet score *Billy the Kid* (1938). Copland also composed memorable **film music** for adaptations of John Steinbeck (*Of Mice and Men*, 1939; *The Red Pony*, 1948), Thornton Wilder (*Our Town*, 1940), and Henry James (*The Heiress*, 1949). In 1940, Koussevitzky founded the Berkshire Music Center at Tanglewood and brought in Copland to teach. He remained head of the composition department until 1964; among his students were **Alberto Ginastera**, **Ned Rorem**, **William Flanagan**, **Jacob Druckman**, **Toshi Ichiyanagi**, **Mario Davidovsky**, **Halim El-Dabh**, **Thea Musgrave**, and **Alvin Lucier**.

Copland entered an extraordinary period of productivity in the 1940s, composing such major works as *Quiet City* (1940) for English horn, trumpet, and strings; Piano Sonata (1941); *Lincoln Portrait* (1942) for narrator and orchestra; *Danzón cubano* (1942) for two pianos (orch. 1946); and two ballet scores, *Rodeo* (1942) and *Appalachian Spring* (1944). The latter, arguably Copland's masterpiece, was originally scored for 13 instruments, and found its greatest success as an orchestral suite (1945). His postwar output was equally impressive: Symphony No. 3 (1946), into which he incorporated his classic *Fanfare for the Common Man* (1942) for brass and percussion; *In the Beginning* (1947) for mezzo-soprano and mixed chorus, a setting from the Book of Genesis; Concerto for Clarinet and String Orchestra (1948) with harp and piano, commissioned by Benny Goodman; and *Four Piano Blues* (1948).

Some of Copland's finest vocal music was composed in the early 1950s, starting with his songs for medium voice and piano—*Twelve Poems of Emily Dickinson* (1950) and the folk-song arrangements *Old American Songs I* (1950) and *II* (1952)—and culminating in an opera, *The Tender Land* (1954). He also renewed his interest in **serial** techniques in the 1950s with the Piano Quartet (1950), which melded tonal and twelve-tone methods. That approach defined his *Piano Fantasy* (1957) and the orchestral pieces *Connotations* (1962) and *Inscape* (1967), which are among his greatest scores. Other important works in these years include the ballet score *Dance Panels* (1959, rev. 1962); Nonet (1960) for three violins, three violas, and three cellos; and *Music for a Great City* (1964) for orchestra.

From the mid-1950s until the early 1980s, Copland enjoyed an international career as a conductor. Although specializing in his own music, he also performed American masters such as **Charles Ives**, **Carl Ruggles**, and **Edgard Varèse**; such contemporaries as **George Gershwin**, **Roy Harris**, and **Virgil Thomson**; and important younger composers, including **Iannis Xenakis**, **Morton Feldman**, and **Toru Takemitsu**. Copland's ability to compose receded over the 1960s, and his last pieces were from the early 1970s, most notably Duo for Flute and Piano (1971) and *Night Thoughts (Homage to Ives)* (1972) for piano. At age 90, Copland contracted pneumonia and died of respiratory failure in a hospital in North Tarrytown, New York.

CORIGLIANO, JOHN (1938–). American composer, musician, and educator. John Corigliano studied with **Otto Luening** at Columbia University and at the Manhattan School of Music and taught at Juilliard and Lehman College. A tuneful **neoromantic** composer, Corigliano has written such notable works as Violin Sonata (1964), the oratorio *A Dylan Thomas Trilogy* (1976, rev. 1999), Clarinet Concerto (1977), three symphonies (1988–2004), the **opera** *The Ghosts of Versailles* (1991), String Quartet (1995), *Chiaroscuro* (1997) for two pianos tuned a **quarter-tone** apart, and *Conjurer* (2008) for percussion and string orchestra. He also scored the **films** *Altered States* (1980), *Revolution* (1985), and *Le violon rouge* (1998).

CORNER, PHILIP (1933–). American composer, musician, and educator. Philip Corner studied piano with Dorothy Taubman, composition with **Henry Cowell** and **Otto Luening**, and analysis with **Olivier Messiaen**. He taught at Rutgers University (1972–1992) and other institutions. A cofounder of Tone Roads Chamber Ensemble and Gamelan Son of Lion, Corner was also part of the **Fluxus** group. He has composed many **indeterminate** works of variable instrumentation, often scored verbally and/or in **graphic notation**, such as *Passionate Expanse of the Law* (1959), *Lovely Music* (1961–1962), *attempting whiteness* (1964), the over 400 pieces in his *Gamelan* series (1972–1989), *Just Another 12-Tone Piece* (1995), *When They Pull the Plug* (2002), and *One Note More Than Once* (2005). *See also* MINIMALISM; POSTMODERNISM.

COUPER, MILDRED (1887–1974). Argentine-born American composer, musician, and educator. Mildred Couper was educated in Germany, Italy, and France, where she studied piano with Moritz Moszkowski and composition with **Nadia Boulanger**. In 1915, she relocated to the United States and taught piano at the Mannes College of Music before settling in California in 1927. Couper wrote vocal and instrumental scores in traditional tunings, as well as works for two pianos tuned a **quarter-tone** apart such as *Xanadu* (1930). Her other **microtonal** music includes *Dirge* (1937) and *Rumba* (c. 1951).

COWELL, HENRY (1897–1965). American composer, musician, and educator. An essential pioneer of experimental **modernism** and **multiculturalism**, Henry Dixon Cowell was born in Menlo Park, California, and took violin lessons as a child. After studying piano for about a year, the 16-year-old Cowell composed *Adventures in Harmony* (1913), in which blocks of keys are played with the entire hand or the forearm. He began studying with composer **Charles Seeger** in 1915 and learned harmony and counterpoint with others. Cowell found further encouragement from **Leo Ornstein**'s piano music, and the densities of *Adventures in Harmony* were extended in *Dynamic Motion* (1916), *Antinomy* (1917), *The Tides of Manaunaun* (1917), and other innovative piano scores. He investigated the harmonic series and used overtone ratios to derive harmonies and complex rhythms that then defied performance.

Seeger urged him to systematize and document his work, and in 1919 Cowell completed his *Two Rhythm-Harmony Quartets*, using new notation techniques, and a treatise explaining his new rhythms and **polyharmony**, which introduced the term *tone-cluster* for piano densities. This influential text was published in 1930 as *New Musical Resources*, but the *Two Rhythm-Harmony Quartets* remained in manuscript until 1975.

In the 1920s, Cowell produced more tone-cluster piano works, such as *The Voice of Lir* (1920), *The Trumpet of Angus Og* (1924), and *Tiger* (1929). *Ensemble* (1924) for string quintet and three Native American thundersticks was an early indication of his interest in the music of other cultures; it also featured **graphic notation** and required improvisation. Cowell developed what he termed the *string piano*—plucking, rubbing, and strumming the strings inside the piano—in *Aeolian Harp* (1923), *The Sword of Oblivion* (1924), and *The Banshee* (1925). He showcased these **extended performance techniques** in *The Irish Suite* (1928), a concerto for string piano with small orchestra. Similarly, he composed his Piano Concerto (1929) as a tour de force in tone-cluster music. Cowell then stepped away from both techniques, having largely exhausted their usefulness for himself.

Cowell became an ardent champion of progressive music with his New Music Society concerts (1925–1936), the scores published by New Music Quarterly (1927–1958), and a series of New Music Quarterly Recordings (1934–1949). He was a cofounder of the Pan-American Association of Composers (1928–1934) and taught at the New School for Social Research (1930–

1936). Cowell aided composers internationally and was especially helpful to Americans native and adopted, including Seeger, Ornstein, **Charles Ives, Carl Ruggles, Edgard Varèse, John Becker, Wallingford Riegger, Dane Rudhyar, William Russell, Paul Bowles, Ruth Crawford Seeger, Nicolas Slonimsky, Henry Brant,** and **Harry Partch.** Cowell also performed his piano music nationwide and made five acclaimed European concert tours between 1923 and 1932; he performed in the Soviet Union in 1929, the first American composer to be invited. **Béla Bartók** and **Alban Berg** expressed to Cowell their interest in using tone-clusters. In 1932, **Arnold Schoenberg** invited Cowell to perform for his master classes in Berlin, and **Anton Webern** conducted Cowell's *Sinfonietta* (1928) in Vienna. In Berlin, Cowell also studied the music of Java, Bali, South India, and other countries.

Cowell's major works of the early 1930s include *Rhythmicana* (1931), an orchestral concerto for **Leon Theremin**'s electronic instrument the rhythmicon (which was tuned to the overtone series and could play complex **polyrhythms**), the dance score *Atlantis* (1931), and *Ostinato pianissimo* (1934) for percussion ensemble. *Mosaic Quartet* (1935, a.k.a String Quartet No. 3) was one of Cowell's **elastic-form** scores, allowing players to alternate the sequence of movements and change phrase lengths. Cowell's use of **dissonance** and **atonal** structures waned in these years, and tonal methods assumed more importance in *Mosaic Quartet* and *United Quartet* (1936, a.k.a. String Quartet No. 4).

In May 1936, Cowell was arrested in California and charged with having had sexual relations with a 17-year-old boy. He pleaded guilty and was sentenced to 15 years in San Quentin prison; while there, he taught music to prisoners, organized performing ensembles, and composed more than 50 pieces, including *Vocalise* (1937) and *Toccanta* (1938), both featuring wordless voice, and the 1939 percussion-ensemble scores *Pulse* and *Return.* Cowell's good behavior and the efforts of his supporters won his parole in June 1940. He married ethnomusicologist Sidney Hawkins Robertson the following year and received a full and unconditional pardon from the governor in 1942.

Cowell resumed teaching at the New School for Social Research (1940–1965) and later taught at Columbia University (1949–1965). He composed prolifically, but kept to traditional tonal structures and mostly avoided his earlier experimentalism. Instead, world music informed his composition: examples include Variations for Orchestra (1956), which featured Indonesian gamelan; *Persian Set* (1957), with Western and Middle Eastern instruments; *Homage to Iran* (1957) for violin and piano; *Ongaku* (1957) for orchestra; Symphony No. 13, "Madras" (1958), with Indian percussion ensemble; and Koto Concertos Nos. 1 (1962) and 2 (1965). Cowell's love of percussion also

CRUMB, GEORGE • 69

flourished, with the "Madras" Symphony, Percussion Concerto (1959), and Symphony No. 14 (1960), featuring 64 percussion instruments.

When he died at age 68 in Shady, New York, Cowell had composed approximately 1,000 scores, including 21 symphonies (1916–1965) and *Hymn and Fuguing Tune Nos. 1–18* (1943–1964) for various instruments. Among his students were **John Cage, Lou Harrison, George Gershwin, Johanna M. Beyer, Dick Higgins**, and **Philip Corner**. *See also* FUTURISM; JUST INTONATION; PLEROMA.

CRAFT, ROBERT (1923–). American musician and critic. Conductor Robert Craft is best known for his connection with **Igor Stravinsky** over the last 24 years of the composer's life. Along with his numerous concerts and recordings of Stravinsky's music, Craft also released important recordings of the works of **Arnold Schoenberg, Anton Webern**, and **Edgard Varèse**. He is the author of many books written either with or about Stravinsky, as well as such collections of criticism as *Prejudices in Disguise* (1974) and *Small Craft Advisories* (1989).

CRAWFORD, RUTH. *See* SEEGER, RUTH CRAWFORD.

CRUMB, GEORGE (1929–). American composer, musician, and educator. George Crumb studied composition with **Ross Lee Finney** in the United States and Boris Blacher in Germany and would later teach at the University of Pennsylvania (1965–1997). Crumb's early works, such as Sonata (1955) for solo cello and *Variazioni* (1959) for orchestra, showed the influences of **Paul Hindemith** and **Béla Bartók**. With *Five Pieces for Piano* (1962), he began to develop his mature style, employing a greater pointillism and compression along with an evocative and original approach to timbre. *Night Music I* (1963) for soprano, piano/celesta, and percussion was his first setting of Spanish poet Federico García Lorca; it also utilized **extended performance techniques**, including **string piano**, which would characterize his music.

Crumb continued to set Lorca with *Madrigals, Books I–IV* (1965–1969) for soprano and instruments; *Songs, Drones, and Refrains of Death* (1968) for baritone, electric guitar, electric contrabass, electric piano, electric harpsichord, and percussion; and *Night of the Four Moons* (1969) for mezzo-soprano, alto flute/piccolo, banjo, electric cello, and percussion. Other major works from these years are *Eleven Echoes of Autumn, 1965* (1966) for alto flute, clarinet, violin, and piano and the **spatial** *Echoes of Time and the River* (1967) for orchestra. His score writing became increasingly idiosyncratic, with **graphic notation**, elaborate visual designs, and poetic performance notations. Nineteen seventy was a breakthrough year for Crumb, with two classics: *Black Angels* for electric string quartet and *Ancient Voices of Children*, another Lorca setting, for soprano, boy soprano, oboe, mandolin, harp, electric piano, toy piano, and percussion.

The musicians wear masks in the 1971 works *Vox Balanae* for electric flute, electric cello, and electric piano and *Lux aeterna* for soprano, bass flute, sitar, and percussion. Theatrical qualities also enhance *Mikrokosmos, Volumes I and II* (1972–1973) for amplified piano. Crumb's notable later works include *Star Child* (1977) for soprano, children's voices, and orchestra; *Pastoral Drone* (1982) for organ; *A Haunted Landscape* (1984) for orchestra; *Easter Dawning* (1991) for carillon; *Mundus canis* (1998) for guitar and percussion; and *American Songbook, Volumes I–IV* (2001–2004) for soprano, percussion quartet, and amplified piano. *See also* ELECTROACOUSTIC MUSIC.

D

DALLAPICCOLA, LUIGI (1904–1975). Italian composer, musician, and educator. Luigi Dallapiccola was born in Pisino, Istria, and studied at the Florence Conservatory (1923–1931). After graduating, he joined the faculty as a piano teacher and continued to teach there until he retired in 1967; he also taught at the Instituto Tarcuato di Tella in Buenos Aires and at Tanglewood. His students included **Luciano Berio**, **Sylvano Bussotti**, **Frederic Rzewski**, **Salvatore Martirano**, **Halim El-Dabh**, and **Richard Maxfield**.

Inspired by the **neoclassicism** of **Ferruccio Busoni**, Dallapiccola used 17th-century forms in *Tre studi* (1932) for soprano and chamber orchestra, *Partita* (1933) for orchestra, and *Divertimento in quattro esercizi* (1934) for soprano and five instruments; his choral work *Cori di Michelangelo Buonarroti il Giovane* (1935) drew from the madrigals of Renaissance Italy. Protesting Benito Mussolini's dictatorship, Dallapiccola composed *Canti di prigioni* (1940) for mixed chorus, two pianos, two harps, and percussion; it became part of a monumental trilogy decrying oppression and enslavement, with his best known work, the one-act **opera** *Il prigioniero* (1948), and *Canti di liberazione* (1955) for mixed chorus and orchestra. Dallapiccola also began using the **twelve-tone** techniques in *Cinque frammenti di Saffo* (1942) for voice and chamber ensemble, but in 1943 was forced to flee Florence and go into hiding until the liberation of Italy in 1944.

In his mature music, Dallapiccola found new ways of melding **dodeca-phony** with tonal and modal techniques, producing such works as the oratorio *Job* (1950), *Quaderno musicale di Annalibera* (1952) for piano, and the 1954 orchestral scores *Variazioni* and *Piccola musica notturna*. His last vocal works include *Preghiere* (1962) for baritone and chamber orchestra, the opera *Ulisse* (1967), *Sicut umbra* (1970) for mezzo-soprano and 12 instruments, and *Commiato* (1972) for soprano and chamber ensemble. *See also* ATONALITY; MODERNISM.

DAVIDOVSKY, MARIO (1934–). Argentine-born American composer and educator. In his native Argentina, Mario Davidovsky studied composition with Guillermo Graetzer, Teodoro Fuchs, Erwin Leuchter, and Ernesto

Epstein. His early compositions adapted certain organizational techniques of **serialism** to his own totally chromatic and **atonal** music such as String Quartet No. 1 (1954), *Concertino for Percussion and String Orchestra* (1954), and *Noneto* (1956). Davidovsky studied with **Aaron Copland** at Tanglewood and two years later relocated to the United States and settled in New York, where he studied with **Otto Luening**. Using the RCA **synthesizer** at the Columbia-Princeton Electronic Music Center, he began composing **electronic music** with *Contrastes No. 1* (1960) for string orchestra and electronic sounds and *Electronic Studies Nos. 1–3* (1961–1965); he also taught the medium to such composers as **Ross Lee Finney** and **Anne LeBaron**.

Davidovsky's *Synchronisms No. 1* (1963) for flute and electronic sounds launched a landmark series of **electroacoustic** scores that established his reputation. Electronic sounds are heard with flute, clarinet, violin, and cello in *Synchronisms No. 2* (1964), cello in *No. 3* (1965), male or mixed chorus in *No. 4* (1967), percussion ensemble in *No. 5* (1969), piano in *No. 6* (1970), orchestra in *No. 7* (1973), and woodwind quintet in *No. 8* (1974). His instrumental and vocal scores during these years include *Inflexions* (1965) for chamber ensemble, *Transientes* (1972) for orchestra, *Scenes from "Shir-Ha-Shirim"* (1975) for four voices and chamber orchestra, and *Pennplay* (1978) for 16 instruments. Davidovsky was also director of the Columbia-Princeton Electronic Music Center (1981–1994), yet he employed electronic sounds only in his later *Synchronisms: No. 9* (1988) with violin, *No. 10* (1992) with guitar, *No. 11* (2005) with contrabass, and *No. 12* (2006) with clarinet. Other notable recent works by Davidovsky include *Consorts* (1980) for symphonic band, *Shulamit's Dream* (1993) for soprano and orchestra, *Cantione sine textu* (2001) for soprano and chamber ensemble, and Piano Septet (2007). *See also* TWELVE-TONE MUSIC.

DAVIES, (SIR) PETER MAXWELL (1934–). English composer, musician, and educator. Peter Maxwell Davies studied at the Royal Manchester College of Music with Richard Hall (1952–1957) and investigated **serialism** and **atonal modernism** with fellow students **Harrison Birtwistle** and **Alexander Goehr**, which led to their becoming known as the Manchester School. Davies also studied with Goffredo Petrassi in Rome (1957–1959) and **Roger Sessions** and Earl Kim (1962–1964) in the United States. He taught at the Royal Academy of Music, among other institutions, and was knighted in 1987.

Davies's *Prolation* (1958) for orchestra was **totally serialized**, but he found his own voice with a freer atonal style in the dramatic monodrama *Revelation and Fall* (1966, rev. 1980) for soprano and instrumental ensemble. Davies and Birtwistle cofounded the new-music group the Pierrot Players in

1967, which became the Fires of London (1970–1987) and performed internationally, led by Davies. His music for the group includes the score for Ken Russell's **film** *The Devils* (1971) and Davies's theatrical works *Eight Songs for a Mad King* (1969), *Vesalii icones* (1969), *Miss Donnithorne's Maggot* (1974), *The Martyrdom of St. Magnus* (1976), *Le jongleur de Notre-Dame* (1978), and *The Lighthouse* (1979). His other important compositions in these years include *Stone Litany* (1973) for mezzo-soprano and orchestra and the ballet score *Salome* (1978).

Davies has also drawn on music of the Renaissance, in techniques and in **quotation** and arrangements: *St. Thomas Wake* (1969) for orchestra is a foxtrot on a pavane by John Bull. His many works for young people include the cantata *The Peat Cutters* (1985), *Six Songs for St. Andrew's* (1988) for voices and instruments, *Shepherds of Hoy* (1993) for voices and piano, and *Six Sanday Tunes* (2001) for violins. Davies's more than 300 scores include Symphonies Nos. 1–7 (1976–2000), *Strathclyde Concertos Nos. 1–10* (1987–1996), and the **operas** *Taverner* (1970), *Resurrection* (1987), and *The Doctor of Myddfai* (1995). His notable recent works include *Veni Creator Spiritus* (2002) for flute and bass clarinet, *Angelus* (2003) for mixed chorus, *A Sad Paven for These Distracted Tymes* (2004) for string quartet, and *Das Rauschende der Farbe* (2006) for orchestra. *See also* GEBRAUCHSMUSIK; TWELVE-TONE MUSIC.

DEBUSSY, CLAUDE (1862–1918). French composer, musician, and critic. One of the crucial figures in the development of 20th-century music, Claude Debussy revolutionized composition with his novel approach to form and staticism and became a focal point for the **impressionist** movement. Born Achille-Claude Debussy in St.-Germain-en-Laye, not far west of Paris, he showed great talent at the piano. He entered the Paris Conservatoire at age 10 and studied piano with Antoine Marmontel and composition with Ernest Guiraud. His music was admired, and his *L'enfant prodigue* (1884), a cantata for three voices and orchestra, was awarded the Prix de Rome. More original was Debussy's *La damoiselle élue* (1888) for soprano, mezzo-soprano, women's chorus, and orchestra, and it earned him an academic warning against his tendencies toward "impressionism"—a term first applied to French painters of the 1870s who had rejected romanticism and academicism in favor of subtler and more sensual colors and textures.

Debussy was a major composer of songs for voice and piano in the 1880s and 1890s, setting Paul Verlaine (*Ariettes*, 1888; *Trois mélodies*, 1891; *Fêtes galantes*, 1892), Charles Baudelaire (*Cinq poèmes*, 1889), and Pierre Louÿs (*Chansons de Bilitis*, 1897). An enthusiasm for the music of Richard Wagner was excited by Debussy's pilgrimages to Bayreuth in 1888 and 1889, but by the mid-1890s he had turned away from Wagner to follow his own path. He drew ideas from numerous sources, including the works of Modest Mussorgsky, with their modal writing, unusual scales, and asymmetrical rhythms and forms. The music of a Javanese gamelan ensemble at the Grande Exposition Universelle in Paris in 1889 also greatly impressed him—as it did his friend **Erik Satie**, whose lively mind and anti-Teutonic attitude further encouraged Debussy.

With his orchestral score *Prélude à l'après-midi d'un faune* (1894), Debussy synthesized his musical attractions and aversions into a sound that was free from the shadow of Wagner and from the techniques of the French academy. Ignoring traditional methods of development through contrast, Debussy created a static atmosphere of subtle effects and emotions, rich in sensuous harmonies and orchestral color. The score was quickly labeled impressionist, and that painterly quality was even more pronounced in Debussy's *Nocturnes* (1899) for orchestra and wordless female chorus. His second great breakthrough came in **opera** with *Pélléas et Mélisande* (1901), a setting of Maurice Maeterlinck's play. Debussy bypassed the genre's conventions and downplayed drama, becoming as revolutionary for the opera house as he had been for the concert hall. Avoiding vocal pyrotechnics and favoring a restrained and hushed orchestration, *Pélléas et Mélisande* soon found its audience and has remained in the repertory.

The 1900s saw perhaps the most popular of all Debussy's orchestral music: *La mer* (1905), an evocative pictorial score in the spirit of his *Nocturnes*. This decade also marked a third major breakthrough in Debussy's composition, with a series of major works for piano: *Estampes* (1903), *L'isle joyeuse* (1904), the first (1905) and second (1907) series of *Images*, and *Children's Corner* (1908). Inspired by the singing tone of Frédéric Chopin, he embraced an antipercussive piano sound and demanded innovative techniques in fingering and pedal, as well as a more acute ear for sonority. (Although a skilled pianist, Debussy concertized infrequently and did not premiere his own works.) He also wrote music criticism for the magazine *La Revue blanche* (1901), the newspaper *Gil Blas* (1903), and the magazines *Musica* (1906–1911) and *SIM* (1912–1914).

Debussy deplored the impressionist pigeonhole, yet he had plainly defined a new compositional sensibility that liberated numerous composers during the first decades of the 20th century—some of whom he befriended, among them **Maurice Ravel**, **Edgard Varèse**, **Igor Stravinsky**, and **Manuel de Falla**. Internationally famous by the 1910s, Debussy produced his final great piano works with *Douze préludes*, first book (1910) and second book (1913); *Six épigraphes antiques* (1914) for piano four-hands; and *En blanc et noir* (1915) for two pianos. He wrote notable music for voice and piano with *Trois* *ballades de François Villon* (1910) and *Trois poèmes de Stéphane Mallarmé* (1913), and three major orchestral scores: *Le martyre de Saint-Sébastien* (1911), *Images* (1912), and the more hard-edged and **dissonant** *Jeux* (1912).

In these years, Debussy also composed his first important chamber music scores since his String Quartet of 1893, starting with *Première rapsodie* (1910) for clarinet and piano and *Syrinx* (1912) for solo flute. The culmination was his Sonata for Cello and Piano (1915); Sonata for Flute, Viola, and Harp (1915); and Sonata for Violin and Piano (1917), in which he attempted to rethink classical forms. They were written as part of a projected cycle of six chamber scores, which was never realized. Debussy died of cancer at age 55 in Paris. *See also* ATONALITY; MODERNISM; MULTICULTURALISM; NEOCLASSICISM; TONE-CLUSTER.

DEGAETANI, JAN (1933–1989). American musician and educator. Mezzo-soprano Jan DeGaetani studied at Juilliard and became a leading interpreter of 20th-century music, premiering and recording works by such composers as **Elliott Carter**, **George Crumb**, **Peter Maxwell Davies**, **William Schuman**, and **Jacob Druckman**. She was also professor of voice at the Eastman School of Music (1973 1989).

DE GLI ANTONI, MARK. *See* ROUGH ASSEMBLAGE.

DELIUS, FREDERICK (1862–1934). English composer. An original composer who developed his own **impressionistic** voice, Frederick Delius is beloved for his single-minded devotion to beauty and nature. Born to a family of wealthy wool merchants in Bradford, Yorkshire, Fritz Theodor Albert Delius studied violin and piano. After two years of college, he worked for a while in the family business, but gave it up and relocated to Florida in 1884, intending to grow oranges. Although Delius did run a plantation there, his greatest experiences were musical, and the evocative harmonies and melodies in the songs of the African Americans who worked the fields made a deep impression on him.

Another breakthrough came to him there in his friendship with composer/musician **Thomas F. Ward**; after studying with Ward, Delius had a sufficient education to get a job teaching music in Virginia in 1885. He then returned to Europe and entered the Leipzig Conservatory (1886–1888). His teachers included Carl Reinecke, but Delius realized that none of his studies there was as useful to him as Ward's had been. With that experience in mind, he composed his first notable score, *Florida Suite* (1887, rev. 1889). Delius visited Paris in 1888 and decided to live there, and by the 1890s his mature style began emerging in his orchestral music, with a more vital sense of nature and locale, be it the English countryside of *Over the Hills and Far Away* (1897), the American South in the Piano Concerto (1897, rev. 1906), or his beloved France in *Paris* (1899). Along with American music, Delius drew upon such varied sources as Frédéric Chopin, Richard Wagner, Edvard Grieg, and the impressionist works of **Claude Debussy** in developing his own rhapsodic music of lush chromatic harmonies and rich orchestrations.

Delius wrote his first **opera**, libretto and music, with the fairy-tale romance *Irmelin* (1892). He also wrote and scored *The Magic Fountain* (1895, rev. 1898), but turned to a libretto by C. F. Keary for *Koanga* (1897, rev. 1898); both operas were tragic dramas of interracial love set in the New World, with Delius drawing upon music he had known in Florida. Neither *Irmelin* nor *The Magic Fountain* would be staged until many years after his death, but the Voodoo-themed *Koanga* found an audience in Germany and was premiered in Elberfeld in 1904. Even though Delius had settled in Grez-sur-Loing, near Fontainebleau, in 1897 and anglicized his first name to Frederick in 1902, his music was taken up by the Germans, and his finest opera, *A Village Romeo and Juliet* (1901, rev. 1906), was premiered in Berlin in 1907. With a libretto by Delius after Gottfried Keller's novella, *A Village Romeo and Juliet* placed its doomed lovers in a pastoral landscape epitomized by the popular orchestral interlude "The Walk to the Paradise Garden."

Delius also found success in Germany with several major works for mixed chorus and orchestra: *Appalachia* (1903), subtitled *Variations on an Old Slave Song*, which returned to the sounds of 1880s Florida; *Sea Drift* (1904), with baritone soloist, a setting of Walt Whitman; *A Mass of Life* (1905), perhaps his greatest choral work, with soprano, contralto, tenor, and baritone soloists, to texts by Friedrich Nietzsche; and the Ernest Dowson setting *Songs of Sunset* (1907), with soprano and baritone soloists. The late 1900s saw two memorable short tone poems for orchestra, *Brigg Fair* (1907) and *In a Summer Garden* (1908, rev. 1912). Delius then spent more than two years writing the libretto and music for his last opera, the austere romantic drama *Fennimore and Gerda* (1911), after which he returned to his compact lyrical form of the previous decade, modifying it for smaller orchestra with the classics *Summer Night on the River* (1911) and *On Hearing the First Cuckoo in Spring* (1912). Similar qualities arose in his more ambitious *The Song of the High Hills* (1912) for orchestra and wordless mixed chorus.

German support for Delius's music ceased with World War I—*Fennimore and Gerda* waited until 1919 for its premiere in Frankfurt—but he continued composing on a large scale with his Double Concerto (1915) for violin, cello, and orchestra; *Requiem* (1916) for soprano, baritone, chorus, and orchestra; Violin Concerto (1916); and such orchestral scores as *North Country Sketches* (1914) and *Eventyr* (1917). His chamber pieces included Sonata

No. 1 for Violin and Piano (1914) and String Quartet (1917). Delius's composition then became increasingly sporadic as his health deteriorated. He was able to complete such efforts as *A Song before Sunrise* (1918) for orchestra, Cello Concerto (1921), and the 1923 scores Sonata No. 2 for Violin and Piano and the incidental music for *Hassan*, but by 1925 Delius had fallen silent, stricken with paralysis and blindness by neurosyphilis.

In 1928, he accepted an offer from English musician Eric Fenby to join him in France and serve as his amanuensis. Together they produced the last of Delius's compositions, including *A Song of Summer* (1929), Sonata No. 3 for Violin and Piano (1930), *Caprice and Elegy* (1930) for cello and chamber orchestra, and two more settings of Whitman: *Songs of Farewell* (1930) for mixed chorus and orchestra and *Idyll* for soprano, baritone, and orchestra (1932). Delius died in Grez-sur-Loing at age 72.

DEL TREDICI, DAVID (1937–). American composer, musician, and educator. A concert pianist as a teenager, David Del Tredici studied composition with **Roger Sessions** and **Iannis Xenakis** and has taught at Harvard University and the City College of New York. His early music used **twelve-tone** methods, as in two James Joyce settings for soprano: *I Hear an Army* (1964) with string quartet and *Syzygy* (1966) with horn and orchestra. Turning to **neoromantic** techniques, he wrote settings of Lewis Carroll for amplified soprano and orchestra, which include *An Alice Symphony* (1969, rev. 1976), *Final Alice* (1975), and *In Memory of a Summer Day* (1980). Among his recent works are such gay-themed scores as his music for John Kelly's *Brother* (1997) and *My Favorite Penis Songs* (2002) for soprano, baritone, and piano. *See also* POSTMODERNISM.

DENISOV, EDISON (1929–1996). Russian composer, musician, and educator. Siberian-born Edison Denisov studied piano and composition at the Moscow Conservatory and later taught there. He used **serial** techniques in *The Sun of the Incas* (1964) for soprano and chamber ensemble, Sonata for Alto Saxophone and Piano (1970), *Five Etudes* (1983) for solo bassoon, and Wind Octet (1991). Denisov's *Crescendo e diminuendo* (1965) for harpsichord and 12 strings featured **graphic notation** and performance freedoms, while *Chant des oiseaux* (1969) was scored for prepared piano or harpsichord and **tape**. His other notable works include *Peinture* (1970) for orchestra; *Requiem* (1980) for soprano, tenor, mixed chorus, and orchestra; the **opera** *L'écume des jours* (1981); a symphony (1987); and Chamber Symphony No. 2 (1994). *See also* ELECTRONIC MUSIC.

DEYHIM, SUSSAN (1956–). Iranian composer and musician. Sussan Deyhim settled in New York in 1980, and with composer/keyboard player

Richard Horowitz she created and starred in the **multimedia opera** *Azax/ Attra* (1981). A dramatic **multicultural** vocalist who uses **extended performance techniques**, Deyhim has also performed with **Ornette Coleman, Elliott Sharp**, and many others. Among her notable solo recordings are *Madman of God: Divine Love Songs of the Persian Sufi Masters* (2000) and *Full Album: City of Leaves* (2011). Her **electroacoustic music** with Horowitz includes the albums *Desert Equations* (1986), *Majoun* (1996), and *Logic of the Birds* (2008). *Soliloquy* and *Possessed* (both 2008) are Deyhim's music and sound design for the video installations of Shirin Neshat. *See also* FREE IMPROVISATION; POSTMODERNISM.

DIAMOND, DAVID (1915–2005). American composer, musician, and educator. David Diamond studied violin and composition at the Eastman School of Music. He also studied with **Roger Sessions** and **Nadia Boulanger** and taught at Juilliard and other institutions. A traditional composer with such admired early works as *Psalms* (1936) for orchestra and *Rounds* (1944) for strings, Diamond developed his melodic gifts in more chromatic and **dissonant** and tonally ambiguous scores, among them Quintet (1950) for clarinet and strings, *The World of Paul Klee* (1957) for orchestra, *The Fall* (1970) for voice and piano, the **opera** *The Noblest Game* (1975), and Concerto for String Quartet and Orchestra (1996). His other notable works include 11 symphonies (1940–1991), 10 string quartets (1940–1968), and three violin concertos (1937–1976). *See also* MODERNISM.

DISSONANCE. Categories of dissonance and consonance can be traced back to the ancient Greek philosopher and mathematician Pythagoras of Samos. Virtually every culture has drawn some distinctions between consonant combinations of tones, experienced as gentle and soothing, and dissonant harmonies, regarded as harsh or grating. The flowering of romanticism during the 1830s gave rise to a radical extension of music's harmonic vocabulary, with composers utilizing 7th, 9th, and 11th chords that had hitherto been mostly avoided. Some found these tonal combinations discordant and objectionable, but audiences soon embraced the music of such innovators as Frédéric Chopin, Robert Schumann, and Franz Liszt. The operas of Richard Wagner used increasingly chromatic harmonies, paving the way for a more provocative treatment of dissonance by such composers as Anton Bruckner, **Richard Strauss**, and **Gustav Mahler**.

Working in this tradition, **Arnold Schoenberg** regarded dissonance as a more remote form of consonance and developed a music with no tonal bias. With his 1909 **atonal** scores *Erwartung* and *Five Orchestral Pieces*, Schoenberg emancipated dissonance and made available all harmonic combinations.

His pupils **Alban Berg** and **Anton Webern** followed his approach and by the mid-1920s were also using his **twelve-tone** method for composing dissonant atonal music.

Other composers of the 1900s and 1910s, such as **Charles Ives, Alexander Scriabin, Sergey Prokofiev, Igor Stravinsky**, and **Béla Bartók**, were less interested in—or in some cases, fundamentally opposed to—late romantic and postromantic German music, yet they, too, felt the need for a harmonic language that was more expressive and relevant to their experience. Some were inspired by folk music and/or French **impressionism**, but they all followed their own paths into dissonance. By the 1920s, this **modernist** harmonic sensibility had taken root; whether the music was tonal, **polytonal**, or atonal, composers such as **Edgard Varèse, Carl Ruggles, Paul Hindemith, Henry Cowell, Aaron Copland**, and **Darius Milhaud** were using dissonant harmonies as a natural feature of their musical expression. A ready resource for later 20th-century composers, dissonance has become a familiar aspect of contemporary harmonic practice. *See also* EXPRESSIONISM; FREE IMPROVISATION; FREE JAZZ; PANTONALITY.

DLUGOSZEWSKI, LUCIA (1934–2000). American composer and musician. Lucia Dlugoszewski studied piano and composition at the Detroit Conservatory of Music, and in 1949 she premiered *Moving Space Theater Piece for Everyday Sounds* in Detroit, consisting of the sounds of daily, so-called unmusical activities. She relocated to New York City in 1952 and gave a similar concert, *Everyday Sounds for e. e. cummings with Transparencies*. She also studied piano with Grete Sultan and composition with Felix Salzer and **Edgard Varèse** and began playing piano for choreographer Erick Hawkins in 1952. Soon she was composing scores for Hawkins, whom she later married.

The novel sonorities of Dlugoszewski's **atonal** scores can be traced back to the **extended performance techniques** she developed in the early 1950s for what she termed the "timbre piano": playing the piano strings with percussion mallets, brushes, and other objects in such pieces as *Archaic Timbre Piano Music* (1957) and *Five Radiant Grounds* (1961), both of which Hawkins choreographed; *Swift Music* (1965) for two timbre pianos; and *Dazzle on a Knife's Edge* (1966) for timbre piano and orchestra. Dlugoszewski also designed more than 100 new percussion instruments in the late 1950s and used them as the sole instrumentation of *Suchness Concert* (1960), *Geography of Noon* (1964), and *Radical Quidditas for an Unborn Baby* (1991).

Dlugoszewski produced much of her finest and best known music in the early 1970s, some of which was choreographed by Hawkins: *The Suchness of Nine Concerts* (1970) for clarinet, violin, two percussion, and timbre piano; *Tender Theatre Flight Nageire* (1971, rev. 1978), a **spatial** work for brass sextet and percussion; and *Densities: Nova, Corona, Clear Core* (1972) for brass quintet. Her major works written for the concert hall include *Space Is a Diamond* (1970) for solo trumpet, *Fire Fragile Flight* (1974) for 17 instruments, and *Abyss and Caress* (1975) for trumpet and chamber orchestra. Among her notable later scores are *Four Attention Spans* (1988) for piano and orchestra or chamber ensemble, *Disparate Stairway Radical Other* (1995) for string quartet, and *Exacerbated Subtlety Concert (Why Does a Woman Love a Man?)* (1997, rev. 2000) for timbre piano. *See also* INSTRUMENT BUILDING; POSTMODERNISM; STRING PIANO.

DODECAPHONY. Greek for "twelve-tone," *dodecaphony* is an alternative name for **Arnold Schoenberg**'s method of **twelve-tone** composition. *See also* SERIALISM.

DODGE, CHARLES (1942–). American composer and educator. Charles Dodge studied with Richard Hervig, **Darius Milhaud**, **Gunther Schuller**, **Arthur Berger**, **Otto Luening**, and **Chou Wen-chung**. His studies of **electronic music** with **Vladimir Ussachevsky** and **computer music** with Godfrey Winham were a turning point, and in 1970 Dodge completed his first works for computer-synthesized sound: *Changes* and *Earth's Magnetic Field*. His real breakthrough came two years later when he synthesized the human voice in *Speech Songs*, settings of the poetry of Mark Strand.

Dodge's speech-synthesis music became increasingly sophisticated and imaginative with *The Story of Our Lives* (1974) and *In Celebration* (1975), two other Strand settings, and *Cascando* (1978), from Samuel Beckett's radio play. *Any Resemblance Is Purely Coincidental* (1980) has a pianist performing with a synthesized voice derived from an early recording of an aria. Other works by Dodge also combine electronic sound on **tape** with live musicians: soprano in *The Waves* (1984), mixed chorus in *Roundelay* (1985), violin in *Etudes* (1994). Dodge's later works strictly for computer-synthesized sound include *Song without Words* (1986) and *Fades, Dissolves, Fizzles* (1996); among his instrumental scores are *Distribution, Redistribution* (1983) for clarinet, violin, and piano and *The One and the Other* (1993) for chamber orchestra. He taught at Columbia University (1970–1980), Brooklyn College (1980–1995), and Dartmouth College (1995–2009), among other institutions. *See also* ELECTROACOUSTIC MUSIC.

DRUCKMAN, JACOB (1928–1996). American composer and educator. Jacob Druckman's teachers included Vincent Persichetti, **Aaron Copland**, and Tony Aubin. His early music was mostly **serial**: for example, *Four Madrigals* (1958) for mixed chorus; the Psalm settings *Dark upon the Harp* (1962) for mezzo-soprano, brass quintet, and percussion; and String Quartet No. 2 (1966). Exposure to **electronic music** led to a more romantic approach, with Druckman emphasizing drama, surprise, and new sonorities in his **atonal** and electronic works. His *Animus* series combined live musicians and **tape**: trombone in *Animus I* (1966), mezzo-soprano and percussion in *Animus II* (1968), and clarinet in *Animus III* (1969). The last work also had theatrical qualities, and Druckman's *Valentine* (1969) for contrabass was even more of a theater piece. *Incenters* (1968, rev. 1972) for trumpet, horn, trombone, and chamber group and *Windows* (1972) for orchestra used **proportional notation** and gave the players **aleatoric** freedoms in creating densities.

Druckman used **quotation** in *Incenters*; *Delizie contente che l'alme beate* (1973) for woodwind quintet and electronic tape; *Lamia* (1975) for soprano and orchestra; *Animus IV* (1977) for tenor, six instruments, and electronic tape; and the orchestral scores *Mirage* (1976), *Aureole* (1979), and *Prism* (1980). He brought **neoromantic** qualities to his String Quartet No. 3 (1981), the oratorio *Vox humana* (1983), *Come Round* (1992) for six players, and *Counterpoise* (1994) for soprano and orchestra. Druckman taught at Juilliard (1956–1972) and Yale University (1976–1996); his students included **Laurie Spiegel** and **David Lang**. *See also* ELECTROACOUSTIC MUSIC; MODERNISM.

DUCKWORTH, WILLIAM (1943–). American composer, musician, and educator. William Duckworth studied with **Ben Johnston** and has taught at Bucknell University since 1973. Especially admired among Duckworth's many compositions are *Time Curve Preludes* (1978) for piano and *Southern Harmony* (1981) for mixed chorus. His ongoing Cathedral Project, begun in 1997, is a collaborative work for the Internet that involves live performances and interactive electronics. He is the author of *Talking Music* (1995), *20/20* (1999), and *Virtual Music* (2005) and coeditor of *John Cage at Seventy-Five* (1989) and *Sound and Light: La Monte Young and Marian Zazeela* (1996). *See also* COMPUTER MUSIC; ELECTROACOUSTIC MUSIC; POSTMODERNISM.

DUFALLO, RICHARD (1933–2000). American musician and educator. Clarinetist Richard Dufallo studied with **Lukas Foss** and was a member of Foss's Improvisation Chamber Ensemble. He studied conducting with William Steinberg and **Pierre Boulez** and went on to lead the premieres of numerous works by major contemporary composers, including **Iannis Xenakis**, **Karlheinz Stockhausen**, **Krzysztof Penderecki**, **George Crumb**, **Luigi Nono**, and **Peter Maxwell Davis**. Dufallo also taught at the State University of New York at Buffalo and wrote the book *Trackings* (1989).

DUREY, LOUIS. *See* GROUPE DES SIX.

E

EASTMAN, JULIUS (1940–1990). American composer, musician, and educator. Julius Eastman studied at the Curtis Institute and taught at the State University of New York at Buffalo. A gifted singer, he premiered **Peter Maxwell Davies**'s *Eight Songs for a Mad King* (1969) and **Pauline Oliveros**'s *Crow Two* (1974) and sang works by **Meredith Monk** and **Barbara Kolb**. Eastman's **minimalist** compositions using repeated patterns called for improvisation; two examples are the octet *Stay on It* (1973), with a savvy use of pop music, and *If You're So Smart, Why Aren't You Rich?* (1977) for chamber orchestra, which fixated on the chromatic scale. In both, unexpected **dissonances** and glissandi and sustained tones serve to blur the repeated phrases. His other early scores include *Piano Pieces I–IV* (1968); *Comp 1* (1971) for solo flute; *Wood in Time* (1972) for metronomes; *440* (1973) for voice, violin, viola, and double bass; *Femenine* (1974) for chamber orchestra; and the **multimedia** works *The Moon's Silent Modulation* (1970) for dancers, vocalists, and chamber ensemble and *Mumbaphilia* (1972) for solo performer and dancers.

Eastman excelled as an improvising pianist and vocalist, and he used improvisation in three scores for unspecified instruments, which also employed some **graphic notation**: *Crazy Nigger* (1978), *Evil Nigger* (1979), and *Gay Guerilla* (1979). In 1980, all three were performed in realizations for four pianos, and the following year, Eastman massed like voices for another major **pleroma** score, *The Holy Presence of Joan d'Arc* for 10 cellos; he also composed and performed a solo vocal *Prelude* for it. Among his late works are *His Most Qualityless Majesty* (1983) for piano and voice, Symphony No. 2 (1983) for orchestra, the three-movement piano sonata *Piano 2* (1986), and *Our Father* (1989) for two men's voices. His 1988 creation of the title role in David Avidor and Nicole V. Gagné's **opera** *Agamemnon* (1992) is believed to be his final recorded performance. Eastman entered an eclipse in his last years, professionally and personally, and was often homeless. He died of cardiac arrest in a Buffalo hospital at age 49. *See also* FREE IMPROVISATION; POSTMODERNISM.

EICHHEIM, HENRY (1870–1942). American composer and musician. Henry Eichheim attended Chicago Musical College and was a violinist with the Boston Symphony Orchestra (1890–1912). His *Gleanings from Buddha Fields* (1906) for piano expressed a **multicultural** interest, and between the mid-1910s and the mid-1930s, Eichheim made five trips to Asia, studying the music and collecting instruments. His *Oriental Impressions* (1918–1922) for piano combined **impressionist** methodologies with techniques from Asian music; orchestrating the piece in 1922, he called for an array of exotic percussion, Burmese, Chinese, and Japanese. Eichheim's orchestral works *Java* (1929) and *Bali* (1933) featured gamelan instruments. His vocal works include the dance score *The Moon, My Shadow, and I* (1926) with soprano and female chorus. *See also* MODERNISM.

EISLER, HANNS (1898–1962). German composer, musician, and educator. Hanns Eisler studied at the New Vienna Conservatory and privately with **Arnold Schoenberg** and **Anton Webern**. He adopted the **twelve-tone** method with *Palmström* (1924) for voice and five instruments, *Zeitungsausschnitte* (1926) for voice and piano, *Kleine Sinfonie* (1932), and other scores, but he also composed works with left-wing political content, including protest songs ("Der rotte Wedding," 1929; "Lied des Kampfbundes," 1932) and choral music ("Auf den Strassen zu singen," 1928; "Der Streikbrecher," 1929). He began a lengthy collaboration with poet Bertolt Brecht in 1931, composing such works as the songs "Solidaritätslied" (1931) and "Einheitsfrontlied" (1934), the musical plays *Die Massnahme* (1930) and *Die Mutter* (1931), *Gegen den Krieg* (1936) for mixed chorus, *Hollywood Songbook* (1947) for voice and piano, *Die Teppichweber von Kujan-Bulak* (1957) for soprano and orchestra, and the *Lenin Requiem* (1937) and *Deutsche Symphonie* (1935–1958), both for soloists, mixed chorus, and orchestra.

Relocating to the United States in 1938, Eisler taught at the New School for Social Research and composed more twelve-tone music: String Quartet (1938), the quintet *Fourteen Ways to Describe Rain* (1941), and Piano Sonata No. 3 (1943). His Chamber Symphony (1940) featured a Novachord **synthesizer** and electric piano. With Theodor Adorno, Eisler wrote the book *Composing for the Films* (1944); among his **film** scores are Fritz Lang's *Hangmen Also Die!* (1943) and Alain Resnais's *Nuit et brouillard* (1955). American anti-Communist politicking resulted in Eisler's deportation in 1948. He taught at the Deutsche Hochschule für Musik in East Berlin and composed the East German national anthem in 1949, as well as *Goethe-Rhapsodie* (1949) for soprano and orchestra and *Ernste Gesänge* (1962) for baritone and string orchestra. *See also* ATONALITY; GEBRAUCHSMUSIK; MODERNISM; SPRECHSTIMME.

ELASTIC FORM. Anticipating **aleatoric** composition, **Henry Cowell** developed what he termed "elastic-form music" in the mid-1930s. Having written dance scores, Cowell was aware of the changing needs of choreographers as they develop new works. Elastic form permitted a wide range of freedoms: expanding and contracting melodic phrases and sentences; rearranging and repeating sections as block units; altering instrumentation and overall duration. Cowell's elastic-form works include *Mosaic Quartet* (1935, a.k.a. String Quartet No. 3), *Sound Form No. 1* (1937) for five players, the 1939 piano scores *Ritournelle* and *Amerind Suite*, and *26 Simultaneous Mosaics* (1963) for five players. *See also* CHANCE MUSIC; INDETERMINACY; OPEN FORM.

EL-DABH, HALIM (1921–). Egyptian-born American composer, musician, and educator. Halim El-Dabh studied at the University of Cairo and with **Aaron Copland, Irving Fine, Luigi Dallapiccola,** and **Leonard Bernstein** at Tanglewood. He became a U.S. citizen in 1961 and taught at Kent State University (1969–1991). A scholar of African music, El-Dabh devised a notational system for the derabucca, a ceramic Egyptian drum featured in his 1965 solo *Sonic No. 7*, and was the soloist who premiered his *Fantasia-Tahmeel* (1959) for derabucca and string orchestra. With such early works as *Ta'abir al-Zaar* (1944, a.k.a. *Wire Recorder Piece*), El-Dabh anticipated **tape music**; at the Columbia-Princeton Electronic Music Center, he created the **electronic** drama *Leiyla and the Poet* (1961). His other music includes the dance scores *Clytemnestra* (1958) and *Lucifer* (1975); the **opera** *Opera Flies* (1971), about the 1970 shootings at Kent State; *Surr-Rah* (2000) for piano and orchestra; and *Symphony for 1,000 Drums* (2006). *See also* MODERNISM; MULTICULTURALISM.

ELECTROACOUSTIC MUSIC. Although one can still find references to **tape music** as "electroacoustic music"—regarding the tape as an electrical manipulation of natural sound—common usage has designated as "electroacoustic" any music that combines electronic technology with natural sound, be it environmental, mechanical, vocal, or instrumental. The first significant breakthroughs came in the 1920s and 1930s, with the invention of the **theremin, ondes martenot, trautonium,** rhythmicon, and other **electronic-music** instruments and their use with traditional instruments by such composers as **Joseph Schillinger, Henry Cowell, Paul Hindemith,** and **Edgard Varèse.**

    John Cage's *Imaginary Landscape No. 1* (1939) used records of constant and variable frequency, anticipating the initial *musique concrète* pieces by **Pierre Schaeffer** in 1948. Further developments in tape music led composers to combine tape and musicians, as with Schaeffer and **Pierre Henry**'s

Orphée 53 (1953), **Vladimir Ussachevsky** and **Otto Luening**'s *Rhapsodic Variations* (1954), and Varèse's classic *Déserts* (1954). Electrically synthesized sound was also heard with live performers, played on magnetic tape, as in **Mario Davidovsky**'s *Synchronisms* series (1963–2006), and created live by such innovators as Cage, **David Tudor**, **Max Neuhaus**, the **AMM** and **MEV** groups, and **Robert Ashley** with the **ONCE Group** and the **Sonic Arts Union**.

The simplest electronic alteration of sound is amplification; at extremes, it transforms familiar timbres, as with Cage's *Music for Amplified Toy Pianos* (1960), and reveals the imperceptible, such as the amplified brain waves that resonate percussion instruments in **Alvin Lucier**'s *Music for Solo Performer* (1965). Increasingly sophisticated electronic modification and processing of sound emerged with technological developments in the 1960s and 1970s. **Karlheinz Stockhausen**'s *Mixtur* (1964, rev. 1967) separated the orchestra into woodwinds, brass, plucked strings, and bowed strings and fed the sound of each group into its own ring modulator, where a musician played sine-wave tones on an oscillator, transforming the group's sound as it played. **Pauline Oliveros**'s *Accordion* (1966) for amplified accordion with tape-delay systems led to her innovative compositions and improvisations with the expanded accordion, using digital delay systems and custom performance controls. **Morton Subotnick**'s ghost-score pieces, such as *Passages of the Beast* (1978) and *An Arsenal of Defense* (1982), had the musicians' live sound modified into electronic sound and played back on tape into the performance.

The 1970s saw **computer-music** technology entering electroacoustic music with such works as **Gordon Mumma**'s *Conspiracy 8* (1970), **Laurie Spiegel**'s *Waves* (1975), and **Roger Reynolds**'s *". . . the serpent-snapping eye"* (1979). Computers soon came to dominate the field, just as they did with electronic music. For his 1982 recording *The Intermediary*, **"Blue" Gene Tyranny** alternated his improvised piano performance with its computer-generated electronic reinventions. **George Lewis**'s *Voyager* (1988) had an interactive computer with a virtual orchestra, which responded to live improvisers in real time. Subotnick's *A Desert Flowers* (1989) gave the orchestra's conductor a computer-modified baton to control the electronics. Other composers who have used computers in performance with instruments include **Pierre Boulez**, **David Behrman**, **Larry Austin**, **Richard Teitelbaum**, **Tania León**, **Phill Niblock**, **Joan La Barbara**, **Jean-Claude Risset**, **Yuji Takahashi**, and **Laurie Anderson**. *See also* AMIRKHANIAN, CHARLES; ATONALITY; BABBITT, MILTON; BERIO, LUCIANO; CONRAD, TONY; CRUMB, GEORGE; DEYHIM, SUSSAN; DODGE, CHARLES; DRUCKMAN, JACOB; DUCKWORTH, WILLIAM; FERRARI, LUC; FLYNT,

HENRY; FREE IMPROVISATION; FRITH, FRED; GABURO, KENNETH; GALÁS, DIAMANDA; GLASS, PHILIP; GOSFIELD, ANNIE; HARVEY, JONATHAN; IBARRA, SUSIE; KOSUGI, TAKEHISA; LEACH, MARY JANE; LEBARON, ANNE; MARTIRANO, SALVATORE; MAXFIELD, RICHARD; MURAIL, TRISTAN; MUSGRAVE, THEA; NONO, LUIGI; PERKINS, PHILIP; REICH, STEVE; RILEY, TERRY; RYLAN, JESSICA; SHEA, DAVID; SUN RA; SYNTHESIZER; TAL, JOSEF; WESTERKAMP, HILDEGARD; XENAKIS, IANNIS; YOUNG, LA MONTE; YUASA, JOJI; ZIMMERMANN, BERND ALOIS.

ELECTRONIC MUSIC. *This entry focuses on the electrical synthesis of sound prior to the advent of computers; separate entries deal with the different types of* **electroacoustic music,** **tape music,** *and* **computer music.**

The vast field of electronic music has roots well into the 19th century. American inventor Elisha Gray played his two-octave polyphonic *musical telegraph* in 1874, using a keyboard to sound single-tone telegraph transmitters. In 1899, English electrical engineer and inventor William Duddell harnessed the whine of carbon-arc streetlamps for his *singing arc*, a monophonic keyboard instrument with circuitry that altered the sound's pitch. Between 1900 to 1906, American musician Thaddeus Cahill built three versions of the *telharmonium*, a polyphonic electric keyboard instrument that used spinning alternators to produce tuned sine-wave tones. The telharmonium failed to catch on, but Cahill's design was eventually vindicated by the success of the electronic Hammond organ, developed in the late 1920s, which also used rotating wheel elements to generate sound.

The vacuum tube, invented in 1906, permitted the creation of electronic sound without moving mechanical parts and launched a new era of electronic instruments. Russian scientist **Leon Theremin** patented the *theremin* in 1921. This instrument employed a heterodyning, or beat-frequency, method for generating electronic sound: Two pitches, nearly equal in frequency, are created by radio-frequency oscillators set above the range of human hearing; together they produce an audible difference tone, or beat frequency, which is played by adjusting its pitch and amplitude. Other monophonic heterodyning instruments followed in the 1920s, most notably the *Sphaerophon* of German musician **Jörg Mager** and the *ondes martenot* of French musician Maurice Martenot. German engineer Friedrich Trautwein replaced beat-frequency with a neon-tube oscillator and produced a more unusual timbre with his *trautonium*. None of these instruments, however, enjoyed more than limited success at best.

Edgard Varèse took on a prophetic role in the 1930s, envisioning electronic music as a profoundly new sonic terrain that would redefine what was possible in the articulation of time, pitch, timbre, and density. The electrical synthesis of sound began to offer such a gateway by the late 1950s, with the birth of the first major electronic-music studios. Most of these facilities had started out as tape-music studios, but one exception was the West-Deutscher Rundfunk (WDR), the radio network in Cologne. Working with an electronic instrument called a *melochord*, composers Herbert Eimert and Robert Beyer and physicist Werner Meyer-Eppler began creating what they called *elektronischen Musik*. After it was broadcast by the WDR in 1951, they formed a studio to pursue the electrical synthesis of sound; **Karlheinz Stockhausen** became a permanent collaborator in 1953 and later served as artistic director and artistic consultant. Other composers who worked at the WDR studio include **Ernst Krenek, György Ligeti**, and **Mauricio Kagel**.

Tokyo's NHK broadcasting system established an electronic-music studio in 1955, and that year **Toshiro Mayuzumi** produced the first electrically synthesized music in Japan. The Columbia-Princeton Electronic Music Center was founded in 1958, joining together as directors **Vladimir Ussachevsky** and **Otto Luening**, with their tape-music facilities at Columbia University, and **Milton Babbitt** and **Roger Sessions**, with the RCA Mark II Synthesizer at Princeton University. The many composers who worked at the center include **Mario Davidovsky, Halim El-Dabh**, and **Luciano Berio**. That same year, the Paris tape-music studio Groupe de Recherches de Musique Concrète became the Groupe de Recherches Musicales, broadening its focus to include electrically synthesized sound; **Henri Pousseur** founded the Studio de Musique Électronique in Brussels; and **Josef Tal** received a UNESCO research fellowship to tour several electronic-music studios, after which he founded the Israel Center for Electronic Music in Jerusalem.

Also in 1958, Russian engineer Yevgeny Murzin established the Moscow Electronic Music Studio, under the auspices of the Scriabin Museum. Although primarily a tape-music center, by 1966 the studio boasted the only electronic instrument then available in the Soviet Union: Murzin's ANS Synthesizer—ANS being the initials of **Alexander Nikolayevich Scriabin**, a musical visionary and inspiration for the new electronic age. With the ANS, Murzin reversed the photo-optic sound-recording techniques of film: Rather than obtain a visible image of a sound wave, it synthesized sound from sound waves drawn by the composer. The first examples of Soviet electronic music were produced with the ANS by such composers as **Edison Denisov, Sofia Gubaidulina, Alfred Schnittke**, and **Alexander Nemtin**. The studio was closed by Soviet authorities in 1975, and not until 1987 was Mikhail Chekalin able to inaugurate its successor.

The landmark year 1958 also saw independent electronic composers: **Pierre Henry** established the Apsone-Cabasse Studio, the first privately owned electronic-music studio in France, and **Robert Ashley** and **Gordon Mumma** launched the Cooperative Studio for Electronic Music in Michigan, which formed the basis for the electronic music theater works presented by the **ONCE Group** and the **Sonic Arts Union**. **Richard Maxfield** built his own equipment for electrical sound synthesis and gave the first American classes in the creation of electronic music in 1959 at the New School for Social Research.

Other composer/musicians in the 1960s played electronic music in real time, from the oscillators of **Pauline Oliveros** and **Charlemagne Palestine** to the electronic systems developed by **David Tudor**, **Salvatore Martirano**, **Jerry Hunt**, and the **AMM** and **MEV** ensembles. With the marketing of **synthesizers** in 1969, real-time performance of electronic music became generally available. By then, electronic music was gaining greater popularity, helped along by **Wendy Carlos**'s transcriptions of Johann Sebastian Bach and such **Morton Subotnick** LPs as *Silver Apples of the Moon* (1967) and *Touch* (1969). Computers, which had been used to generate electronic sound since the late 1950s, developed rapidly over the 1970s, and by the 1980s, they had largely supplanted most other forms of electronic music. *See also* AMACHER, MARYANNE; ATONALITY; AUSTIN, LARRY; BEHRMAN, DAVID; ENO, BRIAN; FILM MUSIC; GRAINGER, PERCY; KOSUGI, TAKEHISA; LE CAINE, HUGH; LUCIER, ALVIN; MIMAROGLU, ILHAN; MUSIQUE CONCRÈTE; NIBLOCK, PHILL; RADIGUE, ELIANE; REYNOLDS, ROGER; RYLAN, JESSICA; SAMPLING; SCHAEFFER, PIERRE; SPIEGEL, LAURIE; SUN RA; TEITELBAUM, RICHARD; TYRANNY, "BLUE" GENE; WUORINEN, CHARLES; XENAKIS, IANNIS; YUASA, JOJI.

ELLINGTON, DUKE (1899–1974). American composer and musician. The preeminent figure in jazz, Edward Kennedy Ellington, better known as "Duke," was one of America's most prolific and influential composers, winning international renown as an arranger, big-band leader, and pianist. He began piano lessons at age seven and by 1918 had organized his first band. Ellington produced an array of classic songs in the 1920s and 1930s, both instrumental ("Black and Tan Fantasy," 1927; "Creole Love Call," 1927; "The Mooche," 1928) and vocal ("Mood Indigo," 1930; "It Don't Mean a Thing [If It Ain't Got That Swing]," 1932; "Sophisticated Lady," 1933). He was adopting Latin American elements in his music by the 1930s and started employing longer forms with such works as *Creole Rhapsody* (1931) and *Reminiscing in Tempo* (1935). These pieces led to his ambitious suites celebrating African-American life: *Black, Brown, and Beige* (1943), *New World A-Comin'* (1945), *The Liberian Suite* (1947), and *Harlem* (1950).

Ellington's collaborations with composer/arranger/musician Billy Strayhorn resulted in numerous songs and two-piano works, as well as *Deep South Suite* (1946), *Such Sweet Thunder* (1957, a.k.a. *Shakespearean Suite*), *The Queen's Suite* (1959), the **multicultural** *Far East Suite* (1966), and arrangements of Pyotr Tchaikovsky (*Nutcracker Suite*, 1960) and Edvard Grieg (*Peer Gynt Suite*, 1961). Their **multimedia** works *Jump for Joy* (1950), *A Drum Is a Woman* (1956), and *My People* (1963) depicted the struggles of African Americans and called for narration and dancers.

Ellington's **modernist** harmonic sensibility incorporated **impressionist** qualities, **dissonance**, and **bitonality**. Anticipating **free jazz**, he employed freely **atonal** harmonies and a free, nonpulsed rhythmic/metric design in *The Clothed Woman* (1947), which also mixed styles with unexpected ragtime features. Also notable is Ellington's series of sacred-music concerts, combining gospel and jazz: *Concert of Sacred Music* (1965), *Second Sacred Concert* (1968), and the third *Concert of Sacred Music* (1973). His other major late works include *Latin American Suite* (1968), *New Orleans Suite* (1970), the ballet score *The River* (1970), *The Afro-Eurasian Eclipse* (1971), and *Toga Brava Suite* (1973). Ellington completed an autobiography, *Music Is My Mistress* (1973), but his **opera** *Queenie Pie* was left unfinished at the time of his death from cancer in New York at age 75. His son Mercer Ellington led the Duke Ellington Orchestra until his death in 1996, after which Mercer's son Paul Ellington took over; he remains its present leader. *See also* MOONDOG; SCHULLER, GUNTHER; SUN RA; TAYLOR, CECIL.

ENO, BRIAN (1948–). English composer and musician. An art student at Winchester Art College, Brian Eno joined the **Portsmouth Sinfonia** in 1970 and performed on clarinet. The following year, he was a vocalist with the **Scratch Orchestra** in a recording of **Cornelius Cardew**'s *The Great Learning*. He also performed with the band Roxy Music (1971–1973), playing **synthesizer** and operating **tape-music** effects. Eno created tape loops for his albums with guitarist Robert Fripp, *No Pussyfooting* (1973) and *Evening Star* (1975), and produced two Portsmouth Sinfonia LPs. His own successful rock albums include *Taking Tiger Mountain (by Strategy)* (1974) and *Another Green World* (1975). He founded Obscure Records (1975–1978) to release new music, from pieces by **Gavin Bryars**, **John Cage**, and **Michael Nyman** to Eno's *Discreet Music* (1975), a **minimalist** work using synthesizer and tape-delay system.

Discreet Music led to Eno's classic album *Music for Airports* (1978), which combined synthesizers with electronically processed voices and instruments. He coined the term *ambient music* to describe his use of quiet and subtle phrases and textures to create a calm background sound for other sounds and activities, a music that could be ignored or enjoyed as one chose. Ambient music became an enduring art-rock genre, fueled in part by Eno's subsequent ambient releases such as *The Plateaux of Mirror* (1979), created with Harold Budd, and *On Land* (1982), which used environmental sound.

Eno has scored numerous movies, including Derek Jarman's *Sebastiane* (1976), *Jubilee* (1978), and *Glitterbug* (1994); his other innovative **film music** has appeared on the recordings *Film Music* (1978) and *Apollo: Atmospheres and Soundtracks* (1983, co-composed with Roger Eno and Daniel Lanois). He has also created numerous video and **sound installations**, their music released in such CDs as *Lightness: Music for the Marble Palace* (1997), *Compact Forest Proposal* (2001), and *77 Million* (2006). Eno has produced albums by **Laurie Anderson**, David Bowie, U2, and the Talking Heads and has worked with many composer/musicians, among them **Fred Frith**, **Terry Riley**, John Cale, and Jon Hassell. *See also* COMPUTER MUSIC; POSTMODERNISM.

EXPRESSIONISM. The term *expressionism* was originally used to designate a **modernist** movement in German painting that arose in the late 1900s and early 1910s and soon transformed German music, poetry, theater, and film, as well. Such artists as Wassily Kandinsky, Franz Marc, Oskar Kokoschka, and Egon Schiele were articulating subjective and unconscious feelings and imagery that had usually been kept hidden: darkness, irrationality, fear, ugliness, confusion, and hallucination. They heightened reality to extreme emotional pitches and severe distortions, with an intense and frequently symbolic use of color, all in opposition to traditional definitions of beauty and form.

Expressionist painting had its forerunners in the 1880s and 1890s, such as James Ensor and Edvard Munch, and there were late 19th-century anticipations of expressionist music as well, starting with two dark and stripped-down piano pieces composed in 1881 by Franz Liszt, *Unstern! Sinistre, disastro* and *Trübe Wolken* (a.k.a. *Nuages gris*). Expressionist qualities are more pronounced in the unresolved **dissonances** and nightmarish scherzo of Anton Bruckner's Symphony No. 9, which was left unfinished at his death in 1896. Grotesquery and dissonance had also been used to dramatic effect in the music of **Richard Strauss** (*Ein Heldenleben*, 1898; *Salome*, 1905; *Elektra*, 1908) and **Gustav Mahler** (Symphony No. 2, 1894; Symphony No. 6, 1904; Symphony No. 7, 1905). But it was **Arnold Schoenberg** who launched expressionism as a distinct musical movement with his 1909 monodrama for soprano and orchestra, *Erwartung*, in which a woman wanders in the woods at night and comes upon the corpse of her unfaithful lover. Schoenberg's dissonant and **atonal** music, with its wide leaps and shrill cries in both voice and instruments, defied traditional standards of ugliness and irrationality as definitively as expressionist painting had. (Kokoschka and Schiele also painted portraits of Schoenberg, who was an accomplished painter himself.)

Béla Bartók brought expressionist qualities to such notable scores as *Duke Bluebeard's Castle* (1911), String Quartet No. 2 (1917), and *The Miraculous Mandarin* (1919); so did **Egon Wellesz** with *Vorfrühling* (1912) for orchestra. Schoenberg's development of **twelve-tone** organizational techniques in the early 1920s enabled him to work more methodically in an atonal idiom and lessened the need for heightened emotional display. After completing the era's definitive expressionist **opera**, *Wozzeck* (1922), **Alban Berg** also wrote twelve-tone music. Other composers who had taken up expressionism by then include **Paul Hindemith, Ernst Krenek**, and **Kurt Weill**, but over the 1920s they turned to **neoclassicism** and *Gebrauchsmusik*. Expressionist qualities also characterize such later atonal composers as **Miriam Gideon** and **Leon Kirchner**. *See also* BRIDGE, FRANK; SPRECHSTIMME.

EXTENDED PERFORMANCE TECHNIQUES. Twentieth-century music gave rise to innovative instrumental techniques that provided new sounds and articulations and redefined the instrument's expressive possibilities. The pioneer in this approach is **Henry Cowell**, whose **tone-cluster** piano music of the 1910s and 1920s required him to develop his own techniques; so did his **string-piano** music, playing the strings with his hands and household objects. **Béla Bartók**, especially in his string quartets, called for unusual string sonorities and a percussive pizzicato, with the string snapping against the fingerboard. **Carlos Salzedo** created an array of new performance methods for the harp in the 1920s.

Lucia Dlugoszewski expanded on the string piano with the timbre piano, introduced in her theater and dance music of 1952 and 1953; she also developed new techniques for brass instruments. Playing multiphonics with traditionally monophonic wind instruments is another important innovation, employed by **Iannis Xenakis, Lukas Foss**, and **Toru Takemitsu**, to name a few. **Joan La Barbara** and others have shown that the voice can also be multiphonic and have utilized circular-breathing techniques for long sustained tones. Many composer/musicians involved in **free improvisation**, including **Fred Frith, John Zorn, George Lewis, Anne LeBaron, Annie Gosfield**, and **Elliott Sharp**, have developed new ways to play their instruments. Other composers whose scores use extended performance techniques include **Sylvano Bussotti, Krzysztof Penderecki, Vinko Globokar, George Crumb, David Hykes**, and **Helmut Lachenmann**. *See also* BRAXTON, ANTHONY; DEYHIM, SUSSAN; GALÁS, DIAMANDA; KAGEL, MAURICIO; POWELL, MEL; RADULESCU, HORATIU; SHEA, DAVID.

F

FALLA, MANUEL DE (1876–1946). Spanish composer and musician. One of Spain's greatest composers, Manuel de Falla brought **impressionist** and **neoclassical** techniques to his lyrical nationalism and captivated audiences internationally. Manuel Maria de Falla y Matheu was born in Cádiz and studied piano with Alejandro Odero and harmony and counterpoint with Enrico Broca; at the Madrid Conservatory, he studied piano with José Tragó. Falla's interest in the music of Andalusia was encouraged by the nationalist composer Felipe Pedrell, with whom he studied privately in the early 1900s. Falla was then composing for Spain's popular music theater, the zarzuela, but with little success. He decided to compose an **opera**, *La vida breve* (1905), depicting the landscape and people of Andalusia, but although the score won praise, it remained unperformed and unpublished.

Falla's *Cuatro piezas españolas* (1906) for piano, more in the impressionist style, premiered in Paris in 1907. Eager to partake of the city's lively music scene, he used the opportunity to relocate there, and in Paris Falla was befriended by Paul Dukas, **Claude Debussy**, **Maurice Ravel**, and Isaac Albéniz. *Trois mélodies* (1909) for voice and piano, to French texts by Théophile Gautier, was composed and premiered there, with Falla as pianist. After he revised *La vida breve*, it was staged to great acclaim in 1913, first in Nice and then at the Opéra Comique in Paris. But with the start of World War I, Falla returned to Madrid to premiere his *Siete canciones populares españolas* (1915) for voice and piano, which transforms folk songs from different regions of Spain.

The nationalist strain in his music flourished back in Madrid, and Falla found success with two great Andalusian-themed works: the gypsy drama *El amor brujo* (1915), a ballet for orchestra and mezzo-soprano, and his score for the farcical pantomime *El corregidor y la moliñera* (1917), which in 1919 became Falla's beloved ballet *El sombrero de tres picos*. Impressionist qualities characterize Falla's other classic from this period, *Noches en los jardines de España* (1915) for piano and orchestra. After moving to Granada in 1920, Falla composed the puppet opera *El retablo de Maese Pedro* (1922), based on a story from Cervantes's *Don Quixote*, which was scored for three voices and a chamber ensemble that included xylophone, lute-harp, and harpsichord. *Psyché* (1924), an impressionist work, set a brief French text for mezzo-soprano, flute, harp, and string trio. Having worked with harpsichord-ist Wanda Landowska in leading the premiere of *El retablo de Maese Pedro*, Falla composed for her his greatest work of the 1920s: the glittering Concerto (1926) for harpsichord, flute, oboe, clarinet, violin, and cello, which melds 15th-century Castilian folk song and the techniques of Domenico Scarlatti with neoclassical techniques inspired by **Igor Stravinsky**'s music.

After the Concerto, Falla completed only a few pieces. In 1927, he composed *Soneto a Córdoba de Luis de Góngora* for soprano and harp or piano, and incidental music for *El gran teatro del mundo*, an auto sacramental by Pedro Calderón de la Barca. For a Chopin Festival in 1933, he set the Catalan poet Jacinto Verdaguer to the *Andantino* of Frédéric Chopin's *Ballade No. 2* and created *Balada de Mallorca* for mixed chorus. The orchestral score *Homenajes* (1938) was pieced together by Falla over the 1930s. He orchestrated his *Hommage pour le tombeau de Paul Dukas* (1935) for piano and earlier *Homenaje "Le tombeau de Claude Debussy"* (1920) for guitar, combined them with his orchestral *Fanfare sobre el nombre de E. F. Arbós* (1934— Arbos had conducted the premiere of *Noches en los jardines de España*), and added a new short piece for orchestra, *Pedrelliana*, dedicated to Felipe Pedrell. Yet Falla was not inactive in the last decades of his life. Since 1926, he had been working on *Atlántida*, a vast scenic cantata for soloists, chorus, and orchestra, with a text he adapted from *L'Atlántida*, Verdaguer's epic account of Atlantis.

In poor health by the start of the Spanish Civil War in 1936, Falla went into seclusion until the war ended three years later. He then relocated to Argentina, conducting the 1939 premiere of *Homenajes* in Buenos Aires shortly after his arrival. It was his last public appearance; after leading two more concerts in the studios of Radio El Mundo in 1942, he retired from performance. Falla made his final home near the village of Alta Garcia and died there of a heart attack at age 69. The score of *Atlántida* was completed in 1961 (rev. 1976) by his former pupil Ernesto Halffter, and the four-hour work was staged at Milan's La Scala the following year. *See also* MODERNISM; POLYTONALITY.

FARWELL, ARTHUR (1872–1952). American composer, musician, educator, and critic. Arthur Farwell's teachers included Engelbert Humperdinck and Hans Pfitzner. He founded the Wa-Wan Press (1901–1912), which championed American composers; wrote criticism (1909–1914) for *Musical America*; and taught at Michigan State College and other institutions. Farwell transcribed Native American music for piano with *American Indian Melo-*

dies (1901) and drew upon it for such works as *Impressions of the Wa-Wan Ceremony of the Omahas* (1905) for piano, *Three Indian Songs* (1908) for voice and piano, and *The Hako* (1922) for string quartet. His arrangements *Folk Songs of the West and South* (1905) for voice and piano used African-American and Spanish-Californian music as well. Farwell's other notable works include *The Gods of the Mountain* (1916) for orchestra, Piano Quintet (1937), *Polytonal Studies* (1940–1952) for piano, and Piano Sonata (1949). *See also* HARRIS, ROY; MULTICULTURALISM; POLYTONALITY.

FELDMAN, BARBARA MONK (1953–). Canadian composer and educator. Barbara Monk studied with Bengt Hambraeus and **Morton Feldman**; she and Feldman were married in 1987, the last year of his life. She brings a sensitive ear for sustained tones and subtle patterns of color to such chamber works as Trio (1984) for violin, cello, and piano, *The Immutable Silence* (1998) for septet, and *Landscape near La Pocatière, Quebec* (2007) for cello and percussion. Her setting of Homer—*Infinite Other* (1992) for two sopranos, mixed chorus, and seven instruments—is also a **multimedia** piece for which Stan Brakhage created his hand-painted film *Three Homerics* (1993). Her works for soloist include *The I and Thou* (1988) for piano, *The Gentlest Chord* (1991) for voice, and *The Loons of Black Sturgeon Lake* (2004) for flute. She has lectured and taught in Germany, Canada, and the United States. *See also* MINIMALISM.

FELDMAN, MORTON (1926–1987). American composer, musician, and educator. One of the major composers of the 20th century, Morton Feldman was an essential figure in **indeterminate** and **minimalist** music who invented new notation techniques and employed greater extremes of quietness and scale. Born in Brooklyn, Feldman began studying piano at age 12 with Vera Maurina-Press, who introduced him to the works of **Alexander Scriabin** and **Ferruccio Busoni**. As a teenager, he studied composition with **Wallingford Riegger** and **Stefan Wolpe**. In his early 20s, he was keen for the music of **Béla Bartók** and **Anton Webern**, and in 1950 Feldman met and befriended **John Cage**. He introduced pianist **David Tudor** to Cage and soon became friends with others in Cage's circle, forming a special bond with **Christian Wolff** and **Earle Brown**. Feldman's composition was also stimulated by the abstract-expressionist painters, such as his friends Willem de Kooning and Philip Guston, who used paint as paint and not as a representation of an object or idea or emotion.

Seeking to avoid the rhetoric of composition and let sounds be themselves, Feldman's music in the 1950s and 1960s was usually brief, quiet, and slow, its delicate pitches projected into space without gelling into a system or statement. At first he relied upon greater performance freedoms to create this sound. His five *Projection* scores (1950–1951) and four *Intersection* scores (1951–1953), written for a range of instruments, introduced a **graphic notation** that permitted musicians certain choices in pitch and rhythm. A later example of this method is *The King of Denmark* (1964) for percussion, where Feldman defined pitch in only three gradations of low, middle, and high, serving as the vertical axis, and designated time at the horizontal axis, in broad increments of one box equaling MM 66–92. The amount of sounds to be played during a time value is indicated by a number in a box (Arabic for sequential sounds, Roman for simultaneities). A letter in a box specifies either a type of instrument, such as *S* for skin and *B* for bell-like, or a gesture, such as *R* for roll. The many empty boxes denote silence.

Free-duration music was another innovation of Feldman's, an indeterminate technique of notating fixed pitches but leaving their time values open, with tempo defined either by a specified metronome range or simply as "Slow." In his 1957 scores *Piece for Four Pianos* and *Two Pianos*, the musicians play from the same part, producing quiet, shimmering mobile-like aggregates with no clear beginnings and endings. The five *Durations* pieces (1960–1961) were all composed for small chamber groups and featured greater complexity, with individual parts for each musician. Feldman sometimes notated the sequencing of pitches in free duration, as in *De Kooning* (1963) for horn, percussion, piano, violin, and cello, where each sound enters as the preceding one fades.

During these years, Feldman also continued to compose in standard notation, as with *Extensions 1* (1952) for violin and piano and *Structures* (1962) for orchestra. An occasional performer of his own works, he grew increasingly skillful at writing down the kind of nonrelational pitch activities that his indeterminate music had created, and he hit his stride with such major pieces as the four *Viola in My Life* scores (1970–1971) and *Rothko Chapel* (1971) for mixed chorus, celesta, percussion, and viola. He also began teaching at the State University of New York at Buffalo in 1972; among his students were **Bernadette Speach**, **Bunita Marcus**, **Elliott Sharp**, and Barbara Monk.

From the early 1970s on, Feldman worked exclusively in traditional notation. Engaging what he saw as the paradox between repetition and change, his music used repeated materials with modest alterations of meter or phrasing that redefine the listener's sense of what's being repeated. In reducing his compositional tools, Feldman intensified his focus on the challenge of scale, and by the late 1970s he was composing lengthy works devoid of preconceived structures or familiar development techniques; instead, he let procedures for sustaining continuity reveal themselves to him through his concentration on his materials. Feldman had also recognized how the recording industry inhibited composers by encouraging them to operate within lengths amenable to the 20 minutes of one side of an LP, and he decided to create single-movement works that resisted such commodification. As the pieces grew even longer, he saw them as also being resistant to performance itself—from which he took further satisfaction.

This search for purity of expression led to an array of major works in the last years of Feldman's life. Many employed a more familiar scale, such as his **opera** for soprano and orchestra *Neither* (1977); *For Aaron Copland* (1981) for solo violin; and the orchestral scores *The Turfan Fragments* (1980), *Coptic Light* (1985), and *For Samuel Beckett* (1987). He also treated scale more aggressively, as in *For John Cage* (1982) for violin and piano and *For Bunita Marcus* (1985) for piano, both around 75 minutes. Others defied all conventions: *For Christian Wolff* (1986) for flute and piano takes about three and a half hours; the trio *For Philip Guston* (1984) for flutes, percussion, and piano/celesta, over four; and *String Quartet II* (1983), about six. Ailing with pancreatic cancer, Feldman married Barbara Monk in June 1987; three months later, he died in a Buffalo hospital at age 61. *See also* ATONALITY; COPLAND, AARON; FELDMAN, BARBARA MONK; POSTMODERNISM.

FERNEYHOUGH, BRIAN (1943–). English composer and educator. Brian Ferneyhough studied at the Birmingham School of Music, the Royal Academy of Music, the Amsterdam Conservatory, and the Basel Academy and has taught at the Freiburg Musikhochschule, Stanford University, and other institutions. Drawing on **total serialism**, he developed his own approach to **atonal** composition, with a penchant for **microtones** and glissandi. Ferneyhough's works include *Transit* (1975) for six amplified voices and chamber orchestra, *Unity Capsule* (1976) for flute, *Lemma-Icon-Epigram* (1981) for piano, *Allgebrah* (1996) for oboe and nine strings, the **opera** *Shadowtime* (2004), and *Plötzlichkeit* (2006) for orchestra. *See also* MODERNISM; TWELVE-TONE MUSIC.

FERRARI, LUC (1929–2005). French composer, musician, and educator. Trained in piano, Luc Ferrari studied composition with **Arthur Honegger** and **Olivier Messiaen** and later taught internationally. After such early **atonal** works as *Antisonate* (1953) for piano and Piano Quartet (1954), Ferrari turned to *musique concrète* with *Visage No. 5* (1959) and *Études concrètes* (1958–1961). His **tape music** grew to incorporate environmental and ambient sound, often with narrative qualities, as in *Hétérozygote* (1964), *Presque rien No. 1* (1970), *Chantal* (1978), and *Les anecdotiques* (2002). Ferrari's other notable works includes *Société II* (1966) for piano, three percussionists, and 16 instruments, and such **electroacoustic** scores as *Cellule*

75 (1975) for piano, percussion, and tape; *Et si tout entière maintenant* (1987) for actress, tapes, and orchestra; *Madame de Shanghai* (1996) for three flutes and digitally stored sounds; and *Après presque rien* (2004) for 14 instruments and two **samplers**. *See also* COMPUTER MUSIC; POSTMODERNISM.

FILM MUSIC. Modernist musical innovations have a long history in the scoring of motion pictures. **Electronic music** begins appearing in film scores in the 1930s. **Arthur Honegger** included an **ondes martenot** in his music for *L'idée* (1932), *Rapt* (1934), *Crime et châtiment* (1935), *Marthe Richard au service de la France* (1937), and *Un seul amour* (1943). Franz Waxman used a **theremin** in scoring Fritz Lang's *Liliom* (1934), and that instrument made its mark in Hollywood with Miklos Rózsa's scores for the 1945 films *The Lost Weekend* and *Spellbound*. **Edgard Varèse**'s first **tape-music** piece was heard in *Around and About Joan Miró* (1955). Louis and Bebe Barron provided electronic music for *Forbidden Planet* (1955). Using the Mixtur-Trautonium, an extension of the **trautonium**, Oskar Sala created electronic effects for Alfred Hitchcock's *The Birds* (1963). The growth of **synthesizer** technology resulted in film music by such composers as **Wendy Carlos** (*A Clockwork Orange*, 1971; *The Shining*, 1980; *TRON*, 1982), Eduard Artmiev (*Solaris*, 1972; *Stalker*, 1979), Giorgio Moroder (*Midnight Express*, 1978; *Scarface*, 1983), and Vangelis (*Chariots of Fire*, 1981; *Blade Runner*, 1982).

Although **Arnold Schoenberg** never composed a film score—his *Begleitungsmusik zu einer Lichtspielszene* (1930) was not created for a specific film—some of his pupils did employ **twelve-tone** methods in scoring films, for example, **Hanns Eisler** (*Regen*, 1929, scored 1940) and Leonard Rosenman (*The Cobweb*, 1955). Another Schoenberg pupil, David Raskin, used **atonal** and **polytonal** techniques in his scores for *Laura* (1944) and *Force of Evil* (1948). Other composers who used **serial** organization composing for films include Ernest Gold (*On the Beach*, 1959), Rózsa (*King of Kings*, 1961), Benjamin Frankel (*The Curse of the Werewolf*, 1961), Jerry Goldsmith (*Freud*, 1962), Johnny Mandel (*Point Blank*, 1967), and David Shire (*The Taking of Pelham One Two Three*, 1974). Noise, **dissonance**, and atonality also inform memorable film music by **Toru Takemitsu** (*Woman in the Dunes*, 1964), **Peter Maxwell Davies** (*The Devils*, 1971), and **Harrison Birtwistle** (*The Offence*, 1973), among others. **Minimalist** composers of film scores include **Philip Glass** (*Koyaanisqatsi*, 1982; *Bent*, 1997; *The Hours*, 2002), **Steve Reich** (*Oh Dem Watermelons*, 1965; *The Dying Gaul*, 2005), **Terry Riley** (*Lifespan*, 1976; *No Man's Land*, 1985), **Brian Eno** (*Sebastiane*, 1976; *Glitterbug*, 1994), and **Michael Nyman** (*The Piano*, 1993; *Man on Wire*, 2008).

Certain filmmakers have used preexisting music rather than a new score. Examples include the music of **Erik Satie** in Orson Welles's *The Immortal Story* (1968); **Gustav Mahler** in Luchino Visconti's *Death in Venice* (1971); **Sergey Prokofiev** in Woody Allen's *Love and Death* (1975); **Aaron Copland** in Spike Lee's *He Got Game* (1998); **György Ligeti** in Stanley Kubrick's *2001: A Space Odyssey* (1968), *The Shining* (1980), and *Eyes Wide Shut* (1999); and **Hildegard Westerkamp** in Gus Van Sant's *Elephant* (2003) and *Last Days* (2005). By the same token, many composers transformed their film scores into concert works, including Prokofiev (*Lieutenant Kizhe*, 1934; *Alexander Nevsky*, 1939), **Virgil Thomson** (*"The Plow That Broke the Plains" Suite*, 1936; *"The River" Suite*, 1937; *"Louisiana Story" Suite*, 1948), Copland (*Our Town*, 1940; *Music for Movies*, 1942; *The Red Pony*, 1948; *Music for a Great City*, 1964), **John Cage** (*Music for Marcel Duchamp*, 1947), **Ralph Vaughan Williams** (Symphony No. 7, 1952), **Harry Partch** (*Daphne of the Dunes*, 1967), and Glass (String Quartet No. 3 [*Mishima*], 1985).

Composers who made and scored their own films include **Mauricio Kagel** (*Ludwig Van*, 1969; *Phonophonie*, 1979), **Frank Zappa** (*200 Motels*, 1971), **Meredith Monk** (*Ellis Island*, 1982; *Book of Days*, 1989), the **Residents** (*Whatever Happened to Vileness Fats?*, 1984), **Laurie Anderson** (*Home of the Brave*, 1986), and **Sylvano Bussotti** (*Biennale Apollo*, 1990). *See also* ANTHEIL, GEORGE; BAX, ARNOLD; BERNSTEIN, LEONARD; BRANCA, GLENN; CORIGLIANO, JOHN; FRITH, FRED; GORDON, MICHAEL; GROUPE DES SIX; HERRMANN, BERNARD; IBERT, JACQUES; KANCHELI, GIYA; MacLISE, ANGUS; MAYUZUMI, TOSHIRO; MILHAUD, DARIUS; REVUELTAS, SILVESTRE; WALTON, WILLIAM; ZORN, JOHN.

FINE, IRVING (1914–1962). American composer, musician, and educator. Irving Fine studied with Edward Burlingame Hill, **Walter Piston**, and **Nadia Boulanger**; he also performed as a pianist and conductor and taught at Harvard University, Tanglewood, and Brandeis University. Fine's notable early works were **neoclassical**, including *The Choral New Yorker* (1944) for mixed chorus and piano, Violin Sonata (1946), *Music for Piano* (1947), and *Toccata concertante* (1947) for orchestra. His lyrical sensibility adapted well to **twelve-tone** procedures, which he blended with tonal techniques in his String Quartet (1952), *Mutability* (1952) for mezzo-soprano and piano, *Serious Song* (1955) for string orchestra, Fantasia for String Trio (1956), and Symphony (1962). Fine died at age 47 after suffering a heart attack. *See also* EL-DABH, HALIM; MODERNISM; SMIT, LEO (1921–1999).

FINE, VIVIAN (1913–2000). American composer, musician, and educator. Vivian Fine studied composition with Ruth Crawford and **Roger Sessions** and taught at Bennington College (1964–1987) and other institutions. She concertized as a pianist and premiered works by **Charles Ives, Aaron Copland, Henry Cowell, Henry Brant**, and **Dane Rudhyar**, as well as her own music. Fine's early scores, such as *Four Polyphonic Pieces for Piano* (1931) and *Four Songs* (1933) for contralto and strings, explored **dissonant** counterpoint and **atonality**. Suite in E-flat (1940) for piano and *Concertante* (1944) for piano and orchestra were tonal, and Fine matured into her own blend of tonal and atonal composition. Notable later works include her String Quartet (1957); the dance score *Alcestis* (1960); *Dreamscape* (1964) for percussion ensemble, three flutes, cello, piano, and lawnmower; *The Nightingale* (1976) for mezzo-soprano who also plays percussion; *Gertrude and Virginia* (1981) for soprano, mezzo-soprano, and quintet; *Drama for Orchestra* (1982); and the chamber **operas** *The Women in the Garden* (1978) and *Memoirs of Uliana* (1994). *See also* MODERNISM; SEEGER, RUTH CRAWFORD.

FINNEY, ROSS LEE (1906–1997). American composer, musician, and educator. An accomplished cellist, guitarist, and folk singer, Ross Lee Finney received his BA from Carlton College in Northfield, Minnesota, and studied with **Nadia Boulanger** in France (1927–1928), Edward Burlingame Hill at Harvard University (1928–1929), **Alban Berg** in Vienna (1931–1932), and **Roger Sessions** in the United States (1935). Finney taught at Smith College (1929–1948) and the University of Michigan (1949–1973). His early music was **neoclassical**, with recurring themes of American folk music, as in Violin Concerto No. 1 (1933, rev. 1952); Symphony No. 1, "Communiqué 1943" (1942); *Pilgrim Psalms* (1945) for soloists, chorus, and orchestra; and *Poor Richard* (1946) for voice and piano.

Finney's composition became increasingly chromatic in the late 1940s, and in his String Quartet No. 6 in E (1950) he used **twelve-tone** organization while retaining his essential melodic and harmonic profile. That approach defined some of his best music in the 1950s: Violin Sonata No. 2 (1951), *Chromatic Fantasy in E* (1957) for cello, String Quintet (1958), and Symphony No. 2 (1959). In 1962, Finney studied **electronic music** with **Mario Davidovsky** at the Columbia-Princeton Electronic Music Center and featured it in two works that same year: *Three Pieces for Strings, Winds, Percussion, and Tape Recorder* and *Still Are New Worlds* for narrator, chorus, orchestra, and **tape**. His twelve-tone technique was at its most rigorous in his 1965 scores *Three Studies in Fours* for percussion orchestra and Concerto for Percussion and Orchestra.

With *Summer in Valley City* (1969) for concert band, Finney launched a series of major works that explored the nature and experience of memory. His personal use of **serial** composition accommodated popular and folk **quotations,** along with unusual rhythms and effects scored in **proportional notation**, in *Two Acts for Three Players* (1970) for clarinet, piano, and percussion; *Landscapes Remembered* (1971) for chamber orchestra; *Spaces* (1971) for orchestra; *Variations on a Memory* (1975) for chamber orchestra; and *Skating Down the Sheyenne* (1978) for band. For choreographer Erick Hawkins, Finney produced the scores *Heyoka* (1981) and *The Joshua Tree* (1984). Finney completed his first **opera** in 1984—*Weep Torn Land*, from his own libretto—and he wrote the text for a second opera, the comedy *Computer Marriage*, which was left incomplete at the time of his death at age 90. His students included **Robert Ashley**, **Gordon Mumma**, **George Crumb**, and **Roger Reynolds**. *See also* ATONALITY; ELECTROACOUSTIC MUSIC; MODERNISM.

FLANAGAN, WILLIAM (1926–1969). American composer and critic. William Flanagan's teachers included **Aaron Copland**, **Arthur Honegger**, and **Arthur Berger**. His melodic and lyric gifts distinguish his vocal works, which include the Herman Melville settings *Time's Long Ago!* (1951) for voice and piano and the one-act **opera** *Bartleby* (1957); *The Lady of Tearful Regret* (1958) for soprano, baritone, and septet; and *Another August* (1967) for soprano and orchestra. They also inform such instrumental works as his Piano Sonata (1950) and the orchestral scores *A Concert Ode* (1951) and *Notations* (1960). Flanagan wrote music criticism for the *New York Herald Tribune* from 1957 to 1960. He took his own life at age 43. *See also* NEO-ROMANTICISM.

FLUXUS. Drawing on conceptual art, theatricality, humor, **indeterminacy**, **minimalism**, and **multimedia**, Fluxus was a loosely organized group of artists and composers who knew each other in New York during the late 1950s and early 1960s. The momentum for the group arose from such new creative activities as the Happenings of Jim Dine, Jackson Mac Low's poetry, **John Cage**'s classes at the New School, and the AG concerts of George Maciunas (1931–1978), who organized the first Fluxus event in 1961. He also coined the name Fluxus, from the Latin for "to flow," and wrote the Fluxus manifesto in 1963, calling for a purge of commercialized and abstract art, the emergence of art that can be grasped by everyone, and a fusion of cultural, social, and political revolution.

Fluxus began finding a wider audience with a concert in Wiesbaden, Germany, in September 1962; other international and American performances followed. George Brecht (1926–2008) became a central figure in Fluxus, with event scores such as *Three Telephone Events* (1961), which had a ringing telephone that was left to ring, hung up on, and answered; his *Drip Music* (1962) listened to water dripping into an empty vessel. This love of everyday things informed other Fluxus works that appropriated noninstruments, such as **Alison Knowles**'s *Make a Salad* (1962) and *Music by Alison* (1964).

Fluxus concerts also made noninstrumental use of instruments. Maciunas's *12 Piano Compositions for Nam June Paik* (1962) called for the piano to be moved in and out, waxed, and polished; **La Monte Young**'s *Piano Piece for David Tudor #1* (1960) gave the piano a bale of hay and a bucket of water.

Other composers who were part of Fluxus include **Richard Maxfield** (Concert Suite from the Ballet *Dromenon*, 1961), **James Tenney** (*"Chamber Music,"* 1964; *Maximusic*, 1965), **Toshi Ichiyanagi** (*Music for Piano 1–7*, 1959–1961), **Yoko Ono** (*Cut Piece*, 1964), **Nam June Paik** (*Composition for Poor Man*, 1961), **Takehisa Kosugi** (*Organic Music*, 1962), **Philip Corner** (*4th Finale*, 1964), and **Dick Higgins** (*Danger Musics*, 1961–1963). Its most influential concerts occurred in the 1960s, but Fluxus has remained a vital art movement, holding meetings on the 10-year anniversaries of the Wiesbaden concert, in 1972, 1982, 1992, and 2002. *See also* GEBRAUCHSMUSIK; POSTMODERNISM.

FLYNT, HENRY (1940–). American composer and musician. Known primarily as a philosopher, mathematician, and artist, Henry Flynt coined the term *concept art* and led an anti-art movement. He also studied violin and initially composed **indeterminate** scores, but became more interested in regional music. He performed with **La Monte Young**, the Velvet Underground, and others in the 1960s and studied raga singing with Pandit Pran Nath in the 1970s. Drawing on ethnic, rock, experimental, **electroacoustic**, and **minimalist** techniques, Flynt's music from these years has been released in such recordings as *Graduation* (2001), *Raga Electric* (2002), *Back Porch Hillbilly Blues, Vols. 1 and 2* (2003), *I Don't Wanna* (2004), and *Henry Flynt & Nova'Billy* (2007). Later performances can be heard in the four-volume series *New American Ethnic Music* (2002–2007). *See also* MULTICULTURALISM; POSTMODERNISM.

FORMALISM. *Formalism defines any approach that adheres strictly to preestablished external forms. This entry, however, focuses on the use of this term in the Soviet Union during the mid-20th century.*

By the early 1930s, the careers of such composers as **Nikolai Roslavets** and **Alexander Mosolov** had been derailed due to the widespread belief in the Soviet Union that **modernism** was counterrevolutionary. Hostility against formalism worsened in 1936, after Soviet leader Joseph Stalin walked out on **Dmitry Shostakovich**'s opera *Lady Macbeth of Mtsensk*. Outraged by its sexual content and **dissonant** music, Stalin decreed that Soviet opera be traditional and folk song–based in its music, impart ideologically correct Socialist content in its libretto, and provide a happy and optimistic ending.

As Socialist Realism, Stalin's values defined not just opera but all other music and art, film, theater, literature, and dance during his reign. Accessibility was fundamental, and alienating devices of **atonality** or dissonance were denounced as formalist—that is, placing structural or experimental considerations above the principles of Socialist Realism. The works of **Igor Stravinsky, Arnold Schoenberg, Paul Hindemith**, and **Béla Bartók** disappeared from Soviet concert halls and radio, and domestic composers—especially experimentalists such as Georgi Mikhailovich Rimsky-Korsakov, who worked with **quarter-tones** and **Jörg Mager**'s kurbelsphärophon—had to adopt the new agenda.

That conformity was a matter of life and death in a police state where denunciations and disappearances had become commonplace. Cultural purity was less of a concern during World War II, but there was another round of housecleaning in 1948 and Shostakovich, **Sergey Prokofiev, Aram Khachaturian**, and Nikolai Myaskovsky—the Soviet Union's "Big Four" composers—were called before the Central Committee of the Communist Party, along with others. All were accused of formalism, which had come to mean anti-Socialist and pro-Western tendencies; all admitted their failure and promised to do better. Also pressured in the 1940s and 1950s were non-Russian composers within the Soviet sphere of influence, such as **Witold Lutoslawski, Alois Hába**, and **György Ligeti**. A thaw began only after Stalin's death in 1953. *See also* ELECTRONIC MUSIC.

FOSS, LUKAS (1922–2009). German-born American composer, musician, and educator. A pianist and composer from childhood, Lukas Foss came to the United States in 1937. He attended the Curtis Institute (1937–1940), studying with Randall Thompson, Rosario Scalero, and Fritz Reiner; he also studied with Serge Koussevitzky at Tanglewood and **Paul Hindemith** at Tanglewood and Yale University. Foss later taught at UCLA (1953–1963), among other institutions; his students included **Richard Dufallo, Barbara Kolb**, and **Alvin Lucier**. He was a pianist with the Boston Symphony Orchestra (1944–1950) and music director and conductor of the Buffalo Philharmonic (1963–1970), Brooklyn Philharmonic (1971–1990), Jerusalem Symphony Orchestra (1972–1976), and Milwaukee Symphony Orchestra (1980–1986). Foss's early music—*The Prairie* (1944), a cantata for soloists, chorus, and orchestra; *Song of Songs* (1946) for voice and orchestra; the two-act **opera**

The Jumping Frog of Calaveras County (1949)—was tonal and melodic, with **neoromantic** and **neoclassical** elements.

There was admiration for Foss's *A Parable of Death* (1952) for narrator, tenor, mixed chorus, and orchestra or chamber orchestra and the three-act fantasy opera *Griffelkin* (1955), but his music changed after he formed the Improvisation Chamber Ensemble at UCLA in 1957. The search for spontaneity transformed his composition, and he produced two important **atonal** scores: *Time Cycle* (1960, rev. 1961) for soprano and orchestra or chamber group, and *Echoi* (1963) for clarinet, cello, piano, and percussion (the lineup of the Improvisation Chamber Ensemble). *Echoi*, despite its **serial** influences, also featured performance freedoms, and Foss further developed this **aleatoric** approach in *Fragments of Archilichos* (1965) for chorus and chamber ensemble and *Paradigm* (1968) for percussionist, electric guitar, and three other instruments capable of sustaining a sound.

Foss employed **quotation** in *Baroque Variations* (1967) for orchestra, multiphonics in *Cave of the Winds* (1972) for woodwind quintet, game techniques in *MAP* (1973) for any four players, and **minimalism** in String Quartet No. 3 (1975). His late works include *Elegy for Anne Frank* (1989) for narrator, piano, and orchestra; *Piano Concerto for the Left Hand* (1993); and *Symphonic Fantasy* (2002) for orchestra. *See also* EXTENDED PERFORMANCE TECHNIQUES; FREE IMPROVISATION; MODERNISM.

FOULDS, JOHN (1880–1939). English composer and musician. John Foulds came from a family of musicians and was largely self-taught. He joined the Hallé Orchestra as a cellist in 1900, by which time he had already begun experimenting with **microtonality** in his composition. **Quarter-tones** appear in such early works as his *The Waters of Babylon* (c. 1905)—later incorporated into his suite *Aquarelles* (c. 1914) for string quartet—and *Mirage* (1910) for orchestra. He also explored ancient Greek modes in the piano suite *Hellas* (1915). Foulds achieved popular success with his lighter pieces, such as the many arrangements of his *Keltic Lament* (1911), but he also won respect for *A World Requiem* (1921) for soloists, mixed chorus, boys' choir, orchestra, and organ, his requiem to all the dead of World War I, which set liturgical, British, and Hindu texts.

Foulds married Irish violinist, singer, and ethnomusicologist Maud MacCarthy in 1915, and her expertise in Indian music informed the rhythmic and modal structures of his *Gandharva-music* (1926) for piano. By the mid-1920s, he had also completed the first two movements of his unfinished *Lyra Celtica*, a concerto for wordless contralto and orchestra, which featured microtonal pitches for the voice. Foulds's socialist politics, Theosophical mysticism, and fascination with the East tended to isolate him from English society, so he moved to Paris in 1927. There he completed seven of his projected series of piano pieces *Essays in the Modes* (1927), which employed scales derived from the 72 South Indian ragas. Those scores led to his piano concerto *Dynamic Triptych* (1929), in which he included Indian modes, quarter-tone passages, and instances of silence. Foulds's attempt at composing the Sanskrit **opera** *Avatara* was abandoned, but he derived from it the remarkable *Three Mantras* (1930) for orchestra and wordless women's chorus.

Foulds returned to London in 1930 and composed a variety of ethnic-themed orchestral works, including *Keltic Overture* (1931), *Fantasie of Negro Spirituals* (1932), and *Chinese Suite* (1935), as well as his *Quartetto intimo* (1932) for string quartet, which used quarter-tones. After publishing his study of **modernist** musical innovations *Music To-day* (1934), he relocated to India in 1935 and served as director of European music at All-India Radio. Foulds founded the Indo-European Orchestra in 1938, but died of cholera the following year in Calcutta at age 58. *See also* MULTICULTURALISM.

FREE DURATION. Free duration is an **indeterminate** compositional method developed by **Morton Feldman** and introduced in *Piece for Four Pianos* (1957), in which pitches are precisely notated but their time values are left open. Other composers who have used free duration include **Cornelius Cardew** (*The Great Learning*, 1968–1971), **John Cage** (*Etudes Australes*, 1975), and **Bernadette Speach** (*Les ondes pour quatre*, 1988). **Christian Wolff** has pauses in free duration in his trio *Flutist (with Percussionists)* (2003). *See also* OPEN FORM.

FREE IMPROVISATION. Free improvisation arose in the United States and Europe during the 1960s and early 1970s, drawing upon the innovations of **free-jazz** composer/musicians **Ornette Coleman**, **Cecil Taylor**, and **Sun Ra**, the amplification and energy of rock music, and the use of simultaneities and noise by such composers as **Edgard Varèse** and **John Cage**. This **postmodern** approach to improvisation embraces more than **dissonance**, **atonality**, and **polyrhythmic** independence within an ensemble. **Extended performance techniques** have been the norm for many, with **Fred Frith** playing his guitar by laying it flat on a table and working the strings with a variety of implements, or **John Zorn** performing on pieces of his clarinet or attaching game calls to the mouthpiece of his saxophone. **Instrument building** also loomed large, with guitarists Frith and **Elliott Sharp** and harpist Zeena Parkins performing on homemade instruments. Percussionists David Moss, Fast Forward, and Charles K. Noyes would play found objects as well as traditional percussion instruments.

Multicultural performances are also frequent, especially with such skilled performers as American percussionist **Susie Ibarra**, Iranian singer **Sussan Deyhim**, and Korean kayagum player Sang-Won Park. **Electroacoustic and electronic music** are essential, too, from the performances of the **AMM** and **MEV** ensembles to the **synthesizers** of **Jessica Rylan**, the turntables of Christian Marclay, and the use of **sampling** by **Bob Ostertag**, **David Shea**, and David Weinstein. Musicians who also perform with electronics include trombonist **George Lewis** and percussionist Ikue Mori.

By the 1980s, free improvisation had become a vital international trend. Among its many notable performers are guitarists Derek Bailey, Eugene Chadbourne, Arto Lindsay, Henry Kaiser, and René Lussier; saxophone players **Anthony Braxton**, **John Oswald**, Ned Rothenberg, and Lol Coxhill; percussionists Chris Cutler, Roger Turner, David Van Teighem, and Greg Bendian; vocalists **Julius Eastman**, Phil Minton, and Shelley Hirsch; keyboard players **Annie Gosfield**, **Bernadette Speach**, Marilyn Crispell, and Anthony Coleman; harpist **Anne LeBaron**; accordionists **Pauline Oliveros** and Guy Kluscevek; and cornetist Butch Morris, who has also devised new methods for leading groups of improving musicians. *See also* FOSS, LUKAS; GLOBOKAR, VINKO; KOSUGI, TAKEHISA; SCRATCH ORCHESTRA.

FREE JAZZ. **Modernist** approaches to harmony, rhythm, and tonal ambiguity were emerging in jazz by the mid-20th century, appearing in the 1947 works *The Clothed Woman* by **Duke Ellington** and *Thermopylae* by **Robert F. Graettinger**. More aggressive treatments of **atonality, dissonance**, **polytonality**, and **polyrhythm** were heard in the 1950s, with the first recordings of **Cecil Taylor** and **Ornette Coleman**. This sensibility in creative African-American music became widely known as "free jazz" after Coleman's groundbreaking 1960 album of the same name, with its group **free improvisation**. The music of **Sun Ra**, both for keyboard and for his Arkestra, embraced **electronic music** and noise. The Association for the Advancement of Creative Musicians, a composer/musician collective founded in Chicago in 1965, pursued these innovations and provided opportunities for such artists as **Muhal Richard Abrams**, **Anthony Braxton**, **Leroy Jenkins**, **Roscoe Mitchell**, and **George Lewis**.

FREE RHYTHM. The term *free rhythm* was used by composer **Alan Hovhaness** to describe a technique he developed in his 1944 score *Lousadzak* for piano and string orchestra. Hovhaness wrote passages of repeated patterns for strings, assigning pitches and rhythms but having each musician play at his or her own tempo, independent of the others. Free rhythm introduced a **chance** element that enabled Hovhaness to create gusts and clouds of sound in numerous compositions, including such major works as his Symphony No. 6, "Celestial Gate" (1959), and Symphony No. 19, "Vishnu" (1966). *See also* ALEATORY; INDETERMINACY; OPEN FORM.

FRITH, FRED (1949–). English composer, musician, and educator. Jeremy Webster Frith, known since childhood as Fred, came from a musical family and was taking violin lessons at age five. Devoted to the guitar by his teens, Frith founded the radical rock-band collective Henry Cow with Tim Hodgkinson in 1968, when both were at Cambridge University. The band's impressive series of recordings started with *Leg End* (1973) and *Unrest* (1974). The group compositions and **free improvisations** of Henry Cow were an essential education for Frith, and after the band's dissolution in 1978, he performed with and composed songs and instrumentals for the band Art Bears on *Hopes & Fears* (1979), *Winter Songs* (1980), and *The World As It Is Today* (1981). These recordings brought new melodic possibilities to Frith's unusual meters and **polyrhythms** and enlivened his **multicultural** interests, which became more vivid and distinctive in Frith's three classic solo albums: *Gravity* (1980), *Speechless* (1981), and *Cheap at Half the Price* (1983).

As an improvising guitarist, Frith had been employing **extended performance techniques** since the early 1970s and extracted an incredible range of sound for his album *Guitar Solos* (1974). By the early 1980s, he was performing with the electric guitar flat on a table, so he could play its strings with a violin bow or coiled springs or drumsticks or scarves or chains—techniques documented in his double LP *Live in Japan* (1984). Frith also built homemade instruments: slabs of wood with a pickup, bridge, and wire strings stretched on metal screws, which were essentially electric guitars although his techniques with them came closer to those of a percussionist than a guitarist.

The 1980s also saw performances by Frith's bands Massacre and the two-person Skeleton Crew with Tom Cora. He has offered his own take on **ambient music** in the band Death Ambient with Ikue Mori (drum machine) and Kato Hideki (bass). Frith has performed internationally for decades, from solos to large groups such as Derek Bailey's Company and Eugene Chadbourne's 2000 Statues. His fellow musicians have included **John Zorn**, the **Residents, Brian Eno, Anthony Braxton, Susie Ibarra, Bob Ostertag, George Lewis, Richard Teitelbaum, John Oswald, Gordon Mumma**, and **Anne LeBaron**.

After creating the dance scores *Jigsaw* (1986) and *The Technology of Tears* (1987), Frith began composing pieces for the Rova Saxophone Quartet in 1987, such as *Song & Dance*. Scores for other performers followed, including *The As Usual Dance towards the Other Flight to What Is Not* (1989) for four electric guitars; *Lelikovice* (1991) for string quartet; the 1992 **graphic** scores *Stone, Brick, Glass, Wood*, and *Wire* for any number of players; and the **spatial** work *Impur* (1996) for 100 musicians. His **film** scores include *The Top of His Head* (1989), *Before Sunrise* (1995), *Rivers and Tides* (2001), and *Rage* (2009).

Since 1999, Frith has taught at Mills College and composed such works as *Landing* (2001) for choir, flamenco singer, cello, saxophone, and **samples**; *The Right Angel* (2003) for electric guitar and orchestra; and *Episodes* (2007) for Baroque ensemble. Frith's recent recordings include the solo-guitar albums *Clearing* (2001) and *To Sail, to Sail* (2008) and the chamber-music collections *Eleventh Hour* (2005) *and Back to Life* (2008). *See also* ELECTROACOUSTIC MUSIC; INDETERMINACY; POSTMODERNISM.

FULLMAN, ELLEN (1957–). American composer and musician. In 1981, Ellen Fullman began to develop her "long string instrument" as a **sound installation** using dozens of wires, 50 or more feet in length, tuned in **just intonation** and played with rosin-coated fingers. She has toured internationally performing on the long string instrument, for which she has also created her own notation. Fullman's recordings include *Suspended Music* (1997) with **Pauline Oliveros** and the Deep Listening Band, and *Staggered Stasis* (2004). *See also* INSTRUMENT BUILDING; POSTMODERNISM.

FUTURISM. The **modernist** aesthetic movement known as futurism began in Italy in the late 1900s, with its first manifesto from poet Filippo Tommaso Marinetti appearing in 1909. Inspired by machinery and mechanical processes, futurism sought to express a greater dynamic energy. It was taken up in painting by Umberto Boccioni and Luigi Russolo (1885–1947), among others, who wrote their own manifesto the following year, and soon found advocates in architecture and cinema. In 1912, Francesco Balilla Pratella (1880–1955) published his "Manifesto of Futurist Musicians," calling for an end to conservatories and music critics and their competitions, and demanding a music freed of all past influences.

After Pratella premiered his *Musica Futurista* for orchestra in 1913, Russolo responded by writing Pratella a letter that outlined his own vision of *bruitismo*, a new music made from noise. Published that year as the manifesto *L'arte dei rumori* (*The Art of Noises*), it extolled noise and machinery, rejected the use of traditional instruments, and urged the development of new instruments to play sounds from what Russolo defined as the six types or families of noises: bangs, hisses, murmurs, the sounds produced by friction and by striking, and human and animal cries. Working with artist Ugo Piatti, Russolo began designing and building his *intonarumori* (noise-intoners): wooden boxes with megaphones, containing electromechanical machinery for producing a type of sound. Some of these intonarumori were used by Pratella in his **opera** *L'aviatore Dro* (1914). Russolo's keyboard instrument the rumorarmonio also produced **microtonal** tunings.

Russolo invented **graphic notation** for *Risveglio di una città* (1914), a score for eight different types of noisemaking machines. He performed his music in Italy and England, attracting the interest of **Igor Stravinsky**, **Sergey Prokofiev**, and **Maurice Ravel** and persuading **Erik Satie** to incorporate mechanical sounds in *Parade* (1916). **Edgard Varèse**, on the other hand, despite his friendship with Russolo, rejected futurism in a 1917 article. He regarded its music as a mere replication of the superficial abrasiveness of everyday sounds and advocated new instruments of greater timbral and rhythmic sophistication.

In the United States, **Henry Cowell** experimented with futurist ideas in his piano scores *Resumé* (1914) and *Dynamic Motion* (1916). He was also very interested in the piano music of **Leo Ornstein**, which the press had labeled futurist. But in the 1920s, Cowell's music developed along multiple lines, while Ornstein's became more conservative.

Arthur Lourié signed the 1914 Russian futurist manifesto "We and the West," and futurist qualities informed his work as well as music by **Alexander Mosolov** and other Russian composers—all of whom were officially silenced by Soviet antimodernism. Western interest in futurist music faded by the 1930s, due at least in part to the objections that Varèse had raised. In their later years, Russolo retired from music and Pratella turned away from futurism. *See also* BUSSOTTI, SYLVANO; FORMALISM; INSTRUMENT BUILDING.

G

GABURO, KENNETH (1926–1993). American composer, musician, and educator. Kenneth Gaburo played jazz piano and studied at the Eastman School of Music and the University of Illinois at Urbana-Champaign; he later taught there and at the University of California, San Diego, among other institutions. Gaburo's study of linguistics led him to develop what he termed *compositional linguistics*, explored in vocal works (*Psalm* for mixed chorus, 1965; *Never 1* for four groups of male voices, 1967; *Maledetto* for seven virtuoso speakers, 1969) and **multimedia** pieces (*In the Can*, 1970; *My, My, What a Wonderful Fall*, 1975; *Ringings*, 1976). Gaburo's 10 *Antiphony* scores (1958–1991) combined voices or instruments with **tape**. *See also* ELECTROACOUSTIC MUSIC.

GALÁS, DIAMANDA (1955–). American composer and musician. Pianist and vocalist Diamanda Galás studied at the University of San Diego. Her singing employs extended vocal techniques and has drawn upon **opera**, **expressionism**, her Greek heritage, jazz, blues, and gospel. Galás achieved international renown with such **electroacoustic** vocal pieces as *Wild Women with Steak Knives* (1981), *Tragouthia Apo to Aima Exoun Fonos* (1981), and *Panoptikon* (1983). Her rage and grief at the HIV/AIDS pandemic define her trilogy *Masque of the Red Death* (1988) and the live recordings *Plague Mass* (1991) and *Vena Cava* (1993). Galás's notable later releases include *Schrei X* (1996), *Malediction and Prayer* (1998), *Defixiones, Will and Testament* (2003), and the covers of *La serpenta canta* (2003) and *Guilty Guilty Guilty* (2008). *See also* EXTENDED PERFORMANCE TECHNIQUES; MULTI-CULTURALISM; POSTMODERNISM.

GANN, KYLE (1955–). American composer, musician, educator, and critic. Kyle Gann studied composition with **Morton Feldman** and **Ben Johnston** and has taught at Columbia University, Brooklyn College, Bucknell University, and Bard College. The composer of such **just-intonation** works such as *Ghost Town* (1994) for **synthesizer** and **computer tape** and the quintet *The Day Revisited* (2005), Gann also wrote music criticism for the *Village Voice*

(1986–2005; collected in *Music Downtown*, 2006) and is the author of *The Music of Conlon Nancarrow* (1995), *American Music in the Twentieth Century* (1997), and *No Such Thing as Silence: John Cage's 4'33"* (2010). *See also* ALTERNATE TUNING SYSTEMS; MICROTONALITY.

GARLAND, PETER (1952–). American composer, musician, and critic. Peter Garland studied with **James Tenney** and Harold Budd at the California Institute of the Arts. As editor and publisher of Soundings Press (1971–1991), he released editions of *Soundings* on such composers as Tenney, **Lou Harrison**, and **Conlon Nancarrow**, along with collections of his own essays: *Americas* (1982) and *In Search of Silvestre Revueltas* (1991). Garland's melodic compositions are mostly **multicultural**, with **minimalist** qualities shaping pop, Native American, Latin American, and Asian music. They include *Three Songs of Mad Coyote* (1973) for percussion ensemble; *Matachin Dances* (1980) for two violins and gourd rattles; *Love Songs* (1994) for violin, piano, marimbula, and maracas; and *After the Wars* (2008) for piano. *See also* POSTMODERNISM.

GEBRAUCHSMUSIK. Originating in Germany during the early 1920s, the term *Gebrauchsmusik* can be translated as "music for use," "utilitarian music," "workaday music," and "music for everyday life." Gebrauchsmusik renounced art-for-art's-sake and embraced a socially conscious intention to compose music that is readily available—attractive, interesting, and even performable—for all people, not just musicians. A key figure in its dissemination was **Paul Hindemith**, whose numerous Gebrauchsmusiken scores include *Schulwerk für Instrumental-Zusammenspiel* (1927) and *Sing-und Spielmusik* (1928). Other German composers of the era, such as **Hanns Eisler**, **Kurt Weill**, and **Stefan Wolpe**, had also written aggressively **modernist** music in their early works and then reconsidered their relationship to society and set out to produce music for everyone.

Many modernist composers also contributed individual Gebrauchsmusik scores, appreciating its values and intrigued by the challenge of achieving simplicity despite having been trained to prize complexity. Writing music to be performed by children, as in Hindemith's *Wir bauen eine Stadt* (1930) or the educational works of **Zoltán Kodály** and **Carl Orff**, is a quintessential Gebrauchsmusik approach. Others who produced such scores include **Aaron Copland** (*The Second Hurricane*, 1936), **Béla Bartók** (*Mikrokosmos*, 1939), and **Benjamin Britten** (*Noye's Fludde*, 1958). A recent example is **Morton Subotnick**'s musicmaking website for children, www.creatingmusic.com.

Beyond pedagogical concerns, however, the composition of Gebrauchsmusik came to be regarded as old hat by the 1950s with the ascendancy of **serialism, indeterminacy**, and **electronic music**. Nevertheless, this approach speaks to a perennial concern for many creative artists in balancing aesthetic and social considerations. Certain avant-garde works, despite their intellectual aspects, can thus be regarded as having Gebrauchsmusik qualities, as with many pieces by the **Fluxus** composers, which were activities for nonmusicians, or the performances of the **Scratch Orchestra** or the **Portsmouth Sinfonia**. Other examples include such scores as **Christian Wolff**'s *Prose Collection* (1968–1971), **Cornelius Cardew**'s *The Great Learning* (1968–1971), and **Pauline Oliveros**'s *Sonic Meditations I–XII* (1971). *See also* DAVIES, PETER MAXWELL; MODERNISM.

GERHARD, ROBERTO (1896–1970). Spanish-born English composer, musician, and educator. Roberto Gerhard studied piano with Enrique Granados and composition with Felipe Pedrell and **Arnold Schoenberg**. He fled the Civil War in Spain in 1938 and settled in England the following year. There he drew upon Spanish folk music in his Symphony "Homenaje a Pedrell" (1941), the ballet score *Don Quixote* (1941, rev. 1949), and the **opera** *The Duenna* (1949), which also used **twelve-tone** techniques. That method had also informed Gerhard's Wind Quintet (1928), and it characterized such later scores as Symphonies Nos. 1 (1951) and 2 (1959, rev. 1968 as *Metamorphosis*) and the cantata *The Plague* (1964). A leader in English **tape music** with such works as *Audiomobiles I–IV* (1958–1959), he also featured tape in Symphony No. 3, "Collages" (1960). Gerhard taught at the University of Michigan, Tanglewood, and other institutions; his students included **Robert Ashley** and **Roger Reynolds**. *See also* ATONALITY; MODERNISM.

GERSHWIN, GEORGE (1898–1937). American composer and musician. George Gershwin studied piano with Charles Hambitzer and composition with Rubin Goldmark, **Joseph Schillinger**, **Henry Cowell**, and **Wallingford Riegger**. His music ran along two parallel tracks. As a songwriter and composer of musicals, Gershwin's success was meteoric. His lively rhythms and imaginative melodies established him as a master with such shows as *La! La! Lucille* (1919), *Lady, Be Good!* (1924), *Oh, Kay!* (1926), *Girl Crazy* (1927), *Strike Up the Band* (1930), *Of Thee I Sing* (1931), and *Let Them Eat Cake* (1933). Gershwin composed concert music, as well, starting with his String Quartet (1919) and the one-act opera *Blue Monday* (1923, a.k.a. *135th Street*). His success in the concert hall soon rivaled that of his Broadway hits, with the classic *Rhapsody in Blue* (1924) for solo piano or piano and orchestra. The work showcased Gershwin's virtuoso technique and brought an exciting jazz sensibility to new audiences.

Other successful pieces followed: Concerto in F (1925) for piano and orchestra, *Three Preludes* (1926) for piano, and *An American in Paris* (1928) for orchestra. In 1932, Gershwin arranged 18 of his songs for solo piano in *George Gershwin's Song Book* and composed a rumba for orchestra, *Cuban Overture*, which featured Latin percussion. One of his greatest works, the **opera** *Porgy and Bess* (1935), drew on blues and jazz in its depiction of the lives of poor African Americans. Coolly received at first, *Porgy and Bess* went on to international acclaim. Gershwin was at the height of his powers when he died from a brain tumor at age 38. *See also* MULTICULTURALISM.

GIDEON, MIRIAM (1906–1996). American composer, musician, and educator. Miriam Gideon's teachers included **Hans Barth**, **Marion Bauer**, and **Roger Sessions**. A pianist and organist, she attended Boston University and Columbia University and taught at Brooklyn College and other institutions. Gideon blended tonal and **expressionist** techniques, composing **dissonant** and freely **atonal** music such as *The Hound of Heaven* (1945) for medium voice, oboe, and string trio; String Quartet (1946); *Symfonia Brevis* (1953); *Mixco* (1957) for voice and piano; and *Of Shadows Numberless* (1966) for piano. Her **multicultural** scores include *Fantasy on a Javanese Motive* (1948) for cello and piano, the chamber **opera** *Fortunato* (1956), and the quartet *Fantasy on Irish Folk Motives* (1975). Among her Jewish-themed works are *Sacred Service for Sabbath Morning* (1970) for tenor, baritone, mixed chorus, organ, and six instruments and *Shirat Miriam L'Shabbat* (1974) for cantor/tenor, mixed chorus, and organ. *See also* MODERNISM.

GINASTERA, ALBERTO (1916–1983). Argentine composer, musician, and educator. Alberto Ginastera studied at the Conservatorio Nacional in Buenos Aires and with **Aaron Copland** at Tanglewood. He taught at several institutions and founded the Conservatorio de Musicá y Arte Escenico. Among his nationalist works are the ballet score *Estancia* (1941) and *Pampeana No. 3* (1954) for orchestra, but Ginastera moved away from folkloristic materials with Piano Sonata No. 1 (1952), using **polytonal** and **serial** procedures. **Aleatoric** and **microtonal** passages inform the **opera** *Don Rodrigo* (1964) and *Cantata Bomarzo* (1964) for narrator, baritone, and orchestra. Other works include *Variaciones concertantes* (1953) for chamber orchestra, *Cantata para América mágica* (1960) for dramatic soprano and percussion orchestra, Piano Concerto No. 1 (1961), the operas *Bomarzo* (1967) and *Beatrix Cenci* (1971), and *Popul Vuh* (1983) for orchestra. In 1971, Ginastera left Argentina's military regime and settled in Switzerland, where he spent the rest of his life. *See also* MODERNISM; TWELVE-TONE MUSIC.

GLANVILLE-HICKS, PEGGY (1912–1990). Australian-born American composer, musician, educator, and critic. Pianist Peggy Glanville-Hicks studied composition with Fritz Hart in Melbourne, **Ralph Vaughan Williams** in London, **Egon Wellesz** in Vienna, and **Nadia Boulanger** in Paris. She settled in the United States in 1941, became a citizen in 1948, and wrote criticism for the *New York Herald Tribune* (1948–1958). Her early works, such as *Choral Suite* (1937) for female voices, oboe, and string orchestra and the quartet *Concertino da Camera* (1946), had **neoclassical** qualities, and her major scores were **multicultural**: Sonata for Harp (1950), *Letters from Morocco* (1952) for tenor and chamber orchestra, *Etruscan Concerto* (1954) for piano and chamber orchestra, *Pre-Columbian Prelude and Presto for Ancient American Instruments* (1957), and the **operas** *The Transposed Heads* (1953), *Nausicaa* (1960), and *Sappho* (1963). Glanville-Hicks relocated to Greece in 1959, and in 1967 underwent surgery for a brain tumor; she survived, but lost her ability to compose, and in 1976 she returned to Australia.

GLASS, PHILIP (1937–). American composer and musician. Philip Glass studied at Juilliard with Vincent Persichetti and William Bergsma and privately with **Darius Milhaud**, **Nadia Boulanger**, and Indian drummer Allah Rakha. His early music was **modernist** and often employed **twelve-tone** techniques. When Indian sitar player Ravi Shankar scored the **film** *Chappaqua* (1966), Glass worked on the music's notation, arrangement, and performance. The additive rhythmic structures of Indian music led him to a **minimalist** composition based on repeated patterns with restrictive pitch relations, invariably with a constant pulse and a static dynamic range. *600 Lines* (1967) was composed for an ensemble of two electric organs, woodwinds and voice, and this arrangement became the basis of his own sound with such breakthrough works as *Music in Fifths* (1969), *Music with Changing Parts* (1970), the four-hour *Music in Twelve Parts* (1974), and *Dance Nos. 1–5* (1979). With the epochal *Einstein on the Beach* (1975), a non-narrative **opera** created with director Robert Wilson, Glass's reputation was secured.

Glass has toured internationally, performing as soloist on piano or organ and playing electric organ with his ensemble. A prolific composer, he has written more than 20 operas, including *Satyagraha* (1979), *Akhnaten* (1983), *The Making of the Representative of Planet 8* (1986), *Hydrogen Jukebox* (1990), *The Voyage* (1992), *In the Penal Colony* (2000), *Waiting for the Barbarians* (2005), and a trilogy adapting Jean Cocteau: *Orphée* (1993), *La Belle et la Bête* (1994), and *Les enfants terribles* (1996). He reunited with Wilson for *the CIVIL warS—Rome* (1983) and *the CIVIL warS—Cologne* (1984) and collaborated with composer **Robert Moran** on *The Juniper Tree* (1984).

Glass has scored numerous films, including *Mishima* (1984), *Bent* (1997), *Kundun* (1997), and Godfrey Reggio's trilogy *Koyaanisqatsi* (1982), *Powaqqatsi* (1988), and *Naqoyqatsi* (2002). He also created a score for Tod Browning's *Dracula* (1931). His other works include Violin Concerto (1987), Cello Concerto (2001), two piano concertos (2000, 2004), five string quartets (1966–1991), and eight symphonies (1992–2005). Glass has also authored an autobiography, *Music by Philip Glass* (1987). *See also* ELECTROACOUSTIC MUSIC; MULTICULTURALISM; POSTMODERNISM.

GLOBOKAR, VINKO (1934–). French-born Slovene composer, musician, and educator. Vinko Globokar studied trombone at the Conservatoire National Supérieur de Paris and composition with **René Leibowitz** and **Luciano Berio**. He taught trombone and composition in Cologne and cofounded the **free-improvisation** quartet New Phonic Art in 1969. Globokar has premiered trombone works by Leibowitz, Berio, **Karlheinz Stockhausen**, **Henri Pousseur**, **Toru Takemitsu**, and **Mauricio Kagel** and has conducted orchestras internationally. **Extended performance techniques** and improvisation characterize his trombone playing as well as such compositions as *Discours II* (1968) for five trombones and *Ausstrahlungen* (1971) for oboe and chamber ensemble. Globokar has explored the relationship between instruments and voice in *Voie* (1966) for narrator, three choruses, and orchestra; Concerto Grosso (1975) for five instruments, chorus, and orchestra; the **multimedia** *Introspection d'un tubiste* (1983) for tuba, electronics, and **tape**; and the **opera** *L'armonia drammatica* (1990). Among his recent works are the theatrical *Kaktus unter Strom* (1999) for oboe, horn, bass, live electronics, and tape; *Les chemins de la liberté* (2004) for orchestra without conductor; and *Damdaj* (2009) for nine improvising musicians. *See also* ELECTROACOUSTIC MUSIC; POSTMODERNISM.

GOEHR, ALEXANDER (1932–). German-born English composer and educator. Alexander Goehr studied at the Royal Manchester College of Music with Richard Hall (1952–1955). Fellow students **Harrison Birtwistle**, **Peter Maxwell Davies**, and Goehr shared an interest in **serialism** and **atonal modernism**, which led to them being dubbed the Manchester School. Goehr also studied with **Olivier Messiaen** in Paris and taught at Leeds and Cambridge Universities. His Piano Sonata (1952) and *The Deluge* (1958) for two voices and octet were strict in the use of serial techniques, but Goehr later turned to juxtaposing serial, tonal, and modal techniques in Symphonies Nos. 1–4 (1963–1987); the **operas** *Arden Must Die* (1966), *Behold the Sun* (1984), and *Arianna* (1995); Piano Concerto (1972); String Quartet No. 3 (1976); the cantata *The Death of Moses* (1992); and *Broken Lute* (2006) for solo violin. *See also* TWELVE-TONE MUSIC.

GORDON, MICHAEL (1956–). American composer and musician. Michael Gordon studied with Martin Bresnick at the Yale School of Music. He cofounded the music collective Bang on a Can in 1987 with his wife **Julia Wolfe** and **David Lang**; the three also co-composed the **operas** *The Carbon Copy Building* (1995), *Lost Objects* (2001), and *Shelter* (2005). Gordon's **postmodern** music has drawn on **minimalism** and rock; among his **multimedia** works with video are *Van Gogh Video Opera* (1991) and *Weather* (1997) for string orchestra. Other scores range from chamber pieces (*Thou Shalt!/Thou Shalt Not!*, 1983; *I Buried Paul*, 1996) to large ensemble works (*Yo Shakespeare*, 1992; *Trance*, 1995). He formed the Michael Gordon Philharmonic in 1983 (renamed the Michael Gordon Band in 2000) and has collaborated with filmmaker Bill Morrison on *Decasia* (2001), *Gotham* (2004), and *Dystopia* (2008). *See also* FILM MUSIC.

GORDON, PETER (1951–). American composer and musician. Saxophonist Peter Gordon studied composition with **Kenneth Gaburo**, **Roger Reynolds**, **Robert Ashley**, and **Terry Riley**. He formed the Love of Life Orchestra in 1977, playing his own and others' music. Among Gordon's tuneful **postmodern** works are the dance score *Secret Pastures* (1984), the **multimedia** piece *The Return of the Native* (1988), and the **operas** *The Strange Life of Ivan Osokin* (1994) and *The Society Architect Ponders the Golden Gate Bridge* (2000). He has also performed with such notable composer/musicians as Ashley, **Laurie Anderson**, **"Blue" Gene Tyranny**, **Ned Sublette**, and **Arthur Russell**.

GÓRECKI, HENRYK (1933–2010). Polish composer, musician, and educator. Henryk Górecki studied at the State Higher School of Music in Katowice and later taught there. His *Eptafium* (1958) for mixed chorus and instruments was a **spatial** score, and the **dissonant** Symphony No. 1 (1959) and *Scontri* (1960) for orchestra employed **serial** techniques, but Górecki found his own voice drawing on Polish folk, medieval, and Renaissance music in such popular modal scores as Symphony No. 3 (1976) for soprano and orchestra, *Already It Is Dusk* (1988) for string quartet, *Concerto-Cantata* (1992) for flute and orchestra, and *Lobgesang* (2000) for chorus and glockenspiel. *See also* MODERNISM.

GOSFIELD, ANNIE (1960–). American composer, musician, and educator. Annie Gosfield studied composition at the University of Southern California and North Texas State University. Her notable works include the quintet *The Manufacture of Tangled Ivory* (1994, rev. 1995), *Blue Serge* (1996) for **sampling** keyboard, the **microtonal** *Four Roses* (1997) for cello and detuned piano, *Lightheaded and Heavyhearted* (2002) for string quartet, *The Harmony of the Body-Machine* (2003) for cello and electronics, and *A Sideways Glance from an Electric Eye* (2006) for a virtual version of **Leon Theremin**'s rhythmicon. Skilled at **extended performance techniques**, Gosfield has improvised on piano and sampler with **John Zorn**, **Fred Frith**, and others. The founder of the Annie Gosfield Ensemble, she has also taught at Mills College and Princeton University. *See also* ELECTROACOUSTIC MUSIC; FREE IMPROVISATION; POSTMODERNISM.

GRAETTINGER, ROBERT F. (1923–1957). American composer and musician. Robert Frederick Graettinger played alto saxophone in bands while in high school and studied composition at the Westlake School of Music in Los Angeles. In 1941, the teenage Graettinger approached bandleader Stan Kenton with some of his arrangements, and Kenton encouraged him to get more experience playing in bands. He then performed and arranged for Benny Carter, Vido Musso, Alvino Rey, and Bobby Sherwood. When Graettinger returned six years later, Kenton started performing his *Thermopylae* (1947).

Graettinger had taken the most controversial qualities of Kenton's music—loudness, **dissonance**, lack of tunefulness, absence of familiar swing rhythms—and pushed them to new extremes. Encouraged by Kenton, he composed pieces too startling for the band's conventional sets; instead, they were performed and recorded by Kenton's Innovations in Modern Music orchestra, which included a string section. Graettinger's notable works for the ensemble include the three-movement *City of Glass* (1947, rev. 1951), *Incident in Jazz* (1949), *House of Strings* (1950), and the six-part suite *This Modern World* (1953).

Graettinger composed in fields or layers of harmony, rhythm, and sonority. He would create his scores on graph paper, reproduce that music in a conventionally notated score, and then tailor the parts to the individual qualities of Kenton's musicians. The result was a razor-sharp big-band music that sounded more like **Edgard Varèse** or **Henry Cowell** than anything heard in the popular music of postwar America. Graettinger pursued more formal **modernist** composition after the dissolution of the Innovations orchestra, but completed only three movements of his Suite for String Trio and Wind Quartet (1957) before he died of lung cancer at age 33. *See also* FREE JAZZ; SCHULLER, GUNTHER.

GRAINGER, PERCY (1882–1961). Australian-born American composer, musician, and educator. A piano prodigy, Percy Aldridge Grainger was concertizing at age 12. He studied at Hoch's Konservatorium in Frankfurt-am-Main and relocated to England in 1901. Along with performing internationally, Grainger also studied and collected folk songs in Great Britain. His many arrangements of these produced his most popular scores, such as *Molly on the Shore* (1907) and *Country Gardens* (1918)—although he later dismissed them as uncharacteristic of his work.

From boyhood, Grainger believed in a **modernist** tonal freedom he called "free music," embracing nonharmonic simultaneities, sliding tones, **polyrhythms**, and nonpulsed events. By 1899, he was investigating beatless music and unusual meters from the rhythms of speech. Some of these qualities can be heard in *Hill Song No. 1* (1902) for 21 winds and *The Warriors* (1916) for orchestra and three pianos. He anticipated **aleatoric** procedures in *Random Round* (1915) for voices and instruments, and **string piano** and **tone-clusters** in the *In a Nutshell Suite* (1914–1916) for piano.

Grainger relocated to the United States in 1914 and became a citizen in 1918. He taught at Chicago Musical College (1919–1928) and studied the folk music of Denmark, which led to his impressive *Danish Folk-Song Suite* (1928, rev. 1941) for orchestra. Regarding **electronic music** as an ideal medium for free music, Grainger used **graphic notation** to compose for multiple **theremins** in *Free Music Nos. 1 and 2* (1936) and *Beatless Music* (1937). Wind and band music was also an important feature of his composition, such as the notable folk-song arrangement *Lincolnshire Posy* (1937).

Devoting more time to free music in his last years, Grainger worked with scientist Burnett Cross in the early 1950s. They built the Oscillator-Playing Tone-Tool, which adapted a Morse-code practice oscillator; the Butterfly piano, tuned **microtonally** in sixth-tones to simulate glissandi; and the Reed-Box Tone-Tool, which used harmonium reeds tuned in eighth-tones and could play gliding chords accurately. Eight valve oscillators and amplifiers were used in his Hills and Dales, or Kangaroo Pouch, machine, which was left unfinished at the time of Grainger's death from cancer in White Plains, New York, at age 78. *See also* INSTRUMENT BUILDING; MULTICULTURALISM.

GRAPHIC NOTATION. The first 20th-century score to dispense completely with the traditional representations of pitch and rhythm and instead use graphics is believed to be Luigi Russolo's **futurist** work *Risveglio di una città* (1914), written for an orchestra of eight different types of noisemaking machines. Among American composers, **Henry Cowell** was once again ahead of the curve when he devised alternative notation systems and other graphics for such pieces as *Two Rhythm-Harmony Quartets* (1919), *Ensemble* (1924), *The Banshee* (1925), and *Tiger* (1929). **Percy Grainger** used graphic notation for his 1936 **theremin** scores *Free Music Nos. 1 and 2*. An actual tradition of writing scores without standard notation, however, did not arise until the 1950s.

The most basic form of graphic notation is a literal graph—typically with the vertical and horizontal axes indicating pitch and time, respectively—which **Morton Feldman** introduced with his series of *Projection* scores (1950–1951). This technique proved useful to other composers involved with randomness, **chance**, and **indeterminacy**, such as **John Cage** (*26'1.1499" for a String Player*, 1955) and **Earle Brown** (*Folio* series, 1952–1954). Clearly an idea was in the air in the early 1950s. **Robert F. Graettinger**, whose innovative music was performed by bandleader Stan Kenton, used graph paper to layer harmonies, rhythms, and sonorities and then translated the result into traditional notation for his scores and parts. **Iannis Xenakis** did likewise working on the score of *Metastasis* (1954), in a compositional method that would also be used by **György Ligeti**.

Brown's graphic score *December 1952* from his *Folio* series is a field of vertical and horizontal lines of varying weights and lengths—his most extreme **open-form** work, although he still retained the relationship of vertical-pitch and horizontal-time from traditional notation. So did most others who utilized graphic notation, such as **Krzysztof Penderecki** (*Polymorphia*, 1961), **Roger Reynolds** (*The Emperor of Ice Cream*, 1962, rev. 1974), **Robert Moran** (*Interiors*, 1964), and **Christian Wolff** (*Edges*, 1968). Graphic notation that dispenses with pitch/time coordinates can require more explanatory comments in the score, but the music—both on the page and in performance—can be inspired, as evidenced by Cage's *Cartridge Music* (1960) and *Variations II* (1961), **Sylvano Bussotti**'s *Siciliano* (1962), **Toru Takemitsu**'s *Corona for Pianists* (1962), **Robert Ashley**'s *In memoriam . . .* series (1963), **Karlheinz Stockhausen**'s *Plus-Minus* (1963), **Cornelius Cardew**'s *Treatise* (1967), **Anthony Braxton**'s *Composition 76* (1977), and **Pauline Oliveros**'s *Portraits* (1987). *See also* ALEATORY; PROPORTIONAL NOTATION.

GRIFFES, CHARLES T. (1884–1920). American composer, musician, and educator. Charles Tomlinson Griffes studied composition with Philippe Bartholomé Rüfer and Engelbert Humperdinck in Berlin in 1903 and taught at the Hackley School in Tarrytown, New York (1907–1919). He brought an individual and lyrical voice to his **impressionist** idiom and is most admired for the piano works *Three Tone-Pictures* (1915), *Fantasy Pieces* (1915), *Roman Sketches* (1916), and Sonata (1919). Along with performing his piano music, he also gained recognition composing for orchestra with the glittering tone poem *The Pleasure-Dome of Kubla Khan* (1917), *Poem* (1918) for flute and orchestra, and *The White Peacock* (1919), a popular orchestration of one of his *Roman Sketches*.

Griffes's **multicultural** music includes the dance score *Sho-Jo* (1917, orch. 1919), composed for Japanese mime artist Michio Ito; *Four Poems of*

Ancient China and Japan (1917) for medium voice and piano; and *Three Javanese Melodies* (1919) for high voice and piano, with Javanese texts. He also explored Native American music in *Two Sketches for String Quartet Based on Indian Themes* (1919). Among his vocal works are *Tone Images* (1915) for mezzo-soprano and piano, *Three Poems* (1916) for high voice and piano, and *Three Poems by Fiona Macleod* (1918) for high voice and piano or orchestra. Griffes was 35 years old when he died of complications from influenza.

GRISEY, GÉRARD (1946–1998). French composer and educator. Gérard Grisey studied in Paris with **Olivier Messiaen** and in Darmstadt with **Karlheinz Stockhausen, György Ligeti**, and **Iannis Xenakis**. He also taught at numerous institutions, European and American. Although his early compositions were **serial**, Grisey's studies of acoustics led him to **spectral music**, in which the acoustic properties of a sound (its spectra) are explored, along with the nature of perception. Grisey's early spectral works include *Dérives* (1974) for small ensemble and large orchestra and *Partiels* (1975) for 18 musicians. His spectral music could also be **microtonal**, and **quarter-tones** are used in *Modulations* (1976) for chamber orchestra. Both *Partiels* and *Modulations* are included in Grisey's cycle of six scores from solo to orchestral, *Les éspaces acoustiques* (1985).

Grisey and his fellow spectralists **Tristan Murail**, Roger Tessier, and Michaël Lévinas cofounded the music collective/ensemble L'Itinéraire in 1973, with a special devotion to **electroacoustic music**. But despite his *Jour, contre-jour* (1978) for electric organ, 13 musicians, and four-channel **tape**, Grisey mostly worked with acoustic sound. He came to resist the spectralist label, having moved beyond that approach with *Talea* (1986) for five instruments. His microtonal composition, however, continued with such works as *L'icône paradoxale* (1994) for two female voices and orchestra divided into two groups and *Quatre chants pour franchir le seuil* (1998) for soprano and 15 instruments. Grisey died in Paris of a ruptured aneurysm at age 52. *See also* ALTERNATE TUNING SYSTEMS; ELECTRONIC MUSIC; MODERNISM; TWELVE-TONE MUSIC.

GROUPE DES SIX. Also known as Les Six, the Groupe des Six was so named by critic Henri Collet in a 1920 article about a concert of the previous year, which had included works by **Darius Milhaud** and Louis Durey (1888–1979). Collet lumped the two together with **Francis Poulenc, Arthur Honegger**, Germaine Taillefaire (1892–1983), and Georges Auric (1899–1983), seeing in these young **modernist** composers a new spirit comparable to that of the Russian Five of the 19th century.

These composers had in fact turned away from **impressionism** and were seeking a different path; another common denominator was their enthusiasm for **Erik Satie**'s use of music-hall tunes and for **Igor Stravinsky's polytonal** and **polyrhythmic** music. Poet Jean Cocteau was also a unifying factor, articulating and promoting their values. Cocteau supplied the show for Milhaud's *Le boeuf sur la toit* (1919) and the libretto for Honegger's **opera** *Antigone* (1927). Poulenc set Cocteau's poetry in *Cocardes* (1919), and Auric scored all of Cocteau's **films**, from *Le sang d'un poète* (1930) to *Le testament d'Orphée* (1960).

The six had indeed been friends since the late 1910s, but their music took them in different directions during the 1920s. Milhaud and Honegger were then at their creative peaks and produced some of their greatest works. Their later decades were a period of decline for both, whereas the music of Poulenc, especially for voice, got better and better, in songs of pop-tune wit and charm as well as in profound expressions of faith. Durey did not care for Cocteau, and he was the only one of the six who did not contribute music to the 1921 production of Cocteau's *Les mariés de la Tour Eiffel*, which brought an un-official end to the informal group. Durey's works include *Carillons et neige* (1918) for piano four-hands, the opera *L'occasion* (1923), and the cantata *La longue marche* (1949).

Neoclassicism strongly impacted Tailleferre in such works as the dance score *Le marchand d'oiseaux* (1923), Piano Concerto No. 1 (1923), and Concertino for Harp and Orchestra (1927); among her later works are the comic opera *Zoulaina* (1931), the dance scores *Paris-Magie* (1948) and *Parisiana* (1953), and Concerto for Two Guitars and Orchestra (c. 1964). Auric found his greatest success in films, composing well over 100 scores between 1930 and 1970, with such standouts as *À nous la liberté* (1931), *Dead of Night* (1945), *Moulin Rouge* (1952), *Roman Holiday* (1953), *Le salaire de la peur* (1953), *Lola Montès* (1955), and *Therese and Isabelle* (1968).

GUBAIDULINA, SOFIA (1931–). Russian composer and musician. Tartar-born Sofia Gubaidulina studied at the Kazan Conservatory and the Moscow Conservatory; in 1992, she relocated to Germany. An early voice in Soviet **electronic music** with *Vivente—Non-vivente* (1970), she also improvises on folk instruments with her ensemble Astraea. Gubaidulina's **multimedia** String Quartet No. 4 (1994), which featured lighting and a prerecorded quartet, and *Music for Flute, Strings, and Percussion* (1994) both featured **quarter-tone** tunings, as did *In the Shadow of the Tree* (1998) for koto, bass koto, zheng, and orchestra. Religious themes are explored in *Offertorium* (1980; rev. 1982, 1986) for violin and orchestra; *Seven Words* (1982) for cello, bayan, and string orchestra; and *Johannes Passion* (2000) and *Jo-*

hannes Ostern (2001), both for soloists, mixed chorus, organ, and orchestra. Gubaidulina's other major works include *Concordanza* (1971) for chamber orchestra, Concerto for Bassoon and Low Strings (1975), *The Unasked Answer* (1988) for three orchestras, *Zeitgestalten* (1994) for orchestra, Viola Concerto (1996), and *Feast during a Plague* (2005) for orchestra. *See also* MULTICULTURALISM.

HÁBA, ALOIS (1893–1973). Czech composer, musician, educator, and theorist. Alois Hába studied at the Prague Conservatory and later taught there (1924–1951). His first published **quarter-tone** composition was String Quartet No. 2 (1920). Hába outlined his theories of **microtonality** in the book *Neue Harmonielehre* (1925) and collaborated with **Ivan Wyschnegradsky** on the design of a quarter-tone piano; he also commissioned a sixth-tone harmonium and quarter-tone trumpets and clarinets. Among his quarter-tone scores are 10 piano fantasies (1923–1926), the **opera** *Matka* (1929), two guitar suites (1943, 1947), and the Violin Suite (1962); works in other tunings include String Quartets Nos. 5 (1923) and 10 (1952) in sixth-tones and No. 16 (1967) in fifth-tones. *See also* ALTERNATE TUNING SYSTEMS; INSTRUMENT BUILDING; MODERNISM.

HANNAN, JOE (1953–). American composer and musician. Pianist Joe Hannan studied composition with **James Tenney** and **Gordon Mumma** at the University of California, Santa Cruz. Frequently combining pop and traditional techniques with a sharp sense of humor, Hannan's compositions include *Elegy/Chaconne* (1988) for viola, tenor saxophone, and piano; *Variations on a Theme of Bill Conti* (1990) for piano; *Fly in Milk* (1992, a.k.a. *Villon Songs*) for mezzo-soprano, baritone, viola, harp, and tenor saxophone; and the short **operas** *Christina the Astonishing* (1994) and *Dwyn: Patron Saint of Lovers and Sick Cattle* (1996). *See also* POSTMODERNISM.

HARDIN, LOUIS. *See* MOONDOG.

HARRIS, ROY (1898–1979). American composer, musician, and educator. Roy Harris studied with **Arthur Farwell** and **Nadia Boulanger**. A tuneful composer with an ear for American folk music and **polytonal** harmonies, Harris composed several notable works: Concerto for Piano, Clarinet, and String Quartet (1926, rev. 1928), Piano Sonata (1928), *Symphony 1933*, *When Johnny Comes Marching Home* (1934) for orchestra, Piano Quintet (1936), String Quartet No. 3 (1937), and his greatest success, Symphony

No. 3 (1938). Among his later scores are Violin Concerto (1949), Symphony No. 7 (1952, rev. 1955), and *Epilogue to Profiles in Courage—JFK* (1964) for orchestra. Harris also taught at such institutions as Juilliard and Indiana University. *See also* MODERNISM.

HARRISON, LOU (1917–2003). American composer, musician, educator, and critic. Lou Harrison took piano and violin lessons as a boy and studied privately with **Henry Cowell**. He started composing percussion music with *France 1917–Spain 1937* (1937, rev. 1968) for string quartet and two percussionists and *Fifth Simfony* (1939) for percussion quartet. Harrison and **John Cage** gave percussion-ensemble concerts from 1939 to 1941, premiering Harrison's scores *Canticle No. 1* (1940), *Song of Quetzecoatl* (1941), and *Simfony No. 13* (1941), as well as his collaboration with Cage, *Double Music* (1941). Harrison studied with **Arnold Schoenberg** in 1943 and began composing **twelve-tone music** that year with his Suite for Piano. Relocating to New York, he wrote criticism for the *New York Herald Tribune* (1944–1947), studied with **Virgil Thomson**, and composed such important works as *First Suite for Strings* (1948, rev. 1995), *Seven Pastorales* (1951) for chamber orchestra, and the **opera** *Rapunzel* (1953, rev. 1996).

Harrison returned to California in 1954 and settled in Aptos. He began composing in **just intonation** with the 1955 scores *Strict Songs* (rev. 1992) for eight baritones and orchestra and *Simfony in Free Style*, which used specially constructed plastic flutes along with viols, harps, tack piano, and trombones. In 1961, he attended a conference in Tokyo, his first trip to Asia; others would follow, with Harrison studying the music of different Eastern cultures and reinventing his own composition. Asian music began informing his work with *Concerto in Slendro* (1961, rev. 1972) for violin, two tack pianos, celesta, and percussion. *Pacifika Rondo* (1963), *Avalokiteshvara* (1964), and *Music for Violin and Various Instruments, European, Asian, and African* (1967, rev. 1969) were **multicultural** scores that combined Eastern and Western instruments. Harrison and William Colvig constructed their American gamelan, first used in two major pieces: the gay-themed puppet opera *Young Caesar* (1971) and the Buddhist choral work *La Koro Sutro* (1972).

Harrison studied gamelan with the master Javanese composer and musician Pak Chokro and with Daniel Schmidt and Jody Diamond, gaining expertise in Javanese, Sudanese, Cirebonese, and Balinese gamelan styles. Some of Harrison's gamelan scores included Western instruments, most notably French horn in *Main Bersama-sama* (1978), baritone and male chorus in *Scenes from Cavafy* (1980), violin and cello in *Double Concerto* (1981), and soprano saxophone in *A Cornish Lancaran* (1986). He also composed numerous pieces purely in gamelan instrumentation, such as *Buburan Robert* (1976, rev. 1981), *Gending Dennis* (1982), *Lagu Victoria* (1983), and *Landrang in Honor of Pak Daliyo* (1986). Harrison's other notable late works include Piano Concerto (1985), a standard opera version of *Young Caesar* (1988), Fourth Symphony (1990, rev. 1995), and the dance score *Rhymes with Silver* (1996). The author of *Lou Harrison's Music Primer* (1971), he also taught at numerous institutions, including Black Mountain College and Mills College. *See also* INSTRUMENT BUILDING; IVES, CHARLES.

HARVEY, JONATHAN (1939–). English composer, musician, and educator. Jonathan Harvey studied at Cambridge University and with **Milton Babbitt** at Princeton University. He was a cellist in the BBC Scottish Symphony Orchestra and has taught at Sussex University and Stanford University. Harvey explored **spectral music** in *Mortuos plango, vivos voco* (1980) for **tape**. His **computer music** includes other tape works (*Ritual Melodies*, 1990; *Mythic Figures*, 2001) and such **electroacoustic** pieces as *Madonna of Winter and Spring* (1986) for orchestra and **synthesizers**; *Soleil noir/Chitra* (1995) for chamber ensemble; *Mothers Don't Cry* (2000) for soloists, female voices, and orchestra; String Quartet No. 4 (2003); and his **opera** *Wagner Dream* (2006). Harvey's nonelectronic scores include String Quartets Nos. 1–3 (1977–1995), Cello Concerto (1990), and the operas *Passion and Resurrection* (1981) and *Inquest of Love* (1992). *See also* ELECTRONIC MUSIC.

HAUER, JOSEF MATTHIAS (1883–1959). Austrian composer, musician, and theorist. Instructed in music by his father, Josef Matthias Hauer began composing highly chromatic works with such scores as *Apokalyptische Phantasie* (1913) for chamber orchestra. He developed his own approach to **atonality** and **twelve-tone** organization in *Nomos* (1919) for piano and detailed his ideas in the books *Vom Wesen des Musikalischen* (1920), *Deutung des Melos* (1923), *Vom Melos zur Pauke* (1925), and *Zwölftontechnik* (1926). His other compositions include *Hölderlin Lieder* (1922) for voice and piano, Violin Concerto (1928), the cantata *Der menschen Weg* (1934), and *Zwölftönespiel I* (1940) for orchestra. *See also* MODERNISM.

HENRY, PIERRE (1927–). French composer. Pierre Henry studied at the Paris Conservatoire with **Olivier Messiaen** and **Nadia Boulanger**. Drawn to **Pierre Schaeffer**'s *musique concrète*, Henry gained access to the equipment at the RTF radio network and created with Schaeffer the landmark *Symphonie pour un homme seul* (1950). In 1951, they established the first **tape-music** studio, Groupe de Recherches de Musique Concrète. Along with his solo pieces *Concerto des ambiguïtés* (1950) and *Voile d'Orpheé* (1953), Henry pursued other collaborations with Schaeffer, including the **electroacoustic opera** *Orphée 53* (1953) for tape, harpsichord, and female voice.

Henry left the Groupe de Recherches in 1958 and established the Apsone-Cabasse Studio. There he worked with electrically synthesized sound as well and created the dance scores *Le voyage* (1963), *Variations pour une porte et un soupir* (1964), and *Messe pour le temps present* (1967). Other important **electronic music** by Henry includes *Messe de Liverpool* (1967), *Apocalypse de Jean* (1968), and *Intérieur/extérieur* (1997). *Mise en musique du Corticalart* (1971) was a **multimedia** work that converted brain waves into audio and visual materials. He incorporated live performance in *Dieu* (1978) and *Futuriste* (1980) and **quoted** the music of Ludwig van Beethoven in *Dixième symphonie* (1979). Henry's *Labyrinthe!* (2003) also employed **spatial** distribution. *See also* COMPUTER MUSIC.

HENZE, HANS WERNER (1926–). German composer, musician, and educator. Hans Werner Henze began studying at the Braunschweig Staats-musikschule in 1942, but in 1944 was conscripted into the German army; eventually he became a prisoner of war. After the war, he studied with Wolfgang Fortner at the Heidelberg Church Music Institute. Henze began composing **twelve-tone music** in the late 1940s and studied the method with **René Leibowitz**. His works from this period include Violin Concerto No. 1 (1948) and Symphony No. 2 (1949). He became artistic director and conductor of the Weisbaden Hessische Staatstheater in 1950, but in 1953 relocated permanently to Italy.

Henze's **serial** music incorporated tonal procedures in the lyric drama *Boulevard Solitude* (1951), using French music-hall tunes and American jazz, and the pop-inflected ballet score *Undine* (1956); popular music also shaped his **opera** *König Hirsch* (1955, rev. 1962), the ballet score *Maratona di danza* (1956), and *Nachtstücke und Arien* (1957) for soprano and orchestra. Henze found success in opera with *Elegie für junge Liebende* (1961, rev. 1987), *Der junge Lord* (1964), and *Die Bassariden* (1965, rev. 1992). His revolutionary socialist beliefs informed his music-theater piece *El Cimarrón* (1970), the stage cantata *Streik bei Mannesmann* (1973), and the opera *We Come to the River* (1976).

Along with the **dissonant** and **modernistic** qualities of his music, as in *Heliogabalus imperator* (1972) for orchestra and *Tristan* (1974) for piano and orchestra, Henze also has a **neoromantic** side that found voice in the operas *The English Cat* (1983), *Das verratene Meer* (1990), and *Phaedra* (2007); as well as in Symphony No. 7 (1984); *Requiem* (1993) for piano, trumpet, and chamber orchestra; and *Sebastian im Traum* (2004) for orchestra. Henze's prolific output includes 10 symphonies (1948–1996), five string quartets

(1947–1977), and three violin concertos (1948–1996). He has taught at the Salzburg Mozarteum (1962–1967), Cologne's Staatliche Hochschule für Musik (1980–1991), and Tanglewood (1983, 1988–1996) and is the author of *Musik und Politik* (1976, rev. 1984) and *Reiselieder mit böhmischen Quinten* (1996).

HERRMANN, BERNARD (1911–1975). American composer and musician. Bernard Herrmann studied at New York University and Juilliard. A respected conductor, he also composed such works as the cantata *Moby Dick* (1938), Symphony No. 1 (1941), the **opera** *Wuthering Heights* (1951), and *Souvenirs de voyage* (1967) for clarinet and string quartet. Herrmann is most prized for his expressive and inventive **film music**, which includes scores for the classics *Citizen Kane* (1941), *The Magnificent Ambersons* (1942), *Vertigo* (1958), *North by Northwest* (1959), *Psycho* (1960), *Jason and the Argonauts* (1963), and *Taxi Driver* (1976). He also consulted on the **electronic-music** effects created for Alfred Hitchcock's *The Birds* (1963). *See also* IVES, CHARLES; THEREMIN.

HESELTINE, PHILIP. *See* WARLOCK, PETER.

HIGGINS, DICK (1938–1998). English-born American composer. Dick Higgins studied with **John Cage** and **Henry Cowell**. As part of the **Fluxus** group, Higgins produced such conceptual scores as *Danger Musics* (1961–1963) and *Music for Stringed Instruments* (1964). Mostly active as a writer and visual artist, he also founded Something Else Press (1963–1974). *See also* POSTMODERNISM.

HILLER, LEJAREN (1924–1994). American composer and educator. Lejaren Hiller studied at Princeton University with **Milton Babbitt** and **Roger Sessions** and received his MMus in 1958 from the University of Illinois at Urbana-Champaign, where he founded and was director of the Experimental Music Studio (1958–1968). He later taught at the University of Buffalo (1968–1989). Hiller became a leader in **computer music** with String Quartet No. 4, "Illiac Suite" (1957, co-composed with Leonard Isaacson), which made the first significant use of a computer to generate composition. He developed the composition programs of *Computer Cantata* (1963, co-composed with Robert Baker) for soprano, chamber ensemble, and **tape**, using **stochastic** procedures for music and text. Those procedures also shaped his series *Algorithms I* (1968), *II* (1972, co-composed with Ravi Kumra), and *III* (1984) for nine instruments and tape; each work has four versions, showing the progressive complexity of the computer program used in their composition.

A lively and original thinker, Hiller worked in numerous styles and genres. He wrote **serial** music with *Twelve-Tone Variations* (1954) for piano and String Quartet No. 5 (1962), the latter composed in **quarter-tones**; he also used **microtonal** tunings in *Seven Electronic Studies* (1963) for two-channel tape. Hiller composed such theatrical pieces as *A Triptych for Hieronymus* (1966) for actors, dancers, projections, tape, and orchestra, and *An Avalanche for Pitchman, Prima Donna, Player Piano, Percussionist, and Pre-recorded Playback* (1968). Collaborating with **John Cage**, he created *HPSCHD* (1968), a **multimedia** work for one to seven harpsichords and one to 51 tapes. He also utilized randomness in String Quartet No. 6 (1972) and *A Portfolio for Diverse Performers and Tape* (1974), scored for up to 10 performers of any sort and eight channels of tape.

Hiller wrote tonal scores with String Quartet No. 3 (1953), Symphony No. 2 (1960), and Violin Sonata No. 3 (1970); Americana such as *Jesse James* (1950) for vocal quartet and piano and *Five Appalachian Ballads* (1958) for voice and guitar or harpsichord; and the **multicultural** *Diabelskie skrzypce* (1978) for stringed instrument and harpsichord and *An Apotheosis for Archaeopterix* (1979) for piccolo and berimbau. His other works include six piano sonatas (1946–1972), seven string quartets (1949–1979), and three symphonies (1953–1987). He coauthored *Experimental Music* (1959) and wrote *Informationstheorie und Computermusik* (1964). Hiller died of Alzheimer's disease in Buffalo, New York, at age 69. *See also* ATONALITY; INDETERMINACY; POSTMODERNISM; TWELVE-TONE MUSIC.

HINDEMITH, PAUL (1895–1963). German-born American composer, musician, and educator. Born in Hanau, Paul Hindemith began playing violin as a child and studied at the Conservatory in Frankfurt (1908–1917). Having made a splash with the **dissonant**, one-act **expressionist operas** *Mörder, Hoffnung der Frauen* (1919), *Das Nusch-Nuschi* (1920), and *Sancta Susanna* (1921), he turned to a preclassical **neoclassicism**, using German Baroque forms with **modernist** harmonies and rhythms in *Kammermusik Nos. 1–7* (1922–1927), mostly for soloist and chamber ensembles. In the 1920s, Hindemith also composed two major song cycles—*Die junge Magd* (1922) for alto and six instruments and *Das Marienleben* (1923, rev. 1948) for soprano and piano—and his String Quartet No. 3 (1921), the dance score *Der Dämon* (1922), and the opera *Cardillac* (1926, rev. 1952).

Hindemith had an experimental streak, and in 1926 he created *Rondo* and *Toccata* for mechanical piano by punching holes directly into a piano roll. Anticipating *musique concrète*, he manipulated phonograph records on variable-speed turntables to create the recording *Grammophonplatteneigene Stücke* (1930). Hindemith taught himself to play the **trautonium**, an elec-

tronic-music keyboard instrument, and composed *Des kleinen Elektromusikers Lieblinge* (1930) for three trautoniums, *Konzertstück* (1931) for trautonium and string orchestra, and the solo *Langsames Stück und Rondo* (1935).

Hindemith taught at the Berlin Hochschule für Musik (1927–1939), and his progressive approach to music education became an international model: In 1935, the Turkish government commissioned him to organize Turkey's musical activities and instruction. An exponent of **Gebrauchsmusik**, he produced numerous didactic pieces for amateur musicians, including *Sing- und Spielmusik* (1928) and *Wir bauen eine Stadt* (1930), a musical game for children. In the 1930s and 1940s, Hindemith wrote a series of sonatas for all the major instruments in the orchestra. Later in life, however, when others used the term to pigeonhole him, he distanced himself from Gebrauchsmusik.

In 1934, Hindemith completed the opera *Mathis der Maler* and derived from it one of his most successful scores, the Symphony *Mathis der Maler*. He followed with two great concertos for viola, *Der Schwanendreher* (1935) with small orchestra and *Trauermusik* (1936) with string orchestra, premiering both as soloist; he also conducted the premieres of his *Symphonische Tänze* (1937) for orchestra and the ballet score *Nobilissimma Visione* (1938). Hindemith's music was banned by the Nazis, and in 1938 he left Germany. After a stay in Switzerland, he moved to the United States in 1940, becoming a U.S. citizen in 1946. He taught principally at Yale University (1940–1955).

Hindemith composed some of his best and most popular scores during his years in the United States: *Theme with Four Variations (According to the Four Temperaments)* (1940) for piano and string orchestra, Cello Concerto (1941), *Ludus tonalis* (1942) for piano, *Symphonic Metamorphoses on Themes by C. M. von Weber* (1943) for orchestra, and his requiem setting of Walt Whitman, *When Lilacs Last in the Dooryard Bloom'd* (1946) for mezzo-soprano, baritone, mixed chorus, and orchestra. Relocating to Zurich in 1953, he began performing more as a conductor, touring with the Vienna Symphony Orchestra in 1956. His last compositions include *Pittsburgh Symphony* (1959), the one-act opera *The Long Christmas Dinner* (1961), and Organ Concerto (1963). Hindemith died in a Frankfurt hospital at age 68 after suffering a series of strokes. *See also* TAPE MUSIC.

HOLST, GUSTAV (1874–1934). English composer, musician, and educator. Gustav Holst studied at London's Royal College of Music and researched English folk music with **Ralph Vaughan Williams** and **George Butterworth** in the 1900s. Best known for his dazzling orchestral suite *The Planets* (1916), Holst also composed such **multicultural** works as *Choral Hymns from the Rig Veda* (1908–1910) for chorus and orchestra and the orchestral scores *Beni Mora Suite* (1910) and *Japanese Suite* (1915). He used **bitonality** in Double

Concerto (1929) for two violins and orchestra, new sonorities in *Hammersmith* (1930) for band or orchestra, and **dissonance** in *A Choral Fantasia* (1930) for soprano, chorus, organ, and orchestra. Other works include *The Hymn of Jesus* (1917) for chorus and orchestra, *First Choral Symphony* (1924), and *Egdon Heath* (1927) for orchestra. Among his eight **operas** are *Savitri* (1908) and *The Perfect Fool* (1922). An instrumentalist and conductor, he also taught at several English institutions and Harvard University. Holst died in London of complications from surgery at age 59. *See also* MODERNISM.

HONEGGER, ARTHUR (1892–1955). French composer and educator. After studying at the Conservatory of Zurich (1909–1911), Arthur Honegger attended the Paris Conservatoire (1911–1918), where his teachers included Charles-Marie Widor and Vincent d'Indy. He befriended fellow student **Darius Milhaud** there, and in the early 1920s both were among the French composers known as the **Groupe des Six**. Honegger, however, was the most austere, serious, and Germanic of Les Six, with the biblical oratorio *Le Roi David* (1921); the tone poem *Pacific 2.3.1* (1923) for orchestra, an age-of-steel depiction of a locomotive; the jazz-inflected *Concertino* (1924) for piano and orchestra; and the **opera** *Antigone* (1927), with libretto by Jean Cocteau. Honegger also wrote music for the classic Abel Gance **films** *La roue* (1923) and *Napoléon* (1927). Some of his 1930s film scores featured the **ondes martentot**, an **electronic-music** instrument he also used in the dramatic oratorio *Jeanne d'Arc au bûcher* (1935). His later works include the opera *L'Aiglon* (1937, co-composed with **Jacques Ibert**), String Quartets Nos. 2 (1935) and 3 (1937), and five symphonies (1930–1950). Honegger also taught at L'École Normale de Musique in Paris; his students included **Ned Rorem, Luc Ferrari, William Flanagan**, and **Iannis Xenakis**. *See also* MODERNISM.

HOVHANESS, ALAN (1911–2000). American composer and musician. Alan Vaness Chakmakjian composed and took piano lessons as a child and studied with Federick Converse at the New England Conservatory of Music (1932–1934). Calling himself Alan Hovhaness, he briefly attended Tanglewood in 1942 and studied with **Bohuslav Martinu**, but left to research the music of his ancestral Armenia. He destroyed most of his scores of the 1930s, keeping only certain successful pieces such as his Cello Concerto (1936). Inspired by the music of Yenovk Der Hagopian and Komitas Vartabed, he made Armenian music the basis of his work with such notable scores as *Armenian Rhapsody No. 1* (1944) for percussion and strings, *Lousadzak* (1944) for piano and strings, and *Khaldis* (1951) for four trumpets (or any multiple thereof), piano, and percussion.

Lousadzak introduced **free-rhythm** passages in his music: repeated note patterns played simultaneously but at different tempi. Other unusual techniques in Hovhaness's composition include drones, rapid repeated figurations, multiple glissandi, and the massing of like voices. Yet his music has always been popular and accessible, thanks to his Armenian-inspired long-lined melodies, as in Symphony No. 2, "Mysterious Mountain" (1955) and Symphony No. 6, "Celestial Gate" (1959). In the late 1950s and early 1960s, Hovhaness studied Asian musical traditions, mainly the orchestral music of Tang-dynasty China, Korean Ah-ak, Japanese Gagaku, and the music of North and South India. Numerous **multicultural** scores resulted, including *Nagooran* (1960) for South Indian orchestra, *Fantasy on Japanese Wood Prints (Hanga Genso)* (1964) for xylophone and orchestra, and *Mountains and Rivers without End* (1968) for 10 players.

Hovhaness was a mystic and a visionary, and those qualities define such major compositions of his as Symphony No. 19, "Vishnu" (1966), *Fra Angelico* (1967) for orchestra, *And God Created Great Whales* (1970) for orchestra with **tape** of whale sounds, *Spirit of Ink* (1970) for three flutes, *O Lord Bless Thy Mountains* (1974) for two pianos tuned a **quarter-tone** apart, and Symphony No. 50, "Mount St. Helens" (1982). A regular performer of his own music as pianist and conductor, Hovhaness was also an extremely prolific composer and left close to 500 works, including seven **operas** (1946–1978) and 67 symphonies (1936–1992). *See also* PLEROMA.

HUNT, JERRY (1943–1993). American composer and musician. Jerry Hunt studied piano and composition at the University of North Texas. He first used electronics in his composition with *Helix 3* (1963) for variable instrumentation. Hunt devised interactive systems to produce real-time **electronic music** such as *Haramand Plane: Continuous* (1972) for electronic information processing systems and *Cantegral Segment 16* (1976) for voice with interactive adaptive electronic system and generalized delay processors. But the obscure technical titles and dry and complex descriptions he gave his pieces belie their eccentricity. By the late 1970s, Hunt's lifelong fascination with the occult led to theatrical and ceremonial solo performances of *Transphalba* (1978), *Lattice* (1979), and *Phalba (Stream)* (1979). His stylized movements and sometimes manic activity would trigger music through unpredictably responsive sensors that were linked to **computers** and **synthesizers**. Often evoking John Dee, the late 16th-century English astrologer and mathematician, Hunt gave shamanistic performances that featured percussion, vocalizations, whistling, and handmade props such as dolls, rattles, bells, and wands.

Birome (ZONE): Cube (1983) was an installation system with interactive video-audio system and adaptive control systems, and *Transphalba (ROTA):*

Monopole (1984) was a system performance using electronic storage and adaptive control with video and audio-scan detection interface. Hunt also composed for piano (*Cantegral Segment 13*, 1975; *Trapani [Stream]*, 1990) and created the electronic *Song Drapes* (1992) for performance artist Karen Finley in "The Hunt/Finley Report" (1993). His later works include *Fluud* (1985), a system of translation derivatives with various instrument and control system implementations, and *CANA (Bed): Overlay* (1992), a composite interactive installation. Suffering from emphysema and lung cancer, Hunt took his own life at age 49. *See also* ATONALITY; INDETERMINACY; INSTRUMENT BUILDING; MULTIMEDIA; POSTMODERNISM.

HYKES, DAVID (1953–). American composer and musician. David Hykes studied at Antioch College and Columbia University and with North Indian raga singer Sheila Dhar and Tibetan master Thuksey Rinpoche. Adopting Central Asian throat-singing methods, he founded David Hykes and the Harmonic Choir in 1975, devoted to ensemble overtone singing. Notable recordings of his music include *Hearing Solar Winds* (1982), *Harmonic Meetings* (1992), *Earth to the Unknown Power* (1996), *Harmonic Meditations* (2005), and *Harmonic Mantra* (2010). *See also* EXTENDED PERFORMANCE TECHNIQUES; JUST INTONATION; MULTICULTURALISM; PLEROMA; POSTMODERNISM.

I

IBARRA, SUSIE (1970–). American composer, musician, and educator. Susie Ibarra attended the Mannes College of Music and studied drum set with jazz musicians Buster Smith of **Sun Ra**'s Arkestra and Milford Graves. She studied Philippine Kulintang with Danongan Kalanduyan and the Kalanduyan family and has taught at numerous American institutions. An accomplished percussionist and improviser, Ibarra often uses Philippine Kulintang and Southeast Asian gong music in her **multicultural** performances and compositions. She has played with **Pauline Oliveros, John Zorn**, and **Fred Frith** and created the electric kulintang by combining the electronics of her husband, composer/percussionist Roberto Rodriguez, with her gong playing. Her compositions include *Fractals* (2000) for drum; *Dancesteps* (2007) for piano; *Pintados Dream* (2007, a.k.a. *The Painted's Dream*), a **multimedia** concerto for drums, visual art, and orchestra; and *A Translation of Silk* (2009) for spoken English, Vietnamese soprano, and violin. *See also* ELECTRO-ACOUSTIC MUSIC; FREE IMPROVISATION; POSTMODERNISM.

IBERT, JACQUES (1890–1962). French composer, musician, and educator. Jacques Ibert studied with Gabriel Fauré at the Paris Conservatoire and was director of the French Academy in Rome (1937–1960). Blending **impressionist** and **neoclassical** techniques, his music includes the orchestral scores *Escales* (1922, a.k.a. *Ports of Call*), the witty *Divertissement* (1930), and Flute Concerto (1934). Among his **operas** are *Angélique* (1926) and *L'Aiglon* (1937, co-composed with **Arthur Honegger**). Ibert also scored such notable **films** as G. W. Pabst's *Don Quixote* (1933), Julien Duvivier's *Golgotha* (1935), and Orson Welles's *Macbeth* (1948). *See also* MODERNISM.

ICHIYANAGI, TOSHI (1933–). Japanese composer and musician. Toshi Ichiyanagi studied composition with Kishio Hirao, **Aaron Copland**, and **John Cage** and piano with Chieko Hara and Beveridge Webster. He used **graphic notation** in *Music for Electric Metronome* (1960) and *Appearance* (1963) for amplified organ, brass instrument, string instrument, and electronics. He also wrote instructional scores for **Fluxus** performances, such as the

1962 pieces *Sapporo* and *Distance*, and composed the **tape** pieces *Music for Tinguely* (1963) and *Appearance* (1967). Among Ichiyanagi's **multicultural** scores are *Engen* (1982, rev. 1986) for koto and orchestra, *Ten, Zui, Ho, Gyaku* (1988) for shakuhachi and **ondes martenot**, and *Cosmos Ceremony* (1993) for ryuteki, sho, and orchestra. In addition, he is the author of *An Ancient Resonance in Contemporary Music* (2007). Other Ichiyanagi works include the **operas** *The Last Will of Fire* (1995), *Momo* (1995, rev. 1998), and *Hikari* (2002); four string quartets (1964–1999); four piano concertos (1981–2009); and six symphonies (1986–2001). *See also* ELECTROACOUSTIC MUSIC; POSTMODERNISM.

IMPRESSIONISM. The term *impressionism* derives from art criticism: Claude Monet's painting *Impression, soleil levant* (1872) met with critical disdain, and by the late 1870s his work and that of Edgar Degas, Camille Pissarro, Edouard Manet, and Auguste Renoir was widely labeled *impressionist*. What these artists had in common was their avoidance of the common romantic rhetoric and academic devices, adopting instead an original and sensual treatment of light, color, and texture. They also sought to evoke subtle emotional and spiritual states in their stylized depictions of people, objects, and above all nature.

Impressionist qualities emerge in Franz Liszt's piano music of the time, most notably *Weihnachtsbaum* (1876, a.k.a. *L'arbre de Noël*) and the glittering *Les jeux d'eaux à la Villa d'Este* (1877). Although chided by the Académie des Beaux-Arts in 1887 for his impressionist tendencies, the young **Claude Debussy** soon departed from the excesses of Richard Wagner and the familiar academicism of Vincent d'Indy. He composed a series of classic works, including *Prélude à l'après-midi d'un faune* (1894) and *Pelléas et Mélisande* (1901), which epitomized impressionist music in the sensuality of their harmonies and tone colors and in Debussy's rejection of drama and development in favor of a static atmosphere and subtle evocations of moods and feelings.

The "impressionist" label stuck to Debussy, who eventually came to hate it. It was also used in some circles to describe other original French composers, such as **Maurice Ravel** and **Erik Satie**, despite their considerable musical differences, as well as the English composer **Frederick Delius**, whose more rhapsodic and elegiac music defined an impressionist sound of his own, and **Charles T. Griffes**, who also had an individual lyrical voice.

As acclaim for Debussy and Ravel spread internationally, other composers embraced this alternative to German romanticism in the 1900s and 1910s. For **Béla Bartók, Igor Stravinsky, Karol Szymanowski**, and **Manuel de Falla**, impressionism opened doors into their own individual **modernist** voices.

By the late 1920s, with the interest in **neoclassicism** and the music of the **Groupe des Six**, impressionism came to be regarded as out of style. Nevertheless, its values have continued to inform a wide range of music. Generations of composers have reflected the impressionist devotion to color and staticism, among them **Albert Roussel, Henry Eichheim, Frank Bridge, Zoltán Kodály, Heitor Villa-Lobos, Olivier Messiaen, Toru Takemitsu, Joan Tower, George Crumb, Barbara Kolb**, and **La Monte Young**. *See also* BECKER, JOHN J.; BOULANGER, LILI; CHÁVEZ, CARLOS; ELLINGTON, DUKE; IBERT, JACQUES; IRELAND, JOHN; OPERA; RUDHYAR, DANE; SEEGER, CHARLES; SMIT, LEO (1900–1943); SORABJI, KAIKHOSRU SHAPURJI.

INDETERMINACY. With his 1951 compositions *Sixteen Dances, Concerto for Prepared Piano and Orchestra*, and *Music of Changes*, **John Cage** began using **chance** procedures in his music, placing material chosen by a random process into a preexisting structure of rhythmic relationships. His *Imaginary Landscape No. 4 (March No. 2)*, also from 1951, followed this approach, but was scored for 12 radios, with two players per radio, adjusting the wavelength and volume knobs to different positions predetermined by chance. Unlike its predecessors, this piece always sounds different in every performance, and thus it brought Cage's music into indeterminacy: the creation of musical situations where the composer has no control over the sounds that are produced. Some of Cage's other notable indeterminate compositions include the tacet score *4'33"* (1952), *Winter Music* (1957), *Atlas Eclipticalis* (1961), and *Variations I–VIII* (1958–1978).

Composers who were friendly with Cage began using indeterminacy as well, starting with **Earle Brown** and his *Folio* series (1952–1954). In 1957, **Christian Wolff** composed *Duo for Pianists I*, in which the performers determine varying degrees of what they actually play, and **Morton Feldman** composed *Piece for Four Pianos*, where the duration of pitches was left open to the musicians. The **operas** of **Robert Ashley** and the expanded-accordion music of **Pauline Oliveros** join indeterminacy with improvisation. Other composers of indeterminate music include **Philip Corner, Richard Maxfield, La Monte Young, Terry Jennings, Larry Austin, Cornelius Cardew, Toru Takemitsu, Gavin Bryars, Jerry Hunt, Lejaren Hiller, Robert Moran, Henri Pousseur, Glenn Branca**, and **Mel Powell**. *See also* ALEATORY; ATONALITY; FLUXUS; FREE DURATION; GEBRAUCHSMUSIK; GRAPHIC NOTATION; OPEN FORM.

INSTRUMENT BUILDING. The instrument-building spirit motivates a good deal of **postmodern** musicmaking, insofar as it informs the appropriation of noninstruments for performance and the deconstruction of familiar instruments through **alternate tuning systems, extended performance techniques,** and the incorporation of electronic systems in **electroacoustic music. Electronic music** and **computer music** draw on this sensibility, too, with composers creating new hardware and software. It is also a major factor in **sound sculpture** and **sound installations.**

In modern times, the tradition of composer/musicians becoming inventor/builders in order to realize a sound world unavailable with traditional instruments can perhaps be traced to **futurist** composer Luigi Russolo, who constructed *intonarumori* (noise-intoners) to perform such noise-music pieces as *Risveglio di una città* (1914). Composers who employed **microtonality,** such as **Julián Carrillo, Alois Hába, Hans Barth,** and **Percy Grainger,** also designed and built instruments in order to hear the tunings. **Harry Partch,** however, saw instrument building as more than just the means to an end. From 1930 until his death in 1974, Partch built and played his own instruments, chiefly string and percussion, which he tuned in **just intonation.** They were designed to serve onstage as sculptural/dramatic presences in his music theater, and they have survived their maker: Originals and replicas continue to be used, not only for his music but also in new works by composers such as **Anne LeBaron** and **John Zorn.**

In the 1950s, **Moondog** was performing on and recording the percussion instruments he built, and **Lucia Dlugoszewski** began playing the more than 100 percussion instruments she designed (built for her by sculptor Ralph Dorazio). **Lou Harrison'**s puppet opera *Young Caesar* (1971) introduced the American gamelan made by William Colvig and Harrison. Other specialized built-instrument ensembles arose in the 1970s. The Glass Orchestra, originated by students at Toronto's York University in the early 1970s, performs on glass instruments. Skip LaPlante and Carole Weber founded the composers collective Music for Homemade Instruments during the mid-1970s; they invent, build, compose for, and play instruments made from trash and found objects. More recent is the Vienna Vegetable Orchestra, begun in 1998, which performs on instruments made of fresh vegetables.

Former Partch assistant Dean Drummond built the zoomoozophone in 1978; **John Cage** and **Joan La Barbara** have composed for this microtonal percussion instrument. **Mauricio Kagel** used homemade instruments in *Acustica* (1970), as did the **Residents** in *Eskimo* (1979). **Ellen Fullman** began developing her long string instrument in 1981. **Glenn Branca** devised mallet guitars for his Symphony No. 2 (1982) and designed keyboard instruments for his Symphonies Nos. 3 and 4 in 1983. Homemade instruments held a special interest for such **free improvisers** as **Fred Frith** and **Elliott Sharp.**

Tan Dun had potter Ragnar Naess construct more than 50 ceramic percussion, wind, and string instruments for Tan's *Nine Songs* (1989) and *Soundshape* (1990). Barry Ransom, Susan Rawcliffe, and Ward Hartenstein have also designed, built, and played ceramic instruments. Darrell De Vore has constructed wind and percussion instruments from bamboo, and **Alison Knowles** has created paper instruments. Other notable instrument-building composer/musicians include Bart Hopkin, Ken Butler, and Tom Nunn.

IRELAND, JOHN (1879–1962). English composer, musician, and educator. John Ireland studied at the Royal College of Music with Sir Charles Villiers Stanford; he also taught there (1920–1939) and was organist and choirmaster at St. Luke's Chelsea. His notable early scores include *Sea Fever* (1913) for voice and piano, *The Holy Boy* (1915) in numerous arrangements, and Violin Sonata No. 2 (1917). Inspired by **Igor Stravinsky** and the French **impressionists**, he brought rhythmic vitality and complex harmonies to his music's sonorities, evoking the English landscape in *London Pieces* (1920) for piano and the orchestral scores *The Forgotten Rite* (1918) and *Mai-Dun* (1921). Despite such major works as his Piano Concerto (1930), *A London Overture* (1936) for orchestra, *Concertino pastorale* (1939) for string orchestra, and *Fantasy Sonata* (1943) for clarinet and piano, Ireland stopped composing in the late 1940s. *See also* MODERNISM.

IVES, CHARLES (1874–1954). American composer and musician. A forward-looking **modernist**, neglected in his day, Charles Ives has come to be recognized as one of America's greatest composers, celebrated for his original approach to **dissonance**, **atonality** and **polytonality**, **polyrhythm**, extreme densities, and the **quotation** of popular, sacred, and classical tunes, which made his music unique and instantly identifiable.

Born in Danbury, Connecticut, Charles Edward Ives was serving regularly as a church organist by age 14. Some of his early compositions reflect the attitudes of his father George Ives (1845–1894), a professional musician with an experimental streak, who explored **microtonality** and **bitonality**. The provocative and funny *Variations on "America"* (1892) for organ by the teenage Charles included polytonal passages. *Song for Harvest Season* (1894) for voice and three brass instruments was completely polytonal, with each musician in a different key, whereas *Psalm 67* (1898) for male and female voices was mostly bitonal.

Ives entered Yale University in 1894 and studied with Horatio Parker. In the idiom of Johannes Brahms and Antonin Dvořák, he produced two tuneful 1898 scores, String Quartet No. 1 and Symphony No. 1, but after graduating, he followed his father's example and chose a business career over the life of a professional musician. He started the Ives & Myrick Agency with Julian Myrick in 1909 and flourished in the insurance industry.

During these years, Ives composed his radical works at home in the evenings and on weekends, largely isolated from other modernist developments in Europe and America. The music of rural Connecticut was celebrated in his Symphonies Nos. 2 (1902) and 3 (1904). Ives also looked ahead to **spatial music**, combining unsynchronized groups of musicians in his 1908 scores for chamber orchestra *The Unanswered Question* and *Central Park in the Dark*. His early *Studies* (1907–1922) for piano and Piano Sonata No. 1 (1909) featured some of the most dense and dissonant music Ives had yet composed.

He pursued that sound as far as he could during the 1910s, with a rich expressive spirit and nostalgic affection for his New England roots, producing his most important and celebrated works: String Quartet No. 2 (1913), *Holidays Symphony* (1913), four sonatas for violin and piano (1914–1917), Piano Sonata No. 2 (1915), Symphony No. 4 (1916), and the orchestral scores *Set for Theater Orchestra* (1911), *Robert Browning Overture* (1914), *Three Places in New England* (1914), and Orchestral Set No. 2 (1919). They are his most extreme music as well and feature unprecedented densities, often thick with quotations. His most ambitious work, however, was left a series of fragments: the multiorchestral *Universe Symphony*, composed mostly in 1915, which included a lengthy movement for percussion ensemble. After Ives's death, the *Universe Symphony* was performed in realizations by **Larry Austin** (1993) and **Johnny Reinhard** (1996).

Ives suffered a severe heart attack at age 43 in 1918 and never fully recovered; his composing came to an end by the mid-1920s. One of his last works was the innovative *Three Quarter-Tone Pieces* (1924) for two pianos. In 1922, Ives self-published *114 Songs*, making available the many songs for voice and piano he had composed in the prior 30 years. He also self-published "Essays before a Sonata" in 1920, which described the Transcendentalist themes in his Piano Sonata No. 2 (subtitled "Concord, Mass., 1840–60"), as well as authoring other essays on music and politics. Thanks to his business success, Ives was also able to help finance the publication of **Henry Cowell**'s New Music Quarterly scores and the construction of **Leon Theremin**'s rhythmicon.

Performances of his music were few when Ives was composing, but by 1927 Cowell had discovered his music and begun championing him. Other composer/conductors who led Ives's scores in the 1930s and 1940s include **John Becker, Nicolas Slonimsky, Anton Webern, Bernard Herrmann,** and **Lou Harrison**. The appreciation of Ives's music grew steadily after **John Kirkpatrick**'s 1939 premiere of the "Concord" Sonata, and his Symphony No. 3 received the Pulitzer Prize after its 1946 premiere. At the time of his death in New York at age 79, Ives had witnessed the beginning of the ascent of his reputation. By the 1960s, he had become for many the quintessential American composer, beloved as much for his avant-garde innovations as for his Yankee fervor, his humor, and the depth of his emotion. Fifty years later, his stature is more secure than ever. *See also* BRANT, HENRY; CARTER, ELLIOTT; COPLAND, AARON; PLEROMA; QUARTER-TONE MUSIC; RUGGLES, CARL; TONE-CLUSTER.

J

JANÁCEK, LEOS (1854–1928). Czechoslovakian composer, musician, educator, critic, and theorist. Born in Hukvaldy, Moravia, Leos Janácek spent most of his life in Brno and studied music with Pavel Krízkovsky; he also attended the Prague Organ School. Janácek founded the Brno Organ School in 1881, where he was director until 1920, and the review-based journal *Hudební listy* in 1884, which published his criticism. His first major scores were the **operas** *Sárka* (1888; rev. 1918, 1925) and *Pocátek Románu* (1891).

Janácek began collecting folk songs in 1888 and by the early 1890s was notating the rhythmic and melodic contours of everyday Czech speech. This research led him to the speech-melodies that transformed his vocal music, starting with the opera *Jenufa* (1903, rev. 1907), a powerful drama of infanticide, which became an international success after being performed in Prague and Vienna in 1916. Janácek's important works during the 1910s include *Pohádka* (1910) for cello and piano; *In the Mists* (1912) for piano; *The Diary of One Who Vanished* (1916) for alto, tenor, women's chorus, and piano; the opera *The Excursions of Mr. Broucek* (1917); and *Taras Bulba* (1918) for orchestra.

Speech-melody encouraged the use of declamatory vocal lines in his operas, with the orchestra creating melody and drama. Janácek's harmonic sense became more **dissonant** in the operas *Kátya Kabanová* (1921), *The Cunning Little Vixen* (1923), *The Makropulos Affair* (1925), and *From the House of the Dead* (1928), as well as in his classic *Glagolitic Mass* (1926) for soloists, mixed chorus, orchestra, and organ. Other notable late works include Concertino for Piano and Chamber Orchestra (1925), *Sinfonietta* (1926) for orchestra, and String Quartets Nos. 1 (1925) and 2 (1928). *See also* MODERNISM.

JENKINS, LEROY (1932–2007). American composer, musician, and educator. Violinist Leroy Jenkins taught in schools in Mobile, Alabama, and Chicago in the 1960s and was a member of the Association for the Advancement of Creative Musicians. He worked with such notable composer/musicians as **Anthony Braxton, Ornette Coleman, Cecil Taylor, Anne LeBaron,**

Richard Teitelbaum, **"Blue" Gene Tyranny**, and **George Lewis**. Among his recordings are *Lifelong Ambitions* (1977) with **Muhal Richard Abrams**, *Solo* (1998), and the **multicultural** *The Art of Improvisation* (2006). Jenkins also drew upon creative African-American music in such compositions as the dance **opera** *The Mother of Three Sons* (1990), the cantata *The Negro Burial Ground* (1996), and the **multimedia** opera *The Three Willies* (2001). *See also* FREE IMPROVISATION; FREE JAZZ; POSTMODERNISM.

JENNINGS, TERRY (1940–1981). American composer and musician. Terry Jennings studied composition with **La Monte Young** in the late 1950s and, by 1960, was composing **minimalist** music with long sustained tones like Young's: String Quartet, *Piano Piece for Christine Jennings*, *Piece for Cello and Saxophone*. As an improviser on alto saxophone and piano, Jennings played with Young on piano and **Dennis Johnson** on Japanese hichiriki in the early 1960s, developing a repetitive modal drone style. Jennings also participated in two pioneering **electroacoustic** works, **Richard Maxfield**'s *Wind for Terry Jennings* (1960) and the first performances of Young's *The Tortoise, His Dreams and Journeys* (1964). Jennings composed a pair of **indeterminate** piano works of extended duration, *Winter Trees* (1965) and *Winter Sun* (1966), in which the pianist selects the material to be repeated. His later music, such as *The Seasons* (1975) for voice and piano, was **neoromantic**. *See also* POSTMODERNISM.

JOHNSON, DENNIS (1938–). American composer and musician. While a student at UCLA during the late 1950s, Dennis Johnson became friends with **La Monte Young** and began composing **minimalist** pieces with long sustained tones. *The Second Machine* (1959) utilized only the four pitches of one of the "dream chords" from Young's *The Four Dreams of China (The Harmonic Versions)* (1962); *Avalanche #1, a Concert Drama* (1960) included a tape of Young's *Trio for Strings* (1958). Johnson's *November* (1959) for piano, a repetitive diatonic work, could last up to six hours. *Din* (1960) for large ensemble distributed the musicians among the audience. In the early 1960s, Johnson was improvising on Japanese hichiriki and piano along with Young on piano and **Terry Jennings** on alto saxophone, in a repetitive modal drone style. He wrote *109 Bar Tune* (1961), a series of chord changes for the trio, as well as conceptual pieces, but not long afterward Johnson gave up music. *See also* MULTICULTURALISM; POSTMODERNISM; SPATIAL MUSIC.

JOHNSON, TOM (1939–). American composer, musician, and critic. Tom Johnson studied at Yale University and privately with **Morton Feldman**. He composed numerous important **minimalist** scores, frequently combining simple forms and limited scales with logical and mathematical techniques—an approach described in his book *Self-Similar Melodies* (1996). Johnson's notable early works include *An Hour for Piano* (1971), *Failing, a Very Difficult Piece for Solo String Bass* (1975), and *Nine Bells* (1979). Johnson was new-music critic for the *Village Voice* (1972–1982); his writings were collected in the book *The Voice of New Music* (1991). Among his later works are *Rational Melodies* (1982) for any melodic instrument(s), *Bonhoeffer Oratorium* (1992) for chorus and orchestra, and the *Tilework* series of solos (2002–2005). *See also* POSTMODERNISM.

JOHNSTON, BEN (1926–). American composer, musician, and educator. Ben Johnston studied at the Cincinnati Conservatory of Music and worked at **Harry Partch**'s California studio in 1950 and 1951, playing and recording Partch's music and absorbing the principles of **just intonation**; he also collaborated with Partch on incidental music for Wilford Leach's play *The Wooden Bird*. Johnston studied with **Darius Milhaud** at Mills College and taught at the University of Illinois at Urbana-Champaign (1951–1984). He met **John Cage** at Illinois and assisted with the **tape** editing of Cage's *Williams Mix* in 1952; he also studied with Cage in 1959. **Microtonality** was featured in Johnston's *Five Fragments* (1960) for alto, oboe, bassoon, and cello and *A Sea Dirge* (1962) for mezzo-soprano, flute, oboe, and violin. String Quartet No. 2 (1964) used **serial** procedures with a 53-note-to-the-octave tuning system. He retuned a piano for his *Sonata for Microtonal Piano* (1965) and brought just intonation to the orchestra with *Quintet for Groups* (1966).

Among Johnston's major works of the 1970s are the vampire-themed **opera** *Carmilla* (1970); String Quartets Nos. 4 (1973) and 5 (1979), just-intonation variations on the hymns "Amazing Grace" and "Lonesome Valley," respectively; and *Suite for Microtonal Piano* (1978). He has become a leader in extended just intonation with such later works as *Sonnets of Desolation* (1980) for eight voices; String Quartet No. 9 (1987); *Calamity Jane to Her Daughter* (1989) for soprano, violin, keyboard, organ, and drum set; String Quartet No. 10 (1995); and Octet (2000). *See also* ALTERNATE TUNING SYSTEMS.

JOLAS, BETSY (1926–). French composer, musician, and educator. Pianist and organist Betsy Jolas studied composition with Paul Boepple in the United States and with **Darius Milhaud** and **Olivier Messiaen** in France. She taught at the Paris Conservatoire and Mills College and is the author of *Molto espressivo* (1999). Avoiding systems, Jolas has explored color and texture in *Quatuor II* (1964) for coloratura soprano and string trio, *J. D. E.* (1966)

for chamber ensemble, *Musique d'hiver* (1971) for organ and orchestra, and the **operas** *Le pavillon au bord de la rivière* (1975), *Le Cyclope* (1986), and *Schliemann* (1993). *D'un opera de poupée en sept musiques* (1982) featured an **ondes martenot** in its ensemble. Notable later works include *Quoth the Raven* (1993) for clarinet and piano, *Sonate à 8* (1998) for eight cellos, *Motet IV* (2002) for soprano and quintet, and *B Day* (2006) for orchestra. *See also* ELECTROACOUSTIC MUSIC.

JOLIVET, ANDRÉ (1905–1974). French composer, musician, and educator. André Jolivet studied composition with Paul Le Flem and **Edgard Varèse**, taught at the Paris Conservatoire (1966–1971), and performed internationally as a conductor. A **modernist** with a mystical strain, he wrote several works for **ondes martenot**: with piano in *Trois poèmes* (1935), within the orchestras of *Danse incantatoire* (1936) and *Suite delphique* (1943), and showcased in an orchestral Concerto (1947). Jolivet's other notable scores include *Mana* (1933) for piano, the North African–inspired *Cinq incantations* (1936) for flute, the one-act **opera** buffa *Dolores* (1942), *Hopi Snake Dance* (1948) for two pianos, Symphonies Nos. 1–3 (1953–1964), Cello Concertos Nos. 1 (1962) and 2 (1966), the oratorio *La vérité de Jeanne* (1956), *Mandala* (1969) for organ, and *Yin-Yang* (1973) for 11 strings. *See also* ELECTROACOUSTIC MUSIC; MULTICULTURALISM.

JOPLIN, SCOTT (1868–1917). American composer and musician. Scott Joplin played piano as a boy and by age 20 was traveling the country as an itinerant musician. He performed the minstrel songs and cakewalks with a popular syncopated approach to rhythm then called "ragged time." As "ragtime," this music made a hit with the public in the late 1890s, and Joplin's tunefulness, charm, and expressivity made his music famous, with such classics as *Maple Leaf Rag* (1899) and *The Entertainer* (1902). He composed memorable works in other genres, too, including the march (*Combination March*, 1896), waltz (*Bethena*, 1905), and tango (*Solace*, 1909); but it was in ragtime that he became a master, producing hit after hit, among them *The Cascades* (1904), *Gladiolus Rag* (1907), *Fig Leaf Rag* (1908), and *Wall Street Rag* (1909), a work that featured **tone-clusters**.

Joplin wrote a ballet score, *The Ragtime Dance* (1899), and orchestrated several of his rags for *The Red Back Book* (c. 1906). He also composed two **operas**: the one-act *A Guest of Honor* (1903) and the three-act *Treemonisha* (1911). He used bolder and more original harmonies in his final masterpieces *Scott Joplin's New Rag* (1912) and *Magnetic Rag* (1914), but by then the public's interest in ragtime was fading. Joplin financed a 1915 concert performance of *Treemonisha* and its failure broke him, materially and spiritually. The following year, he announced that he was working on a music comedy drama called *If* and a symphony, but he was no longer able to compose. His mental condition deteriorated and Joplin died in a New York hospital at age 49. *Treemonisha*, orchestrated by **Gunther Schuller**, was finally staged in 1975.

JUST INTONATION. Just intonation is an **alternate tuning system** derived from the intervals of the overtone, or harmonic, series. When any pitch, or *fundamental*, is sounded, there occurs naturally a specific sequence of less audible pitches, known as *partial tones*, *overtones*, or *harmonics*, in an ascending series of intervals (and, theoretically at least, an equivalent descending series). The frequency of each higher partial is equal to the frequency of the fundamental times the number of that partial in the overtone series. For example, when middle C is the fundamental (the first partial), it vibrates at a rate of 256 beats per second and produces a second partial with a frequency of 512 beats, which is a C one octave higher in equal temperament. The third partial has a frequency of 768 beats (3 × 256), which is a G above the second C, an interval of a perfect fifth; the fourth partial has 1,024 beats, which is another C. Four more partials follow, the last of which has a frequency of 2,048 beats, or yet another C; then eight partials to the next highest C, followed by 16, 32, and 64. The partials extend and on and on, into intervals too minute for the human ear to discriminate.

Lou Harrison, Ben Johnston, Terry Riley, James Tenney, Tony Conrad, and **Pauline Oliveros** have used traditional instruments in just tunings. **Harry Partch**, the great champion of just intonation, devoted himself to designing and building instruments tuned to a just system. Other composers who followed him out of equal temperament were drawn to the aural phenomena that just intonation makes available: The pitches reinforce and strengthen the natural resonance of their higher partials and generate prominent overtone activity unavailable in equal-tempered music. The **pleroma** music of **La Monte Young, Rhys Chatham**, and **Glenn Branca** has involved working with amplified densities of pitches tuned to the ratios of higher just-intonation octaves. *See also* COWELL, HENRY; FULLMAN, ELLEN; HYKES, DAVID; MOONDOG; REINHARD, JOHNNY; SCRIABIN, ALEXANDER; STOCKHAUSEN, KARLHEINZ.

K

KAGEL, MAURICIO (1931–2008). Argentine composer and musician. Born in Buenos Aires of German and Russian parents, Mauricio Kagel relocated to Europe in 1957. Settling in Cologne, he created *Transición I* (1960) at the WDR Electronic Music Studio. Language was the sound source of *Anagrama* (1958) for four voices, speaking choir, and chamber ensemble, which used innovative vocal techniques. Building on *Anagrama*'s dramatic qualities, Kagel became one of Europe's leading composers of theatrical music. Musicians performed with recordings of themselves in *Transición II* (1959) for piano, percussion, and two **tape** recorders, which used **extended performance techniques** with **string piano**. A lecture sinks into unintelligibility in *Sur scène* (1960) for singer, speaker, mime, three instrumentalists, and tape. The score of *Sonant (1960/ . . .)* (1960) for guitar, harp, double bass, and membranophones included **graphic notation** and texts for the musicians to speak. In the 1960s, Kagel began teaching in Europe and the United States; his students included **Anne LeBaron** and **Horatiu Radulescu**.

The deconstructing of performance norms brought a surrealistic quality to Kagel's music. *Match* (1964) had two competing cellists with a percussionist referee, in a reproduction of music that Kagel had heard in a recurring dream. He composed precise scores for imprecise instruments, compelling audiences to consider how the music was being played. Invented and esoteric instruments were used with noninstruments in *Der Schall* (1968). *Acustica* (1970) featured homemade instruments, as did *1898* (1973, rev. 1996), in which children's choruses sing out of tune. *Exotica* (1972) had Western musicians performing pseudo world music on non-Western instruments. Players imitated old blues recordings in *Blue's Blue* (1979). Kagel's song-**opera** *Aus Deutschland* (1979) set texts used by Franz Schubert, Robert Schumann, and Johannes Brahms, while *Quodlibet* (1988) for female voice and orchestra used 15th-century French chanson lyrics.

Among Kagel's later works are *Liturgien* (1990) for solo voices, double choir, and large orchestra; *Entführung im konzertsaal* (1999) for an abducted orchestra; *Broken Chords* (2001) for large orchestra; and a farce for ensemble, *Divertimento* (2006). Kagel also created numerous radio plays, including

Guten Morgen! (1971) and *Rrrrrrr* . . . (1982), and was a prolific filmmaker, deriving from his music theater such **films** and videos as *Antithese* (1965), *Hallelujah* (1968), *Ludwig Van* (1969), and *Phonophonie* (1979). *See also* ELECTRONIC MUSIC; INSTRUMENT BUILDING; MULTICULTURALISM; MULTIMEDIA; POSTMODERNISM.

KANCHELI, GIYA (1935–). Georgian composer, musician, and educator. Giya Kancheli studied at the Georgian State Conservatory at Tbilisi and later taught there; in 1995, he settled in Belgium. A prolific composer of **film** scores, Kancheli has employed extreme contrasts, particularly in dynamics, in such concert works as Symphonies Nos. 6 (1980) and 7 (1986). His other notable works include Symphonies Nos. 1–5 (1967–1977); the **opera** *Music for the Living* (1983); *Night Prayers* (1992) for string quartet and **tape**; *Diplipito* (1997) for countertenor, cello, and orchestra; and the orchestral scores *Ergo* (2000) and *Warzone* (2002). *See also* MODERNISM.

KHACHATURIAN, ARAM (1903–1978). Armenian composer, musician, and educator. Aram Ilyich Khachaturian studied at the Moscow Conservatory with Reinhold Glière and Nikolai Myaskovsky and later taught there. Also a conductor, he composed colorful **neoromantic** pieces with a special feeling for an array of Soviet folk music: Armenian, Georgian, Ukrainian, Russian, Turkmenian, and Irano-Azerbaijani. Among his notable early works are the Piano Concerto (1936), Violin Concerto (1940), and the ballet score *Gayaneh* (1942), with its popular "Sabre Dance." But when Khachaturian's music was denounced as **formalist** in 1948, along with that of his fellow "Big Four" Soviet composers Myaskovsky, **Sergey Prokofiev**, and **Dmitry Shostakovich**, as well as many others, he was compelled like the rest to acknowledge his errors and mend his ways. Khachaturian's later works include the ballet score *Spartacus* (1954) and the Concerto-Rhapsody for Cello and Orchestra (1963). *See also* MULTICULTURALISM.

KIRCHNER, LEON (1919–2009). American composer, musician, and educator. Leon Kirchner studied with **Arnold Schoenberg** and **Roger Sessions** and taught at Mills College and Harvard University; his students included **Morton Subotnick** and **John Adams**. Also active as a pianist and conductor, Kirchner composed chiefly in an **expressionist**-inspired **atonal** idiom, producing such notable scores as Piano Trio No. 1 (1954), String Quartet No. 3 (1966) with **electronic music** on **tape**, the **opera** *Lily* (1977), *Music for Twelve* (1985), *Music for Cello and Orchestra* (1992), and *The Forbidden* (2008) for orchestra. *See also* MODERNISM.

KIRKPATRICK, JOHN (1905–1991). American musician and educator. Devoted to American music, pianist John Kirkpatrick championed **Aaron Copland** and **Roy Harris** in the 1930s, and his 1939 premiere of **Charles Ives**'s "Concord" Sonata was a turning point in the recognition of that composer. Kirkpatrick was also curator of the Ives Collection at Yale University and taught at Yale and Cornell University. *See also* RUGGLES, CARL.

KNOWLES, ALISON (1933–). American composer. Alison Knowles studied fine arts at the Pratt Institute. Her involvement with the **Fluxus** group resulted in her composing such event scores as *Shuffle* (1961), *Make a Salad* (1962), *Shoes of Your Choice* (1963), *Music by Alison* (1964), and *Wounded Furniture* (1965). Although primarily a visual artist and writer, Knowles has continued to produce **indeterminate** and conceptual music, including *The Bean Garden* (1976) and *Loose Pages* (1986–present). Among the paper instruments she has created are the Giant Bean Turner, Wrist Rubber, and Bamboo & Flax Accordion. *See also* INSTRUMENT BUILDING; POST-MODERNISM.

KNUSSEN, OLIVER (1952–). Scottish composer and musician. Oliver Knussen studied privately with John Lambert and at Tanglewood with **Gunther Schuller**. Prodigious as both composer and conductor, at age 15 he led the London Symphony Orchestra in the 1968 premiere of his partially **twelve-tone** Symphony No. 1. Knussen is admired for his Symphony No. 2 (1971) for soprano and small orchestra, the nonet *Ophelia Dances, Book I* (1975), *Cantata* (1977) for oboe and string trio, and his chamber-**opera** settings of Maurice Sendak: *Where the Wild Things Are* (1981) and *Higglety Pigglety Pop!* (1990). His recent works include the octet *Songs without Voices* (1992) and *Requiem: Songs for Sue* (2006) for soprano and chamber ensemble. *See also* MODERNISM.

KODÁLY, ZOLTÁN (1882–1967). Hungarian composer, musician, and educator. Zoltán Kodály studied at the Budapest Academy of Music and began investigating folk music in 1905 with **Béla Bartók**; they also co-composed *Twenty Hungarian Folksongs* (1906) for voice and piano. Kodály became an important ethnomusicologist, and his nationalist compositions blended folk, **impressionist**, romantic, and neomedieval qualities. Major works include the oratorio *Psalmus hungaricus* (1923); *Missa brevis* (1944) for soloists, mixed chorus, and organ or orchestra; and the orchestral scores *Háry János Suite* (1926), *Variations on a Hungarian Folk Song* (1939, a.k.a. *Peacock Variations*), and Concerto for Orchestra (1940). Kodály also taught at the Budapest Academy and served as its director; his Kodály Method for developing children's musicality has been adopted internationally. *See also* GEBRAUCHSMUSIK; MODERNISM.

KOLB, BARBARA (1939–). American composer. Barbara Kolb studied with **Gunther Schuller** and **Lukas Foss**. Inspired by **impressionism**, Kolb's static yet colorful music has utilized **aleatoric** and **serial** techniques along with other **atonal** structures. Among her orchestral compositions are *Soundings* (1978), *All in Good Time* (1993), and *The Web Spinner* (2004). Kolb's other notable works include *Three Place Settings* for narrator and four musicians (1968), *Trobar Clus* for chamber orchestra (1970), *Related Characters* for trumpet and piano (1980), *Voyants* for piano and chamber orchestra (1991), and *Sidebars* for bassoon and piano (2004). Kolb has also combined **tape** with piano in *Solitaire* (1971), with two pianos in *Spring River Flowers Moon Night* (1975), and with chamber orchestra in *Millefoglie* (1985). *See also* ELECTROACOUSTIC MUSIC; MODERNISM.

KOSUGI, TAKEHISA (1938–). Japanese composer and musician. Takehisa Kosugi studied musicology at the Tokyo University of Arts. Seeking new forms of improvisation, he cofounded Group Ongaku (1958–1962) and Taj Mahal Travellers (1969–1975) and as an improvising violinist with electronics has performed such pieces as *Catch-Wave* (1975), *Violin Improvisations* (1990), *Violin Solo 1980* (1998), and *Catch-Wave '97* (2008). With the **Fluxus** group, Kosugi produced such event scores as *Organic Music* (1962), *South Nos. 1–3* (1962–1965), *Theatre Music* (1963), and *Anima 7* (1964). Among his **multimedia** pieces are *South No. 8* (1979) and *75 Letters and Improvisation* (1987). Music director of the Merce Cunningham Dance Company since 1995, Kosugi has created such live **electronic-music** works as *S.E. Wave/E.W. Song* (1976), *Cycles* (1981), *Spacings* (1984), *Transfigurations* (1993), and *Wave Code A–Z* (1997). His **sound installations** include *Islands* (1991) and *Illuminated Summer* (1996). *See also* ATONALITY; ELECTROACOUSTIC MUSIC; FREE IMPROVISATION; MINIMALISM; POSTMODERNISM.

KOTIK, PETR (1942–). Czechoslovakian composer and musician. Flutist and conductor Petr Kotik studied music in Europe and settled in the United States in 1969. He founded the S.E.M. Ensemble in 1970, specializing in **modern** and contemporary music. His compositions include the **open-form** vocal works *Many Many Women* (1978) and *Explorations in the Geometry of Thinking* (1982), lengthy **minimalist** settings of Gertrude Stein and Buckminster Fuller, respectively, and the orchestral scores *Quiescent Form* (1996) and *Music in Two Movements* (2003). *See also* POSTMODERNISM.

KRENEK, ERNST (1900–1991). Austrian-born American composer, musician, and educator. Ernst Krenek, a child prodigy as composer and pianist, studied at the Vienna Musikhochschule and conducted **opera** in Germany. A **modernist** with his **dissonant** String Quartet No. 1 (1921), **atonal** Symphony No. 2 (1922), and **expressionist** opera *Orpheus und Eurydike* (1923), Krenek was also drawn to **neoclassicism** and composed the popular jazz-inflected opera *Jonny spielt auf* (1926). He turned to **neoromanticism** in the opera *Leben des Orest* (1929), *Reisebuch aus den österreichischen Alpen* (1929) for medium voice and piano, and String Quartet No. 5 (1930) and then embraced **twelve-tone music** with the opera *Karl V* (1933, rev. 1954), String Quartet No. 6 (1936), *Lamentatio Jeremiae prophetae* (1942) for mixed chorus, and Piano Sonata No. 3 (1943, rev. 1960). *Sestina* (1957) for soprano and octet and *Quaestio temporis* (1959) for orchestra were **totally serialized**. Krenek settled in the United States in 1938, becoming a citizen in 1945; he taught at Vassar College and Hamline University and wrote the books *Music Here and Now* (1939), *Exploring Music* (1966), and *Horizons Circled* (1974).

Krenek combined **electronic music** with voices in *Spiritus intelligentiae, Sanctus* (1956), with orchestra in *Exercises of a Late Hour* (1967), and with organ in *Orga-Nastro* (1971). **Aleatoric** techniques informed *Fibonacci Mobile* (1964) for string quartet and piano four-hands and the orchestral scores *From Three Make Seven* (1961, rev. 1968) and *Horizon Circled* (1967). His later scores include the autobiographical *Spätlese* (1972) for baritone and piano, String Quartet No. 8 (1981), and the oratorio *Opus sine nomine* (1988). A prolific composer, Krenek wrote seven piano sonatas (1919–1988), eight string quartets (1921–1981), five symphonies (1921–1949), 19 operas (1923–1969), and four piano concertos (1923–1950). *See also* ELECTRO-ACOUSTIC MUSIC.

KURTÁG, GYÖRGY (1926–). Hungarian composer, musician, and educator. György Kurtág studied at the Franz Liszt Academy of Music, where he later taught (1967–1993), and in Paris with **Olivier Messiaen** and **Darius Milhaud**. Melding the rhythmic vigor of **Béla Bartók** with the sparseness and compression of **Anton Webern**, Kurtág composed such notable works as his String Quartet (1959), *The Sayings of Péter Bornemisza* (1968) for soprano and piano, *Messages of the Late R. V. Troussova* (1980) for soprano and chamber ensemble, and the **spatial** scores . . . *quasi una fantasia* . . . (1988) for piano and chamber ensemble, *Grabstein für Stephan* (1989) for guitar and instrumental groups, and Double Concerto (1990). Kurtág left Hungary in 1993 and settled in Berlin. His recent compositions include the orchestral scores *Stele* (1994) and *Messages* (1996); . . . *pas à pas—nulle part* . . . (1997) for baritone, string trio, and percussion; and *Six moments musicaux* (2005) for string quartet. *See also* MODERNISM.

L

LA BARBARA, JOAN (1947–). American composer, musician, and educator. Joan La Barbara studied voice with Helen Boatwright, Phyllis Curtin, and Marian Szekely-Fresch, and she has taught at several American institutions and the Hochschule der Kunst in Berlin. A virtuoso singer with a command of **extended performance techniques**, La Barbara has premiered works by **Steve Reich**, **Philip Glass**, **Robert Ashley**, **John Cage**, **Morton Feldman**, and her husband **Morton Subotnick**. Her compositions are mostly **electro-acoustic**, such as *Shadow Song* (1979) for voice and multitrack **tape**, *The Solar Wind III* (1984) for amplified voice and orchestra, the **opera** *Events in (the) Elsewhere* (1990), and *Der Wassergeister* (2006) for voice, violin, **sampled** sounds, **computer**, and surround sound. *See also* INSTRUMENT BUILDING; POSTMODERNISM.

LACHENMANN, HELMUT (1935–). German composer, musician, and educator. Helmut Lachenmann studied composition with Johann Nepomuk David and **Luigi Nono** and piano with Jürgen Uhde; he has also taught at several German institutions. Exploring delicate and unusual sonorities through **extended performance techniques**, Lachenmann has used novel methods of playing string instruments in such works as *Pression* (1969) for solo cello and String Quartet No. 2 (1989). The piano lid is fanned to produce waves of sound in *Zwei Gefühle* (1992) for two speakers and chamber ensemble. His other notable music includes the music-theater piece *Das Mädchen mit den Schwefelhölzern* (1996, rev. 1999), the piano scores *Guero* (1970, rev. 1988) and *Serynade* (1998, rev. 2000), and the orchestral works *Fassade* (1973), *Tableau* (1988), and *Schreiben* (2003).

LAM, BUN-CHING (1954–). Chinese composer, musician, and educator. Macao-born Bun-Ching Lam studied piano at the Chinese University of Hong Kong and composition with **Roger Reynolds** and **Pauline Oliveros**. She has performed internationally as pianist and conductor and taught at Cardiff College of the Arts and other institutions. Lam wrote for Chinese instruments in *Impetus* (1987) and combined them with Western ensembles in *Omni Hakkei*

(2000) and *Atlas* (2004, also with Middle Eastern instruments), and with voices in *Walking Walking Keep Walking* (1991), *The Journey* (2002), and her **operas** *The Child God* (1993) and *Wenji* (2001). Lam's music for Western instruments includes *After Spring* (1983) for two pianos; . . . *Like Water* (1991) for violin/viola, piano, and percussion; and the orchestral scores *Lang Tao Sha* (1981, with solo violin) and *Saudades de Macau I* (1989) and *II* (2005). *See also* MULTICULTURALISM.

LANG, DAVID (1957–). American composer and musician. David Lang studied with **Jacob Druckman**, **Roger Reynolds**, **Morton Subotnick**, **Hans Werner Henze**, and Martin Bresnick. He cofounded the music collective Bang on a Can in 1987 with **Julia Wolfe** and **Michael Gordon**, and the three also co-composed the **operas** *The Carbon Copy Building* (1995), *Lost Objects* (2001), and *Shelter* (2005). Lang's **postmodern** works frequently combine **minimalist** and rock techniques. Notable works include *are you experienced?* (1987) for large ensemble; *the passing measures* (1998) for orchestra; the music-theater piece *the difficulty of crossing a field* (2002) for five vocal soloists, small choir, and string quartet; and *the little match girl passion* (2007) for four singers who also play percussion.

LEACH, MARY JANE (1949–). American composer and musician. Mary Jane Leach studied at Columbia University with Mark Zuckerman. Her **pleroma** composition deals with difference, combination, and interference tones. Leach massed like voices in *4BC* (1984) for four bass clarinets and *Bare Bones* (1989) for four trombones/bass trombones. Other works combined soloists with eight **taped** versions of themselves: oboe in *Xanthippe's Rebuke* (1993), countertenor in *Tricky Pan* (1995), and cello in *Bach's Set* (2007). Her music for women's voices includes *Ariadne's Lament* (1993) and *The Great Goddess* (2001). *The Upper Room* (1990) is a **sound installation** for **synthesizer**. Leach has performed *Dido Remembered* (2002) and *Gulf War Syndrome* (2006) for synthesizer and tape. *See also* ELECTROACOUSTIC MUSIC; POSTMODERNISM.

LEBARON, ANNE (1953–). American composer, musician, and educator. Anne LeBaron's composition teachers included Frederic Goossen, **Chou Wen-chung**, **Mario Davidovsky**, **György Ligeti**, and **Mauricio Kagel**. She studied harp privately with Alice Chalifoux. As an improviser, she has developed **extended performance techniques** for the harp and has performed with numerous improvisers, including **Anthony Braxton**, **Muhal Richard Abrams**, **Fred Frith**, **George Lewis**, Lionel Hampton, Derek Bailey, Shelley Hirsch, Davey Williams, LaDonna Smith, and her Anne LeBaron Quintet.

A leading **postmodern** composer, LeBaron has embraced a wide range of media and styles. Her music has readily combined tonal and **atonal** techniques; featured blues, jazz, classical, and world music elements; and employed theatricality. A rich vein of humor can also arise, as in *Concerto for Active Frogs* (1975) for voices, three instruments, and **tape**. Her music for voice with instruments includes the solos *Lamentation/Invocation* (1984), *Dish* (1990), and *Is Money Money* (2000); the choral scores *Light Breaks Where No Sun Shines* (1977) and *Nightmare* (1999); the **operas** *The E&O Line* (1991), *Croak (The Last Frog)* (1996), *Wet* (2005), and *Crescent City* (2010); and music-theater pieces for soprano and chamber musicians such as *Pope Joan* (2000), *Transfiguration* (2003), and *Sucktion* (2008). LeBaron has composed for orchestra (*Strange Attractors*, 1987; Double Concerto for Harp and Chamber Orchestra, 1995; *American Icons*, 1996; *Traces of Mississippi*, 2000), chamber ensembles (*The Sea and the Honeycomb*, 1979; *Noh Reflections*, 1986; *Devil in the Belfry*, 1993), and solo musicians (*After a Dammit to Hell* for bassoon, 1982; *Hsing* for harp, 2002; *Los murmullos* for piano, 2006). *Southern Ephemera* (1993) was scored for a consort of **Harry Partch** instruments.

Among LeBaron's tape music works are *Quadratura Circuli* (1978) and *Eurydice Is Dead* (1983). She has combined tape with harp in *Planxty Bowerbird* (1982) and *I Am an American . . . My Government Will Reward You* (1988), with electric harp and clarinet/bass clarinet in *Bodice Ripper* (1999), with flute in *Sachamama* (1995), and with contrabass in *Inner Voice* (2002). Her **multimedia** *Way of Light* (2006) for trumpet featured video. LeBaron has taught at the University of Pittsburgh, California Institute of the Arts, and other institutions. *See also* ELECTROACOUSTIC MUSIC; FREE IMPROVISATION.

LE CAINE, HUGH (1914–1977). Canadian composer and musician. An engineer and scientist who studied at Queen's University, Hugh Le Caine began building **electronic** instruments in his home studio in the late 1940s, such as the Electronic Sackbut, the first voltage-controlled **synthesizer**. He moved his studio to the National Research Council of Canada (NRC) in 1954 and built more than 20 instruments; he also invented the Multi-track, on which he created **tape music** such as *Dripsody* (1955) and *Invocation* (1957). *Ninety-Nine Generators* (1956) was played on his Touch Sensitive Organ, *Nocturne* (1962) on his Conductive Keyboard, and *Music for Expo* (1967) on his Serial Sound Structure Generator, which he had designed to create **totally serialized** electronic music. Le Caine's *Mobile: The Computer Laughed (Perpetual Motion)* (1970) was for the NRC Computer Music System. *See also* COMPUTER MUSIC; INSTRUMENT BUILDING; MODERNISM.

LEIBOWITZ, RENÉ (1913–1972). Polish-born French composer, musician, and educator. René Leibowitz studied conducting with Pierre Monteux; despite his claims to the contrary, he never studied with **Anton Webern** or **Arnold Schoenberg**. Nevertheless, after World War II, Leibowitz did play an essential role in reigniting European interest in **twelve-tone music**. He conducted Schoenberg's works, taught the method to such students as **Pierre Boulez** and **Hans Werner Henze**, and wrote the books *Schoenberg et son école* (1947), *Qu'est-ce que la musique de douze sons?* (1948), and *Introduction à la musique de douze sons* (1949). He also coined the term *serial*, due to the use of a specific series of pitches arranged in a set, or row, in twelve-tone music. Leibowitz's many scores include nine string quartets (1940–1972) and three **operas** (1953–1971). He also wrote the books *L'évolution de la musique de Bach à Schoenberg* (1952) and *Schoenberg* (1969). *See also* MODERNISM.

LEÓN, TANIA (1943–). Cuban-born American composer, musician, and educator. After receiving her musical education in Havana, Tania León relocated to the United States in 1967. She became a cofounder of the Dance Theater of Harlem and its first music director in 1969, and by the 1970s she was performing internationally as a conductor. She has also taught at numerous institutions, including Brooklyn College and the City University of New York. León's **multicultural** music has combined **atonal** materials with a Caribbean rhythmic sensibility. Among her orchestral scores are *Batá* (1985, rev. 1988), *Carabalí* (1991), *Desde . . .* (2001), and *Ácana* (2008). Her chamber music includes *Elegia a Paul Robeson* (1987) for violin, cello, and piano; *Saóko* (1997) for brass quintet; and the septet *Toque* (2006), as well as **electroacoustic** works such as *Tau* (1995) for electric oboe, electric bass, and electronic keyboards and *Axon* (2002) and *Abanico* (2007), both for violin and interactive **computer**. Other works include *A Row of Buttons* (2002) for female voices, the **opera** *Scourge of Hyacinths* (1999), and the ballet scores *The Beloved* (1972), *Belé* (1981), and *Inura* (2009). *See also* POSTMODERNISM.

LES SIX. *See* GROUPE DES SIX.

LEWIS, GEORGE (1952–). American composer, musician, and educator. George Lewis, also known as George E. Lewis, studied composition with **Muhal Richard Abrams** and trombone with Dean Hay. A **free-jazz** composer and improviser, Lewis has been a member of the Association for the Advancement of Creative Musicians (AACM) since 1971. He has used closed and **open forms**, **extended performance techniques**, and electronics and

computers in his music, working with such composer/musicians as Abrams, **Leroy Jenkins, Roscoe Mitchell, Laurie Anderson, Anthony Braxton, John Zorn, Richard Teitelbaum, Anne LeBaron, Phill Niblock, Frederic Rzewski,** and **Fred Frith.** His **electroacoustic music** includes *The Kim and I* (1979) for trombone and computer; *Voyager,* conceived and programmed in 1986–1988, with an interactive computer creating a virtual orchestra that is responsive to an improviser in real time; and *Virtual Discourse* (1993), blending infrared-controlled virtual percussion with percussion quartet.

Among Lewis's instrumental works are *Endless Shout* (1994) for piano and *Signifying Riffs* (1998) for string quartet and percussion. He has released the recordings *The George Lewis Solo Trombone Record* (1976), *Chicago Slow Dance* (1977), and *Homage to Charles Parker* (1979). His large-ensemble compositions are heard on *The Shadowgraph Series* (2001), and works for voice and instruments are collected on *Changing with the Times* (1993). Lewis has also created **sound installations** such as *Kalimbascope* (1985–1986), with interactive computer graphics. He is the author of *A Power Stronger Than Itself: The AACM and American Experimental Music* (2008) and has taught at Mills College and Columbia University. *See also* FREE IMPROVISATION; POSTMODERNISM.

LIGETI, GYÖRGY (1923–2006). Hungarian-born Austrian composer and educator. György Ligeti studied at the Budapest Academy of Music (1945–1949) and taught there from 1950 to 1956. In Hungary, Ligeti composed in traditional and **neoclassical** idioms, except for the purely static *Visiok* for orchestra. *Visiok* was written just months before the Hungarian Revolution in 1956, after which Ligeti fled the country. At the WDR Electronic Music Studio at Cologne, he created **electronic music** (*Glissandi,* 1957) and **tape music** (*Artikulation,* 1958). His orchestral scores *Apparitions* (1960) and *Atmosphères* (1961) developed a static sound world of **tone-clusters** and complex polyphonic webs that he called micropolyphony. Ligeti also taught at Darmstadt (1959–1972) and other European institutions; his students included **Gérard Grisey, Anne LeBaron,** and **Unsuk Chin.** In 1967, he became an Austrian citizen. His son is composer/percussionist Lukas Ligeti.

Ligeti's music grew increasingly radical with his 1962 works *Volumina* for organ, *Poème symphonique* for 100 metronomes, and the seriocomic *Aventures* and *Nouvelles aventures* for three singers and seven instrumentalists (performed in a scenic version in 1966). With his *Requiem* (1963) for soprano, mezzo-soprano, two mixed choirs, and orchestra, Ligeti moved away from tone-clusters and developed a new idiomatic sound that he pursued in *Lux aeterna* (1966) for 16-part mixed chorus, Cello Concerto (1966), and *Lontano* (1967) for orchestra.

Ligeti's String Quartet No. 2 (1968) included **microtonal** tunings, as did *Volumina* and *Requiem*. *Ramifications* (1968) was scored for two string ensembles tuned a **quarter-tone** apart. His other notable orchestral scores include *Melodien* (1971), Double Concerto for Flute and Oboe (1972), and *San Francisco Polyphony* (1973). He also composed a satiric **opera**, *Le grand macabre* (1974, rev. 1996), which used collage. In the early 1980s, Ligeti's composition left staticism for new **polyrhythmic** complexes with a harmonic approach neither tonal nor **atonal**, as in the Trio for Horn, Violin, and Piano (1982). In his *Piano Etudes, Books 1–3* (1985–2001), he superimposed rhythmic grids of varying densities. Despite failing health, Ligeti pursued these rhythmic complexes in his Piano Concerto (1986), Violin Concerto (1992), and *Hamburgisches Konzert* (1998, rev. 2002) for horn and chamber orchestra. *See also* GRAPHIC NOTATION; MODERNISM.

LOCKWOOD, ANNEA (1939–). New Zealand–born American composer and educator. Annea Lockwood studied at the Royal College of Music in London and at Darmstadt; she settled in the United States in 1973 and taught at Hunter College and Vassar College. Lockwood has explored unusual timbres in such works as *The Glass Concert* (1967) for amplified glass, *Amazonia Dreaming* (1987) for snare drum and voice, and the **multicultural** scores *The Angle of Repose* (1991) for baritone, alto flute, and khaeen and *Thousand Year Dreaming* (1990), also a **multimedia** piece, for four woodwinds, two brass, four didjeridus, two conch-shell trumpets, percussion, voice, and slide projections. Her **tape music** includes *Tiger Balm* (1970) and *Thirst* (2008). Among her **sound installations** are *A Sound Map of the Hudson River* (1982) and *A Sound Map of the Danube* (2005). *See also* POSTMODERNISM.

LORIOD, YVONNE (1924–2010). French musician and educator. Yvonne Loriod studied piano with Lazare Lévy at the Paris Conservatoire and was in the first class taught by **Olivier Messiaen** after his repatriation to France in 1941. Loriod and Messiaen premiered his *Visions de l'Amen* for two pianos in 1943, and she went on to premiere all his piano works and toured internationally with his music. They were married in 1961. Loriod also performed scores by other **modern** and contemporary composers, recorded works by **Manuel de Falla**, **Pierre Boulez**, and **Jean Barraqué**, and taught at the Badische Musikhochschule in Karlsruhe.

Yvonne's sister Jeanne Loriod (1928–2001) was a master of the **ondes martenot**, having studied with its maker, Maurice Martenot. Jeanne recorded works by Messiaen, **Darius Milhaud**, **André Jolivet**, and **Tristan Murail** and was professor of ondes martenot at the Paris Conservatoire. *See also* MODERNISM.

LOURIÉ, ARTHUR (1892–1966). Russian composer and musician. Arthur Sergeyevich Lourié studied piano and composition at the St. Petersburg Conservatory (1909–1913). Inspired by **futurism**, **Claude Debussy**, and **Alexander Scriabin**, Lourié's **modernist** piano music anticipated **twelve-tone** methodology in *Synthèses* (1914). *Masques* (1913) and *Formes en l'air* (1915) employed notational innovations. Lourié left Russia in 1922 and settled in Paris. He brought a modal approach to **neoclassicism** in such works as Symphony No. 1 (1930) and the **opera**-ballet *Le festin pendant la peste* (1935). Fleeing the Nazi occupation, in 1941 Lourié relocated to the United States, where he wrote the opera *The Blackamoor of Peter the Great* (1948–1961). He is also the author of *Sergei Koussevitzky and His Epoch* (1931) and *Profanation et sanctification du temps—Journal musical: Saint-Pétersbourg, Paris, New York, 1910–1960* (1966). *See also* ATONALITY.

LUCIER, ALVIN (1931–). American composer, musician, and educator. Alvin Lucier studied at Yale University, Tanglewood, and Brandeis University; his teachers include **Aaron Copland**, **Lukas Foss**, and **Arthur Berger**. His early music, such as *Arioso and Allegro* (1955) for piano, was **neoclassical**, but his mature works have been **minimalist** and experimental. *Action Music for Piano* (1962) notated the player's physical gestures. *Music for Solo Performer* (1965) used amplified brain waves to resonate percussion instruments. In 1966, Lucier cofounded the **Sonic Arts Union**, a **multimedia electronic-music** group, with **Robert Ashley**, **Gordon Mumma**, and **David Behrman**.

Lucier's *Vespers* (1967) explored the acoustic character of the performance space with echo-location devices. In *I Am Sitting in a Room* (1970) for voice and **tape**, a speech is simultaneously played back and recorded over and over, with the space acting as a filter for speech that gradually becomes pure sound. *Chambers* (1968) sounded the acoustic properties of thimbles, seashells, and other portable resonant environments. *Music for Gamelan Instruments, Microphones, Amplifiers, and Loudspeakers* (1994) treated the bonang instruments as resonating environments. In *The Queen of the South* (1972), Lucier used sound to generate visual imagery in strewn media such as sugar or iron filings. His other multimedia works include *Intervals* (1983) for chorus and sound-sensitive lights, *Self-Portrait* (1989) for flute and anemometer, and *Heavier Than Air* (1999) for any number of players with carbon dioxide–filled balloons. *Music on a Long Thin Wire* (1977) was a **sound installation** with a resounding monochord; among his later installations are *Sferics* (1981) and *Music for Piano with Half-Closed Lid* (1993).

Beating effects are created in *Crossings* (1982) for small orchestra and slow-sweep pure-wave oscillator, with musicians playing against the oscillator's changing frequency. Lucier also explored interference phenomena in other **electroacoustic** pieces combining musicians and oscillators, such as *A Tribute to James Tenney* (1986), *Sol 432* (1993), and *Ever Present* (2002). *Silver Streetcar for the Orchestra* (1988) revealed the dense acoustic characteristics of an amplified triangle. His recent works include *Sierpinski Lines* (1994), composed for saxophonist **Anthony Braxton** and 12 strings; *Skin, Meat, Bone* (1994), a collaborative theater work with Robert Wilson; *Diamonds* (1999) for one, two, or three orchestras; and *Fan* (2003) for four kotos. Lucier taught at Wesleyan University and is the coauthor of *Chambers* (1980). *See also* ATONALITY; POSTMODERNISM.

LUENING, OTTO (1900–1996). American composer, musician, and educator. In the late 1910s, Otto Luening studied composition, flute, and conducting at the Staatliche Hochschule für Musik in Munich and the Zurich Conservatory; he also studied privately with **Ferruccio Busoni**. Luening later taught at Columbia University, among other institutions, and was a cofounder of the Columbia-Princeton Electronic Music Center; his students included **Chou Wen-chung, Charles Wuorinen, Charles Dodge, Harvey Sollberger, Philip Corner, Wendy Carlos, John Corigliano,** and **Mario Davidovsky**. Luening showed a **modernist** bent with the **polytonal** and **atonal** passages in his Sextet (1918) and String Quartet No. 1 (1919). After returning to the United States in 1920, he composed his String Quartets Nos. 2 (1922) and 3 (1928), *Two Symphonic Interludes* (1935) for orchestra, and the **opera** *Evangeline* (1931, rev. 1948). Using his own **open-form** approach in the last movement of the Trio for Flute, Violin, and Soprano (1923), he notated only pitches and left phrasing, rhythmic, and dynamic decisions to the musicians.

Drawn to the possibilities of **tape music**, Luening composed the 1952 pieces *Fantasy in Space, Low Speed,* and *Invention in Twelve Tones,* all using the flute as their sound source. In collaboration with **Vladimir Ussachevsky**, he created *Incantation for Tape Recording* (1953). Their *Rhapsodic Variations* (1954) was the first work to combine orchestra and tape; they also composed *A Poem in Cycles and Bells for Tape Recorder and Orchestra* (1954) and *Concerted Piece for Tape Recorder and Orchestra* (1960). Luening's solo music united electronically synthesized sounds with violin in *Gargoyles* (1960) and with orchestra in *Synthesis* (1962). His later instrumental works include *Lyric Scene* (1958) for flute and string orchestra, *Trio for Three Flutists* (1966), and the cantata *No Jerusalem but This* (1982). He is the author of *Modern Music* (1943) and *The Odyssey of an American Composer* (1980). *See also* ELECTROACOUSTIC MUSIC.

LUTOSLAWSKI, WITOLD (1913–1994). Polish composer, musician, and educator. A pianist and violinist, Witold Lutoslawski studied at the Warsaw Conservatory. His *Symphonic Variations* (1938) for orchestra won acclaim, but Symphony No. 1 (1947), also **neoclassical**, was declared **formalist** and banned in Soviet-dominated Poland. Lutoslawski turned to Polish folk themes in his Concerto for Orchestra (1954). He composed **twelve-tone music** with *Five Songs* (1957) for female voice and piano or chamber orchestra. *Musique funèbre* (1958) for string orchestra was neither tonal nor **serial**. Lutoslawski first used **aleatoric** techniques in *Jeux venitiens* (1961) for chamber orchestra and featured them in such orchestral works as *Novelette* (1979) and Symphony No. 3 (1983). Notable later works include Piano Concerto (1988), *Interludium* (1990) for orchestra, and Symphony No. 4 (1992). Lutoslawski also taught at numerous institutions and performed internationally as a conductor. *See also* ATONALITY; MODERNISM.

MACHT, ROBERT (1958–). American composer and musician. Robert Macht studied composition with **Henry Brant** and acoustics with Gunnar Schonbeck at Bennington College; he also composed for the new instruments designed and built by Schonbeck. Macht studied gamelan in Java with Pak Walika and founded the Robert Macht Gamelan Ensemble. His **multicultural** compositions include *Kreasi Baru* (1995) for gamelan and orchestra; *Suite for Javanese Gamelan and Synthesizer* (1998); *Vishnu* (1999) for coloratura soprano, gamelan percussion, and non-Western instruments; and *Waterwalk: Surface and Depth* (2000), a music-theater work for soprano and gamelan orchestra. *Waniugo* (1999) for chamber orchestra melded Carl Philipp Emanuel Bach's harmonies with African pop rhythms. *See also* INSTRUMENT BUILDING; POSTMODERNISM.

MACIUNAS, GEORGE. *See* FLUXUS.

MacLISE, ANGUS (1938–1979). American composer and musician. An innovative **multicultural** hand-drummer, Angus MacLise performed with **La Monte Young** on sopranino saxophone in 1963 and 1964. Their repetitive modal improvisations, with drones played by **Tony Conrad, Marian Zazeela**, and John Cale, evolved into Young's landmark **minimalist** work *The Tortoise, His Dreams and Journeys* (1964). MacLise performed with Young's Theater of Eternal Music throughout the 1960s. He also scored Ron Rice's **film** *Chumlum* (1964), playing cembalom, and was a cofounder of the rock band the Velvet Underground. MacLise studied percussion traditions in the Middle East and South Asia in 1964–1965 and 1971–1976; he began performing his *Swayambhu Opera* in Nepal in 1977. Two years later, he died there at age 41.

MADERNA, BRUNO (1920–1973). Italian-born German composer, musician, and educator. Bruno Maderna studied at the Rome Conservatory and Venice Conservatory. He wrote **serial** works—such as his 1952 scores *Improvvisazione No. 1* for orchestra and *Musica su due dimensioni* for flute, cymbal, and **tape**—and **totally serialized** music, including *Serenata No. 2* (1954, rev. 1956) for 11 instruments and String Quartet (1955). Maderna collaborated with **Luciano Berio** on *Ritratto di città* (1954) for tape, and in 1955 they founded the Studio di Fonologia Musicale where Maderna created *Notturno* (1956) and *Continuo* (1957). He explored **tone-clusters** and **string-piano** techniques in *Honeyrêves* (1961) for flute and piano and **graphic notation** in Oboe Concerto No. 1 (1962).

Maderna taught at numerous European institutions, including Darmstadt, where he relocated in 1963, becoming a German citizen. An internationally respected conductor, he led premieres of works by himself, **Karlheinz Stockhausen, Earle Brown, Iannis Xenakis, Jacob Druckman**, and many others. Maderna moved away from serialism in composing the theatrical pieces of *Hyperion* (1964–1973), an unfinished music drama, and the **aleatoric** *Quadrivium* (1969) for percussion quartet and four orchestral groups. His notable late works include *Juilliard Serenade* (1971) for chamber orchestra and tape and the **opera** *Satyricon* (1973). Maderna died of lung cancer in Darmstadt at age 53. *See also* ATONALITY; MODERNISM; TWELVE-TONE MUSIC.

MAGER, JÖRG (1880–1939). German musician. Interested in both **microtonality** and **electronic music**, Jörg Mager invented the Electrophon in the early 1920s, which used the heterodyning method to generate sound. This electronic instrument offered a continuous glissando, controlled by a handle. It was modified by Mager in 1923 as the Kurbelsphärophon, with two handles that freed it from the glissando, along with timbre and volume controls. Introduced in 1926, the Kurbelsphärophon was also used by Georgi Mikhailovich Rimsky-Korsakov. In 1928, Mager completed his Klatvitursphärophon, or Sphaerophon, a monophonic keyboard instrument tuned in **quarter-tones**, which was featured in a 1931 production of Richard Wagner's *Parsifal* at Bayreuth. Mager redesigned the Sphärophon as the polyphonic Partituophon in 1935 and completed his Kaleidophon shortly before his death. None of his instruments survived World War II. *See also* INSTRUMENT BUILDING; MODERNISM.

MAHLER, GUSTAV (1860–1911). Bohemian-born Austrian composer and musician. Gustav Mahler entered the Vienna Conservatory in 1875, where Anton Bruckner was one of his teachers. Mahler began conducting in Austria in 1880 and soon led orchestras in Prague, Leipzig, and Budapest. Inspired by Bruckner and Richard Wagner, Mahler composed his first important scores in these years: *Das klagende Lied* (1880) for soprano, mezzo-soprano, tenor, mixed chorus, and orchestra; *Lieder eines fahrenden Gesellen* (1884) for voice and piano (orch. 1893); and Symphony No. 1 (1888). All are distinguished by Mahler's gift for song and his expressive and imaginative orchestration, which gave resonance to his depictions of nature and his recurring themes of sorrow, loss, and death.

Mahler's music became more grandiose and unconventional during his years as music director of the Hamburg Opera (1891–1897). The lengthy, five-movement Symphony No. 2, "Resurrection" (1894), called for soprano, mezzo-soprano, mixed chorus, large orchestra, and organ, as well as the **spatial** treatment of a distant ensemble of trumpets and percussion. The lengthier six-movement Symphony No. 3 (1896) included mezzo-soprano, boys' chorus, and women's chorus. Mahler won international renown as artistic director of the Vienna Opera (1897–1907) and went on to conduct the New York Philharmonic (1907–1910). Performances of his music, however, were infrequent, even though his composition became more concise and less programmatic with Symphony No. 4 (1901), which included a soprano, and Symphony No. 5 (1903). A greater use of **dissonance** characterizes Symphonies Nos. 6 (1904) and 7 (1905)—longer and more macabre scores that feature an expanded and innovative use of percussion.

The joyous Symphony No. 8 (1906), which set the hymn "Veni, Creator Spiritus" and the final scene of Johann Wolfgang von Goethe's *Faust*, was premiered by Mahler with a complement of 858 singers (eight soloists, two mixed choruses, boy's chorus) and 171 instrumentalists (large orchestra and organ). Mortality became the focus of his last years with two classic scores, *Das Lied von der Erde* (1909) for mezzo-soprano or baritone, tenor, and orchestra, and Symphony No. 9 (1910). Mahler completed the sketch of his Symphony No. 10, but died in Vienna of bacterial endocarditis at age 50 before finishing the orchestration. Approaching **expressionism** in its anguished dissonance and amorphous tonality, the entire work went unheard until Deryck Cooke's performing version of the sketch was premiered in 1964. Mahler's music deeply impacted his younger Viennese admirers **Arnold Schoenberg**, **Anton Webern**, and **Alban Berg** and opened doors for such 20th-century composers as **Aaron Copland, Dmitry Shostakovich,** and **Benjamin Britten**. *See also* ATONALITY; MODERNISM.

MAMLOK, URSULA (1923–). German-born American composer, musician, and educator. Ursula Mamlok studied piano and composition with Gustav Ernest. Her family fled Nazi Germany in 1939 and settled in the United States the following year; she lived there until 2006, when she returned to her native Berlin. In America, her teachers included **Roger Sessions, Stefan Wolpe, Ernst Krenek,** and **Ralph Shapey,** and she taught at New York University, Temple University, and the Manhattan School of Music. Mamlok's personal approach to the **twelve-tone** method informs such notable works as

String Quartets Nos. 1 (1962) and 2 (1998); *Grasshoppers* (1957) for piano or orchestra; *Cantata Based on the First Psalm* (1958) for mixed chorus and piano or organ; Sextet (1977); *Panta Rhei (Time in Flux)* (1981) for violin, cello, and piano; and Concerto for Oboe and Chamber Orchestra (2003). *See also* ATONALITY; MODERNISM.

MARCUS, BUNITA (1952–). American composer and musician. Bunita Marcus studied composition with **Morton Feldman**. As a conductor and pianist, she has played her own music and Feldman's. Her *Two Pianos and Violin* (1981) gave each instrument its own time unit. *Music for Japan* (1983) for flute, clarinet, harp, piano, and percussion avoided repetition, while the sextet *Adam and Eve* (1987) used repetition effectively, as did the string quartet *The Rugmaker* (1986), with minor alterations to repeated motives after the method of Feldman. *Julia* (1989) for piano was based on a 1968 **Beatles** song. Marcus has also composed **multimedia** works (*Perhaps a Woman Would Know*, 1976), theatrical pieces (*Women's Work*, 1990), and **tape music** (*Tape Piece*, 1975; *Ice Falling*, 1990). Her 2007 series of music for two pianos includes *Counter Points* and *Expedition. See also* MINIMALISM; POSTMODERNISM.

MARTIN, FRANK (1890–1974). Swiss composer, musician, and educator. Frank Martin studied at the University of Geneva and later taught at the Geneva Conservatory of Music and the Cologne Conservatory; he also performed and recorded his music as pianist and conductor. Martin's Piano Concerto No. 1 (1934), String Trio (1936), and Symphony (1937) were **twelve-tone** works; he started melding tonal and twelve-tone methods with such scores as *Le vin herbé* (1941) for 12 solo voices, seven strings, and piano and *Petite symphonie concertante* (1945) for harp, harpsichord, piano, and two string orchestras. Martin's later works include his Violin Concerto (1951); the **opera** *Der Sturm* (1955); the oratorios *Golgotha* (1948) and *Mystère de la Nativité* (1960); String Quartet (1967); *Maria-Triptychon* (1968) for soprano, violin, and orchestra; and *Ballade* (1972) for viola and wind orchestra. *See also* ATONALITY; MODERNISM.

MARTINU, BOHUSLAV (1890–1959). Bohemian-born American composer, musician, and educator. Bohuslav Martinu studied at the Prague Conservatory and was a violinist with the Czech Philharmonic. He drew upon folk materials in such early works as the cantata *Czech Rhapsody* (1918) and in 1923 relocated to France, where he studied with **Albert Roussel**. Martinu used jazz elements in the ballet score *La revue de cuisine* (1927) and *Jazz Suite* (1928) for small orchestra and **neoclassical** techniques in *Sinfonia* *concertante* for two orchestras (1932) and Concerto Grosso for chamber orchestra (1937). He immigrated to the United States in 1940 and became a citizen in 1952. Martinu taught at Tanglewood and other institutions; his students include **Chou Wen-chung** and **Alan Hovhaness**. Notable later works by Martinu include *Memorial to Lidice* (1943) for orchestra; *Fantasia* (1944) for **theremin**, oboe, string quartet, and piano; and the oratorio *The Epic of Gilgamesh* (1955). A prolific composer, he also produced seven string quartets (1918–1947), five piano concertos (1925–1958), six symphonies (1942–1953), and 13 **operas** (1927–1959). *See also* MODERNISM.

MARTIRANO, SALVATORE (1927–1995). American composer, musician, and educator. Salvatore Martirano studied at Oberlin College and the Eastman School of Music, and with **Luigi Dallapiccola** in Italy, and he taught at the University of Illinois at Urbana-Champaign (1963–1995). Martirano combined jazz and **serialism** in *O, O, O, O, That Shakespeherian Rag* (1958) for mixed chorus and chamber ensemble and *Ballad* (1966) for voice and septet. He composed the **tape** works *Buffet* (1965) and *Shoptalk* (1974) and created a **multimedia** classic with the theatrical *L's G.A.* (1968). Martirano also built the **electronic** composing/performing systems SAL-MAR Construction, on which he improvised, and yahaSALmaMAC, which he used with violin in *Sampler* (1985) and with amplified flute in *Phleu* (1990). *See also* COMPUTER MUSIC; ELECTROACOUSTIC MUSIC; POSTMODERNISM.

MAW, NICHOLAS (1935–2009). English composer and educator. Nicholas Maw studied with Sir Lennox Berkeley at London's Royal Academy of Music and with **Nadia Boulanger** in France; he later taught at Yale University, Cambridge University, and other institutions. Maw blended tonal and **atonal** techniques in *Essay* (1961) for organ and the theatrical *Scenes and Arias* for three female voices and orchestra (1962). He went on to compose such **neoromantic** works as *Life Studies* for strings (1976), String Quartet No. 2 (1982), *Odyssey* for orchestra (1987), Violin Concerto (1993), and the **operas** *One Man Show* (1964), *The Rising of the Moon* (1970), and *Sophie's Choice* (2002).

MAXFIELD, RICHARD (1927–1969). American composer and educator. Richard Maxfield studied in the United States with **Roger Sessions**, **Milton Babbitt**, and **Aaron Copland**, and in Europe with **Ernst Krenek**, **Luigi Dallapiccola**, and **Bruno Maderna**. Although his early instrumental music had been mostly **serial**, by the late 1950s Maxfield was attracted to ideas of **indeterminate** composition, which he encountered through **Christian Wolff**,

David Tudor, and **John Cage**; he was also drawn to **electronic music**. In 1958, Maxfield studied with Cage at the New School for Social Research, and the following year he began teaching a course there in making music from electronically generated sound—quite likely the first such pedagogue in America.

One of the first American composers to build his own equipment for the electrical synthesis of sound, Maxfield produced such landmark compositions as *Sine Music (A Swarm of Butterflies Encountered over the Ocean)* (1959), *Trinity Piece* (1960), *Pastoral Symphony* (1960), and *Night Music* (1961). A **minimalist** sensibility shaped the static sounds in his electronic music, and Maxfield was also involved then with the **Fluxus** composers and their performances, which included his *Concert Suite from the Ballet "Dromenon"* (1961). Equally pioneering in **tape music**, he created an array of notable works, among them *Amazing Grace* (1960), *Cough Music* (1961), *Radio Music* (1961), *Steam IV* (1961), and *Bacchanale* (1963). His tape music typically combined deliberate methods of recording and processing sound with random selections in editing the results, and he often kept these works in fluid states, playing different versions in concerts.

Maxfield broke new ground in **electroacoustic music** with *Wind for Terry Jennings* (1960), *Piano Concert for David Tudor* (1961), and *Perspectives for La Monte Young* (1962): He taped each of these composer/musicians performing and then electronically altered the tapes to create new music to accompany them in live performance. Maxfield created similar pieces for ensembles, such as *Toy Symphony* (1962). He left New York in 1966, taught at San Francisco State College until 1967, and relocated to Los Angeles in 1968. The following year, Maxfield took his life there at age 42. *See also* POSTMODERNISM.

MAYUZUMI, TOSHIRO (1929–1997). Japanese composer. Toshiro Mayuzumi was an avant-garde composer in the 1950s, with such works as *Tone Pleromas 55* (1955) for five saxophones, piano, and musical saw. A pioneer in **electronic music**, in 1955 he created Japan's first **tape music**, *X, Y, Z*, and first electrically synthesized music, *Shusaku I*. Mayuzumi's interest in Buddhism and the Japanese musical tradition led to a more conservative music, starting with *Nirvana Symphony* (1958); other Buddhist-themed works include *Mandala Symphony* (1960), *Samsara* (1962) for orchestra, and the cantata *Geka (Pratidesana)* (1963). The ballet score *Bugaku* (1962) had a Western orchestra re-create the sound of the eponymous Japanese court dance; *Showa Tenpyo-raku* (1970) was scored for *gagaku* ensemble. Mayuzumi composed music for the ballets *Kabuki* (1986) and *M* (1993) and two **operas**: the Yukio Mishima adaptation *Kinkakuji* (1976), which uses **serial**

procedures, and *Kojiki* (1996), based on Japanese mythology. Mayuzumi also scored more than 100 **films**, including Kenji Mizoguchi's *Street of Shame* (1956), Mikio Naruse's *When a Woman Ascends the Stairs* (1960), Yasujiro Ozu's *The End of Summer* (1961), and John Huston's *The Bible* (1966) and *Reflections in a Golden Eye* (1967). *See also* MODERNISM; PLEROMA; TWELVE-TONE MUSIC.

McPHEE, COLIN (1901–1964). Canadian composer, musician, educator, and critic. Colin McPhee studied piano and composition at the Peabody Conservatory and in Paris; he was also a private student of **Edgard Varèse**. McPhee used **polytonal** and **polyrhythmic** devices in the **neoclassical** *Concerto for Piano, with Wind Octette Acc.* (1928). He lived in Bali (1933–1938) and studied gamelan music, which characterized his classic **multicultural** score *Tabu-Tabuhan* (1936) for two pianos and orchestra. He also wrote the two-piano transcription *Balinese Ceremonial Music* (1938), which he recorded with **Benjamin Britten** in 1941, and used Balinese elements in his Symphony No. 2 (1957). His other notable works include *Four Iroquois Dances* (1944) for orchestra and Concerto for Wind Orchestra (1960). The author of *A House in Bali* (1947) and *Music in Bali* (1966), McPhee also wrote criticism for *Modern Music* (1939–1945) and taught at UCLA (1960–1964).

MENOTTI, GIAN CARLO (1911–2007). Italian composer, musician, and educator. Gian Carlo Menotti studied with Rosario Scalero at the Curtis Institute of Music, where he later taught. Although he also wrote instrumental scores, Menotti is best known as a prolific and popular composer of **opera** in the tradition of Giacomo Puccini, writing his own librettos and frequently staging the productions; his operas include *The Medium* (1946), *The Consul* (1950), *Amahl and the Night Visitors* (1951), and *The Saint of Bleecker Street* (1954). Menotti founded the Two Worlds music festival in Spoleto, Italy, and was its director (1958–1999); he also led Spoleto Festival USA (1977–1993).

MESSIAEN, OLIVIER (1908–1992). French composer, musician, and educator. A unique and innovative composer who was also greatly influential as a teacher, Olivier Eugène Prosper Charles Messiaen was born in Avignon. His parents nurtured their son's talent, and by age eight Messiaen had taught himself to play piano and was composing. He also discovered and embraced Catholicism around that age, and his music and his faith soon united and defined each other. **Claude Debussy**'s *Pelléas et Mélisande* profoundly impressed him at age 10, and Messiaen entered the Paris Conservatoire the next year; his teachers included Marcel Dupré and Paul Dukas. He excelled there in all fields and at age 22 became principal organist at La Sainte Trinité in Paris.

Messiaen took an individual approach to tempo and modal harmony in his early works *Le banquet céleste* (1928) for organ, *Préludes* (1929) for piano, *Les offrandes oubliées* (1930) for orchestra, and *Trois mélodies* (1930) for soprano and piano. His tendency toward a static nondevelopmental music, inspired by **impressionism**, was further encouraged by his first encounter with the Balinese gamelan in 1931 and his studies of ancient Greek and Hindu rhythms. These different streams merged with Messiaen's enthusiasm for Gregorian plainchant and church modes in his first major organ scores— *L'ascension* (1934, also for orchestra), *La Nativité du Seigneur* (1935), and *Les corps glorieux* (1939)—as well as in his songs for soprano and piano *Poèmes pour mi* (1936) and *Chants de terre et de ciel* (1938) (both using his own texts, as in all his later vocal music). Attracted to the electronic **ondes martenot**, he composed *Fête des belles eaux* (1937) for six of them, and the **microtonal** solo *Deux monodies en quarts de ton* (1938).

Messiaen began studying birdsong in the 1930s, and the sound of birds characterized his later works. He experienced visual color associations when hearing or reading music, and the evocation of color also informed his composition. Just when his musical sensibility was crystallizing, Messiaen was summoned into the French army, and in June 1940 he was captured by the Nazis. While confined in a POW camp in Germany, he composed a masterpiece: *Quatuor pour la fin du Temps* (1941) for clarinet, violin, cello, and piano. Messiaen also premiered it there in 1941, playing with three other prisoners for an audience of their fellow prisoners and their German captors. The next month, he was repatriated to France and resumed his position as organist at La Sainte Trinité, which he held until his death. Messiaen also taught at the Paris Conservatoire (1941–1978), where his students included **Pierre Boulez, Karlheinz Stockhausen, Betsy Jolas, Iannis Xenakis, György Kurtág, Philip Corner, Alexander Goehr, William Bolcom, Tristan Murail, Luc Ferrari, Gérard Grisey, Jean Barraqué, Pierre Henry,** and **Horatiu Radulescu.**

With the lengthy *Quatuor pour la fin du Temps*, Messiaen pulled together the diverse qualities of his music, and the scale of his composition grew in a series of classic works over the 1940s. He premiered *Visions de l'Amen* (1943) for two pianos with his student **Yvonne Loriod,** who would premiere all Messiaen's subsequent piano music and in 1961 would become his wife. To Loriod, Messiaen entrusted the two-hour-plus *Vingt regards sur l'Enfant-Jésus* (1944) for piano. She was also featured in *Trois petites liturgies de la Présence Divine* (1944) for female voices, piano, ondes martenot, percussion, and strings and *Turangalîla-symphonie* (1948) for piano, ondes martenot, and orchestra.

By the end of the decade, Messiaen was extending the techniques of **serial** organization from pitch to rhythm, timbre, and dynamics in his influential

Quatre études de rythme (1950) for piano; he also composed the **musique concrète** piece *Timbres-durées* (1952). More fundamental to his music of the 1950s, however, was birdsong. Along with the massive *Catalogue d'oiseaux* (1958) for piano, birdsong also shaped a series of shorter scores for piano and chamber orchestra: *Réveil des oiseaux* (1953), *Oiseaux exotiques* (1956), *Sept haïki* (1962), and *Couleurs de la cité céleste* (1963). Messiaen's other notable scores of the 1960s include *Chronochromie* (1960) for orchestra; *Et exspecto resurrectionem mortuorum* (1964) for winds, brass, and metallic percussion; and *Méditations sur le mystère de la Sainte Trinité* (1969) for organ.

The pace of Messiaen's composition slowed in the late 1960s. *La Transfiguration de Notre-Seigneur Jésus-Christ* for mixed chorus, seven solo instruments, and orchestra was composed from 1965 to 1969; *Des canyons aux étoiles . . .* for piano and chamber orchestra, from 1971 to 1974; and the epic **opera** *Saint François d'Assise*, from 1975 to 1983. After the vast *Livre du Saint Sacrament* (1984) for organ, Messiaen wrote shorter scores: *Petites esquisses d'oiseaux* (1985) for piano; *Un vitrail et des oiseaux* (1986) for piano and orchestra; *La ville d'en-haut* (1987) for 31 winds, piano, and percussion; *Un sourire* (1989) for orchestra; and *Pièce pour piano et quatuor à cordes* (1991). From 1988 to 1992, he also composed *Éclairs sur l'au-delà* for orchestra, the last work Messiaen finished before his death in a Paris hospital at age 83. Loriod and George Benjamin completed the orchestration of his *Concert à quatre* (1994) for flute, oboe, cello, piano, and orchestra. *See also* ELECTRONIC MUSIC; QUARTER-TONE MUSIC; TONE-CLUSTER.

METRIC MODULATION. Seeking a more smooth and efficient method of employing **polyrhythms**, **Elliott Carter** began modulating tempi in a step-by-step manner with his Sonata for Cello and Piano (1948), much as had been done with the modulation of key signatures. Employing metric modulation, Carter could compose with different tempi simultaneously, at constant speeds as well as accelerating and decelerating, as in his Concerto for Orchestra (1969). Other composers who have used metric modulation include **George Perle** (Wind Quintet No. 3, 1967), **Steve Reich** (*Vermont Counterpoint*, 1982), **Gunther Schuller** (*Diptych*, 1964), and **John Adams** (Violin Concerto, 1993).

MEV. Musica Elettronica Viva, better known as MEV, was founded in Rome in 1966 by Allan Bryant, Alvin Curran, Jon Phetteplace, Carol Plantamura, **Frederic Rzewski**, **Richard Teitelbaum**, and Ivan Vandor. Dedicated to playing composed and improvised **electronic music**, the group used everything from **synthesizers** and photocell devices to contact microphones and homemade circuitry. MEV has performed internationally, with Curran,

Rzewski, and Teitelbaum as the core members. Recordings include *The Sound Pool* (1969), *Leave the City* (1970), and *MEV 40* (2008). *See also* COMPUTER MUSIC; ELECTROACOUSTIC MUSIC; FREE IMPROVISATION; POSTMODERNISM.

MICROTONALITY. *Microtonality* refers to the use of intervals smaller than the semitone of equal temperament. **Ferruccio Busoni** proposed sixth-tones in *Sketch of a New Esthetic of Music* (1907), but a more common approach has been **quarter-tones**. Although its use in 19th-century Western composition was rare, by the late 1890s this **alternate tuning system** was being seriously investigated by **John Foulds** in England and **Julián Carrillo** in Mexico. The 1910s and 1920s heard their early microtonal works and those of **Alois Hába, Hans Barth,** and **Ivan Wyschnegradsky.** Georgi Mikhailovich Rimsky-Korsakov founded the Society for Quarter-Tone Music in Petrograd in 1923 and conducted concerts of microtonal music from 1925 to 1932, playing works by himself, Hába, and others. The desire to hear and perform microtonal tunings also led many of these composers to design and/ or build new instruments. In 1928, German **electronic-music** pioneer **Jörg Mager** created his Sphaerophon, a monophonic keyboard instrument, to play quarter-tones. That same year, French musician Maurice Martenot introduced his monophonic electronic instrument, the **ondes martenot,** in a performance that included quarter- and eighth-tones. *See also* INSTRUMENT BUILDING; REINHARD, JOHNNY.

MIKHASHOFF, YVAR (1941–1993). American composer, musician, and educator. Yvar Mikhashoff studied piano and composition at the University of Houston and the University of Texas at Austin; he also studied with **Nadia Boulanger** and taught at the State University of New York at Buffalo. A pianist who specialized in contemporary music, Mikhashoff premiered works written for him by such composers as **John Cage, Bernadette Speach, Lukas Foss, Christian Wolff,** and **"Blue" Gene Tyranny.** He also made piano and instrumental arrangements of works by **Conlon Nancarrow** and others. His compositions include Viola Concerto (1968, rev. 1976), *Pipes of Colchis* (1973) for clarinet and piano, the quintet *Twilight Dances* (1986), and *Elemental Figures* (1987–1990) for piano. Mikhashoff died in Buffalo at age 52 of complications from AIDS.

MILHAUD, DARIUS (1892–1974). French composer, musician, and educator. Darius Milhaud entered the Paris Conservatoire at age 17, where his teachers included Paul Dukas and Charles-Marie Widor; he also studied privately with Vincent d'Indy. He independently discovered the music of **Claude Debussy**, **Béla Bartók**, **Erik Satie**, **Arnold Schoenberg**, and **Igor Stravinsky**. Milhaud's early **polytonal** music could be highly **dissonant**, as in *Agamemnon* (1913), *Les choéphores* (1915), which featured extended passages for voices and percussion, and *Les euménides* (1922)—three **opera**-oratorios based on the *Oresteia* of Aeschylus, with librettos by poet Paul Claudel. In 1916, Claudel was appointed minister to Brazil, and Milhaud accompanied him as secretary in the French legation at Rio de Janeiro. This exposure to Brazilian music in 1917 and 1918 brought greater rhythmic invention to Milhaud's music, reflected in *Le boeuf sur la toit* (1919) for chamber orchestra and *Saudades do Brasil* (1921) for piano or orchestra.

In the early 1920s, Milhaud was known with other French composers of his generation as the **Groupe des Six**, but his was an individual voice. The **polyrhythmic** dance score *L'homme et son désir* (1918) for four voices and chamber orchestra anticipated **spatial music** by subdividing and relocating its players into six groups. American jazz informs *La création du monde* (1923) for chamber orchestra. Other important early works include six chamber symphonies (1917–1923), *Trois rag-caprices* (1922) for chamber orchestra, and *Cinq études* (1921) and *Le carnaval d'Aix* (1926), both for piano and orchestra. His noteworthy later music includes Concerto for Percussion and Small Orchestra (1930), Suite (1932) for **ondes martenot** and piano, *Scaramouche* for two pianos (1937), and the **neoclassical** *Fantaisie pastorale* (1939) for piano and orchestra. *Étude Poétique* (1954) for mezzo-soprano, two narrators, and orchestra included his **musique concrète** work *La rivière endormie*. Many of Milhaud's vocal pieces explored his Jewish faith; these include *Poèmes juifs* (1916), *Six chants populaires hébraïques* (1925), *Trois psaumes de David* (1954), *Cantata from Job* (1965), and *Ani maamin* (1972). Among his **film** scores are two 1933 classics: Luis Buñuel's *Land without Bread* and Jean Renoir's *Madame Bovary*.

Milhaud produced well over 400 scores by the time of his death in Geneva at age 81. His music includes 12 symphonies (1939–1962); 18 string quartets (1912–1950); five piano concertos (1933–1955); the **operas** *Les malheurs d'Orphée* (1924), *Christopher Colomb* (1928), *Maximilien* (1930), *Bolivar* (1943), *David* (1953), and *La mère coupable* (1965); and the opera-oratorio *Saint-Louis, Roi de France* (1972). A cellist and pianist, Milhaud was also a frequent conductor of his own music. He taught in France and the United States; among his pupils were **Iannis Xenakis**, **Philip Glass**, **Larry Austin**, **Joan Tower**, **Arthur Berger**, **Morton Subotnick**, **Ben Johnston**, **Steve Reich**, **Betsy Jolas**, **William Bolcom**, **Charles Dodge**, **Robert Moran**, **György Kurtág**, Pete Rugolo, and Burt Bacharach. *See also* ELECTRO-ACOUSTIC MUSIC.

MIMAROGLU, ILHAN (1926–). Turkish composer. Ilhan Mimaroglu studied at Columbia University, settled in New York City in 1959, and worked at the Columbia-Princeton Electronic Music Center, mentored by **Vladimir Ussachevsky.** Mimaroglu's electronic works include *Twelve Preludes for Magnetic Tape* (1966–1967), *Tract* (1975) for magnetic **tape**, *The Offering* (1979), *Immolation Scene* (1983), and *The Last Largo* (1989). Among his instrumental compositions are *Idols of Perversity* (1974) for solo viola and string ensemble, *Rosa* (1978) for piano, and *Monologue* (1997) for clarinet and viola. Mimaroglu is the founder of Finnadar Records (1975–1981), which focused on contemporary music, and the website www .mimaroglumusicsales.com, a wide-ranging source of recordings of **electronic, computer**, and tape music.

MINIMALISM. Despite a flurry of anticipations in France during the 1920s—for example, **Erik Satie**'s *Musique d'ameublement* scores of 1920 and 1923, the silences of **George Antheil**'s *Ballet mécanique* (1925), **Virgil Thomson**'s drama-free settings of Gertrude Stein, **Ezra Pound**'s neomedieval settings of François Villon, and **Maurice Ravel**'s *Boléro* (1928) and its hypnotic repetitions—there are no true prototypes for minimalism in **modernist** music. Not until the second half of the 20th century did it flourish, developing methodologies in several parallel streams during the 1960s and 1970s. Most familiar is the use of repeated patterns, especially in such pulse-driven works as **Terry Riley**'s *In C* (1964), **Philip Glass**'s *Music in Fifths* (1969), and **Steve Reich**'s *Drumming* (1971), where the sustained activity becomes a static sound. Another approach is gradual-process music, magnifying the sound's transformation, as in **Charlemagne Palestine**'s *Holy 1 & Holy 2* (1967), **Frederic Rzewski**'s *Les moutons de Panurge* (1969), **Alvin Lucier**'s *I Am Sitting in a Room* (1970), and **James Tenney**'s *Clang* (1972).

Minimalism also exalts the singular event, making something fleeting into the focus of attention, as some of the **Fluxus** composers did: **La Monte Young** called for the player to build a fire in *Composition 1960 No. 2*; George Brecht had a flute disassembled and reassembled in *Flute Solo* (1962). Instructing the player to perform any action as slowly as possible, **Takehisa Kosugi**'s *Anima 7* (1964) combined this aesthetic with gradual process. Reducing his materials drastically, **Giacinto Scelsi** composed *Quattro pezzi su una nota sola* (1959). Another minimalist device is to expand the scale of the music; Young, **Dennis Johnson**, **Terry Jennings**, and **Morton Feldman** all composed works lasting several hours.

What all these approaches have in common is that they are essentially nondramatic: The music coheres without traditional or modernist techniques of contrast and development. Minimalism can thus be seen as originating with the **chance music** of **John Cage**, which banished drama by removing hierarchies of importance—all the sounds are equally important. That is why Cage's music can be full of contrast, as in *Etudes Australes* (1975) or *Europeras I/II* (1987), yet remain nondramatic, because none of those changes express any narrative, programmatic or structural. Associating with Cage helped free up Feldman, **Earle Brown**, and **Christian Wolff** to compose **indeterminate** scores with their own minimalist qualities. Feldman fully notated his subtle alterations of nonpulsed repeated patterning in his later works such as *Neither* (1977) and *For Philip Guston* (1984). Cage's music and ideas invigorated the minimalist works of other important composers, as well, including Young, **Pauline Oliveros**, and **Robert Ashley**.

Nevertheless, minimalism also represents a reaction *against* indeterminacy— and **serial** organization and traditional tonality. In this **postmodern** approach, many composers sought a new drive and energy in their music, reflecting their varying experiences of jazz, blues, pop, and rock. Note also its **multicultural** strain, with Riley, Young, Palestine, and Glass impacted by Indian music, and Reich by African drumming. Minimalist music has also encouraged such related developments as **sound installations** and **sound sculpture**.

By the 1970s, minimalism had taken root in Western composition. It has informed the music of such notable composers as **Philip Corner, Tony Conrad, Julius Eastman, Gavin Bryars, Tom Johnson, Henry Flynt, Eliane Radigue, Arthur Russell, Rhys Chatham, John Adams, Bunita Marcus, Robert Moran, John Luther Adams, Louis Andriessen, Brian Eno, Beata Moon, Glenn Branca, Barbara Monk Feldman, Arvo Pärt, Peter Garland, John Tavener, Richard Maxfield, John Zorn, Lois V. Vierk, Petr Kotik, Michael Gordon, David Lang, Julia Wolfe, Michael Nyman, Phill Niblock**, and **Meredith Monk**.

MITCHELL, ROSCOE (1940–). American composer, musician, and educator. A multi-instrumentalist on woodwinds, Roscoe Mitchell is a leading exponent of **free jazz** and cofounder of the Association for the Advancement of Creative Musicians and the Art Ensemble of Chicago. Among his notable recordings are *Congliptious* (1968), *Nonaah* (1977), *Snurdy McGurdy and Her Dancin' Shoes* (1980), *Sound Songs* (1997), and *Solo 3* (2004). His compositions include *Variations and Sketches from the Bamboo Terrace* (1988) for chamber orchestra, *Fallen Heroes* (1998) for baritone and orchestra, and *The Bells of 59th Street* (2000) for alto saxophone and gamelan. Mitchell has played with such composer/musicians as **Anthony Braxton, George Lewis**, and **Muhal Richard Abrams** and taught at the University of Wisconsin, the California Institute for the Arts, and other institutions. *See also* MULTICULTURALISM; POSTMODERNISM.

MODERNISM. Every generation has regarded itself as modern in comparison to preceding generations; examples date back to the Renaissance of commentaries that refer to the modern music of their day. But in the early 20th century, a distinct movement that came to be called "modernist" transformed virtually every area of aesthetic expression, most notably art, literature, architecture, dance, and music.

Musical modernism developed along two parallel tracks. One approach expanded on the German romanticism of Richard Wagner, extending his chromaticism into new realms of **dissonance** and tonal ambiguity and amplifying the drama and emotion of Wagnerian opera to the extreme exaggerations of **expressionism**. **Richard Strauss** and **Gustav Mahler** were important precursors to this development, which came into its own with the music of **Arnold Schoenberg**. The other approach rejected Wagnerian excess. French composers **Claude Debussy**, **Maurice Ravel**, and **Erik Satie** sought to create a new music that relied upon staticism, repetition, and subtlety. Portentous philosophical content was avoided; emotional expression, if present at all, was nuanced and muted.

Modernism was an international movement in music by the 1910s. Schoenberg, **Alexander Scriabin**, **Charles Ives**, **Béla Bartók**, **Igor Stravinsky**, **Anton Webern**, **Alban Berg**, **Henry Cowell**, **Edgard Varèse**, **Dane Rudhyar**, **Carl Ruggles**, and Ruth Crawford represented an extreme modernism over the 1910s and 1920s, often referred to as "ultramodernism," which was highly dissonant and could be **polytonal** or **atonal**. Melodic lines became more angular and fragmentary, with wide leaps and asymmetrical designs. Rhythm gained a new complexity in the form of **polyrhythm** and polymeter. Unusual sonorities proliferated and percussion became more prominent in both orchestration and pianism. In the 1920s and 1930s, some of these composers began employing more familiar tonal structures in their music, seeking to invigorate and redefine the past rather than escape it—an approach they shared with **Manuel de Falla**, **Sergey Prokofiev**, **Paul Hindemith**, **Darius Milhaud**, and **Aaron Copland**.

Although the 1940s and 1950s saw a heightened interest in Schoenberg's **twelve-tone** method of atonal composition, modernism was by then reaching a plateau, and a cultural shift into **postmodernism** was beginning. Anticipated by Satie and launched by the American innovators **Harry Partch** and **John Cage**, postmodernism built upon modernist freedoms while avoiding familiar modernist materials. Although such composers as **Elliott Carter**, **Olivier Messiaen**, **Milton Babbitt**, **Conlon Nancarrow**, **Iannis Xenakis**, **Pierre Boulez**, and **Karlheinz Stockhausen** continued to pursue modernism into the late 20th and early 21st centuries, in what has been called "high modernism," they came to represent an aesthetic minority within the postmodern activity going on around them, typified by **minimalist, multicultural,** and pop-influenced new music.

See also ANTHEIL, GEORGE; BARRAQUÉ, JEAN; BARTH, HANS; BAUER, MARION; BECKER, JOHN J.; BERIO, LUCIANO; BEYER, JOHANNA M.; BIRTWISTLE, HARRISON; BLITZSTEIN, MARC; BOULANGER, NADIA; BRIDGE, FRANK; BUSONI, FERRUCCIO; CARRILLO, JULIÁN; CATURLA, ALEJANDRO; CERHA, FRIEDRICH; CHÁVEZ, CARLOS; CHOU WEN-CHUNG; DALLAPICCOLA, LUIGI; DAVIES, PETER MAXWELL; DIAMOND, DAVID; DRUCKMAN, JACOB; EICHHEIM, HENRY; EISLER, HANNS; EL-DABH, HALIM; ELLINGTON, DUKE; FERNEYHOUGH, BRIAN; FILM MUSIC; FINE, IRVING; FINE, VIVIAN; FINNEY, ROSS LEE; FORMALISM; FOSS, LUKAS; FOULDS, JOHN; FREE JAZZ; FUTURISM; GEBRAUCHSMUSIK; GERHARD, ROBERTO; GIDEON, MIRIAM; GINASTERA, ALBERTO; GOEHR, ALEXANDER; GÓRECKI, HENRYK; GRAETTINGER, ROBERT F.; GRAINGER, PERCY; GRIFFES, CHARLES T.; GRISEY, GÉRARD; GROUPE DES SIX; HÁBA, ALOIS; HARVEY, JONATHAN; HAUER, JOSEF MATTHIAS; HENRY, PIERRE; HENZE, HANS WERNER; HOLST, GUSTAV; HONEGGER, ARTHUR; IBERT, JACQUES; IMPRESSIONISM; IRELAND, JOHN; JANÁCEK, LEOS; JOLIVET, ANDRÉ; KANCHELI, GIYA; KIRCHNER, LEON; KNUSSEN, OLIVER; KODÁLY, ZOLTÁN; KOLB, BARBARA; KRENEK, ERNST; KURTÁG, GYÖRGY; LE CAINE, HUGH; LEIBOWITZ, RENÉ; LIGETI, GYÖRGY; LOURIÉ, ARTHUR; LUENING, OTTO; LUTOSLAWSKI, WITOLD; MADERNA, BRUNO; MAMLOK, URSULA; MARTIN, FRANK; MARTINU, BOHUSLAV; MAW, NICHOLAS; MAYUZUMI, TOSHIRO; MOSOLOV, ALEXANDER; MURAIL, TRISTAN; MUSGRAVE, THEA; NEOCLASSICISM; NEOROMANTICISM; NIELSEN, CARL; NONO, LUIGI; OPERA; ORNSTEIN, LEO; PENDERECKI, KRZYSZTOF; PERLE, GEORGE; PISTON, WALTER; POULENC, FRANCIS; POUND, EZRA; POWELL, MEL; REVUELTAS, SILVESTRE; RIEGGER, WALLINGFORD; ROCHBERG, GEORGE; ROLDÁN, AMADEO; ROSLAVETS, NIKOLAI; ROUSSEL, ALBERT; RUSSELL, GEORGE; RUSSELL, WILLIAM; SALZEDO, CARLOS; SCHAEFFER, PIERRE; SCHILLINGER, JOSEPH; SCHNITTKE, ALFRED; SCHULLER, GUNTHER; SEEGER, CHARLES; SEEGER, RUTH CRAWFORD; SESSIONS, ROGER; SHAPEY, RALPH; SHOSTAKOVICH, DMITRY; SLONIMSKY, NICOLAS; SMIT, LEO (1900–1943); SOLLBERGER, HARVEY; SZYMANOWSKI, KAROL; TAKEMITSU, TORU; TAL, JOSEF; TALMA, LOUISE; TAYLOR, CECIL; THOMSON, VIRGIL; TOWER, JOAN; USSACHEVSKY, VLADIMIR; VILLA-LOBOS, HEITOR; WALTON,

WILLIAM; WEBER, BEN; WEILL, KURT; WELLESZ, EGON; WOLPE, STEFAN; WUORINEN, CHARLES; WYSCHNEGRADSKY, IVAN; ZIMMERMANN, BERND ALOIS; ZWILICH, ELLEN TAAFFE.

MONK, BARBARA. See FELDMAN, BARBARA MONK.

MONK, MEREDITH (1942–). American composer and musician. Meredith Monk graduated from Sarah Lawrence College in 1964, where she first developed her own unique blend of composition, singing, choreography, and theater. Her music-theater piece *16 Millimeter Earrings* (1966) included **film**; later works have also utilized video. *Juice* (1969) was performed in installments at three different locations. By then, Monk was also working regularly as a solo artist, focusing on her singing and releasing such recordings as *Key* (1970) and *Our Lady of Late* (1974). Her **minimalist** modal music has a fondness for ostinati, **dissonance**, and **polytonal** inflections. The 1970s and 1980s saw international performances of her **operas**, large-scale theatrical works such as *Vessel: An Opera Epic* (1971), *Education of the Girlchild* (1972), *Quarry* (1976), *Recent Ruins* (1979), *Specimen Days* (1981), and *The Games* (1983), a collaboration with Ping Chong.

In 1978, she formed her performance group Meredith Monk and Vocal Ensemble, composing for it *Dolmen Music* (1979) for six voices, piano, violin, cello, and percussion. Also a filmmaker, Monk has written and directed *Ellis Island* (1982) and *Book of Days* (1989). The operas *Magic Frequencies* (1998) and *Mercy* (2001) were scored for six voices, two keyboards, percussion, violin, and **theremin**. Among her other notable recent operas are *Atlas* (1991), *The Politics of Quiet* (1996), *The Impermanence Project* (2004), and *Songs of Ascension* (2008). Monk has also composed her first orchestral score, *Possible Sky* (2003), and her first string quartet, *Stringsongs* (2004). Her other pieces include the two-piano scores *Parlour Games* (1988) and *Phantom Waltz* (1990), the piano solo *Steppe Music* (1997), and *WEAVE* (2010) for two voices, chorus, and chamber orchestra. *See also* POSTMODERNISM.

MOON, BEATA (1969–). American composer, musician, and educator. Beata Moon studied piano at Juilliard and is self-taught as a composer. Her **postmodern** scores have incorporated elements of **modernism**, **minimalism**, jazz, and pop; notable works include *Mary* (1996) for soprano, piano, violin, and drum; *Moonpaths* (1998) for clarinet, violin, and piano; *Illusions* (2000) for marimba; *The Beatitudes* (2003) for baritone and piano; Wind Quintet (2004); Piano Sonata (2006); and *Locomotion* (2008) for double bass and piano. A teaching artist at New York's Lincoln Center Institute, she founded the all-female Beata Moon Ensemble in 2002, which performs music composed by women.

MOONDOG (1916–1999). American composer and musician. Louis Hardin lost his eyesight at age 16 when a dynamite cap exploded in his face. He started his musical training at the Iowa School for the Blind and later studied with Burnet Tuthill at the Memphis Conservatory of Music. Hardin came to New York in 1943 and befriended conductor Artur Rodzinski, who let him attend rehearsals with the New York Philharmonic. By the late 1940s, Hardin had adopted the name Moondog and was a familiar presence on the streets of Manhattan wearing Viking regalia. His lodgings, both in the city and upstate, were intermittent, and he lived mostly on the street for the next three decades.

During the 1950s, Moondog supported himself as a street musician, often playing instruments that he had built such as trimbas (triangular drums), a yukh (a suspended log struck with rubber mallets), or an oo (a triangular stringed instrument struck with a clave). He would type out his compositions in Braille and have them transcribed into conventional notation.

Moondog's music relied upon unusual meters and intricate and rigorous canonic procedures, and it featured refined and evocative melodies. He also recorded the urban sounds around him and sometimes incorporated them into his music. On his trio of notable LPs released by Prestige (*Moondog*, 1956; *More Moondog*, 1957; *The Story of Moondog*, 1957), he frequently played all the instruments. Equally impressive were his Columbia albums, *Moondog* (1969) and *Moondog 2* (1971), in which he led groups of musicians and singers. During these years, he received support and encouragement from composer/musicians such as **Duke Ellington**, **Igor Stravinsky**, **Steve Reich**, and **Philip Glass**.

Moondog went to Germany for a concert of his music in 1974 and was invited to live with Ilona Goebel and her family in Oer-Erkenshwick. She became an indispensable part of his life, serving as manager, assistant, and publisher of his scores, poetry, and essays through her company Managarm. His music flourished in Europe in his last years, and the overtone series became more important to his composition. He also released several impressive CDs, including *H'Art Songs* (1989) and *Elpmas* (1991). A prolific composer, Moondog's opus list numbers 898 compositions, most of which are still being cataloged and dated. His works include at least 80 symphonies, 70 songs, and 50 works for saxophone ensemble. *See also* JUST INTONATION; POST-MODERNISM.

MORAN, ROBERT (1937–). American composer, musician, and educator. Robert Moran studied with Hans Apostel, **Luciano Berio**, and **Darius**

Milhaud. His early compositions include the graphic scores *Interiors* (1964) for variable ensemble and *L'après-midi du Dracoula* (1966) for any sound-producing instruments, as well as the city-wide works *39 Minutes for 39 Autos* (1969), *Hallelujah* (1971), and *Pachelbel Promenade* (1975). **Minimalism** informs *Ten Miles High over Albania* (1983) for eight harps, the **opera** *The Juniper Tree* (1984), which Moran co-composed with **Philip Glass**, and *Open Veins* (1986) for amplified violin and variable ensemble. Also notable are Moran's 1990 operas *Desert of Roses* and *From the Towers of the Moon* and his scores for chorus and instruments, *Requiem: Chant du cygne* (1989), *Winni Ille Pu* (1994), *Night Passage* (1994), *Stimmen des letzten Siegels* (2000), and *Gitanjali* (2001). He taught at the San Francisco Conservatory of Music and directed the San Francisco New Music Ensemble. *See also* GRAPHIC NOTATION; INDETERMINACY; POSTMODERNISM.

MOSOLOV, ALEXANDER (1900–1973). Russian composer and musician. Pianist Alexander Mosolov studied composition at the Moscow Conservatory with Nikolai Myaskovsky and privately with Reinhold Glière. Drawing on the late works of **Alexander Scriabin** as well as **futurist** ideas, Mosolov used registral extremes, driving ostinati, and harsh **dissonances** in such notable works as Piano Sonatas Nos. 2 (1924) and 5 (1925), String Quartet No. 1 (1926), *Turkmenian Nights* (1928) for piano, and *Zavod* (1928, a.k.a. *Iron Foundry*) for orchestra, which was played internationally. But Mosolov's **modernist** music was denounced as antirevolutionary by the Russian Union of Proletarian Musicians, and he fell into disfavor with the regime of Joseph Stalin. By the early 1930s, Mosolov's works were no longer published or performed in the Soviet Union, and in 1937 he was arrested and sentenced to a gulag. The efforts of Glière, Myaskovsky, and others secured Mosolov's release the following year. His later works, which include Cello Concerto (1946), *Song-Symphony* (1950), and Symphony No. 5 (1965), were traditional scores that reflected his folk-song expeditions into Turkmenistan, Kyrgyzstan, and other regions in the 1930s and 1940s. *See also* FORMALISM.

MULTICULTURALISM. The conviction that the music of other cultures is available for use in one's own music can be traced back at least as far as the American composer and pianist Louis Moreau Gottschalk (1829–1869). Its impact on European music, however, was more subtle and internalized in the later 19th century, as with the 1889 performances of Javanese gamelan in Paris, which revealed new possibilities to the young composers **Claude Debussy** and **Erik Satie**. In the first decades of the 20th century, **Béla Bartók**'s composition drew upon his research into the folk music of not just his native Hungary but also Slovakia, Romania, Turkey, and the Middle East. Other composers of the era who were drawn to music outside their own tradition include **Ferruccio Busoni, Arthur Farwell, Darius Milhaud, Charles T. Griffes, Dane Rudhyar, Gustav Holst, Albert Roussel, Henry Eichheim, John Foulds, Colin McPhee,** and **Benjamin Britten.**

When **Henry Cowell** was studying and teaching world music in the early 1930s, his composition became less aggressively **modernist**; at the same time, **George Gershwin, William Russell,** and others were being impacted by the Latin American music that they were hearing in popular venues. Multicultural composition is essentially **postmodern**, involving the appropriation, deconstruction, and recontextualization of another culture's music, and it was not fully articulated in the West until the second half of the 20th century. By the late 1950s and early 1960s, major composers such as Cowell, **Alan Hovhaness, Harry Partch,** and **Lou Harrison** were using Eastern instruments and techniques in their scores. Perhaps the 20th century's greatest advocate of multicultural music, Harrison also embraced the gamelan and helped stimulate international enthusiasm for it. Other composers who wrote for gamelan include **James Tenney, Henry Brant, Pauline Oliveros, Alvin Lucier, Roscoe Mitchell,** and **Robert Macht.**

Several American **minimalist** composer/musicians also have multicultural roots: **Steve Reich** studied African drumming, and **Philip Glass, La Monte Young, Charlemagne Palestine,** and **Terry Riley** turned to Indian music. Compositions specifically about multiculturalism include **Karlheinz Stockhausen's** *Hymnen* (1967) and **John Cage's** *Apartment House 1776* (1975). It has also informed creative African-American music in the work of **Duke Ellington, Sun Ra, Ornette Coleman, Anthony Braxton, Leroy Jenkins,** and others. Some first-generation Americans have explored their own heritage in multicultural works, from **Aaron Copland's** *Vitebsk* (1928) and the Armenian-themed scores of Hovhaness and **Richard Yardumian** to music by **Diamanda Galás** and **Susie Ibarra.** Other multicultural composers include **Peggy Glanville-Hicks, Halim El-Dabh, Bun-Ching Lam, Toru Takemitsu, John Zorn, Henry Flynt, Chou Wen-chung, Tania León, Yuji Takahashi, David Hykes, Toshi Ichiyanagi, Richard Teitelbaum, Peter Garland, Sussan Deyhim, Tan Dun, Unsuk Chin,** and **Fred Frith.**

MULTIMEDIA. Had **Alexander Scriabin** lived and been able to realize his visionary *Mysterium*, he would have presided over the first major multimedia composition, combining instrumentalists and vocalists with dancers and actors as well as specialized treatments of color, texture, and scent. **John Becker** composed pioneering multimedia music in *A Marriage with Space* (1935) for orchestra, dancers, actors, and manipulated colors and lights—which has yet to be performed. In the first half of the 20th century, few dared to follow the path that Scriabin and Becker had anticipated.

In 1951, **Toru Takemitsu** and **Joji Yuasa** were among the cofounders of Japan's Experimental Workshop, established to perform multimedia pieces, and by the 1960s, multimedia music was enjoying a vital period internationally. **Robert Ashley**'s involvement with the **ONCE Group**, and later the **Sonic Arts Union**, brought theater, dance, and film into his composition; in Ashley's **operas** *Perfect Lives* (1980) and *Atalanta (Acts of God)* (1982–1987), video played an essential role. **La Monte Young** was another important figure in multimedia music through his collaborations with visual designer **Marian Zazeela**, whose slide projections and lighting effects (and later, sculpted mobiles) became an integral facet of Young's music. **Lejaren Hiller** and **John Cage** created *HPSCHD* (1968) for one to seven harpsichords and one to 51 **tapes**, which premiered in 1969 using film and slide projections. Other multimedia composers include **Salvatore Martirano, Larry Austin, Mauricio Kagel, Pauline Oliveros, Laurie Anderson, Tan Dun, Sussan Deyhim, Kenneth Gaburo, Morton Subotnick, Sun Ra, Duke Ellington, Roger Reynolds, Alvin Lucier, Takehisa Kosugi, David Tudor, Iannis Xenakis, Michael Gordon**, and **Phill Niblock**. *See also* FLUXUS; POSTMODERNISM.

MUMMA, GORDON (1935–). American composer, musician, and educator. A pianist and horn player, Gordon Mumma studied with **Ross Lee Finney** at the University of Michigan and later taught at Mills College, the University of Victoria, and the University of California, Santa Cruz, among other institutions. Mumma formed the Cooperative Studio for Electronic Music with **Robert Ashley** in 1958; he was also a founding member of the legendary **ONCE Group**, a composer/musician for the Merce Cunningham Dance Company, and a founding member of the **Sonic Arts Union**.

Mumma has specialized in designing and building his own electronic circuitry, and his **electroacoustic music** employs live **electronics**. A cybersonic console is used with piano four-hands in *Medium Size Monograph* (1963), bandoneon or three chromatic harmonicas in *Mesa* (1966), and solo modified horn in *Hornpipe* (1967). The **tape** piece *Cybersonic Cantilevers* (1973) utilized sound materials contributed by visitors to Mumma's sound-capturing installation. A digital **computer** was combined with a variable group of live performers in *Conspiracy 8* (1970), a collaboration with Stephen Smoliar. His *Than Particle* (1985) was for percussionist and computer-percussionist. Mumma has also collaborated with such composer/musicians as **David Tudor, Anthony Braxton, Fred Frith, Pauline Oliveros, Frederic Rzewski**, and **Christian Wolff**. His notable recent works include the piano scores

Graftings (1996) and *Sixpac Sonatas* (1985–1997). *See also* POSTMOD-ERNISM; SOUND INSTALLATION.

MURAIL, TRISTAN (1947–). French composer and educator. Tristan Murail studied at the Paris Conservatoire with **Olivier Messiaen** and cofounded the **electroacoustic-music** ensemble/collective L'Itineraire. A leading figure in **spectral music**, with such compositions as *Mémoires/Erosion* (1976) for French horn and nine instruments and *Gondwana* (1980) for orchestra, Murail adapted **computer music** to spectral analysis and synthesis, as in *Désintégrations* (1982) for 17 instruments and **electronics**. He has written for **ondes martenot**, sextet (*March 2,5*, 1976) and solo (*La conquête de l'Antarctique*, 1982). The **multicultural** *L'esprit des dunes* (1994) used Mongolian overtone singing and traditional Tibetan instruments. Since 1997, Murail has lived and taught in the United States. His recent works include *Terre d'ombre* (2004) for orchestra and electronics and *Liber fulguralis* (2008) for ensemble, electronics, and video. *See also* GRISEY, GÉRARD; MODERNISM.

MUSGRAVE, THEA (1928–). Scottish composer, musician, and educator. Thea Musgrave studied with Hans Gal at the University of Edinburgh, **Nadia Boulanger** at the Paris Conservatoire, and **Aaron Copland** at Tanglewood. She settled in the United States in 1972 and taught at the University of California, Santa Barbara (1970–1978), and at Queens College, City University of New York (1987–2002). As pianist and conductor, Musgrave has performed her works internationally. She wrote **twelve-tone music** with such scores as *Triptych* (1959) for tenor and orchestra, *Colloquy* (1960) for violin and piano, and *Sinfonia* (1963) for orchestra, but went on to develop her own lyrical chromatic style with a greater feeling for melody, as in her **opera** *The Decision* (1965).

Dramatic effects have frequently informed Musgrave's music: Instrumental insurrections arise in the Concerto for Orchestra (1967); the viola section stands for the soloist in the Viola Concerto (1973); different chamber-orchestra soloists compete in *Points of View* (2007). Other works have programmatic qualities, such as *The Seasons* (1988) for orchestra, *Autumn Sonata* (1993) for bass clarinet and orchestra, and *Turbulent Landscapes* (2003) for orchestra. Musgrave's ballet score *Beauty and the Beast* (1969) included **tape music** that she created with Daphne Oram. *Echoes through Time* (1988) for five soloists, five speakers, three dancers, women's chorus, spoken chorus, and orchestra has an optional prologue and epilogue of **electronic music**. Her other **electroacoustic** works include *From One to Another I* (1970) for viola and tape, *Orfeo I* (1975) for flute and tape, and *Narcissus* (1987) for clarinet and digital delay system.

Musgrave has utilized **spatial** resources in such works as Clarinet Concerto (1969), with the soloist moving through the orchestra and leading subgroups, and Horn Concerto (1971), in which she positioned the orchestra's horns around the hall. She found success in opera with *The Voice of Ariadne* (1973), *Mary, Queen of Scots* (1977), *A Christmas Carol* (1979), *Harriet, the Woman Called Moses* (1984), *Simón Bolívar* (1992), and *Pontalba* (2003). Her recent compositions include the spatial work *Phoenix Rising* (1997) for orchestra; *Three Women* (1998) for soprano, narrator, and orchestra; and the dramatic choral piece *Voices of Power and Protest* (2006). *See also* MODERNISM.

MUSIQUE CONCRÈTE. French composer **Pierre Schaeffer** coined the term *musique concrète* in 1948 to distinguish music created with prerecorded sounds, in which he heard a unique "concreteness" that instrumental and vocal sound lacked. He inaugurated the medium with *Étude aux chemins de fer* (1948) and collaborated with **Pierre Henry** on the first major musique concrète work, *Symphonie pour un homme seul* (1950). With further developments in **tape music**, the term came to specify music made from natural sounds on tape, as distinct from electrically synthesized sound. Other important composers of musique concrète include **Karlheinz Stockhausen, Edgard Varèse, Iannis Xenakis, Toru Takemitsu, Luc Ferrari, Darius Milhaud, Jean Barraqué, Jean-Claude Risset**, and **Laurie Spiegel**. *See also* ELECTROACOUSTIC MUSIC; ELECTRONIC MUSIC; HINDEMITH, PAUL.

N

NANCARROW, CONLON (1912–1997). American-born Mexican composer. One of the most original 20th-century composers, Conlon Nancarrow articulated new **polyrhythms**, tempo relationships, and densities in his *Studies for Player Piano*. Born in Texarkana, Arkansas, Samuel Conlon Nancarrow studied trumpet but was mostly self-taught as a composer; his earliest surviving piece is the lively *Sarabande and Scherzo* (1930) for oboe, bassoon, and piano. Nancarrow played jazz trumpet in the early 1930s, and after a semester at the Cincinnati College Conservatory of Music, he was in Boston by 1934, studying with **Roger Sessions** and finding encouragement from **Nicolas Slonimsky** and **Walter Piston**. Nancarrow completed his Toccata, for violin and piano, and Prelude and *Blues*, both for piano, in 1935, but his speedy tempi and jazz-inspired rhythms were so demanding that the pieces had to be arranged for piano four-hands when premiered in 1939.

Nancarrow went to Spain in 1937 to fight in the civil war with the Abraham Lincoln Brigade. The following year, Slonimsky published the Toccata, Prelude, and *Blues* in a New Music Edition. **Aaron Copland** praised these scores in *Modern Music* and got Nancarrow to write for the magazine after he returned from Spain in 1939. But when the government refused to issue Nancarrow a passport because of his Communist affiliations, he left the United States and settled in Mexico City in 1940; he became a Mexican citizen in 1955.

Most of Nancarrow's **modernist** music in the early 1940s—Septet (1940); *Three 2-Part Studies* (c. 1940) for piano; *Sonatina* (1941) for piano; Trio No. 1 (1942) for clarinet, bassoon, and piano; *Piece for Small Orchestra No. 1* (1943); String Quartet No. 1 (1945)—had jazz and blues strains. But his tempi and rhythms became even more challenging, and performances were few and unsatisfactory. Seeking to explore further extremes in rhythm and tempo, Nancarrow followed **Henry Cowell**'s suggestion in his book *New Musical Resources* that rhythms too complex for a human to play could easily be cut onto a player-piano roll. Nancarrow tried to build a percussion machine after the principle of a player piano, using a pneumatic device to read holes on a paper roll and operate beaters that struck drumheads and wood blocks. But it never worked properly, so he went to New York in 1947 and bought a player piano and a roll-punching machine.

In 1951, New Music Edition published Nancarrow's *Rhythm Study No. 1 for Player Piano*. By then, he was working on other *Studies* ("Rhythm" was dropped from the titles), in a series that became his exclusive focus for decades. Although meticulous in numbering (and sometimes renumbering) the studies, Nancarrow disregarded their dates. Research indicates that Studies Nos. 1–30 were created from the late 1940s to the late 1950s. Nancarrow then stopped composing and turned to creating legible scores of his studies for about five years, after which his music resumed, with Studies Nos. 31–41 from 1965 to 1978 and Nos. 42–50 in the 1980s. Nancarrow's fondness for boogie-woogie and Spanish guitars are reflected in early studies; later ones are more single-minded, especially those employing canonic procedures. Study No. 21, "Canon-X," has a slow pattern of bass notes that constantly accelerates, played against the same material in an extremely fast treble voicing that continuously slows down. Study No. 24 has three voices playing against each other at tempo ratios of 14 against 15 against 16. Study No. 33 used irrational numbers for its tempi, playing the square root of 2 against 2.

Nancarrow's music was promoted by **Elliott Carter** and **John Cage** in the 1950s and 1960s and championed in the 1970s by younger composers such as **Peter Garland** and **Charles Amirkhanian**. The Studies were eventually heard and appreciated worldwide, and Nancarrow toured the United States and Europe in the 1980s. Pianists such as **Yvar Mikhashoff** began performing certain of the Studies, and some were arranged by Mikhashoff and others in versions for piano four-hands or for chamber ensembles. The composer and inventor Trimpin digitalized the Studies into MIDI information, so a **computer** could drive his vorsetzer, a device placed on a piano keyboard that plays the studies "live."

Nancarrow began accepting instrumental commissions with *Tango?* (1984) for piano, String Quartet No. 3 (1988; a second string quartet was never completed), and *Three Canons for Ursula* (1989) for piano. Study No. 50 (1988) was his player-piano arrangement of *Piece for Small Orchestra No. 2* (1986), while *Study for Orchestra* (1991) was adapted from Study No. 49; originally envisioned as a concerto for player piano and orchestra, it included a computer-driven Disklavier for player-piano tempi and effects.

Despite suffering a stroke in 1990, Nancarrow completed *Para Yoko* (1991) for his wife Yoko Sugiura—his only non-Study composition for player piano—and Study No. 51 (1992). Trio No. 2 (1991) for oboe, bassoon, and piano used the instrumentation of the *Sarabande and Scherzo* he had composed as a teenager. *Three Movements for Chamber Orchestra* (1993) was an arrangement made by Nancarrow and his assistant Carlos Sandoval, using material from abandoned piano rolls. His final composition was *Contraption No. 1* (1993), written for Trimpin's Contraption IPP. Study No. 52

for Player Piano was left unfinished when Nancarrow died at his home in Mexico City at age 84. *See also* ATONALITY; INSTRUMENT BUILDING.

NEMTIN, ALEXANDER (1936–1999). Russian composer. Alexander Nemtin studied at the Moscow Conservatory. In the 1960s, he used the ANS Synthesizer at the Moscow Electronic Music Studio to realize Johann Sebastian Bach's C Major Choral Prelude and to create *Tears*. Nemtin spent more than 25 years completing a three-hour realization of **Alexander Scriabin**'s *The Prefatory Act* (1996). He also orchestrated Scriabin's piano music for the ballet score *Nuances* (1975). Nemtin's other music includes *Japanese Songs* (1964) for tenor and five instruments; Symphony No. 2, "War and Peace" (1974); and *Three Poems* (1987) for piano. *See also* ELECTRONIC MUSIC.

NEOCLASSICISM. Rejecting romanticism's dramatic and personalized expression, many **modernist** composers practiced a new devotion to classical principles and techniques, writing for smaller groups of performers and employing classical and Baroque forms. **Ferruccio Busoni** began articulating this new classicism with his orchestral scores *Turandot* (1905) and *Berceuse élégiaque* (1909) and his *Fantasia contrappuntistica* (1910) for piano. **Claude Debussy** turned to classical forms in his last compositions, three chamber sonatas (1915–1917). **Sergey Prokofiev** composed his Symphony No. 1 (1917) as a structurally classical work with modernist harmonies and rhythms.

But Prokofiev moved on to other devices, and Busoni died in 1924; when neoclassicism ignited in the 1920s, its leader was **Igor Stravinsky**, with such scores as his Octet (1923), Piano Concerto (1924), and *Oedipus Rex* (1927). **Paul Hindemith** was another important figure, evoking the great German Baroque composers with his *Kammermusik* series (1922–1927). Nevertheless, it was Stravinsky's articulation of a new impersonality and precision that proved most directly helpful to the French composers who had defined their music outside of **impressionism,** such as **Darius Milhaud, Francis Poulenc,** and their fellow composers known as the **Groupe des Six**; it aided Spaniard **Manuel de Falla,** as well. The influential teacher **Nadia Boulanger** embraced Stravinskian neoclassicism, and it informed the early works of many of her American pupils, including **Virgil Thomson, Louise Talma, Ross Lee Finney, Walter Piston, Irving Fine, Elliott Carter,** and **Arthur Berger.**

With the **twelve-tone music** of **Arnold Schoenberg, Alban Berg,** and **Anton Webern** attracting attention during the 1930s, neoclassicism was championed as the modernist option for composers who rejected **atonality.** Opposing camps formed in support of either Schoenberg or Stravinsky, just as earlier generations had felt obliged to choose between Richard Wagner and

Giuseppe Verdi, or Johannes Brahms and Anton Bruckner. Such obligations are unreal from an inclusive **postmodern** perspective, but neoclassicism is not postmodern; it is modernist classicism, the use of classical disciplines to give form to modernist **dissonance** and **polyrhythm**.

Stravinsky enjoyed great success, both material and artistic, with a series of major neoclassical scores, including *Symphony of Psalms* (1930), Violin Concerto (1931), Symphony in C (1940), and Symphony in Three Movements (1945). Far more audience friendly than twelve-tone music could ever be, neoclassicism became internationally popular and accommodated such different composers as **Roger Sessions, Paul Bowles, Dmitry Shostakovich, Arthur Lourié, Witold Lutoslawski, Peggy Glanville-Hicks, Ernest Bloch, Luigi Dallapiccola, Albert Roussel, Colin McPhee**, and **Bohuslav Martinu**.

But the 1940s saw a greater appreciation of twelve-tone music, stimulated by Schoenberg's residence in the United States and the postwar fascination with the music of Webern. By the 1950s, Dallapiccola, Sessions, Finney, Talma, Berger, Fine, and even Stravinsky himself were composing twelve-tone music. Exclusively neoclassical composition largely faded with the postmodern willingness to combine modernist and traditional methods along with other techniques. *See also* CHÁVEZ, CARLOS; LIGETI, GYÖRGY; LUCIER, ALVIN; IBERT, JACQUES; NEOROMANTICISM; POWELL, MEL; SMIT, LEO (1900–1943); ZIMMERMANN, BERND ALOIS.

NEOROMANTICISM. Nineteenth-century romanticism celebrated the appeal to emotion, the relaxation of classical forms, the use of programmatic and literary ideas, and the appetite for beauty and fantasy—all of which were rejected by **modernist** composers in the early-20th century. But the 1920s and 1930s saw a reconsideration of romanticism, which followed the lead of **neoclassicism** and brought a modernist sensibility to romantic materials, as in the music of **Carl Orff, William Walton, Ernst Krenek, Samuel Barber**, and **Virgil Thomson**. Many neoromantic works, however, tended to feature **dissonance** and **polyrhythm** less aggressively than a lot of neoclassical music did. Baroque and classical forms gave piquant contrast to modernist materials; the formal freedoms and nuanced melodic lines of romanticism tended to be obscured by advanced harmonies and rhythms. Neoromanticism had a revival in the 1980s as the New Romanticism, with such composers as **Krzysztof Penderecki, Jacob Druckman, Hans Werner Henze, George Rochberg**, and **David Del Tredici**. *See also* BISCARDI, CHESTER; CORIGLIANO, JOHN; MAW, NICHOLAS; WELLESZ, EGON.

NEUHAUS, MAX (1939–2009). American composer and musician. Percussionist Max Neuhaus studied at the Manhattan School of Music and specialized in contemporary works, often using his own **electroacoustic** instruments. He won renown as the creator of site-specific **sound installations**, a term that Neuhaus coined. *Public Supply I* (1966) in New York joined radio and telephone systems for an interactive aural space of some 300 square miles. The weather-sensitive *Walkthrough* (1973–1977) brought shifting sonic zones to a Brooklyn subway entrance. *River Grove* (1988) used the sound of Roaring Fork River in Aspen. The indoor *Intersection I* (1999) in Venice created interpenetrating diagonals of sound. *Times Square* was installed in a Manhattan traffic island in 1977; it ran until 1992 and was reinstated in 2002. Other ongoing works include *Three "Similar" Rooms* (installed 1990 in Turin), *Suspended Sound Line* (1999, Bern), *Auracle* (2004, www.auracle.org), and *Sound Figure* (2008, Houston). *See also* POSTMODERNISM.

NIBLOCK, PHILL (1933–). American composer and musician. Phill Niblock has explored textures and densities in **minimalist** compositions of **electronically** processed **microtonal** drones in *Held Tones* (1982, rev. 1994) for flute, *Wintergreen* (1990) for **computer**-controlled **synthesizers**, *Hurdy Hurry* (1999) for hurdy gurdy, and *Organ* (2007) for church organ. His works are often **multimedia** events utilizing film, video, and slides. Niblock joined the Experimental Intermedia Foundation in 1968 and has served as its director since 1985. *See also* POSTMODERNISM.

NIELSEN, CARL (1865–1931). Danish composer and musician. Carl Nielsen studied at the Copenhagen Conservatory of Music and was conductor of the Royal Theater (1908–1914) and head of the Copenhagen Music Society (1915–1927). His postromantic music offers an original approach to tonality, progressing into distant areas from the work's key signature in Symphonies Nos. 5 (1922) and 6, "*Sinfonia semplice*" (1925); the former also featured **polytonal** passages. Nielsen's timbral and rhythmic imagination was lively, too, and his innovations anticipate **spatial music**: Symphony No. 3, "*Sinfonia espansiva*" (1911), seated a baritone and soprano in the orchestra, singing wordlessly and blending with the instruments; Symphony No. 4, "The Inextinguishable" (1916), climaxes with a battle between two timpanists at opposite sides of the stage. Nielsen's other notable works include Symphonies Nos. 1 (1892) and 2, "The Four Temperaments" (1902); Flute Concerto (1926); and Clarinet Concerto (1928). *See also* MODERNISM.

NONO, LUIGI (1924–1990). Italian composer, musician, and educator. Luigi Nono studied with Gian Francesco Malipiero at the Venice Conservatory (1943–1945) and with **Bruno Maderna** and Hermann Scherchen after the war. Nono also taught at numerous institutions and conducted many of his own works. He began composing **serial** music with *Variazioni canoniche sulla serie dell'op. 41 di Arnold Schoenberg* (1950) for orchestra and the octet *Polifonica–monodia–ritmica* (1951). Nono's **totally serialized** music grew more dramatic with *Incontri* (1955) for 24 instruments and *Diario polacco '58* (1959) for orchestra with 16 percussionists, and in works for chorus and instruments: *Epitaffio per Federico García Lorca* (1953), *La victoire de Guernica* (1954), *Il canto sospeso* (1956), *La terra e la compagna* (1958), and *Cori di Didone* (1958). This music won Nono international recognition and culminated with the **opera** *Intolleranza 1960* (1961), from which he derived an orchestral Suite in 1969. *Intolleranza 1960* included radical left-wing political content, a cause Nono championed in his music and activism.

Nono created **tape music** with *Omaggio a Emilio Vedova* (1960) and used tape in *La fabbrica illuminata* (1964) for female voices; *Y entonces comprendió* (1970) for six female voices and chorus; *Coma una ola de fuerza y luz* (1972) for soprano, piano, and orchestra; the opera *Al gran sole carico d'amore* (1974); and . . . *sofferte onde sereme . . .* (1976) for piano. Nono began combining musicians and live electronics with the percussion-ensemble piece *Con Luigi Dallapiccola* (1979); other **electroacoustic** works followed: *Omaggio a György Kurtág* (1983, rev. 1986) for contralto, flute, clarinet, and bass tuba; *Guai ai gelidi mostri* (1983) for two contraltos and six instruments; the opera *Prometeo* (1985); *Post-prae-ludium No. 1 per Donau* (1987) for tuba; and *Post-prae-ludium No. 3 "BAAB-ARR"* (1988) for piccolo. *See also* ATONALITY; MODERNISM; TWELVE-TONE MUSIC.

NYMAN, MICHAEL (1944–). English composer, musician, and critic. Michael Nyman studied at the Royal Academy of Music and at King's College, London. The author of *Experimental Music* (1974), Nyman also wrote criticism for such publications as *The Spectator*. He was a member of the **Portsmouth Sinfonia** and the **Scratch Orchestra**, and in 1976 he founded the Campiello Band, which later became the Michael Nyman Band. Works by this prolific **minimalist** composer include four string quartets (1985–1995), *For John Cage* (1992) for brass ensemble, *Melody Waves* (2005) for Chinese instruments, and six **operas** (1986–2005). Among his many **film** scores are *A Zed & Two Naughts* (1985), *The Piano* (1993), *Gattaca* (1997), and *Man on Wire* (2008). *See also* MULTICULTURALISM; POSTMODERNISM.

O

OLIVEROS, PAULINE (1932–). American composer, musician, and educator. One of the most influential **postmodern** composers and improvisers, Pauline Oliveros has been a leader in **electroacoustic** improvisation; the real-time performance of **electronic music**; the composition of **indeterminate**, **minimalist**, theatrical, **multimedia**, and ceremonial music; and the musical use of meditation techniques. Born in Houston, Texas, Oliveros played piano, French horn, and accordion as a child. An accordion major at the University of Texas (1949–1952), where she studied composition with Paul Koepke, she received her BA in composition from San Francisco State College in 1957 and studied with Robert Erickson at the San Francisco Conservatory of Music (1957–1960).

In 1957, Oliveros began giving improvised performances (mostly on French horn) with **Terry Riley** and Loren Rush, using **serial** techniques in her compositions *Concert Piece* for accordion and *Three Songs* for soprano and piano. But she moved away from those methods and began incorporating drones and superimposing different tempi in *Variations for Sextet* (1960) and *Trio for Flute, Piano, and Page Turner* (1961), her last traditionally notated score. Along with Ramon Sender, Oliveros formed Sonics in 1960, a center for **tape** and electronic music, which was then part of the San Francisco Conservatory of Music. Sonics grew into the San Francisco Tape Music Center by 1962, with the participation of **Morton Subotnick**, and was later relocated to Mills College with Oliveros as its first director (1966–1967). She then taught electronic music and experimental studies at the University of California, San Diego (1967–1981); her students include **Wendy Mae Chambers** and **Bun-Ching Lam**.

Oliveros's *Sound Patterns* (1961) for mixed chorus evoked electronic densities and textures through performance freedoms and novel vocal effects. Improvisation was featured in *Outline* (1963) for flute, percussion, and string bass and *Fifteen for an Ensemble of Performers* (1964). Theatrical elements were developed in such scores as *Pieces of Eight* (1964) for nine instruments, *Duo for Bandoneon and Accordion with Possible Mynah Bird Obligato, Seesaw Version* (1965), and *Theater Piece for Trombone Player* (1966). She incorporated film and tape into her 1965 works *A Theater Piece* for 15 actors, *George Washington Slept Here* for amplified violin, and *Light Piece for David Tudor* for electronically modified piano. During these years, Oliveros also devised methods for real-time improvised electronic music and produced such classic works as *Bye Bye Butterfly* (1965) and *I of IV* (1966). Her use of tape-delay systems in these works was adapted to other instruments in 1966 with *Accordion* for amplified accordion and *Hallo* for electronically modified piano, violins, voice, actor, lights, and dancers.

Exploration of different aspects of consciousness and meditation in the late 1960s informed Oliveros's groundbreaking minimalist works *Meditation on the Points of the Compass* (1970), *Sonic Meditations I–XII* (1971) and *XIII–XXV* (1973), and *Sonic Images* (1972). Written for specialized and nonspecialized musicians, these pieces also involve audience participation. In the 1970s, she refined her theatrical compositions into a memorable series of elaborate ceremonial pieces, many of which also put the audience to work: *Phantom Fathom (II)* (1972), *A Ceremony of Sounds* (1974), *Crow Two—A Ceremonial Opera* (1974), *Rose Moon* (1977), *The Yellow River Map* (1977), and *Crow's Nest (The Tuning Meditation)* (1979). Oliveros also developed methods for improvised performances by large ensembles in *To Valerie Solanas and Marilyn Monroe in Recognition of Their Desperation* (1970) for orchestra, chorus, organ, electronics, and lights; *Willowbrook Generations and Reflections* (1976) for mixed winds, brasses, and voices (20 or more) or chorus alone; and *Tashi Gomang* (1981) for orchestra.

Also in the 1970s, Oliveros further developed what she called the "expanded accordion," modifying the instrument with multiple delays and custom performance controls. She created several notable electroacoustic works for the expanded accordion, both with voice (*Horse Sings from Cloud*, 1975; *Rattlesnake Mountain*, 1982) and without (*Crone Music*, 1989), as well as *The Wanderer* (1982) for accordion ensemble and percussion. Oliveros won international renown as an improviser on the expanded accordion, especially after she formed the Deep Listening Band with Stuart Dempster (trombone) and Panaiotis (voice and electronic processing) in 1988. By then, her accordion had been retuned in **just intonation**. She has also played with such creative composer/musicians as **Cecil Taylor**, **Susie Ibarra**, **Gordon Mumma**, **David Tudor**, **Ellen Fullman**, and **Tony Conrad**.

She formed the Pauline Oliveros Foundation in 1985 (later the Deep Listening Institute) to foster creativity in artists of all ages and abilities. As its president, she has performed music and led classes, workshops, and retreats. Oliveros's notable later works include *Gathering Together* (1983) for piano eight-hands; *Lion's Eye* (1985) for Javanese gamelan and **sampler**; *Portraits* (1987) for solo or any ensemble, which is a mandala in **graphic notation**;

Dream Horse Spiel (1988) for voices and sound effects; *Njinga the Queen King* (1993), a play with music and pageantry; *Four Meditations for Orchestra* (1997); *Sound Patterns and Tropes* (2001) for chorus and percussion; and *Ringing for Healing: For All Victims of Violence All over the World* (2004) for bells. *See also* GEBRAUCHSMUSIK; MULTICULTURALISM; SPATIAL MUSIC.

ONCE GROUP. The celebrated ONCE Group was organized by composer **Robert Ashley** in 1960 and brought together an array of creative talent in Ann Arbor, Michigan: his wife Mary Ashley, who was both a visual and performance artist; Milton Cohen who sculpted in light; filmmaker George Manupelli; architects Harold Borkin and Joseph Wehrer; poet Jackie Mumma; performer Anne Wehrer; and composers **Gordon Mumma**, **Roger Reynolds**, George Cacioppo, and Donald Scavarda. Robert Sheff, later to be known as **"Blue" Gene Tyranny**, arrived in Ann Arbor in 1962 and became involved as well. They gave the first ONCE Festival in 1961, which became an annual event throughout the 1960s and featured many innovative composers as guests, including **La Monte Young, Terry Jennings, Alvin Lucier, Pauline Oliveros, Christian Wolff, Morton Feldman, John Cage, David Tudor, Luciano Berio, Cathy Berberian, David Behrman, Mauricio Kagel, Max Neuhaus, Lukas Foss**, and Eric Dolphy. *See also* ELECTROACOUSTIC MUSIC; ELECTRONIC MUSIC; MULTIMEDIA.

ONDES MARTENOT. The ondes martenot (French for "Martenot waves") is a monophonic **electronic-music** instrument invented by French musician Maurice Martenot (1898–1980), which utilizes the heterodyning method to produce sound. Pitch is controlled over a seven-octave range by a lateral-moving finger ring, played with the right hand; Martenot later added a keyboard with keys responsive to vibrato. At the left hand are filtering keys for timbral variation and a pressure-sensitive key that controls volume. Martenot debuted the ondes martenot in 1928 when he premiered Dimitri Levidis's *Symphonic Poem*, an orchestral concerto for the instrument which featured its **microtonal** capabilities. The ondes martenot was used by **Darius Milhaud, André Jolivet, Arthur Honegger**, and **Pierre Boulez** (who also performed on it), but it was **Olivier Messiaen** who assured the instrument's survival with two of his greatest works: *Trois petites liturgies de la Présence Divine* (1944) and *Turangalîla-symphonie* (1948). Others who have composed for ondes martenot include **Ivan Wyschnegradsky, Toshi Ichiyanagi, Giacinto Scelsi, Betsy Jolas**, and **Tristan Murail**. *See also* ELECTROACOUSTIC MUSIC; INSTRUMENT BUILDING; LORIOD, YVONNE.

ONO, YOKO (1933–). Japanese-born American composer and musician. Yoko Ono studied at Sarah Lawrence College and began creating conceptual pieces, often with the **Fluxus** group, such as the 1964 works *Cut Piece* and *Hide-and-Seek Piece*. With John Lennon of the **Beatles**, she created the **tape-music** album *Two Virgins* (1968). A singer whose performances include noise and shrieking, Ono made her name in rock music with such recordings as *Approximately Infinite Universe* (1972), *Season of Glass* (1981), and *Open Your Box* (2007). *See also* POSTMODERNISM.

OPEN FORM. A compositional approach that employs **chance**, **indeterminate**, and/or improvisational techniques so that the same score can sound different in every performance. *See also* ALEATORY; ELASTIC FORM; FREE DURATION; FREE IMPROVISATION; FREE RHYTHM; GRAPHIC NOTATION.

OPERA. Opera entered a new era with **Claude Debussy**'s *Pélléas et Mélisande* (1901), which eschewed the grand drama and familiar musical materials and gestures of 19th-century opera in favor of intimacy and subtlety; a similar quality also defined **Frederick Delius**'s *A Village Romeo and Juliet* (1901). Drama and **dissonance** were intensified in the **modernist** operas of **Richard Strauss** (*Salome*, 1905; *Elektra*, 1908), **Béla Bartók** (*Duke Bluebeard's Castle*, 1911), **Darius Milhaud** (*Les choéphores*, 1915), **Paul Hindemith** (*Das Nusch-Nuschi*, 1920), **Ferruccio Busoni** (*Doktor Faust*, 1924), and **Leos Janácek** (*From the House of the Dead*, 1928). **Atonal** opera entered the repertory with **Alban Berg**'s *Wozzeck* (1922). **Arnold Schoenberg**'s **twelve-tone** method was used in Schoenberg's *Moses und Aron* (1932), **Ernst Krenek**'s *Karl V* (1933), Berg's *Lulu* (1935), and such later operas as **Luigi Dallapiccola**'s *Il prigioniero* (1948), **Lousie Talma**'s *The Alcestiad* (1958), **Roger Sessions**'s *Montezuma* (1962), **Bernd Alois Zimmermann**'s *Die Soldaten* (1965), and **Toshiro Mayuzumi**'s *Kinkakuji* (1976).

In the United States, **Scott Joplin**'s operas *A Guest of Honor* (1903) and *Treemonisha* (1911) used popular forms; ragtime was also used by **Maurice Ravel** in *L'enfant et les sortilèges* (1925). **Virgil Thomson quoted** the hymns and folk tunes of his youth in Missouri in *Four Saints in Three Acts* (1928). Jazz elements entered opera with Krenek's *Jonny spielt auf* (1927), **George Antheil**'s *Transatlantic* (1928), **Bohuslav Martinu**'s *Les larmes du couteau* (1928), **Kurt Weill**'s *Aufstieg und fall der Stadt Mahagonny* (1929), and **George Gershwin**'s *Porgy and Bess* (1935).

Another innovation was restricting opera to a few singers and instruments, in staged or semistaged performances. The results range from the puppet operas of **Erik Satie** (*Geneviève de Brabant*, 1900) and **Manuel de Falla** (*El retablo de Maese Pedro*, 1922) to **Ezra Pound**'s neomedieval *Le testament* (1933) and **Pierre Schaeffer** and **Pierre Henry**'s *musique concrète* opera *Orphée 53* (1953). This reductiveness also defines the groundbreaking operas of **Robert Ashley** and **Meredith Monk**, as well as such recent works as **John Zorn**'s *Rituals* (1998) and **Anne LeBaron**'s *Pope Joan* (2000) and *Transfiguration* (2003). **Karlheinz Stockhausen**'s monumental seven-opera cycle *Licht* (1978–2003) has a foot in this category as well, insofar as each opera is comprised of numerous works for varying forces, which can also be performed individually. A similar sensibility informs **Anthony Braxton**'s *Trillium* series (1984–present), 36 one-act operas that can be interconnected in any combination.

Postmodern composers redefined opera radically in the second half of the 20th century. Collaborating with director Robert Wilson on the lengthy **minimalist** opera *Einstein on the Beach* (1975), **Philip Glass** dispensed with traditional operatic singing and instrumentation almost entirely. Ashley used video, improvisation, and **electroacoustic music** in such **multimedia** works as *Perfect Lives* (1977–1980) and *Atalanta (Acts of God)* (1982–1987). Monk largely eschewed electronics and emphasized choreography in *Education of the Girlchild* (1972), *The Games* (1983), and *Atlas* (1991). **John Cage** provided the last word in the deconstruction of opera with *Europeras I/II* (1987), using **chance** procedures to collage the music of European opera. Other notable composers of minimalist opera include **Morton Feldman** (*Neither*, 1977), **John Adams** (*Nixon in China*, 1987), and **Louis Andriessen** (*La commedia*, 2008).

More traditional forms of tonal opera, of course, remained a constant throughout the 20th century, most notably from **Benjamin Britten**, whose major works include *Peter Grimes* (1945), *Billy Budd* (1951), *The Turn of the Screw* (1954), *A Midsummer Night's Dream* (1960), and *Death in Venice* (1973). Among the many composers who have produced important tonal operas are Strauss (*Der Rosenkavalier*, 1910; *Die frau ohne schatten*, 1917), **Ralph Vaughan Williams** (*Sir John in Love*, 1928; *Riders to the Sea*, 1932), **Sergey Prokofiev** (*The Love for Three Oranges*, 1919; *War and Peace*, 1943, rev. 1952), **Francis Poulenc** (*Les mamelles de Tirésias*, 1944; *Les dialogues des Carmélites*, 1955; *La voix humaine*, 1958), **Gian Carlo Menotti** (*The Medium*, 1946; *Amahl and the Night Visitors*, 1951), and **Michael Tippett** (*The Midsummer Marriage*, 1952; *The Knot Garden*, 1970).

See also BARBER, SAMUEL; BARTH, HANS; BECKER, JOHN J.; BERG, CHRISTOPHER; BERIO, LUCIANO; BERNSTEIN, LEONARD; BIRTWISTLE, HARRISON; BISCARDI, CHESTER; BLITZSTEIN, MARC; BOLCOM, WILLIAM; BOWLES, PAUL; BRYARS, GAVIN; BUSSOTTI,

SYLVANO; CARTER, ELLIOTT; CERHA, FRIEDRICH; CHÁVEZ, CAR-
LOS; CHIN, UNSUK; COPLAND, AARON; CORIGLIANO, JOHN; DA-
VIES, PETER MAXWELL; DENISOV, EDISON; DEYHIM, SUSSAN;
DIAMOND, DAVID; EL-DABH, HALIM; FERNEYHOUGH, BRIAN;
FINE, VIVIAN; FINNEY, ROSS LEE; FLANAGAN, WILLIAM; FOSS,
LUKAS; FUTURISM; GERHARD, ROBERTO; GIDEON, MIRIAM;
GINASTERA, ALBERTO; GLANVILLE-HICKS, PEGGY; GLOBOKAR,
VINKO; GOEHR, ALEXANDER; GORDON, MICHAEL; GORDON,
PETER; HÁBA, ALOIS; HANNAN, JOE; HARRISON, LOU; HARVEY,
JONATHAN; HENZE, HANS WERNER; HERRMANN, BERNARD;
HOLST, GUSTAV; HONEGGER, ARTHUR; HOVHANESS, ALAN;
IBERT, JACQUES; ICHIYANAGI, TOSHI; JENKINS, LEROY; JOHN-
STON, BEN; JOLAS, BETSY; JOLIVET, ANDRÉ; KAGEL, MAURI-
CIO; KANCHELI, GIYA; KIRCHNER, LEON; KNUSSEN, OLIVER; LA
BARBARA, JOAN; LAM, BUN-CHING; LANG, DAVID; LEIBOWITZ,
RENÉ; LEÓN, TANIA; LIGETI, GYÖRGY; LOURIÉ, ARTHUR; LUEN-
ING, OTTO; MADERNA, BRUNO; MARTIN, FRANK; MAW, NICHO-
LAS; MESSIAEN, OLIVIER; MORAN, ROBERT; MUSGRAVE, THEA;
NONO, LUIGI; NYMAN, MICHAEL; ORFF, CARL; PENDERECKI,
KRZYSZTOF; REICH, STEVE; ROCHBERG, GEORGE; ROREM, NED;
ROUSSEL, ALBERT; SCHNITTKE, ALFRED; SCHULLER, GUNTHER;
SCHUMAN, WILLIAM; SHOSTAKOVICH, DMITRY; SMIT, LEO
(1921–1999); STILL, WILLIAM GRANT; STRAVINSKY, IGOR; SZY-
MANOWSKI, KAROL; TAL, JOSEF; TAN DUN; TAVENER, JOHN;
TEITELBAUM, RICHARD; VILLA-LOBOS, HEITOR; WALTON, WIL-
LIAM; WELLESZ, EGON; WOLFE, JULIA; WOLPE, STEFAN; WUO-
RINEN, CHARLES.

OPPENS, URSULA (1944–). American musician and educator. A pianist
specializing in **modern** and contemporary music, Ursula Oppens has pre-
miered numerous works, commissioning such composers as **Elliott Carter**,
Conlon Nancarrow, **György Ligeti**, **Frederic Rzewski**, and **Anthony
Braxton**. She also cofounded the contemporary-music ensemble Speculum
Musicae (1971–present) and has taught at Northwestern University.

ORFF, CARL (1895–1982). German composer, musician, and educator.
Carl Orff studied at the Akademie der Tonkunst in Munich and founded
the Güntherschule in 1924, where he developed his innovative Schulwerk
music-education program. A tuneful **neoromantic**, Orff is best known for
his cantatas *Carmina Burana* (1936), *Catulli Carmina* (1942), and *Tronfo
di Afrodite* (1951) and the **operas** *Der Mond* (1938, rev. 1941), *Die Kluge*

(1942), *Antigonae* (1949), and *De temporum fine comoedia* (1972, rev. 1979). *See also* GEBRAUCHSMUSIK.

ORNSTEIN, LEO (1893–2002). Russian-born American composer, musician, and educator. Already a piano prodigy, the young Leo Ornstein fled Russia's anti-Semitic violence and immigrated with his family to the United States in 1906. By 1911, Ornstein was concertizing, and in 1913–1914 he composed radical piano works with themes in **dissonant** clumps of two or three keys such as *Wild Men's Dance* (a.k.a. *Danse Sauvage*), *Three Moods*, and *Suicide in an Airplane*. His other innovative scores of the 1910s include Sonata for Violin and Piano (1915) and *The Corpse* (1918) for soprano and piano.

Ornstein toured internationally performing his own music, which was dubbed **futurist** by others, as well as works by such composers as **Claude Debussy, Alexander Scriabin, Béla Bartók, Maurice Ravel, Darius Milhaud,** and **Arnold Schoenberg**. Ornstein's composition became more conservative with his Piano Concerto (1920) and Piano Quintet (1927). By then, he was burned out as a performer, and eventually he left the stage permanently. In Philadelphia, he taught at the Academy of Music. He and his wife also founded the Ornstein School of Music. Late in life, Ornstein produced such noteworthy scores as his String Quartet No. 3 (1976) and Piano Sonatas Nos. 6 (1981), 7 (1988), and 8 (1990). *See also* COWELL, HENRY; MODERNISM; TONE-CLUSTER.

OSTERTAG, BOB (1957–). American composer, musician, and educator. By the end of the 1970s, Bob Ostertag was **sampling** before there were samplers, utilizing **tape** recorders to improvise with such composer/musicians as **Anthony Braxton, Fred Frith,** and **John Zorn**. He combined his own **electronic** instruments with samplers and digital editing in his music—solo (*Like a Melody, No Bitterness*, 1997), with his ensemble Say No More (*Say No More Project*, 2002), and in his compositions *Sooner or Later* (1991), *All the Rage* (1992) for string quartet and tape, and the **multimedia** pieces *Hunting Crows* (1997) and *Yugoslavia* (1999). His other works include *Dear Prime Minister* (1999) for voices and *Desert Boy on a Stick* (2001) for cello, slides, and spoken word. Ostertag teaches at the University of California, Davis, and is the author of *Creative Life* (2009) and other books. *See also* COMPUTER MUSIC; ELECTROACOUSTIC MUSIC; FREE IMPROVISATION; POST-MODERNISM.

OSWALD, JOHN (1953–). Canadian composer and musician. As a saxophonist, John Oswald has performed with **Fred Frith**, Henry Kaiser, Roger

Turner, and others. In his **electronic music**, he took **quotation** into what he called "plunderphonics": working with altered but not unrecognizable fragments of other recordings of pop, rock, jazz, and traditional and **modern** concert music. Oswald's witty and imaginative use of **sampling** includes the recordings *Plunderphonics EP* (1988), *Grayfolded* (1994), and *69plunderphonics96* (2000). *Aparenthesi* (2000–2003), in studio and concert versions, avoids plunderphonics and combines piano with electronic and recorded environmental sound. *See also* COMPUTER MUSIC; FREE IMPROVISATION; POSTMODERNISM.

P

PAIK, NAM JUNE (1932–2006). Korean-born American composer. Nam June Paik studied at the University of Tokyo and the Freiburg Conservatory. Paik's provocative conceptual pieces with the **Fluxus** group include *One for Violin Solo* (1964). His *Opéra sextronique* (1967) with cellist Charlotte Moorman resulted in her arrest for indecent exposure at its New York premiere. Paik is best known for his video-based art; among his **sound installations** are *Megatron Matrix* (1995) and *Modulation in Sync* (2000). *See also* POSTMODERNISM.

PALESTINE, CHARLEMAGNE (1947–). American composer and musician. Charlemagne Palestine became a legend in the **minimalist** scene by the early 1970s, giving lengthy performances with an ecstatic endurance-art quality. On piano or organ (or, more rarely, tubular bells or carillon), he would aggressively hammer chords or strum the keys and generate overtone activity. A student of the North Indian master singer Pandit Pran Nath, Palestine would sustain a vocal drone while walking or running throughout the performance space, or sing a slow continuing crescendo as he threw himself against the walls and floor. He created **tape music** such as *Holy 1 & Holy 2* (1967) and used sine-tone generators in *Negative Sound Study* (1969) to produce pure sound waves as **electronic** drones that he then gradually altered, adding or filtering overtones and white noise. He also built a machine of oscillators and filters on which he performed drones.

Palestine composed *Birth of a Sonority* (1977) for string orchestra, but by the mid-1970s he had turned away from what he regarded as the commercialization of minimalist music. He eventually relocated to Europe and stopped performing and composing. Over the 1980s, he began reintroducing his music, and now he performs mostly in Europe. His CD releases include such reissues as his 1974 recordings *Strumming Music* and *Four Manifestations on Six Elements*, as well as recent performances such as *Godbear* (1998) and *From Etudes to Cataclysms* (2008). *See also* MULTICULTURALISM; PLEROMA; POSTMODERNISM; TONE-CLUSTER.

PANTONALITY. The term *pantonality* has been used with two different meanings. **Arnold Schoenberg** thought that his music should be described as pantonal—the 12 tones of the chromatic scale being equally important and available, with no single tone dominating—rather than **atonal**, which suggested a music devoid of tones. **Béla Bartók** used *pantonality* to define his music's evocation of a key signature through repeated or sustained tones, while in fact avoiding tonal structures and thereby remaining free to utilize any and all pitches or sounds. Hence, confusion still surrounds the term, with some sources insisting that it is a synonym for atonality, and others using it to designate music that shifts in and out of specific key centers but is *not* atonal.

PÄRT, ARVO (1935–). Estonian-born Austrian composer, musician, and educator. Arvo Pärt studied at the Tallinn Conservatory, where he later taught. He employed **serial** methods in such orchestral pieces as *Nekrolog* (1960) and *Perpetuum mobile* (1966), but found his own voice with a stripped-down, quasi-**minimalist** music, launched in 1977 with *Fratres* for chamber ensemble of early or modern instruments and *Tabula rasa* for two violins (or violin and viola), string orchestra, and prepared piano. Pärt immigrated to Austria in 1980, became a citizen, and then settled in Germany the following year. He has since composed mostly religious-themed works, most notably for mixed chorus either solo (*Magnificat*, 1989; *Tribute to Ceasar*, 1997), with organ (*The Beatitudes*, 1990; *Salve Regina*, 2002), or with orchestra (*Cecilia, vergine romana*, 2000, rev. 2002; *In principio*, 2003). *See also* TWELVE-TONE MUSIC.

PARTCH, HARRY (1901–1974). American composer and musician. The breakthrough figure in the fields of **just intonation** and **instrument building**, Harry Partch also played an essential role in **postmodern** music, deconstructing and reinventing Western musical techniques. Born in Oakland, California, and raised mostly in Arizona and New Mexico, Partch studied briefly at the University of Southern California in 1920 and 1922 and composed a symphonic poem in 1924. The following year, he began investigating just intonation and wrote a string quartet in that **alternate tuning system**, for which he built new violin and viola fingerboards. In 1930, Partch destroyed all his scores and hired an instrument maker to construct his Adapted Viola. Requiring an extra-long fingerboard, it was played like a cello and tuned to a scale that divided the octave into 37 tones, for which Partch devised his own notation system. (He would further develop that notation in later years, as his tunings and instruments changed.)

Weary of the unintelligible melismatic singing that had dominated Western composition, Partch created a vocal music that truly projected the words being sung, starting with a series of songs to the poetry of Li Po. During the early 1930s, he also gave lecture-recitals of what he termed "corporeal" (as opposed to abstract) music, singing and accompanying himself on the Adapted Viola. He built a keyboard instrument, the Ptolemy Organ, in 1933, tuning it to a 39-note-to-the-octave scale, and his first Adapted Guitar in 1934. Later that year, he met Irish poet and playwright W. B. Yeats, demonstrated his music, and received permission to adapt Yeats's translation of Sophocles' *Oedipus Tyrannos*. Funding, however, proved so difficult that by 1935 Partch abandoned his efforts. He became a hobo and worked at federal camps—a life chronicled in a journal published in 1991 as *Bitter Music*. He found employment again in 1936 and resumed building just-intonation instruments, completing his 72-string kithara in 1938.

Using a scale of 43 tones to the octave, Partch modified a harmonium into his first Chromelodeon in 1941. That same year, he composed *Barstow*, a setting of hitchhiker graffiti for Adapted Guitar and voice, and hopped freight trains to travel to Chicago. Partch described that journey in *U.S. Highball* (1943) for Adapted Guitar, kithara, Chromelodeon, and voices, and he revised *Barstow* for a similar ensemble. His lecture-recitals in the early 1940s attracted research support at the University of Wisconsin, Madison, and Partch relocated there in 1944. He built the 44-string Harmonic Canon, demonstrated in his *Two Studies on Ancient Greek Scales* (1946), and his first percussion instrument, the wood-block Diamond Marimba in 1946. The University of Wisconsin Press also published Partch's *Genesis of a Music* in 1949, but by then he was in a new studio in Gualala, California, composing, building instruments, and making recordings.

Partch built two of his most memorable percussion instruments in 1950: the Cloud Chamber Bowls, using suspended sections of 12-gallon Pyrex carboys, and the Spoils of War, combining wood, metal, bamboo, gourd, and Pyrex percussion. He also constructed two more wooden marimbas, the Bass Marimba and the Marimba Eroica, in 1950 and 1951, respectively. All the Partch instruments were designed as objects of sculptural beauty, and in his music theater, the instruments were always onstage, played by costumed musicians who would also sing and perform with the other players. That phase of his music began in 1952 when Partch premiered *Oedipus* at Mills College; he also established a studio there, but left the following year. At a new facility in Sausalito, California, he composed the dance score *Plectra and Percussion Dances* (1953), for which he built his Surrogate Kithara. Partch revised *Barstow* again in 1954 and *U.S. Highball* the following year. He built his first bamboo marimba, the Boo, in 1955 and completed his music-theater work *The Bewitched* as well as a chamber piece, *Ulysses at the Edge*.

Partch relocated again in 1956, this time to Illinois, and premiered *The Bewitched* at the University of Illinois at Urbana-Champaign the following year. He followed with *Revelation in the Courthouse Park* (1960), his adaptation of Euripides' *The Bacchae*, and *Water! Water!* (1961). Partch then left Illinois for a new studio in Petaluma, California, where in 1963 he built the percussion instruments the Zymo-Xyl—using woodblocks, empty wine and liquor bottles, and automobile hubcaps—and the Mazda Marimba, made of light globes. After composing *And on the Seventh Day Petals Fell in Petaluma* (1964), he left Petaluma and worked in various California studios for the rest of the decade.

Partch constructed his Gourd Tree in 1964, with Chinese temple bells bolted to gourds, and his grand Quadrangularis Reversum, incorporating five wooden marimbas, in 1965. His last and greatest music-theater piece was *Delusion of the Fury* (1966), an adaptation of Japanese and African folk tales, premiered in 1969 at UCLA. *The Dreamer That Remains*, his final composition, was written in 1972 and featured in a documentary on Partch of the same title. The revised and expanded edition of *Genesis of a Music* was published in 1974, a few months before Partch's death from a heart attack in San Diego at age 73. *See also* JOHNSTON, BEN; MICROTONALITY; MULTICULTURALISM.

PEARS, (SIR) PETER (1910–1986). English musician and educator. Tenor Peter Pears studied at Oxford University and the Royal College of Music, and in 1937 he met **Benjamin Britten** who became his lifetime companion. Britten composed numerous outstanding concert works for Pears's voice, including *Les illuminations* (1939), *Seven Sonnets of Michelangelo* (1940), *Serenade* (1943), and *War Requiem* (1962); his operas also have many notable roles composed specifically for Pears, such as the title role in *Peter Grimes* (1945), Captain Vere in *Billy Budd* (1951), the Madwoman in *Curlew River* (1964), and Aschenbach in *Death in Venice* (1973). Pears performed music by other important 20th-century composers, as well, and recorded works by **Frederick Delius**, **Ralph Vaughan Williams**, **Igor Stravinsky**, **William Walton**, **Frank Martin**, **Michael Tippett**, **Witold Lutoslawski**, and **Percy Grainger**. He taught at the Britten-Pears School for Advanced Musical Studies and was knighted in 1978.

PENDERECKI, KRZYSZTOF (1933–). Polish composer, musician, and educator. Krzysztof Penderecki played violin and piano from his youth and attended the Kraków Academy of Music, where he later served as principal (1972–1978). He also taught at Yale University (1973–1978) and developed an active career as a conductor. A sensitive orchestral colorist, Penderecki utilized **graphic notation**, **extended performance techniques**, glissandi, **tone-clusters**, and **quarter-tones** in his gripping and expressive works. He achieved international recognition with two 1960 scores, *Anaklasis* for strings and percussion and *Threnos* (a.k.a. *Threnody for the Victims of Hiroshima*) for 52 strings.

Penderecki has composed numerous large-scale liturgical scores for soloists, mixed chorus, and orchestra: *St. Luke Passion* (1966), *Dies Irae* (1967), *Utrenja I* (1970), *Utrenja II* (1971), *Magnificat* (1974), *Te Deum* (1980), *Polish Requiem* (1984; rev. 1993, 2005), and *Credo* (1998). Also noteworthy are his **operas** *The Devils of Loudon* (1969), *Paradise Lost* (1976, rev. 1978), *Die schwarze Maske* (1986), and *Ubu Rex* (1991) and his eight symphonies (1973–2007). He had a **neoromantic** phase in the 1970s and 1980s, with such pieces as the Violin Concerto No. 1 (1977, rev. 1988) and Cello Concerto No. 2 (1982). Penderecki's recent works include Concerto Grosso (2001) for three cellos and orchestra and "Resurrection" Piano Concerto (2002, rev. 2007). *See also* MODERNISM.

PERKINS, PHILIP (1951–). American composer and musician. The co-founder of the label Fun Music, Philip Perkins has made expressive use of environmental sound and location recordings, often with **synthesizers** and instruments. His notable works include *Neighborhood with a Sky* (1982), *King of the World* (1984), *Drive Time* (1985), *Virgo Ramayana* (1994), and *At the Other End of the Day* (2005). In *Shapiro Songs* (1989), he combined voice and **tape**. Perkins has also collaborated with **"Blue" Gene Tyranny** and the **Residents**. *See also* ELECTROACOUSTIC MUSIC; POSTMODERNISM.

PERLE, GEORGE (1915–2009). American composer, musician, educator, and theorist. George Perle studied with **Ernst Krenek** and at New York University. Blending **atonal**, **twelve-tone**, and tonal techniques, his music includes *Six Etudes* (1976) for piano, *Serenade No. 3* (1983) for piano and chamber ensemble, Wind Quintet No. 4 (1984), *Transcendental Modulations* (1993) for orchestra, *Phantasyplay* (1995) for piano, and the sextets *Critical Moments* (1996) and *Critical Moments 2* (2001). He taught at Columbia University, Queens College, and other institutions and is the author of *Serial Composition and Atonality* (1962, sixth edition 1991), *Twelve-Tone Tonality* (1977, rev. 1996), *The Operas of Alban Berg* (1980–1985), and *The Listening Composer* (1990). *See also* METRIC MODULATION; MODERNISM.

PISTON, WALTER (1894–1976). American composer, musician, and educator. Walter Piston studied with **Nadia Boulanger** and Paul Dukas and taught at Harvard University (1926–1960); his students included **Elliott**

Carter, Leonard Bernstein, Irving Fine, and **Arthur Berger**. Piston's textbooks *Principles of Harmonic Analysis* (1933), *Harmony* (1941), *Counterpoint* (1947), and *Orchestration* (1955) have been widely used for decades. A **neoclassical** composer with a lyrical voice, Piston is especially admired for his Concerto for Orchestra (1933), the ballet score *The Incredible Flutist* (1938), Symphony No. 3 (1947), and *Three New England Sketches* (1959) for orchestra. **Twelve-tone** and tonal techniques are blended in his *Chromatic Fantasy on the Name of BACH* (1940) for organ and such later scores as Symphony No. 8 (1965) and Variations for Cello and Orchestra (1966). Piston's other works include eight symphonies (1937–1965) and five string quartets (1933–1962). *See also* MODERNISM.

PLEROMA. From the Greek word for "fullness" or "completeness," *pleroma* came to mean within Gnostic Christianity both the spiritual universe of the Creator and the totality of that divine power. Its application to 20th-century music can be traced to **Alexander Scriabin**, who was familiar with Gnosticism. His classic *Prométhée—Le poème du feu* (1910) was built upon a six-tone chord that he referred to as the "chord of the pleroma": C, F-sharp, B-flat, E, A, and D. (Only after Scriabin's death did it come to be called in English the "mystic chord.") Such music is intended not only to describe the movement toward transcendent revelation but to energize and actualize that experience as well.

　　Dane Rudhyar, in his book *The Magic of Tone and the Art of Music*, defined a pleroma as a specialized musical aggregate in which different relationships interpenetrate to produce a singular resonance or meaning. The densities in **Charles Ives**'s music make him one of the first and greatest pleroma composers; so is **Henry Cowell**, with his **tone-cluster** and **string-piano** works. Scriabin had selected the pitches of the chord of the pleroma from higher partials in the overtone series, and composers who create dense fields of overtones and resultant tones—such as **La Monte Young, Charlemagne Palestine, Rhys Chatham, Glenn Branca, David Hykes**, and **Mary Jane Leach**—are creating pleromas. This quality can also define music that masses like voices, whether in small groups (**Toshiro Mayuzumi**'s *Tone Pleromas 55*, 1955; **Alan Hovhaness**'s *Spirit of Ink*, 1970; **Julius Eastman**'s *Gay Guerilla*, 1979; **Lois V. Vierk**'s *Simoom*, 1986) or large (**Henry Brant**'s *Orbits*, 1979; **Pauline Oliveros**'s *The Wanderer*, 1982; **Wendy Mae Chambers**'s *A Mass for Massed Trombones*, 1993). **Free jazz** can be pleromatic, as in the piano and ensemble music of **Cecil Taylor** and **Sun Ra**. *See also* JUST INTONATION.

POLYHARMONY. In his book *New Musical Resources*, **Henry Cowell** described the use of polyharmony as a succession of polychords—chords in which certain overtones and/or undertones of each pitch are also sounded. Polyharmony permits more tones to be introduced within the harmonic vocabulary while avoiding overcomplexity, insofar as they can be grouped within the harmony into related units. Cowell composed polyharmonic music with his *Two Rhythm-Harmony Quartets* in 1919, but the music was of such rhythmic complexity that it was not performed until 1964. *See also* JUST INTONATION; SPECTRAL MUSIC.

POLYMETER. *See* POLYRHYTHM.

POLYRHYTHM. The simultaneous use of two or more different rhythmic patterns that conflict, insofar as their accents fail to coincide. The piling up of different rhythms typifies many of the greatest works of **Charles Ives**, such as *The Unanswered Question* (1908), Piano Sonatas Nos. 1 (1909) and 2 (1915), String Quartet No. 2 (1913), *Three Places in New England* (1914), and Symphony No. 4 (1916). While avoiding the extreme densities of Ives's music, other composers also compounded rhythms with new daring in the early 20th century, most notably **Alexander Scriabin, Igor Stravinsky,** and **Béla Bartók. Henry Cowell**'s *Two Rhythm-Harmony Quartets* (1919) went unplayed and unpublished, but his fascination with complex polyrhythms also led him to compose *Rhythmicana* (1931), a concerto with a machine as soloist: the rhythmicon, built by **Leon Theremin**.

These **modernist** composers were also using polymeters, another device usually associated with polyrhythmic music, in which the time signature in a score can change from bar to bar—a necessity in the **totally serialized** music of such composers as **Milton Babbitt** and **Pierre Boulez**, who organized durations as well as pitch. Others who took polyrhythmic music in new directions include **Conlon Nancarrow, Olivier Messiaen, John Cage, Elliott Carter, Henry Brant,** and **György Ligeti,** as well as such innovative figures in creative African-American music as **Sun Ra, Cecil Taylor,** and **Anthony Braxton.** *See also* METRIC MODULATION; NEOCLASSICISM.

POLYTONALITY. The simultaneous use of two or more different key signatures. Examples occur at the end of the 19th century with the more daring scores of the young **Charles Ives,** most notably *Song for Harvest Season* (1894); his music of the 1900s and 1910s delved even more deeply into simultaneities and densities. **Béla Bartók** began incorporating polytonality in his music with such works as Violin Concerto No. 1 (1908) and String Quartet No. 1 (1909). This **dissonant modernist** device became more frequent in the 1910s, after the success of **Igor Stravinsky**'s *Petrushka* (1911), and found a major exponent in **Darius Milhaud.** Other notable composers of polytonal music in the 1910s and 1920s include **Erik Satie**, **Ferruccio Busoni**, **Karol Szymanowski**, **Sergey Prokofiev**, **Carl Nielsen**, and **Manuel de Falla**. *See also* BITONALITY.

PORTSMOUTH SINFONIA. The Portsmouth Sinfonia was founded collectively in 1970 by **Gavin Bryars**, conductor John Farley, and art students from Portsmouth (England) Polytechnic. Their aim was to perform orchestral standards despite the fact that all their members were either nonmusicians or unskilled on their assigned instrument. The resulting deconstructions of the repertory's warhorses were full of surprises and humor; they also invited music lovers to reassess their understanding of that music. The group soon attracted more players, including **Brian Eno** and **Michael Nyman**, and released the albums *Portsmouth Sinfonia Plays the Popular Classics* (1973) and *Hallelujah!* (1974), both produced by Eno. The LP *20 Classic Rock Classics*, sending up orchestral versions of rock music, was released in 1979, the Portsmouth Sinfonia's final year. *See also* GEBRAUCHSMUSIK; POSTMODERNISM.

POSTMODERNISM. Postmodernism is a reaction to and critique of **modernism**. By finding beauty in **atonality**, **dissonance**, and **polyrhythm**, modernist music revealed the arbitrary nature of traditional tonality, harmony, and rhythm; postmodern music turns modernism's x-ray upon itself and explores modernist freedoms without relying on modernist conceptualizations. Whereas modernism shattered traditional music into individualized styles and methods, postmodernism develops techniques to appropriate, deconstruct, and recontextualize what is available in today's unprecedented range of musical expression.

That spectrum of music goes beyond traditional and modernist—the materials of jazz, blues, rock, and other popular-music forms are also used, either transformed or in **quotation**, without pursuing the conventions of their native genres, as **Erik Satie** had anticipated in the 1910s and 1920s. A **multicultural** interest in world music is another factor. All these elements proved essential for **La Monte Young**, **Terry Riley**, **Philip Glass**, and **Steve Reich**, whose **minimalist** music is a postmodern response to the limitations of traditionalism and modernism. **Spatial music**, exemplified by the works of **Henry Brant**, can be seen as a further critique that redefines the relationship between performer and listener and enables different kinds of music to be performed simultaneously.

Postmodernism also redefines earlier work. **John Cage** took Satie literally and had *Vexations* performed 840 times in a row. **John Zorn** studied Carl Stalling's cartoon scores. The **Portsmouth Sinfonia** and the **Scratch**

Orchestra performed classical works they did not know how to play. The **Residents'** covers of 1960s pop tunes in *The Third Reich 'n' Roll* (1976) and Elvis Presley in *The King & Eye* (1989) were scathing accounts of American consumerism. With **computer** and **sampling** technology, as in the music of **John Oswald** and **David Shea**, composers have the ideal equipment for borrowing and reinventing other recorded sounds.

Along with its tradition of **instrument building**—stretching from the pioneering works of **Harry Partch** to pieces by **Glenn Branca, Tan Dun**, and many others—postmodern music also deconstructs traditional instruments. One method for this is the use of **alternate tuning systems**, championed by Partch and used in works by **Lou Harrison, Pauline Oliveros, James Tenney**, and **Ben Johnston**, among others. There are also **extended performance techniques**, such as **Lucia Dlugoszewski**'s timbre piano or the dismantled instruments played by Zorn and **George Lewis**. Another approach is the appropriation of noninstruments for performance, as in the percussion-ensemble pieces of **William Russell**, Cage, and Harrison and the music of Partch, Z'ev, Charles K. Noyes, and Fast Forward. Certain **Fluxus** composers focused on the noninstrumental character of the sounds they made: George Brecht's *Comb Music* (1962, a.k.a. *Comb Event*) plucked the teeth of a comb; **Alison Knowles**'s *Music by Alison* (1964) listened to fabric being waved.

Everyday objects can also have their sounds altered through amplification, from Eugene Chadbourne improvising on a rake to Cage using plant materials in *Branches (Improvisation IB)* (1976). Note Cage's subtitle: playing such unfamiliar "instruments" requires an improviser's spontaneity and openness. Improvisation with appropriated and/or deconstructed instruments has been essential to the work of such outstanding postmodern composer/musicians as Young, Oliveros, Riley, Lewis, Zorn, **Robert Ashley, Anne LeBaron, "Blue" Gene Tyranny, Fred Frith, Anthony Braxton, Susie Ibarra, Elliott Sharp, David Tudor, Jerry Hunt**, and **Laurie Spiegel**.

Postmodernism views the options of music as encompassing the entire world of sound: the full spectrum of noise and the infinity of **microtonalities**, not just the pitches of equal temperament; any instrument that anyone has ever played or could ever build or adapt, not just the complement of the orchestra. It also encompasses the assimilation of other arts in **multimedia** works. This fundamental shift in Western musical thought had two highly influential exponents: Partch, who built instruments that were tuned to his own system, and Cage, whose use of **chance** procedures and **indeterminacy** stripped his musical materials of their cultural baggage. Partch and Cage offered both an attitude and a methodology for making music beyond the notion of a mainstream, into a delta or ocean of innumerable possibilities—the quintessential postmodern situation.

See also ADAMS, JOHN; ADAMS, JOHN LUTHER; AMBIENT MUSIC; AMM; ANDERSON, LAURIE; ANDRIESSEN, LOUIS; AUSTIN, LARRY; BEATLES, THE; BEHRMAN, DAVID; BOLCOM, WILLIAM; BROWN, EARLE; BRYARS, GAVIN; CHAMBERS, WENDY MAE; CHATHAM, RHYS; CONRAD, TONY; CORNER, PHILIP; DEL TREDICI, DAVID; DEYHIM, SUSSAN; DUCKWORTH, WILLIAM; EASTMAN, JULIUS; ENO, BRIAN; FELDMAN, MORTON; FERRARI, LUC; FLYNT, HENRY; FREE IMPROVISATION; FULLMAN, ELLEN; GARLAND, PETER; GLOBOKAR, VINKO; GORDON, MICHAEL; GORDON, PETER; GOS-FIELD, ANNIE; HANNAN, JOE; HIGGINS, DICK; HILLER, LEJAREN; HYKES, DAVID; ICHIYANAGI, TOSHI; JENKINS, LEROY; JENNINGS, TERRY; JOHNSON, DENNIS; JOHNSON, TOM; KAGEL, MAURICIO; KOSUGI, TAKEHISA; KOTIK, PETR; LA BARBARA, JOAN; LANG, DAVID; LEACH, MARY JANE; LEÓN, TANIA; LOCKWOOD, ANNEA; LUCIER, ALVIN; MACHT, ROBERT; MARCUS, BUNITA; MARTI-RANO, SALVATORE; MAXFIELD, RICHARD; MEV; MITCHELL, ROSCOE; MONK, MEREDITH; MOON, BEATA; MOONDOG; MORAN, ROBERT; MUMMA, GORDON; NEUHAUS, MAX; NIBLOCK, PHILL; NYMAN, MICHAEL; ONO, YOKO; OSTERTAG, BOB; PAIK, NAM JUNE; PALESTINE, CHARLEMAGNE; PERKINS, PHILIP; RADIGUE, ELIANE; ROCHBERG, GEORGE; ROUGH ASSEMBLAGE; RUSSELL, ARTHUR; RYLAN, JESSICA; RZEWSKI, FREDERIC; SPEACH, BER-NADETTE; SUN RA; TAKAHASHI, YUJI; TAVENER, JOHN; TEITEL-BAUM, RICHARD; VIERK, LOIS V.; WESTERKAMP, HILDEGARD; WOLFE, JULIA; WOLFF, CHRISTIAN; ZAPPA, FRANK.

POULENC, FRANCIS (1889–1963). French composer and musician. Francis Poulenc studied piano with Ricardo Viñes in the 1910s and composition with Charles Koechlin in the 1920s. A sense of humor distinguished Poulenc's early works, such as *Rapsodie nègre* (1917) for baritone and seven instruments, Sonata for Two Clarinets (1918, rev. 1945), and *Trois mouvements perpétuels* (1918, rev. 1962) for piano. In the early 1920s, Poulenc was known as a member of the **Groupe des Six,** but he went on to attract attention for such **neoclassical** pieces as the dance score *Les biches* (1923), *Aubade* (1929) for piano and 18 instruments, Sextet (1932, rev. 1940) for piano and winds, and Concerto for Two Pianos and Orchestra (1932). Humor and light-ness also defined his songs for voice and piano, a genre in which he excelled, for example, *Le bestiaire* (1919), *Poèmes de Ronsard* (1925), *Quatre poèmes de Guillaume Apollinaire* (1931), *Tel jour, telle nuit* (1937), *Banalités* (1940), *Chansons villageoises* (1942), and *Caligrammes* (1948). Poulenc also per-formed internationally as a pianist, principally in recitals of his songs.

Although Poulenc's music was inflected with **polytonal** and other **dissonant** procedures, he was essentially a tonal composer whose melodic gifts were best served by a familiar harmonic vocabulary. Religious music became important to him in the 1930s, with such choral works as *Litanies à la Vierge noire* (1936) for women's or boys' chorus and organ and two works for mixed chorus: the Mass in G (1937) and *Quatre motets pour un temps de pénitence* (1939). Poulenc's **opera** *Les mamelles de Tirésias* (1944) was comic, but a greater seriousness characterized his Concerto for Organ, Strings, and Percussion (1938), *Sinfonietta* (1947) for orchestra, and Piano Concerto (1949).

Among the religious scores of Poulenc's later years are *Figure humaine* (1943) for double mixed chorus and *Stabat Mater* (1950) and *Gloria* (1958), both for soprano, mixed chorus, and orchestra. One of Poulenc's finest scores, the opera *Les dialogues des Carmélites* (1955), was also religious-themed. His other notable vocal works are the songs of *Parisiana* (1954), *Le travail du peintre* (1956), and *La courte paille* (1960) and the one-act one-voice opera *La voix humaine* (1958). Poulenc's last instrumental scores were his Flute Sonata (1957), *Elégie* (1957) for horn and piano, Clarinet Sonata (1962), and Oboe Sonata (1962). *See also* MODERNISM.

POUND, EZRA (1885–1972). American composer and critic. One of the great poets and translators of his era, Ezra Pound was an autodidact in music. He began publishing music criticism in England in 1908 and, as "William Atheling," was a critic for the London weekly *The New Age* (1917–1921). Pound relocated to Paris in 1920, where he connected with two American musicians: violinist Olga Rudge and composer **George Antheil**. Pound composed several solo-violin scores for Rudge, including *Sujet* (1923) and *Fiddle Music* (1924). In Antheil's music, Pound discerned innovative techniques of rhythmic organization, and he published his study *Antheil and the Treatise on Harmony* in 1924.

Pound's approach to rhythm and prosody was showcased in *Le testament*, settings of 15th-century French poet François Villon as a one-act **opera** for tenor, bass-baritone, violin, harpsichord, two trombones, kettledrums, and *cornet de dessus*, a medieval horn. Excerpts were performed privately in Paris in 1926, and its final version of 1933 called for nine or more singers and 10 to 12 instruments. This neomedieval opera anticipated **minimalist** attitudes toward drama and singing. So, too, did *Cavalcanti*, also completed in 1933, which set the 13th-century Italian poets Guido Cavalcanti and Sordello da Goito as a three-act opera for tenor, bass-baritone, three sopranos, flute, English horn, bassoon, trombone, violin, cello, contrabass, and percussion. Pound sketched a third opera, *Collis o Heliconii*, in 1932 but left these settings of Catullus and Sappho unfinished.

Pound moved to Italy in 1924, and in Rapallo he produced a series of concerts from 1933 to 1939 featuring works by such **modernists** as **Béla Bartók**, **Igor Stravinsky**, and **Paul Hindemith**—composers whom he also promoted in the newspaper *Il mare*. World War II ended his musical activities, and in 1945 Pound was taken prisoner by American authorities, charged with treason for having made wartime radio broadcasts in support of the Axis. Brought back to the United States, he was declared psychologically unfit to stand trial and placed in a mental hospital. Upon his discharge in 1958, all charges against him were dropped, and Pound returned to Italy. He continued to work at his poetry despite failing health and died in Venice two days after his 87th birthday.

POUSSEUR, HENRI (1929–2009). Belgian composer and educator. Henri Pousseur attended the Liège Conservatoire, where he later taught and served as director. He used an **Anton Webern**–derived **serial** technique in *Trois chants sacrés* (1951) for soprano and string trio and the **microtonal** *Prospection* (1953) for three pianos tuned in sixth-tones. His Quintet (1955) was **totally serialized**, but *Exercices* (1956) for piano was freely **atonal**. Pousseur began composing **electronic music** with *Séismogrammes* (1954); *Scambi* (1957), an **open-form** work, was created exclusively from white noise. In 1958, he founded the Studio de Musique Électronique in Brussels. *Rimes* (1958) was a **spatial** piece combining three orchestral groups with magnetic **tape**; Pousseur's other tape music includes the dance score *Électre* (1960) and *Trois visages de Liège* (1961). Among his music-theater works are *Votre Faust* (1961–1968) and *Leçons d'Enfer* (1990–1991).

Pousseur's innovations covered a spectrum of musical expression. He devised the improvisation systems of *Mnémosyne II* (1969) and *Icare apprenti* (1970). He cofounded the Centre de Recherches et de Formation Musicales de Wallonie in Liège in 1970 (renamed Centre Henri Pousseur in 2010), devoted to electronic and **multimedia** music. His **electroacoustic** *Crosses of Crossed Colors* (1970) was scored for amplified female voice, two to five pianos, two tape recorders, two turntables, and two radios. *Racine 19e de 8/4* (1976) was for solo cello tuned in 19th-tones. *Les îles déchaînées* (1980), a collaboration with his son Denis, called for jazz septet, four **synthesizers**, and orchestra.

The author of *Fragments Théoriques I* (1970), *Musiques croisées* (1997), and other books, Pousseur also founded the review *Marsyas* in Paris in 1987 and taught at Darmstadt, the Basel Conservatory, the State University of New York at Buffalo, and other institutions. His late works include *Figure et ombres* (1988), of **indeterminate** instrumentation and duration; *Suite du massacre des innocents* (1997) for large wind orchestra and unison chorus ad lib; and the three-and-a-half-hour electronic suite *Seize paysages planétaires* (2000), from which he derived the **sound installation** *Un jour du monde en 280 minutes* (2002) and the multimedia *Voix et vues planétaires* (2004). He died in Brussels of bronchial pneumonia at age 79. *See also* POSTMODERNISM.

POWELL, MEL (1923–1998). American composer, musician, and educator. Mel Powell's teachers included **Joseph Schillinger** and **Paul Hindemith**; he later taught at Yale University and the California Institute for the Arts. Powell played jazz piano and arranged for Benny Goodman and others in the 1940s. He used **neoclassical** and **serial** techniques in his Piano Trio (1954) and *Divertimento* (1955) for wind quintet. *Filigree Setting* (1959) for string quartet was **totally serialized** and had **extended performance techniques**, as did *Haiku* (1961) for soprano and piano. *Events for Tape Recorder* (1963) blended **tape music** and **electronically** synthesized sound, and the *Immobiles* series (1967–1969) used tape with an **indeterminate** number of musicians and offered performance freedoms. Powell's late works include *Strand Settings: Darker* (1983) for soprano and tape, *Duplicates* (1987) for two pianos and orchestra, *Sonatina for Flute Alone* (1995), and *Seven Miniatures, Women Poets of China* (1998) for mezzo-soprano and harp. *See also* ALEATORY; ATONALITY; ELECTROACOUSTIC MUSIC; MODERNISM.

PRATELLA, FRANCESCO BALILLA. *See* FUTURISM.

PROKOFIEV, SERGEY (1891–1953). Russian composer and musician. Sergey Prokofiev's humor, expressivity, and passion made his music internationally successful, from the fiery **modernism** of his youth to the more conservative works of his years in the Soviet Union. Sergey Sergeyevich Prokofiev was born in the Ukrainian estate of Sontsovka and received piano lessons from his mother. Composing by age five, he began studying piano and composition with Reinhold Glière at 11. Prokofiev was 13 when he entered the St. Petersburg Conservatory, where his teachers included Nikolay Rimsky-Korsakov and Alexander Glazunov. Embracing influences as diverse as Richard Wagner, **Alexander Scriabin**, Edvard Grieg, Modest Mussorgsky, and Max Reger, Prokofiev produced his first important works, *Suggestion diabolique* (1908) for piano and Piano Sonata No. 1 (1909). His **dissonant**, percussive, sometimes shocking approach to the piano was showcased in his Piano Concertos Nos. 1 (1911) and 2 (1913, rev. 1923), both of which he premiered as pianist. He included **bitonality** in his *Sarcasms* for piano, completed in 1914, the same year in which he graduated and began to travel.

In France, Prokofiev worked on *Ala i Lolli* for the Ballets Russes of impresario Serge Diaghilev. It was never completed or staged, but the music resulted in his barbaric *Scythian Suite* (1915, rev. 1922) for orchestra. Back in Russia, he completed *The Gambler*, an **opera** adapted from Fyodor Dostoevsky's novel, in 1917. It was left unstaged in that year of revolution, when Prokofiev composed some of his greatest scores: *Visions fugitives* for piano, the lyrical Violin Concerto No. 1, and his Symphony No. 1, the charming and ever youthful "Classical Symphony." Prokofiev had anticipated **neoclassicism** by redefining classical techniques for modern harmonies and rhythms, but he remained uninvolved in the 1920s trend that **Igor Stravinsky** and others embraced.

After reprising the savagery of the *Scythian Suite* with his cantata *They Are Seven* (1918) for tenor, mixed chorus, and orchestra, Prokofiev began living and concertizing in the United States. But his comic opera *The Love for Three Oranges* (1919) failed there in 1921, despite its popular orchestral suite (1919, rev. 1924), and Prokofiev relocated to France where he completed his Piano Concerto No. 3 (1921). His comic ballet *Chout* (1915) was successfully premiered by Diaghilev's company in 1922, but the dark opera *The Fiery Angel* (1923, rev. 1927) was never staged in Prokofiev's lifetime. His Symphony No. 2 (1924), an abrasive "Age of Steel" score, was received coolly, but the machine-themed *Le pas d'acier* (1925), for the Ballets Russes, was celebrated.

Although Prokofiev was acclaimed when he concertized in the Soviet Union in 1927, he returned to France to complete his Symphony No. 3 (1928), which utilized themes from *The Fiery Angel*. *L'enfant prodigue* (1929), a dramatic dance for Diaghilev, in turn yielded material for his Symphony No. 4 (1930, rev. 1947). He also composed his Piano Concertos Nos. 4 (1931, for the left hand) and 5 (1932) in France, but in 1936 Prokofiev settled with his family in Moscow. That year, he completed two internationally popular scores: the evening-length ballet *Romeo and Juliet* and the children's fable *Peter and the Wolf* for narrator and orchestra. Two of his 1930s **film** scores also resulted in some of Prokofiev's best concert music. The farcical *Lieutenant Kizhe* led to a sprightly and popular orchestral suite in 1934, and Sergey Eisenstein's patriotic classic *Alexander Nevsky* yielded a powerful 1939 cantata for mezzo-soprano, chorus, and orchestra.

By then, Prokofiev was feeling the pressure to produce music in praise of the Soviet Union, and he complied with a series of flag-wavers. His horror and grief at living in a police state found voice in three piano sonatas, Nos. 6 (1940), 7 (1942), and 8 (1944), all begun in 1939; his Violin Sonata No. 1 (1946), begun in 1938, also shares the same anguished sensibility. During the early years of World War II, he also labored on his epic opera *War and Peace*, from Leo Tolstoy's novel. The first version, completed in 1943, met with official interference, although it was performed in concert in 1945; revisions affected the score until 1952. But Prokofiev triumphed with two accomplished and popular works completed in 1944, the fairy-tale ballet *Cinderella* and the defiant Symphony No. 5.

In these scores, as in all the music Prokofiev was writing, he largely avoided dissonance, tonal ambiguity, or other modernist devices that were then being denounced as **formalist** in the Soviet Union. Nevertheless, after his mournful Symphony No. 6 (1947), he was subjected to a scathing official denunciation in 1948, with his Piano Sonata No. 6 and *War and Peace* declared formalist. Along with his fellow "Big Four" composers **Dmitry Shostakovich**, **Aram Khachaturian**, and Nikolai Myaskovsky, Prokofiev had to apologize to Joseph Stalin and promise to do better. His ballet *The Stone Flower* (1949) was criticized and withdrawn, and Prokofiev resumed his celebratory obligations.

Despite poor health, he was able to complete his 1952 scores *Sinfonia concertante* for cello and orchestra and Symphony No. 7. In Moscow on 5 March 1953, the 61-year-old Prokofiev was fatally stricken by a brain hemorrhage. Less than an hour later, the same fate befell Stalin, and the news of Prokofiev's death was initially withheld by the Soviet government so as not to distract from its leader's demise. *See also* FUTURISM.

PROPORTIONAL NOTATION. Proportional notation is a form of **graphic notation** for unpulsed events; it is also known as "analog notation," insofar as space on the score is analogous to duration. **Earle Brown**'s Music for Cello and Piano (1955) mostly replaced noteheads with horizontal lines, their lengths proportional to time lengths. In **Luciano Berio**'s *Sequenza I* (1958), the length of the beam between two note stems indicates how long the first note is held. A wavy line in **Ross Lee Finney**'s Symphony No. 4 (1972) notates how long an ostinato phrase is repeated. Proportional notation also occurs in scores by **Roger Reynolds** (*Traces*, 1969) and **Jacob Druckman** (*Windows*, 1972).

QIN, ERIC. *See* ROUGH ASSEMBLAGE.

QUARTER-TONE MUSIC. Quarter-tone music splits the 12 more or less equivalent intervals of the chromatic scale into 24 more or less equivalent **microtonal** intervals. Heard in works by **John Foulds, Julián Carrillo, Alois Hába, Ivan Wyschnegradsky**, and **Hans Barth**, quarter-tones were also used in the music of **Ernest Bloch** (Piano Quintet No. 1, 1923), **Charles Ives** (*Three Quarter-Tone Pieces*, 1924), **Alban Berg** (Chamber Concerto, 1925), **Aaron Copland** (*Vitebsk*, 1928), **Mildred Couper** (*Xanadu*, 1930), **Olivier Messiaen** (*Deux monodies en quarts de ton*, 1938), **Béla Bartók** (Violin Concerto No. 2, 1938; Sonata for Solo Violin, 1944), and **Pierre Boulez** (*Le visage nuptial*, 1946). Later composers who occasionally used quarter-tones include **Lejaren Hiller** (String Quartet No. 5, 1962), **Luciano Berio** (*E vó*, 1972), **Alan Hovhaness** (*O Lord Bless Thy Mountains*, 1974), **Toru Takemitsu** (*Bryce*, 1976), and **John Corigliano** (*Chiaroscuro*, 1997). Others have employed them more extensively, such as **Giacinto Scelsi, Iannis Xenakis, Krzysztof Penderecki, György Ligeti, Sofia Gubaidulina**, and **Gérard Grisey**. *See also* ALTERNATE TUNING SYSTEMS.

QUOTATION. The device of musical quotation had a major exponent in composer **Charles Ives**. Although his Piano Sonata No. 2 (1915) is built around the opening theme of Ludwig van Beethoven's Symphony No. 5, Ives's most vigorous use of quotation involved the hymn, pop, and folk tunes of his youth, frequently collaged into unusual densities in his orchestral, chamber, and piano music. Other early **modernist** composers tended to pursue either allusions to classical music—such as the quotations of Johann Sebastian Bach in **Ferruccio Busoni**'s Violin Sonata No. 2 (1898) and **Alban Berg**'s Violin Concerto (1935)—or pop-music quotations, as in **Erik Satie**'s *Embryons desséchés* (1913) and **George Antheil**'s *Sonata No. 2 for Violin and Piano with Drums* (1923). For his memorable 1928 scores *Symphony on a Hymn Tune* and *Four Saints in Three Acts*, **Virgil Thomson** devised sly and original combinations of hymns and folk music.

Quotation became more frequent in the **postmodern** era, with its openness to appropriating, deconstructing, and recontextualizing other music. **George Rochberg** began quoting earlier music in his 1965 works *Contra mortem et tempus* and *Music for the Magic Theater*, and he eventually was composing original works in earlier styles. The third movement of **Luciano Berio**'s classic *Sinfonia* (1968) was built around the third movement of **Gustav Mahler**'s Symphony No. 2 and included a spectrum of quotations from other composers throughout the history of Western music. **John Cage**'s *Europeras I/II* (1987) used only quoted music. Other composers who have used quotation include **Ross Lee Finney**, **Jacob Druckman**, **Alfred Schnittke**, **Lukas Foss**, **Pierre Henry**, **Peter Maxwell Davies**, **Bernd Alois Zimmermann**, **John Zorn**, and **John Oswald**.

R

RADIGUE, ELIANE (1932–). French composer and musician. Eliane Radigue studied with **Pierre Schaeffer** and **Pierre Henry**. Her early **tape music** includes *Elemental I* (1968) and the **open-form** work *vice versa, etc. . . .* (1970). Using the Arp **synthesizer**, she has created a **minimalist** and meditative **electronic music** characterized by her feeling for atmosphere and texture, most notably in her Buddhist-themed works *Triptych* (1978), *Adnos II* (1980), *Adnos III* (1981), *Songs of Milarepa* (1983), *Jetsun Mila* (1986), and *Trilogy de la mort*, which consists of *Kyema* (1988), *Kailasha* (1991), and *Koume* (1993). Radigue's instrumental scores include *Naldjorak I* (2005) for cello and *Naldjorak II* (2007) for two basset horns. *See also* POSTMODERNISM; SOUND INSTALLATION.

RADULESCU, HORATIU (1942–2008). Romanian-born French composer and musician. After graduating from the Bucharest Academy of Music in 1969, Horatiu Radulescu left Romania and settled in Paris, becoming a French citizen in 1974. In the early 1970s, he studied with **John Cage**, **György Ligeti**, **Karlheinz Stockhausen**, **Iannis Xenakis**, **Mauricio Kagel**, and **Olivier Messiaen**. The author of *Sound Plasma* (1973) and *Musique des mes univers* (1985), he founded the ensemble European Lucero in 1983, which he has led in performances of his music. Radulescu composed **spectral music** but bypassed polyphony in favor of creating ever-changing textures, drawing out upper partials, and generating difference tones through **microtonal** tunings, as in *Unde incotro* (1984) for 11 strings and String Quartet No. 4 (1987). His other **pleroma** works include *Credo* (1969, rev. 1976) for nine cellos, *Everlasting Longings* (1972) for 24 strings, *Doruind* (1976) for 48 voices, and *Byzantine Prayer* (1980) for 40 flutists with 72 flutes. In *A Doini* (1974) and *Clepsydra* (1983), the piano became a sound icon, turned on its side with its strings bowed or struck. Taoist themes characterized Radulescu's Piano Sonatas Nos. 2–6 (1991–2006) and String Quartets Nos. 5 (1990, rev. 1995) and 6 (1992). Romanian folk music informed his piano sonatas, *The Quest* (1996) for piano and orchestra, and other late works. *See also* EXTENDED PERFORMANCE TECHNIQUES; STRING PIANO.

RAVEL, MAURICE (1875–1937). French composer and musician. One of the 20th century's great composers for piano, Maurice Ravel was also a brilliant orchestrator who brought a new clarity and classicism to **impressionist** techniques. Joseph Maurice Ravel was born in the village of Ciboure in France's southwestern Basque territory, to a mother of Basque origin and a Swiss father. The family soon relocated to Paris, and at age seven he began taking piano lessons and studying harmony, counterpoint, and composition; at 14, he gave his first public recital. Ravel attended the Paris Conservatoire (1889–1905), where his teachers included Gabriel Fauré. His first important compositions were for piano: *Pavane pour une Infante défunte* (1899, orch. 1910) and the impressionist *Jeux d'eau* (1901), which predated the piano music of his sometimes friend **Claude Debussy**.

For all the sensuality and sonorousness of his music, however, Ravel was devoted to melody and the clear, precise lines of classical forms, and he resisted the impressionist label. Nevertheless, that style characterized his String Quartet in F Major (1903); *Shéhérazade* (1903) for voice and orchestra or piano; *Sonatine* (1905) for piano; *Miroirs* (1905) for piano; *Introduction and Allegro* (1905) for harp accompanied by string quartet, flute, and clarinet; and perhaps his finest work for piano, the fantastical *Gaspard de la nuit* (1908). Ravel's lifelong enthusiasm for Spain defined two other works of this period, *Rapsodie espagnole* (1908) for orchestra and the comic **opera** *L'heure espagnole* (1909).

Ravel found success with scores for the ballet during the 1910s, although the music was usually composed for the recital hall first. *Ma Mère l'Oye* (1910), subtitled "Five Children's Pieces for Piano Four-Hands," was expanded and orchestrated in 1911 and staged as a ballet the following year. A similar trajectory occurred with *Valses nobles et sentimentales* (1911) for piano, orchestrated and choreographed in 1912. That work was also Ravel's first significant appearance as a conductor, and he led many performances of his orchestral music over the next 20 years. He concertized as a pianist, too, but refrained from premiering his own piano music, performing more frequently as accompanist in his songs; he also played piano works by such composers as Fauré, Debussy, and **Erik Satie**.

With *Daphnis et Chloé* for orchestra, completed in 1912, Ravel achieved what for many is his masterpiece—his most extended composition, lasting close to an hour, and his only score written specifically for the ballet. He also derived two popular concert suites from *Daphnis et Chloé* in 1911 and 1913. On the eve of World War I, Ravel completed two notable chamber works, *Trois poèmes de Stéphane Mallarmé* (1913) for voice and chamber ensemble and Trio (1914) for piano, violin, and cello. During the war, he joined the motor transport corps and served near the front in the Verdun sector until his discharge due to poor health in 1917. The immediate effect of the war on

Ravel can be seen in two major scores: *Le tombeau de Couperin* for piano, completed in 1917 (and orchestrated for the ballet in 1919), with each of its six pieces dedicated to a comrade fallen in the war, and *La valse* for orchestra (or piano or two pianos), completed in 1920, which inflated waltz conventions into a quasi-surreal evocation of Teutonic decadence.

The 1920s marked Ravel's final creative period. In 1922, he composed the Sonata for Violin and Cello and completed his beloved orchestration of Modest Mussorgsky's piano score *Pictures at an Exhibition*. Impressed by American popular music, he incorporated ragtime into the fantasy opera *L'enfant et les sortilèges* (1925) and featured jazz and blues techniques in his Sonata for Violin and Piano (1927). Other important pieces from this period are the gypsy-inspired *Tzigane* (1924) for violin and piano or orchestra and *Chansons madécasses* (1926) for voice, flute, cello, and piano. Ravel ended the decade with a classic: *Boléro* (1928) for orchestra. One of his most radical scores, *Boléro* was a quasi-**minimalist** attempt to replace development with thematic repetition and a relentless growing intensity. Internationally respected after a decade of concert tours throughout Europe and North America, Ravel sealed that success with two more acclaimed works, his *Concerto for the Left Hand* (1930) for piano and orchestra and his Piano Concerto (1931), both of which demonstrated his interest in jazz.

Injured in an automobile accident in 1932, Ravel recovered fairly quickly and completed *Don Quichotte et Dulcinée* for voice and piano or orchestra (1933). But by then he was already having lapses in his speech, memory, and motor control, and soon he was left incapable of playing the piano or composing. After undergoing exploratory brain surgery in 1937, he fell into a coma; nine days later, Ravel died in a Paris hospital at age 62. *See also* FUTURISM; MODERNISM; VAUGHAN WILLIAMS, RALPH.

REICH, STEVE (1936–). American composer and musician. Steve Reich studied composition with Vincent Persichetti, **Darius Milhaud**, and **Luciano Berio**. He began creating **tape music** with such pieces as *It's Gonna Rain* (1965) and *Come Out* (1966), **minimalist** works in which a repeating fragment of sound was overdubbed and gradually moved out of phase with itself. Reich created more phase music in *Reed Phase* (1966) for soprano saxophone and tape, *Violin Phase* (1967) for four violins or violin and tape, and *Piano Phase* (1967) for two pianos or two marimbas. In *Pendulum Music* (1968), three or more microphones were suspended upside down, pulled back, and left to swing over their loudspeakers, producing feedback that phased as they gradually slowed down. These gradual-process pieces led Reich to *Four Organs* (1970) for four electric organs and maracas, in which the musicians play a single chord that is slowly lengthened in duration.

After studying African drumming in 1970, Reich composed his final phase work, *Drumming* (1971) for eight small tuned drums, three marimbas, three glockenspiels, two female voices, whistling, and piccolo. He employed repeated musical phrases that rhythmically realigned on specific beats in the 1973 scores *Six Pianos* and *Music for Mallet Instruments, Voices, and Organ*. The culmination was the classic *Music for Eighteen Musicians* (1976), which brought greater harmonic and timbral variety to Reich's music. By then, he had been performing with his own ensemble, Steve Reich and Musicians, for over a decade. He composed for other performers with *Variations for Winds, Strings, and Keyboards* (1979) for chamber orchestra or orchestra and the Psalm settings *Tehillim* (1981) for four female voices and orchestra. Reich's *Counterpoint* series combined an amplified solo instrument with tape: flute in *Vermont Counterpoint* (1982), clarinet in *New York Counterpoint* (1985), and guitar in *Electric Counterpoint* (1987).

Reich's later works include *The Desert Music* (1984) for mixed chorus and orchestra, *The Four Sections* (1987) for orchestra, *Different Trains* (1988) for string quartet and tape, *Proverb* (1995) for voices and ensemble, *Variations for Vibes, Pianos, and Strings* (2005), and *Double Sextet* (2007) for 12 instruments or six instruments and prerecorded tape. The **multimedia** *The Cave* (1993) is a music and video theater work, and *Three Tales* (2002) is a video **opera**. He is the author of *Writings on Music, 1965–2000* (2002). *See also* ELECTROACOUSTIC MUSIC; MULTICULTURALISM; POST-MODERNISM.

REINHARD, JOHNNY (1956–). American composer, musician, and educator. Bassoonist and conductor Johnny Reinhard studied at the Manhattan School of Music and Columbia University; his teachers include Pandit Pran Nath and **Chou Wen-chung**. He formed the American Festival of Microtonal Music in 1981, which has produced concerts of **microtonal** and **just-intonation** music internationally. The editor of the journal *Pitch*, he has also taught at New York University and other institutions. Reinhard's notable compositions include *Dune* (1990) for bassoon; *Cosmic Rays* (1995) for string quartet; *Middle-Earth* (1999) for orchestra; *Talibanned Buddhas* (2000) for contrabassoon, cello, metal bowls, and gong; and *Semantics of Tone* (2007) for bass trombone. *See also* ALTERNATE TUNING SYSTEMS; IVES, CHARLES; QUARTER-TONE MUSIC.

RESIDENTS, THE. American composers and musicians. The Residents have worked in anonymity since the group's inception around 1970. Based in California, they formed the label Ralph Records in 1972 and began releasing their music with a package of two 45s called *Santa Dog* (1972) and the LP

Meet the Residents (1974, rev. 1977). The Residents' unique sound featured **tape** distortions and electronic treatments of voices and instruments, rather than guitars and drums. They favored **dissonances** and other grating effects and eschewed song format, making eccentric segues into strange new realms of sound, always with a rich sense of jet-black humor. Their second album, released in 1978 as *Not Available*, was a bleak look at a failed love affair between one woman and several men. Seeking to break the social and personal control exerted by the commodification of music for corporate profit, they released *The Third Reich 'n' Roll* (1976), covering 1960s pop tunes in a series of funny and savage dissections. *The Third Reich 'n' Roll* also freed up the Residents to work more in short-song format, and they released the surrealistic tunes of *Fingerprince* (1977) and *Duck Stab/Buster & Glen* (1978).

Fingerprince also included an 18-minute composition, *Six Things to a Cycle* (1975). Inspired by **Harry Partch**, it featured **instrument building**, unusual tunings, and rhythmic chanting—all of which fed into their most popular album, *Eskimo* (1979). For all its humor, *Eskimo*'s programmatic depictions of life in the Frozen North achieved passages of startling visceral intensity and haunting beauty. Working within conceptual restraints is a hallmark of the Residents' music, and they followed *Eskimo* with a disco version, *Diskomo*, in a 1980 EP backed with *Goosebumps*, a deconstruction of nursery rhymes performed on toy instruments. The LP *Commercial Album* (1980) was a tour de force in which each song was exactly 60 seconds long.

Building on their original use of **synthesizers**, the Residents turned to **sampling** technology for their atypically somber narrative *Mark of the Mole* (1981), a fantasy of exploitation and displacement based on American history. That work generated several Mole-themed efforts, most notably their classic *The Tunes of Two Cities* (1982), which examined the music of both the Haves and the Have-Nots in the Mole Saga. *Mark of the Mole* was also staged by the Residents and performed internationally in 1982 and 1983; more live appearances followed with the 13th Anniversary Tour in 1985. The Residents also reinvented the music of **George Gershwin** and James Brown in *George & James* (1984) and John Philip Sousa and Hank Williams in *Stars & Hank Forever!* (1986).

In adapting the CD format, the Residents produced two of their finest works: *God in Three Persons* (1988), a dark tale of sexual repression and the huckstering of religion, and *The King & Eye* (1989), which recast Elvis Presley as an epic commercialization of emotional need. *The King & Eye* was also performed live, along with the Residents' versions of cowboy and early African-American songs, as the *Cube-E Show*. Some of their subsequent releases have also spawned elaborate live shows: *Wormwood* (1998), *Demons Dance Alone* (2002), and *The Bunny Boy* (2008). With *Freak Show*

(1994), *The Gingerbread Man* (1995), and *Bad Day on the Midway* (1995), they explored new interactive possibilities in the CD-ROM format. Musicians who have performed with the Residents include **Fred Frith**, **Philip Perkins**, Chris Cutler, Don Preston, Lene Lovich, and Philip Lithman, a.k.a. Snakefinger, a frequent collaborator until his death in 1987. *See also* FILM MUSIC; POSTMODERNISM.

REVUELTAS, SILVESTRE (1899–1940). Mexican composer, musician, and educator. A child prodigy as a violinist, Silvestre Revueltas studied composition with Rafael J. Tello in Mexico and Felix Borowski in the United States. He performed violin and piano recitals with **Carlos Chávez** in the mid-1920s and served as Chávez's assistant conductor with the Orquesta Sinfónica de México (1929–1935); in the 1930s, Revueltas taught violin and composition at the Conservatorio Nacional. He had a brief creative arc, his mature music spanning from 1930 to 1940, when he died of pneumonia in Mexico City at age 40.

Although he composed noteworthy chamber music (four string quartets, 1930–1932; *Three Pieces for Violin and Piano*, 1932) and songs for voice and piano (*Ranas* and *El tecolote*, 1937; *Siete canciones*, 1938), Revueltas's real forte was the orchestra. **Bitonal** qualities and a lively rhythmic sensibility invigorate his use of Indian and mestizo materials in a series of orchestral works, starting with *Cuauhnáhuac* (1930), *Esquinas* (1930), *Ventanas* (1931), *Alcancías* (1932), and *Colorines* (1933). In *Janitzio* (1933, rev. 1936) and *Danza geométrica* (1934), Revueltas's music became more aggressively percussive and **modernist**. The mournful *Homenaje a García Lorca* (1936) for chamber orchestra included an expressive use of glissandi and **dissonance**; the compressed *Tres sonetos* (1938) for 10 instruments featured darker and more sustained sonorities. *Sensemayá* (1937, rev. 1938), his best known score, brought Afro-Cuban qualities into his music. Revueltas also composed several **film** scores, most notably for *Redes* (1935) and *La noche de los Mayas* (1939).

REYNOLDS, ROGER (1934–). American composer and educator. Roger Reynolds studied composition with **Ross Lee Finney** and **Roberto Gerhard**. He was a founding member of the **ONCE Group**, for which he wrote his first major work, *The Emperor of Ice Cream* (1962, rev. 1974), scored in **graphic notation** for eight voices, contrabass, piano, and percussion. Other important pieces from these years include *Quick Are the Mouths of Earth* (1965) for chamber ensemble, *Blind Men* (1966) for 24 voices and chamber ensemble, and *Threshold* (1967) for orchestra. He also excelled in **electroacoustic music** with . . . *between* . . . (1968) for orchestra and electronics; *Traces* (1969) for solo piano, flute, cello, electronics, and **tape**; and *". . . from behind the unreasoning mask"* (1975) for trombone, percussionist and assistant, and tape. In the 1979 pieces *Less Than Two* for two pianos and two percussionists and *". . . the serpent-snapping eye"* for trumpet, piano, and percussion, **computers** generated **electronic** sound.

Some of Reynolds's electroacoustic works have been **multimedia** pieces: *Ping* (1968) for flute, piano, percussion, electronics, tape, slides, and film; *I/O: A Ritual for 23 Performers* (1970); *The Palace* (1980) for baritone, tape, and lighting; and *Vertigo* (1985) for computer-processed sound and video. His recent music includes *Dreaming* (1992) for orchestra and tape, *The Image Machine* (2005) for real-time interactive computer music, and the **spatial** works *The Red Act Arias* (1997) for narrator, chorus, orchestra, and computer-processed sound and *22* (2005) for computer-processed sound. The author of *Mind Models: New Forms of Musical Experience* (1975, rev. 2005) and *Form and Method: Composing Music* (2002), Reynolds has taught at the University of California, San Diego, since 1969; his students included **Wendy Mae Chambers** and **Bun-Ching Lam**. *See also* ATONALITY; PROPORTIONAL NOTATION.

RIEGGER, WALLINGFORD (1885–1961). American composer, musician, and educator. Wallingford Riegger studied at the Institute of Musical Art in New York, the Hochschule für Musik in Berlin, and the Cincinnati Conservatory. He taught at numerous institutions, including the Ithaca Conservatory and the New School for Social Research; his students included **George Gershwin, Henry Brant, Morton Feldman,** and **Robert Ashley**. A cellist with the St. Paul Symphony Orchestra (1910–1913), he also conducted opera and orchestral concerts in Germany (1914–1916). Riegger's **modernist** approach to tonality, **dissonance,** and texture emerged in *A Study in Sonority* (1927) for 10 (or multiples of 10) violins. He began using **twelve-tone** techniques in his *Suite for Flute Alone* (1930) and *Dichotomy* (1932) for chamber orchestra. His later scores include String Quartets Nos. 1 (1938) and 2 (1949), *Music for Brass Choir* (1949), Woodwind Quintet (1951), and Symphonies Nos. 3 (1947, rev. 1957) and 4 (1956). *See also* ATONALITY.

RILEY, TERRY (1935–). American composer, musician, and educator. Terry Riley took violin and piano lessons as a boy; his composition teachers included Seymour Shifrin and Robert Erickson. In the late 1950s, Riley formed an improvising trio with **Pauline Oliveros** and Loren Rush. Soon he was playing saxophone, too, and composing **tape music** such as his dance score *The Five-Legged Stool* (1960). He also performed on tape-delay system with jazz trumpeter Chet Baker. All this work fed into Riley's epochal *In C*

(1964) for large ensemble, a **minimalist** classic that used repeated patterns, with the musicians selecting the number of repetitions. *The Keyboard Studies* (1965) also had improvisation with repetitive thematic materials. Riley played in **La Monte Young**'s Theater of Eternal Music in the mid-1960s. He also began performing internationally as an improviser on soprano saxophone and electronic keyboards, as documented in his LPs *Poppy Nogood and the Phantom Band* (1967) and *A Rainbow in Curved Air* (1968). In 1970, he became a disciple of the North Indian master singer Pandit Pran Nath.

Riley used **just-intonation** tunings in the electronic-keyboard LPs *Shri Camel* (1978) and *The Descending Moonshine Dervishes* (1982) and in his composition for retuned piano, *The Harp of New Albion* (1984). He returned to composing scores for musicians with his string-quartet works *Sunrise of the Planetary Dream Collector* (1981), *Cadenza on the Night Plain* (1984), and *Salome Dances for Peace* (1986). These in turn led him to the orchestra: *The Jade Palace Orchestral Dances* (1989), *The Sands* (1991) with string quartet, *June Buddhas* (1991) with mixed chorus. Riley also blended raga and Western techniques, singing and playing electronic keyboards in *Song from the Old Country* (1980) and *The Ethereal Time Shadow* (1982), and in sets with his **multicultural** band Khayal. His notable recent works include *ArchAngels* (2003) for eight cellos and *The Cusp of Magic* (2004) for string quartet and pipa. Riley has taught at such institutions as Stockholm's Royal Academy of Music, New York University, and Mills College. *See also* ELECTROACOUSTIC MUSIC; POSTMODERNISM; SYNTHESIZER.

RISSET, JEAN-CLAUDE (1938–). French composer, musician, and educator. Jean-Claude Risset studied composition with **André Jolivet** and worked at Bell Labs with Max Mathews. A pioneer in **computer music**, Risset produced such notable works as *Computer Suite from "Little Boy"* (1968) and *Mutations* (1969), and he developed methods for synthesizing the sound of a trumpet. He taught at the Université d'Aix–Marseille and was director of computer music at IRCAM (1975–1979). Risset has composed *musique concrète* (*Songes*, 1979; *Sud*, 1985; *Invisible Irène*, 1995) and a variety of **electroacoustic** scores: *Mutations II* (1973) for ensemble and electronics, *Inharmonique* (1977) for soprano and **tape**, *Passages* (1982) for flute and tape, *Trois études en duo* (1991) for Disklavier and computer, *Variants* (1994) for violin and digital processing, and *Échappées* (2004) for Celtic harp and computer. Among his instrumental works are *Prélude* (1963) for orchestra, *Trois esquisses* (1988) for organ, *Triptyque* (1991) for clarinet and orchestra, and *Escalas* (2001) for orchestra. *See also* ELECTRONIC MUSIC.

ROCHBERG, GEORGE (1918–2005). American composer and educator. George Rochberg studied with George Szell and Leopold Mannes at the Mannes School of Music (1939–1942), and with Rosario Scalero and **Gian Carlo Menotti** at the Curtis Institute of Music (1945–1948); he also studied at the University of Pennsylvania and subsequently taught there (1960–1983). Rochberg's early tonal scores include Trio (1947, rev. 1980) for clarinet, horn, and piano; Symphony No. 1 (1948; rev. 1977, 2003); and *Night Music* for orchestra (1949). His first **twelve-tone** work was *Twelve Bagatelles* for piano (1952), and he achieved distinction with this method in *Chamber Symphony for Nine Instruments* (1953), Symphony No. 2 (1956), and String Quartet No. 2 (with soprano, 1961).

In 1964, Rochberg experienced a personal tragedy that triggered an aesthetic crisis: His grief at the death of his 20-year-old son Paul revealed to him his own dissatisfaction with the expressive limits of his **serial** composition. Rochberg collaged music in *Contra mortem et tempus* (1965) for flute, clarinet, violin, and piano; *Music for the Magic Theater* (1965) for orchestra; *Nach Bach* (1966) for harpsichord or piano; and *Passions (According to the 20th Century)* (1967) for singers, jazz quintet, brass ensemble, percussion, piano, and **tape**. He contrasted cultures and expressed feelings of wonder, loss, and nostalgia through his **quotations** of music by Johann Sebastian Bach, Wolfgang Amadeus Mozart, Ludwig van Beethoven, **Gustav Mahler**, **Edgard Varèse**, and **Anton Webern**. In Symphony No. 3 (1969), Rochberg included tonal methods, and the Violin Concerto (1974, rev. 2001) alternated and combined tonal and **atonal** structures.

Quotation freed up Rochberg to compose **neoromantic** music in the style of earlier composers in his String Quartet No. 3 (1972) and the three "Concord" String Quartets (Nos. 4, 1977; 5, 1977; and 6, 1978). *Electrikaleidoscope* (1972) for amplified chamber ensemble used elements of rock music, but by the late 1970s Rochberg's music had become more homogeneous and tonal. His later works include the Herman Melville **opera** *The Confidence Man* (1982), Oboe Concerto (1984), Symphony No. 5 (1985), Clarinet Concerto (1996), and *Eden: Out of Time and Out of Space* (1998) for guitar and chamber ensemble. *See also* MODERNISM; POSTMODERNISM.

ROLDÁN, AMADEO (1900–1939). French-born Cuban composer and musician. Born in Paris of Cuban parents, Amadeo Roldán y Gardes entered the Madrid Conservatory at age five. He returned to Cuba in 1919 and became concertmaster of Havana's Orquesta Filarmonica and later its conductor. Roldán's composition was groundbreaking in its use of Afro-Cuban music, with such works as *Tres pequeños poemas* (1926) for orchestra, the ballet scores *La rebambaramba* (1928) and *El milagro de Anaquillé* (1929), *Tres* *toques* (1931) for chamber orchestra, and *Motivos de son* (1934) for voice and 11 instruments. **Polyrhythmic** qualities inform his six *Ritmicas* (1930), the first four of which were scored for five winds and piano; the last two were for percussion ensemble—another breakthrough in 20th-century music. Roldán's *Piezas infantiles* (1937) for piano was his last composition before his death from cancer at age 38. *See also* MODERNISM.

ROREM, NED (1923–). American composer, musician, educator, and critic. A skilled pianist, Ned Rorem studied composition with **Virgil Thomson** and **Aaron Copland**, among others; he also attended the Curtis Institute and later taught there. His 1947 works *Four Madrigals* for mixed chorus and *The Lordly Hudson* for voice and piano won respect, and in 1949 he went to France to study with **Arthur Honegger**. Rorem lived in Paris until 1958; his works from these years include *Cycle of Holy Songs* (1951) for voice and piano and *Four Dialogues* (1954) for two voices and two pianos. A melodic and tonal composer, he wrote some of his best music back in the United States: *Eagles* (1958) for orchestra, *Two Poems of Theodore Roethke* (1959) for voice and piano, Trio (1960) for flute, cello, and piano, *Lions* (1963) for orchestra, *Poems of Love and the Rain* (1963) for mezzo-soprano and piano, and the **opera** *Miss Julie* (1965, rev. 1978).

In 1966, Rorem published diaries that he had kept in Paris. His witty and articulate prose, peppered with his provocative comments on matters aesthetic, political, and sexual, generated acclaim and controversy, and diaries written afterward in New York were released the following year. Subsequent volumes include *The Later Diaries* (1974) and *Lies* (2000); an autobiography, *Knowing When to Stop*, appeared in 1993. Among his collections of music criticism are *Setting the Tone* (1983) and *Settling the Score* (1988).

With such works as *Some Trees* (1968) for three voices and piano; *Ariel* (1971) for soprano, clarinet, and piano; *Last Poems of Wallace Stevens* (1972) for voice, cello, and piano; and *Women's Voices* (1976) for soprano and piano, Rorem solidified his reputation as a master composer of art song. His instrumental music also continued to impress, with *Air Music* (1972) for orchestra, *A Quaker Reader* (1976) for organ, and *Sunday Morning* (1977) for orchestra. Rorem's notable later works include *Pilgrim Strangers* (1984) for six male voices, *String Symphony* (1985), Third String Quartet (1991), *Concerto for Mallet Instruments* (2004), and the opera *Our Town* (2005).

ROSLAVETS, NIKOLAI (1881–1944). Russian composer and musician. Nikolai Andreyevich Roslavets studied violin and composition at the Moscow Conservatory (1901–1912). Building on **Alexander Scriabin**'s music, he developed **atonal** techniques similar to **twelve-tone** organization in such scores as String Quartet No. 1 (1912), Violin Sonata No. 1 (1913), Piano Sonatas Nos. 1 (1914) and 2 (1916), and *Five Preludes* (1921) for piano. Roslavets's **modernist** works were attacked as antirevolutionary, and he turned to composing Socialist Realist music, such as the cantata *October* (1927). But by 1930, he was no longer able to obtain any official position, even though he had publicly renounced his earlier works. Roslavets's later scores—orchestral, chamber, and vocal—went unperformed; not until 1989 did the official suppression of his music end. *See also* FORMALISM.

ROUGH ASSEMBLAGE. The composers collective Rough Assemblage was formed around 1991 by Mark Degliantoni (1962–), Eric Qin (1967–1993), and Norman Yamada (1962–). All from New York's Mannes College of Music, these composer/musicians shared a **postmodern** interest in pop-music forms, **minimalist** procedures, noise, densities, and performance freedoms, as well as a lively sense of humor. An imaginative performer on **sampler**, Degliantoni included the instrument in his duo with percussion *Mit starken Schlägen streckt' ich dich* and his sextet *Ring 'Em*, both 1992 scores. Qin utilized open structures in his 1991 scores *Februarys* for solo viola and *Music in Grey* for six musicians, and he embraced both traditional and experimental techniques in *Construction et demolition* (1992) for two percussionists and *Music for Dancing #1–4, 5* (1993), a group of short and elegant piano works. Yamada employed pointillistic effects in *Mundane Dissatisfactions* (1991) for brass quintet and *Year One* (1993) for guitar, bass, and two percussionists; he also conducted many Rough Assemblage concerts.

The collective was terminated after the death of Qin in 1993 at age 25, struck by an automobile while riding his bicycle. Degliantoni played in the rock band Soul Coughing (1992–2000) as Mark De Gli Antoni and has created numerous **film** scores. Yamada's later works were released on the CD *Being and Time* (1998).

ROUSSEL, ALBERT (1869–1937). French composer, musician, and educator. Albert Roussel studied with Vincent d'Indy at the Schola Cantorum; he later taught there, and his students included **Erik Satie, Edgard Varèse**, and **Bohuslav Martinu**. Working within an **impressionist** idiom, Roussel found his own voice in such works as the orchestral *Suite from "Le festin de l'araignée"* (1912) and the **opera** *Padmâvatî* (1918), which drew upon Indian music. His later **neoclassical** works became his most admired scores: Suite in F (1926) for orchestra, the ballet scores *Bacchus et Ariane* (1930) and *Aeneas* (1935), Symphony No. 3 (1930), String Quartet (1932), Symphony No. 4 (1934), and String Trio (1937). *See also* MODERNISM; MULTICULTURALISM.

RUDHYAR, DANE (1895–1985). French-born American composer and musician. Born in Paris, Daniel Chennevière began playing piano at age seven. At 18, he published some of his **impressionist** piano music and the book *Claude Debussy et son ouevre*. That year, he also heard **Igor Stravinsky**'s *Le sacre du printemps* and began composing **dissonant**, **polytonal** orchestral music. He immigrated to the United States in 1916 and changed his name to Dane Rudhyar; he became a U.S. citizen in 1926. His **modernist** orchestral works *Three Metochoric Poems*, *Poèmes ironiques*, and *Vision végétale* were performed in New York in 1917, and Rudhyar began investigating the music of **Alexander Scriabin**. He also studied Indian, Japanese, and Chinese music, as well as Eastern and occult philosophy, and lectured on and wrote about modernist and Eastern music. His book *The Rebirth of Hindu Music* was published in India in 1928.

Interested in densities and resonances, Rudhyar scored *The Surge of Fire* (1924) for small orchestra with three pianos. He then stepped away from tonality and composed his best known piano music: *Pentagrams Nos. 1–4* (1924–1926), *Tetragrams Nos. 2–8* (1924–1929), *Three Paeans* (1925–1927), and *Granites* (1929). These **atonal** works employed rhythmic patterns derived from speech and a resonant textural approach that included **tone-clusters** and made the piano sound like gongs and bells. Rudhyar performed at the piano in these years, as both composer and improviser, and he found support from such American composers as **Henry Cowell**, **Ruth Crawford Seeger**, and **Charles Ives**. He also composed the orchestral scores *Five Stanzas* (1927) for string orchestra, Sinfonietta (1928, rev. 1979), *Desert Chant* (1932), and *Threshold of Light* (1934).

Rudhyar's music became more sporadic due to health problems and the demands of his other creative pursuits—he was also a painter, poet, novelist, and author of many books on astrology. After he turned 80, composition became his primary focus, resulting in such piano works as *Transmutation* (1976), *Three Cantos* (1977), *Rites of Transcendence* (1981), and *Processional* (1983). He also composed *Encounter* (1977) for piano and orchestra, two string quartets (1978, 1979), *Cosmic Cycle* (1981) for orchestra, and the quintet *Nostalgia* (1983). He created orchestral works from earlier scores, such as *The Warrior* (1921/1976) and *Poems of Youth* (1921–1933/1983–1984), and wrote the book *The Magic of Tone and the Art of Music* (1982). Rudhyar died in San Francisco at age 90. *See also* BRANCA, GLENN; MULTICULTURALISM; PLEROMA.

RUGGLES, CARL (1876–1971). American composer, musician, and educator. Carl Ruggles was a groundbreaking **modernist** whose **atonal** music was championed by **Henry Cowell**, **Edgard Varèse**, and **Charles**

Ives. Born Charles Sprague Ruggles in Marion, Massachusetts, he played the violin from boyhood, and in the late 1890s began studying privately with John Knowles Paine and others. Ruggles's earliest compositions were songs for voice and piano in a late romantic style. He reviewed concerts for newspapers and played in theater orchestras in the early 1900s. Adopting the first name Carl, he relocated to Winona, Minnesota, in 1907 and taught violin at the Mar d'Mar School of Music. The next year, Ruggles founded the Winona Symphony Orchestra, for which he was music director and conductor (1908–1917). In 1912, he began writing an opera based on Gerhart Hauptmann's play *The Sunken Bell*, but abandoned the project after a few years. Although Ruggles eventually destroyed almost all of his early scores, surviving sketches of *The Sunken Bell* show his growing use of **dissonance** and tonal ambiguity, as do the 1918 sketches of *Mood* for violin and piano (completed in 1975 by **John Kirkpatrick**).

Ruggles embraced this more aggressive direction in his first mature work, *Toys* (1919) for soprano and piano, a setting of his own text. By then, he was in New York as organizer and director of the Rand School of Social Science's symphony orchestra (1918–1921). He joined the International Composers' Guild in 1922, and that year one of his finest works, *Angels* for six muted trumpets, was premiered at a Guild concert. This brief, dense piece, even more dissonant than *Toys*, was originally composed in 1921 as part of a symphonic poem entitled *Men and Angels*, which was never completed. Instead, Ruggles produced three short atonal scores, all premiered by the Guild, in which he refined his personal approach to dissonant polyphony and developed techniques similar to **Arnold Schoenberg**'s **twelve-tone** method. *Vox clamans in deserto* (1923) was a trio of songs for mezzo-soprano and 14 instruments. The dramatic *Men and Mountains* (1924) for 18 instruments followed, highlighted by its slow movement, "Lilacs" for seven strings. Ruggles further elaborated on that idiom with his visionary *Portals* for 12 strings (1926).

All these works are imbued with Ruggles's passionate mystical spirit and sense of awe and grandeur and mystery—qualities that epitomize his masterpiece, the apocalyptic *Sun-Treader* (1933) for orchestra. His most extreme and exacting achievement in the realm of dissonant counterpoint, *Sun-Treader* is, at 16 minutes, his lengthiest composition as well. A ferocious perfectionist, Ruggles would labor for years over a score, and he often revised his music. He spent a decade working on the four chants of *Evocations* (1934–1943) for piano, which he also orchestrated during the 1940s. He revised *Men and Mountains* for full symphony orchestra in 1935 and recast *Angels* for four muted trumpets and three muted trombones in 1938. *Organum* (1945), his last orchestral work, was also rescored for two pianos in 1947. Ruggles was in his early 70s by then, and the intensity of his vision had receded. In 1957, he lost Charlotte Snell Ruggles, his wife of almost 50 years; in her honor, he composed *Exaltation* (1958), a 16-measure wordless hymn in G Major. Ruggles entered a nursing home in Bennington, Vermont, in 1966, and died there of pneumonia five years later at age 95.

RUSSELL, ARTHUR (1951–1992). American composer and musician. Arthur Russell studied at the Ali Akbar Khan School and the Manhattan School of Music. A cellist and vocalist, Russell worked in pop and avant-garde idioms; he blended the two for the songs of his albums *World of Echo* (1986) and *Another Thought* (1994). Among his **minimalist** compositions are *Reach One* (1973) for two Fender Rhodes pianos and the orchestral scores *Instrumentals, Volume 1* (1974) and *Tower of Meaning* (1981). Russell died at age 40 of complications from AIDS. *See also* GORDON, PETER; POST-MODERNISM.

RUSSELL, GEORGE (1923–2009). American composer, musician, educator, and theorist. A jazz drummer in the early 1940s, George Russell turned to composition and conducting with his theory of modal tonality, set forth in his influential book *The Lydian Chromatic Concept of Tonal Organization* (1953; fourth edition, 2001). He also taught at the New England Conservatory of Music (1969–2004). Russell drew upon the music of Charlie Parker and **Igor Stravinsky** in *A Bird in Igor's Yard* (1949), blending jazz and **modernist** techniques. In the 1960s, he began using **aleatoric** scoring methods in his notation and creating his **polyrhythmic** "Vertical Form" scores, which include *Othello Ballet Suite* (1967) and *Vertical Form VI* (1976) for jazz orchestra. Among his notable recordings are *The Jazz Workshop* (1956), *The African Game* (1983), and *It's About Time* (1995). *See also* SCHULLER, GUNTHER.

RUSSELL, WILLIAM (1905–1992). American composer and musician. Russell William Wagner took violin lessons as a boy and attended the Quincy Conservatory of Music in Illinois. He relocated to New York in 1928, where he changed his name to William Russell. Impressed by a performance of African drumming, Russell composed his first work, *Fugue for Eight Percussion Instruments* (1932), in which he treated rhythmic themes contrapuntally and featured **tone-clusters**. His subsequent scores, all for percussion ensemble, relied more on pop and jazz. *Three Dance Movements* (1933) had rhythmic reinventions of popular forms: "Waltz" in 7/4, "March" in 3/4, and "Foxtrot" in 5/4. Marches were also reworked in Russell's five-movement *March Suite* (1936, rev. 1984).

Multiculturalism is another **postmodern** anticipation in Russell's percussion music. A 1932 trip to Haiti led to his *Ogou Badagri* (1933), a ballet score based on Haitian voodoo rites. For performances of *Three Cuban Pieces* (1935, a.k.a. *Studies in Cuban Rhythms*), Russell had to supply some of the more exotic percussion instruments, such as a marimbula and a rattling quijada, or jawbone of an ass. *Made in America* (1936, rev. 1990) is an ode to appropriation, scored for auto brake drums, suitcase, washboard, tin cans, lion's roar, and a drum kit made of found objects. It was also **electroacoustic** and included a Baetz's Rhythm Rotor: a mechanical device similar to **Leon Theremin**'s rhythmicon, which produced **polyrhythmic** ticks. In *Chicago Sketches* (1940), Russell evoked music that he had heard throughout that city, from the blues to a washboard band, and called for finger-snapping and foot-stomping from the percussionists.

By the 1940s, Russell's interest in New Orleans jazz had displaced his composition. He founded the label American Music (1944–1957), recording and releasing more than 60 jazz records, and became curator of Tulane University's jazz archive in 1958. Russell returned to composition in his last years, writing *Prelude* and *Chorale* in 1985 to precede his 1932 *Fugue*. In 1990, he completed his Trumpet Concerto, which he had set aside in the mid-1930s, and composed "Tango" for percussion, which he added to his 1933 work, renaming it *Four Dance Movements. See also* MODERNISM.

RUSSOLO, LUIGI. *See* FUTURISM.

RYLAN, JESSICA (1974–). American composer and musician. Jessica Rylan studied at Bard College. A performer of live and improvised **electronic music**, often augmented by her processed and/or natural vocals, Rylan has designed and constructed her own **synthesizers**. Her recordings include *Interior Design* (2007) and, as the one-woman noise band Can't, *Private Time Part 2* (2008). Among Rylan's **sound installations** are *Red Sky at Night, Sailor's Delight* (2002) and *The Voice of the Theatre* (2004). *See also* ELECTROACOUSTIC MUSIC; FREE IMPROVISATION; POSTMODERNISM.

RZEWSKI, FREDERIC (1938–). American composer, musician, and educator. Frederic Rzewski studied with **Roger Sessions**, **Milton Babbitt**, and **Luigi Dallapiccola** and has taught at the Yale School of Music, Mills College, and the Conservatoire Royal de Musique in Belgium. A virtuoso pianist and improviser, Rzewski is a cofounder of **MEV** and has also performed with such composer/musicians as **Anthony Braxton, Gordon Mumma**, and **George Lewis**. Among his early compositions are the **minimalist** *Les moutons de Panurge* (1969) for melody instruments, *Coming Together* (1971) for speaker and variable ensemble, and *The People*

United Will Never Be Defeated (1975) for piano. *The Price of Oil* (1980) for voices and instruments utilized **graphic notation**, and *The Persians* (1985), a music-theater piece, adopted **twelve-tone** methods. His recent scores include *De profundis* (1992) for solo pianist playing and reciting and the eight-hour *The Road* (1995–2003) for piano. *See also* FREE IMPROVISATION; POSTMODERNISM.

S

SALZEDO, CARLOS (1885–1961). French-born American composer, musician, and educator. Carlos Salzedo studied in France and settled in New York in 1909. A virtuoso harpist, he composed almost exclusively for that instrument and developed revolutionary **extended performance techniques** in such scores as Sonata (1922) for harp and piano and Concerto (1926) for harp and seven woodwinds. Salzedo founded the International Composers' Guild (1921–1927) with **Edgard Varèse**, the modern-music magazine *Eolian Review* (later *Eolus*, 1921–1933), and the Salzedo Harp Colony, where he taught; he also taught at the Curtis Institute and wrote *Modern Study of the Harp* (1921). His notable works for solo harp include *Variations sur un thème dans le style ancien* (1911) and *Suite of Eight Dances* (1943). *See also* MODERNISM.

SAMPLING. Defined broadly, sampling is the recording of a fragment, or sample, of a sound, which is then reused in a new context. **Tape music** thus represents a form of sampling; so does the manipulation of phonograph records, as in the music of Christian Marclay. More specifically, sampling refers to **synthesizer** innovations of the late 1970s, such as the Synclavier, which incorporated **computer**-based technology for converting a sound into digital information that can then be altered and played. This technology became generally available by the early 1980s, with the Fairlight and the Emulator in the marketplace, and samplers soon displaced the use of tape. Notable composers of music created with sampling include **Vladimir Ussachevsky**, **John Oswald**, the **Residents**, **Frank Zappa**, **Bob Ostertag**, and **David Shea**. *See also* ELECTRONIC MUSIC.

SATIE, ERIK (1866–1925). French composer and musician. An inspiration for generations of experimental composers, Satie anticipated **postmodern** developments such as **ambient music** and the use of pop materials for non-pop purposes, and he brought a bracing humor and imagination to his work. Eric Alfred Leslie Satie was born in Honfleur in northern France and entered the Paris Conservatoire at age 13. He accomplished little there and got out by joining the army in 1886; he then quickly got himself discharged for health reasons. Rejecting the romantic excesses of Richard Wagner, Satie began using slow chordal progressions to achieve a static quality in his 1886 songs for voice and piano, *Trois mélodies* and *Élégie*. His four *Ogives* for piano, also of that year, drew on medieval plainsong, with each one written in four barless lines.

By 1887, Satie had taken the first name Erik and was performing as a cabaret pianist; he also composed his *Trois sarabandes* for piano, introducing what would be a lifelong enthusiasm for dance forms. He expanded on the sarabandes' modal structures and irregular phrasing in the piano scores *Trois Gymnopédies* (1888) and *Trois Gnossiennes* (1890), replacing development with repetition, tempered by slight rhythmic alterations—anticipating what would become a familiar **minimalist** technique. Both scores also evoked classical Greece with his invented terms *Gymnopédie* and *Gnossienne*, and that conceptual wit informs *Trois Gnossiennes'* performance notations as well, with Satie calling for amazement and right thinking alongside more traditional expression markings.

Trois Gnossiennes reflects Satie's sense of new possibilities after hearing the Javanese gamelan in Paris in 1889. In the early 1890s, his neomedieval interests also became more prominent with Satie's involvement in Rosicrucian mysticism. As official composer of the Paris Rose + Croix Temple, he took the techniques of the *Ogives* and *Gymnopédies* further, producing such important piano works as *Le fils des étoiles* (1891, also for flute and harps), *Sonneries de la Rose + Croix* (1892), *Danses gothiques* (1893), and *"Pages mystiques"* (1895), as well as the memorable *Messe des pauvres* (1895) for piano or organ with unison mixed chorus. His cryptic humor also persisted, and in *Vexations*, the second of the *"Pages mystiques,"* he has a suggestion for playing the piece 840 times in succession.

Satie left Rosicrucianism in the mid-1890s and began composing for wider audiences with two scores completed in 1900: *Jack in the Box* for piano, which was incidental music for a pantomime, and the puppet **opera** *Geneviève de Brabant* for soloists, chorus, and piano. Despite having composed the accomplished *Trois morceaux en forme de poire* (1903) for piano four-hands, Satie decided at age 39 to repair the gaps in his education by enrolling in the Schola Cantorum (1905–1908). He proved a diligent pupil with Vincent d'Indy and **Albert Roussel** and, after graduating, entered a new creative period, in which staticism and repetition—and bar lines and key signatures—gave way to richer **bitonal** harmonies, livelier rhythms, and zanier titles and commentaries. Satie wed the music hall with the concert hall, **quoting** popular tunes in such piano works as *Embryons desséchés* (1913), *Chapitres tournés en tout sens* (1913), and *Sports et divertissements* (1914). He wrote *Choses vues à droite et à gauche (sans lunettes)* (1914) for violin and piano, and *Cinq grimaces pour "Un songe d'une nuit d'été"* (1915) was his first work for orchestra.

The music-hall and circus qualities of the *Cinq grimaces* dominated Satie's 1916 ballet score *Parade*, which included a ragtime dance. *Parade* used a large orchestra with augmented percussion, including a *bouteillophone* of tuned bottles, as well as noises such as typing and gunfire. The young composers who would be known as the **Groupe des Six** were drawn to the alternative that *Parade* represented. Although as resolutely non-Germanic and antiacademic as his friend **Claude Debussy**, Satie operated outside the **impressionist** orbit and favored the angular vitality of the cabaret over lush harmonies and textures. *Parade* was anything but static, yet Satie was still ignoring development, this time by using symmetrical mosaiclike structures of time units, within which he juxtaposed different musical blocks. This form also defines perhaps his greatest work: *Socrate* (1918) for one to four sopranos and piano or orchestra, in which a conversational vocal line is supported by blocks of ostinati and somewhat **dissonant** chords.

Satie foresaw the idea of ambient music with his *Musique d'ameublement* ("furniture music") in 1920 and 1923. Seeking to fill in ambient sound rather than mask it, he composed asymmetrically phrased ostinati and fragments of quotations for musicians to play in public spaces. The pop sound of *Parade* continued with *Trois petites pièces montées* (1919) and *La belle excentrique* (1920), both for music-hall orchestra, and his 1924 dance scores *Mercure* and *Relâche*. As an interlude for *Relâche*, director René Clair made the classic dada short *Entr'acte* (1924), in which Satie appeared. Satie also scored the **film**—his final composition. Suffering from cirrhosis of the liver with complications of pleurisy, he died in a Paris hospital at age 59. *See also* FUTURISM; MODERNISM.

SCELSI, GIACINTO (1905–1988). Italian composer and musician. Although he pursued some studies in Italy, Switzerland, and Germany, Giacinto Scelsi was largely self-taught. Some of his early scores, such as *Quattro poemi* (1936–1939) for piano, used **twelve-tone** techniques, but Scelsi's music changed radically in his later years. His **minimalist** works, rich in **microtonal** inflections, described a personal spiritual esotericism and were usually based on his recorded and transcribed improvisations. Notable scores include *Quattro pezzi su una nota sola* (1959) for chamber orchestra; *Hymnos* (1963) for organ and two orchestras; String Quartet No. 4 (1964); *Anahit* (1965) for violin and 18 instruments; *Uaxuctum* (1966) for mixed chorus, chamber orchestra, and **ondes martenot**; *Canti dei capricorno* (1972) for female voice and instruments; *Aitsi* (1974) for amplified piano; and *Dharana* (1975) for cello and double bass. Scelsi also wrote such solo works as *Trilogy* (1956–1965) for cello, *Hô* (1960) for soprano, *Xnoybis* (1964) for violin, *Nuits* (1972) for double bass, and *Maknongan* (1976) for bass voice or instrument. *See also* QUARTER-TONE MUSIC; TONE-CLUSTER.

SCHAEFFER, PIERRE (1910–1995). French composer and theorist. An engineer and announcer for France's RTF radio network, Pierre Schaeffer created *Étude aux chemins de fer* in 1948 by manipulating gramophone recordings of locomotives. Calling the results **musique concrète**, he created other **tapes** using prerecorded sounds—*Étude pour orchestre*, *Étude au piano*, *Étude aux casseroles*, and *Étude aux tourniquets*—for his *Cinq études de bruit* (rev. 1971 as *Quatre études de bruit*). Schaeffer's music was broadcast in 1948, and the RTF made studio space and equipment available to him. There he collaborated with **Pierre Henry** on the first major musique concrète work, *Symphonie pour un homme seul* (1950), and in 1951 he and Henry were able to establish the Groupe de Recherches de Musique Concrète at the RTF, the first tape-music studio.

Schaeffer's subsequent collaborations with Henry include *Bidule en ut* (1950) and *Orphée 53* (1953), a musique concrète **opera** for tape, harpsichord, and female voice. He also created such solo works as *Diapason Concerto* (1948), *Variations sur une flûte mexicaine* (1949), *L'oiseau RAI* (1950), and *Les paroles dégelées* (1952) and wrote a book about the new medium, *À la recherche d'une musique concrète* (1952). In 1958, the studio became the Groupe de Recherches Musicales (GRM), with a commitment to electrically synthesized sound as well as tape music. But by then Schaeffer was nearing the end of his involvement with composition. After his *Étude aux allures* (1958), *Étude aux sons animés* (1958), and *Étude aux objets* (1959), Schaeffer retired from the GRM.

GRM members formed the Groupe Solfège to pursue musical experiments based on Schaeffer's phenomenological theories, and he compiled the results in his book *Traité des objets musicaux* (1966). Schaeffer, Guy Reibel, and Beatriz Ferreyra created a two-hour musique concrète piece, *Solfège de l'objet sonore*, issued in 1967 as an extension of the *Traité*. Schaeffer's work in psychoacoustic research led him to a final musique concrète work, *Le trièdre fertile* (1975), and *Bilude* (1979) for harpsichord or piano and tape. *See also* ATONALITY; ELECTROACOUSTIC MUSIC; ELECTRONIC MUSIC.

SCHILLINGER, JOSEPH (1895–1943). Russian-born American composer, educator, and theorist. A student of the Petrograd Conservatory, Joseph Schillinger immigrated to the United States in 1928 and became a citizen in 1936. He taught at the New School for Social Research and Columbia

University Teachers College, with students including **Mel Powell, George Gershwin**, Tommy Dorsey, Glenn Miller, and Benny Goodman. Schillinger developed a mathematical system of composition, using melody, harmony, rhythm, and orchestration in geometric relationships. But he wrote just a few works in the United States: *North Russian Symphony* (1930), the ballet score *The People and the Prophet* (1931), and *Study in Rhythm I* (1935) for piano. He also composed for **theremin**, with orchestra in *First Airphonic Suite* (1929), with piano in *Melody* (1929) and *Mouvement électrique et pathétique* (1932), and with piano and voice in *Bury Me, Bury Me Wind* (1930). His books *The Schillinger System of Musical Composition* (1946) and *The Mathematical Basis of the Arts* (1948) were compiled and published after Schillinger's death from lung cancer at age 47. *See also* BROWN, EARLE; ELECTROACOUSTIC MUSIC; MODERNISM.

SCHNITTKE, ALFRED (1934–1998). Russian composer, musician, and educator. Alfred Schnittke studied at the Moscow Conservatory, where he later taught. He used **twelve-tone** techniques in such works as *Music for Piano and Chamber Orchestra* (1964) and composed **electronic music** with *Stream* (1969). A penchant for humor and **quotation** led Schnittke to collage different musical styles in Violin Sonata No. 2 (1968), Symphony No. 1 (1972), and other scores. His Piano Quintet (1976), which featured **microtonal tone-clusters**, was more stylistically unified, as were the darker and more introspective works written after his health began to deteriorate, such as String Quartet No. 4 (1989) and Symphony No. 6 (1992). In 1990, Schnittke relocated to Germany, where he died of a stroke at age 63. His many compositions include Symphonies Nos. 0–8 (1957–1995), four violin concertos (1957–1984), six concerti grossi (1977–1994), and three **operas** (1990–1994). *See also* MODERNISM.

SCHOENBERG, ARNOLD (1874–1951). Austrian-born American composer, musician, educator, and theorist. One of the great **modernists**, Arnold Schoenberg defined the seismic shift away from tonality and developed the widely used method of **twelve-tone** composition. Born in Vienna, Arnold Franz Walter Schönberg started violin lessons in 1882, was composing at age eight, and taught himself the cello, but in 1890 was compelled to leave school and work as a bank clerk to help support his family. Not until 1895 did Schönberg quit the bank and fully devote himself to music, despite having no formal education other than his lessons with Alexander von Zemlinsky in 1893. Immersed in the work of Johannes Brahms, Schönberg composed his (unnumbered) String Quartet in D Major in 1897. But the greater chromaticism and ambiguous tonality of Richard Wagner also had a profound impact on him, reflected in the programmatic and expressive *Verklärte Nacht* (1899) for string sextet, which became his most popular score (especially in his version for string orchestra, arranged in 1917 and revised in 1944).

The postromantic sensibility of *Verklärte Nacht* also characterized Schönberg's symphonic poem *Pelleas und Melisande* (1903) and String Quartet No. 1 (1905). By then, he had begun teaching private composition students. **Alban Berg** and **Anton Webern** were among them, and Schönberg's professional and personal relationship with Berg and Webern led to their being identified as the Second Viennese School. In Schönberg's Chamber Symphony No. 1 (1906), the tonal center became unclear, and it was even more elusive in the **dissonant** String Quartet No. 2 (1908), which included a soprano.

In 1909, he completed four major scores in a fully **atonal** and dissonant idiom: *Das buch der hängenden Gärten* for voice and piano, *Three Piano Pieces*, the monodrama *Erwartung* for soprano and orchestra, and *Five Orchestral Pieces* (rev. 1949). After this extraordinary burst of creativity, Schönberg came to be regarded as the leading exponent of **expressionist** music, even though in 1911 he completed a treatise on tonal harmony, *Harmonielehre*, and the score of *Gurrelieder*, a vast postromantic work for soloists, reciter, chorus, and orchestra, composed mostly between 1900 and 1902. Shunning the anti-Semitism and poor employment prospects in Vienna, he moved to Berlin, and there in 1912 he composed and conducted the premiere of the epochal *Pierrot lunaire* for soprano and quintet. This masterpiece took the vocal techniques of ***Sprechstimme*** into new realms and established Schönberg as the most important modernist composer of his day.

After completing his one-act **opera** *Die glückliche Hand* (1913), Schönberg responded to the war in Europe by volunteering for the Austrian army in 1915. Discharged for health reasons two years later, he moved to the Viennese suburb of Mödling in 1918 and resumed teaching, accepting as pupils **Hanns Eisler** and **Roberto Gerhard**. Schönberg's composition, however, was quiescent for several years as he developed a method for providing greater form and structure in atonality—or, as he preferred to call it, **pantonality**: the shared importance and availability of all 12 tones in the chromatic scale. Schönberg introduced procedures from his twelve-tone, or **dodecaphonic**, method in 1923 with the *Five Piano Pieces* and the Serenade for baritone and septet. The Piano Suite of that year was his first completely twelve-tone score, followed by the Wind Quintet (1924).

Schönberg returned to Berlin in 1926, where his students included **Marc Blitzstein**. He composed more twelve-tone music with the String Quartet No. 3 (1927), Variations for Orchestra (1928), and *Begleitungsmusik zu einer Lichtspielszene* (1930) for orchestra. But after two years' work on the libretto and music for *Moses und Aron*, he was unable to complete the third act of his Old Testament opera and left the score incomplete in 1932. The rise of Nazism forced Schönberg to flee Germany; in 1933, he changed the spelling of his name to Schoenberg and relocated to the United States, becoming a citizen in 1941. By 1935, he was teaching at the University of Southern California, before moving to UCLA, where he worked until his retirement in 1944. Among his American students were **John Cage**, **Leon Kirchner**, **Lou Harrison**, Leonard Stein, Alfred Newman, and Oscar Levant.

Schoenberg adapted well to his new homeland, and America adapted well to him. His enduring reputation was established in the United States, where he brought a greater understanding of his music to numerous composers and musicians, through his work as an educator and through the force of his late compositions, in which he achieved a new mastery and eloquence. That breakthrough was unmistakable with two outstanding twelve-tone scores in 1936, the Violin Concerto and String Quartet No. 4. Schoenberg wrote noteworthy tonal music as well—including the Suite for String Orchestra (1934) and Chamber Symphony No. 2 (1939), a work that he had started in 1906—but his dodecaphonic music, vitalized by the urgency of World War II, produced masterpieces.

In 1942, Schoenberg composed a denunciation of all dictators, *Ode to Napoleon Buonaparte* for reciter, piano, and string quartet or string orchestra; that year also saw the evocative Piano Concerto with its subtext of displacement and endurance. Even more autobiographical was the String Trio of 1946. Schoenberg suffered a near-fatal heart attack that year, and while recovering, he incorporated a programmatic account of the episode into the score. *A Survivor from Warsaw* (1947) for narrator, men's chorus, and orchestra looked at the horror of genocide during the war.

Although his health declined in his last years, Schoenberg's creative vision never slackened, and he continued to explore new ground with his *Phantasy for Violin with Piano Accompaniment* (1949). Schoenberg died of heart failure at age 76 in his Los Angeles home. *See also* LEIBOWITZ, RENÉ.

SCHULLER, GUNTHER (1925–). American composer, musician, and educator. Gunther Schuller studied at the Manhattan School of Music, where he later taught (1950–1963); he also taught at Yale University (1964–1967) and was president of the New England Conservatory of Music (1967–1977) and director of the Berkshire Music Center at Tanglewood (1970–1985). Schuller played French horn with the Metropolitan Opera Orchestra (1944–1959) and with jazz greats Miles Davis and Gil Evans. He has also achieved an international reputation as a conductor and has championed the music of such diverse composers as Charles Mingus, **Arnold Schoenberg**, **Duke Ellington**, **Scott Joplin**, **Robert F. Graettinger**, **George Russell**, and **Milton Babbitt**.

In what he termed his "third stream" works, Schuller blended jazz with such **modernist** techniques as **twelve-tone** organization and **metric modulation**; examples include *Seven Studies on Themes of Paul Klee* (1959) for orchestra, *Variants on a Theme of Thelonious Monk* (1960) for 13 instruments, *Diptych* (1964) for brass quintet and orchestra, and the **opera** *The Visitation* (1965). The author of *Early Jazz* (1968), *The Swing Era* (1988), and *The Compleat Conductor* (1997), Schuller also founded the music-publishing firms Margun Music in 1975 and Gun-Mar Music in 1979, and the GM Recordings label in 1981. His other notable works include *Deaï* (1978) for eight voices and three orchestras, Piano Trio (1984), the opera *A Question of Taste* (1989), *Concerto for Piano Three Hands* (1990), the orchestral scores *Of Reminiscences and Reflections* (1993) and *Where the World Ends* (2007), and *Encounters* (2003) for six voices (optional), alto saxophone, tenor saxophone, trumpet, jazz band, and orchestra. *See also* ATONALITY.

SCHUMAN, WILLIAM (1910–1992). American composer, musician, and educator. William Schuman's composition teachers included **Roy Harris**. He taught at Sarah Lawrence College (1935–1945) and was president of Juilliard (1962–1969). Schuman composed traditional tonal music with a special feel for Americana in the orchestral scores *American Festival Overture* (1939), *New England Triptych* (1956), and *American Hymn* (1981); *Mail Order Madrigals* (1971) for mixed chorus; and the cantatas *Casey at the Bat* (1976), adapted from his 1953 **opera** *The Mighty Casey*, and *On Freedom's Ground* (1985). Schuman's other works include 10 symphonies (1935–1975), five string quartets (1936–1987), *A Song of Orpheus* (1961) for cello and orchestra, and the ballet scores *Undertow* (1945), *Night Journey* (1947), and *Judith* (1949).

SCRATCH ORCHESTRA. Drawing on the musicians professional and nonprofessional who had performed **Cornelius Cardew**'s *The Great Learning*, the Scratch Orchestra was founded in 1969 by Cardew, Michael Parsons, and Howard Skempton. In its Draft Constitution, Cardew outlined the group's areas of musicmaking: *Scratch Music*, notated accompaniments written by the players and performed together; *Popular Classics*, performed not from scores but from memory and imagination; *Improvisation Rites*, verbal instructions for group improvisations, including **free improvisation**; *Compositions*, works by **La Monte Young, Karlheinz Stockhausen, John Cage**, and others; and *Research Project*, independent investigations that were experiential and nonacademic. Each member could design and coordinate a concert, and between 1969 and 1970 the Scratch Orchestra gave more than 50 performances. Internal contradictions within the group led to its 1971 reinvention as the Scratch Ideological Group, focusing on revolutionary political theories. *See also* ENO, BRIAN; GEBRAUCHSMUSIK; NYMAN, MICHAEL; POSTMODERNISM.

SCRIABIN, ALEXANDER (1872–1915). Russian composer and musician. Alexander Scriabin composed one of the most important bodies of piano music in the 20th century and blazed his own path from lush postromanticism to an extreme **modernism** that was heightened by his mystical sensibility. Born in Moscow, Alexander Nikolayevich Scriabin studied piano as a boy with Nikolai Zverev and was composing at an early age; by 14, he had completed, as part of his Op. 2, the impressive Étude in C-sharp Minor (1886), inspired by Frédéric Chopin. Scriabin attended the Moscow Conservatory (1888–1892), studying piano with Vassily Sofonov and composition with Anton Arensky and Sergei Taneyey, and in the late 1890s he made a splash concertizing in Russia and Europe. His programs included works by Chopin, Franz Liszt, Robert Schumann, Felix Mendelssohn, and Johann Sebastian Bach, along with selections from his own compositions, such as the Op. 8 Études (1894) and Opp. 11 and 15 sets of Préludes, both completed in 1896— talented scores mostly after the models of Chopin and Liszt.

Scriabin's Piano Sonatas Nos. 1 (1892) and 2 (1897) were more ambitious works that featured autobiographical content. In 1898, he began teaching piano at the Moscow Conservatory, and that year his music became more pointillistic and enigmatic with Piano Sonata No. 3, "*États d'âme.*" He had begun writing large-scale compositions by then, and in his Piano Concerto (1897) and Symphony No. 1 (1900) for mezzo-soprano, tenor, mixed chorus, and orchestra, Scriabin's debts to Liszt, Richard Wagner, and Pyotr Tchaikovsky are apparent. A more personal voice emerged in the tonal ambiguities of *Réverie* (1898) for orchestra and Symphony No. 2 (1902), which were enlivened by Scriabin's characteristic alternation of languid sensuality with energetic striving. That approach also characterized his Piano Sonata No. 4 (1903) and Symphony No. 3, "*Le divin poème*" (1904), which utilized chords based on fourths. These were also his last movement-form works; all of his subsequent music would be single-movement pieces.

After quitting the Moscow Conservatory in 1903, Scriabin relocated to Europe and lived in Switzerland, France, and Belgium; he also toured the United States with success. His involvement with Theosophy in the mid-1900s transformed the erotic longings of Scriabin's music into a search for mystical ecstasy, described in two major 1907 scores: Piano Sonata No. 5, his most densely chromatic effort to date, and the sensual *Le poème de l'extase* (rev. 1908), written for a large orchestra with organ. Scriabin experienced color associations with music, and he worked out a series of correspondences between pitches and colors for his finest orchestral work, *Prométhée—Le poème du feu* (1910), which included piano and wordless mixed chorus. It was also supposed to feature a color organ that produced tones and flashes of color in synchronization, but the instrument was never realized. Both *Poèmes* achieved a greater concision and harmonic daring, with a broader spectrum of instrumental color, and became his most popular orchestral music.

Scriabin returned to Russia in 1910, and his composition grew more radical with his last five piano sonatas: Nos. 6 and 7, "*La Messe blanche*," from 1911, and Nos. 8, 9, and 10 from 1913. Like his orchestral music, these works moved toward compression: The total duration of all five is less than an hour. They use harsh **dissonances**, extremes in register, unusual sonorities, and startling visceral arpeggios; their tonal bases can be elusive, with No. 10 approaching **atonality**. In these sonatas and his other later piano music, such as *Vers la flamme* (1914), Scriabin was also generating and reinforcing overtones through loudness, sharpness of attack, trills, and tremolos. He had used partials in the overtone series to derive the six pitches of his "chord of the **pleroma**" (C, F-sharp, B-flat, E, A, D), more commonly known as the "mystic chord," which permeates *Prométhée* and all his late piano music in a manner that anticipates **twelve-tone** procedures.

For years, Scriabin had also been working on *Mysterium*, an apocalyptic **multimedia** score to be performed in India and last for days. Colors, textures, and aromas would combine with the sights and sounds of dancers, actors, singers, orchestra, and piano, and *Mysterium*'s performance would result in the spiritual and physical transformation of reality. Scriabin was composing *The Prefatory Act*, an orchestral piece to prepare the way for *Mysterium*, when he developed blood poisoning from an abscess and died in Moscow at age 43. **Alexander Nemtin** began constructing a realization of *The Prefatory Act* from Scriabin's surviving sketches and earlier music in 1970; he completed the three-hour work in 1996, scored for orchestra, soprano, chorus, piano, and organ. *See also* ELECTRONIC MUSIC; JUST INTONATION.

SEEGER, CHARLES (1886–1979). Mexican-born American composer, educator, and theorist. Born in Mexico City of American parents, Charles Seeger was raised in Boston and studied at Harvard University (1904–1908), where he wrote the orchestral overture *The Shadowy Waters* (1908). He then lived in Germany and composed the **impressionistic** Seven Songs (1911) for high voice and piano. Seeger taught at the University of California, Berkeley (1912–1918), where **Henry Cowell** was one of his students. In these years, Seeger wrote his String Quartet (1913), Violin Sonata (1913), the pageants *Derdra* (1914) and *The Queen's Masque* (1915) for orchestra and chorus, and *Parthenia* (1915) for orchestra.

Seeger largely abandoned composition in the 1920s and turned to musicology. Ruth Crawford began studying with him at the end of the decade and absorbed his **modernist** theories of **dissonant** counterpoint. But after marrying in 1932, Seeger and Crawford turned away from modernism and became involved with radical-left politics, with Seeger composing the workers' songs "Lenin! Who's That Guy?" "Mount the Barricades," and "Song of the Builders" in the mid-1930s. He joined Crawford in transcribing and arranging American folk songs and contributed to *Treasury of American Folklore* (1943) and *Folk Song U.S.A.* (1947). His son from a previous marriage, Pete Seeger, became one of America's most popular folksingers. After Crawford's death in 1953, Seeger devoted himself to ethnomusicology. *See also* SEEGER, RUTH CRAWFORD.

SEEGER, RUTH CRAWFORD (1901–1953). American composer, musician, and educator. A skilled pianist by her teens, Ruth Crawford taught piano throughout her life. She studied at the American Conservatory in Chicago (1921–1924) and composed the **dissonant** *Kaleidoscopic Changes on an Original Theme, Ending with a Fugue* (1924) for piano; she also explored the music of **Alexander Scriabin** and composed two preludes for piano. In 1925, three more preludes were written, which included **tone-clusters**. That year, she also became friends with **Dane Rudhyar** and **Henry Cowell**, who championed her music. Crawford turned to chamber music with the 1926 scores Sonata for Violin and Piano and *Music for Small Orchestra*. She composed four more preludes in 1928, making a set of nine, and wrote the Suite No. 1 (1928, rev. 1929) for five winds and piano and *Five Songs to Poems by Carl Sandburg* (1929) for contralto and piano.

Crawford began studying with **Charles Seeger** late in 1929 and adopted his notions of dissonant counterpoint to her **atonal** composition with four chamber pieces she called the *Diaphonic Suites* (1930–1931) and her remarkable *Piano Study in Mixed Accents* (1930). Crawford's masterpiece, *String Quartet 1931*, employed certain **twelve-tone** procedures and a contrapuntal treatment of dynamics. She also wrote *Three Chants for Women's Chorus* (1930), using texts of phoneme and vowel sounds, and *Three Songs to Poems by Carl Sandburg for Contralto, Oboe, Piano, and Percussion with Optional Orchestral Ostinati for Strings and Winds* (1932). Crawford and Seeger married in 1932, and she joined him in radical-left politics, leaving **modernism** behind with her *Two Ricercare* (1932) for mezzo-soprano and piano, "Sacco, Vanzetti" and "Chinaman, Laundryman."

In the mid-1930s, Crawford turned to the study and documentation of American folk song. She made hundreds of transcriptions of field recordings for the anthology *Our Singing Country* (1941) and composed more than 100 piano accompaniments for her transcriptions, published as *Folk Song U.S.A.* (1947). The audience-friendly *Rissolty, Rossolty* (1939) for orchestra was her only original composition in the years she devoted to ethnomusicology. Crawford returned to her own composition in 1952 with the Suite for Wind Quintet, but fell ill with intestinal cancer and died the following year at age 52.

SERIALISM. Noting the importance of the fundamental series of pitches that are arranged in a set, or row, in **Arnold Schoenberg**'s **twelve-tone** method of composition, **René Leibowitz** began using the word *serial* for this music around 1947. **Olivier Messiaen, Pierre Boulez**, and **Karlheinz Stockhausen** narrowed its meaning just a few years later, drawing a distinction between the serial music of **Anton Webern**, which they saw leading to **total serialism**, and the **dodecaphonic** music of Webern's teacher, Schoenberg. Although the word retains this connotation in German, its common usage in English, French, and Italian has been as a synonym for twelve-tone music.

SESSIONS, ROGER (1896–1985). American composer and educator. Roger Sessions entered Harvard University at age 14, received his degree, and then entered Yale University, where he studied with Horatio Parker and received another degree. In 1921, he studied with **Ernest Bloch** at the Cleveland Institute of Music and worked as his assistant. Sessions's **neoclassical** music for the play *The Black Maskers* became a successful orchestral suite in 1923. Living mostly in Europe from 1926 to 1933, he wrote his Symphony No. 1 in E Minor (1927) and Piano Sonata No. 1 (1930). Back in the United States, he started teaching at Princeton University in 1933 and composed his Violin Concerto in B Minor (1935), String Quartet No. 1 in E Minor (1936), *Three Dirges* (1938) for orchestra, and *From My Diary* (1940) for piano. Sessions left Princeton in 1944 to teach at the University of California, Berkeley (1945–1952). There he wrote his Symphony No. 2 (1946), Piano Sonata No. 2 (1946), the one-act **opera** *The Trail of Lucullus* (1947), and String Quartet No. 2 (1951).

Sessions's music had grown increasingly chromatic, and his friendships with **Arnold Schoenberg, Luigi Dallapiccola**, and **Milton Babbitt** helped excite his interest in **twelve-tone** composition. He produced his first **dodecaphonic** work, *Sonata for Solo Violin*, in 1953; that same year, he returned to Princeton, where he taught until 1965. Sessions adapted readily to twelve-tone techniques and worked within the idiom for the rest of his life. This approach was especially congenial to his vocal writing, with such major works as *Idyll of Theocritus* (1954) for soprano and orchestra, the three-act opera *Montezuma* (1962), and the cantata *When Lilacs Last in the Dooryard Bloom'd* (1970) for soloists, chorus, and orchestra. His orchestral music also flourished, with his Piano Concerto (1956); *Divertimento* (1960); *Double Concerto* (1970) for violin, cello, and orchestra; *Rhapsody* (1970); *Concerto for Orchestra* (1981); and Symphonies Nos. 3–9 (1957–1979). Other scores include his String Quintet (1958), Piano Sonata No. 3 (1965), and *Five Pieces for Piano* (1975). A diverse array of composers studied with Sessions throughout his teaching career, including Babbitt, **Miriam Gideon, Leon Kirchner, Ross Lee Finney, David Diamond, Conlon Nancarrow, Vivian Fine, Paul Bowles, Lejaren Hiller, Peter Maxwell Davies, Elaine Taaffe Zwilich, Frederic Rzewski, David Del Tredici, Ursula Mamlok, Richard Maxfield,** and **John Adams**. *See also* ATONALITY; MODERNISM.

SHAPEY, RALPH (1921–2002). American composer, musician, and educator. Ralph Shapey studied violin with Emmanuel Zetlin, conducted the Philadelphia National Youth Administration Symphony Orchestra, and studied composition with **Stefan Wolpe**. Shapey's early music, which includes his first four string quartets (1946–1953) and *Challenge: The Family of Man* (1955) for orchestra, employed more traditional forms, but he became increasingly dissatisfied with 19th-century development techniques.

Seeking a music that was fully itself, like a sculpted object, rather than an essay in growth that attains its full identity over time, Shapey worked in a more **dissonant** and **atonal** style with *Ontogeny* (1958) for orchestra; *Evocation* (1959) for violin, piano, and percussion; and *Rituals* (1959) for orchestra, which included improvisation. His composition matured in this direction with such major works as *Incantations* (1961) for soprano and 10 instruments, String Quartet No. 6 (1963), and *Songs of Ecstasy* (1967) for soprano, piano, percussion, and **tape**. In 1964, Shapey joined the University of Chicago, serving as music director of the Contemporary Chamber Players and teaching composition; his students include **Ursula Mamlok** and **Joan Tower**.

Frustrated with music publishers, audiences, musicians, and critics, Shapey declared a moratorium on all performances of his music in the late 1960s, but continued to compose, producing *Praise* (1971) for bass-baritone, mixed chorus, and chamber orchestra; String Quartet No. 7 (1972); *Fromm Variations* (1973) for piano; and *Songs of Eros* (1975) for soprano, orchestra, and tape. He lifted his moratorium with a 1976 performance of *Praise* and conducted his own and other **modern** and contemporary music for the rest of his career. Shapey's notable late works include *21 Variations* (1978) for piano; Double Concerto for Violin and Cello (1982); Concerto for Cello, Piano, and Two String Orchestras (1986); *Images* (1998) for oboe, piano, and percussion; and String Quartet No. 10 (2000). He is the author of *A Basic Course in Music Composition* (2001).

SHARP, ELLIOTT (1951–). American composer and musician. Elliott Sharp's teachers included **Morton Feldman** and **Lejaren Hiller.** A guitarist and reed player who has employed **extended performance techniques,** Sharp has played with such **free improvisers** as **John Zorn, Sussan Deyhim,** Zeena Parkins, and Butch Morris. His band Carbon used homemade instruments and expanded into Orchestra Carbon; Sharp has also played in the bands Tectonics and Terraplane. His compositions draw on art-rock and new-music methods and have used mathematical models and **alternate tuning systems**; notable works include the string quartets *Tessalation Row* (1984) and *Dispersion of Seeds* (2003), the sextet *Marco Polo's Argali* (1985), and *Skew* (1991) for orchestra. *See also* INSTRUMENT BUILDING; POSTMODERNISM.

SHEA, DAVID (1965–). American composer and musician. David Shea studied at the Oberlin Conservatory of Music. An improvising vocalist who used **extended performance techniques,** Shea turned to playing **samplers,** turntables, CD players, and **computers.** His compositions combining sampled sound with live musicians include *Shock Corridor* (1992), *The Tower of Mirrors* (1995), *Hsi-Yu Chi* (1996), *Satyricon* (1997), Chamber Symphonies Nos. 1 (1998) and 2 (2002), and *The Book of Scenes* (2004). Among Shea's works made totally through sampling are *Alpha* (1995) and *Satyricon 2000* (2000). *See also* ELECTROACOUSTIC MUSIC; FREE IMPROVISATION; POSTMODERNISM.

SHOSTAKOVICH, DMITRY (1906–1975). Russian composer, musician, and educator. One of the giants of 20th-century music, Dmitry Shostakovich is beloved for his symphonies and string quartets, written mostly in a postromantic idiom. His struggles with the Soviet government mark a tragic period in his life and in the history of his country.

Dmitry Dmitryevich Shostakovich was born in St. Petersburg and grew up amid the throes of the Russian Revolution. His mother began teaching him piano at age eight, and soon he was composing. Shostakovich was 13 when he entered the St. Petersburg Conservatory, where he studied with Maximilian Steinberg. His breakthrough came at age 18 with Symphony No. 1 (1925), a witty and exuberant score that caused a sensation at its premiere in 1926.

Shostakovich confirmed his stature as a major composer in the late 1920s and early 1930s, employing **neoclassical** and other **modernist** techniques in such works as his Piano Sonata No. 1 (1926) and Piano Concerto No. 1 (1933), both of which he also premiered as part of a busy performing career. *The Nose* (1928), his satiric **opera** adapted from Nikolai Gogol, featured an interlude for percussion ensemble, and **polytonal** passages highlight his

Symphony No. 2, "To October" (1927), and *Five Fragments for Orchestra* (1935). Like the second, Symphony No. 3, "The First of May" (1931), was a one-movement work with chorus that featured political content praising the Revolution. State authorities had commissioned Shostakovich to write it, but he soon became the state's target with his opera *Lady Macbeth of Mtsensk* (1932). Harsh **dissonances** informed this grim drama of adultery and murder, and although popular internationally, *Lady Macbeth of Mtsensk* offended Joseph Stalin. It was condemned in the official media in 1936 and no longer performed. Shostakovich then withdrew his Symphony No. 4 (1936), another dissonant and tragic work, one of many by him with roots in the music of **Gustav Mahler**; it would remain unperformed until 1961.

Modernist music was denounced as **formalist** and anti-Soviet in these years, and Shostakovich found himself in considerable danger. But he reasserted his reputation with the dynamic and accessible Symphony No. 5 (1937); subtitled "A Soviet Artist's Response to Just Criticism," it was an international success and perhaps his most popular work. Shostakovich began teaching at the Leningrad Conservatory in 1937, and the next year composed his String Quartet No. 1, launching his admired cycle of quartets. His Symphony No. 6 (1939) met with a mixed response, but all was forgiven during the war years. Shostakovich's 1940 Piano Quintet received the Stalin Prize First Grade, and he won again the following year for his Symphony No. 7, "Leningrad" (1941), a work that was championed in the Allied nations, increasing Shostakovich's stature abroad. He left the Leningrad Conservatory in 1941 and taught at the Moscow Conservatory from 1943 to 1948, during which time he composed his Symphony No. 8 (1943), String Quartet No. 2 (1944), Symphony No. 9 (1945), and String Quartet No. 3 (1946).

Despite having been presented with the Order of Lenin in 1946, Shostakovich was officially denounced once again in 1948. The darkness and pessimism of the Eighth Symphony were again reviled as formalist—but so were the lightness and humor of the Ninth. Shostakovich, along with the other erring "Big Four" composers **Sergey Prokofiev**, **Aram Khachaturian**, and Nikolai Myaskovsky, had to apologize and rehabilitate themselves. Shostakovich wrote the patriotic music demanded by the state and confided his deeper feelings about the oppression around him in his Violin Concerto No. 1 (1948, rev. 1955); *From Jewish Folk Poetry* (1948) for soprano, contralto, tenor, and piano; String Quartets Nos. 4 (1949) and 5 (1952); and Symphony No. 10 (1953)—all premiered after Stalin's death in 1953.

Named People's Artist of the Union of Soviet Socialist Republics in 1954, Shostakovich received the Order of Lenin again in 1956 and produced his String Quartet No. 6 (1956), Piano Concerto No. 2 (1957), Symphony No. 11, "The Year 1905" (1957), and Cello Concerto No. 1 (1959). Shostakovich's health deteriorated severely over the 1960s, yet he composed an array of major works, starting with String Quartets Nos. 7 and 8 (1960) and Symphony No. 12, "The Year 1917" (1961). Symphony No. 13, "Babi Yar" (1962), and the cantata *The Execution of Stepan Razin* (1964), both scored for bass soloist, male chorus, and orchestra, were settings of Yevgeny Yevtushenko's poetry and not without controversy.

Shostakovich's expression became even more personal and intense with String Quartets Nos. 9–12 (1964–1968), Cello Concerto No. 2 (1966), and Violin Concerto No. 2 (1967). After Symphony No. 14 (1969), a meditation on death for soprano, bass, and chamber orchestra, his music achieved a new serenity and calm, for all its sadness, with String Quartet No. 13 (1970), Symphony No. 15 (1971), String Quartets Nos. 14 (1973) and 15 (1974), and Sonata for Viola and Piano (1975). Shostakovich died of cancer at age 68 in a Moscow hospital; mourned throughout the Soviet Union, he was given a hero's funeral.

SLONIMSKY, NICOLAS (1894–1995). Russian-born American composer, musician, and educator. Nicolas Slonimsky studied at the St. Petersburg Conservatory and came to the United States in 1923; he became a citizen in 1931 and taught at UCLA (1964–1967). As a conductor, Slonimsky premiered major works by **Edgard Varèse**, **Carl Ruggles**, **Charles Ives**, **Henry Cowell**, and other **modernists**. His compositions include the **bitonal** *Studies in Black and White* (1928) for piano, *My Toy Balloon* (1942) for orchestra and 100 colored balloons, *Gravestones* (1945) for voice and piano, and *Minitudes* (1971–1977) for piano. Slonimsky compiled the *Thesaurus of Scales and Melodic Patterns* (1947) and *Lexicon of Musical Invective* (1952) and wrote the books *Music since 1900* (1937; fifth edition, 1986), *Music in Latin America* (1945), and an autobiography, *Perfect Pitch* (1988). *See also* MULTIMEDIA.

SMIT, LEO (1900–1943). Dutch composer, musician, and educator. Leo Smit studied composition and piano at the Amsterdam Conservatory; he also taught theory and composition there shortly after graduating in 1924. **Impressionist** elements characterize Smit's early orchestral works *Silhouetten* (1922) and his overture to *De vertraagde film* (1923), which also showed the impact of jazz. In 1927, he relocated to Paris. Drawn to the music of **Maurice Ravel**, **Igor Stravinsky**, and the **Groupe des Six**, Smit wrote such works as the Sextet (1928), the ballet score *Schemselnihar* (1929), Concertino for Harp and Orchestra (1933), and the often **dissonant** *Symphonie in C* (1936). In 1937, he returned to Amsterdam, where he composed the impressionist *La mort* (1938) for soprano, alto, and piano; *De bruid* (1939) for female chorus;

and *Divertimento* (1942) for piano four-hands. Concerto for Viola and Strings (1940) was a **neoclassical** work with jazz inflections. He had completed the Sonata for Flute and Piano in 1943 and was working on a string quartet when the Nazis arrested Smit, who was Jewish, and sent him to the Sobibor concentration camp in Poland, where he was killed. *See also* MODERNISM.

SMIT, LEO (1921–1999). American composer, musician, and educator. Pianist Leo Smit studied as a boy with Dmitri Kabalevsky, José Iturbi, and Nicolas Nabokov. As pianist or conductor, he premiered works by Kabalevsky, Nabokov, **Aaron Copland**, **Béla Bartók**, **Paul Hindemith**, and **Irving Fine**. He taught at Sarah Lawrence College, UCLA, and the State University of New York at Buffalo. Smit's music, tonal with **neoromantic** qualities, includes the ballet score *Virginia Sampler* (1947, rev. 1960); three symphonies (1955–1981); two **operas**, *The Alchemy of Love* (1969) and *Magic Water* (1978); and *The Ecstatic Pilgrimage* (1992), 80 songs for voice and piano to poems by Emily Dickinson.

SOLLBERGER, HARVEY (1938–). American composer, musician, and educator. Flutist and conductor Harvey Sollberger studied with **Otto Luening** at Columbia University. With **Charles Wuorinen**, he cofounded and codirected the Group for Contemporary Music. He has also taught at the University of California, San Diego, among other institutions. Sollberger's compositions include *Chamber Variations* (1964) for 12 players and conductor, *The Two and the One* (1972) for cellist and two percussionists, and *Angel and Stone* (1981) for flute and piano. *See also* MODERNISM.

SONIC ARTS UNION. Originally known as the Sonic Arts Group, the Sonic Arts Union was a composers collective formed in 1966 by **Robert Ashley**, **Gordon Mumma**, **David Behrman**, and **Alvin Lucier**. Essentially a live-performance **electronic** ensemble, their **multimedia** music extended into theater, film, television, and dance. Touring and performing in the United States and Europe, they maintained the Sonic Arts Union until 1976. The group also commissioned **Pauline Oliveros**'s theater piece *Valentine* (1968) for four players with amplification. *See also* ELECTROACOUSTIC MUSIC.

SORABJI, KAIKHOSRU SHAPURJI (1892–1988). English composer, musician, and critic. Born to a Parsi father and an English mother, Kaikhosru Shapurji Sorabji was a virtuoso pianist who drew in part upon **impressionism** in his early works—lengthy, highly chromatic scores that were virtuosic in their technical requirements. He was extremely prolific throughout the late 1910s and 1920s, producing eight piano concertos (1916–1928), four piano sonatas (1919–1929), and Symphony (1922) for piano, orchestra, chorus, and organ, among many other works. The culmination was *Opus clavicembalisticum* (1930) for piano, a 250-page score that takes about five hours to perform; unlike later **minimalist** works of such duration, Sorabji's music utilized traditional techniques on a vast scale, with complex fugues and themes with dozens of variations. He also drew upon Iranian, Chinese, and Indian influences in his approach to scale and ornamentation, especially in such nocturne-like piano scores as *In the Hothouse* (1919) and *Le jardin parfumé* (1923).

Sorabji retired from concertizing in 1936 and withdrew his music from performance for several decades. A legend by the 1970s, he attracted a new generation of performers and audiences who could meet the demands of his music. Among Sorabji's later works are *Symphonic Variations* (1937) for piano; six piano symphonies (1939–1976); *Sequentia cyclica super "Dies irae"* (1949) for piano; the 1,001-page score *Messa alta sinfonica* (1961) for soloists, mixed chorus, orchestra, and organ; and *Opus secretum* (1981) for piano. He also authored the music criticism collections *Around Music* (1932) and *Mi contra fa* (1947). *See also* MULTICULTURALISM.

SOUND INSTALLATION. Installation art, in which the exhibition space becomes an art object itself, can be traced back to the 1910s and 1920s, although the term did not come into the nomenclature until the 1960s. The transformation of an interior space into a continuous musical experience also emerged then, along with other forms of **minimalist** music. **Max Neuhaus** coined the term *sound installation* to describe such pioneering works as his *Drive-in Music* (1967), with weather-sensing radio transmitters playing over the radios of passing vehicles along a specially prepared stretch of highway. Other exterior installations interact not with the listener but with the environment: Leif Brush's "terrain instruments," for example, are outdoor structures that respond audibly to environmental conditions. The structures of Patrick Zentz have used wind, sunlight, water, and traffic to trigger sound production.

Many interior installations are simply zones of sound into which one enters. *Chords from "The Tortoise, His Dreams and Journeys"* (1967) was the first of many sound environments of electronic drones created by **La Monte Young** and **Marian Zazeela**. **Earle Brown** used suspended cassette recorders in his interactive *Wikiup* (1979). **Iannis Xenakis** designed the curved architectural space in which his **tape music** *La légende d'Eer* (1978) was premiered as an installation.

Sound installations and site-specific works also have an **instrument-building** quality, insofar as they create an oversized resonating "instrument" out of a preexisting space, as with Bill Fontana's works within the Washington Cathedral's bell tower or the clockworks of Big Ben, or **Ellen**

Fullman's "long string instrument." Other composers who have made sound installations include **Alvin Lucier**, **John Luther Adams**, **Annea Lockwood**, **Takehisa Kosugi**, **David Behrman**, **Maryanne Amacher**, **David Tudor**, **Eliane Radigue**, **Brian Eno**, **Jessica Rylan**, **George Lewis**, and **Nam June Paik**. *See also* SOUND SCULPTURE.

SOUND SCULPTURE. An offshoot of 20th-century **instrument building** is the genre of sound sculpture: art objects that produce sound through an energy source, be it natural, mechanical, or human. Some of these sculptors have created works that are also **sound installations**: Norman A. Andersen reconstructed found objects and musical instruments to function in a mechanical/behavioral mode in *Rainmaker's Baggage* (2005) and *Koo-Koo* (2007); Bill Fontana has used sensors, microphones, and **tape** for certain works, such as *Speeds of Time* (2004) or *Pigeon Soundings* (2005). Other builders of sound sculpture have produced interactive pieces that exist in a gray area between instrument and sculpture. Among the many examples is composer/musician Butch Morris, who has collaborated with different visual artists to create "music machines"—essentially, music boxes combining an original design with an original composition. Richard Lerman's amplified screens are sculpture as "Sound-Seen," but can also be played as transducers. Reinhold Marxhausen's "Stardust" series and "Cosmic Cubes" produce music audible only when shaken close to the ear. Fred "Spaceman" Long has used pickups for his series of unique junk-metal constructions he calls "Jokers."

SPATIAL MUSIC. The tradition of composers assigning the physical placement of a work's performers goes back to Adrian Willaert, Giovanni Gabrieli, and the other 16th-century Venetian polyphonists who heightened patterns of antiphonal response and clarified polyphonic lines by situating their musicians in unusual places within St. Mark's Basilica. This approach faded in the later 17th century, but stirred again in the 19th, when certain composers literalized their music's transcendent spiritual themes by devising new and transformative listening experiences: Hector Berlioz employed multiple instrumental groups in a distinct arrangement for his *Requiem* (1837), and Giuseppe Verdi's *Requiem* (1874) and **Gustav Mahler**'s Symphony No. 2 (1894) included offstage ensembles.

The 20th-century breakthrough in creating music with a specialized spatial arrangement occured in 1908 with **Charles Ives**'s *The Unanswered Question* and *Central Park in the Dark*, chamber-orchestra scores with independent subgroups of musicians. **Carl Nielsen**, in his Symphonies Nos. 3 (1911) and 4 (1916), anticipated certain spatial ideas, and **Darius Milhaud**'s *L'homme* *et son désir* (1918) and **Béla Bartók**'s *Music for Strings, Percussion, and Celesta* (1936) called for their own spatial design.

Yet the real interest in spatial music has been essentially **postmodern**, and this deconstruction of the traditional listening experience did not really gain momentum until the 1950s. Teo Macero spatially reconfigured the five jazz ensembles of *Areas* (1952). **Henry Brant** adapted Ives's approach of physically separating the musicians and not maintaining rhythmic ensemble with *Antiphony One* (1953, rev. 1968), and went on to devote himself to spatial music. With *Gesang der jünglinge* (1956) and *Gruppen* (1957), **Karlheinz Stockhausen** incorporated spatial considerations into his music.

By the 1960s and 1970s, spatial music was exploring further possibilities. Audiences were seeded with musicians in **Dennis Johnson**'s *Din* (1960), **Luciano Berio**'s *Passagio* (1962), and **Iannis Xenakis**'s *Terretektorh* (1966). Performers moved about the space in **George Crumb**'s *Echoes of Time and the River* (1967) and **Lucia Dlugoszewski**'s *Tender Theatre Flight Nageire* (1971, rev. 1978). **Electronic music** became spatial in quadraphonic recordings, such as **Morton Subotnick**'s *Sidewinder* (1971). Spatial assignment evoked ritual in **Pauline Oliveros**'s ceremonial works *Crow Two* (1974) and *Rose Moon* (1977). Other composers of spatial works include **Gyorgy Kurtág, Thea Musgrave, Henri Pousseur, Henryk Górecki, Toru Takemitsu, Roger Reynolds, Fred Frith**, and **Pierre Henry**.

SPEACH, BERNADETTE (1948–). American composer and musician. Pianist Bernadette Speach studied with **Morton Feldman, Lejaren Hiller**, and Leo Smit at the State University of New York at Buffalo. Her *Les ondes pour quatre* (1988) for string quartet notated time in fixed and **free durations**. *Boppin' Again* (1989, rev. 1991) for 10-piece ensemble displayed her jazz roots, and *When It Rains, Llueve* (1995) was a **multicultural** work with Latin rhythms and melodies. Her **multimedia** piece *TreeSing* (2007) for bass clarinet and marimba used video processing. Among Speach's large-scale works are *Within* (1990) for piano and orchestra and *Embrace the Universe* (2001) for mezzo-soprano, viola, piano, mixed chorus, and orchestra. Her collaborations with poet and writer Thulani Davis include *Telepathy Suite* (1987) for chamber ensemble and *Woman without Adornment* (1994) for piano and reciter. Also an improviser, Speach has performed frequently with her husband, guitarist/composer Jeffrey Schanzer. *See also* FREE IMPROVISATION; POSTMODERNISM; SMIT, LEO (1921–1999).

SPECTRAL MUSIC. More a compositional approach than a methodology, spectral music investigates the spectra, or acoustic properties, of a sound, with new harmonies derived from the overtones of specific pitches. It is also concerned with the perception of both individual sounds and overall compositional form. Spectralism developed in France in the 1970s. Composer Hughes Dufour coined the term *musique spectrale*, but its best-known exponent was **Gérard Grisey** with *Les espaces acoustiques* (1985). Other composers of spectral music include **James Tenney, Horatiu Radulescu, Unsuk Chin,** and **Tristan Murail**. *See also* JUST INTONATION; POLYHARMONY.

SPIEGEL, LAURIE (1945–). American composer, musician, and educator. Laurie Spiegel studied guitar and composition with J. W. Duarte in London; in the United States, her composition teachers included Vincent Persichetti and **Jacob Druckman**. She has taught at Bucks County Community College and New York University. Spiegel's work in **electronic music** began with pieces created in 1971 on the Buchla **synthesizer,** such as *Orchestras* and *Harmonic Spheres*. Her *musique concrète* includes *Introit* (1973) and *Water Music* (1974). At Bell Laboratories, she created such **computer-music** pieces as *The Unquestioned Answer* (1974), *Appalachian Grove* (1974), *The Expanding Universe* (1975), and *A Voyage* (1976). *Kepler's "Harmony of the Planets"* (1977), her computer realization of Kepler's 17th-century treatise, was the opening track of the "Sounds of Earth" recording that the National Aeronautics and Space Administration sent into space on the *Voyager* spacecraft in 1977.

Spiegel's **electroacoustic** works include *Waves* (1975) for nine instruments and computer-generated **tape,** the **multimedia** *Guadalcanal Requiem* (1977), *A Canon* (1980) for chamber ensemble and computer, and *Lyric for MIDI Guitar* (1987) for classical guitar with computer interface. An innovator in computer technology, Spiegel helped design the AlphaSyntauri synthesizer for use with Apple II microcomputers and, in the mid-1980s, designed her breakthrough Macintosh software *Music Mouse*, enabling the performance of real-time computer music without an instrumental keyboard or acoustic or **sampled** sounds. She has improvised on *Music Mouse* and used it to compose such notable pieces as *Cavis muris* (1986), *Three Sonic Spaces* (1989), and *Sound Zones* (1990). She has also composed for classic guitar (*After Dowland,* 1979; *Fantasy on a Theme from Duarte's "English Suite,"* 1990) and piano (*À la recherche du temps perdu,* 1976, rev. 1990; *After Clementi,* 1981; *Returning East,* 1988). Spiegel's recent music includes the multimedia electronic work *Lift Off* (1999), *Conversational Paws* (2001) for recorded processed dog sounds, and *A Stream* (2007) for solo violin. *See also* POSTMODERNISM.

SPRECHSTIMME. In the 19th century, operas and melodramas had notated rhythmic speech as *Sprechstimme* ("speech voice"), and by the 1890s a more precise indication of pitch emerged within this practice: a *Sprechgesang* ("speech song"), as in Engelbert Humperdinck's melodrama *Königskinder* (1897). **Arnold Schoenberg** adopted this modification of Sprechstimme for the reciting voice in *Gurrelieder* (1911), a declamation somewhere between spoken and sung that provides greater clarity while remaining heightened and musical. With his classic *Pierrot lunaire* (1912), Schoenberg made Sprechstimme his own, having the soprano's voice always rise to or fall from the assigned pitches, rather than sustain them. He also featured Sprechstimme in his **operas** *Die glückliche Hand* (1913) and *Moses und Aron* (1932) and simplified it for *Ode to Napoleon Buonaparte* (1942)—using not the full five-line stave of *Pierrot lunaire* but a single line, augmented with ledger lines to indicate higher and lower intervals. Other composers who used Sprechstimme include **Alban Berg** (*Wozzeck*, 1922) and **Hanns Eisler** (*Palmström*, 1924).

STILL, WILLIAM GRANT (1895–1978). American composer and musician. William Grant Still studied at the Oberlin Conservatory of Music, the New England Conservatory of Music, and with **Edgard Varèse**. He also performed and arranged for W. C. Handy and composed pieces for Paul Whiteman and Artie Shaw. A conductor and multi-instrumentalist, Still was the most celebrated African-American composer of his day, bringing spirituals and other folk idioms to the concert tradition in evocations of black America. Among his many works are five symphonies (1933–1958), most notably No. 1, "Afro-American Symphony"; seven **operas**, including *Troubled Island* (1938) and *Highway 1 U.S.A.* (1962); *And They Lynched Him on a Tree* (1940) for narrator, alto, black and white mixed choruses, and orchestra; and such orchestral scores as *Darker America* (1925), *Africa* (1930), and *Pages from Negro History* (1943).

STOCHASTIC MUSIC. In probability theory, the term *stochastic* refers to a system of time parameters used to define a process that employs random variables. A stochastic process is nondeterministic: the previous state of the environment cannot fully determine the following state. Its use in music was coined by **Iannis Xenakis** regarding *Pithoprakhta* (1956). He had shaped the score with a controlled random process that gave the work a logical and perceptible form and a coherent overall musical effect, despite individual moment-to-moment activities that could not be determined or fully perceived.

Stochastic composition relies on mathematical procedures from statistics and probabilities to guide randomness, and so it can be regarded as another response to **John Cage**'s **chance music**. Like **aleatory**, stochastic methods enable composers to use randomness without the abandonment of their tastes and memories, which Cage had advocated. The enormous amount of calculation invariably demanded by stochastic techniques is ordinarily handled by **computers**; and such composers as **Lejaren Hiller** and **James Tenney**, who utilized computers to generate sound and compositional material, also worked with stochastic techniques. *See also* TAKAHASHI, YUJI.

STOCKHAUSEN, KARLHEINZ (1928–2007). German composer, musician, and educator. One of the most influential figures in late 20th-century music, Karlheinz Stockhausen was a leader in **serial** composition, **spatial music**, *musique concrète*, **electronic music**, **electroacoustic music**, extended time scales, and new performance freedoms. Born in Mödrath, near Cologne, Stockhausen began studying piano at age six. In 1941, he entered the teachers' training college in Xanten, where he also studied violin and played the oboe. Stockhausen attended the State Academy of Music in Cologne (1947–1951), studying composition with **Frank Martin**, and began to write **totally serialized** music in 1951 with the sextet *Kreuzspiel* and *Formel* for chamber orchestra. The following year, he moved to Paris and studied with **Olivier Messiaen** (1952–1953). Stockhausen also worked at **Pierre Schaeffer**'s RTF studio, creating his first **tape music**, *Etude* (1952). His instrumental music became more pointillistic in the 1952 scores *Spiel* for orchestra, *Schlagtrio* for piano and percussion, and *Punkte* for orchestra (rev. 1962).

After Stockhausen returned to Germany in 1953, he became a permanent collaborator at the WDR electronic music studio in Cologne, where he created electrically synthesized music with *Studie I* (1953) and *Studie II* (1954); he would later become the studio's artistic director (1963–1977) and artistic consultant (1977–1990). *Kontra-Punkte* (1953) for 10 instruments attracted international attention, as did both *Zeitmasze* (1956) for woodwind quintet and the piano series *Klavierstücke* (*I–IV*, 1952; *V–X*, 1954–1955). By then, Stockhausen was coeditor of the new-music publication *Die reihe* (1954–1959) and a lecturer at the International Summer Courses for New Music at Darmstadt (1954–1974). He produced two major compositions in 1956: *Klavierstücke XI*, where the pianist selects what is played, and *Gesang der jünglinge*, a tape piece using vocal and electronic sounds, with **microtonal** scales and the spatial distribution of five loudspeaker groups. Spatial concerns defined one of Stockhausen's finest works, *Gruppen* (1957) for three orchestras and three conductors. In 1958, he began a series of annual tours, conducting, playing, and talking about his music.

The performance freedoms of *Klavierstücke XI* were extended in Stockhausen's 1959 scores *Zylkus* for solo percussionist and *Refrain* for piano, vibraphone, and celesta. In 1960, he completed *Kontakte*, a microtonal piece combining electronic sounds with piano and percussion, and *Carré* for four orchestras and four choirs. *Plus-Minus* (1963), written in **graphic notation**, was of open duration and instrumentation. Over the decade of the 1960s, Stockhausen worked on the many sections of *Momente* (1969) for soprano, four choirs, and 13 instrumentalists, which can be performed in numerous different versions. He also taught at the Basel Academy of Music (1963), the University of Pennsylvania (1965), the University of California, Davis (1966–1967), and the State Academy of Music in Cologne (1971–1977). His students included **La Monte Young**, **Maryanne Amacher**, **Gérard Grisey**, **Richard Teitelbaum**, and **Horatiu Radulescu**.

In 1964, Stockhausen formed a group to perform live electronic music, for which he composed the sextets *Mikrophonie I* (1964), for tam-tam, two microphones, and two filters with potentiometers, and *Prozession* (1967) and *Kurzwellen* (1968), both for tam-tam, viola, electronium or **synthesizer**, piano, and live electronics. His other electroacoustic works included *Mixtur* (1964) for orchestra with four sine-wave generators and four ring modulators; *Solo* (1966) for melody instrument with feedback; *Mikrophonie II* (1965) for 12 singers, Hammond organ or synthesizer, four ring modulators, and tape; and *Spiral* (1968) for soloist with shortwave receiver. The **multicultural** tape piece *Hymnen* (1967) yielded a 1969 version for tape and orchestra. Even *Stimmung* (1968) amplified the six vocalists who sang harmonics of a low B-flat fundamental.

Stockhausen's live electronic music led him to spontaneous performance, explored in *Aus den sieben Tagen* (1968). Designated "15 Text Compositions for Intuitive Music," this purely verbal score is to be performed only by a special electroacoustic ensemble without conductor and can take upwards of seven hours. Another work in this vein is *Für kommende Zeiten* (1970). Otherwise, Stockhausen kept to notated scores, as with the five-hour *Fresco* (1969), subtitled "Wall-Sounds for Meditation," for four orchestra groups and four conductors; *Mantra* (1970) for two pianos and live electronics; and *Inori* (1974) for one or two soloists and orchestra or tape, with dancer-mimes as the soloists.

The culmination of Stockhausen's work in electronic and electroacoustic music, microtonality, performance freedoms, spatial music, extended durations, and theater was his 29-hour music-drama cycle *Licht*—a monumental series of **operas**, one for each day of the week: *Donnerstag* (1978–1980), *Samstag* (1981–1983), *Montag* (1984–1988), *Dienstag* (1987–1991), *Freitag* (1991–1994), *Mittwoch* (1995–1997), and *Sonntag* (1998–2003). Each opera was a sequence of smaller works, written for various forces and individually performable. The 127 scores include *Donnerstag-Abschied* (1980) for five trumpets; *Luzifers Zorn* (1987) for bass, actor, synthesizer player, and tape; *Ave* (1985) for basset-horn and flute; *Pietà* (1991) for flugelhorn, soprano, and electronic music; *Chor-Spirale* (1994) for 12 voices and live electronics; *Helikopter-Streichquartett* (1993); *Hoch-Zeiten* (2002) for choir and orchestra; and *Klavierstücke XII–XIX* (1979–2004).

In his last years, Stockhausen worked on *Klang*, a series of pieces for each hour of the day. Mostly scored for soloists or chamber forces, invariably with live electronics, they ranged from *Freude* (2005) for two harps and *Himmelstür* (2005) for a percussionist and a little girl to the purely electronic *Cosmic Pulses* (2007). He completed the 21st hour, *Paradies* for flute and electronic music, shortly before his death at age 79 at his home in Kuerten-Kettenberg, Germany. *See also* ALEATORY; AMBIENT MUSIC; BEATLES, THE; CARDEW, CORNELIUS; JUST INTONATION; OPEN FORM.

STRAUSS, RICHARD (1864–1949). German composer and musician. Richard Strauss studied composition with Friedrich Wilhelm Mayer in 1875 and wrote conservative but skillful works in the 1880s, including his Serenade (1881) for wind ensemble, Suite (1884) for 13 winds, *Burleske* (1886) for piano and orchestra, and *Aus Italien* (1886) for orchestra. Upon absorbing the music of Hector Berlioz, Franz Liszt, and Richard Wagner, Strauss developed a livelier and more imaginative orchestral voice, beginning with *Don Juan* (1888) for orchestra. This programmatic tone poem in the Lisztian tradition used unusual melodic material and featured wide and sudden leaps. Strauss became an international sensation with the orchestral scores that followed—*Tod und Verklärung* (1889), *Till Eulenspiegels lustige Streiche* (1895), *Also sprach Zarathustra* (1896), *Don Quixote* (1897), *Ein Heldenleben* (1898)—and also established himself as a conductor.

His tone poems ended with *Sinfonia domestica* (1903) and *Ein Alpensinfonie* (1915), but Strauss won further renown with two landmark **operas**, *Salome* (1905) and *Elektra* (1908). They featured harsh **dissonances** and dramatic extremes of **expressionist** intensity, but their orchestral brilliance and vocal bravura secured their place in the repertory. With the tuneful and lighthearted *Der Rosenkavalier* (1910), Strauss composed his most popular opera. Hugo von Hofmannsthal wrote the librettos of *Elektra* and *Der Rosenkavalier*, but his later collaborations with Strauss—*Ariadne auf Naxos* (1912; rev. 1916), *Die Frau ohne Schatten* (1917), *Die ägyptische Helena* (1927), *Arabella* (1932)—were not as startling or affecting as their earlier work had been. The novelty of Strauss's tone poems had worn off by then, too, and the man who had seemed the last word in **modernism** at the turn of the century came to be recognized as a true postromantic.

Strauss coauthored the libretto for his final opera, *Capriccio* (1941). By then the grand old man of German music, he had formed an uneasy alliance with the Nazi government. Most of the autumnal works of his final years

were intimate pieces for smaller forces—Concerto No. 2 for horn and orchestra (1942), *Metamorphosen* (1945) for 23 strings, Concerto for oboe and
orchestra (1945)—but Strauss scored the beloved *Vier letzte Lieder* (1948)
for soprano with full orchestra. *See* also TRAUTONIUM.

STRAVINSKY, IGOR (1882–1971). Russian-born American composer
and musician. Arguably the definitive **modernist**, Igor Stravinsky brought
a genius for rhythmic innovation to all his music—nationalist, **neoclassical**,
and **serial**—and became one of the most admired composers in the history
of Western music. Igor Fyodorovich Stravinsky was born on the estate of
Oranienbaum (now Lomonosov), not far west of St. Petersburg. He began
piano lessons at age nine and was composing by his teens. Preparing for a
career in law, he entered St. Petersburg University in 1901, but began studying privately with composer Nikolai Rimsky-Korsakov in 1903. Stravinsky
produced a Symphony in E-flat (1907, rev. 1914), which was indebted to
Pyotr Tchaikovsky and Alexander Glazunov. More original were his colorful
1908 orchestral scores *Scherzo Fantastique* and *Fireworks*.

Impressed by *Fireworks*, impresario Serge Diaghilev had Stravinsky
compose a ballet on the Firebird legend. The result, *L'oiseau de feu* (*The
Firebird*, 1910), met with enormous acclaim. Stravinsky brought brilliant
orchestral color and a lively rhythmic sensibility to materials from Russian folk music, and *The Firebird* ultimately proved to be his most popular
work, especially in the orchestral suites that he derived from it in 1911
(rev. 1919) and 1945. Diaghilev called for two more Russian-nationalist
ballets—although Stravinsky was by then living in Europe, chiefly Switzerland. *Petrushka* (1911, rev. 1947) was well received despite its provocative **polytonal** passages. The premiere of the epochal *Le sacre du
printemps* (1913, rev. 1947), however, was the most notorious scandal in
music history. Stravinsky's savage **polyrhythms**, thunderous percussion,
and **dissonant** harmonies created an uproar that sealed his reputation. *Le
sacre du printemps* joined its two predecessors in the repertory and proved
widely influential for decades.

Russian folk music informed other theater works by Stravinsky in the
1910s and early 1920s, such as the **opera** *Le rossignol* (1914, rev. 1962),
which he reworked as the ballet score *Le chant du rossignol* in 1917; the
burlesque *Renard* (1916) for two tenors, two basses, and chamber ensemble;
and the one-act comic opera *Mavra* (1922). It is also present in the beloved
musical fable *L'histoire du soldat* (1918, rev. 1924) for three speakers,
dancer, and seven instruments and *Symphonies of Wind Instruments* (1920,
rev. 1947). Stravinsky's masterpiece *Les noces* (1923), scored for soprano,
mezzo-soprano, tenor, bass, mixed chorus, four pianos, and 17 percussion

instruments, was perhaps his most radical marriage of nationalism and modernism, topping even *Le sacre.*

Stravinsky relocated to France in 1920 and started utilizing Baroque and classical forms to strip the romantic rhetoric that still clung to modernist rhythmic and harmonic techniques. With the Octet (1923, rev. 1952), he made his first use of the sonata form since his 1907 symphony. Stravinsky's neoclassicism was fueled by his passion for clarity, polyrhythmic invention, and smaller mixed ensembles, and a series of major scores ensued. The first, Concerto for Piano and Wind Instruments (1924, rev. 1950), also launched his lifelong career as pianist or conductor of his own music. His love of older music also led to his arrangements for ballet scores, recasting Giovanni Pergolesi in *Pulcinella* (1920, rev. 1965) and Tchaikovsky in *Le baiser de la fée* (1928, rev. 1950).

Giuseppe Verdi and George Frideric Handel loomed large behind Stravinsky's oratorio *Oedipus Rex* (1927, rev. 1948), but its tragic impact was undeniable and it became one of his most performed works. So did *Symphony of Psalms* (1930, rev. 1948) for chorus and orchestra—in its purity and vigor, perhaps Stravinsky's finest music of the era, which includes such major scores as his two ballets choreographed by George Balanchine, *Apollon-Musagète* (1928, rev. 1947) and *Jeu de cartes* (1936), as well as the Violin Concerto (1931), *Duo Concertant* (1932) for violin and piano, Concerto for Two Solo Pianos (1935), and the *Dumbarton Oaks Concerto* (1938) for chamber orchestra.

Shortly after World War II ignited in 1939, Stravinsky left Europe and settled in the United States; the following year, he applied for citizenship. American life invigorated his music, and he composed the Symphony in C (1940) and Symphony in Three Movements (1945). He reunited with Balanchine for *Danses concertantes* (1942) and *Orpheus* (1947) and composed the jazz-inspired *Ebony Concerto* (1945) for clarinetist Woody Herman and his band. Stravinsky's vocal writing also found renewed power with the Mass (1948) for mixed chorus and double wind quintet and his opera *The Rake's Progress* (1951).

Stravinsky by then had become the most highly regarded contemporary composer in the world. Some admirers were confounded, however, when he began using serial techniques in the Cantata (1952) for soprano, tenor, female chorus, and ensemble; the Septet (1953); and *Three Songs by William Shakespeare* (1953) for mezzo-soprano, flute, clarinet, and viola. Having come to these methods largely through his interest in the music of **Anton Webern**, Stravinsky fully embraced serialism in *Canticum sacrum* (1955) for tenor, baritone, chorus, and orchestra and the ballet score *Agon* (1957).

Serialism dominated Stravinsky's late music, with such scores as *Threni* (1958) for six solo voices, mixed chorus, and orchestra; *Movements* (1959) for piano and orchestra; *A Sermon, a Narrative, and a Prayer* (1961) for alto, tenor, speaker, chorus, and orchestra; Variations for Orchestra (1964); and *Requiem Canticles* (1966) for contralto, bass, chorus, and orchestra. He also made two of his finest arrangements: *Monumentum pro Gesualdo di Venosa ad CD annum* (1960), a tribute to Don Carlo Gesualdo, and *Two Sacred Songs* (1968) of Hugo Wolf. Declining health circumscribed Stravinsky's last years, but at age 88, he moved into his new home in New York City. One week later, he died there. *See also* ATONALITY; FUTURISM; WUO-RINEN, CHARLES.

STRING PIANO. Henry Cowell coined the term *string piano* to describe his innovative techniques for performing directly on the strings of a piano. He first strummed and plucked and struck the strings in his coyly titled solo *Piece for Piano with Strings* (1923). *Aeolian Harp* (1923) and *The Banshee* (1925) were also popular string-piano works. Cowell began using implements within the piano—such as a pencil or thimble or darning egg—to produce new textures. *The Irish Suite* (1928), a string-piano concerto with small orchestra, summed up the possibilities for him. Other **extended performance techniques** for piano, developed by later composers, owed much to Cowell, from the "prepared piano" of **John Cage** and the "timbre piano" of **Lucia Dlugoszewski** to works by **George Crumb**, **Mauricio Kagel**, **Bruno Maderna**, and the sound-icon pieces of **Horatiu Radulecscu**. Creative African-American composer/musicians such as **Cecil Taylor** and **Sun Ra** have also played string piano.

SUBLETTE, NED (1951–). American composer and musician. Ned Sublette studied with **Kenneth Gaburo**, **Pauline Oliveros**, and **La Monte Young**. A producer, guitarist, and vocalist, Sublette has worked with such creative composer/musicians as Young, **John Cage**, **Robert Ashley**, **Glenn Branca**, **Peter Gordon**, and **"Blue" Gene Tyranny**. His recordings include *Western Classics* (1982) and the **multicultural** *Cowboy Rumba* (1999). Sublette is also the author of *Cuba and Its Music* (2004) and *The World That Made New Orleans* (2008). *See also* POSTMODERNISM.

SUBOTNICK, MORTON (1933–). American composer and educator. Morton Subotnick studied with **Darius Milhaud** and **Leon Kirchner** at Mills College and began creating **tape-music** scores for theater and dancers in 1960. He cofounded the San Francisco Tape Music Center with Ramon Sender in 1962 and composed his first **multimedia** works: *Mandolin* (1963) for viola, tape, and film and *Play! No. 3* (1965) for pianist/mime, tape, and film. In the mid-1960s, Subotnick supplied **electronic music** for New York's legendary discotheque the Electric Circus. Commissioned by Nonesuch Records to compose an electronic work for LP, Subtonick created the landmark *Silver Apples of the Moon* (1967). A series of memorable records followed: *The Wild Bull* (1968), *Touch* (1969), *Sidewinder* (1971), *Four Butterflies* (1973), and *Until Spring* (1975).

With *Two Life Histories* (1977) for clarinet, male voice, and electronics, Subotnick began creating **electroacoustic** works that he termed "ghost scores," in which the players are accompanied by electronic sound that is generated from their own music, created by a tape recorder with outputs attached to different modules to alter their sounds. His other ghost-score works include *Liquid Strata* (1977) for piano and *Axolotl* (1981) for cello. Subotnick began using **computers** in his music with *Ascent into Air* (1981) for chamber ensemble and computer. *The Key to Songs* (1985) combined live musicians with an interactive computer that imitated their instruments. *Return* (1986) was purely electronic, made with a computer-controlled digital **synthesizer**. In *A Desert Flowers* (1989) for orchestra and computer, the conductor used a computer-modified baton that controlled the electronics. Subotnick achieved another breakthrough in 1992 with *Five Scenes from an Imaginary Ballet*, the first work conceived specifically for CD-ROM.

Subotnick collaborated with his wife **Joan La Barbara** and Mark Coniglio on the multimedia work *The Misfortune of the Immortals* (1995). Balinese dancers join the voices, instruments, computers, and lights of his *Hungers* (1986) and *Intimate Immensity* (1997). Subotnick's recent music includes *Echoes from the Silent Call of Girona* (1998) for string quartet and CD-ROM and the electronic work *Gestures: It Starts with Colors* (2000). He has taught at Mills College and Yale University, and his students have included **Rhys Chatham** and **David Lang**. Subotnick has also developed a series of CD-ROMs and the website www.creatingmusic.com to teach composition to children. *See also* ATONALITY; GEBRAUCHSMUSIK; MULTICULTURALISM.

SUN RA (1914–1993). American composer and musician. Herman "Sonny" Blount began playing piano at age 11 and, by the early 1930s, was leading his own band and touring the South. In 1946, he served as pianist and arranger for Fletcher Henderson in Chicago. His studies of Egyptology, the Bible, and outer space merged into a dynamic personal philosophy, and in 1952 he changed his name and began performing as Le Sony'r Ra, or more simply Sun Ra; he also formed his own group, called the Arkestra, which he would continue to lead for 40 years. Several key players stayed with the Arkestra for good, too, most notably saxophonists John Gilmore (tenor), Pat Patrick (baritone), and Marshall Allen (alto). Sun Ra released his first LP, *Jazz by*

Sun Ra, in 1956, and shortly thereafter formed his own record label, Saturn, through which he would document his music.

In 1961, Sun Ra relocated the Arkestra to New York, and their sets there established the band's character. Dressed in colorful and glittering costumes, the musicians often marched around the audience while playing or singing. Performances were **multimedia** events that included dancers and light shows. Sun Ra's music became more **dissonant** and **polyrhythmic**, and his sets evolved into unpredictable excursions through the history of African-American music—past (Sun Ra's arrangements of classics by Henderson, Jelly Roll Morton, **Duke Ellington**, and others), present (his driving hard-bop originals), and future (roof-raising collective **free jazz** improvisations). The Arkestra musicians became multi-instrumentalists, and the percussion section grew **multiculturally**, with Brazilian and Indian drumming. Original instruments were also included, such as the "lightning log drum," made by bassoonist James Jacson from a tree that had been hit by lightning.

A gifted pianist, Sun Ra improvised and composed in numerous idioms. He could play free and create dissonances, **tone-clusters**, noise, and over-tone resonances; he also played **string piano**. But he nourished a special devotion for electric keyboards, playing one of the first Moog **synthesizers**, a preproduction Mini-Moog bought in 1969. Over the years, his arsenal included Solovox, Wurlitzer organ, Farfisa organ, Rocksichord, Yamaha organ, Spacemaster, electronic celeste, and DMX, and his imagination and virtuosity at the synthesizer resulted in one of the great bodies of work in real-time **electronic music**.

Sun Ra's vast discography includes such notable releases as *The Magic City* (1965), *Nothing Is* (1967), *Pictures of Infinity* (1974), *Live at Montreux* (1978), *Aurora Borealis* (1980), *Strange Celestial Road* (1980), *Nuits de la Fondation Maeght* (1981), *Stars That Shine Darkly* (1985), *John Cage Meets Sun Ra* (1986), *A Night in East Berlin* (1987), *Live London 1990* (1990), and *The Singles* (1996). The Arkestra settled in Philadelphia in 1968 and performed nationwide and internationally. It survived Sun Ra's death at age 80 and continues to play under the guidance of Marshall Allen. See also ELECTROACOUSTIC MUSIC; FREE IMPROVISATION; PLEROMA; POSTMODERNISM.

SYNTHESIZER. A synthesizer is a single device that contains the resources needed to generate and modify electronic sound. Along with synthesizing sound, such a machine also synthesizes an **electronic-music** studio, bringing together a panoply of equipment into a single unit (or a group of linked units). From 1938 to 1942, the Hammond Organ Company produced more than a thousand Novachord keyboard instruments, but this all-tube, 72-note polyphonic synthesizer with oscillators failed to catch on (although **Hanns Eisler** featured it in his 1940 Chamber Symphony). The Electronic Sackbut of Canadian composer **Hugh Le Caine**, developed in 1948, is considered the first voltage-controlled synthesizer. In the United States in 1955, Harry Olsen and Herbert Belar first demonstrated their Mark I Synthesizer developed at the RCA studios, and in 1959, the RCA Mark II was installed at the Columbia-Princeton Electronic Music Center.

The breakthrough came in the mid-1960s with keyboard-operated synthesizers developed by Donald Buchla and Robert Moog, working independently. The first synthesizers entered the marketplace in 1969 and transformed the experience of playing real-time electronic music. One of the first Moogs was purchased by **Sun Ra**, who soon was giving virtuoso performances on synthesizer. The **Beatles** were also ahead of the curve, using a synthesizer on *Abbey Road* (1969), and the instrument quickly found a home in rock music. As the technology has continued to develop, synthesizers have been marketed by an array of manufacturers. They have also been used by many innovative electronic and **electroacoustic** composer/musicians, including **Wendy Carlos, Morton Subotnick, La Monte Young, Karlheinz Stockhausen, Robert Ashley, Eliane Radigue, Jerry Hunt, Terry Riley, Richard Teitelbaum, Jessica Rylan, Brian Eno, "Blue" Gene Tyranny, Laurie Anderson, Mary Jane Leach**, and the **Residents**. *See also* COMPUTER MUSIC; FILM MUSIC; SAMPLING.

SZYMANOWSKI, KAROL (1882–1937). Ukrainian-born Polish composer, musician, and educator. Karol Szymanowski studied piano at the Warsaw Conservatory and later served as its director (1927–1930). His early scores, such as Symphony No. 2 (1910) and the **opera** *Hagith* (1913), showed the impact of Richard Wagner and **Richard Strauss**. But Szymanowski's exposure to the music of **Claude Debussy, Alexander Scriabin**, and **Igor Stravinsky** led him to an **impressionist** idiom invigorated with **polytonal** techniques, as in *Mythes* (1915) for violin and piano, Symphony No. 3 (1916), and the opera *Król Roger* (1924). His later compositions drew upon Polish folk music, for example, *Stabat Mater* (1928) for tenor or soprano, mixed chorus, and orchestra; the ballet score *Harnasie* (1931); Symphony No. 4 (1932, a.k.a. *Symphonie concertante*) for piano and orchestra; Violin Concerto No. 2 (1933). After a long struggle with tuberculosis, Szymanowski died in a Swiss sanitarium at age 54. *See also* MODERNISM.

T

TAILLEFERRE, GERMAINE. *See* GROUPE DES SIX.

TAKAHASHI, YUJI (1938–). Japanese composer, musician, and educator. Yuji Takahashi studied piano with Hiroshi Ito and composition with Shibata Minao, Ogura Roh, and **Iannis Xenakis**; he has taught at Indiana University and other institutions. A virtuoso pianist, he has championed the works of **Erik Satie, Toru Takemitsu,** and Xenakis. **Stochastic** techniques inform Takahashi's septet *Chromamorphe 1* (1964) and *Metatheses 1* (1968) for piano. He has composed **tape music** (*Time*, 1963; *Tadori*, 1972) and **electroacoustic** scores (*Bridges 1* for electric harpsichord or piano, amplified cello, bass drum, and castanets, 1967; *Kafka* for three voices, saxophone, keyboards, and live electronics, 1990) and also performed protest songs with Suigyu Band (1978–1985). By the early 1980s, Takahashi was improvising on piano and **computer**. Among his **multicultural** scores are *Mimi no ho* (1994) for sho, viola, and reciter and the **indeterminate** *Koto nado asobi* (2000) for koto and ensemble of any instruments. Takahashi's other compositions include *For You I Sing This Song* (1976) for clarinet, violin, cello, and piano; *Kwang-ju, May 1980* (1980) for piano; *Viola of Dmitry Shostakovich* (2002) for solo viola; and *Yoru, ame, samusa* (2006) for mixed chorus. His sister Aki Takahashi, also a virtuoso pianist, has premiered scores by **Morton Feldman, Toshi Ichiyanagi, John Cage, Joji Yuasa, Takehisa Kosugi,** and her brother, among others. *See also* ATONALITY; ELECTRONIC MUSIC; FREE IMPROVISATION; POSTMODERNISM.

TAKEMITSU, TORU (1930–1996). Japanese composer and educator. The first Japanese composer to achieve an international audience, Takemitsu created a sound world of subtle textures, delicate harmonies, and eloquent silences, unsurpassed in its austere beauty. Toru Takemitsu was born in Tokyo and raised in Dalian, China, where his father was employed; not until 1937 did he return to Japan. Drafted into the Japanese army during the war, he was working on the construction of an army camp at age 14 when he first heard a recording of a French song, despite the official ban on Western music.

Moved by its beauty, he resolved to become a musician and did so mostly on his own; composition lessons with Yasuji Kiyose in 1948 were his only formal training.

In 1951, with composer **Joji Yuasa** and others, Takemitsu cofounded the Experimental Workshop, which gave performances of **multimedia** works. The facility enabled him to produce **tape music** such as *Static Relief* (1955), *Tree, Sky, Bird* (1956), and *Sky, Horse, and Death* (1958). In *Vocalism A-1* (1956), he used inflections of the Japanese word for "love" as his only sound source; *Water Music* (1960) used dripping water similarly. *Requiem for Strings* (1957) was the first of Takemitsu's instrumental pieces to be taken up in the West; others soon followed, such as *Tableau noir* (1958) for speaker and chamber orchestra, *Coral Island* (1962) for soprano and orchestra, and *Textures* (1965) for piano and orchestra. Takemitsu's Western admirers in the 1960s included **Igor Stravinsky** and **John Cage**, and **Aaron Copland** conducted the premiere of Takemitsu's *The Dorian Horizon* (1966) for 17 strings. In 1970, Takemitsu organized the Music Today festival in Osaka and designed its Space Theater with lighting effects, lasers, and **sound sculptures**. Music Today brought international music to Japan for the next two decades; during these years, Takemitsu also lectured at Harvard, Yale, and other institutions.

Takemitsu's love of French **modernism**, especially the music of **Claude Debussy** and **Olivier Messiaen**, was reflected in his own **impressionistic** use of slow tempi and subtle textures and harmonies. He drew upon Japan's traditional court music *gagaku*, as well as Western concert music, jazz, and experimental music, invariably with a refined feeling for silence. Rather than begin with a formal structure or methodology, Takemitsu would typically assemble his sonic elements, with their varying degrees of stillness and activity, in cycles of differing lengths, not unlike the arrangement of a Japanese garden.

Takemitsu developed his own approach to silence and **indeterminacy** with the graphic score *Ring* (1961), for flute, terz guitar, and lute; *Sacrifice* (1962), for alto flute, lute, and vibraphone with antique cymbals; and the septet *Sonant* (1965, rev. 1969), which he soon renamed *Varelia*. During these years, Takemitsu was also creating **film music**. He scored more than 90 movies in his career, among them such classics as *Woman in the Dunes* (1964), *Kwaidan* (1964), and *Ran* (1985). His film scores encouraged Takemitsu to employ Japanese instruments compositionally in *Eclipse* (1966) for shakuhachi and biwa, for which he devised a **graphic notation**; in *November Steps* (1967), a popular **multicultural** score, he combined those two instruments with a Western orchestra.

Experimental features characterize other music by Takemitsu from the 1960s and 1970s. The 1962 works *Corona for Pianists* and *Corona II* for string orchestra are graphic scores; *Stanza II* (1971) for tape and harp also includes graphic notation. *Stanza I* (1969) for female voice, guitar, harp, vibraphone, and piano/celesta offered performance freedoms, and Takemitsu incorporated it into his next piece, *Crossing* (1969), having it played in combination with two large orchestras. *Toward* (1970) and *Wonder World* (1972) are purely electronic works. *Gémeaux* (1971, rev. 1986) was scored for oboe solo, trombone solo, two orchestras, and two conductors. *Voice* (1971) for solo flute imitated the shakuhachi and called for multiphonics and other **extended performance techniques**. *In an Autumn Garden* (1973) is a full-fledged gagaku score. The quintet *Bryce* (1976) is built on three tones and the eight **quarter-tones** that surround them.

Natural sound appeared in Takemitsu's composition with birdsong in *Stanza II* and the 1986 environmental tape pieces *A Minneapolis Garden* and *The Sea Is Still*. A feeling for nature also pervaded his purely instrumental music, as in *A Flock Descends into the Pentagonal Garden* (1977) for orchestra, *From Far beyond Chrysanthemums and November Fog* (1983) for violin and piano, *How Slow the Wind* (1991) for chamber orchestra, and its companion piece *And Then I Knew 'Twas Wind* (1992) for flute, viola, and harp. In *Archipelago S.* (1994), the 21 musicians are divided into five subgroups distributed through the performance space. *Spirit Garden* (1994) for orchestra utilized his own version of **serial** procedures. Takemitsu had begun his first **opera** when he died of pneumonia in a Tokyo hospital at age 65 while undergoing treatment for bladder cancer. *See also* ELECTROACOUSTIC MUSIC; MICROTONALITY; SPATIAL MUSIC.

TAL, JOSEF (1910–2008). Polish-born Israeli composer, musician, and educator. Born Joseph Grünthal in what is now Poland, Josef Tal was raised in Berlin and studied with **Paul Hindemith** at the Hochschule für Musik. He immigrated to Palestine in 1934 and taught at the Jerusalem Academy of Music and the Hebrew University, where he founded the Israel Center for **Electronic Music** in 1961. Blending tonal, **atonal**, and **twelve-tone** techniques, Tal's music includes six symphonies (1953–1991), *Five Essays* (1986–2000) for piano, the **operas** *Ashmedai* (1968) and *Josef* (1993), and the electronic *Variations* (1970) and *Frequencies 440–462* (1972). He replaced the orchestra with **tape** in his Harpsichord Concerto (1964, rev. 1977), Piano Concerto No. 6 (1970), Harp Concerto (1971, rev. 1980), and the opera *Massada 967* (1972). A pianist and conductor, Tal also wrote the autobiographies *Der Sohn des Rabbiners* (1985), *Reminiscences, Reflection, Summaries* (1997), and

Tonspur (2005) and developed with Shlomo Markel the Talmark notation system for electronic music. *See also* ELECTROACOUSTIC MUSIC.

TALMA, LOUISE (1906–1996). French-born American composer, musician, and educator. Lousie Talma relocated from France to New York with her family in 1914. At the American Conservatory at Fontainebleau, she studied piano with Isidore Philipp and composition with **Nadia Boulanger**; she also taught there and at Hunter College. Her early works, which include *Four-Handed Fun* (1939) for two pianos and *Toccata* (1944) for orchestra, were **neoclassical**, but she turned to **twelve-tone music** with her String Quartet (1954), the **opera** *The Alcestiad* (1958), and *Dialogues* (1963) for piano and orchestra. Talma's later **serial** music became less strict and more freely **atonal**, as in *Thirteen Ways of Looking at a Blackbird* (1979) for voice, oboe, and piano; *The Ambient Air* (1981) for four instruments; and *Full Circle* (1985) for orchestra. *See also* MODERNISM.

TAN DUN (1957–). Chinese composer and musician. Tan Dun studied at the Central Conservatory of Beijing and Columbia University. Among his **multicultural** scores are Concerto for String Quartet and Pipa (1999), Concerto for Zheng and String Orchestra (1999), and the **operas** *Marco Polo* (1995), *Peony Pavilion* (1998), and *The First Emperor* (2006). Other notable works include *On Taoism* (1985) for voice, bass clarinet, contrabassoon, and orchestra; the **multimedia** *Orchestral Theatre I–IV* (1990–1999); and *Water Concerto* (1998), *Paper Concerto* (2003), and *Earth Concerto* (2009), which employed new instruments. *See also* INSTRUMENT BUILDING; POSTMODERNISM.

TAPE MUSIC. Tape music actually began before magnetic tape: In Cairo in 1944, **Halim El-Dabh** composed *Ta'abir al-Zaar* using a wire recorder, and in 1948, French radio engineer **Pierre Schaeffer** created *Étude aux chemins de fer*, the first of his *Cinq études de bruit*, using disk recordings—a technique anticipated by **Paul Hindemith**'s *Grammophonplatteneigene Stücke* (1930). Schaeffer called the new medium *musique concrète*, and the French radio network RTF broadcast his music and gave him further access to its facilities. In collaboration with **Pierre Henry**, Schaeffer created the breakthrough work *Symphonie pour un homme seul* (1950). By then, magnetic tape recorders were generally available, and Schaeffer and Henry established the Groupe de Recherches de Musique Concrète at the RTF in 1951, becoming the first **tape-music** studio, and thus the first **electronic-music** studio. With sound engineer Jacques Poullin, the group developed the studio's musicmaking capabilities and produced musique concrète by such composers as **Ed-**

gard **Varèse, Karlheinz Stockhausen, Pierre Boulez, Luc Ferrari, Jean Barraqué, Olivier Messiaen, Darius Milhaud,** and **Iannis Xenakis.**

Making music with tape became an international activity. In the United States, **Vladimir Ussachevsky** premiered a concert of his tape works in 1952 and then began collaborating with **Otto Luening.** Eschewing the European jargon, they called their pieces "tape music" and created *Rhapsodic Variations* (1954), the first work combining tape and orchestra. In Italy in 1954, **Luciano Berio** and **Bruno Maderna** collaborated on a tape piece, *Ritratto di città*; the following year, they founded the Studio di Fonologia Musicale of the Italian Radio in Milan, where Berio, Maderna, **Luigi Nono,** and others composed tape music. **Toshiro Mayuzumi** made the first Japanese tape piece—*X, Y, Z* (1955)—at the electronic-music studios of the NHK, Japan's broadcasting system; **Toru Takemitsu** and **Joji Yuasa** also created tape music at Tokyo's Experimental Workshop. **Roberto Gerhard** pioneered English tape music, composing at the BBC Radiophonic Workshop. Canadian engineer and composer **Hugh Le Caine** in 1955 invented the Multi-track, which could replay six tapes simultaneously, each with variable speed and direction.

Electroacoustic music combining taped sounds with live musicians became a permanent feature of 20th-century music, but the type of music on the tape continued to change. By the 1960s, the sounds were more frequently electrically synthesized—magnetic tape was no longer the medium, but rather the messenger. Eventually it was supplanted almost completely by innovations in **computer music** and **sampling,** which became commonly available in the 1980s and provided greater ease in selecting and manipulating sounds. *See also* ATONALITY.

TAVENER, (SIR) JOHN (1944–). English composer. John Tavener studied with Sir Lennox Berkeley at London's Royal Academy of Music (1961–1965). He attracted attention with his avant-garde retelling of Jonah— *The Whale* (1966) for soloists, mixed chorus, and orchestra—and the **opera** *Thérèse* (1973). *Ultimos ritos* (1972) for soloists, mixed chorus, orchestra, and **tape** explored stillness and meditation. The **minimalist** qualities of Tavener's music crystallized after he was received into the Eastern Orthodox Church in 1976, and stillness characterized *Akhmatova rekviem* (1980) for soprano, baritone, and orchestra and *Prayer for the World* (1981) for mixed chorus, his half-hour setting of a 12-word prayer. Tavener's static, melodic music includes such notable scores as *The Protecting Veil* (1987) for cello and string orchestra, the opera *Mary of Egypt* (1991), and the orchestral works *Theophany* (1993) and *Mystagogia* (1998).

After Tavener was knighted in 2000, his music became more **multicultural** and explored other religions. He combined Christian, Hindu, and Islamic texts in *The Veil of the Temple* (2002), scored for soprano, boys' choir, and Eastern and Western instruments and composed in versions of two-and-a-half and seven hours, and in *Requiem* (2007) for cello, soprano, tenor, mixed chorus, and orchestra. *See also* POSTMODERNISM.

TAYLOR, CECIL (1929–). American composer and musician. Cecil Taylor started playing piano at age five. He studied at the New York College of Music and New England Conservatory of Music, but found his real education on his own, principally in the music of **Duke Ellington**, Thelonious Monk, Bud Powell, and Horace Silver. Taylor played in bands during the early 1950s and formed his own quartet in 1953. His lengthy, heavily chromatic, **dissonant**, and frequently **atonal** post-bop piano music became longer and more visceral and **polyrhythmic** in the early 1960s and included **tone-clusters**.

Despite such noteworthy recordings as *The World of Cecil Taylor* (1961) and *Unit Structures* (1966), Taylor's music often met with incomprehension and hostility. Nevertheless, by the 1980s, he was recognized internationally as a master of **free jazz**, and he began composing for large ensembles. He adapted his densities and cross-tempi and sense of spirit to a broad canvas in such works as the 10-musician recording *Segments II* (1985); the 1988 sessions of *Legba Crossing* and *Alms/Tiergarten (Spree)*, for 15 and 17 musicians, respectively, released on *Cecil Taylor in Berlin '88* (1990); his 1990 sessions for 11 musicians released on *Melancholy* (1999); and his 2000 recordings with the 18-musician Italian Instabile Orchestra, released on *The Owner of the River Bank* (2004).

Taylor has performed with numerous improvising composer/musicians in his career, including the Art Ensemble of Chicago, Max Roach, Derek Bailey, **Leroy Jenkins**, and **Pauline Oliveros**. His other notable recordings include the solos *Silent Tongues* (1975), *For Olim* (1987), and *The Tree of Life* (1998), and the group performances *3 Phasis* (1979), *Live in Bologna* (1988), *In Florescence* (1990), and *Nailed* (2000). *See also* FREE IMPROVISATION; MODERNISM; PLEROMA; STRING PIANO.

TEITELBAUM, RICHARD (1939–). American composer, musician, and educator. Richard Teitelbaum studied with **Mel Powell**, **Luigi Nono**, **György Ligeti**, **Karlheinz Stockhausen**, and **Milton Babbitt** and taught at Bard College. A pioneer in live **electronic music**, Teitelbaum co-founded **MEV** and has improvised on **synthesizers** and electronic systems with **Anthony Braxton**, **Fred Frith**, **George Lewis**, **Leroy Jenkins**, and others. His **electroacoustic** works include *Ode* (1980) for voice and Harmonizer, *Solo for Pianos* (1982) for digital piano system, the **operas** *Golem* (1994) and *Z'vi* (2005), and the **multicultural** scores *Blends* (1977) for shakuhachi and two synthesizers, *Man Made Ears* (1987) for synthesizers, violin, and shamisen, *Intera* (1991) for yokobue, Western reeds, and interactive **computer** system, and *Trio* (2001) for sho, hichiriki, **sampler**, and computer. *See also* FREE IMPROVISATION; POSTMODERNISM.

TELHARMONIUM. American musician Thaddeus Cahill (1867–1934) studied at the Oberlin Conservatory of Music and patented a polyphonic electric keyboard instrument in 1896. Called the telharmonium or dynamophone, it used the electromechanical action of spinning alternators to produce sine-wave tones that were tuned to the chromatic scale. It included a touch-sensitive keyboard for dynamic control, filters to create wind and string timbres, and a telephone—its sound was fed into telephone wires and heard through amplified phone receivers. Cahill built three telharmoniums between 1900 and 1906 and gave public performances of the third and most ambitious model, which spanned five octaves. The telharmonium was discussed by **Ferruccio Busoni** in *Sketch of a New Esthetic of Music* (1907) and praised by Mark Twain, but the elaborate and unwieldy instrument met with no success, and Cahill gave up **electronic music** in the early 1910s.

TENNEY, JAMES (1934–2006). American composer, musician, educator, and theorist. James Tenney studied piano with Edward Steuermann, conducting with **Henry Brant, electronic music** with **Lejaren Hiller**, and composition with **Chou Wen-chung, Carl Ruggles, Kenneth Gaburo**, and **Edgard Varèse**. He also held an assistantship with **Harry Partch** in the early 1960s. An associate member of technical staff at Bell Laboratories (1961–1964), he created such landmark **computer-music** works as *Analog #1: Noise Study* (1961), *Stochastic Studies* (1962), *Phases* (1963), and *Ergodos II* (1964), often employing **stochastic** procedures. He collaborated with George Brecht on the electronic *Entrance/Exit Music* (1962) and became involved with **Fluxus** performances in the mid-1960s, creating *"Chamber Music"* (1964) for any number of instruments, players, objects, or events and his series *Postal Pieces* (1965–1971), which included *Swell Piece #1* (1967) for any number of sustained-tone instruments. Tenney was also a cofounder and conductor of the new-music group Tone Roads Chamber Ensemble (1963–1970).

Along with his conceptual scores, Tenney composed **minimalist** electronic music with *For Ann (Rising)* (1969) and such gradual-process pieces as *Clang* (1972) for orchestra, *Saxony* (1978) for one or more saxophone players and tape-delay system, and *Voice(s)* (1983) for variable instrumental ensemble, one or more voices, and multiple tape-delay system. Tenney's other major works from these years include *Quiet Fan* (1971) for chamber ensemble, a tribute to **Erik Satie**; *Spectral CANON for CONLON Nancarrow* (1974, rev.

1991) for harmonic player piano; *Chromatic Canon* (1980, rev. 1983) for two pianos, a blend of **twelve-tone** and minimalist procedures; and *Bridge* (1984) for two **microtonal** pianos eight-hands, which merged the ideas of Partch and **John Cage**.

Tenney composed **multicultural** scores with *The Road to Ubud* (1986) for gamelan and prepared piano and *Last Spring in Toronto* (2000) for gamelan and orchestra. *Critical Band* (1988) for variable ensemble and tape-delay system used interval ratios from the harmonic series. *Flecking* (1993) for two pianos tuned a **quarter-tone** apart utilized **graphic notation**. *Spectrum 1–8* (1995–2001) was a series of **spectral** works for various instruments. Tenney wrote the theoretical studies *META+HODOS* (1961) and *META Meta+Hodos* (1975), as well as *A History of "Consonance" and "Dissonance"* (1988). He taught at York University, the California Institute of the Arts, and other institutions; his students include **Peter Garland**, **Joe Hannan**, and **John Luther Adams**. *See also* ATONALITY; JUST INTONATION; POSTMODERNISM.

THEREMIN. Patented in 1921 by Russian scientist **Leon Theremin**, the theremin was the first **electronic-music** instrument to be used internationally. The monophonic theremin generates sound through the heterodyning method. The right hand controls a vertical antenna for pitch; the left, a horizontal antenna for dynamics. But the theremin is unique in that it is never touched: Frequency and amplitude are altered by moving one's hands within the electromagnetic fields of the antennae.

Despite notable efforts from **Joseph Schillinger**, **Edgard Varèse**, **Percy Grainger**, and **Bohuslav Martinu**, the theremin never attracted much interest from composers, although the outstanding performer Clara Rockmore (1911–1998) kept it before audiences, usually playing transcriptions. Its sound became most familiar in **film** scores: Miklos Rózsa used the theremin to evoke madness in two 1945 dramas—Billy Wilder's *The Lost Weekend* and Alfred Hitchcock's *Spellbound*—and **Bernard Herrmann** gave it a new home in science fiction with his score for *The Day the Earth Stood Still* (1951). With its memorable appearance in the Beach Boys' classic "Good Vibrations" (1966), the theremin excited a new generation of music lovers. It has since enjoyed something of a renaissance, with performances by such virtuosi as Youssef Yancy, Lydia Kavina, and Armen Ra. *See also* ELECTROACOUSTIC MUSIC.

THEREMIN, LEON (1896–1993). Russian scientist and inventor. Lev Sergeyevich Teremen came upon the heterodyning method for synthesizing sound electronically when he was building a radio in 1918. Three years later, as Leon Theremin, he patented the **theremin**, a monophonic **electronic-music** instrument with antennae for controlling pitch and dynamics. Theremin emigrated to the United States in 1928 and found a protégée in the teenage Clara Rockmore who became the preeminent theremin virtuoso of her time. Along with variations on his instrument such as the Keyboard Theremin and Electronic Cello, he also constructed the rhythmicon, which produced pitches tuned to the overtone series as well as difficult new **polyrhythms** for **Henry Cowell**'s *Rhythmicana* (1931). In 1938, Theremin was kidnapped by Soviet agents and forcibly returned to the Soviet Union to develop eavesdropping and surveillance technology. Not until 1991, at age 95, did he revisit the United States and Rockmore. *See also* GOSFIELD, ANNIE; IVES, CHARLES.

THOMSON, VIRGIL (1896–1989). American composer, musician, and critic. Already proficient at piano and organ, Virgil Thomson studied with Edward Burlingame Hill at Harvard University (1919–1923), with **Nadia Boulanger** in Paris in 1922, and with Rosario Scalero back in the United States the following year. Returning to Paris in 1925, he composed the **neoclassical** scores *Synthetic Waltzes* (1925) for piano four-hands and *Sonata de chiesa* (1926) for five instruments. Thomson also became friends with American writer Gertrude Stein and demonstrated a flair for setting her poetry with *Susie Asado* (1926) for voice and piano and *Capital Capitals* (1927) for four male voices and piano.

Inspired by the use of popular tunes in **Erik Satie**'s nonrhetorical music, Thomson **quoted** the hymns and folk music he had heard growing up in Missouri. He used familiar materials in unfamiliar ways, bringing humor, charm, and invention to his diatonic idiom in *Variations on Sunday School Tunes* (1927) for organ, *Symphony on a Hymn Tune* (1928), and Piano Sonata No. 1 (1929, orch. 1931 as Symphony No. 2, rev. 1941). In the **opera** *Four Saints in Three Acts* (1928), Thomson's greatest work, this technique approached **minimalism**, eschewing drama as sweepingly as Stein did in her libretto.

In the late 1920s, Thomson began composing short portraits of people with his subjects sitting for him. He ultimately produced more than 100 portraits and, in 1982, orchestrated 11 of the best. Thomson explored **neoromantic** qualities with Sonata for Violin and Piano (1930), String Quartet No. 2 (1931, rev. 1957, orch. 1972 as Symphony No. 3), *Stabat Mater* (1931) for soprano and string quartet, the ballet *Filling Station* (1937), and the orchestral suites from his scores for the Pare Lorentz **films** *The Plow That Broke the Plains* (1936) and *The River* (1937).

A frequent conductor of his own music, Thomson was also chief music critic for the *New York Herald Tribune* (1940–1954) and a teacher for **Lou**

Harrison, **Ned Rorem**, **Paul Bowles**, and **Richard Yardumian**. His notable later works include a second opera to a Stein libretto, *The Mother of Us All* (1947), the score for Robert Flaherty's film *Louisiana Story* (1948), Cello Concerto (1949), *Three Pictures* (1952) for orchestra, *Mostly about Love* (1959) for voice and piano, the opera *Lord Byron* (1968), the ballet score *Parson Weems and the Cherry Tree* (1975), and *Thoughts for Strings* (1981) for string orchestra. *See also* MODERNISM.

TIPPETT, (SIR) MICHAEL (1905–1998). English composer and musician. Michael Tippett studied composition and conducting at the Royal College of Music. A lyrical tonal composer, he was admired for his Concerto for Double String Orchestra (1939) and the oratorio *A Child of Our Time* (1941). He found special success in **opera** with *The Midsummer Marriage* (1952), *King Priam* (1961), *The Knot Garden* (1970), *The Ice Break* (1976), and *New Year* (1989). Tippet's other vocal music includes *Boyhood's End* (1943) for tenor and piano, *The Heart's Assurance* (1951) for high voice and piano, *Songs for Dov* (1970) for tenor and small orchestra, and the oratorio *The Mask of Time* (1982). The author of *Moving into Aquarius* (1959) and *Those Twentieth-Century Blues* (1991), Tippet was knighted in 1966. Among his other works are five string quartets (1935–1991), four piano sonatas (1937–1984), and four symphonies (1945–1977).

TONE-CLUSTER. Henry Cowell coined the term *tone-cluster* in his book *New Musical Resources* (1930), describing a **modernist** technique that he had employed in his piano music since the mid-1910s: building up chords from major and minor seconds, often in such densities that groups of adjacent keys are played with the flat of the hand or the forearm. These methods had also appeared in the music of **Claude Debussy**, **Alban Berg**, **Percy Grainger**, **Charles Ives**, and **Leo Ornstein**, but Cowell used them the most extensively, producing such notable works as *Dynamic Motion* (1916) and his Piano Concerto (1929). He also educated musicians and the public about tone-clusters and came to be identified with the technique when he toured internationally during the 1920s. **Béla Bartók** adopted tone-clusters, in part through his interest in Cowell's music, as did Cowell's pupils **Johanna M. Beyer**, **Lou Harrison**, and **John Cage**.

In his later years, Cowell deemphasized the radical nature of his innovations and referred to tone-clusters by the more traditional terminology of *secundal harmony*. Yet the subsequent generations of composers who adopted tone-clusters in keyboard and/or ensemble music, among them **Olivier Messiaen**, **George Crumb**, **Iannis Xenakis**, **Krzysztof Penderecki**, **Glenn Branca**, **György Ligeti**, **Charlemagne Palestine**, **Giacinto Scelsi**, and **Alfred Schnittke**, were exploring not harmony so much as density and resonance—the qualities that had first excited Cowell. Creative African-American music also has a long tradition of piano tone-clusters, from "Blind" Tom Bethune to **Scott Joplin** and Jelly Roll Morton to Thelonius Monk, Art Tatum, Horace Silver, **Cecil Taylor**, **Sun Ra**, and **Muhal Richard Abrams**. *See also* DISSONANCE; PLEROMA.

TOTAL SERIALISM. Total serialism, or integral serialism, is the extension of **serial** methods of pitch organization to rhythm, dynamics, and attack/timbre. *See also* TWELVE-TONE MUSIC.

TOWER, JOAN (1938–). American composer, musician, and educator. Joan Tower's teachers included **Henry Brant**, **Ralph Shapey**, **Darius Milhaud**, and **Chou Wen-chung**. She was founder and pianist of the Da Capo Chamber Players (1969–1984) and has taught at Bard College since 1972. Her early scores such as *Breakfast Rhythms I and II* (1974) for clarinet and five players were **serial**, but Tower developed her own colorful and **impressionist**-inspired approach to tonality with such notable works as the quintet *Petroushskates* (1980); the orchestral scores *Sequoia* (1981), *Silver Ladders* (1986), and *Made in America* (2004); and the string quartets *Night Fields* (1994) and *Incandescent* (2003). *See also* MODERNISM; TWELVE-TONE MUSIC.

TRAUTONIUM. The trautonium is a monophonic **electronic** keyboard instrument designed in the late 1920s by German engineer Dr. Friedrich Trautwein (1888–1956). It used a neon-tube oscillator rather than the heterodyning method by which the **theremin** and **ondes martenot** generated sound, giving it a more distinctive timbre. **Paul Hindemith** wrote a trio of works for it in the 1930s, and **Richard Strauss** used it in his *Japanische festmusik* (1940). Trautwein revised the trautonium as the Monochord in the late 1940s, and in the 1950s his assistant Oskar Sala, a noted trautonium player, developed an expanded version for the recording studio, the Mixtur-Trautonium. *See also* ELECTROACOUSTIC MUSIC; FILM MUSIC.

TUDOR, DAVID (1926–1996). American composer, musician, and educator. David Tudor studied piano with Irma Wolpe Rademacher and composition with **Stefan Wolpe**. In 1950, he was introduced to **John Cage** by **Morton Feldman** and soon became part of their circle, along with **Earle Brown** and **Christian Wolff**. Tudor premiered many of their important pieces, as well as works by Wolpe, **Pierre Boulez**, **La Monte Young**, **Karlheinz Stockhausen**, **Sylvano Bussotti**, and **Mauricio Kagel**. His technical virtuosity brought clarity to these innovative works, and Tudor became an international champion of new music. By the end of the 1950s, he was developing equipment and techniques for live **electronic music**. Tudor became a leader in the field, as an improviser and as a composer, and by the end of the 1960s, he had stopped concertizing as a pianist.

Tudor's music could also take on qualities of a **sound installation**, as with *Rainforest IV* (1973), and he used **sound sculpture** in *Web for John Cage II* (1989). **Multimedia** works such as *Bandoneon!* (1966) and *Reunion* (1968) could utilize lighting, television, dance, and video. He also performed with other composer/musicians, including **Pauline Oliveros** and **Gordon Mumma**. Tudor's dance scores for Merce Cunningham include *Rainforest I* (1968), *Weatherings* (1978), *Webwork* (1987), and *Soundings: Ocean Diary* (1994). He taught at Mills College and other institutions. After suffering a series of strokes, Tudor died in his sleep at age 70 in his home on Tompkins Cove, New York. *See also* ATONALITY; ELECTROACOUSTIC MUSIC; POSTMODERNISM.

TWELVE-TONE MUSIC. Also known as **dodecaphony**, the twelve-tone method of composition was developed in the early 1920s by **Arnold Schoenberg**, who first made complete use of the system with his Piano Suite (1923). Seeking greater precision and a more formalized structure in his **atonal** music, Schoenberg patterned the 12 tones of the chromatic scale in a specific sequence, known as the twelve-tone set, or row, which is used forward and backward (known as its retrograde), as well as upside down, both forward (inversion) and backward (retrograde inversion). All the tones in the set are equally important, with no single one exerting a tonal pull or dominance. Melodic, harmonic, and polyphonic expressions of the set are developed through a variety of traditional techniques, including transposition, augmentation, and diminution.

Similar methods had been explored during the 1910s and 1920s by **Josef Matthias Hauer, Alexander Scriabin, Arthur Lourié, Nikolai Roslavets, Béla Bartók**, and **Carl Ruggles**, but it was Schoenberg who defined twelve-tone music for the era. He also disseminated the method, and his pupils **Hanns Eisler, Alban Berg, Anton Webern**, and **Roberto Gerhard** also began using these techniques. After Schoenberg settled in the United States in 1933, appreciation of his methodology steadily grew. Accommodating a wide range of expression, it informed the work of geographically and stylistically diverse composers in the 1930s, among them **Ernst Krenek, Wallingford Riegger, Ben Weber, Frank Martin, Stefan Wolpe, John Cage**, Ruth Crawford, and **Aaron Copland**.

The interest in Schoenberg's method was further invigorated after World War II by a new enthusiasm for Webern's music. **René Leibowitz** began writing about, teaching, and performing twelve-tone music in Europe. From Schoenberg's idea of the set as a premotivic series of pitches, Leibowitz coined the term *serial* for this music. By the late 1940s, **Milton Babbitt** in America and **Olivier Messiaen** in France had extended twelve-tone techniques and were composing with sets of not just tones but serialized rhythmic patterns, dynamic levels, and attacks/timbres as well. This approach of **total serialism** attracted numerous composers in the 1950s, including Krenek, **Pierre Boulez, Karlheinz Stockhausen, Luciano Berio, Bruno Maderna**, and **Luigi Nono**.

During those years, many **neoclassical** composers turned to twelve-tone music, among them **Igor Stravinsky, Roger Sessions, Ross Lee Finney, Louise Talma, Irving Fine**, and **Arthur Berger**. There was also the development of combining twelve-tone organization with tonal structures and techniques, as in the music of **Luigi Dallapiccola, George Perle, Hans Werner Henze, Walter Piston, Samuel Barber, Egon Wellesz**, Martin, Copland, Finney, and Fine. Younger composers who took to stricter methods include **Jean Barraqué, Charles Wuorinen, Gunther Schuller**, and **Brian Ferneyhough**. Twelve-tone techniques were also used by such jazz composers as John Coltrane, Bill Evans, and Yusef Lateef. Over the 1960s, twelve-tone composition secured itself in the American academy, where its minuscule audience proved no hindrance to the music's commission, performance, or recording and its increasingly complex mathematics could be developed along with realizations in **electronic music**.

Other composers began rejecting the limitations of twelve-tone music. **Earle Brown, Pauline Oliveros, La Monte Young, Henri Pousseur, George Rochberg, Richard Maxfield, Thea Musgrave, Jacob Druckman, Gérard Grisey, Peter Maxwell Davies, Henryk Górecki, Joan Tower, Philip Glass, Arvo Pärt, Alfred Schittke**, and **David Del Tredici** used the method in early works and then abandoned it to pursue more personal paths. With the cultural shift toward a **postmodern** sensibility, the hegemony of this **modernist** technique receded, and strict twelve-tone composition became infrequent; more common is an inclusive approach, moving freely among different methods and styles. Composers who have used twelve-tone techniques in this manner include **Lejaren Hiller, Ben Johnston, Toru Takemitsu, Frederic Rzewski**, and **James Tenney**. *See also* BERNSTEIN, LEONARD; CERHA, FRIEDRICH; DENISOV, EDISON; FILM MUSIC; GOEHR, ALEXANDER; HARRISON, LOU; MAMLOK, URSULA; POWELL, MEL; SEEGER, RUTH CRAWFORD; ZIMMERMANN, BERND ALOIS.

TYRANNY, "BLUE" GENE (1945–). American composer, musician, and educator. Robert Sheff studied piano with Meta Hertwig and Rodney Hoare, harmony and orchestration with Otto Wick, and composition with Frank Hughes. As both pianist and composer, Sheff was prodigious, and at age 13 he created a **tape** piece, *Music for Three Begins* (1958). Two years later, he and Philip Krumm were giving concerts in his native San Antonio, performing their own music along with works by **John Cage, La Monte Young, Christian Wolff,**

and **Terry Jennings**. Sheff also played such **modernists** as **Béla Bartók, Erik Satie, Charles Ives, Arnold Schoenberg**, and **Anton Webern**.

Upon relocating to Ann Arbor, Michigan, in 1962, Sheff became involved with the legendary **ONCE Group**. The following year, several of his works were performed at ONCE and ONCE Friends concerts, including his **graphic** scores *Meditation* (1962), played by chamber orchestra, and *Diotima* (1963), realized for flutes and tape. While in Michigan in 1967, Sheff created two interrelated pieces that continued to engage his music over the years: *Country Boy Country Dog* for tape and the procedural score *How to Discover Music in the Sounds of Your Daily Life*. He began teaching at Mills College in California in 1970 and around that time adopted the name "Blue" Gene Tyranny, inaugurating it while performing as a pianist in jazz and rock bands. Among his notable 1970s compositions were *A Letter from Home* (1976) for voices and electronics and two tape works, *Harvey Milk (Portrait)* (1978) and *The White Night Riot* (1979).

Tyranny's music exemplifies the **postmodern** belief in using modernist techniques without modernist materials. He has drawn upon jazz, rock, and pop as improviser and composer, evoking emotion yet remaining nondramatic and nonrepresentational. This sensibility made him the perfect collaborator on piano and **synthesizer** for **Robert Ashley**'s video **opera** *Perfect Lives* (1980); their subsequent work together includes Ashley's *Atalanta (Acts of God)* (1982–1987), *el/Aficionado* (1987), *Dust* (1998), and *Celestial Excursions* (2003). Tyranny recorded a breakthrough piano improvisation in 1981, which he then used to derive the **electronic music** that alternates with this performance in his LP *The Intermediary* (1982). The early 1980s also saw more *Country Boy Country Dog* activity: *The CBCD Concert* (1980) for soloist(s) and electronics, *The CBCD Variations* (1980) for soloist and orchestra, and *The CBCD Intro* (1984)—work that fed into his 1994 recording *Country Boy Country Dog*.

Tyranny's later piano CDs *Free Delivery* (1990) and *Take Your Time* (2003) include interactive electronics, as have many of his performances. He has also composed piano music for other players, such as *Nocturne with and without Memory* (1988), *We All Watch the Sun and the Moon (for a Moment of Insight)* (1992), and the piano duos *Great Seal (Transmigration)* (1990) and *The De-certified Highway of Dreams* (1991). *The Driver's Son* has been an ongoing project since 1989, envisioned not as an opera but rather as an audio storyboard. Tyranny's notable recent compositions include *The Somewhere Songs* (1988–2001) for voice and electronic orchestra; *The Invention of Memory* (2004) for voice, piano, guitar, and five strings; and two major works in 2010: *Scriabin's Chord* for violin and piano and *George Fox Searches* for piano. *See also* COMPUTER MUSIC; ELECTROACOUSTIC MUSIC.

U

ULTRAMODERN. *See* MODERNISM.

USSACHEVSKY, VLADIMIR (1911–1990). Manchurian-born American composer, musician, and educator. The son of Russians in Manchuria, Vladimir Ussachevsky settled in the United States in 1930 and studied at the Eastman School of Music (1936–1939) with Bernard Rogers and Howard Hanson. He taught at Columbia University, the University of Utah, and the Peabody Institute and was a cofounder of the Columbia-Princeton Electronic Music Center. His students included **Charles Wuorinen**, **Wendy Carlos**, and **Charles Dodge**. Ussachevsky's early compositions were mostly **neoromantic**, with elements of Russian sacred music, as in his *Jubilee Cantata* (1938) for baritone, reader, mixed chorus, and orchestra. He started experimenting with a tape recorder in 1951 and a year later premiered his **tape music**, which included *Underwater Valse* (1952). Ussachevsky composed for tape almost exclusively over the next 20 years, with such works as *Piece for Tape Recorder* (1955), *Wireless Fantasy* (1960), and *Computer Piece No. 1* (1968). He collaborated with **Otto Luening** on *Incantation for Tape Recording* (1953); *Rhapsodic Variations* (1954), the first work to combine orchestra and tape; *A Poem in Cycles and Bells for Tape Recorder and Orchestra* (1954); and *Concerted Piece for Tape Recorder and Orchestra* (1960).

Ussachevsky resumed nonelectronic composition in 1972 with *Missa brevis* for soprano, chorus, and brass. Many of his works also combined instruments and tape, such as *Colloquy for Symphony Orchestra, Tape Recorder, and Various Chairs* (1976) and *Dialogues and Contrasts* (1983) for brass quintet and tape. He adapted readily to the use of **synthesizers** and **computers** in **electronic music** and eventually came to prefer the computer for manipulating natural sound. In the early 1980s, Ussachevsky composed for Nyle Steiner's **electroacoustic** electronic valve instrument (EVI), which produced electronic sounds but was controlled by trumpet-valve technique and had a seven-octave range, with timbres from traditional brass and woodwinds to electronic sounds. EVI compositions by Ussachevsky include *Celebration for String Orchestra and Electronic Valve Instrument* (1980) and *Novelette pour Bourges* (1983) for EVI and piano. Among his other late works are *Dances and Fanfares for a Festive Occasion* (1980) for orchestra and *Triskelion* (1982) for oboe and piano. *See also* ATONALITY; MODERNISM.

V

VARÈSE, EDGARD (1883–1965). French-born American composer and musician. An essential figure in the early generation of **modernists**, Edgard Varèse established the importance of percussion in 20th-century music and was a leader in the development of **electronic music**. Born Edgard Victor Achille Charles Varèse in Paris to a French mother and an Italian father, he spent most of his childhood in the village of Villars in Burgundy, raised by his grandfather and other relatives. He was reunited with his parents in 1892 when they relocated to Turin, where he studied privately with Giovanni Bolzoni, director of the Turin Conservatory. At this time, he discovered the music of **Claude Debussy** and **Richard Strauss**, whose innovations opened doors for his own composition.

Varèse returned to Paris in 1903 and was accepted at the Schola Cantorum the following year, where he studied composition and conducting with Vincent d'Indy and counterpoint with **Albert Roussel**. He was also accepted at the Paris Conservatoire in 1905 and studied with Charles-Marie Widor. Varèse was composing orchestral music by the mid-1900s, but eventually found the musical atmosphere in Paris too conservative and stifling. He moved to Berlin in 1908 and there became friends with **Ferruccio Busoni**; later that year, during his trips to Paris, Varèse also befriended Debussy. Both men encouraged him in the orchestral and operatic music he was writing, as did Strauss after meeting Varèse in 1909. Varèse's first job as a conductor came in 1914, leading an orchestra in Prague. When World War I began, he was in Paris and unable to retrieve his scores in Berlin; all were subsequently lost in a fire.

Varèse immigrated to the United States late in 1915 and settled in New York; he became a U.S. citizen in 1927. By the late 1910s, Varèse was conducting American orchestras, and in 1921, with **Carlos Salzedo**, he founded the International Composers' Guild, which gave numerous American premieres of important European composers. The guild disbanded in 1927, and the next year Varèse founded the Pan-American Association of Composers with **Henry Cowell** and **Carlos Chávez**; it lasted until 1934. With *Amériques* (1921) for large orchestra, Varèse defined his mature music: **atonal**, **dissonant**, crystalline, revolving around winds and percussion, driven by rhythm and densities and sonorities. *Amériques* also redefined the role of percussion in orchestral music, calling for 11 percussionists playing more than 20 instruments, including a siren, whip, and lion's roar.

Like *Amériques*, Varèse's other 1920s scores brought a new physicality and immediacy to the concert hall, a heightened sense of sound, with *Offrandes* (1922) for soprano and small orchestra, *Hyperprism* (1923) for nine winds and seven percussionists, and *Intégrales* (1925) for 11 winds and four percussionists. The 120-musician orchestra of *Arcana* (1927) included eight percussionists playing 40 instruments. Only *Octandre* (1924) for seven winds and double bass was percussion free. The culmination came with Varèse's *Ionisation* (1931) for 13 percussionists playing an arsenal of instruments, only three of which—chimes, glockenspiel, and piano—produce equal-tempered pitches. No one in Europe or the United States had yet written an all-percussion score, and this conceptual advance liberated countless composers. After *Ionisation*, music for percussion ensemble became a staple of modern and contemporary composition.

Despite this breakthrough, Varèse's creative output came to a halt in the 1930s. He followed *Ionisation* with *Ecuatorial* (1934) for bass voices, eight brass, piano, organ, six percussionists, and two **theremins**—his first use of electronic music. By then, he was deeply concerned with the creation of new densities, tempi, tunings, and partial tones, all of which were unavailable from conventional instruments, and after composing *Densité 21.5* (1936) for solo flute, Varèse fell silent. The only score to emerge from a long dark period was *Étude pour espace* (1947) for mixed chorus, two pianos, and percussion, a fragment of a large work that he had abandoned; in 2009, **Chou Wen-chung**, his former pupil, created an orchestrated **spatial-music** version of this rarely performed piece.

Encouraged by developments in *musique concrète*, Varèse resumed composing in 1950 and completed the four instrumental sections of *Déserts* two years later. Around this time, he received the anonymous gift of an Ampex 400 tape recorder, which he used to create a brief section of **tape music**, *La procession de Vergès*, for Thomas Bouchard's **film** *Around and about Joan Miró* (1955). Varèse then recorded an array of industrial sounds and percussion instruments and, at **Pierre Schaeffer**'s RTF studio in Paris, reworked the tapes into three more sections of *Déserts*. Scored for 14 winds, piano, five percussionists, and two channels of magnetic tape, *Déserts* (1954) alternates sections of instrumental music and "organized sound"—Varèse's preferred term, as he resisted the label of *musique concrète*. Interest and support came more readily now, and he was also able to create the tape piece *Poème électronique* (1958).

Varèse's *Nocturnal* for soprano, bass voices, and orchestra was premiered in 1961, but he never completed a manuscript score for the work. Four years later, Varèse contracted an infection after undergoing surgery at a New York hospital and died at age 81. A performing score of *Nocturnal*, published in 1972, was prepared by Chou. Others composers who studied with Varèse include **André Jolivet, Colin McPhee, William Grant Still, Lucia Dlugo-szewski**, and **James Tenney**. *See also* ELECTROACOUSTIC MUSIC.

VAUGHAN WILLIAMS, RALPH (1872–1958). English composer, musician, and educator. One of the most important symphonists of the 20th century, Ralph Vaughan Williams produced tonal nationalist works, but achieved universality through his love of folk song, his lyrical gifts, and his wide range of expression. Vaughan Williams was born in Down Ampney, Gloucestershire, where his father was the vicar; his mother was a niece of Charles Darwin. He received his first piano lessons from his aunt and by age six was composing. Violin lessons began the following year, and he entered the Charterhouse School at age 14, where he also became proficient at organ and viola.

Vaughan Williams studied with Sir Charles Hubert Parry at the Royal College of Music (1890–1892) and earned degrees in both music and history at Trinity College, Cambridge (1892–1895). Rejoining the Royal College (1895–1897), he studied with Sir Charles Villiers Stanford and befriended fellow student and composer **Gustav Holst**, who would provide Vaughan Williams with valuable compositional advice until Holst's death almost 40 years later. Vaughan Williams also studied privately with Max Bruch in Berlin in 1898, then returned to Cambridge and received his DMus in 1901.

Already an enthusiast of early modal forms, Elizabethan madrigal, and the great Tudor polyphonists, Vaughan Williams first began listening to and transcribing English folk song late in 1903. Considerable fieldwork followed in the 1900s, often with Holst and **George Butterworth**. Although folk song helped free up a more individual voice in Vaughan Williams's music, he was slow to develop as a composer. After completing his first important orchestral scores—*In the Fen Country* (1904; rev. 1905, 1907, 1935) and *Norfolk Rhapsody No. 1* (1906)—he went to France in 1908 to study with **Maurice Ravel**. His composition then flowed more freely, producing String Quartet No. 1 (1908, rev. 1921); *On Wenlock Edge* (1909) for tenor, piano, and string quartet; and incidental music for a 1909 production of Aristophanes' *The Wasps*, which became a popular orchestral suite.

Vaughan Williams composed some of his best music in the early 1910s, starting in 1910 with *Fantasia on a Theme by Thomas Tallis* for double string orchestra and solo quartet and his Symphony No. 1, "A Sea Symphony," for soprano, baritone, mixed chorus, and orchestra. He followed with *Five Mystical Songs* (1911) for baritone, mixed chorus, and orchestra; the popular Symphony No. 2, "A London Symphony" (1913, rev. 1919); and his classic *The Lark Ascending* (1914, rev. 1920) for violin and orchestra. Just before the outbreak of World War I in 1914, Vaughan Williams completed his first **opera**, *Hugh the Drover*; he then enlisted and served in the Medical Corps in England and France.

Returning to civilian life in 1919, Vaughan Williams began a 20-year teaching stint at the Royal College of Music. There, his composition resumed with the elegiac Symphony No. 3, "A Pastoral Symphony" (1921), for orchestra with wordless soprano or tenor, and the *Mass* (1922) for soloists and double chorus, with organ ad lib. He orchestrated *On Wenlock Edge* in 1923 and completed three major works in 1925: *Flos Campi* for viola, small wordless chorus, and small orchestra; *Sancta Civitas*, an oratorio for soloists, mixed chorus, and orchestra; and *Concerto accademico* for violin and string orchestra. By then, Vaughan Williams was a regular conductor of his own music and had begun two more operas: the four-act comedy *Sir John in Love* (1928), adapted from Shakespeare's *The Merry Wives of Windsor*, and *Riders to the Sea* (1932), a one-act setting of John Millington Synge's drama.

Riders was also part of a darker strain that emerged in Vaughan Williams's music in the early 1930s, which had begun with the orchestral score *Job: A Masque for Dancing* (1930). A thornier, more percussive and jazz-inflected sound entered his music with his Piano Concerto (1931, rev. 1946), which he later arranged for two pianos and orchestra. The **dissonant** and uncompromising Symphony No. 4 (1934) was his most aggressive work to date, yet Vaughan Williams was made a member of the Order of Merit in 1935. His music of the later 1930s was less extreme; it includes two major scores for soloists, mixed chorus, and orchestra—*Five Tudor Portraits* (1935) and *Dona nobis pacem* (1936)—and the folk song–based *Five Variants of Dives and Lazarus* (1939) for strings and harp.

Vaughan Williams evoked confidence and serenity in his indomitable Symphony No. 5 (1943), composed during the dark days of World War II. Not until after the war could he create the bleak and chilling Symphony No. 6 (1947). In the 1950s, Vaughan Williams composed three major cantatas for mixed chorus and orchestra: *The Sons of Light* (1950); the Christmas-themed *Hodie* (1954), which also featured soloists, boys' voices, and optional organ; and *Epithalamion* (1957) for smaller orchestra with baritone soloist. After more than four decades of work, Vaughan Williams completed *The Pilgrim's Progress*, his final opera, in 1952. That same year, he also adapted one of his **film** scores for the eerie and evocative Symphony No. 7, "Sinfonia Antartica," with wordless soprano and women's chorus. Two more symphonies followed: the colorful but enigmatic No. 8 (1955) and the darker, more provocative No. 9 (1957). Vaughan Williams was at his home in London when he died in his sleep at age 85. *See also* GLANVILLE-HICKS, PEGGY.

VIERK, LOIS V. (1951–). American composer and musician. Lois V. Vierk studied piano and ethnomusicology at UCLA; composition with Leonard Stein, **Mel Powell**, and **Morton Subotnick** at the California Institute of the Arts; *gagaku* with Suenobu Togi; and *ryuteki* with Sukeyasu Shiba. She has written **minimalist** scores that mass like voices and explore densities and glissandi in *Go Guitars* (1981) for five electric guitars; *Simoom* (1986) for eight cellos; *Jagged Mesa* (1990) for two or more trumpets, trombones, and bass trombones; and *Dark Bourn* (1995) for four bassoons and four cellos. Vierk's works for mixed ensembles include the string quartets *River beneath the River* (1993) and *Into the Brightening Air* (1994, rev. 1999), *Silversword* (1996) for gagaku orchestra, and *In Memory* (2004) for cello and piano. *See also* MULTICULTURALISM; PLEROMA; POSTMODERNISM.

VILLA-LOBOS, HEITOR (1887–1959). Brazilian composer, musician, and educator. Heitor Villa-Lobos learned cello from his father and studied at the Instituto Nacional de Música in his native Rio de Janeiro. He later served as Rio's director of music education and founded its Academia Brasileira de Música; he also performed internationally as a conductor. Villa-Lobos combined Brazilian, Indian, and pop idioms, most notably with the 12 pieces of his *Chôros* series (1920–1929), which range from solo guitar to orchestra and chorus. He also used **polytonal, impressionist**, and **neoromantic** techniques. His major works include *Suite populaire brésilienne* (1912) for guitar and the nine suites of his *Bachianas brasileiras* (1930–1948) for instruments and voices, a **multicultural** take on Johann Sebastian Bach. Villa-Lobos was prolific and produced more than 500 scores, including six **operas** (1914–1958), 17 string quartets (1915–1957), 12 symphonies (1916–1957), and five piano concertos (1945–1954). *See also* MODERNISM.

W

WALTON, (SIR) WILLIAM (1902–1983). English composer and musician. William Walton studied at Oxford University and found his first success with two witty scores: the jazz-inspired *Façade* (1921; rev. 1926, 1942) for reciter and six instruments, a setting of poems by Dame Edith Sitwell; and *Portsmouth Point* (1925) for orchestra. Walton's popular Viola Concerto (1929, rev. 1961) was **neoromantic**, as were *Belshazzar's Feast* (1931) for baritone, mixed chorus, and orchestra, Symphony No. 1 (1935), Violin Concerto (1939), and String Quartet No. 2 (1946). Walton is also prized for his **film** scores, especially those for actor/director Laurence Olivier: *Henry V* (1944), *Hamlet* (1948), *Richard III* (1955), and *Three Sisters* (1970). Walton was knighted in 1951 and made a member of the Order of Merit in 1968. Among his later works are the **operas** *Troilus and Cressida* (1954; rev. 1963, 1976) and *The Bear* (1967), his Cello Concerto (1956), Symphony No. 2 (1960), and *Façade 2* (1978) for reciter and six instruments.

WARD, THOMAS F. (1855 or 1856–1912). American composer, musician, and educator. Thomas Francis Ward composed, played piano and organ, and taught in his native Brooklyn until tuberculosis forced his relocation to Florida in 1884. Ward arrived around the same time as English composer **Frederick Delius** and soon became his teacher. Delius left in 1885 to teach music in Virginia, and the two lost contact. Although Delius later studied at the Leipzig Conservatory, he would always insist that only Ward's instruction had been of any use to him as a composer. Ward remained in Florida and entered a Benedictine monastery in 1891; except for a four-measure miniature he composed there, none of his music is extant. He left after five years and resumed working as a musician and church organist in Texas, where he died of pulmonary tuberculosis.

WARLOCK, PETER (1894–1930). English composer, musician, musicologist, and critic. Philip Heseltine studied piano at Eton College. Mostly self-taught as a composer, he drew from Elizabethan music and Celtic folk song, publishing scores and criticism under the name Peter Warlock. He wrote *As Dew in Aprylle* (1918), *Three Dirges of Webster* (1925), *Bethlehem Down* (1927), and other works for mixed chorus, as well as notable songs for voice and piano such as *My Gostly Fader* (1918), *Lilygay* (1922), *Three Belloc Songs* (1927), *The Frostbound Wood* (1929), and *The Fox* (1930); *The Curlew* (1922) was scored for tenor and sextet. Among his few instrumental works are *Serenade* (1922) for string orchestra and *Capriol Suite* (1926) for two pianos or string orchestra (orch. 1928). At age 36, Warlock was found dead of gas poisoning in his London flat; no final verdict was reached as to whether his death was an accident, murder, or suicide.

WEBER, BEN (1916–1979). American composer and musician. Ben Weber studied piano and voice at DePaul University and showed a special flair for piano and vocal composition, usually in a lyrical **twelve-tone** idiom. His notable works include Fantasia for Piano (1946), Second Piano Suite (1948), *Concert Aria after Solomon* (1949) for soprano and chamber ensemble, *Symphony in Four Movements on Poems of William Blake* (1950) for baritone and orchestra, Violin Concerto (1954), Piano Concerto (1961), and *Dolmen, an Elegy* (1964) for orchestra. *See also* ATONALITY; MODERNISM.

WEBERN, ANTON (1883–1945). Austrian composer and musician. Anton Webern was a great early **modernist** composer who brought a personal approach to **twelve-tone music** and greatly impacted later 20th-century composition. Born Anton Friedrich Wilhelm von Webern in Vienna, he received his first piano lessons from his mother when he was a child and was also studying cello by age 11. He entered the University of Vienna in 1902, where his teachers included musicologist Guido Adler, and in 1904 he began studying privately with **Arnold Schoenberg**, who remained his teacher and advisor for the next 20 years. **Alban Berg** also began studying with Schoenberg then, and the working friendship of these three composers came to be known as the Second Viennese School.

Webern did not produce his Op. 1 until 1908—the *Passacaglia* for orchestra, a Brahmsian study in variation that shows signs of the unusual sound world he would soon develop. That same year, he conducted his first orchestra, leading an ensemble in Bad Ischl in mostly operettas and light music; similar work followed over the 1910s. Inspired by developments in Schoenberg's music, Webern moved away from tonal references in his settings of Stefan George: *Entflieht auf leichten Kähnen* for chorus (1908) and the 10 songs for voice and piano that became his Opp. 3 and 4 in 1909. He began composing **atonal** scores that year, with *Five Movements* for string quartet and *Six Pieces* for orchestra. The already pronounced concision of Webern's music became even more extreme in the *Six Bagatelles* for string quartet and

Five Pieces for orchestra, composed between 1911 and 1913—one of the *Five Pieces* is only seven measures long. Webern had distilled his own music of fragmentary and aphoristic gestures, where subtle adjustments of tempo and the use of silence achieved new prominence, and the moment-to-moment assignment of pitch, timbre, and dynamics was thrown into heightened relief.

The presence of a text helped Webern compose athematic and atonal music, and writing for voice became his focus for more than a decade. Using folk, sacred, and secular texts, he developed a vocal style of wide leaps and unexpected intimacy in *Four Songs* (1918) for soprano and orchestra, *Six Songs* (1921) for high voice and instruments, *Five Sacred Songs* (1922) for soprano and instruments, and *Five Canons on Latin Texts* (1924) for soprano, clarinet, and bass clarinet. His conducting career took off with the Vienna Workers' Symphony (1922–1934) and Vienna Workers' Chorus (1923–1934); he also conducted for Austrian radio (1927–1938). Along with the masters of the Viennese repertory, Webern performed works by **Gustav Mahler**, **Charles Ives**, **Henry Cowell**, **Darius Milhaud**, Schoenberg, and Berg, and some of his own music, too.

Webern's static, stripped-down music avoided the lurid emotionalism of Schoenberg's and Berg's **expressionist** works. Schoenberg's new method of twelve-tone organization, however, began informing Webern's composition with *Three Sacred Folksongs* (1924) for voice, violin, clarinet, and bass clarinet; *Three Songs* (1925) for voice, clarinet, and guitar; and *Two Choral Songs* (1926) for mixed chorus and instruments. This method fit well with the polyphonic procedures of medieval and Renaissance music, which were lifelong passions of Webern's, and gave him a path into purely instrumental composition. A series of masterpieces ensued: String Trio (1927); Symphony (1928); Quartet (1930) for clarinet, saxophone, violin, and piano; Concerto for Nine Instruments (1934); Variations for Piano (1936); String Quartet (1938); and Variations for Orchestra (1940).

Restricting himself to texts by his friend, poet Hildegard Jone, Webern also wrote for voice with a new eloquence in the twelve-tone scores *Three Songs* (1934) for medium voice and piano, *Three Songs* (1935) for high voice and piano, *Das Augenlicht* (1935) for mixed chorus and orchestra, and perhaps most notably, *First Cantata* (1939) and *Second Cantata* (1943), both for soloists, mixed chorus, and orchestra. At just over 10 minutes, *Second Cantata* was his lengthiest composition. It would also be his last.

After the Austrian government officially turned fascist in 1934, the workers' associations were terminated and Webern's orchestra and chorus were disbanded. The *Anschluss* uniting Austria with Nazi Germany was finalized four years later, and Webern's radio position was withdrawn, ending his livelihood as a conductor. He did editorial work for Universal Edition and during the war retreated into seclusion at Mödling. Webern relocated to Mittersill in 1945 and that September was erroneously shot and killed by an American soldier five months after hostilities had ceased.

When he died at age 61, Webern's obscurity as a composer was complete. But almost immediately a new generation of composers discovered his work, attracted by its lack of postromantic rhetoric—it was the music of Webern that drew **Igor Stravinsky** into **serial** composition in the 1950s. Webern was lionized by young European composers who embraced **total serialism**, such as **Pierre Boulez** and **Karlheinz Stockhausen**, who saw in him anticipations of the serialized use of nonpitch elements. That aura faded from Webern as the focus on serial methods diminished in late 20th-century composition. What remained was a body of music unrivaled in its beauty, precision, and purity. *See also* EISLER, HANNS; LEIBOWITZ, RENÉ; WOLPE, STEFAN.

WEILL, KURT (1900–1950). German-born American composer. Kurt Weill attended Berlin's Staatliche Hochschule für Musik in 1918 and studied with Engelbert Humperdinck; he also studied privately with **Ferruccio Busoni** (1920–1924). Weill's impressive early scores include the single-movement Symphony No. 1 (1921), *Frauentanz* (1923) for soprano and five instruments, and Concerto for Violin and Wind Ensemble (1924). He found success with two **expressionist** works: his one-act **opera** *Der Protagonist* (1925) and the cantata *Der neue Orpheus* (1926) for soprano, violin, and orchestra, into which Weill incorporated elements of traditional and popular music.

Energized by *Gebrauchsmusik* social concerns, this cross-fertilization defined a series of major dramatic works that Weill created with the poet and playwright Bertolt Brecht, starting with *Mahagonny Songspiel* (1927) for two sopranos, two tenors, two basses, and 11 instruments. Folk song, dance-band tunes, and jazz streamed together into Weill's **modernist** composition and made an indelible fit with Brecht's savage political commentaries. Turning to music theater, they had an international sensation with their classic *Die Dreigroschenoper* (*The Threepenny Opera*, 1928). Weill's score was even finer, more expressive, and more original in their follow-up, *Happy End* (1929). Their other efforts include the operas *Aufstieg und Fall der Stadt Mahagonny* (1929) and *Der Jasager* (1930) and the cantatas *Das Berliner Requiem* (1928) for tenor, baritone, male chorus, and wind orchestra and *Der Lindberghflug* (1929) for tenor, baritone, bass, mixed chorus, and orchestra.

After his dramatic musical *Der Silbersee* (1932), Weill was forced to flee Nazi Germany. He relocated to France in 1933 and completed two of his finest works: the sung ballet *Die Sieben Todsünden der Kleinbürger* (1933)—his final collaboration with Brecht—and the ominous and desperate Symphony

No. 2 (1934), his last instrumental score for the concert hall. Weill settled in the United States in 1935 and became a citizen in 1943. He composed *The Eternal Road* (1935), a dramatic oratorio to an epic account of Hebrew scripture, and the opera *Street Scene* (1947), but otherwise focused on musicals, writing beloved scores for *Knickerbocker Holiday* (1938), *Lady in the Dark* (1941), *One Touch of Venus* (1943), *Love Life* (1948), and *Lost in the Stars* (1949). Weill died of a heart attack at age 50 in New York City. *See also* BLITZSTEIN, MARC.

WEISBERG, ARTHUR (1931–2009). American composer, musician, and educator. A bassoonist and conductor, Arthur Weisberg created and led the Contemporary Chamber Ensemble (1960–1988). His compositions include Duo for Cello and Piano (1985) and Concerto for Bassoon and Strings (1998). Weisberg taught at Juilliard and Yale University and wrote the books *The Art of Wind Playing* (1975) and *Performing 20th-Century Music: A Handbook for Conductors and Instrumentalists* (1993).

WELLESZ, EGON (1885–1974). Austrian-born English composer, educator, and musicologist. Egon Wellesz studied musicology at the University of Vienna, where he later taught; he also studied composition with **Arnold Schoenberg**. Wellesz's *Vorfrühling* (1912) for orchestra and his Euripides **operas** *Alkestis* (1924) and *Die Bakchantinnen* (1929) were **dissonant** and had **expressionist** qualities; more traditional techniques informed *Prosperos Beschwörungen* (1936) for orchestra. Wellesz moved to England in 1938 and became a citizen in 1946. A **neoromantic** spirit characterized his Symphonies Nos. 1 (1945) and 2 (1948) and Octet (1949). With Symphony No. 4 (1953) and String Quartet No. 8 (1957), he combined **serialism** and tonality. Wellesz's works include nine string quartets (1912–1966), nine symphonies (1945–1971), and the operas *Die Prinzessin Girnara* (1920), *Die Opferung des Gefangenen* (1925), *Scherz, List und Rache* (1927), and *Incognita* (1950). *See also* MODERNISM; TWELVE-TONE MUSIC.

WESTERKAMP, HILDEGARD (1946–). German-born Canadian composer and educator. Hildegard Westerkamp left Germany for Canada in 1968 and studied at Simon Fraser University, where she later taught. She has explored urban and natural soundscapes in such works for two-channel **tape** as *A Walk through the City* (1981), *Cricket Voice* (1987), *Beneath the Forest Floor* (1992), *Talking Rain* (1997), and *Attending to Sacred Matters* (2002). Westerkamp's **electroacoustic music** includes *École polytechnique* (1990) for eight church bells, mixed choir, bass clarinet, trumpet, percussion, and tape; *Like a Memory* (2002) for piano and two digital soundtracks; and

Liebes-Lied/Love Song (2005) for cello and eight digital soundtracks. Among her **sound installations** are *Nada* (1998) and *At the Edge of Wilderness* (2000). *See also* POSTMODERNISM.

WOLFE, JULIA (1958–). American composer and educator. Julia Wolfe studied with Martin Bresnick at the Yale University School of Music and has taught at New York University. A **postmodern** composer who combines **minimalist**, folk, classical, and rock techniques, she cofounded the music collective Bang on a Can in 1987 with her husband **Michael Gordon** and **David Lang**; the three also co-composed the **operas** *The Carbon Copy Building* (1995), *Lost Objects* (2001), and *Shelter* (2005). Wolfe's music includes *Lick* (1994) for chamber ensemble; the string quartets *Four Marys* (1991), *Early That Summer* (1993), and *Dig Deep* (1995); *Steam* (1995) for flute, electric organ, cello, and three **Harry Partch** instruments; the orchestral scores *The Vermeeer Room* (1989), *Window of Vulnerability* (1991), and *Thirst* (2008); and *Cruel Sister* (2004) for string orchestra.

WOLFF, CHRISTIAN (1934–). French-born American composer, musician, and educator. Christian Wolff left France at age seven and immigrated with his family to New York. He began composing in the late 1940s and, around 1950, met **John Cage**, with whom he studied for a short time. The teenage Wolff soon became part of Cage's circle, along with **David Tudor**, **Morton Feldman**, and **Earle Brown**. Having composed proto-**minimalist** scores such as *String Trio* (1950) and *For Prepared Piano* (1951), Wolff was drawn to Cage's ideas: He used **chance** procedures in *For Piano I* (1952) and composed **indeterminate** works such as *Duo for Pianists I* (1957) and *II* (1958). *Duo II* also employed cueing techniques, with the musicians listening for certain sounds from each other, which would signal what was to happen next. Wolff went on to use cueing without specifying instrumentation in *For Five or Ten Players* (1962), *In Between Pieces* (1963) for three players, and *For One, Two or Three People* (1964). His *Prose Collection* (1968–1971) is all verbal instructions with no musical notation. In the mid-1960s, Wolff began playing electric guitar and included it in the chamber ensembles of *Electric Spring Nos. 1* (1966), *2* (1966–1970), and *3* (1967). He also taught classics at Harvard University (1962–1970) and classics, comparative literature, and music at Dartmouth College (1971–1999).

In *Edges* (1968) for any number of players, Wolff combined traditional and **graphic notation**, but after *Burdocks* (1971) for one or more groups of five or more players and *Lines* (1972) for string quartet or other string ensembles, he felt he had gone as far as he could with indeterminacy. Inspired by **Cornelius Cardew**, Wolff engaged democratic-socialist political content in his music with *Accompaniments* (1972) for piano and *Changing the System* (1973) for eight or more instruments. He set political texts in many works, including *Wobbly Music* (1978) for mixed chorus and instruments and *"I Like to Think of Harriet Tubman"* (1985) for woman's voice and three instruments. Older political songs were incorporated into *Bread and Roses* (1976) for piano, *Preludes 1–11* (1981) for piano, *Mayday Materials* (1989) for synclavier/**synthesizer**-generated sound, and *Aarau Songs* (1994) for clarinet and string quartet. His notable recent pieces include *Ordinary Matter* (2001) for three orchestras and *Microexercises* (2006) for one or more players. *See also* AMM; ATONALITY; GEBRAUCHSMUSIK; POSTMODERNISM.

WOLPE, STEFAN (1902–1972). German-born American composer, musician, and educator. Wolpe produced a multifaceted and expressive body of work, from **Gebrauchsmusik** to **atonality**, which ranks with the finest of his time. Born in Berlin, Stefan Wolpe entered the Berlin Conservatory at age 14. He then attended the Staatliche Hochschule für Musik (1920–1921) and studied privately with **Ferruccio Busoni**. In the song cycle *Hölderlin Lieder* (1924) for mezzo-soprano or alto and piano, Wolpe used modal, tonal, and atonal techniques. Popular music informed his *Blues and Tango* (1926) for piano and the jazz-inspired chamber **operas** *Zeus und Elida* (1928) and *Schöne Geschichten* (1929). He also played piano for socialist gatherings and composed political songs and piano works throughout the 1920s.

Drawn to the era's Gebrauchsmusik spirit, Wolpe pursued a simpler tonal style in the 1930s with such didactic works as *Cantata about Sport* (1932) for voices and brass band. He also composed and played for the left-wing theater group Die Truppe 31 until it was shut down by the Nazi chief of police in 1933. Wolpe fled Germany soon afterward and went to Vienna, where he studied with **Anton Webern**. The following year, he arrived in Palestine and taught at the Palestine Conservatory (1934–1938). While there, Wolpe explored his Jewish heritage in his music, with *Two Songs from the Song of Songs* (1936) for alto and piano and *Songs from the Hebrew* (1938) for mezzo-soprano or baritone and piano. He also investigated **twelve-tone** methods in his 1936 scores *Duo im Hexachord* for oboe and clarinet and *Four Studies on Basic Rows* for piano.

Wolpe's **modernist** composition and progressive politics were not welcome at the conservatory, so Wolpe left Palestine in 1938 and settled in the United States, becoming a citizen in 1945. He produced several notable scores in the 1940s, including two Old Testament–themed works: the ballet *The Man from Midian* (1942) for two pianos and the cantata *Yigdal* (1945) for baritone, mixed chorus, and organ. Although he lived mostly in New York, Wolpe taught at numerous American institutions, including the Philadelphia

Academy of Music (1949–1952), Black Mountain College in North Carolina (1952–1956), and C. W. Post College (1957–1968). His students included **David Tudor**, **Morton Feldman**, **Ralph Shapey**, **Ursula Mamlok**, and Johnny Mandel.

By the late 1940s, with such compositions as *Battle Piece* (1947) for piano, Sonata (1949) for violin and piano, and Quartet (1950, rev. 1954) for trumpet, tenor saxophone, percussion, and piano, Wolpe had turned more to the articulation of simultaneities and the opposition of contrary materials. Chromatic circulation was coordinated with structural transformation in several of his major scores in the 1950s: *Enactments* (1953) for three pianos; Piece for Oboe, Cello, Percussion, and Piano (1955); Symphony (1956); and *Quintet with Voice* (1957). After these daunting complexities, Wolpe developed a leaner, more condensed and succinct music with his *Form* (1959) for piano. This approach defined his composition in the early 1960s, as seen in *Piece in Two Parts* (1960) for flute and piano; Piece for Piano and 16 Players (1961); *In Two Parts for Six Players* (1962); the cantata *Street Music* (1962) for baritone, speaker, and five instruments; *Piece for Two Instrumental Units* (1963); Cantata (1963) for mezzo-soprano, three women's voices, and nine instruments; and *Trio in Two Parts* (1964) for flute, cello, and piano.

In 1963, Wolpe was diagnosed with Parkinson's disease, which would claim his life a decade later in New York at age 69. But in his final years, he achieved a new clarity and originality in *Chamber Pieces Nos. 1* (1964) and 2 (1967) for 14 players; *Piece in Two Parts for Violin Alone* (1964); *Second Piece for Violin Alone* (1966); *Solo Piece for Trumpet* (1966); String Quartet (1969); *From Here on Farther* (1969) for violin, clarinet, bass clarinet, and piano; *Form IV: Broken Sequences* (1969) for piano; and *Piece for Trumpet and Seven Instruments* (1971).

WUORINEN, CHARLES (1938–). American composer, musician, and educator. Charles Wuorinen studied with **Otto Luening** and **Vladimir Ussachevsky**. As a pianist or conductor, he has performed the music of many **modern** and contemporary composers, and with **Harvey Sollberger**, he cofounded and codirected the Group for Contemporary Music (1962–present). With such early pieces as Concertante Nos. 1 (1957) and 2 (1958) for violin and orchestra, Wuorinen drew upon the tonal works of **Igor Stravinsky**. By the 1960s, he was combining Stravinskian techniques with the **twelve-tone music** of **Arnold Schoenberg** and **Milton Babbitt** in such scores as Chamber Concerto for Cello and Ten Players (1963) and *Making Ends Meet* (1966) for piano four-hands. *A Reliquary for Igor Stravinsky* (1975) for orchestra utilized Stravinsky's last musical sketches.

Despite the praise for his electronic work *Time's Encomium* (1969), there is little **electronic music** in Wuorinen's prolific output. Instrumental music has been his primary focus, with a special flair for percussion; examples include *Janissary Music* (1966), *Ringing Changes* (1970), *Percussion Symphony* (1976), *Percussion Quartet* (1994), and *Marimba Variations* (2009). His later works blend twelve-tone and tonal methods. Wuorinen also began composing more for voice, as in *Lightenings VIII* (1994) for soprano and piano, *Stanzas before Time* (2001) for tenor and harp, and *The Long Boat* (2003) for mezzo-soprano and English horn.

Wuorinen's music includes eight symphonies (1958–2006), four string quartets (1971–2000), four piano sonatas (1958–2007), and four piano concertos (1966–2003). Among his recent works are the ballet score *Dante Trilogy* (1996), the **opera** *Haroun and the Sea of Stories* (2001), and *Time Regained* (2008) for piano and orchestra. The author of *Simple Composition* (1979), he has taught at such institutions as Columbia University, the Mannes School of Music, and Rutgers University. *See also* ATONALITY.

WYSCHNEGRADSKY, IVAN (1893–1979). Russian composer, musician, and theorist. Ivan Wyschnegradsky studied at the St. Petersburg Conservatory and began investigating **microtonal** music in the late 1910s. He relocated to France in 1919 and composed such **quarter-tone** works as String Quartets Nos. 1 (1924) and 2 (1931); he also wrote *Manuel d'harmonie à quarts de ton* (1932). Wyschnegradsky commissioned a quarter-tone harmonium in the 1920s and collaborated with **Alois Hába** on the design of a quarter-tone piano. *Also sprach Zarathustra* (1930) featured both keyboards, along with clarinet and strings, but Wyschnegradsky came to prefer using multiple pianos tuned a quarter-tone apart. He arranged *Zarathustra* for four pianos and composed 24 preludes (1934, rev. 1970) for two pianos, *Cosmos* (1940) for four pianos, and *Transparence I* (1953) and *II* (1963) for **ondes martenot** and two pianos. Among his scores in other microtonal tunings are *Arc-en-ciel* (1956) for six pianos in 12th-tones, *Étude ultrachromatique* (1959) for 31-tone organ, *Prélude et danse* (1966) for third-tone piano, and *Dialogue à trois* (1974) for three pianos in sixth-tones. *See also* INSTRUMENT BUILDING; MODERNISM.

XENAKIS, IANNIS (1921 or 1922–2001). Romanian-born French composer and educator. A highly influential composer, Iannis Xenakis created **stochastic** processes and other musical structures derived from higher mathematics and played an essential role in the development of **computer music**. Born of Greek parents in Braïla, Romania, Xenakis was sent to the Greek island of Spetsai in 1932 for his education and began studying music. Fighting with the Communist Resistance during World War II, Xenakis was badly wounded, but he recovered and graduated from the Polytechnic School of Athens in 1947 with an engineering diploma. That same year, he was arrested by the Greek regime for his continued guerrilla activities, but managed to escape and flee the country. In Greece, he was sentenced to death in absentia and stripped of his citizenship.

Xenakis settled in Paris, becoming a French citizen in 1965. He worked with architect Le Corbusier until 1959 and pursued his musical education, studying with **Arthur Honegger** and **Darius Milhaud** (1949) and **Olivier Messiaen** (1951–1953). Xenakis recognized that the polyphony of deterministic **serial** composition was mostly imperceptible to the ear; he also rejected the surrender of control inherent in **chance music**. Seeking a structural coherence that could be heard in performance, he utilized graphic designs of parabolas in *Metastasis* (1955) for orchestra. To write the score, he had a computer calculate the variable-speed glissandi. Computer calculations also informed *Pithoprakhta* (1956) for string orchestra, two trombones, and percussion, in which Xenakis introduced the use of stochastic procedures from probability theory. These controlled random processes brought unpredictability to the music as it unfolded, yet gave it a recognizable form and character of its own. The long, slow glissandi, clouds of pointillistic sounds, **tone-clusters**, and **microtonal** densities in Xenakis's works of these years soon became familiar sounds in the music of other composers internationally.

A member of **Pierre Schaeffer**'s Groupe de Recherches de **Musique Concrète** from 1955 to 1962, Xenakis created **tape music** derived from acoustic sounds, which often existed in multiple versions: *Concret PH* (1956), *Diamorphoses* (1957), *Orient-Occident* (1960), and *Bohor* (1962). He also produced his first **electroacoustic** work: *Analogiques A & B* (1959) for nine strings and tape. In 1962, Xenakis completed his three *ST* pieces (*ST* indicating stochastic music): *ST/48, 1-240162* for 48 instruments, *ST/10, 1-080262* for 10 instruments, and *ST/4, 1-080262* for string quartet. His other stochastic works include *Kraanerg* (1969) for 23 musicians and tape and *Mikka* (1971) for solo violin.

Xenakis also combined ideas of set theory with stochastic materials in *Herma* (1961) for piano and *Eonta* (1963) for piano and brass instruments, in which the musicians move around the space. Further theoretical studies led to his use of group theory in *Akrata* (1964) for eight woodwinds and eight brass, which employed **quarter-tones**, and *Nomos gamma* (1968) for orchestra, a **spatial** piece that distributed its 98 musicians throughout the audience. Game theory informed *Stratégie* (1962) for two orchestras with two conductors using controlled improvisation. In his vocal music, Xenakis's Greek heritage emerged with *Polla ta dhina* (1962) for children's chorus and orchestra, a setting of Sophocles with the young voices singing on one note. *Oresteïa* (1966) for children's chorus, mixed chorus, and 12 musicians attempted to re-create aspects of music from the time of Aeschylus's trilogy in fifth-century-B.C.E. Athens. *Aïs* (1980) for amplified baritone, solo percussion, and orchestra used texts from Homer and Sappho. *Les Bacchantes* (1993) for baritone, women's chorus, and orchestra adapted Euripides.

Xenakis published two collections of his writings on music, *Musiques formelles* (1963) and *Musique, architecture* (1971). He taught at Tanglewood (1963), Indiana University (1967–1972), and the University of Paris I (1972–1989), among other institutions; his students included **Yuji Takahashi**, **David Del Tredici**, and **Gérard Grisey**. *Polytope de Montréal* (1967) launched Xenakis's **multimedia** spectacles of light and tape. He called for four ensembles of 14 players in *Polytope de Montréal*, but more often created tape music for these international events, which also used lasers; others included *Hibiki hana ma* (1970), *Persepolis* (1971), and *Polytope de Cluny* (1972). *La légende d'Eer* (1978) was a **sound installation** in a curved architectural space that Xenakis designed.

From the mid-1970s to the mid-1980s, Xenakis developed the UPIC system, in which an electromagnetic ballpoint draws graphics that are transformed into sound by a computer. With UPIC, Xenakis created *Mycenae alpha* (1978), *Pour la paix* (1981), *Taurhiphanie* (1987), and *Voyage absolu des Unari vers Andromède* (1989). His notable instrumental music in these years included *Nyuyo* (1985), a **multicultural** score for Japanese instruments (shakuhachi, sanger, and two kotos), and *Epicycle* (1989) for 12 cellos.

In the 1990s, Xenakis introduced stochastic parameters into sound synthesis with the GENDY-N computer program, creating *Gendy3* (1991) and *S. 709* (1994). His other late works include the string quartets *Tetora* (1990) and *Ergma* (1996), *Knephas* (1990) and *Sea Nymphs* (1994) for mixed chorus and orchestra, *Dox-orkh* (1991) for violin and orchestra, and *Sea Change* (1997) for orchestra. Xenakis's composition ended when his health began to fail in his last years, and he died in his Paris home at age 78. *See also* ELECTRONIC MUSIC.

Y

YAMADA, NORMAN. *See* ROUGH ASSEMBLAGE.

YARDUMIAN, RICHARD (1917–1985). American composer and musician. Mostly self-taught, Richard Yardumian studied piano with George Boyle, conducting with Pierre Monteux, and composition with **Virgil Thomson**. Drawing on the folk and sacred music of his Armenian heritage, he composed such notable works as the orchestral scores *Armenian Suite* (1936, rev. 1954), *Desolate City* (1944), and Symphonies Nos. 1 (1950, rev. 1961) and 2 (1964); *Chromatic Sonata* (1946) for piano; Violin Concerto (1949, rev. 1960) and *Passacaglia, Recitative and Fugue* (1957) for piano and orchestra; *Cantus animae et cordis* (1955) for string quartet or string orchestra; *Come, Creator Spirit* (1966) for mezzo-soprano or baritone, mixed chorus, congregation, and orchestra or organ, the **multimedia** oratorio *The Story of Abraham* (1971, rev. 197); and *Hrashapar* (1984) for mixed chorus, organ, and orchestra. *See also* MULTICULTURALISM.

YOUNG, LA MONTE (1935–). American composer, musician, and educator. As a composer and improviser, La Monte Young has been at the forefront of **minimalist** music since its beginnings and is a major figure in the use of **just intonation**. Born in Berne, Idaho, Young relocated with his family to Los Angeles and studied saxophone and clarinet at the Los Angeles Conservatory of Music (1951–1954). He began studying with Leonard Stein in 1953 and continued while attending UCLA in 1957–1958. During these years, Young's interests shifted from jazz to **serial** composition, which he employed in his own way, starting with the brief and static *Five Small Pieces for String Quartet* (1956).

Young used long, sustained tones in *for Brass* (1957) for brass octet and the solo-guitar score *for Guitar* (1958), and they defined *Trio for Strings* (1958) for violin, viola, and cello, a landmark minimalist work in the extremity of its held pitches. He studied with Andrew Imbrie and Seymour Shifrin at the University of California, Berkeley, and in 1959 Young produced serial music of a more traditional complexity and activity with *Study I* and *Study II* for piano. While attending **Karlheinz Stockhausen**'s Advanced Composition Seminar at

Darmstadt later that year, he wrote *Study III*, which included long silences and sustained tones.

Young was stimulated by the **indeterminate** music of **John Cage**, and his score *Vision* (1959) for 12 instruments was mostly verbal, with some **graphic notation**. *Poem for Chairs, Tables, Benches, etc.* (1960) listened to the sound of furniture being dragged across the floor. Although he studied **electronic music** with **Richard Maxfield** at the New School for Social Research (1960–1961), Young composed mostly performance pieces then, including *Compositions 1960* and *Compositions 1961*. He was drawn into the **Fluxus** orbit, and during a 1961 Fluxus concert, he inserted a rendition of his *Composition 1960 No. 2* and burned his violin. The following year, he hit a frying pan 923 times to perform *Arabic Numeral (Any Integer) to H. F.* (1960), dedicated to **Henry Flynt**.

In the early 1960s, Young was improvising on piano and sopranino saxophone, using blues forms in a static and modal drone-like style. These sessions with such musicians as **Terry Jennings** and **Angus MacLise** led to the compositions for which Young is most well known: *The Four Dreams of China (The Harmonic Versions)* (1962) for tunable sustaining instruments of like timbre in multiples of four; *The Tortoise, His Dreams and Journeys* (1964) for voices, various instruments, and sine waves; and *The Well-Tuned Piano* (1964) for piano retuned in just intonation. Both *The Tortoise* and *The Well-Tuned Piano* were ongoing pieces that became lifetime projects as Young developed and expanded them. All three works involved improvisation techniques, just intonation, sustained tones, and a lengthy time scale— the qualities that have defined Young's music.

Those improvisations also led Young to initiate the Theater of Eternal Music in 1962, and over the years its performers of his music have included Jennings, MacLise, **Marian Zazeela**, **Dennis Johnson**, **Terry Riley**, **Tony Conrad**, John Cale, Jon Gibson, and Jon Hassell. Beyond singing and playing instruments, Zazeela also served as visual designer, and with her *Ornamental Lightyears Tracery* series of slide projections, Young's music became a **multimedia** experience. For *The Well-Tuned Piano*, Zazeela made *The Magenta Lights*, using colored lighting and curved mobiles to transform the performance spaces. She and Young married in 1963, and her lighting has been essential to his music, in concert and with such sound environments as *Betty Freeman Commission* (1967), *The Big Dream* (1984), and *The Young Prime Time Twins* (1991).

Young and Zazeela became disciples of master singer Pandit Pran Nath in 1970, studying North Indian classical vocal music until his death in 1996; they have also performed ragas and taught students of their own. Raga heightened Young's approach of organically evolving improvisation, leading him to give five- and six-hour performances of *The Well-Tuned Piano* in the 1980s and 1990s. He also produced versions of *Trio for Strings* for string quartet and string orchestra in 1983 and composed *The Subsequent Dreams of China* (1980) for tunable sustaining instruments of like timbre in multiples of eight. In 1984, he wrote *Melodic Versions* of both the *Subsequent Dreams* and the original *Four Dreams of China*, calling for the same forces. That interest in massing like voices also characterized one of Young's greatest works: *The Lower Map of the Eleven's Division in the Romantic Symmetry (over a 60-Cycle Base) in Prime Time from 144 to 112 with 119* (1990), scored for tunable sustaining instruments in sections of like timbre, playing within a sine-wave drone sound environment. It was premiered by an ensemble of four voices, 15 brass instruments, two electric guitars, and two electric basses, with the musicians articulating pitches that generated epic overtone and resultant-tone activity, even mightier than the marvels Young has produced playing *The Well-Tuned Piano*.

The fully notated *Chronos kristalla* (1990) for string quartet was in just intonation, as was the music of the Forever Bad Blues Band, which Young formed in 1993, playing minimalist blues on Korg Synthesizer accompanied by electric guitar, electric bass, and drums. He revised the string-orchestra version of *Trio for Strings* into just intonation in 2001 and composed *Just Charles and Cello in the Romantic Chord* (2003) for cello and prerecorded cello drones, with a live **computer** part. Young, Zazeela, and Jung Hee Choi founded the Just Alap Raga Ensemble in 2002, which became Young's primary vehicle for performance and composition with *Raga Sundara* (2004) for voices, sarangi, cello, and tabla. *See also* ELECTROACOUSTIC MUSIC; MULTICULTUR-ALISM; PLEROMA; POSTMODERNISM; SOUND INSTALLATION.

YUASA, JOJI (1929–). Japanese composer and educator. A cofounder of Tokyo's Experimental Workshop in 1951, Joji Yuasa has created **tape music** (*Aoi-no-ue*, 1961; *Moment Grand-Guignolesques*, 1962), **electronic music** (*Projection Essemplastic for White Noise*, 1964; *My Blue Sky [No. 1]*, 1975), **multicultural** music (*Projection for Kotos and Orchestra*, 1967; *Suite Fushi Gyo-un* for Japanese traditional instruments, alto, and tenor, 1988), **multi-media** works (*Music for Space Projection*, 1970), **electroacoustic** pieces (*Triplicity for Contrabass* for contrabass and tape, 1979; *Scenes with a Harp* for harp and tape, 1999), and **computer music** (*A Study in White*, 1987). His many instrumental scores include *Cosmos Haptic* (1957) for piano, *Chrono-plastic for Orchestra* (1972), Violin Concerto (1996), and *Four Imaginary Landscapes from Basho* (2007) for violin and piano. Yuasa has taught at Nihon University, the Tokyo College of Music, and the University of California, San Diego. *See also* TAKEMITSU, TORU.

Z

ZAPPA, FRANK (1940–1993). American composer and musician. Mostly self-taught, Frank Zappa brought a provocative wit and avant-garde sensibility to rock music. He released albums with the band the Mothers of Invention (*Freak Out!*, 1966; *We're Only in It for the Money*, 1968; *Weasels Ripped My Flesh*, 1970) and such solo recordings as *Hot Rats* (1969), *Zoot Allures* (1976), *Shut Up 'n' Play Yer Guitar* (1981), and the Synclavier pieces of *Jazz from Hell* (1986). Zappa also produced Captain Beefheart's classic double LP *Trout Mask Replica* (1969). Drawing inspiration from **Igor Stravinsky** and **Edgard Varèse** as well as jazz and rock, he composed large-ensemble works heard on the albums *Lumpy Gravy* (1967), *The Grand Wazoo* (1972), and *Orchestral Favorites* (1979), some of which he arranged for full orchestra. Zappa died of prostate cancer at age 52. *See also* FILM MUSIC; POSTMODERNISM; SAMPLING.

ZAZEELA, MARIAN (1940–). American musician and educator. Along with serving as its visual designer, Marian Zazeela has participated in performances of **La Monte Young**'s Theater of Eternal Music, most often as singer or playing bowed gong. Her lighting has been fundamental to Young's sound environments and concert music, and the two have been married since 1963. A disciple of the master North Indian singer Pandit Pran Nath from 1970 until his death in 1996, Zazeela has sung and taught raga and was a cofounder of the Just Alap Raga Ensemble in 2002.

ZIMMERMANN, BERND ALOIS (1918–1970). German composer, musician, and educator. Bernd Alois Zimmermann studied at the Cologne Hochschule für Musik, where he later taught. He merged techniques of **neoclassical** tonality and **polyrhythm** with **atonality**, **serialism**, the collaging of **quotations**, and jazz elements in such notable scores as Symphony (1951, rev. 1953), *Dialoge* (1965) for two pianos and orchestra, and *Stille und Umkehr* (1970) for orchestra. His two major vocal works, the **opera** *Die Soldaten* (1963, rev. 1965) and the oratorio *Requiem für einen jungen Dichter* (1969), included **electronic music**. Zimmermann took his own life in Königsdorf at age 52. *See also* ELECTROACOUSTIC MUSIC; MODERNISM; TWELVE-TONE MUSIC.

ZORN, JOHN (1953–). American composer and musician. John Zorn studied composition with Kendall Stallings at Webster College, where he researched the music of Carl Stalling, who scored hundreds of cartoons at Warner Bros. Also drawn to the music of such innovators as **Anthony Braxton** and **Mauricio Kagel**, Zorn developed his own genre-defying, **multicultural** sound of rapidly changing material, combining techniques from jazz, rock, world music, and experimental music. He composed scores for improvising musicians such as *Lacrosse* (1977), *Fencing* (1978), *Archery* (1979), *Go!* (1981), *Track & Field* (1982), and *Cobra* (1984). For several years, Zorn also played sections of his disassembled clarinet and often used game calls in place of reeds in his alto saxophone. He became an essential figure among the **free improvisers** and worked with numerous musicians, including **Fred Frith, George Lewis, Annie Gosfield, Bob Ostertag, Susie Ibarra,** and **Elliott Sharp.** Zorn has also formed and played in such bands as Painkiller, News for Lulu, and Masada. His music for Naked City varied from noise, hardcore rock, and instrumental covers to the **minimalist** *Qûê Trán* (1989) for two keyboards and Vietnamese narration and the **ambient** album *Absinthe* (1993).

After *The Big Gundown* (1986), an album of arrangements of Ennio Morricone's **film music,** Zorn began composing fully notated nonimprovisational scores such as the **quotation**-filled *For Your Eyes Only* (1989) for chamber orchestra, *Carny* (1991) for piano, and the string quartets *Cat o' Nine Tails* (1988), *The Dead Man* (1990), and *Memento mori* (1992). *The Wanderers* (1993) was scored for a consort of **Harry Partch** instruments. Zorn created impressive works in the studio as well, such as *Spillane* (1986), *Elegy* (1991), and *Kristallnacht* (1995). One of the most influential **postmodern** composers of his generation, Zorn has also scored such films as *She Must Be Seeing Things* (1987), *The Elegant Spanking* (1995), *Trembling before G-d* (2001), and *Jack Smith and the Destruction of Atlantis* (2006). His recent concert works include *Aporias* (1994) for piano, orchestra, and children's choir; the **opera** *Rituals* (1998) for mezzo-soprano and 10 instruments; and *Gris-Gris* (2000) for solo percussionist. He composed **electronic music** (*American Magus*) and **computer music** (*The Nerve Key*) in 2001. Among his notable recent studio albums are *Six Litanies for Heliogabalus* (2007), *Femina* (2009), and *Interzone* (2010). *See also* ATONALITY; CHANCE MUSIC; EXTENDED PERFORMANCE TECHNIQUES; INSTRUMENT BUILDING.

ZUKOFSKY, PAUL (1943–). American musician and educator. A violinist and conductor devoted to contemporary music, Paul Zukofsky has premiered works by such composers as **Philip Glass, Milton Babbitt,** and **John Cage.**

He founded the CD label CP2 and has taught at the Manhattan School of Music and Reykjavik College of Music.

ZWILICH, ELLEN TAAFFE (1939–). American composer, musician, and educator. Pianist, trumpet player, and violinist Ellen Taaffe Zwilich studied at Juilliard with **Elliott Carter** and **Roger Sessions** and has taught at Florida State University. Among her early works are *Symposium* (1973) for orchestra and *String Quartet 1974.* Zwilich's **modernist** use of continuous variation shaped her melodic sensibility in Symphony No. 1 (1983, a.k.a. *Three Movements for Orchestra*). Her other notable works include Symphonies Nos. 2–5 (1985–2008), *Peanuts Gallery* (1996) for piano and orchestra, String Quartet No. 2 (1998), *Lament* (1999) for piano, *Rituals* (2003) for five percussionists and orchestra, Quartet for Oboe and Strings (2004), and concertos for piano (1986), flute (1988), oboe (1990), bassoon (1992), violin (1997), and clarinet (2002).

Bibliography

CONTENTS

INTRODUCTION

Although the dictionary includes entries on certain innovators in pop, jazz, and rock, along with some postromantic composers who had modernist qualities, this bibliography of English-language books, journals, and websites focuses more narrowly on modern and contemporary music. The books listed here reflect the growth over the years in appreciation of this music: More than three-quarters of these titles were written after 1970. Not only have the *scandales* of the 1910s become the classics of the 2010s, producing generations of research and commentary, but there has also been a great amount of scholarship in the last 40 years devoted to contemporary practices— note the numerous interview books, none of which predate the 1970s.

Theodor W. Adorno's *Essays on Music* and Donald Mitchell's *The Language of Modern Music* remain intelligent and thought-provoking considerations of modernist music in general. The composer's perspective is cogently expressed in the essays of Gregory Battcock's *Breaking the Sound Barrier* and Benjamin Boretz and Edward T. Cone's *Perspectives on Contemporary Music Theory*. *The Cambridge Companion to Twentieth-Century Opera*, edited by Mervyn Cooke, and *The Symphony*, volume 2, edited by Robert Simpson, provide valuable surveys, as do the writings of Kyle Gann in *Music Downtown*, Paul Griffiths in *The Substance of Things Heard*, and Alex Ross in *The Rest Is Noise*.

The Cambridge History of Twentieth-Century Music, edited by Nicholas Cook and Anthony Pople, and *The Cambridge Companion to Electronic Music*, edited by Nick Collins and Julio d'Escrivan, are thorough and reliable histories. Other accomplished works include Thomas B. Holmes's *Electronic and Experimental Music*, Joseph Machlis's *Introduction to Contemporary Music*, and H. H. Stuckenschmidt's *Twentieth-Century Music*. More specialized are the insightful studies of Michael Nyman's *Experimental Music* and Edward Strickland's *Minimalism: Origins*. *Composers' Voices from Ives to Ellington: An Oral History of American Music*, edited by Vivian Perlis and Libby Van Cleeve, is an invaluable primary source.

Among the essential writings by composers are *Béla Bartók Essays*, Pierre Boulez's *Orientations*, Ferruccio Busoni's *Sketch of a New Esthetic of Music*, John Cage's *Silence*, Aaron Copland's *Music and Imagination* and *The New Music: 1900–1960*, Henry Cowell's *New Musical Resources*, *Debussy on Music*, Charles Ives's *Essays before a Sonata, The Majority, and Other Writings*, Olivier Messiaen's *The Technique of My Musical Language*, Pauline Oliveros's *Deep Listening*, Harry Partch's *Genesis of a Music*, Dane Rudhyar's *The Magic of Tone and the Art of Music*, Erik Satie's *A Mammal's Notebook*, Arnold Schoenberg's *Theory of Harmony* and *Style and Idea*, Igor Stravinsky's *Poetics of Music*, and Iannis Xenakis's *Formalized Music*.

The numerous books about composers provide an array of perspectives. Invaluable personal insights characterize *Stravinsky: Chronicle of a Friendship* by Robert Craft, *Delius as I Knew Him* by Eric Fenby, *Bartók Remembered*, edited by Malcolm Gillies, *Forces in Motion: Anthony Braxton and the Meta-Reality of Creative Music* by Graham Lock, *Schoenberg Remembered* by Dika Newlin, *Charles Ives Remembered* by Vivian Perlis, *Varèse: A Looking-Glass Diary* by Louise Varèse, and *RVW: A Biography of Ralph Vaughan Williams* by Ursula Vaughan Williams.

Thoughtful compositional analysis is offered by *On the Music of Stefan Wolpe*, edited by Austin Clarkson, Allan Forte's *The Harmonic Organization of "The Rite of Spring,"* *The Bartók Companion*, edited by Malcolm Gillies, Paul Griffiths's *Olivier Messiaen and the Music of Time*, George Perle's *The Operas of Alban Berg, Vols. 1 and 2*, and E. Robert Schmitz's *The Piano Works of Claude Debussy*.

Illuminating and well-researched biographies and studies include Sabine Feisst's *Schoenberg's New World: The American Years*, Don C. Gillespie's *The Search for Thomas F. Ward, Teacher of Frederick Delius*, Allan B. Ho and Dmitry Feofanov's *Shostakovich Reconsidered*, Rita Mead's *Henry Cowell's New Music, 1925–1936*, Howard Pollack's *Aaron Copland*, Rebecca Rischin's *For the End of Time: The Story of the Messiaen Quartet*, Arbie Orenstein's *Ravel: Man and Musician*, Vera Stravinsky and Robert Craft's *Stravinsky in Pictures and Documents*, and Judith Tick's *Ruth Crawford Seeger*.

Most of the journals and reviews listed remain in publication, in print or online. The websites compiled at the end of this bibliography indicate the vitality that the Internet has brought to disseminating information about modern and contemporary music. Many of these websites continue to evolve along with their subjects. Like the journals and reviews, they are liable to cease operations for varying reasons, but all were operational shortly before publication of this book in 2011.

BOOKS

General

Adorno, Theodor W. *Essays on Music*. Edited by Richard Leppert. Berkeley: University of California Press, 2002.

Ashby, Arved, ed. *The Pleasure of Modernist Music: Listening, Meaning, Intention, Ideology*. Rochester, N.Y.: University of Rochester Press, 2004.

Bandur, Markus. *Aesthetics of Total Serialism*. Basel, Switzerland: Mirkhäuser, 2001.

Battcock, Gregory, ed. *Breaking the Sound Barrier*. New York: Dutton, 1981.

Boretz, Benjamin, and Edward T. Cone, eds. *Perspectives on Contemporary Music Theory*. New York: Norton, 1972.

——. *Perspectives on Notation and Performance*. New York: Norton, 1976.

Bruhn, Siglind. *Images and Ideas in Modern French Piano Music*. New York: Pendragon, 1997.

——, ed. *Voicing the Ineffable: Musical Representations of Religious Experience*. New York: Pendragon, 2002.

Burge, David. *Twentieth-Century Piano Music*. Metuchen, N.J.: Scarecrow Press, 2004.

Cooke, Mervyn, ed. *The Cambridge Companion to Twentieth-Century Opera*. Cambridge: Cambridge University Press, 2006.

Downes, Stephen. *Music and Decadence in European Modernism*. Cambridge: Cambridge University Press, 2010.

Duckworth, William. *20/20: 20 New Sounds of the 20th Century*. New York: Schirmer, 1999.

——. *Virtual Music: How the Web Got Wired for Sound*. New York: Routledge, 2005.

Emerson, Isabelle. *Twentieth-Century American Music for the Dance*. Westport, Conn.: Greenwood, 1996.

Everett, Yayoi Uno, and Frederick Lau, eds. *Locating East Asia in Western Art Music*. Middletown, Conn.: Wesleyan University Press, 2004.

Fink, Robert. *Repeating Ourselves: American Minimal Music as Cultural Practice*. Berkeley: University of California Press, 2005.

Forte, Allen. *The Structure of Atonal Music*. New Haven, Conn.: Yale University Press, 1999.

Gann, Kyle. *Music Downtown*. Berkeley: University of California Press, 2006.

Grant, M. J. *Serial Music, Serial Aesthetics: Compositional Theory in Post-War Europe*. Cambridge: Cambridge University Press, 2005.

Griffiths, Paul. *The Substance of Things Heard: Writings about Music*. Rochester, N.Y.: University of Rochester Press, 2005.

Hinton, Stephen. *The Idea of Gebrauchsmusik*. New York: Garland, 1989.

Jones, Evans, ed. *Intimate Voices: The Twentieth-Century String Quartets*. 2 vols. Rochester, N.Y.: University of Rochester Press, 2009.

Licata, Thomas. *Electroacoustic Music: Analytical Perspectives*. Westport, Conn.: Greenwood, 2002.

Lochhead, Judy, and Joseph Auner, eds. *Postmodern Music, Postmodern Thought*. New York: Routledge, 2001.

Mabry, Sharon. *Exploring Twentieth-Century Vocal Music: A Practical Guide to Innovations in Performance and Repertoire*. New York: Oxford University Press, 2002.

Marquis, G. Welton, *Twentieth-Century Music Idioms*. Westport, Conn.: Greenwood, 1981.

Metzer, David. *Quotation and Cultural Meaning in Twentieth-Century Music*. Cambridge: Cambridge University Press, 2003.

Mitchell, Donald. *The Language of Modern Music*. New York: St. Martin's, 1970.

Moreno, Enrique. *Expanded Tunings in Contemporary Music*. Lewiston, N.Y.: Mellen, 1992.

Paddison, Max, and Irène Deliège, eds. *Contemporary Music: Theoretical and Philosophical Perspectives*. Burlington, Vt.: Ashgate, 2010.

Pendergast, Roy M. *Film Music: A Neglected Art*. New York: Norton, 1992.

Perle, George. *Twelve-Tone Tonality*. Berkeley: University of California Press, 1996.

Peyser, Joan. *The Music of My Time*. White Plains, N.Y.: Pro/Am Music Resources, 1995.

Rahn, John, ed. *Perspectives on Musical Aesthetics*. New York: Norton, 1995.

Read, Gardner. *Modern Rhythmic Notation*. Bloomington: Indiana University Press, 1978.

———. *20th-Century Microtonal Notation*. Westport, Conn.: Greenwood, 1990.

Reti, Rudolph Richard. *Tonality, Atonality, Pantonality*. Westport, Conn.: Greenwood, 1978.

Ross, Alex. *The Rest Is Noise: Listening to the Twentieth Century*. New York: Picador, 2007.

Rufer, Josef. *Composition with Twelve Tones Related Only to One Another*. London: Rockliff, 1954.

Schaefer, John. *New Sounds: A Listener's Guide*. New York: Harper & Row, 1987.

Schuijer, Michiel. *Analyzing Atonal Music: Pitch-Class Set Theory and Its Contexts*. Rochester, N.Y.: University of Rochester Press, 2008.

Simpson, Robert, ed. *The Symphony*. Vol. 2. Middlesex, U.K.: Penguin, 1967.

Stone, Kurt. *Music Notation in the Twentieth Century*. New York: Norton, 1980.

Sutherland, Roger. *New Perspectives in Music*. London: Sun Tavern Fields, 1994.

Voegelin, Salomé. *Listening to Noise and Silence: Towards a Philosophy of Sound Art*. New York: Continuum, 2010.

Whitall, Arnold. *Exploring Twentieth-Century Music*. Cambridge: Cambridge University Press, 2003.

Histories

Appleton, John H., and Ronald C. Perera. *The Development and Practice of Electronic Music*. Englewood Cliffs, N.J.: Prentice-Hall, 1975.

Collins, Nick, and Julio d'Escrivan, eds. *The Cambridge Companion to Electronic Music*. Cambridge: Cambridge University Press, 2008.

Cook, Nicholas, and Anthony Pople, eds. *The Cambridge History of Twentieth-Century Music*. Cambridge: Cambridge University Press, 2004.

Cooke, Mervyn. *A History of Film Music*. Cambridge: Cambridge University Press, 2008.

Doctor, Jennifer. *The BBC and Ultra-Modern Music, 1922–1936*. Cambridge: Cambridge University Press, 2007.

Fearn, Raymond. *Italian Opera since 1945*. Amsterdam: Harwood, 1997.

Gann, Kyle. *American Music in the Twentieth Century*. New York: Schirmer, 1997.

Graf, Max. *Modern Music*. Westport, Conn.: Greenwood, 1978.

Hartog, Howard. *European Music in the Twentieth Century*. Westport, Conn.: Greenwood, 1976.

Hegarty, Paul. *Noise/Music: A History*. New York: Continuum, 2007.

Holmes, Thomas B. *Electronic and Experimental Music*. New York: Routledge, 2002.

Howard, John Tasker, and James Lyons. *Modern Music*. Westport, Conn.: Greenwood, 1979.

Lewis, George E. *A Power Stronger Than Itself: The AACM and American Experimental Music*. Chicago: University of Chicago Press, 2008.

Machlis, Joseph. *Introduction to Contemporary Music*. New York: Norton, 1979.

Mackay, Andy. *Electronic Music*. Minneapolis, Minn.: Control Data, 1981.

Manning, Peter. *Electronic and Computer Music*. Oxford, U.K.: Clarendon, 1985.

McLoskey, Lansing. *Twentieth-Century Danish Music*. Westport, Conn.: Greenwood, 1998.

Mellers, Wilfred. *Music in a New Found Land*. New York: Hillstone, 1975.

Messing, Scott. *Neoclassicism in Music*. Rochester, N.Y.: University of Rochester Press, 1988.

Mikkonen, Simo. *Music and Power in the Soviet 1930s: A History of Composers' Bureaucracy*. Lewiston, N.Y.: Mellen, 2009.

Nicholls, David. *American Experimental Music, 1890–1940*. Cambridge: Cambridge University Press, 1991.

Nyman, Michael. *Experimental Music: Cage and Beyond*. New York: Schirmer, 1974.

Oja, Carol J. *Making Music Modern: New York in the 1920s*. New York: Oxford University Press, 2000.

Olkhovsky, Andrey Vasilyevich. *Music under the Soviets*. Westport, Conn.: Greenwood, 1975.

Packer, Renée Levine. *This Life of Sounds: Evenings for New Music in Buffalo*. New York: Oxford University Press, 2010.

Perlis, Vivian, and Libby Van Cleeve. *Composers' Voices from Ives to Ellington: An Oral History of American Music*. New Haven, Conn.: Yale University Press, 2005.

Peyser, Joan. *To Boulez and Beyond*. Metuchen, N.J.: Scarecrow Press, 2007.

———. *Twentieth-Century Music: The Sense behind the Sound*. New York: Schirmer, 1980.

Pinch, Trevor, and Frank Trocco. *Analog Days: The Invention and Impact of the Moog Synthesizer*. Cambridge, Mass.: Harvard University Press, 2002.

Prendergast, Mark. *The Ambient Century: From Mahler to Trance: The Evolution of Sound in the Electronic Age*. New York: Bloomsbury USA, 2001.

Rappoport-Gelfand, Lidia. *Musical Life in Poland: The Postwar Years, 1945–1977*. New York: Gordon & Breach, 1991.

Riley, Matthew, ed. *British Music and Modernism, 1895–1960*. Burlington, Vt.: Ashgate, 2010.

Russcol, Herbert. *The Liberation of Sound*. Englewood Cliffs, N.J.: Prentice-Hall, 1972.

Salazar, Adolfo. *Music in Our Time*. Westport, Conn.: Greenwood, 1970.

Saunders, James, ed. *The Ashgate Research Companion to Experimental Music*. Burlington, Vt.: Ashgate, 2009.

Schwartz, Elliott. *Electronic Music: A Listener's Guide to New Music*. New York: Praeger, 1975.

Sitsky, Larry. *Australian Piano Music of the Twentieth Century*. Westport, Conn.: Greenwood, 2005.

———. *Music of the Repressed Russian Avant-Garde, 1900–1929*. Westport, Conn.: Greenwood, 1994.

———, ed. *Music of the Twentieth-Century Avant-Garde: A Biocritical Sourcebook*. Westport, Conn.: Greenwood, 2002.

Smith Brindle, Reginald. *The New Music*. London: Oxford University Press, 1975.

Stradling, Robert, and Meirion Hughes. *The English Musical Renaissance, 1860–1940*. New York: Routledge, 1993.

Straus, Joseph N. *Twelve-Tone Music in America*. Cambridge: Cambridge University Press, 2009.

Strickland, Edward. *Minimalism: Origins*. Bloomington: Indiana University Press, 2000.

Strimple, Nick. *Choral Music in the Twentieth Century*. Portland, Ore.: Amadeus, 2005.

Struble, John Warthen. *The History of American Classical Music*. New York: Facts on File, 1995.

Stuckenschmidt, H. H. *Twentieth-Century Music*. New York: McGraw-Hill, 1969.

Thomas, Adrian. *Polish Music since Szymanowski*. Cambridge: Cambridge University Press, 2008.

Tomoff, Kiril. *Creative Union: The Professional Organization of Soviet Composers, 1939–1953*. Ithaca, N.Y.: Cornell University Press, 2006.

Vander Weg, John D. *Serial Music and Serialism: A Research and Information Guide*. New York: Routledge, 2000.

Whitall, Arnold. *The Cambridge Introduction to Serialism*. Cambridge: Cambridge University Press, 2008.

——. *Music since the First World War*. New York: Oxford University Press, 1988.
Wick, Robert L. *Electronic and Computer Music*. Westport, Conn.: Greenwood, 1997.
Yates, Peter. *Twentieth-Century Music*. Westport, Conn.: Greenwood, 1981.
Zaimont, Judith Lang, and Karen Famera. *Contemporary Concert Music by Women*. Westport, Conn.: Greenwood, 1981.

Individual Composers

Anderson, Laurie

Anderson, Laurie. *Empty Places*. New York: Harper, 1991.
——. *Night Life*. Gottingen, Germany: Steidl, 2006.
——. *Stories from the Nerve Bible: 1972–1992, a Retrospective*. New York: Harper, 1994.
——. *United States*. New York: Harper, 1984.
Anderson, Laurie, and Germano Celant. *Laurie Anderson: Dal Vivo*. Milan: Fondazione Prada, 1999.
Goldberg, Roselee. *Laurie Anderson*. New York: Abrams, 2000.
Howell, John. *Laurie Anderson*. New York: Thunder's Mouth, 1992.

Andriessen, Louis

Adlington, Robert. *Louis Andriessen: De Staat*. Burlington, Vt.: Ashgate, 2004.
Andriessen, Louis. *The Art of Stealing Time*. Edited by Mirjam Zegers. Todmorden, Lancashire, U.K.: Arc, 2002.
Everett, Yayoi Uno. *The Music of Louis Andriessen*. Cambridge: Cambridge University Press, 2007.
Trochimczyk, Maja, ed. *The Music of Louis Andriessen*. New York: Routledge, 2002.

Babbitt, Milton

Babbitt, Milton. *The Collected Essays of Milton Babbitt*. Edited by Stephen Peles, Stephen Dembski, Andrew Mead, and Joseph N. Straus. Princeton, N.J.: Princeton University Press, 2003.
Dembski, Stephen, and Joseph N. Straus. *Milton Babbitt: Words about Music*. Madison: University of Wisconsin Press, 1987.
Mead, Andrew. *An Introduction to the Music of Milton Babbitt*. Princeton, N.J.: Princeton University Press, 1994.

Barber, Samuel

Broder, Nathan. *Samuel Barber*. Westport, Conn.: Greenwood, 1985.
Dickinson, Peter. *Samuel Barber Remembered: A Centenary Tribute*. Rochester, N.Y.: University of Rochester Press, 2010.

Hennessee, Don A. *Samuel Barber: A Bio-Bibliography.* Westport, Conn.: Greenwood, 1985.

Heyman, Barbara B. *Samuel Barber: A Thematic Catalogue of the Complete Works.* New York: Oxford University Press, 2011.

——. *Samuel Barber: The Composer and His Music.* New York: Oxford University Press, 1994.

Larson, Thomas. *The Saddest Music Ever Written: The Story of Samuel Barber's Adagio for Strings.* New York: Pegasus, 2010.

Wentzel, Wayne. *Samuel Barber: A Research and Information Guide.* New York: Routledge, 2010.

Bartók, Béla

Antokoletz, Elliott. *Béla Bartók: A Guide to Research.* New York: Garland, 1997.

——. *The Music of Béla Bartók.* Berkeley: University of California Press, 1984.

Antokoletz, Elliott, Victoria Fischer, and Benjamin Suchoff, eds. *Bartók Perspectives: Man, Composer, and Ethnomusicologist.* New York: Oxford University Press, 2000.

Antokoletz, Elliott, and Paolo Susanni. *Béla Bartók: A Research and Information Guide.* New York: Routledge, 1997.

Bartók, Béla. *Béla Bartók Essays.* Edited by Benjamin Suchoff. London: Faber, 1976.

——. *Béla Bartók Letters.* Edited by János Demény. London: Faber, 1971.

——. *Studies in Ethnomusicology.* Edited by Benjamin Suchoff. Lincoln: University of Nebraska Press, 1997.

Bayley, Amanda, ed. *The Cambridge Companion to Bartók.* Cambridge: Cambridge University Press, 2001.

Bónis, Ferenc. *Béla Bartók: His Life in Pictures and Documents.* Budapest: Corvina, 1972.

Brown, Julie. *Bartók and the Grotesque.* Burlington, Vt.: Ashgate, 2007.

Chalmers, Kenneth. *Béla Bartók.* London: Phaidon, 2008.

Cooper, David. *Bartók: Concerto for Orchestra.* Cambridge: Cambridge University Press, 1996.

Fassett, Agatha. *Béla Bartók: The American Years.* New York: Dover, 1970.

Frigyesi, Judit. *Béla Bartók and Turn-of-the-Century Budapest.* Berkeley: University of California Press, 1998.

Gillies, Malcolm, ed. *The Bartók Companion.* Portland, Ore.: Amadeus, 1994.

——, ed. *Bartók Remembered.* New York: Norton, 1990.

Griffiths, Paul. *Bartók.* London: Dent, 1984.

Helm, Everett. *Bartók.* New York: Crowell, 1972.

John, Nicholas, ed. *The Stage Works of Béla Bartók.* London: Calder, 1991.

Karpati, Janos. *Bartók's Chamber Music.* New York: Pendragon, 1994.

Laki, Peter, ed. *Bartók and His World.* Princeton, N.J.: Princeton University Press, 1995.

Leafstedt, Carl S. *Inside Bluebeard's Castle: Music and Drama in Béla Bartók's Opera.* New York: Oxford University Press, 1999.

Lendvai, Ernö. *Béla Bartók: An Analysis of His Music*. London: Kahn & Averill, 2005.

Milne, Hamish. *Bartók: His Life and Times*. New York: Hippocrene, 1982.

Moreux, Serge. *Béla Bartók*. New York: Vienna House, 1974.

Nissman, Barbara. *Bartók and the Piano*. Metuchen, N.J.: Scarecrow Press, 2002.

Seiber, Mátyás. *The String Quartets of Béla Bartók*. London: Boosey & Hawkes, 1945.

Somfai, László. *Béla Bartók: Composition, Concepts, and Autograph Scores*. Berkeley: University of California Press, 1996.

Stevens, Halsey. *The Life and Music of Béla Bartók*. Edited by Malcolm Gillies. New York: Oxford University Press, 1993.

Suchoff, Benjamin. *Bartók, Concerto for Orchestra: Understanding Bartók's World*. New York: Schirmer, 1995.

———. *Bartók's Mikrokosmos: Genesis, Pedagogy, and Style*. Metuchen, N.J.: Scarecrow Press, 2004.

———. *Béla Bartók: A Celebration*. Metuchen, N.J.: Scarecrow Press, 2003.

———. *Béla Bartók: Life and Work*. Metuchen, N.J.: Scarecrow Press, 2001.

Szabolcsi, Bence. *Béla Bartók: His Life in Pictures*. Edited by Ferenc Bónis. London: Boosey & Hawkes, 1964.

Tallian, Tibor. *Béla Bartók: The Man and His Work*. Budapest: Corvina, 1981.

Wilson, Paul. *The Music of Béla Bartók*. New Haven, Conn.: Yale University Press, 1974.

Yeomans, David. *Bartók for Piano: A Survey of His Solo Literature*. Bloomington: Indiana University Press, 2000.

Bax, Arnold

Bax, Arnold. *Farewell, My Youth, and Other Writings by Arnold Bax*. Edited by Lewis Foreman. Brookfield, Vt.: Scolar, 1987.

Foreman, Lewis. *Bax: A Composer and His Times*. Woodbridge, Suffolk, U.K.: Boydell, 2007.

Parlett, Graham. *A Catalogue of the Works of Sir Arnold Bax*. Oxford, U.K.: Clarendon, 1999.

Scott-Sutherland, Colin. *Arnold Bax*. London: Dent, 1973.

Berg, Alban

Adorno, Theodor W. *Alban Berg: Master of the Smallest Link*. Cambridge: Cambridge University Press, 1994.

Bañuelos, Diego. *Beyond the Spectrum of Music: Exploration through Spectral Analysis of Sound Color in the Alban Berg Violin Concerto*. Saarbrücken, Germany: VDM, 2008.

Berg, Alban. *Alban Berg: Letters to His Wife*. Edited by Bernard Grun. London: Faber, 1971.

Bruhn, Siglind, ed. *Encrypted Messages in Alban Berg's Music*. New York: Garland, 1998.

Carner, Mosco. *Alban Berg: The Man and the Work*. New York: Holmes & Meier, 1983.

Floros, Constantin. *Alban Berg and Hanna Fuchs: The Story of a Love in Letters*. Bloomington: Indiana University Press, 2007.

Gable, David, and Robert P. Morgan, eds. *Alban Berg: Historical and Analytical Perspectives*. New York: Oxford University Press, 1991.

Hailey, Christopher, ed. *Alban Berg and His World*. Princeton, N.J.: Princeton University Press, 2010.

Hall, Patricia. *Berg's Wozzeck*. New York: Oxford University Press, 2011.

———. *A View of Berg's Lulu through the Autograph Sources*. Berkeley: University of California Press, 1996.

Headlam, Dave. *The Music of Alban Berg*. New Haven, Conn.: Yale University Press, 1996.

Jarman, Douglas. *Alban Berg: Lulu*. Cambridge: Cambridge University Press, 1991.

———. *Alban Berg: Wozzeck*. Cambridge: Cambridge University Press, 1989.

———, ed. *The Berg Companion*. Boston: Northeastern University Press, 1990.

———. *The Music of Alban Berg*. Berkeley: University of California Press, 1985.

Lonitz, Henri, ed. *Theodor W. Adorno and Alban Berg: Correspondence, 1925–1935*. Malden, Mass.: Polity, 2005.

Monson, Karen. *Alban Berg*. Boston: Houghton Mifflin, 1979.

Perle, George. *The Operas of Alban Berg*. Vol. 1: *Wozzeck*. Berkeley: University of California Press, 1980. Vol. 2: *Lulu*. Berkeley: University of California Press, 1985.

———. *Style and Idea in the Lyric Suite of Alban Berg*. New York: Pendragon, 2001.

Pople, Anthony. *Berg: Violin Concerto*. Cambridge: Cambridge University Press, 1991.

———, ed. *The Cambridge Companion to Berg*. Cambridge: Cambridge University Press, 1997.

Redlich, H. F. *Alban Berg: The Man and His Music*. London: Calder, 1957.

Reich, Willi. *Alban Berg*. New York: Harcourt, Brace & World, 1965.

Schmalfeldt, Janet. *Berg's Wozzeck: Harmonic Language and Dramatic Design*. New Haven, Conn.: Yale University Press, 1983.

Simms, Bryan R. *Alban Berg: A Research and Information Guide*. New York: Routledge, 2009.

Tucker, Gary. *Tonality and Atonality in Alban Berg's Four Songs, Op. 2*. Lewiston, N.Y.: Mellen, 2001.

Berio, Luciano

Berio, Luciano. *Remembering the Future*. Cambridge, Mass.: Harvard University Press, 2006.

Dalmonte, Rosana, and Bálint András Varga. *Luciano Berio: Two Interviews*. New York: Marion Boyars, 1985.

Halfyard, Janet K., ed. *Berio's Sequenzas: Essays on Performance, Composition and Analysis.* Burlington, Vt.: Ashgate, 2007.

Osmond-Smith, David. *Berio.* New York: Oxford University Press, 1991.

———. *Playing on Words: A Guide to Luciano Berio's Sinfonia.* London: Royal Musical Association, 1985.

Bernstein, Leonard

Bernstein, Burton, and Barbara B. Haws. *Leonard Bernstein: American Original.* New York: Collins, 2008.

Bernstein, Leonard. *Findings.* New York: Simon & Schuster, 1982.

———. *The Infinite Variety of Music.* New York: Simon & Schuster, 1966.

———. *The Joy of Music.* New York: Simon & Schuster, 1959.

———. *The Unanswered Question.* Cambridge, Mass.: Harvard University Press, 1976.

Blashfield, Jean F. *Leonard Bernstein: Composer and Conductor.* Chicago: Ferguson, 2000.

Briggs, John. *Leonard Bernstein: The Man, His Work and His World.* New York: World, 1961.

Burton, Humphrey. *Leonard Bernstein.* New York: Doubleday, 1994.

Burton, William W., ed. *Conversations about Bernstein.* New York: Oxford University Press, 1995.

Chapin, Schuyler. *Leonard Bernstein: Notes from a Friend.* New York: Walker 1992.

Fluegel, Jane, ed. *Bernstein Remembered: A Life in Pictures.* New York: Carroll & Graf, 1991.

Freedland, Michael. *Leonard Bernstein.* London: Harrap, 1987.

Gradenwitz, Peter. *Leonard Bernstein: The Infinite Variety of a Musician.* New York: Berg, 1987.

Gruen, John. *The Private World of Leonard Bernstein.* New York: Viking, 1968.

Laird, Paul. *The Chichester Psalms of Leonard Bernstein.* New York: Pendragon, 2010.

———. *Leonard Bernstein: A Guide to Research.* New York: Routledge, 2001.

Myers, Paul. *Leonard Bernstein.* London: Phaidon, 1998.

Peyser, Joan. *Bernstein: A Biography.* New York: Billboard, 1998.

Secrest, Meryle. *Leonard Bernstein: A Life.* New York: Knopf, 1994.

Seiler, Thomas R. *Leonard Bernstein: The Last Ten Years.* New York: Stemmle, 2000.

Seldes, Barry. *Leonard Bernstein: The Political Life of an American Musician.* Berkeley: University of California Press, 2009.

Sherman, Steve J. *Leonard Bernstein at Work: His Final Years, 1984–1990.* Milwaukee, Wis.: Amadeus, 2010.

Simeone, Nigel. *Leonard Bernstein: West Side Story.* Burlington, Vt.: Ashgate, 2009.

Swan, Claudia, ed. *Leonard Bernstein: The Harvard Years, 1934–1939.* New York: Eos Music, 1999.

Birtwistle, Harrison

Adlington, Robert. *The Music of Harrison Birtwistle*. Cambridge: Cambridge University Press, 2006.
Cross, Jonathan. *Harrison Birtwistle: Man, Mind, Music*. Ithaca, N.Y.: Cornell University Press, 2000.
——. *Harrison Birtwistle: The Mask of Orpheus*. Burlington, Vt.: Ashgate, 2009.

Boulez, Pierre

Born, Georgina. *Rationalizing Culture: IRCAM, Boulez, and the Institutionalization of the Musical Avant-Garde*. Berkeley: University of California Press, 1995.
Boulez, Pierre. *Boulez on Conducting*. London: Faber, 2003.
——. *Boulez on Music Today*. Cambridge, Mass.: Harvard University Press, 1971.
——. *Notes of an Apprenticeship*. New York: Knopf, 1968.
——. *Orientations*. Cambridge, Mass.: Harvard University Press, 1986.
——. *Pierre Boulez: Conversations with Célestin Deliège*. London: Eulenburg, 1976.
Breatnach, Mary. *Boulez and Mallarmé: A Study in Poetic Influence*. Brookfield, Vt.: Scolar, 1996.
Campbell, Edward. *Boulez, Music and Philosophy*. Cambridge: Cambridge University Press, 2010.
Di Pietro, Rocco. *Dialogues with Boulez*. Metuchen, N.J.: Scarecrow Press, 2000.
Glock, William, ed. *Pierre Boulez: A Symposium*. London: Eulenburg, 1986.
Goldman, Jonathan. *The Musical Language of Pierre Boulez*. Cambridge: Cambridge University Press, 2011.
Jameux, Dominique. *Pierre Boulez*. Cambridge, Mass.: Harvard University Press, 1990.
Koblyakov, Lev. *Pierre Boulez: A World of Harmony*. Chur, Switzerland: Harwood, 1990.
Peyser, Joan. *Boulez: Composer, Conductor, Enigma*. New York: Schirmer, 1976.
Stacey, Peter F. *Boulez and the Modern Concept*. Lincoln: University of Nebraska Press, 1987.
Vermeil, Jean. *Conversations with Boulez*. Portland, Ore.: Amadeus, 1996.

Braxton, Anthony

Braxton, Anthony. *Composition Notes, Vols. A–E*. Lebanon, N.H.: Frog Peak Music, 1988.
——. *Tri-axium Writings*. 3 vols. Lebanon, N.H.: Frog Peak Music, 1985.
Broomer, Stuart. *Time and Anthony Braxton*. Toronto: Mercury, 2009.
Heffley, Mike. *The Music of Anthony Braxton*. Westport, Conn.: Greenwood, 1996.
Lock, Graham. *Forces in Motion: Anthony Braxton and the Meta-reality of Creative Music*. London: Quartet, 1988.

——, ed. *Mixtery: A Festschrift for Anthony Braxton.* Devoran, Cornwall, U.K.: Stride, 1995.

Radano, Ronald M. *New Musical Figurations: Anthony Braxton's Cultural Critique.* Chicago: University of Chicago Press, 1993.

Britten, Benjamin

Banks, Paul, ed. *Britten's Gloriana: Essays and Sources.* Woodbridge, Suffolk, U.K.: Boydell, 1993.

——, ed. *Britten's Peter Grimes: Essays and Sources.* Woodbridge, Suffolk, U.K.: Boydell, 1997.

Brett, Philip. *Benjamin Britten: Peter Grimes.* Cambridge: Cambridge University Press, 1983.

Britten, Benjamin. *Journeying Boy: The Diaries of the Young Benjamin Britten, 1928–1938.* Edited by John Evans. London: Faber, 2010.

——. *Letters from a Life: Selected Letters and Diaries of Benjamin Britten.* Vol. 1: *1923–1939.* Vol. 2: *1939–1945.* Edited by Donald Mitchell and Philip Reed. London: Faber, 1998.

——. *Letters from a Life: The Selected Letters of Benjamin Britten.* Vol. 3: *1946–1951.* Edited by Donald Mitchell, Philip Reed, and Mervyn Cooke. London: Faber, 2004.

——. *Letters from a Life: The Selected Letters of Benjamin Britten, 1913–1976.* Vol. 4: *1952–1957.* Edited by Philip Reed, Mervyn Cooke, and Donald Mitchell. Woodbridge, Suffolk, U.K.: Boydell, 2008.

——. *Letters from a Life: The Selected Letters of Benjamin Britten, 1913–1976.* Vol. 5: *1958–1965.* Edited by Philip Reed and Mervyn Cooke. Woodbridge, Suffolk, U.K.: Boydell, 2010.

Carpenter, Humphrey. *Benjamin Britten.* London: Faber, 2003.

Cooke, Mervyn. *Britten: War Requiem.* Cambridge: Cambridge University Press, 1996.

——. *Britten and the Far East: Asian Influences in the Music of Benjamin Britten.* Woodbridge, Suffolk, U.K.: Boydell, 1998.

——, ed. *The Cambridge Companion to Benjamin Britten.* Cambridge: Cambridge University Press, 1999.

Cooke, Mervyn, and Philip Reed. *Benjamin Britten: Billy Budd.* Cambridge: Cambridge University Press, 1993.

Craggs, Stewart R. *Benjamin Britten: A Bio-Bibliography.* Westport, Conn.: Greenwood, 2001.

Graham, Elliott. *Benjamin Britten: The Spiritual Dimension.* London: Oxford University Press, 2006.

Hodgson, Peter J. *Benjamin Britten: A Guide to Research.* New York: Routledge, 1996.

Howard, Patricia. *Benjamin Britten: The Turn of the Screw.* Cambridge: Cambridge University Press, 1985.

Johnson, Graham. *Britten, Voice and Piano*. Edited by George Odam. Burlington, Vt.: Ashgate, 2003.

Kendall, Alan. *Benjamin Britten*. London: Macmillan, 1973.

Matthews, David. *Britten*. London: Haus, 2003.

Mitchell, Donald. *Benjamin Britten: Death in Venice*. Cambridge: Cambridge University Press, 1987.

——. *Britten and Auden in the Thirties: The Year 1936*. Woodbridge, Suffolk, U.K.: Boydell, 1981.

Parsons, Charles H. *A Benjamin Britten Discography*. Lewiston, N.Y.: Mellen, 1990.

Rupprecht, Philip. *Britten's Musical Language*. Cambridge: Cambridge University Press, 2006.

Seymour, Claire. *The Operas of Benjamin Britten: Expression and Evasion*. Woodbridge, Suffolk, U.K.: Boydell, 2007.

Walker, Lucy, ed. *Benjamin Britten: New Perspectives on His Life and Work*. Woodbridge, Suffolk, U.K.: Boydell, 2009.

Wintle, Christopher. *All the Gods: Benjamin Britten's Night-Piece in Context*. London: Plumbago, 2006.

Busoni, Ferruccio

Beaumont, Antony. *Busoni the Composer*. Bloomington: Indiana University Press, 1986.

Busoni, Ferruccio. *The Essence of Music, and Other Papers*. New York: Philosophical Library, 1957.

——. *Ferruccio Busoni: Letters to His Wife*. Edited by Friedrich Schnapp. London: Edward Arnold, 1938.

——. *Selected Letters*. Edited by Antony Beaumont. New York: Columbia University Press, 1987.

——. *Sketch of a New Esthetic of Music*. New York: G. Schirmer, 1911.

Couling, Della. *Ferruccio Busoni: A Musical Ishmael*. Metuchen, N.J.: Scarecrow Press, 2004.

Dent, Edward Joseph. *Ferruccio Busoni*. Oxford: Oxford University Press, 1933.

Fleet, Paul. *Ferruccio Busoni: A Phenomenological Approach to His Music and Aesthetic*. Saarbrücken, Germany: LAP, 2009.

Kogan, Grigory. *Busoni as Pianist*. Rochester, N.Y.: University of Rochester Press, 2010.

Levitz, Tamara. *Teaching the New Classicality: Ferruccio Busoni's Master Class in Composition*. Frankfurt: Peter Lang, 1996.

Roberge, Marc-André. *Ferruccio Busoni: A Bio-Bibliography*. Westport, Conn.: Greenwood, 1991.

Sitsky, Larry, ed. *Busoni and the Piano*. New York: Pendragon, 2009.

Stuckenschmidt, H. H. *Ferruccio Busoni: Chronicle of a European*. New York: St. Martin's, 1970.

Cage, John

Bernstein, David W., and Christopher Hatch, eds. *Writings through John Cage's Music, Poetry, and Art.* Chicago: University of Chicago Press, 2001.

Cage, John. *Anarchy.* Middletown, Conn.: Wesleyan University Press, 2001.

——. *Composition in Retrospect.* Cambridge, Mass.: Exact Change, 1993.

——. *Empty Words.* Middletown, Conn.: Wesleyan University Press, 1979.

——. *I–VI.* Cambridge, Mass.: Harvard University Press, 1990.

——. *John Cage, Writer: Selected Texts.* Edited by Richard Kostelanetz. New York: Cooper Square, 2000.

——. *M.* Middletown, Conn.: Wesleyan University Press, 1973.

——. *MUSICAGE.* Joan Retallack, contributor. Middletown, Conn.: Wesleyan University Press, 1996.

——. *Silence.* Middletown, Conn.: Wesleyan University Press, 1973.

——. *X.* Middletown, Conn.: Wesleyan University Press, 1986.

——. *A Year from Monday.* Middletown, Conn.: Wesleyan University Press, 1967.

Cage, John, and Daniel Charles. *For the Birds: John Cage in Conversation with Daniel Charles.* Salem, N.H.: Marion Boyars, 1981.

DeLio, Thomas. *The Amores of John Cage.* New York: Pendragon, 2010.

Dickinson, Peter, ed. *CageTalk: Dialogues with and about John Cage.* Rochester, N.Y.: University of Rochester Press, 2006.

Fetterman, William. *John Cage's Theatre Pieces: Notations and Performances.* Amsterdam: Harwood, 1996.

Fleming, Richard, and William Duckworth, eds. *John Cage at Seventy-Five.* Lewisburg, Pa.: Bucknell University Press, 1989.

Gann, Kyle. *No Such Thing as Silence: John Cage's 4'33".* New Haven, Conn.: Yale University Press, 2010.

Gena, Peter, and Jonathan Brent, eds. *A John Cage Reader.* Assisted by Don C. Gillespie. New York: C. F. Peters, 1982.

Griffiths, Paul. *John Cage.* Oxford: Oxford University Press, 1981.

Herzogenrath, Wulf. *Sounds of the Inner Eye: John Cage, Mark Tobey, and Morris Graves.* Seattle: University of Washington Press, 2002.

Kostelanetz, Richard, ed. *Conversing with Cage.* New York: Limelight, 1988.

——, ed. *John Cage.* London: Penguin, 1971.

——. *John Cage (Ex)plain(ed).* New York: Schirmer, 1996.

——, ed. *Writings about Cage.* Ann Arbor: University of Michigan Press, 1993.

Nicholls, David, ed. *The Cambridge Companion to John Cage.* Cambridge: Cambridge University Press, 2002.

——. *John Cage.* Urbana: University of Illinois Press, 2007.

Patterson, David W., ed. *John Cage: Music, Philosophy, and Intention, 1933–1950.* New York: Routledge, 2002.

Perloff, Marjorie, and Charles Junkerman, eds. *John Cage: Composed in America.* Chicago: University of Chicago Press, 1994.

Pritchett, James. *The Music of John Cage.* Cambridge: Cambridge University Press, 1996.

Revill, David. *The Roaring Silence: John Cage, a Life.* New York: Arcade, 1992.

Shultis, Christopher. *Silencing the Sounded Self: John Cage and the American Experimental Tradition.* Boston: Northeastern University Press, 1998.

Silverman, Kenneth. *Begin Again: A Biography of John Cage.* New York: Knopf, 2010.

Cardew, Cornelius

Cardew, Cornelius. *Cornelius Cardew: A Reader.* Edited by Edwin Prévost. Harlow, Essex, U.K.: Copula, 2006.

———, ed. *Scratch Music.* Cambridge, Mass.: MIT Press, 1972.

———. *Stockhausen Serves Imperialism, and Other Articles.* London: Latimer New Dimensions, 1974.

Tilbury, John. *Cornelius Cardew: A Life Unfinished.* Harlow, Essex, U.K.: Copula, 2008.

Carter, Elliott

Carter, Elliott. *Elliott Carter: Collected Essays and Lectures, 1937–1995.* Edited by Jonathan W. Bernard. Rochester, N.Y.: University of Rochester Press, 1996.

Doering, William T. *Elliott Carter: A Bio-Bibliography.* Westport, Conn.: Greenwood, 1993.

Edwards, Allen. *Flawed Words and Stubborn Sounds: A Conversation with Elliott Carter.* New York: Norton, 1972.

Jackson, Richard, ed. *Elliott Carter: Sketches and Scores in Manuscript.* New York: New York Public Library, 1973.

Link, John F. *Elliott Carter: A Guide to Research.* New York: Routledge, 2000.

Meyer, Felix, and Anne C. Shreffler. *Elliott Carter: A Centennial Portrait in Letters and Documents.* Rochester, N.Y.: University of Rochester Press, 2008.

Ponthus, Marc, ed. *Elliott Carter: A Centennial Celebration.* New York: Pendragon, 2008.

Rosen, Charles. *The Musical Languages of Elliott Carter.* Washington, D.C.: Library of Congress, 1984.

Schiff, David. *The Music of Elliott Carter.* Ithaca, N.Y.: Cornell University Press, 1998.

Chávez, Carlos

Chávez, Carlos. *Musical Thought.* Cambridge, Mass.: Harvard University Press, 1961.

———. *Toward a New Music: Music and Electricity.* New York: Norton, 1937.

Parker, Robert. *Carlos Chávez: A Guide to Research.* New York: Garland, 1998.

———. *Carlos Chávez: Mexico's Modern-Day Orpheus.* Boston: Twayne, 1983.

Weinstock, Herbert. *Carlos Chávez: North American Press, 1936–1950.* New York: Herbert Barrett, 1951.

Copland, Aaron

Berger, Arthur. *Aaron Copland*. New York: Oxford University Press, 1953.

Butterworth, Neil. *The Music of Aaron Copland*. London: Toccata Press, 1985.

Copland, Aaron. *Aaron Copland: A Reader: Selected Writings, 1923–1972*. Edited by Richard Kostelanetz. New York: Routledge, 2004.

——. *Copland on Music*. New York: Norton, 1968.

——. *Music and Imagination*. Cambridge, Mass.: Harvard University Press, 1952.

——. *The New Music: 1900–1960*. New York: Norton, 1963.

——. *The Selected Correspondence of Aaron Copland*. Edited by Elizabeth B. Crist and Wayne Shirley. New Haven, Conn.: Yale University Press, 2006.

——. *What to Listen For in Music*. New York: McGraw-Hill, 1957.

Copland, Aaron, and Vivian Perlis. *Copland: 1900 through 1942*. New York: St. Martin's/Marek, 1984.

——. *Copland: Since 1943*. New York: St. Martin's/Marek, 1989.

Dickinson, Peter. *Copland Connotations: Studies and Interviews*. Woodbridge, Suffolk, U.K.: Boydell, 2004.

Oja, Carol J., and Judith Tick, eds. *Aaron Copland and His World*. Princeton, N.J.: Princeton University Press, 2005.

Pollack, Howard. *Aaron Copland: The Life and Work of an Uncommon Man*. New York: Henry Holt, 1999.

Robertson, Marta, and Robin Armstrong. *Aaron Copland: A Guide to Research*. New York: Routledge, 2001.

Skowronski, JoAnn. *Aaron Copland: A Bio Bibliography*. Westport, Conn.: Greenwood, 1985.

Smith, Julia Frances. *Aaron Copland: His Work and Contribution to American Music*. New York: Dutton, 1955.

Starr, Larry. *The Dickinson Songs of Aaron Copland*. New York: Pendragon, 2003.

Cowell, Henry

Cowell, Henry, ed. *American Composers on American Music*. New York: Ungar, 1962.

——. *Essential Cowell: Selected Writings on Music by Henry Cowell, 1921–1964*. Edited by Dick Higgins. New York: McPherson, 2002.

——. *New Musical Resources*. New York: Knopf, 1930.

Cowell, Henry, and Sidney Cowell. *Charles Ives and His Music*. New York: Oxford University Press, 1955.

Hicks, Michael. *Henry Cowell, Bohemian*. Chicago: University of Illinois Press, 2002.

Lichtenwanger, William. *The Music of Henry Cowell: A Descriptive Catalog*. Brooklyn, N.Y.: ISAM, 1986.

Manion, Martha L. *Writings about Henry Cowell: An Annotated Bibliography*. Brooklyn, N.Y.: ISAM, 1982.

Mead, Rita. *Henry Cowell's New Music, 1925–1936*. Ann Arbor, Mich.: UMI Research Press, 1981.

Nicholls, David, ed. *The Whole World of Music: A Henry Cowell Symposium*. New York: Routledge, 1998.

Sachs, Joel. *Henry Cowell: A Biography*. New York: Oxford University Press, 2011.

Saylor, Bruce. *The Writings of Henry Cowell: A Descriptive Bibliography*. Brooklyn, N.Y.: ISAM, 1977.

Weisgall, Hugo. *The Music of Henry Cowell*. New York: G. Schirmer, 1959.

Crumb, George

Bruns, Steven, and Ofer Ben-Amots, eds. *George Crumb: The Alchemy of Sound*. Colorado Springs: Colorado College Music, 2005.

Cohen, David. *George Crumb: A Bio-Bibliography*. Westport, Conn.: Greenwood, 2002.

Gillespie, Don C., ed. *George Crumb: Profile of a Composer*. New York: C. F. Peters, 1986.

Dallapiccola, Luigi

Alegant, Brian. *The Twelve-Tone Music of Luigi Dallapiccola*. Rochester, N.Y.: University of Rochester Press, 2010.

Dallapiccola, Luigi. *Dallapiccola on Opera*. Edited by Rudy Shackelford. London: Toccata Press, 1987.

Fearn, Raymond. *The Music of Luigi Dallapiccola*. Rochester, N.Y.: University of Rochester Press, 2003.

——, ed. *Selected Letters of Luigi Dallapiccola*. Burlington, Vt.: Ashgate, 2009.

MacDonald, Malcolm. *Luigi Dallapiccola: A Complete Catalogue*. London: Boosey & Hawkes, 1978.

Nathan, Hans. *The Twelve-Tone Compositions of Luigi Dallapiccola*. New York: G. Schirmer, 1958.

Vlad, Roman. *Luigi Dallapiccola*. Milan: Suvini Zerboni, 1957.

Davies, Peter Maxwell

Bayliss, Colin, ed. *The Music of Sir Peter Maxwell Davies: An Annotated Catalogue*. Beverley, North Humberside, U.K.: Highgate, 1991.

Craggs, Stewart R., ed. *Peter Maxwell Davies: A Source Book*. Burlington, Vt.: Ashgate, 2002.

Gloag, Kenneth, and Nicolas Jones, eds. *Peter Maxwell Davies Studies*. Cambridge: Cambridge University Press, 2011.

Griffiths, Paul. *Peter Maxwell Davies*. London: Robson, 1982.

McGregor, Richard, ed. *Perspectives on Peter Maxwell Davies*. Burlington, Vt.: Ashgate, 2000.

Seabrook, Mike. *Max: The Life and Music of Peter Maxwell Davies*. London: Gollancz, 1995.

Smith, Carolyn J. *Peter Maxwell Davies: A Bio-Bibliography*. Westport, Conn.: Greenwood, 1995.

Debussy, Claude

Bathori, Jane. *On the Interpretation of the Melodies of Claude Debussy*. New York: Pendragon, 1998.

Briscoe, James R., ed. *Debussy in Performance*. New Haven, Conn.: Yale University Press, 2000.

Cobb, Margaret G., and Richard Miller, eds. *The Poetic Debussy: A Collection of His Song Texts and Letters*. Rochester, N.Y.: University of Rochester Press, 1982.

Code, David J. *Claude Debussy*. London: Reaktion, 2010.

Debussy, Claude. *Debussy on Music*. Edited by Richard Langham Smith; collected by François Lesure. New York: Knopf, 1977.

——. *Debussy's Letters to Inghelbrecht: The Story of a Musical Friendship*. Edited by Margaret G. Cobb. Rochester, N.Y.: University of Rochester Press, 2005.

Devoto, Mark. *Debussy and the Veil of Tonality*. New York: Pendragon, 2004.

Fulcher, Jane F., ed. *Debussy and His World*. Princeton, N.J.: Princeton University Press, 2001.

Hartmann, Arthur. *Claude Debussy As I Knew Him, and Other Writings*. Edited by Samuel Hsu, Sidney Grolnic, and Mark Peters. Rochester, N.Y.: University of Rochester Press, 2004.

Howat, Roy. *Debussy in Proportion: A Musical Analysis*. Cambridge: Cambridge University Press, 1986.

Nichols, Roger. *The Life of Debussy*. Cambridge: Cambridge University Press, 1998.

Nichols, Roger, and Richard Langham Smith. *Claude Debussy: Pelléas et Mélisande*. Cambridge: Cambridge University Press, 1989.

Orledge, Robert. *Debussy and the Theatre*. Cambridge: Cambridge University Press, 2009.

Raad, Virginia. *The Piano Sonority of Claude Debussy*. Lewiston, N.Y.: Mellen, 1994.

Schmitz, E. Robert. *The Piano Works of Claude Debussy*. New York: Duell, Sloan & Pearce, 1950.

Smith, Richard Langham, ed. *Debussy Studies*. Cambridge: Cambridge University Press, 2009.

Trezise, Simon, ed. *The Cambridge Companion to Debussy*. Cambridge: Cambridge University Press, 2003.

——. *Debussy: La Mer*. Cambridge: Cambridge University Press, 1995.

Vallas, Léon. *Claude Debussy: His Life and Works*. New York: Oxford University Press, 1933.

Wheeldon, Marianne. *Debussy's Late Style*. Bloomington: Indiana University Press, 2008.

Delius, Frederick

Beecham, Thomas. *Frederick Delius*. London: Hutchinson, 1959.

Carley, Lionel, ed. *Delius: A Life in Letters, 1862–1908*. Brookfield, Vt.: Scolar, 1983.

——, ed. *Delius: A Life in Letters, 1909–1934*. Brookfield, Vt.: Scolar, 1988.

——. *Delius: The Paris Years*. Rickmansworth, U.K.: Triad, 1975.

——, ed. *Frederick Delius: Music, Art and Literature*. Burlington, Vt.: Ashgate, 1998.

——, ed. *Grieg and Delius: A Chronicle of Their Friendship in Letters*. London: Boyars, 2000.

Carley, Lionel, and Robert Threlfall. *Delius: Life in Pictures*. London: Oxford University Press, 1977.

Chop, Max. *The Collected Writings of German Musicologist Max Chop on the Composer Frederick Delius*. Edited by Philip Jones. Lewiston, N.Y.: Mellen, 2002.

Delius, Clare. *Memories of My Brother*. London: Nicholson & Watson, 1935.

Fenby, Eric. *Delius*. London: Faber, 1971.

——. *Delius as I Knew Him*. London: Cambridge University Press, 1981.

——. *Fenby on Delius*. London: Thames, 1996.

Gillespie, Don C. *The Search for Thomas F. Ward, Teacher of Frederick Delius*. Gainesville: University Press of Florida, 1996.

Heseltine, Philip. *Frederick Delius*. Westport, Conn.: Greenwood, 1974.

Huismann, Mary Christison. *Frederick Delius: A Research and Information Guide*. New York: Routledge, 2009.

Hutchings, Arthur. *Delius*. Westport, Conn.: Greenwood, 1970.

Jefferson, Alan. *Delius*. Abingdon, Oxfordshire, U.K: Everyman, 1972.

Jenkins, Lyndon. *While Spring and Summer Sang: Thomas Beecham and the Music of Frederick Delius*. Burlington, Vt.: Ashgate, 2005.

Johoda, Gloria. *The Road to Samarkand: Frederick Delius and His Music*. New York: Scribner, 1969.

Jones, Philip. *The American Source of Delius' Style*. New York: Routledge, 1990.

Montgomery, Robert, and Robert Threlfall. *Music and Copyright: The Case of Delius and His Publishers*. Burlington, Vt.: Ashgate, 2007.

Palmer, Christopher. *Delius: Portrait of a Cosmopolitan*. New York: Holmes & Meier, 1976.

Redwood, Christopher, ed. *A Delius Companion*. London: Calder, 1980.

Redwood, Dawn. *Flecker and Delius: The Making of Hassan*. London: Thames, 1978.

Smith, Barry, ed. *Frederick Delius and Peter Warlock: A Friendship Revealed*. New York: Oxford University Press, 2000.

Smith, John Boulton. *Frederick Delius and Edvard Munch: Their Friendship and Their Correspondence*. Rickmansworth, U.K.: Triad, 1983.

Eisler, Hanns

Betz, Albrecht. *Hanns Eisler, Political Musician*. Cambridge: Cambridge University Press, 2006.

Blake, David, ed. *Hanns Eisler: A Miscellany*. Amsterdam: Harwood, 1995.

Eisler, Hanns. *Hanns Eisler: A Rebel in Music: Selected Writings*. Edited by Manfred Grabs. Berlin: Seven Seas, 1978.

Eisler, Hanns, and Theodor W. Adorno. *Composing for the Films*. New York: Oxford University Press, 1947.

Falla, Manuel de

Armero, Gonzalo, and Jorge de Persia, eds. *Manuel de Falla: His Life and Works.* London: Omnibus, 1999.

Chase, Gilbert. *Manuel de Falla: A Bibliography and Research Guide.* New York: Garland, 1986.

Christofordis, Michael. *Studies on Manuel de Falla.* Burlington, Vt.: Ashgate, 2008.

Crichton, Ronald. *Manuel de Falla.* Wappingers Falls, N.Y.: Beekman, 1992.

Demarquez, Suzanne. *Manuel de Falla.* Philadelphia, Pa.: Chilton, 1968.

Falla, Manuel de. *Miniature Essays.* London: J&W Chester, 1922.

Franco, Enrique. *Manuel de Falla in the Centenary of His Birth, 1876–1976.* Granada, Spain: Fundación Rodriguez-Acosta, 1976.

Harper, Nancy Lee. *Manuel de Falla: A Bio-Bibliography.* Westport, Conn.: Greenwood, 1998.

———. *Manuel de Falla: His Life and Music.* Metuchen, N.J.: Scarecrow Press, 2005.

Hess, Carol A. *Manuel de Falla and Modernism in Spain, 1898–1936.* Chicago: University of Chicago Press, 2001.

———. *Sacred Passions: The Life and Music of Manuel de Falla.* New York: Oxford University Press, 2005.

James, David Burnett. *Manuel de Falla and the Spanish Musical Renaissance.* Worthing, West Sussex, U.K.: Littlehampton, 1979.

Pahissa, Jaime. *Manuel de Falla: His Life and Works.* Westport, Conn.: Hyperion, 1979.

Suarez-Pajares, Javier. *Manuel de Falla, 1876–1946.* Madrid: Fundación Autor, 1999.

Trend, J. B. *Manuel de Falla and Spanish Music.* New York: Knopf, 1934.

Feldman, Morton

DeLio, Thomas. *The Music of Morton Feldman.* Westport, Conn.: Greenwood, 1996.

Feldman, Morton. *Give My Regards to Eighth Street: Collected Writings of Morton Feldman.* Edited by B. H. Friedman. Cambridge, Mass.: Exact Change, 2004.

———. *Morton Feldman Essays.* Edited by Walter Zimmermann. Kerpen, Germany: Beginner, 1985.

———. *Morton Feldman in Middleburg: Words on Music: Lectures and Conversations.* 2 vols. Edited by Raoul Mörchen. Cologne, Germany: MusikTexte, 2007.

———. *Morton Feldman Says: Selected Interviews and Lectures, 1964–1987.* Edited by Chris Villars. London: Hyphen, 2006.

Kissane, Sean, ed. *Vertical Thoughts: Morton Feldman and the Visual Arts.* Dublin: Irish Museum of Modern Art, 2011.

Finney, Ross Lee

Finney, Gretchen. *Facts and Memories.* New York: C. F. Peters, 1990.

Finney, Ross Lee. *Analysis and the Creative Process.* Claremont, Calif.: Scripps College, 1958.

——. *Profile of a Lifetime: A Musical Autobiography*. New York: C. F. Peters, 1992.

——. *Thinking about Music: The Collected Writings of Ross Lee Finney*. Edited by Frederic Goosen. Tuscaloosa: University of Alabama Press, 1991.

Hitchens, Susan Hayes. *Ross Lee Finney: A Bio-Bibliography*. Westport, Conn.: Greenwood, 1996.

Foulds, John

Foulds, John. *Music To-day*. London: Nicholson & Watson, 1934.

MacDonald, Malcolm. *John Foulds: His Life in Music*. Rickmansworth, U.K.: Triad, 1975.

——. *John Foulds and His Music: An Introduction*. White Plains, N.Y.: Pro/Am Music Resources, 1989.

Gershwin, George

Armitage, Merle, ed. *George Gershwin*. New York: Longmans, Green, 1938.

Carnovale, Norbert. *George Gershwin: A Bio-Bibliography*. Westport, Conn.: Greenwood, 2000.

Ewen, David. *George Gershwin: His Journey to Greatness*. New York: Ungar, 1986.

Gilbert, Steven E. *The Music of Gershwin*. New Haven, Conn.: Yale University Press, 1995.

Goldberg, Isaac. *George Gershwin: A Study in American Music*. Supplemented by Edith Garson. New York: Ungar, 1958.

Greenberg, Rodney. *George Gershwin*. London: Phaidon, 1998.

Hyland, William G. *George Gershwin: A New Biography*. Westport, Conn.: Praeger, 2003.

Jablonski, Edward. *Gershwin Remembered*. Portland, Ore.: Amadeus, 1992.

Kendall, Alan. *George Gershwin: A Biography*. New York: Universe, 1987.

Kimball, Robert, and Alfred Simon. *The Gershwins*. New York: Bonanza, 1973.

Leon, Ruth. *Gershwin*. London: Haus, 2004.

Peyser, Joan. *The Memory of All That: The Life of George Gershwin*. New York: Simon & Schuster, 1993.

Pollack, Howard: *George Gershwin: His Life and Work*. Berkeley: University of California Press, 2006.

Rimler, Walter: *George Gershwin: An Intimate Portrait*. Urbana: University of Illinois Press, 2009.

Schiff, David: *Gershwin: Rhapsody in Blue*. Cambridge: Cambridge University Press, 1997.

Schneider, Wayne, ed. *The Gershwin Style: New Looks at the Music of George Gershwin*. New York: Oxford University Press, 1999.

Starr, Larry. *George Gershwin*. New Haven, Conn.: Yale University Press, 2010.

Wood, Eam: *George Gershwin: His Life and Music*. London: Sanctuary, 1996.

Wyatt, Robert, and John Andrew Johnson, eds. *The George Gershwin Reader*. New York: Oxford University Press, 2007.

Glanville-Hicks, Peggy

Beckett, Wendy. *Peggy Glanville-Hicks*. Pymble, Australia: Angus & Robertson, 1992.

Hayes, Deborah. *Peggy Glanville-Hicks: A Bio-Bibliography*. Westport, Conn.: Greenwood, 1990.

Murdoch, James. *Peggy Glanville-Hicks: A Transposed Life*. Hillsdale, N.Y.: Pendragon, 2003.

Rogers, Victoria. *The Music of Peggy Glanville-Hicks*. Burlington, Vt.: Ashgate, 2009.

Glass, Philip

Glass, Philip. *Music by Philip Glass*. Edited by Robert T. Jones. New York: Da Capo, 1995.

Kostelanetz, Richard, and Robert Flemming, eds. *Writings on Glass: Essays, Interviews, Criticism*. New York: Schirmer, 1997.

Maycock, Robert. *Glass: A Biography of Philip Glass*. Port Jefferson, N.Y.: Sanctuary, 2002.

Richardson, John. *Reflections of Masculinity: Ambivalence and Androgyny in Philip Glass's Opera "Akhnaten" and Selected Recent Works*. Jyväskylä, Finland: University of Jyväskylä Press, 1995.

———. *Singing Archeology: Philip Glass's Akhnaten*. Middletown, Conn.: Wesleyan University Press, 1999.

Grainger, Percy

Balough, Teresa. *A Complete Catalogue of the Works of Percy Grainger*. Nedlands: University of Western Australia Press, 1975.

———, ed. *Comrades in Art: Correspondence of Ronald Stevenson and Percy Grainger, 1957–1961*. London: Toccata, 2010.

———, ed. *A Musical Genius from Australia: Selected Writings by and about Percy Grainger*. Nedlands: University of Western Australia Press, 1982.

Bird, John. *Percy Grainger*. New York: Oxford University Press, 1999.

Blacking, John. *A Commonsense View of All Music: Reflections on Percy Grainger's Contribution to Ethnomusicology and Music Education*. Cambridge: Cambridge University Press, 1989.

Dorum, Eileen. *Percy Grainger: The Man behind the Music*. White Plains, N.Y.: Pro/Am Music Resources, 1989.

Dreyfus, Kay. *Music by Percy Aldridge Grainger: First Supplementary List and Index*. Melbourne, Australia: University of Melbourne Press, 1995.

Foreman, Lewis. *The Percy Grainger Companion*. London: Thames, 1981.

Gillies, Malcolm, and David Pear, eds. *Portrait of Percy Grainger*. Rochester, N.Y.: University of Rochester Press, 2002.

Gillies, Malcolm, David Pear, and Mark Carroll, eds. *Self-Portrait of Percy Grainger*. New York: Oxford University Press, 2006.

Grainger, Percy. *The All-Around Man: Selected Letters of Percy Grainger, 1914–1961*. Edited by Malcolm Gillies and David Pear. New York: Oxford University Press, 1994.

———. *The Farthest North of Humanness: Letters of Percy Grainger, 1901–1914*. Edited by Kay Dreyfus. Saint Louis: MMB Music, 1985.

———. *Grainger on Music*. Edited by Malcolm Gillies and Bruce Clunies Ross. Oxford: Oxford University Press, 1999.

Lewis, Thomas P., ed. *A Source Guide to the Music of Percy Grainger*. London: Kahn & Averill, 1991.

Mellers, Wilfrid. *Percy Grainger*. New York: Oxford University Press, 1992.

Simon, Robert. *Percy Grainger: The Pictorial Biography*. Troy, N.Y.: Whitston, 1984.

Slattery, Thomas C. *Percy Grainger: The Inveterate Innovator*. Evanston, Ill.: Instrumentalist, 1974.

Thwaites, Penelope, ed. *The New Percy Grainger Companion*. Woodbridge, Suffolk, U.K.: Boydell, 2010.

Wilson, Brian Scott. *Orchestrational Archetypes in Percy Grainger's Wind Band Music*. Lewiston, N.Y.: Mellen, 2001.

Harris, Roy

Paquin, Ethel. *Johana Harris: A Biography*. Metuchen, N.J.: Scarecrow Press, 2011.

Stehman, Dan. *Roy Harris: A Bio-Bibliography*. Westport, Conn.: Greenwood, 1991.

———. *Roy Harris: An American Musical Pioneer*. Boston: Twayne, 1984.

Harrison, Lou

Garland, Peter, ed. *A Lou Harrison Reader*. Santa Fe, N.Mex.: Soundings, 1987.

Harrison, Lou. *Lou Harrison's Music Primer*. New York: C. F. Peters, 1971.

Miller, Leta E., and Frederic Lieberman. *Lou Harrison*. Urbana: University of Illinois Press, 2006.

———. *Lou Harrison: Composing a World*. New York: Oxford University Press, 1998.

von Gunden, Heidi. *The Music of Lou Harrison*. Metuchen, N.J.: Scarecrow Press, 1995.

Henze, Hans Werner

Henze, Hans Werner. *Bohemian Fifths: An Autobiography*. Princeton, N.J.: Princeton University Press, 1999.

———. *Music and Politics*. London: Faber, 1982.
———. *Ondine: Diary of a Ballet*. Hightstown, N.J.: Princeton Book Co., 2004.

Hindemith, Paul

Bruhn, Siglind. *Musical Ekphrasis in Rilke's Marien-Leben*. Amsterdam: Rodopi, 2000.
———. *The Musical Order of the World: Kepler, Hesse, Hindemith*. New York: Pendragon, 2005.
———. *The Temptation of Paul Hindemith*. New York: Pendragon, 1998.
Hindemith, Paul. *A Composer's World: Horizons and Limitations*. Cambridge, Mass.: Harvard University Press, 1952.
———. *The Craft of Musical Composition*. London: Schott, 1945.
———. *Selected Letters of Paul Hindemith*. Edited by Geoffrey Skelton. New Haven, Conn.: Yale University Press, 1995.
Kemp, Ian. *Hindemith*. London: Oxford University Press, 1970.
Luttmann, Stephen. *Paul Hindemith: A Research and Information Guide*. New York: Routledge, 2009.
Neumeyer, David. *The Music of Paul Hindemith*. New Haven, Conn.: Yale University Press, 1986.
Noss, Luther. *Paul Hindemith in the United States*. Urbana: University of Illinois Press, 1989.
Skelton, Geoffrey. *Paul Hindemith: The Man behind the Music*. London: Gollancz, 1975.

Holst, Gustav

Greene, Richard. *Holst: The Planets*. Cambridge: Cambridge University Press, 1995.
Holmes, Paul. *Holst: His Life and Times*. London: Omnibus, 1997.
Holst, Imogen. *Gustav Holst: A Biography*. London: Faber, 1969.
———. *Holst*. London: Faber, 1981.
———. *The Music of Gustav Holst and Holst's Music Reconsidered*. New York: Oxford University Press, 1981.
———. *A Thematic Catalogue of Gustav Holst's Music*. London: Faber Music, 1974.
Huismann, Mary Christison. *Gustav Holst: A Research and Information Guide*. New York: Routledge, 2010.
Mitchell, Jon Ceander. *A Comprehensive Biography of Composer Gustav Holst*. Lewiston, N.Y.: Mellen, 2001.
Rubbra, Edmund. *Collected Essays on Gustav Holst*. Rickmansworth, U.K.: Triad, 1974.
Short, Michael. *Gustav Holst: The Man and His Music*. New York: Oxford University Press, 1990.
———. *Gustav Holst, 1874–1934: A Centenary Documentation*. London: White Lion, 1974.

Honegger, Arthur

Halbreich, Harry. *Arthur Honegger.* Portland, Ore.: Amadeus, 1999.
Honegger, Arthur. *I Am a Composer.* New York: St. Martin's, 1966.
Spratt, Geoffrey. *The Music of Arthur Honegger.* Cork, Ireland: Cork University Press, 1987.
Waters, Keith. *Rhythmic and Contrapuntal Structures in the Music of Arthur Honegger.* Burlington, Vt.: Ashgate, 2002.

Ives, Charles

Block, Geoffrey. *Charles Ives: A Bio-Bibliography.* Westport, Conn.: Greenwood, 1988.
———. *Ives: Concord Sonata.* Cambridge: Cambridge University Press, 1996.
Block, Geoffrey, and J. Peter Burkholder. *Charles Ives and the Classical Tradition.* New Haven, Conn.: Yale University Press, 1996.
Burk, James Mack, and Michael J. Budds, eds. *A Charles Ives Omnibus.* New York: Pendragon, 2008.
Burkholder, J. Peter. *All Made of Tunes: Charles Ives and the Use of Musical Borrowing.* New Haven, Conn.: Yale University Press, 2004.
———, ed. *Charles Ives and His World.* Princeton, N.J.: Princeton University Press, 1996.
Feder, Stuart. *Charles Ives, "My Father's Songs": A Psychoanalytic Biography.* New Haven, Conn.: Yale University Press, 1992.
———. *The Life of Charles Ives.* Cambridge: Cambridge University Press, 1999.
Henderson, Clayton W. *The Charles Ives Tunebook.* Bloomington: Indiana University Press, 2008.
Hitchcock, H. Wiley, and Vivian Perlis, eds. *An Ives Celebration.* Urbana: University of Illinois Press, 1977.
Ives, Charles. *Charles E. Ives: Memos.* Edited by John Kirkpatrick. New York: Norton, 1972.
———. *Essays before a Sonata, The Majority, and Other Writings.* New York: Norton, 1961.
Lambert, Philip, ed. *Ives Studies.* Cambridge: Cambridge University Press, 2006.
———. *The Music of Charles Ives.* New Haven, Conn.: Yale University Press, 1997.
Magee, Gayle Sherwood. *Charles Ives: A Research and Information Guide.* New York: Routledge, 2010.
———. *Charles Ives Reconsidered.* Urbana: University of Illinois Press, 2008.
Owens, Tom C., ed. *Selected Correspondence of Charles Ives.* Berkeley: University of California Press, 2007.
Perlis, Vivian. *Charles Ives Remembered.* New Haven, Conn.: Yale University Press, 1974.
Reed, Alice S. *Charles Edward Ives and His Piano Sonata No. 2, "Concord, Mass. 1840–1860."* Victoria, B.C.: Trafford, 2005.
Rossiter, Frank. *Charles Ives and His America.* New York: Liveright, 1975.

Sinclair, James B. *A Descriptive Catalogue of the Music of Charles Ives*. New Haven, Conn.: Yale University Press, 1999.
Swafford, Jan. *Charles Ives: A Life with Music*. New York: Norton, 1996.
Zobel, Mark. *The Third Symphony of Charles Ives*. New York: Pendragon, 2009.

Kodály, Zoltán

Breuer, János. *Guide to Kodály*. Budapest: Corvina, 1990.
Choksy, Lois. *The Kodály Method*. Englewood Cliffs, N.J.: Prentice-Hall, 1988.
Eosze, Laszlo. *Zoltán Kodály: His Life and Works*. Boston: Crescendo, 1962.
———. *Zoltán Kodály: His Life in Pictures and Documents*. Budapest: Corvina, 1971.
Houlahan, Michael, and Philip Tacka. *Zoltán Kodály: A Guide to Research*. New York: Routledge, 1998.
Kodály, Zoltán. *The Selected Writings of Zoltán Kodály*. Edited by Ferenc Bónis. London: Boosey & Hawkes, 1974.
Ranki, Gyorgy, ed. *Bartók and Kodály Revisited*. Budapest: Akadémiai Kiadó, 1987.
Young, Percy Marshall. *Zoltán Kodály: A Hungarian Musician*. London: Benn, 1964.

Krenek, Ernst

Bowles, Garrett H. *Ernst Krenek: A Bio-Bibliography*. Westport, Conn.: Greenwood, 1989.
Krenek, Ernst. *Exploring Music*. London: Calder, 1966.
———. *Horizons Circled*. Berkeley: University of California Press, 1974.
———. *Music Here and Now*. New York: Norton, 1939.
Stewart, John L. *Ernst Krenek: The Man and His Music*. Berkeley: University of California Press, 1991.

Ligeti, György

Griffiths, Paul. *György Ligeti*. London: Robson, 1997.
Ligeti, György. *György Ligeti in Conversation with Peter Varnai, Josef Hausler, Claude Samuel and Himself*. London: Eulenburg, 1983.
Lobanova, M. *György Ligeti: Style, Ideas, Poetics*. Berlin: Kuhn, 2002.
Richart, Robert W. *György Ligeti: A Bio-Bibliography*. Westport, Conn.: Greenwood, 1990.
Sallis, Friedemann. *An Introduction to the Early Works of György Ligeti*. Cologne, Germany: Studio, 1996.
Searby, Michael D. *Ligeti's Stylistic Crisis: Transformation in His Musical Style, 1974–1985*. Metuchen, N.J.: Scarecrow Press, 2009.
Steinitz, Richard. *György Ligeti: Music of the Imagination*. London: Faber, 2003.
Toop, Richard. *György Ligeti*. London: Phaidon, 1999.

Lutoslawski, Witold

Bedkowski, Stanislaw, and Stanislaw Hrabia. *Witold Lutoslawski: A Bio-Bibliography.* Westport, Conn.: Greenwood, 2001.

Bodman Rae, Charles. *The Music of Lutoslawski.* London: Omnibus, 1999.

Kaczynski, Tadeusz. *Conversations with Lutoslawski.* London: Chester Music, 1980.

Lutoslawski, Witold. *Lutoslawski on Music.* Edited by Zbigniew Skowron. Metuchen, N.J.: Scarecrow Press, 2007.

Skowron, Zbigniew, ed. *Lutoslawski Studies.* New York: Oxford University Press, 2001.

Stucky, Steven. *Lutoslawski and His Music.* Cambridge: Cambridge University Press, 2009.

Martinu, Bohuslav

Beckerman, Michael, ed. *Martinu's Mysterious Accident.* New York: Pendragon, 2007.

Crump, Michael. *Martinu and the Symphony.* London: Toccata, 2010.

Lodge, Brian. *Martinu.* London: Gerald Duckworth, 1975.

Martinu, Bohuslav. *Martinu's Letters Home: Five Decades of Correspondence with Family and Friends.* Edited by Isa Popelka. London: Toccata, 2010.

Martinu, Charlotte. *My Life with Bohuslav Martinu.* Prague: Orbis, 1978.

Mihule, Jaroslav. *Bohuslav Martinu.* Prague: Orbis, 1978.

Rybka, F. *Bohuslav Martinu: The Compulsion to Compose.* Metuchen, N.J.: Scarecrow Press, 2011.

Safranek, Milos. *Bohuslav Martinu: His Life and Works.* London: Allan Wingate, 1962.

———. *Bohuslav Martinu: The Man and His Music.* New York: Knopf, 1944.

Messiaen, Olivier

Bell, Carla Huston. *Olivier Messiaen.* Boston: Twayne, 1984.

Benitez, Vincent. *Olivier Messiaen: A Research and Information Guide.* New York: Routledge, 2007.

Bruhn, Siglind. *Messiaen's Contemplations of Covenant and Incarnation.* New York: Pendragon, 2007.

———. *Messiaen's Explorations of Love and Death.* New York: Pendragon, 2008.

———. *Messiaen's Interpretations of Holiness and Trinity.* New York: Pendragon, 2008.

———, ed. *Messiaen's Language of Mystical Love.* New York: Garland, 1998.

Dingle, Christopher. *The Life of Messiaen.* Cambridge: Cambridge University Press, 2007.

Dingle, Christopher, and Nigel Simeone, eds. *Olivier Messiaen: Music, Art and Literature.* Burlington, Vt.: Ashgate, 2007.

Gillock, Jon. *Performing Messiaen's Organ Music: 66 Masterclasses.* Bloomington: Indiana University Press, 2009.

Griffiths, Paul. *Olivier Messiaen and the Music of Time*. Ithaca, N.Y.: Cornell University Press, 1985.

Hill, Peter, ed. *The Messiaen Companion*. Portland, Ore.: Amadeus, 1994.

Hill, Peter, and Nigel Simeone. *Messiaen*. New Haven, Conn.: Yale University Press, 2005.

——. *Olivier Messiaen: Oiseaux Exotiques*. Burlington, Vt.: Ashgate, 2007.

Johnson, Robert Sherlaw. *Messiaen*. London: Omnibus, 2008.

Messiaen, Olivier. *Music and Color: Conversations with Claude Samuel*. Portland, Ore.: Amadeus, 1986.

——. *The Technique of My Musical Language*. Paris: Alphonse Leduc, 1956.

Nichols, Roger. *Messiaen*. Oxford: Oxford University Press, 1986.

Pople, Anthony. *Messiaen: Quatuor pour la Fin du Temps*. Cambridge: Cambridge University Press, 1998.

Rischin, Rebecca. *For the End of Time: The Story of the Messiaen Quartet*. Ithaca, N.Y.: Cornell University Press, 2003.

Shenton, Andrew, ed. *Messiaen the Theologian*. Burlington, Vt.: Ashgate, 2010.

——. *Olivier Messiaen's System of Signs*. Burlington, Vt.: Ashgate, 2008.

Sholl, Robert, ed. *Messiaen Studies*. Cambridge: Cambridge University Press, 2011.

Milhaud, Darius

Collaer, Paul. *Darius Milhaud*. London: Macmillan, 1988.

Kelly, Barbara L. *Tradition and Style in the Works of Darius Milhaud, 1912–1939*. Burlington, Vt.: Ashgate, 2003.

Mawer, Deborah. *Darius Milhaud: Modality and Structure in Music of the 1920s*. Brookfield, Vt.: Scolar, 1997.

Milhaud, Darius. *My Happy Life*. New York: Marion Boyars, 1995.

Milhaud, Darius, and Claude Rostand. *Darius Milhaud: Interviews with Claude Rostand*. Oakland, Calif.: Center for the Book at Mills College, 2002.

Oliveros, Pauline

Mockus, Martha. *Sounding Out: Pauline Oliveros and Lesbian Musicality*. New York: Routledge, 2007.

Oliveros, Pauline. *Deep Listening: A Composer's Sound Practice*. New York: iUniverse, 2005.

——. *The Roots of the Moment: Collected Writings, 1980–1996*. New York: Drogue, 1998.

——. *Software for People: Collected Writings, 1963–1980*. Baltimore, Md.: Smith, 1984.

——. *Sounding the Margins: Collected Writings, 1992–2009*. Edited by Lawton Hall. Kingston, N.Y.: Deep Listening, 2010.

Oliveros, Pauline, and Becky Cohen. *Initiation Dream*. Los Angeles: Astro Artz, 1981.

von Gunden, Heidi. *The Music of Pauline Oliveros*. Metuchen, N.J.: Scarecrow Press, 1983.

Partch, Harry

Dunn, David, ed. *Harry Partch: An Anthology of Critical Perspectives*. Amsterdam: Harwood, 2000.

Gilmore, Bob. *Harry Partch: A Biography*. New Haven, Conn.: Yale University Press, 1998.

Harlan, Brian. *One Voice: A Reconciliation of Harry Partch's Disparate Musical Theories*. Saarbrücken, Germany: VDM, 2008.

McGreary, Thomas. *The Music of Harry Partch: A Descriptive Catalog*. Monograph No. 31. Brooklyn, N.Y.: ISAM, 1991.

Partch, Harry. *Bitter Music*. Edited by Thomas McGreary. Urbana: University of Illinois Press, 1991.

———. *Genesis of a Music*. New York: Da Capo, 1974.

Penderecki, Krzysztof

Bylander, Cindy. *Krzysztof Penderecki: A Bio-Bibliography*. Westport, Conn.: Greenwood, 2004.

Penderecki, Krzysztof. *Labyrinth of Time: Five Addresses for the End of the Millennium*. Chapel Hill, N.C.: Hinshaw Music, 1998.

Robinson, Ray. *Krzysztof Penderecki: A Guide to His Works*. Secaucus, N.J.: Summy-Birchard, 1983.

Robinson, Ray, and Regina Chlopicka, eds. *Studies in Penderecki*. Princeton, N.J.: Prestige, 1998.

Robinson, Ray, and Allen Winold. *A Study of the Penderecki St. Luke Passion*. Secaucus, N.J.: Summy-Birchard, 1983.

Schwinger, Wolfram. *Krzysztof Penderecki: His Life and Works*. London: Schott, 1989.

Poulenc, Francis

Bernac, Pierre. *Francis Poulenc: The Man and His Songs*. London: Gollancz, 1977.

Buckland, Sidney, and Myriam Chimènes, eds. *Francis Poulenc: Music, Art and Literature*. Burlington, Vt.: Ashgate, 1999.

Burton, Richard D. E. *Francis Poulenc*. Bath, U.K.: Absolute, 2004.

Hell, Henri. *Francis Poulenc*. New York: Grove, 1959.

Ivry, Benjamin. *Francis Poulenc*. London: Phaidon, 1996.

Keck, George R. *Francis Poulenc: A Bio-Bibliography*. Westport, Conn.: Greenwood, 1990.

Mellers, Wilfrid. *Francis Poulenc*. Oxford: Oxford University Press, 1993.

Poulenc, Francis. *Diary of My Songs*. London: Gollancz, 1986.

———. *Echo and Source: Selected Correspondence, 1915–1963*. Edited by Sidney Buckland. London: Gollancz, 1992.

———. *My Friends and Myself: Conversations with Francis Poulenc*. Edited by Stephane Audel. London: Dobson, 1978.

Schmidt, Carl B. *Entrancing Muse: A Documented Biography of Francis Poulenc.* New York: Pendragon, 2001.

———. *The Music of Francis Poulenc: A Catalogue.* New York: Oxford University Press, 1995.

Prokofiev, Sergey

Berman, Boris. *Prokofiev's Piano Sonatas: A Guide for the Listener and the Performer.* New Haven, Conn.: Yale University Press, 2008.

Fiess, Stephen C. E. *The Piano Works of Serge Prokofiev.* Metuchen, N.J.: Scarecrow Press, 1994.

Gutman, David. *Prokofiev: His Life and Times.* New York: Hippocrene, 1985.

Hanson, Lawrence, and Elizabeth Hanson. *Prokofiev: A Biography in Three Movements.* New York: Random House, 1964.

Jaffé, Daniel. *Sergey Prokofiev.* London: Phaidon, 2008.

Kaufman, Helen L. *The Story of Sergei Prokofiev.* Philadelphia: Lippincott, 1971.

Minturn, Neil. *The Music of Sergei Prokofiev.* New Haven, Conn.: Yale University Press, 1997.

Morrison, Simon. *The People's Artist: Prokofiev's Soviet Years.* New York: Oxford University Press, 2009.

———, ed. *Sergey Prokofiev and His World.* Princeton, N.J.: Princeton University Press, 2008.

Nestyev, Israel V. *Prokofiev.* Palo Alto, Calif.: Stanford University Press, 1961.

Nice, David. *Prokofiev: A Biography: From Russia to the West, 1891–1935.* New Haven, Conn.: Yale University Press, 2003.

Park, Junghee. *A Performer's Perspective: A Performance History and Analysis of Sergei Prokofiev's Ten Piano Pieces, Op. 12.* Saarbrücken, Germany: VDM, 2009.

Press, Stephen D. *Prokofiev's Ballets for Diaghilev.* Burlington, Vt.: Ashgate, 2006.

Prokofiev, Sergey. *Autobiography, Articles, Reminiscences.* Edited by Rose Prokofieva and S. Shlifstein. Honolulu: University Press of the Pacific, 2000.

———. *Diaries, 1907–1914: Prodigious Youth.* Edited by Anthony Phillips. Ithaca, N.Y.: Cornell University Press, 2006.

———. *Diaries, 1915–1923: Behind the Mask.* Edited by Anthony Phillips. Ithaca, N.Y.: Cornell University Press, 2008.

———. *Prokofiev by Prokofiev: A Composer's Memoir.* New York: Doubleday, 1979.

———. *Selected Letters of Sergei Prokofiev.* Edited by Harlow Robinson. Boston: Northeastern University Press, 1998.

———. *Soviet Diary 1927, and Other Writings.* Edited by Olga Prokofiev and Christopher Palmer. Boston: Northeastern University Press, 1991.

Robinson, Harlow. *Sergei Prokofiev: A Biography.* Boston: Northeastern University Press, 2002.

Samuel, Claude. *Prokofiev.* London: Marion Boyars, 1971.

Schipperges, Thomas. *Prokofiev.* London: Haus, 2003.

Seroff, Victor Ilyitch. *Sergei Prokofiev: A Soviet Tragedy.* New York: Taplinger, 1969.

Ravel, Maurice

Demuth, Norman. *Ravel*. Westport, Conn.: Hyperion, 1979.

James, Burnett. *Ravel*. London: Omnibus, 1987.

——. *Ravel: His Life and Times*. New York: Hippocrene, 1983.

Kaminsky, Peter, ed. *Unmasking Ravel: New Perspectives on the Music*. Rochester, N.Y.: University of Rochester Press, 2011.

Mawer, Deborah. *The Ballets of Maurice Ravel*. Burlington, Vt.: Ashgate, 2006.

——, ed. *The Cambridge Companion to Ravel*. Cambridge: Cambridge University Press, 2000.

——, ed. *Ravel Studies*. Cambridge: Cambridge University Press, 2010.

Nichols, Roger, ed. *Ravel Remembered*. New York: Norton, 1988.

Orenstein, Arbie. *Ravel: Man and Musician*. New York: Columbia University Press, 1975.

Ravel, Maurice. *A Ravel Reader: Correspondence, Articles, Interviews*. Edited by Arbie Orenstein. New York: Columbia University Press, 1990.

Zank, Stephen. *Irony and Sound: The Music of Maurice Ravel*. Rochester, N.Y.: University of Rochester Press, 2009.

——. *Maurice Ravel: A Guide to Research*. New York: Routledge, 2004.

Reynolds, Roger

Gillespie, Don C., ed. *Roger Reynolds: Profile of a Composer*. New York: C. F. Peters, 1982.

Reynolds, Roger. *Form and Method: Composing Music*. Edited by Stephen McAdams. New York: Routledge, 2002.

——. *Mind Models: New Forms of Musical Experience*. New York: Routledge, 2005.

Rochberg, George

Dixon, Joan Devee. *George Rochberg: A Bio-bibliographic Guide to His Life and Works*. New York: Pendragon, 1992.

Gillmor, Alan M., ed. *Eagle Minds: Selected Correspondence of István Anhalt and George Rochberg, 1961–2005*. Waterloo, Ont.: Wilfrid Laurier University Press, 2007.

Rochberg, George. *The Aesthetics of Survival: A Composer's View of Twentieth-Century Music*. Ann Arbor: University of Michigan Press, 2004.

——. *Five Lines, Four Spaces: The World of My Music*. Edited by Gene Rochberg and Richard Griscom. Urbana: University of Illinois Press, 2009.

——. *The Hexachord and Its Relation to the Twelve-Tone Row*. King of Prussia, Pa.: Theodore Presser, 1955.

Rorem, Ned

McDonald, Arlys L. *Ned Rorem: A Bio-Bibliography*. Westport, Conn.: Greenwood, 1989.

Rorem, Ned. *An Absolute Gift.* New York: Simon & Schuster, 1978.
———. *Critical Affairs: A Composer's Journal.* New York: Braziller, 1970.
———. *Facing the Night: A Diary (1999–2005) and Musical Writings.* Emeryville, Calif.: Avalon, 2006.
———. *Knowing When to Stop: A Memoir.* New York: Simon & Schuster, 1994.
———. *The Later Diaries of Ned Rorem, 1961–1972.* San Francisco: North Point, 1983.
———. *Lies: A Diary, 1986–1999.* New York: Da Capo, 2000.
———. *Music and People.* New York: Braziller, 1968.
———. *Music from Inside Out.* New York: Braziller, 1967.
———. *The Nantucket Diary, 1973–1985.* San Francisco: North Point, 1987.
———. *A Ned Rorem Reader.* New Haven, Conn.: Yale University Press, 2001.
———. *Other Entertainment.* New York: Simon & Schuster, 1996.
———. *The Paris and New York Diaries of Ned Rorem, 1951–1961.* San Francisco: North Point, 1983.
———. *Paul's Blues.* New York: Red Ozier, 1984.
———. *Pure Contraption.* New York: Holt, Rinehart & Winston, 1974.
———. *Setting the Tone.* New York: Limelight, 1983.
———. *Settling the Score.* New York: Harcourt Brace Jovanovich, 1988.
———. *Wings of Friendship: Selected Letters, 1944–2003.* Emeryville, Calif.: Avalon, 2005.

Satie, Erik

Davis, Mary E. *Erik Satie.* London: Reaktion, 2007.
Gillmor, Alan M. *Erik Satie.* New York: Norton, 1988.
Harding, James. *Erik Satie.* London: Secker & Warburg, 1975.
Myers, Rollo H. *Erik Satie.* London: Dobson, 1948.
Orledge, Robert, ed. *Satie Remembered.* Portland, Ore.: Amadeus, 2003.
———. *Satie the Composer.* New York: Oxford University Press, 1999.
Perloff, Nancy. *Art and the Everyday: Popular Entertainment and the Circle of Erik Satie.* New York: Oxford University Press, 1993.
Satie, Erik. *A Mammal's Notebook: Collected Writings of Erik Satie.* Edited by Ornella Volta. London: Serpent's Tail, 1997.
Templier, Pierre-Daniel. *Erik Satie.* Cambridge, Mass.: MIT Press, 1969.
Volta, Ornella. *Erik Satie.* Paris: Hazan, 1997.
———. *Satie Seen through His Letters.* New York: Boyars, 1989.
Whiting, Steven Moore. *Satie the Bohemian: From Cabaret to Concert Hall.* New York: Clarendon, 1992.

Schoenberg, Arnold

Armitage, Merle, ed. *Schoenberg.* New York: Schirmer, 1937.
Auner, Joseph. *A Schoenberg Reader.* New Haven, Conn.: Yale University Press, 2003.

Bailey, Walter B., ed. *The Arnold Schoenberg Companion*. Westport, Conn.: Greenwood, 1998.

Boehmer, Konrad. *Schönberg and Kandinsky: An Historic Encounter*. Amsterdam: Harwood, 1997.

Brand, Juliane, and Christopher Hailey, eds. *Constructive Dissonance: Arnold Schoenberg and the Transformations of Twentieth-Century Culture*. Berkeley: University of California Press, 1997.

Brinkmann, Reinhold, and Christoph Wolff, eds. *The Music of My Future: The Schoenberg Quartets and Trio*. Cambridge, Mass.: Harvard University Press, 2001.

Bryn-Julson, Phyllis, and Paul Matthews. *Inside "Pierrot Lunaire": Performing the Sprechstimme in Schoenberg's Masterpiece*. Metuchen, N.J.: Scarecrow Press, 2009.

Bujic, Bojan. *Arnold Schoenberg*. London: Phaidon, 2011.

Cherlin, Michael. *Schoenberg's Musical Imagination*. Cambridge: Cambridge University Press, 2009.

Christensen, Jean. *From Arnold Schoenberg's Literary Legacy: A Catalog of Neglected Items*. Warren, Mich.: Harmonie Park, 1988.

Christensen, Jean, and Jespe Christensen. *Arnold Schoenberg*. New York: Routledge, 2004.

Cross, Charlotte M., and Russell A. Berman, eds. *Political and Religious Ideas in the Works of Arnold Schoenberg*. New York: Garland, 2000.

———, eds. *Schoenberg and Words: The Modernist Years*. New York: Garland, 2000.

Dahlhaus, Carl. *Schoenberg and the New Music*. Cambridge: Cambridge University Press, 1989.

Dudeque, Norton. *Music Theory and Analysis in the Writings of Arnold Schoenberg*. Burlington, Vt.: Ashgate, 2005.

Dunsby, Jonathan. *Schoenberg: Pierrot Lunaire*. Cambridge: Cambridge University Press, 1992.

Feisst, Sabine. *Schoenberg's New World: The American Years*. New York: Oxford University Press, 2011.

Frisch, Walter. *The Early Works of Arnold Schoenberg, 1893–1908*. Berkeley: University of California Press, 1993.

———, ed. *Schoenberg and His World*. Princeton, N.J.: Princeton University Press, 1999.

Gilmor, Alan M., and James K. Wright, eds. *Schoenberg's Chamber Music, Schoenberg's World*. New York: Pendragon, 2009.

Gould, Glenn. *Arnold Schoenberg: A Perspective*. Cincinnati, Ohio: University of Cincinnati Press, 1964.

Hahl-Koch, Jelena, ed. *Arnold Schoenberg, Wassily Kandinsky: Letters, Pictures and Documents*. London: Faber, 1984.

Haimo, Ethan. *Schoenberg's Serial Odyssey: The Evolution of His Twelve-Tone Method, 1914–1928*. Oxford: Clarendon, 1990.

———. *Schoenberg's Transformation of Musical Language*. Cambridge: Cambridge University Press, 2009.

Kallir, Jane. *Arnold Schoenberg's Vienna*. New York: Rizzoli International, 1984.

Kimmey, John, ed. *The Arnold Schoenberg–Hans Nachod Collection*. Warren, Mich.: Harmonie Park, 1979.

Leibowitz, René. *Schoenberg and His School*. New York: Philosophical Library, 1949.

MacDonald, Malcolm. *Schoenberg*. New York: Oxford University Press, 2008.

Milstein, Silvina. *Arnold Schoenberg: Notes, Sets, Forms*. Cambridge: Cambridge University Press, 2009.

Newlin, Dika. *Schoenberg Remembered: Diaries and Recollections, 1938–1976*. New York: Pendragon, 1980.

Reich, Willi. *Schoenberg: A Critical Biography*. New York: Praeger, 1971.

Ringer, Alexander L. *Arnold Schoenberg: The Composer as Jew*. New York: Oxford University Press, 1993.

Rosen, Charles. *Arnold Schoenberg*. Chicago: University of Chicago Press, 1996.

Rufer, Josef. *The Works of Arnold Schoenberg: A Catalogue of His Compositions, Writings, and Paintings*. London: Faber, 1962.

Schoenberg, Arnold. *Arnold Schoenberg Correspondence*. Edited by Egbert M. Ennulat. Metuchen, N.J.: Scarecrow Press, 1991.

———. *Catalogue Raisonné*. Edited by Therese Muxeneder. London: Thames & Hudson, 2005.

———. *Coherence, Counterpoint, Instrumentation, Instruction in Form*. Edited by Severine Neff. Lincoln: University of Nebraska Press, 1993.

———. *Fundamentals of Musical Composition*. Edited by Gerald Strang and Leonard Stein. London: Faber, 1999.

———. *Letters*. Edited by Erwin Stein. New York: St. Martin's, 1965.

———. *The Musical Idea and the Logic, Technique and Art of Its Presentation*. Edited by Patricia Carpenter and Severine Neff. Bloomington: Indiana University Press, 2006.

———. *Structural Functions of Harmony*. Edited by Leonard Stein. New York: Norton, 1969.

———. *Style and Idea*. Edited by Leonard Stein. Berkeley: University of California Press, 1992.

———. *Theory of Harmony*. Berkeley: University of California Press, 2010.

Schoenberg-Nono, Nuria, ed. *Arnold Schoenberg Self-Portrait*. Pacific Palisades, Calif.: Belmont Music, 1988.

Shaw, Jennifer, and Joseph Auner, eds. *The Cambridge Companion to Schoenberg*. Cambridge: Cambridge University Press, 2010.

Shawn, Allen. *Arnold Schoenberg's Journey*. Cambridge, Mass.: Harvard University Press, 2001.

Simms, Bryan R. *The Atonal Music of Arnold Schoenberg, 1908–1923*. New York: Oxford University Press, 2000.

Smith, Joan Allen. *Schoenberg and His Circle: A Viennese Portrait*. New York: Schirmer, 1986.

Soder, Aidan. *Sprechstimme in Arnold Schoenberg's Pierrot Lunaire: A Study of Vocal Performance Practice*. Lewiston, N.Y.: Mellen, 2008.

Sterne, Colin C. *Arnold Schoenberg: The Composer as Numerologist*. Lewiston, N.Y.: Mellen, 1993.

Stuckenschmidt, H. H. *Arnold Schoenberg: His Life, World and Work*. London: Calder, 1977.

Thomson, William. *Schoenberg's Error*. Philadelphia: University of Pennsylvania Press, 1991.

Trenkamp, Anne, and John G. Seuss, eds. *Studies in the Schoenbergian Movement in Vienna and the United States*. Lewiston, N.Y.: Mellen, 1990.

Wellesz, Egon. *Arnold Schoenberg: The Formative Years*. London: Clarendon, 1925.

Schuller, Gunther

Carnovale, Norbert. *Gunther Schuller: A Bio-Bibliography*. Westport, Conn.: Greenwood, 1987.

Schuller, Gunther. *Gunther Schuller: An Autobiography*. Rochester, N.Y.: University of Rochester Press, 2011.

———. *Musings*. New York: Oxford University Press, 1986.

Schuman, William

Adams, Gary K. *William Schuman: A Bio-Bibliography*. Westport, Conn.: Greenwood, 1998.

Polisi, Joseph W. *American Muse: The Life and Times of William Schuman*. Portland, Ore.: Amadeus, 2008.

Rheta, Flora, and Vincent Persichetti. *William Schuman*. New York: G. Schirmer, 1954.

Swayne, Steve. *Orpheus in Manhattan: William Schuman and the Shaping of America's Musical Life*. New York: Oxford University Press, 2011.

Seeger, Ruth Crawford

Allen, Ray, and Ellie M. Hisama, eds. *Ruth Crawford Seeger's Worlds*. Rochester, N.Y.: University of Rochester Press, 2007.

Seeger, Ruth Crawford. *The Music of American Folk Song, and Selected Other Writings on American Folk Music*. Edited by Larry Polansky with Judith Tick. Rochester, N.Y.: University of Rochester Press, 2001.

Straus, Joseph N. *The Music of Ruth Crawford Seeger*. Cambridge: Cambridge University Press, 2003.

Tick, Judith. *Ruth Crawford Seeger: A Composer's Search for American Music*. New York: Oxford University Press, 1997.

Sessions, Roger

Olmstead, Andrea. *Conversations with Roger Sessions*. Boston: Northeastern University Press, 1987.

———, ed. *The Correspondence of Roger Sessions*. Boston: Northeastern University Press, 1992.

———. *Roger Sessions: A Biography*. New York: Routledge, 2007.

———. *Roger Sessions and His Music*. Rochester, N.Y.: University of Rochester Press, 1985.

Prausnitz, Frederik. *Roger Sessions: How a "Difficult" Composer Got That Way*. New York: Oxford University Press, 2002.

Sessions, Roger. *The Composer and His Message*. Chicago: University of Chicago Press, 1965.

———. *Harmonic Practice*. New York: Harcourt, Brace, & World, 1951.

———. *The Musical Experience of Composer, Performer, Listener*. Princeton, N.J.: Princeton University Press, 1974.

———. *Questions about Music*. Cambridge, Mass.: Harvard University Press, 1970.

———. *Reflections on the Music Life in the United States*. New York: Merlin, 1956.

———. *Roger Sessions on Music: Collected Essays*. Edited by Edward T. Cone. Princeton, N.J.: Princeton University Press, 1979.

Shostakovich, Dmitry

Bartlett, Rosamund, ed. *Shostakovich in Context*. New York: Oxford University Press, 2000.

Brown, Malcolm Hamrick, ed. *A Shostakovich Casebook*. Bloomington: Indiana University Press, 2004.

Fairclough, Pauline, ed. *Shostakovich Studies 2*. Cambridge: Cambridge University Press, 2010.

———. *A Soviet Credo: Shostakovich's Fourth Symphony*. Burlington, Vt.: Ashgate, 2006.

Fairclough, Pauline, and David Fanning, eds. *The Cambridge Companion to Shostakovich*. Cambridge: Cambridge University Press, 2008.

Fanning, David. *Shostakovich: String Quartet No. 8*. Burlington, Vt.: Ashgate, 2004.

———, ed. *Shostakovich Studies*. Cambridge: Cambridge University Press, 2006.

Fay, Laurel E. *Shostakovich: A Life*. New York: Oxford University Press, 2004.

———, ed. *Shostakovich and His World*. Princeton, N.J.: Princeton University Press, 2004.

Ho, Allan B., and Dmitry Feofanov. *Shostakovich Reconsidered*. London: Toccata, 1998.

Hulme, Derek C. *Dmitri Shostakovich: A Catalogue, Bibliography, and Discography*. Metuchen, N.J.: Scarecrow Press, 2002.

Hurwitz, David. *Shostakovich Symphonies and Concertos: An Owner's Manual*. Milwaukee, Wis.: Hal Leonard, 2006.

Jackson, Stephen. *Dmitri Shostakovich: An Essential Guide to His Life and Works*. London: Pavilion, 1997.

Kuhn, Judith. *Shostakovich in Dialogue: Form, Imagery and Ideas in Quartets 1–7*. Burlington, Vt.: Ashgate, 2010.

Lesser, Wendy. *Music for Silenced Voices: Shostakovich and His Fifteen Quartets.* New Haven, Conn.: Yale University Press, 2011.

MacDonald, Malcolm. *Dmitri Shostakovich: A Complete Catalogue.* London: Boosey & Hawkes, 1985.

Martynov, Ivan. *Dmitri Shostakovich: The Man and His Work.* New York: Philosophical Library, 1947.

Mazullo, Mark. *Shostakovich's Preludes and Fugues: Contexts, Style, Performance.* New Haven, Conn.: Yale University Press, 2010.

Morton, Brian. *Shostakovich: His Life and Music.* London: Haus, 2006.

Moshevich, Sofia. *Dmitri Shostakovich, Pianist.* Montreal: McGill–Queen's University Press, 2004.

Norris, Christopher, ed. *Shostakovich: The Man and His Music.* London: Lawrence & Wishart, 1982.

Ottaway, Hugh. *Shostakovich Symphonies.* Seattle: University of Washington Press, 1978.

Reinhardt, Sarah. *Composing the Modern Subject: Four String Quartets by Dmitri Shostakovich.* Burlington, Vt.: Ashgate, 2008.

Riley, John. *Shostakovich: A Life in Film.* London: I. B. Tauris, 2005.

Roseberry, Eric. *Shostakovich: His Life and Times.* New York: Hippocrene, 1982.

Shostakovich, Dmitry. *Story of a Friendship: The Letters of Dmitry Shostakovich to Isaak Glikman, 1941–1975.* Edited by Anthony Phillips. Ithaca, N.Y.: Cornell University Press, 2001.

———. *Testimony: The Memoirs of Dmitri Shostakovich.* Edited by Solomon Volkov. New York: Harper & Row, 1979.

Sollertinsky, Dmitri, and Ludmilla Sollertinsky. *Pages from the Life of Dmitri Shostakovich.* London: Hale, 1981.

Volkov, Solomon. *Shostakovich and Stalin.* New York: Knopf, 2004.

Wilson, Elizabeth. *Shostakovich: A Life Remembered.* London: Faber, 2006.

Slonimsky, Nicolas

Slonimsky, Nicolas. *Nicolas Slonimsky: The First Hundred Years.* Edited by Richard Kostelanetz. New York: Schirmer, 1994.

———. *Perfect Pitch: An Autobiography.* New York: Schirmer, 2002.

———. *Writings on Music.* 4 vols. Edited by Electra Slonimsky Yourke. New York: Routledge, 2003–2004.

Sorabji, Kaikhosru Shapurji

Rapoport, Paul, ed. *Sorabji: A Critical Celebration.* Brookfield, Vt.: Scolar, 1992.

Sorabji, Kaikhosru Shapurji. *Around Music.* London: Unicorn, 1932.

———. *Mi contra Fa: The Immoralisings of a Machiavellian Musician.* London: Porcupine, 1947.

Stockhausen, Karlheinz

Cott, Jonathan. *Stockhausen: Conversations with the Composer*. New York: Simon & Schuster, 1973.

Harvey, Jonathan. *The Music of Stockhausen*. London: Faber, 1975.

Heikinheimo, Seppo. *The Electronic Music of Karlheinz Stockhausen*. Helsinki: Suomen Musiikkitieteellinen Seura, 1972.

Kurtz, Michael. *Stockhausen: A Biography*. London: Faber, 1993.

Maconie, Robin. *Other Planets: The Music of Karlheinz Stockhausen*. Metuchen, N.J.: Scarecrow Press, 2005.

Nagel, Hans-Jurgen, ed. *Stockhausen in Calcutta*. Calcutta: Seagull, 1984.

Stockhausen, Karlheinz. *Stockhausen on Music: Lectures and Interviews*. Edited by Robin Maconie. New York: Marion Boyars, 2000.

———. *Towards a Cosmic Music*. Shaftesbury, U.K.: Element, 1990.

Tannenbaum, Mya. *Conversations with Stockhausen*. New York: Oxford University Press, 1988.

Wörner, Karl. *Stockhausen: Life and Work*. Berkeley: University of California Press, 1973.

Stravinsky, Igor

Albright, Daniel. *Stravinsky: The Music Box and the Nightingale*. New York: Gordon & Breach, 1989.

Andriessen, Louis, and Elmer Schönberger. *The Apollonian Clockwork: On Stravinsky*. Oxford: Oxford University Press, 1989.

Boucourechliev, André. *Stravinsky*. London: Gollancz, 1987.

Carr, Maureen A. *Multiple Masks: Neoclassicism in Stravinsky's Works on Greek Subjects*. Lincoln: University of Nebraska Press, 2002.

Corle, Edwin, ed. *Stravinsky*. New York: Duell, Sloan & Pearce, 1949.

Craft, Robert. *Bravo Stravinsky*. Cleveland, Ohio: World, 1967.

———. *Igor and Vera Stravinsky: A Photograph Album*. London: Thames & Hudson, 1982.

———. *Stravinsky: Chronicle of a Friendship, 1948–1971*. Nashville, Tenn.: Vanderbilt University Press, 1994.

———. *Stravinsky: Glimpses of a Life*. London: Lime Tree, 1992.

———. *A Stravinsky Scrapbook, 1940–1971*. London: Thames & Hudson, 1983.

Cross, Jonathan, ed. *The Cambridge Companion to Stravinsky*. Cambridge: Cambridge University Press, 2003.

———. *The Stravinsky Legacy*. Cambridge: Cambridge University Press, 2005.

Dobrin, Arnold. *Igor Stravinsky: His Life and Times*. New York: Crowell, 1970.

Druskin, Mikhail. *Igor Stravinsky: His Life, Works and Views*. Cambridge: Cambridge University Press, 1983.

Forte, Allan. *The Harmonic Organization of "The Rite of Spring."* New Haven, Conn.: Yale University Press, 1978.

Griffiths, Paul. *Igor Stravinsky: The Rake's Progress*. Cambridge: Cambridge University Press, 1982.

——. *Stravinsky*. New York: Schirmer, 1993.

Haimo, Ethan, and Paul Johnson, eds. *Stravinsky Retrospectives*. Lincoln: University of Nebraska Press, 1987.

Hill, Peter. *Stravinsky: The Rite of Spring*. Cambridge: Cambridge University Press, 2000.

Horgan, Paul. *Encounters with Stravinsky*. New York: Farrar, Straus & Giroux, 1972.

Joseph, Charles M. *Stravinsky and Balanchine: A Journey of Invention*. New Haven, Conn.: Yale University Press, 2002.

——. *Stravinsky Inside Out*. New Haven, Conn.: Yale University Press, 2001.

Keller, Hans, and Milein Cosman. *Stravinsky the Music-Maker*. London: Toccata, 2011.

Lang, Paul Henry, ed. *Stravinsky: A New Appraisal of His Work with a Complete List of Works*. New York: Norton, 1963.

Ledermann, Minna, ed. *Stravinsky in the Theatre*. New York: Farrar, Straus & Giroux, 1949.

Lubaroff, Scott. *An Examination of the Neo-classical Wind Works of Igor Stravinsky*. Lewiston, N.Y.: Mellen, 2004.

Oliver, Michael. *Igor Stravinsky*. London: Phaidon, 1995.

Routh, Francis. *Stravinsky*. London: Dent, 1975.

Siohan, Robert. *Stravinsky*. New York: Vienna House, 1965.

Straus, Joseph N. *Stravinsky's Late Music*. Cambridge: Cambridge University Press, 2004.

Stravinsky, Igor. *An Autobiography*. New York: Simon & Schuster, 1936.

——. *Miniature Essays*. London: J. & W. Chester, 1921.

——. *Poetics of Music*. Cambridge, Mass.: Harvard University Press, 1942.

——. *Stravinsky: Selected Correspondence*. 3 vols. Edited by Robert Craft. New York: Knopf, 1982–1985.

Stravinsky, Igor, and Robert Craft. *Conversations with Igor Stravinsky*. New York: Doubleday, 1959.

——. *Dialogues and a Diary*. New York: Doubleday, 1963.

——. *Expositions and Developments*. New York: Doubleday, 1962.

——. *Memories and Commentaries*. New York: Doubleday, 1960.

——. *Retrospectives and Conclusions*. New York: Knopf, 1969.

——. *Themes and Conclusions*. London: Faber, 1972.

——. *Themes and Episodes*. New York: Knopf, 1966.

Stravinsky, Igor, and Vera Stravinsky. *Dearest Bubushkin: The Correspondence of Vera and Igor Stravinsky, 1921–1954*. Edited by Robert Craft. London: Thames & Hudson, 1985.

Stravinsky, Theodore. *Catherine and Igor Stravinsky: A Family Album*. London: Boosey & Hawkes, 1973.

Stravinsky, Theodore, and Denise Stravinsky. *Catherine and Igor Stravinsky: A Family Chronicle, 1906–1940*. New York: Music Sales, 1973.

Stravinsky, Vera, and Robert Craft. *Stravinsky in Pictures and Documents*. New York: Simon & Schuster, 1978.

Taruskin, Richard. *Stravinsky and the Russian Traditions: A Biography of the Works through Mavra*. 2 vols. Berkeley: University of California Press, 1996.

Vlad, Roman. *Stravinsky*. London: Oxford University Press, 1967.

Wachtel, Andrew, ed. *Petrushka: Sources and Contexts*. Evanston, Ill.: Northwestern University Press, 1998.

Walsh, Stephen. *The Music of Stravinsky*. Oxford: Oxford University Press, 1998.

———. *Stravinsky: A Creative Spring: Russia and France, 1882–1934*. New York: Knopf, 1999.

———. *Stravinsky: Oedipus Rex*. Cambridge: Cambridge University Press, 1993.

———. *Stravinsky: The Second Exile: France and America, 1934–1971*. New York: Knopf, 2006.

Wenborn, Neil. *Stravinsky*. London: Omnibus, 1999.

White, Eric Walter. *Stravinsky: A Critical Survey*. New York: Philosophical Library, 1948.

———. *Stravinsky: The Composer and His Works*. Berkeley: University of California Press, 1966.

Takemitsu, Toru

Burt, Peter. *The Music of Toru Takemitsu*. Cambridge: Cambridge University Press, 2006.

de Ferranti, Hugh, and Yoko Narazaki, eds. *A Way a Lone: Writings on Toru Takemitsu*. Tokyo: Academia Music, 2002.

Ohtake, Noriko. *Creative Sources for the Music of Toru Takemitsu*. Brookfield, Vt.: Scolar, 1993.

Siddons, James. *Toru Takemitsu: A Bio-Bibliography*. Westport, Conn.: Greenwood, 2001.

Takemitsu, Asaka. *A Memoir of Toru Takemitsu*. New York: iUniverse, 2010.

Tenney, James

Garland, Peter, ed. *The Music of James Tenney*. Santa Fe, N.Mex.: Soundings, 1984.

Tenney, James. *A History of "Consonance" and "Dissonance."* New York: Routledge, 1988.

———. *META-HODOS and META Meta-Hodos*. Edited by Larry Polansky. Lebanon, N.H.: Frog Peak Music, 2000.

Thomson, Virgil

Hoover, Kathleen, and John Cage. *Virgil Thomson: His Life and Music*. New York: Thomas Yoseloff, 1959.

Meckna, Michael. *Virgil Thomson: A Bio-Bibliography.* Westport, Conn.: Greenwood, 1986.

Thomson, Virgil. *American Music since 1910.* New York: Holt, Rinehart & Winston, 1971.

——. *Everbest Ever: Correspondence with Bay Area Friends.* Edited by Charles Shere and Margery Tede. Metuchen, N.J.: Scarecrow Press, 1996.

——. *Music Reviewed 1940–1954.* New York: Vintage, 1967.

——. *Music, Right and Left.* Westport, Conn.: Greenwood, 1969.

——. *Music with Words: A Composer's View.* New Haven, Conn.: Yale University Press, 1989.

——. *Selected Letters of Virgil Thomson.* Edited by Tim Page and Vanessa Weeks Page. New York: Summit, 1988.

——. *Virgil Thomson.* New York: Knopf, 1966.

Tommasini, Anthony. *Virgil Thomson: Composer on the Aisle.* New York: Norton, 1997.

——. *Virgil Thomson's Musical Portraits.* New York: Pendragon, 1986.

Watson, Steven. *Prepare for Saints.* Berkeley: University of California Press, 1998.

Tippett, Michael

Bowen, Meirion. *Michael Tippett.* London: Robson, 1999.

——. *Shaping the Harmonies of Our Time: Michael Tippett.* Birmingham, U.K.: Delos, 2003.

Clarke, David. *The Music and Thought of Michael Tippett.* Cambridge: Cambridge University Press, 2006.

——, ed. *Tippett Studies.* Cambridge: Cambridge University Press, 2006.

Gloag, Kenneth. *Tippett: A Child of Our Time.* Cambridge: Cambridge University Press, 1999.

Jones, Richard Elfyn. *The Early Operas of Michael Tippett.* Lewiston, N.Y.: Mellen, 1996.

Kemp, Ian, ed. *Michael Tippett: A Symposium on His Sixtieth Birthday.* London: Faber, 1965.

——. *Tippett: The Composer and His Music.* New York: Oxford University Press, 1987.

Lewis, Geraint. *Michael Tippett, O.M.: A Celebration.* Tunbridge Wells, U.K.: Baton, 1985.

Matthews, David. *Michael Tippett.* London: Faber, 1980.

Robinson, Suzanne, ed. *Michael Tippett: Music and Literature.* Burlington, Vt.: Ashgate, 2002.

Sheppach, Margaret. *Dramatic Parallels in the Operas of Michael Tippett.* Lewiston, N.Y.: Mellen, 1990.

Theil, Gordon. *Michael Tippett: A Bio-Bibliography.* Westport, Conn.: Greenwood, 1989.

Tippett, Michael. *Moving into Aquarius.* New York: HarperCollins, 1974.

——. *Music of the Angels: Essays and Sketchbooks of Michael Tippett.* Edited by Meirion Bowen. New York: Da Capo, 1982.

——. *The Selected Letters of Michael Tippett.* Edited by Thomas Schuttenhelm. London: Faber, 2005.

——. *Those Twentieth-Century Blues: An Autobiography.* London: Hutchinson, 1991.

——. *Tippett on Music.* Edited by Meirion Bowen. London: Oxford University Press, 1995.

White, Eric Walter. *Tippett and His Operas.* New York: Da Capo, 1981.

Varèse, Edgard

Bernard, Jonathan W. *The Music of Edgard Varèse.* New Haven, Conn.: Yale University Press, 1987.

——. *A Theory of Pitch and Register for the Music of Edgard Varèse.* New Haven, Conn.: Yale University Press, 1977.

Clayson, Alan. *Edgard Varèse.* London: Sanctuary, 2002.

MacDonald, Malcolm. *Varèse: Astronomer in Sound.* London: Kahn & Averill, 2003.

Meyer, Felix, and Heidy Zimmermann, eds. *Edgard Varèse: Composer, Sound Sculptor, Visionary.* Woodbridge, Suffolk, U.K.: Boydell, 2006.

Ouellette, Fernand. *Edgard Varèse.* New York: Orion, 1968.

Parks, Anne F. *Edgard Varèse: A Guide to Research.* New York: Garland, 1993.

Sprowles, Michael David. *Geometric Pitch Structure and Form in "Déserts" by Edgard Varèse.* Saarbrücken, Germany: VDM, 2008.

Treib, Marc. *Space Calculated in Seconds: The Philips Pavilion, Le Corbusier, Edgard Varèse.* Princeton, N.J.: Princeton University Press, 1996.

Varèse, Louise. *Varèse: A Looking-Glass Diary.* New York: Norton, 1972.

Vaughan Williams, Ralph

Adams, Byron, and Robin Wells, eds. *Vaughan Williams Essays.* Burlington, Vt.: Ashgate, 2003.

Frogley, Alain, ed. *Vaughan Williams Studies.* Cambridge: Cambridge University Press, 2008.

Heffer, Simon. *Vaughan Williams.* Boston: Northeastern University Press, 2000.

Holmes, Paul. *Vaughan Williams: His Life and Times.* London: Omnibus, 1997.

Howes, Frank Stewart. *The Music of Ralph Vaughan Williams.* Westport, Conn.: Greenwood, 1975.

Kennedy, Michael. *A Catalogue of the Works of Ralph Vaughan Williams.* New York: Oxford University Press, 1996.

——. *The Works of Ralph Vaughan Williams.* New York: Clarendon, 1992.

Mellers, Wilfrid. *Vaughan Williams and the Vision of Albion.* London: Travis & Emery, 2009.

Ottaway, Hugh. *Vaughan Williams Symphonies.* London: BBC Publications, 1972.

Pike, Lionel. *Vaughan Williams and the Symphony*. London: Toccata, 2003.

Vaughan Williams, Ralph. *National Music, and Other Essays*. New York: Oxford University Press, 1987.

——. *Vaughan Williams on Music*. Edited by David Manning. New York: Oxford University Press, 2008.

Vaughan Williams, Ursula. *RVW: A Biography of Ralph Vaughan Williams*. New York: Oxford University Press, 1964.

Villa-Lobos, Heitor

Appleby, David P. *Heitor Villa-Lobos: A Bio-Bibliography*. Westport, Conn.: Greenwood, 1988.

——. *Heitor Villa-Lobos: A Life*. Metuchen, N.J.: Scarecrow Press, 2002.

Peppercorn, Lisa M. *Villa-Lobos*. London: Omnibus, 1989.

——. *Villa-Lobos: Collected Studies*. Burlington, Vt.: Ashgate, 1992.

——. *Villa-Lobos, the Music: An Analysis of His Style*. London: Kahn & Averill, 1991.

——. *The World of Villa-Lobos in Pictures and Documents*. Burlington, Vt.: Ashgate, 1996.

Tarasti, Eero. *Heitor Villa-Lobos: The Life and Works, 1887–1959*. Jefferson, N.C.: McFarland, 1995.

Villa-Lobos, Heitor. *The Villa-Lobos Letters*. Edited by Lisa M. Peppercorn. London: Toccata, 1994.

Wright, Simon. *Villa-Lobos*. New York: Oxford University Press, 1992.

Walton, William

Burton, Humphrey, and Maureen Murray. *William Walton: The Romantic Loner: A Centenary Portrait*. Oxford: Oxford University Press, 2002.

Craggs, Stewart R, ed. *William Walton: A Catalogue*. New York: Oxford University Press, 1990.

——. *William Walton: A Source Book*. Brookfield, Vt.: Scolar, 1993.

——, ed. *William Walton: Music and Literature*. Burlington, Vt.: Ashgate, 1999.

Howes, Frank Stewart. *The Music of William Walton*. London: Oxford University Press, 1973.

Kennedy, Michael. *Portrait of Walton*. Oxford, U.K.: Clarendon, 1998.

Lloyd, Stephen. *William Walton: Muse of Fire*. Woodbridge, Suffolk, U.K.: Boydell, 2001.

Petrocelli, Paolo. *The Resonance of a Small Voice: William Walton and the Violin Concerto in England between 1900 and 1940*. Newcastle upon Tyne, U.K.: Cambridge Scholars, 2010.

Smith, Carolyn J. *William Walton: A Bio-Bibliography*. Westport, Conn.: Greenwood, 1988.

Tierney, Neil. *Sir William Walton*. London: Hale, 1984.

Walton, Susana. *William Walton: Behind the Façade*. New York: Oxford University Press, 1988.

Walton, William. *The Selected Letters of William Walton*. Edited by Malcolm Hayes. London: Faber, 2002.

Warlock, Peter

Collins, Brian. *Peter Warlock the Composer*. Burlington, Vt.: Ashgate, 1996.

Copley, I. A. *The Music of Peter Warlock*. London: Dobson, 1979.

Cox, David, and John Bishop, eds. *Peter Warlock: A Centenary Celebration*. London: Thames, 1994.

Gray, Cecil. *Peter Warlock: A Memoir of Philip Heseltine*. London: Jonathan Cape, 1934.

Heseltine, Nigel. *Capriol for Mother: A Memoir of Philip Heseltine (Peter Warlock)*. London: Thames, 1992.

Parrott, Ian. *The Crying Curlew: Peter Warlock, Family and Influences, Centenary 1994*. Llandysul, Wales: Gomer, 1994.

Smith, Barry. *Peter Warlock: The Life of Philip Heseltine*. London: Oxford University Press, 1994.

Warlock, Peter. *The Collected Letters of Peter Warlock (Philip Heseltine)*. 4 vols. Edited by Barry Smith. Woodbridge, Suffolk, U.K.: Boydell, 2005.

———. *The Occasional Writings of Philip Heseltine (Peter Warlock)*. 4 vols. Edited by Barry Smith. London: Thames, 1998.

Webern, Anton

Bailey, Kathryn. *The Life of Webern*. Cambridge: Cambridge University Press, 1998.

———. *The Twelve-Note Music of Anton Webern*. Cambridge: Cambridge University Press, 2006.

———, ed. *Webern Studies*. Cambridge: Cambridge University Press, 2009.

Forte, Allen. *The Atonal Music of Anton Webern*. New Haven, Conn.: Yale University Press, 1999.

Hayes, Malcolm. *Anton von Webern*. London: Phaidon, 1995.

Irvine, Demar, ed. *Anton von Webern: Perspectives*. Compiled by Hans Moldenhauer. Seattle: University of Washington Press, 1966.

Johnson, Julian. *Webern and the Transformation of Nature*. Cambridge: Cambridge University Press, 2006.

Kolneder, Walter. *Anton Webern: An Introduction to His Work*. Westport, Conn.: Greenwood, 1982.

Moldenhauer, Hans. *The Death of Anton Webern: A Drama in Documents*. New York: Philosophical Library, 1961.

Moldenhauer, Hans, and Rosaleen Moldenhauer. *Anton von Webern: A Chronicle of His Life*. London: Gollancz, 1978.

Roman, Zoltan. *Anton von Webern: An Annotated Bibliography*. Detroit: Information Coordinators, 1983

Shreffler, Anne C. *Webern and the Lyric Impulse: Songs and Fragments on Poems of Georg Trakl*. New York: Oxford University Press, 1995.

Webern, Anton. *Letters to Hildegard Jone and Josef Humplik*. Edited by Josef Polnauer. Bryn Mawr, Pa.: Theodore Presser, 1967.

——. *The Path to the New Music*. Bryn Mawr, Pa.: Theodore Presser, 1963.

Wildgans, Friedrich. *Anton Webern*. New York: October House, 1967.

Weill, Kurt

Drew, David. *Kurt Weill: A Handbook*. London: Faber, 1987.

Farneth, David, with Elmar Juchem and Dave Stein. *Kurt Weill: A Life in Pictures and Documents*. Woodstock, N.Y.: Overlook, 2000.

Hinton, Stephen, ed. *Kurt Weill: The Threepenny Opera*. Cambridge: Cambridge University Press, 1990.

Hirsch, Foster. *Kurt Weill on Stage: From Berlin to Broadway*. New York: Knopf, 1990.

Jarman, Douglas. *Kurt Weill: An Illustrated Biography*. Bloomington: Indiana University Press, 1983.

Kowalke, Kim H., ed. *The New Orpheus: Essays on Kurt Weill*. New Haven, Conn.: Yale University Press, 1990.

McClung, Bruce. *Kurt Weill: A Guide to Research*. New York: Routledge, 2002.

Sanders, Ronald. *The Days Grow Short: The Life and Music of Kurt Weill*. New York: Holt, Rinehart & Winston, 1980.

Schebera, Jürgen. *Kurt Weill: An Illustrated Life*. New Haven, Conn.: Yale University Press, 1997.

Symonette, Lys, and Kim H. Kowalke, eds. *Speak Low (When You Speak Love): The Letters of Kurt Weill and Lotte Lenya*. Berkeley: University of California Press, 1996.

Taylor, Ronald. *Kurt Weill: Composer in a Divided World*. Boston: Northeastern University Press, 1992.

Xenakis, Iannis

Bois, Mario. *Iannis Xenakis: The Man and His Music*. Westport, Conn.: Greenwood, 1980.

Gibson, Benoît. *The Instrumental Music of Iannis Xenakis: Theory, Practice, Self-Borrowing*. New York: Pendragon, 2011.

Harley, James. *Xenakis: His Life in Music*. New York: Routledge, 2004.

Kanach, Sharon, ed. *Performing Xenakis*. New York: Pendragon, 2010.

Varga, Bálint András. *Conversations with Iannis Xenakis*. London: Faber, 2003.

Xenakis, Iannis. *Arts/Sciences: Alloys*. New York: Pendragon, 2010.

——. *Formalized Music: Thoughts and Mathematics in Music*. New York: Pendragon, 2001.

——. *Music and Architecture*. New York: Pendragon, 2008.

Other Individual Composers

Adams, John. *Hallelujah Junction: Composing an American Life*. New York: Farrar, Straus & Giroux, 2008.

Adams, John Luther. *The Place Where You Go to Listen: In Search of an Ecology of Music*. Middletown, Conn.: Wesleyan University Press, 2009.

———. *Winter Music: Composing the North*. Middletown, Conn.: Wesleyan University Press, 2004.

Adrian, Thomas. *Górecki*. Oxford: Oxford University Press, 1997.

Antheil, George. *Bad Boy of Music*. Garden City, N.Y.: Doubleday, Doran, 1945.

Ap Siôn, Pwyll. *The Music of Michael Nyman*. Burlington, Vt.: Ashgate, 2007.

Ashley, Robert. *Outside of Time: Ideas about Music*. Edited by Ralf Dietrich. Cologne, Germany: MusikTexte, 2009.

———. *Perfect Lives, an Opera*. Garden City, N.Y.: Arthur Fields, Burning Books, 1991.

Austin, Larry, and Thomas Clark. *Learning to Compose: Modes, Materials, and Models of Musical Invention*. Dubuque, Iowa: William C. Brown, 1989.

Baker, James M. *The Music of Alexander Scriabin*. New Haven, Conn.: Yale University Press, 1986.

Barlow, Michael. *Whom the Gods Love: The Life and Music of George Butterworth*. London: Toccata, 1997.

Bauer, Marion. *Twentieth-Century Music*. New York: G. P. Putnam's Sons, 1947.

Beckles Willson, Rachel. *György Kurtág: The Sayings of Péter Bornemisza, Op. 7*. Burlington, Vt.: Ashgate, 2004.

Benser, Caroline Cepin. *Egon Wellesz (1885–1974): Chronicle of a Twentieth-Century Musician*. New York: Peter Lang, 1985.

Berger, Arthur. *Reflections of an American Composer*. Berkeley: University of California Press, 2002.

Bohn, James Matthew. *The Music of American Composer Lejaren Hiller*. Lewiston, N.Y.: Mellen, 2004.

Bowers, Faubion. *Scriabin: A Biography*. New York: Dover, 1996.

Bowles, Paul. *Paul Bowles on Music*. Berkeley: University of California Press, 2003.

Brackett, John. *John Zorn: Tradition and Transgression*. Bloomington: Indiana University Press, 2009.

Brant, Henry. *Textures and Timbres: An Orchestrator's Handbook*. New York: Carl Fischer, 2009.

Bruhn, Siglind. *Frank Martin's Musical Reflections on Death*. New York: Pendragon, 2011.

Burbank, Richard D. *Charles Wuorinen: A Bio-Bibliography*. Westport, Conn.: Greenwood, 1993.

Carl, Robert. *Terry Riley's "In C."* New York: Oxford University Press, 2009.

Chase, Stephen, and Philip Thomas, eds. *Changing the System: The Music of Christian Wolff*. Burlington, Vt.: Ashgate, 2010.

Clarkson, Austin, ed. *On the Music of Stefan Wolpe*. New York: Pendragon, 2003.

Cody, Judith. *Vivian Fine: A Bio-Bibliography*. Westport, Conn.: Greenwood, 2002.

Craggs, Stewart R., ed. *John Ireland: A Catalogue, Discography and Bibliography*. Burlington, Vt.: Ashgate, 2007.

Culbertson, Evelyn Davis. *He Heard America Singing: Arthur Farwell, Composer and Crusading Music Educator.* Metuchen, N.J.: Scarecrow Press, 1992.

Dodge, Charles, and Thomas A. Jerse. *Computer Music: Synthesis, Composition, and Performance.* New York: Schirmer, 1997.

Duckworth, William, and Richard Fleming, eds. *Sound and Light: La Monte Young and Marian Zazeela.* Lewisburg, Pa.: Bucknell University Press, 1996.

Ertan, Deniz. *Dane Rudhyar: His Music, Thought, and Art.* Rochester, N.Y.: University of Rochester Press, 2009.

Farwell, Arthur. *Wanderjahre of a Revolutionist, and Other Essays on American Music.* Edited by Thomas Stoner. Rochester, N.Y.: University of Rochester Press, 1996.

Fearn, Raymond. *Bruno Maderna.* Chur, Switzerland: Harwood, 1990.

Ferneyhough, Brian. *Brian Ferneyhough: Collected Writings.* Edited by James Boros and Richard Toop. London: Routledge, 1998.

Finley, Patrick D. *A Catalogue of the Works of Ralph Shapey.* New York: Pendragon, 1997.

Fisher, Margaret. *Ezra Pound's Radio Operas: The BBC Experiments, 1931–1933.* Cambridge, Mass.: MIT Press, 2002.

Follet, Robert. *Albert Roussel: A Bio-Bibliography.* Westport, Conn.: Greenwood, 1988.

Gann, Kyle. *The Music of Conlon Nancarrow.* Cambridge: Cambridge University Press, 2006.

Garland, Peter, ed. *Conlon Nancarrow: Selected Studies for Player Piano.* Berkeley, Calif.: Soundings, 1977.

———. *In Search of Silvestre Revueltas.* Santa Fe, N.Mex.: Soundings, 1991.

Gerhard, Roberto. *Gerhard on Music.* Edited by Meirion Brown. Burlington, Vt.: Ashgate, 2000.

Gloag, Kenneth. *Nicholas Maw: Odyssey.* Burlington, Vt.: Ashgate, 2008.

Goehr, Alexander. *Finding the Key.* London: Faber, 1997.

Gordon, Eric A. *Mark the Music: The Life and Work of Marc Blitzstein.* New York: St. Martin's, 1989.

Green, Jonathan D. *Carl Ruggles: A Bio-Bibliography.* Westport, Conn.: Greenwood, 1995.

Greer, Taylor Aitken. *A Question of Balance: Charles Seeger's Philosophy of Music.* Berkeley: University of California Press, 1998.

Griffiths, Paul. *The Sea on Fire: Jean Barraqué.* Rochester, N.Y.: University of Rochester Press, 2003.

Grolman, Ellen K. *Joan Tower: The Comprehensive Bio-Bibliography.* Metuchen, N.J.: Scarecrow Press, 2007.

Hartsock, Ralph. *Otto Luening: A Bio-Bibliography.* Westport, Conn.: Greenwood, 1991.

Hartsock, Ralph, and Carl Rahkonen. *Vladimir Ussachevsky: A Bio-Bibliography.* Westport, Conn.: Greenwood, 2000.

Heile, Björn. *The Music of Mauricio Kagel.* Burlington, Vt.: Ashgate, 2006.

Hiller, Lejaren, and Leonard Isaacson. *Experimental Music: Composition with an Electronic Computer.* New York: McGraw-Hill, 1959.

Hillier, Paul. *Arvo Pärt*. Oxford: Oxford University Press, 1997.

Hixon, Donald L. *Gian Carlo Menotti: A Bio-Bibliography*. Westport, Conn.: Greenwood, 2000.

———. *Thea Musgrave: A Bio-Bibliography*. Westport, Conn.: Greenwood, 1984.

Hoek, D. J. *Steve Reich: A Bio-Bibliography*. Westport, Conn.: Greenwood, 2001.

Johnston, Ben. *Maximum Clarity, and Other Writings on Music*. Edited by Bob Gilmore. Urbana: University of Illinois Press, 2006.

Joseph, Branden W. *Beyond the Dream Syndicate: Tony Conrad and the Arts after Cage*. Cambridge, Mass.: MIT Press, 2008.

Jowitt, Deborah, ed. *Meredith Monk*. Baltimore: Johns Hopkins University Press, 1997.

Kholopov, Yuri, and Valeria Tsenova. *Edison Denisov*. Amsterdam: Harwood, 1995.

King, Charles W. *Frank Martin: A Bio-Bibliography*. Westport, Conn.: Greenwood, 1990.

Korstvedt, Benjamin M. *Listening for Utopia in Ernest Bloch's Musical Philosophy*. Cambridge: Cambridge University Press, 2010.

Kurtz, Michael. *Sofia Gubaidulina: A Biography*. Bloomington: Indiana University Press, 2007.

Lai, Eric C. *The Music of Chou Wen-chung*. Burlington, Vt.: Ashgate, 2009.

Lehrman, Leonard. *Marc Blitzstein: A Bio-Bibliography*. Westport, Conn.: Greenwood, 2005.

Liess, Andreas. *Carl Orff: His Life and His Music*. London: Calder, 1971.

Little, Karen R. *Frank Bridge: A Bio-Bibliography*. Westport, Conn.: Greenwood, 1991.

Lourié, Arthur. *Sergei Koussevitzky and His Epoch*. New York: Knopf, 1931.

Lucier, Alvin. *Reflections: Interviews, Notations, Scores, Texts, 1963–1994*. Edited by Gisela Gronemeyer and Reinhard Oehlschlägel. Cologne, Germany: Musik-Texte, 2005.

Lucier, Alvin, and Douglas Simon. *Chambers*. Middletown, Conn.: Wesleyan University Press, 1981.

Maisel, Edward. *Charles T. Griffes: The Life of an American Composer*. New York: Knopf, 1984.

May, Thomas, ed. *The John Adams Reader*. Portland, Ore.: Amadeus, 2006.

Oja, Carol J. *Colin McPhee: Composer in Two Worlds*. Champaign: University of Illinois Press, 2004.

Orff, Carl. *Carl Orff/Documentation: His Life and Works*. Vol. 3: *The Schulwerk*. New York: Schott, 1978.

Ostertag, Bob. *Creative Life: Music, Politics, People, and Machines*. Urbana: University of Illinois Press, 2009.

Palmer, John. *Jonathan Harvey's Bhakti for Chamber Ensemble and Electronics*. Lewiston, N.Y.: Mellen, 2001.

Perle, George. *The Listening Composer*. Berkeley: University of California Press, 1990.

———. *The Right Notes: 23 Selected Essays on 20th-Century Music*. New York: Pendragon, 1995.

Perone, Karen L. *Lukas Foss: A Bio-Bibliography*. Westport, Conn.: Greenwood, 1991.

Pound, Ezra. *Ezra Pound and Music: The Complete Criticism.* Edited by R. Murray Schafer. London: Faber, 1978.

Ramey, Philip. *Irving Fine: An American Composer in His Time.* New York: Pendragon, 2005.

Reich, Steve. *Writings on Music, 1965–2000.* Edited by Paul Hillier. New York: Oxford University Press, 2002.

Richards, Fiona. *The Music of John Ireland.* Burlington, Vt.: Ashgate, 2000.

Riggs, Robert. *Leon Kirchner: Composer, Performer, and Teacher.* Rochester, N.Y.: University of Rochester Press, 2010.

Rosenstiel, Léonie. *The Life and Works of Lili Boulanger.* Cranbury, N.J.: Fairleigh Dickinson University Press, 1978.

———. *Nadia Boulanger: A Life in Music.* New York: Norton, 1982.

Rudhyar, Dane. *The Magic of Tone and the Art of Music.* Boulder, Colo.: Shambhala, 1982.

Russolo, Luigi. *The Art of Noises.* New York: Pendragon, 1987.

Rzewski, Frederic. *Nonsequiturs: Writings and Lectures.* Edited by Gisela Gronemeyer and Reinhard Oehlschlägel. Cologne, Germany: MusikTexte, 2007.

Schnittke, Alfred. *A Schnittke Reader.* Edited by Alexander Ivashkin. Bloomington: Indiana University Press, 2002.

Schwartz-Kates, Deborah. *Alberto Ginastera: A Research and Information Guide.* New York: Routledge, 2010.

Scotto, Robert. *Moondog: The Viking of Sixth Avenue.* Los Angeles: Process, 2007.

Seachrist, Denise A. *The Musical World of Halim El-Dabh.* Kent, Ohio: Kent State University Press, 2003.

Shapey, Ralph. *A Basic Course in Music Composition.* King of Prussia, Pa.: Theodore Presser, 2001.

Shapiro, Robert. *Germaine Tailleferre: A Bio-Bibliography.* Westport, Conn.: Greenwood, 1993.

Slottow, Stephen. *A Vast Simplicity: The Music of Carl Ruggles.* New York: Pendragon, 2009.

Smith, Catherine Parsons, ed. *William Grant Still: A Study in Contradictions.* Berkeley: University of California Press, 2000.

Smith, Stephen C. *A Heart at Fire's Center: The Life and Music of Bernard Herrmann.* Berkeley: University of California Press, 1991.

Spycket, Jérôme. *Nadia Boulanger.* New York: Pendragon, 1992.

Still, Judith Anne, Michael J. Dabrishus, and Carolyn L. Quin. *William Grant Still: A Bio-Bibliography.* Westport, Conn.: Greenwood, 1996.

Swan, Claudia, ed. *Paul Bowles: Music.* New York: Eos Music, 1995.

Szymanowski, Karol. *Szymanowski on Music.* Edited by Alistair Wightman. London: Toccata, 1999.

Tavener, John. *The Music of Silence: A Composer's Testament.* Edited by Brian Keeble. London: Faber, 1999.

von Gunden, Heidi. *The Music of Ben Johnston.* Metuchen, N.J.: Scarecrow Press, 1986.

———. *The Music of Vivian Fine.* Metuchen, N.J.: Scarecrow Press, 1999.

Whittall, Arnold. *Jonathan Harvey*. London: Faber, 1999.

Wightman, Alistair. *Karol Szymanowski: His Life and Work*. Edited by Meirion Brown. Burlington, Vt.: Ashgate, 1999.

Wolff, Christian. *Cues: Writings and Conversations*. Edited by Gisela Gronemeyer and Reinhard Oehlschlägel. Cologne, Germany: MusikTexte, 1998.

Wuorinen, Charles. *Simple Composition*. New York: Longman, 1979.

Yung, Bell, and Helen Rees, eds. *Understanding Charles Seeger, Pioneer in American Musicology*. Urbana: University of Illinois Press, 1999.

Ziffrin, Marilyn. *Carl Ruggles: Composer, Painter, and Storyteller*. Urbana: University of Illinois Press, 1994.

Multiple Composers

Beckles Willson, Rachel. *Ligeti, Kurtág, and Hungarian Music during the Cold War*. Cambridge: Cambridge University Press, 2007.

Boretz, Benjamin, and Edward T. Cone, eds. *Perspectives on American Composers*. New York: Norton, 1971.

——. *Perspectives on Schoenberg and Stravinsky*. New York: Norton, 1972.

Boroff, Edith. *Three American Composers*. Lanham, Md.: University Press of America, 1986.

Brand, Juliane, Christopher Hailey, and Donald Harris, eds. *The Berg–Schoenberg Correspondence: Selected Letters*. New York: Norton, 1987.

Burns, Christine H. *Women and Music in America since 1900*. Westport, Conn.: Greenwood, 2002.

Cook, Susan C. *Opera for a New Republic: The Zeitopern of Krenek, Weill, and Hindemith*. Rochester, N.Y.: University of Rochester Press, 1988.

Cooke, Deryck. *Vindications*. Cambridge: Cambridge University Press, 1982.

Craft, Robert. *Down a Path of Wonder*. Franklin, Tenn.: Naxos, 2006.

Foreman, Lewis, ed. *From Parry to Britten: British Music in Letters*. London: Batsford, 1987.

Garland, Peter. *Americas*. Santa Fe, N.Mex.: Soundings, 1982.

Harding, James. *The Ox on the Roof: Scenes from Musical Life in Paris in the Twenties*. London: MacDonald, 1972.

Hinkle-Turner, Elizabeth. *Women Composers and Music Technology in the United States*. Burlington, Vt.: Ashgate, 2006.

Hisama, Ellie M. *Gendering Musical Modernism: The Music of Ruth Crawford, Marion Bauer, and Miriam Gideon*. Cambridge, Mass.: Cambridge University Press, 2001.

Johnson, Barrett Ashley. *Training the Composer: A Comparative Study between the Pedagogical Methodologies of Arnold Schoenberg and Nadia Boulanger*. Newcastle upon Tyne, U.K.: Cambridge Scholars, 2010.

Kostelanetz, Richard. *On Innovative Music(ian)s*. New York: Da Capo, 1989.

Mertens, Wim. *American Minimal Music*. New York: Broude, 1983.

Nattiez, Jean-Jacques, and Robert Samuels, eds. *The Boulez–Cage Correspondence*. Cambridge: Cambridge University Press, 1995.

Newlin, Dika. *Bruckner, Mahler, Schoenberg.* London: Marion Boyars, 1979.

Perle, George. *Serial Composition and Atonality: An Introduction to the Music of Schoenberg, Berg and Webern.* Berkeley: University of California Press, 1991.

Pollack, Howard. *Harvard Composer: Walter Piston and His Students, from Elliott Carter to Frederic Rzewski.* Metuchen, N.J.: Scarecrow Press, 1992.

Potter, Caroline. *Nadia and Lili Boulanger.* Burlington, Vt.: Ashgate, 2006.

Potter, Keith. *Four American Minimalists.* Cambridge: Cambridge University Press, 2002.

Rapp, Willis M. *The Wind Band Masterworks of Holst, Vaughan Williams, and Grainger.* Galesville, Md.: Meredith Music, 2005.

Rich, Alan. *American Pioneers: Ives to Cage and Beyond.* London: Phaidon, 1995.

Rickard, Guy. *Hartmann, Hindemith, and Henze.* London: Phaidon, 1995.

Roberts, Peter Deane. *Modernism in Russian Piano Music: Skriabin, Prokofiev, and Their Russian Contemporaries.* Bloomington: Indiana University Press, 1993.

Rockwell, John. *All American Music.* New York: Knopf, 1983.

Rorem, Ned, and Paul Bowles. *Dear Paul, Dear Ned: The Correspondence of Paul Bowles and Ned Rorem.* North Pomfret, Vt.: Elysium, 1997.

Rosensthal, Manuel. *Satie, Ravel, Poulenc.* New York: Hanuman, 1987.

Schartz, K. Robert. *Minimalists.* London: Phaidon, 2008.

Schiller, David M. *Bloch, Schoenberg, and Bernstein: Assimilating Jewish Music.* New York: Oxford University Press, 2003.

Schonberg, Harold G. *The Lives of the Great Composers.* New York: Norton, 1997.

Schwartz, Elliott, and Barney Childs, eds. *Contemporary Composers on Contemporary Music.* New York: Holt, Rinehart & Winston, 1967.

Simms, Bryan R., ed. *Schoenberg, Berg and Webern: A Companion to the Second Viennese School.* Westport, Conn.: Greenwood, 1999.

Smith, Barry, ed. *Frederick Delius and Peter Warlock: A Friendship Revealed.* London: Oxford University Press, 1994.

Varga, Bálint András. *György Kurtág: Three Interviews and Ligeti Homages.* Rochester, N.Y.: University of Rochester Press, 2009.

Vaughan Williams, Ursula, and Imogen Holst, eds. *Heirs and Rebels: Letters and Occasional Writings by Ralph Vaughan Williams and Gustav Holst.* London: Oxford University Press, 1959.

Whittall, Arnold. *The Music of Britten and Tippett.* Cambridge: Cambridge University Press, 1990.

Zorn, John, ed. *Arcana: Musicians on Music.* New York: Granary, 2000.

——. *Arcana II: Musicians on Music.* New York: Tzadik, 2007.

——. *Arcana III: Musicians on Music.* New York: Tzadik, 2008.

——. *Arcana IV: Musicians on Music.* New York: Tzadik, 2009.

——. *Arcana V: Music, Magic, and Mysticism.* New York: Tzadik, 2010.

Interviews

Biggs, Hayes, and Susan Orzel, eds. *Musically Incorrect: Conversations about Music at the End of the 20th Century.* New York: C. F. Peters, 1998.

Duckworth, William. *Talking Music.* New York: Schirmer, 1995.

Dufalo, Richard. *Trackings.* New York: Oxford University Press, 1989.

Gagne, Cole. *Sonic Transports: New Frontiers in Our Music.* New York: de Falco Books, 1990.

———. *Soundpieces 2: Interviews with American Composers.* Metuchen, N.J.: Scarecrow Press, 1993.

Gagne, Cole, and Tracy Caras. *Soundpieces: Interviews with American Composers.* Metuchen, N.J.: Scarecrow Press, 1982.

Griffiths, Paul. *New Sounds, New Personalities: British Composers of the 1980s.* London: Faber, 1985.

McCutchan, Ann. *The Muse That Sings: Composers Speak about the Creative Process.* New York: Oxford University Press, 1999.

Rodgers, Tara. *Pink Noises: Women on Electronic Music and Sound.* Durham, N.C.: Duke University Press, 2010.

Steenhuisen, Paul. *Sonic Mosaics: Conversations with Composers.* Edmonton: University of Alberta Press, 2009.

Strickland, Edward. *American Composers: Dialogues on Contemporary Music.* Bloomington: Indiana University Press, 1991.

Sumner, Melody, Kathleen Burch, and Michael Sumner, eds. *The Guests Go In to Supper.* Oakland, Calif.: Burning Books, 1986.

Varga, Bálint András. *Three Questions for Sixty-Five Composers.* Rochester, N.Y.: University of Rochester Press, 2011.

Zimmermann, Walter. *Desert Plants: Conversations with 23 American Musicians.* Vancouver, B.C.: A.R.C., 1976.

JOURNALS AND REVIEWS

1/1. Just Intonation Network, 1985.

21st-Century Music. San Anselmo, Calif.: 21st-Century Music, 1994.

Computer Music Journal. Cambridge, Mass.: MIT Press, 1977.

Ear. Berkeley, Calif.: New Wilderness Foundation, 1973–1991.

Experimental Musical Instruments. 1985–1999.

The Improvisor. Birmingham, Ala.: 1980.

Journal of Mathematics and Music. Abingdon, Oxford, U.K.: Taylor & Francis, 2007.

Modern Music. New York: League of Composers, 1924–1946.

Musicworks. Toronto: Musicworks Society of Ontario, 1978.

Op. Olympia, Wash.: Lost Music Network, 1980–1984.

Perspectives of New Music. Seattle: University of Washington School of Music, 1962.

Pitch. New York, 1986–1990.

Soundings. Santa Fe, N.Mex.: Soundings Press, 1971–1991.

Source. Sacramento, Calif.: Composer/Performer Edition, 1967–1973.

Tempo. Cambridge: Cambridge University Press. 1939.

Xenharmonikôn. Lebanon, N.H.: Frog Peak Music, 1974.

WEBSITES

General

Alternate Tuning Systems

http://www.afmm.org
http://www.huygens-fokker.org
http://www.justintonation.net
http://www.microtonal.freeservers.com
http://www.tonalsoft.com

Ambient Music

http://www.ambientmusicguide.com
http://www.ambientvisions.com
http://www.dreamstate.to

Computer Music

http://www.computermusic.org
http://www.computermusicjournal.org

Electroacoustic Music

http://www.ems-network.org
http://www.seamusonline.org

Electronic Music

http://120years.net
http://www.emf.org
http://www.theremin.info
http://www.trautonium.com

Instrument Building

http://windworld.com
http://www.oddmusic.com

Individual Composers

Adams, John: http://www.earbox.com
Adams, John Luther: http://www.johnlutheradams.com

Amacher, Maryanne: http://www.maryanneamacher.org

Anderson, Laurie: http://www.laurieanderson.com

Antheil, George: http://www.antheil.org; http://www.paristransatlantic.com/antheil/frameset.html

Ashley, Robert: http://www.robertashley.org

Austin, Larry: http://cemi.music.unt.edu/larry_austin/

Behrman, David: http://www.dbehrman.net

Berger, Arthur: http://www.arthurvberger.com

Berio, Luciano: http://www.lucianoberio.org/en

Bernstein, Leonard: http://www.leonardbernstein.com

Biscardi, Chester: http://www.chesterbiscardi.com

Blitzstein, Marc: http://www.marcblitzstein.com

Bloch, Ernest: http://www.ernestbloch.org

Bolcom, William: http://www.williambolcom.com

Boulanger, Nadia: http://www.nadiaboulanger.org

Bowles, Paul: http://www.paulbowles.org

Branca, Glenn: http://www.glennbranca.com

Braxton, Anthony: http://www.wesleyan.edu/music/braxton

Britten, Benjamin: http://www.brittenpears.org

Brown, Earle: http://www.earle-brown.org

Bryars, Gavin: http://www.gavinbryars.com

Busoni, Ferruccio: http://www.rodoni.ch/busoni/indexx.html

Cage, John: http://www.johncage.info; http://www.xs4all.nl/~cagecomp/1912–1971.htm

Carlos, Wendy: http://www.wendycarlos.com

Carrillo, Julián: http://paginas.tol.itesm.mx/campus/L00280370/julian.html

Carter, Elliott: http://www.carter100.com

Cerha, Friedrich: http://www.friedrich-cerha.com

Chambers, Wendy Mae: http://www.wendymae.com

Chatham, Rhys: http://www.rhyschatham.net

Chou Wen-chung: http://www.chouwenchung.org

Conrad, Tony: http://tonyconrad.net

Corigliano, John: http://www.johncorigliano.com

Cowell, Henry: http://www.henrycowell.org

Crumb, George: http://www.georgecrumb.net

Davies, Peter Maxwell: http://www.maxopus.com

Delius, Frederick: http://thompsonian.info/delius.html; http://www.delius.org.uk

Del Tredeci, David: http://www.daviddeltredici.com

Deyhim, Sussan: http://sussandeyhim.com

Diamond, David: http://www.daviddiamond.org

Duckworth, William: http://www.billduckworth.com

Eastman, Julius: http://www.mjleach.com/eastman.htm

Eisler, Hanns: http://www.eislermusic.com; http://www.hanns-eisler.com

El-Dabh, Halim: http://www.halimeldabh.com

Falla, Manuel de: http://www.manueldefalla.com

Ferrari, Luc: http://www.lucferrari.org

Fine, Vivian: http://www.vivanfine.org

Flynt, Henry: http://henryflynt.org

Foulds, John: http://www.bluntinstrument.org.uk/foulds

Frith, Fred: http://www.fredfrith.com

Fullman, Ellen: http://www.ellenfullman.com

Gaburo, Kenneth: http://www.angelfire.com/mn/gaburo/indexpage.html

Galás, Diamanda: http://www.diamandagalas.com

Gann, Kyle: http://www.kylegann.com

Gershwin, George: http://www.gershwin.com

Glass, Philip: http://www.philipglass.com

Gordon, Michael: http://www.michaelgordonmusic.com

Gordon, Peter: http://www.petergordon.com

Gosfield, Annie: http://www.anniegosfield.com

Grainger, Percy: http://www.percygrainger.org.uk

Harris, Roy: http://www.royharrisamericancomposer.com

Harvey, Jonathan: http://www.vivosvoco.com

Herrmann, Bernard: http://www.bernardherrmann.org

Hiller, Lejaren: http://ublib.buffalo.edu/libraries/units/music/spcoll/hiller/index.html

Hindemith, Paul: http://www.paul-hindemith.org

Holst, Gustav: http://www.gustavholst.info

Honegger, Arthur: http://www.arthur-honegger.com

Hovhaness, Alan: http://www.hovhaness.com

Hunt, Jerry: http://www.jerryhunt.org

Hykes, David: http://www.harmonicworld.com

Ibarra, Susie: http://www.susieibarra.com

Ives, Charles: http://www.charlesives.org

Johnson, Tom: http://editions75.com

Jolas, Betsy: http://www.betsyjolas.com

Jolivet, André: http://www.jolivet.asso.fr

Kagel, Mauricio: http://www.mauricio-kagel.com; http://www.sussex.ac.uk/Users/bh25/kagel.htm

Knowles, Alison: http://www.aknowles.com

Kodály, Zoltán: http://www.iks.hu

Kotik, Petr: http://www.pkotik.com

Krenek, Ernst: http://www.ernstkrenek.com; http://www.krenek.com

La Barbara, Joan: http://www.joanlabarbara.com

Lam, Bun-Ching: http://www.bunchinglam.com

Lang, David: http://www.davidlangmusic.com

Leach, Mary Jane: http://www.mjleach.com

LeBaron, Anne: http://www.annelebaron.com

Le Caine, Hugh: http://www.hughlecaine.com

León, Tania: http://www.tanialeon.com

Lockwood, Annea: http://www.annealockwood.com

Lourié, Arthur: http://www.lourie.ch

Lucier, Alvin: http://alucier.web.wesleyan.edu

Mamlok, Ursula: http://www.ursulamamlok.com
Marcus, Bunita: http://www.bunitamarcus.com
Martin, Frank: http://www.frankmartin.org
Martinu, Bohuslav: http://www.martinu.cz/english/novinky.php
Messiaen, Olivier: http://oliviermessiaen.net; http://www.oliviermessiaen.org
Mikhashoff, Yvar: http://www.mikhashofftrust.org
Monk, Meredith: http://www.meredithmonk.org
Moon, Beata: http://www.beatamoon.com
Moran, Robert: http://members.macconnect.com/users/r/rbtmoran/
Mumma, Gordon: http://brainwashed.com/mumma/
Murail, Tristan: http://www.tristanmurail.com
Musgrave, Thea: http://www.theamusgrave.com
Nancarrow, Conlon: http://www.fuerst-heidtmann.de
Neuhaus, Max: http://www.max-neuhaus.info
Niblock, Phill: http://www.phillniblock.com
Nono, Luigi: http://www.luiginono.it/en
Nyman, Michael: http://www.michaelnyman.com
Oliveros, Pauline: http://paulineoliveros.us
Orff, Carl: http://www.orff.de/en.html
Ornstein, Leo: http://www.poonhill.com
Ostertag, Bob: http://bobostertag.com
Palestine, Charlemagne: http://www.charlemagnepalestine.org
Pärt, Arvo: http://www.arvopart.info
Partch, Harry: http://www.corporeal.com; http://www.harrypartch.com
Perkins, Philip: http://www.philper.com
Perle, George: http://www.georgeperle.net
Poulenc, Francis: http://www.poulenc.fr/index_en.php
Pound, Ezra: http://www.ezrapoundmusic.com
Pousseur, Henri: http://www.scambi.mdx.ac.uk
Prokofiev, Sergey: http://www.prokofiev.org
Radulescu, Horatiu: http://www.horatiuradulescu.com
Ravel, Maurice: http://www.maurice-ravel.net
Reich, Steve: http://www.stevereich.com
Reynolds, Roger: http://www.rogerreynolds.com
Riley, Terry: http://terryriley.net
Rorem, Ned: http://www.nedrorem.com
Rudhyar, Dane: http://www.khaldea.com/rudhyar
Rylan, Jessica: http://www.irfp.net
Schoenberg, Arnold: http://www.schoenberg.at
Schuman, William: http://www.williamschuman.org
Scriabin, Alexander: http://www.scriabinsociety.com
Sharp, Elliott: http://www.elliottsharp.com
Shostakovich, Dmitry: http://shostakovich.hilwin.nl/index.html
Sorabji, Kaikhosru Shapurji: http://www.sorabji-archive.co.uk
Spiegel, Laurie: http://retiary.org
Still, William Grant: http://www.williamgrantstill.com

Stockhausen, Karlheinz: http://www.stockhausen.org
Subotnick, Morton: http://www.mortonsubotnick.com
Takahashi, Yuji: http://www.suigyu.com/yuji/Yuji_Takahashi_en.html
Talma, Louise: http://www.omnidisc.com/Talma.html
Teitelbaum, Richard: http://inside.bard.edu/teitelbaum
Thomson, Virgil: http://www.virgilthomson.org
Tudor, David: http://www.davidtudor.org
Vaughan Williams, Ralph: http://www.rvwsociety.com
Villa-Lobos, Heitor: http://www.villalobos.ca
Walton, William: http://www.williamwalton.net
Warlock, Peter: http://www.peterwarlock.org
Webern, Anton: http://www.antonwebern.com
Weill, Kurt: http://www.kwf.org
Westerkamp, Hildegard: http://www.sfu.ca/~westerka/
Wolfe, Julia: http://www.juliawolfemusic.com
Wolpe, Stefan: http://www.wolpe.org
Wuorinen, Charles: http://www.charleswuorinen.com
Xenakis, Iannis: http://www.iannis-xenakis.org

Multiple Composers

http://www.composers21.com
http://www.kallistimusic.com
http://www.melafoundation.org
http://www.newmusicbox.org
http://www.therestisnoise.com
http://www.sequenza21.com

Organizations and Resources

http://bangonacan.org
http://www.deeplistening.org
http://www.downtownmusicgallery.com
http://www.experimentalintermedia.org
http://www.frogpeak.org
http://www.hathut.com
http://www.ircam.fr/?L=1
http://www.lovely.com
http://www.mimaroglumusicsales.com
http://www.moderecords.com
http://www.newalbion.com
http://www.otherminds.org
http://www.portsmouthsinfonia.com
http://www.synthmuseum.com
http://www.tzadik.com

About the Author

Nicole V. Gagné is the coauthor of *Soundpieces: Interviews with American Composers* (1982) and the author of *Sonic Transports: New Frontiers in Our Music* (de Falco, 1990) and *Soundpieces 2: Interviews with American Composers* (1994). She is also a contributor to *The New Grove II* and has written articles about music for *BMI* magazine, *Ear*, *Keyboard Classics*, *Op*, *Option*, and Newmusicbox.org. Her essay "The Beaten Path" (2004), a history of percussion in American music, won ASCAP's Deems Taylor Award in 2004. In addition to writing about music, she is the librettist and co-composer of the opera *Agamemnon* (1992).

CPSIA information can be obtained at www.ICGtesting.com
Printed in the USA
270291BV00003B/6/P

9 780810 867659